Sacrificial Worship
of the
Old Testament

Sacrificial Worship of the Old Testament

J. H. Kurtz
Translated by James Martin

BAKER BOOK HOUSE
Grand Rapids, Michigan

Reprinted 1980 by
Baker Book House Company
from the 1863 edition issued by
T. & T. Clark
ISBN: 0-8010-5419-2

PHOTOLITHOPRINTED BY CUSHING - MALLOY, INC.
ANN ARBOR, MICHIGAN, UNITED STATES OF AMERICA

PREFACE

TWENTY years have passed since I was prompted by the appearance of *Bähr's Symbolik* to publish my work on "*Das Mosaische Opfer, Mitau* 1842." As this work was sold off in the course of a few years, I cherished the desire and intention of meeting the questions that were continually arising, by preparing a new edition, as soon as I should have finished another work which I had then in hand. But the longer this task was postponed, the greater the obstacles to its execution appeared. For year after year writings upon this subject were constantly accumulating, which for the most part were strongly opposed to the standpoint and results of my own work, both in their fundamental view and in their interpretation of various details. These writings had also shown me much that was weak and unsatisfactory in my own work, particularly in the elaboration of the separate parts; though opposition had only convinced me more and more of the entire correctness of my earlier opinions, which were no other than the traditional and orthodox views. But this did not render me insensible to the fact, that if the work was to be taken up again, it must be in the form of a thoroughly new book. On the former occasion I had simply to overthrow the views of one single opponent, which were as unscriptural as they were unorthodox, and to raise by the side a new edifice upon the old, firm foundation of the Church. Now, on the contrary, not only is there a whole forest of opposing standpoints and opinions to be dealt with, that differ quite as much from one another, as they do from the view which I have advocated; but so many breaches have been made in the edifice erected by me, that simply repairing the injured and untenable posts is quite out of the question, and it is much better to pull down the old building altogether and erect a new one in its place. The foundation, indeed, still remains the same, and many of the stones formerly employed prove themselves still sound; but even these require fresh chiselling, and such as are not usable have to be laid aside for new ones.

For so extensive a work, however, I could find neither time nor leisure, especially as my studies lay in other directions, in consequence of a change that had taken place in the meantime in my official post and duties. It was not till a year and a half ago, when my academical labours led once more in the direction of Biblical Antiquities, that I had to enter *ex professo* into the Sacrificial Worship of the Old Testament. With this there arose so strong a desire to work once more at the subject with a view to publication, and thus, so to speak, to wipe off old debts, that I could not refrain any longer. Hence the present volume, which has assumed a totally different form from the earlier one, and therefore is to be regarded as an entirely new and independent work.

Thomasius, when speaking of the Old Testament Sacrifices in his well-known work on Scripture Doctrines (III. 1, p. 39), says: " It ought, indeed, to be possible to appeal in this case to the *consensus* of expositors; but how widely do the views of modern writers differ from one another as to the meaning of this institution !" It seems to me, however, that there are but a few prominent points of Biblical Theology in which such a demand can possibly be made, and in *this* point perhaps least of all. Yet there is certainly hardly any other case, in which the complaints that are made as to the confusion of contradictory views are so perfectly warranted as they are here. How widely, for example, are theologians separated, who generally stand closest together when questions relating to the Church, the Bible, or Theology are concerned, *e.g.*, *Hofmann* and *Baumgarten*, *Delitzsch* and *Kliefoth*, *Oehler* and *Keil!* To what an extent doctrinal standpoints, that are in other respects the most opposed, may be associated here, is evident from the fact, that in answering the most essential and fundamental question of all, viz., whether the slaughtering of the expiatory sacrifice had the signification of a *pœna vicaria*, it is possible for me to stand by the side, not of *Hofmann*, *Keil*, *Oehler*, and *Delitzsch*, but of *Gesenius*, *De Wette*, and *Knobel*.

In this state of affairs, a monograph upon this subject would not be complete, without examining the theories of opponents, however great their confusion may frequently be, as well as building up one's own. Even where there is so little agreement, so little common ground, and on the other hand, so much opposition in details and in general principles, in the foundation as well as in the superstructure, it appears to me to be the duty of an author towards his readers, not only to tell them his own views and to defend them by rebutting unwarrantable and unsuccessful attacks, but to give them a full explanation of the opposite views, and his reason for not adopting them, in order that they may be placed in circumstances to survey the whole ground of the questions in dispute, and to form their own independent judgment, even though they may be led to differ from the views and conclusions of the author himself.

My reason for giving a secondary title to this book,[1] by which

[1] The present volume is published in the original with two separate title-pages. One is the title prefixed to this Translation; the other, " History of the Old Covenant; Supplement to the second volume: The Giving of the Law; Part I. The Law of Worship." As the author expressly states that he has written this as an independent work, there was no necessity to publish the second title-page in the English Translation. The reader will be able to assign it to its proper connection with the " History of the Old Covenant."—TR.

I connect it with my " History of the Old Covenant," is the following :—According to the original plan of that work, the second volume, which describes the historical circumstances of the Mosaic age, was to be followed by a systematic account of the Mosaic laws.[1] But I had not the time to carry out the present work on so extensive a scale. Moreover, as I have already stated, it has not arisen from the necessity for going on with the work just mentioned (a necessity which unquestionably does press most powerfully upon me), but from the necessity for returning to a subject upon which I had already written twenty years ago, and which had been taken up since from so many different points of view, in order that I might remove such faults and imperfections in my former work as I had been able to discover, and avail myself of new materials for establishing and elaborating my views. At the same time, by the publication of this volume, the substance of which was to have formed an integral part of my larger work, I have precluded the possibility of carrying out the latter upon the plan originally proposed. I have thought it desirable, therefore, that the *third* volume of that work should continue the history itself (as far as the establishment of the kingdom); and that the present volume should appear as the first part of a supplementary work, embracing the various parts of the Mosaic legislation.

[1] This plan is referred to at vol. ii. p. 328 of the original, vol. iii. p. 192 of the English Translation.—Tr.

TABLE OF CONTENTS

BOOK I

GENERAL BASIS OF THE SACRIFICIAL WORSHIP OF THE OLD TESTAMENT

BOOK II

THE BLEEDING SACRIFICE

PART I

THE RITUAL OF THE SACRIFICE

PART II

VARIETIES OF THE BLEEDING SACRIFICE

BOOK III

THE BLOODLESS SACRIFICE

BOOK IV

MODIFICATION OF THE SACRIFICIAL WORSHIP IN CONNECTION WITH SPECIAL SEASONS AND CIRCUMSTANCES

LIST OF WORKS

MOST FREQUENTLY REFERRED TO

———————◆———————

BÆHR, K. CHR. W. F., *Symbolik des Mosaischen Cultus.* 2 Bde. Heidelb.
    1837, 39.

—— Der salomonische Tempel. Karlsruhe 1848.

BAUMGARTEN, M., Theologischer Commentar zum Pentateuch. Zweiter Bd.
    Kiel 1844.

BUNSEN, CHR. C. J., Vollständiges Bibelwerk. Erster Bd. Leipzig 1858.

DELITZSCH, FR., *Commentar zum Hebräerbrief.* Leipzig 1857.

—— System der biblischen Psychologie. Leipzig 1855.

DIESTEL, Set-Typhon, Asahel und Satan. In Niedner's Zeitschrift für histor.
    Theologie. 1860. Heft ii.

EBRARD, J. H. A., Die Lehre von der stellvertretenden Genugthuung. Königsb.
    1857.

EWALD, H., Die Alterthümer des Volkes Israel. 2. Aufl. Göttingen 1854.

FUERST, J., Hebräisches und Chaldäisches Handwörterbuch. Leipzig 1857 ff.

GESENIUS, Thesaurus philol. crit. linguæ Hebr. et Chald. Lipsiæ 1835 sqq.

HÆVERNICK, Vorlesungen über die Theologie des A. T., herausg. von H. A.
    Hahn. Erlangen 1848.

HENGSTENBERG, E. W., *Die Opfer der heil. Schrift.* Ein Vortrag. Berlin 1852.

—— Das Passa. Evangel. Kirchenzeitung. Jahrg. 1852. No. 16–18.

—— Das Ceremonialgesetz. In his Beiträge zur Einleit. ins A. Test. Bd. iii.
    Berlin 1839. (Dissertations on the Pentateuch, 2 vols. Translated
    by Ryland. Clark 1847.)

—— Die Bücher Mose's und Aegypten. Berlin 1841. (Egypt and the Books
    of Moses. Clark 1845.)

HOFMANN, J. CHR. K. VON, *Der Schriftbeweis.* Zweite Hälfte, erste Abth. 2
    Aufl. Nördlingen 1859.

—— Weissagung und Erfüllung. Nördlingen 1841.

KAHNIS, K. F. A., Lutherische Dogmatik. Bd. i. Leipzig 1862.

KARCH, G., Die mosaischen Opfer als vorbildliche Grundlage der Bitten im Vaterunser. 2 Theile. Würzburg 1856 f.

KEIL, K. FR., *Handbuch der bibl. Archäologie.* Erste Hälfte: Die gottesdienstlichen Verhältnisse der Israeliten. Frankfurt 1858.

—— Die Opfer des A. Bundes nach ihrer symbolischen und typischen Bedeutung. Luth. Zeitschrift 1856, iv., 1857, i. ii. iii.

—— Biblischer Commentar über die Bücher Mose's. Bd. i. Gen. und Exod. Leipzig 1861.

KLIEFOTH, TH., Liturgische Abhandlungen. Bd. iv. Auch u. d. Titel: Die ursprüngl. Gottesdienstordnung u. s. w. Bd. i. 2 Aufl. Schwerin 1858.

KNOBEL, A., *Die Bücher Exodus und Leviticus erklärt.* Leipzig 1857.

—— Die Bücher Numeri, Deuteron. und Josua erklärt. Leipzig 1861.

NEUMANN, W., *Die Opfer des alten Bundes.* Deutsche Zeitschr. für christl. Wissenschaft von Schneider. Jahrg. 1852, 1853.

—— Sacra V. T. Salutaria. Lipsiæ 1854.

OEHLER, *Der Opfercultus des Alten Test.* In Herzog's theolog. Realencyclop. Bd. x. Gotha 1858.

—— Priesterthum im A. Test. Bd. xii. Gotha 1860.

OUTRAM, G., De sacrificiis ll. 2. Amstelod. 1678.

RIEHM, E., Ueber das Schuldopfer. Theol. Studien und Kritiken. 1854.

RINCK, S. W., Ueber das Schuldopfer. Theol. Studien und Kritiken. 1855.

SCHOLL, G. H. F., Ueber die Opferidee der Alten, insbesondere der Juden. In the Studien der evangel. Geistlichkeit Würtembergs. Bd. iv. Heft 1–3. Stuttgart 1832.

SCHULTZ, FR. W., Das Deuteronomium erklärt. Berlin 1859.

SOMMER, J. G., Biblische Abhandlungen. Bd. i. Bonn 1846. Vierte Abhandl.: Rein und Unrein nach dem mosaisch. Gesetze S. 183 ff.

STEUDEL, J. CHR. FR., Vorlesungen über die Theologie des A. Test. herausg. von G. Fr. Oehler. Berlin 1840.

STŒCKL, A., Das Opfer, nach seinem Wesen und seiner Geschichte. Mainz 1860.

THALHOFER, V., Die unblutigen Opfer des mosaischen Cultus. Regensburg 1848.

THOLUCK, A., Das alte Testament im neuen Testament. 5 Aufl. Gotha 1861.

THOMASIUS, G., Christi Person und Werk. Bd. iii. Erlangen 1859.

WELTE, B., Mosaische Opfer. Kirchenlexicon von Wetzer und Welte. Bd. x. Freiburg 1851.

WINER, G. B., Biblisches Realwörterbuch. 2 Bde. Leipzig 1847 f.

SACRIFICIAL WORSHIP

OF

THE OLD TESTAMENT

BOOK I

GENERAL BASIS OF THE SACRIFICIAL WORSHIP OF THE OLD TESTAMENT

S the subject in hand is the sacrificial *worship* of the *Old Testament*, that is to say, of the Israelites before Christ, we have no need to raise the question: *To whom* were the sacrifices presented? By worship (*cultus*) we mean the worship of GOD; and from the very fact that the sacrifices of which we are speaking formed an essential ingredient in the Old Testament worship, they also formed a part of that service which Israel was required to render to its GOD.—A general answer is also thus obtained to the further question: *By whom* were the sacrifices presented? At the same time, we must inquire somewhat minutely into the peculiar position and organization of the Israelitish nation, so far as they affected the worship offered, in order to secure the necessary basis for our investigation of the precise nature of the sacrificial worship of the Old Testament. With this we shall also have to connect an inquiry into the nature and importance of the *place* in which the sacrifices were presented, since this affected the sacrificial worship in various ways. And, lastly, we shall also have to discuss the questions: *What* was sacrifice, and what were the different *modes* of sacrificing?—In this introductory part, therefore, we shall have to treat: 1. Of the persons sacrificing; 2. Of the place of sacrifice; and 3. Of the different varieties of sacrifice. We shall take them in the order thus given, for the simple reason that the arrangement of the place of sacrifice was affected by the organization of the persons sacrificing, and the varieties of sacrifice were affected by them both.

CHAPTER I

THE PERSONS SACRIFICING

A. THE PEOPLE

§ 1. When Jehovah had delivered His chosen people Israel (His "first-born," Ex. iv. 22) out of the bondage of Egypt, and brought them as on eagles' wings to Sinai—the eternal altar erected for that purpose at the creation of the world, where He was about to renew the covenant, which He had made with the fathers of this people, with their descendants who were now a great nation, and to establish them on a firm and immovable foundation by giving them His law,—He first directed His servant Moses (Ex. xix. 4–6) to lay before the people the *preliminaries* of that law, in which the future calling of Israel was declared to be this : to be *Jehovah's possession before all nations*, and as such to be a *kingdom of priests* and a *holy nation.*

This expressed, on the *negative* side, the selection and separation of Israel from all other nations, and its obligation to be unlike them ; and on the *positive* side, its obligation to belong to Jehovah alone, to be holy, because and as He Himself is holy (Lev. xix. 2), and in all it did and left undone throughout its entire history, to act in subservience to the saving designs of Jehovah, as the only way by which it could become the medium of salvation to all nations (Gen. xii. 3, xxviii. 14).[1]

In the destination of Israel to be peculiarly "a kingdom of priests," so that the whole nation was to consist of nothing but priests, it was distinctly taught that every Israelite was to bear a priestly character, and to possess and exercise the specific privileges and duties of the priesthood. But it was soon manifest that Israel, as then constituted, and in the existing stage of the history of sal-

---

[1] For a thorough and careful examination of the contents of these preliminaries of the covenant, see History of the Old Covenant, vol. iii. pp. 102 sqq. (translation).

vation, was not in a condition to enter at once upon its priestly vocation, and fulfil its priestly work of conveying salvation to the rest of the nations. For it speedily furnished a practical proof of its unfitness even for the first and most essential preliminary to this vocation, viz., that it should draw near to Jehovah, and hold personal and immediate intercourse with Him (Num. xvi. 5), by turning round and hurrying away in terror and alarm when it was led up to the sacred mountain, and Jehovah descended amidst thunder and lightning, and proclaimed to the assembled congregation out of the fire and blackness of the mountain the ten fundamental words of the covenant law. On that occasion they said to Moses (Ex. xx. 19), " Speak thou with us, and we will hear ; but let not God speak with us, lest we die" (cf. Deut. v. 22 sqq.). By these words they renounced the great privilege of the priesthood, that of drawing near to God, and holding personal and immediate intercourse with Him. With their consciousness of unholiness, they felt that they were not ripe or qualified for entering upon the fulness of their priestly vocation. They felt rather that they needed a mediator themselves to carry on their intercourse with God. The designs of God Himself with reference to the covenant had from the very first contemplated this (Ex. xx. 20) ; but it was necessary that the people themselves should discover and clearly discern, that for the time it could not be otherwise. Jehovah therefore expressed His approval of the people's words (Deut. v. 28, " They have well said all that they have spoken") ; and from that time forth Moses was formally appointed on both sides as the mediator of the covenant for the period of its first establishment and early development in the giving of the law, and at a later period the family of his brother Aaron was called and set apart by the law itself as a permanent priesthood for the priestly nation.

But even after thus declining the specific work of the priesthood, Israel still remained the holy, chosen nation, which was not to be like other nations, but holy, as Jehovah is holy. It continued to be the possession of Jehovah above all nations ; and it still stood out as a priest of God, distinct from them in life and conduct, in the possession of divine revelation, of divine institutions, and of the means of salvation, as well as in the calling to become the vehicle of salvation to all mankind. The qualifications for this calling it first truly received through the conclusion of the covenant and its consecration at Sinai. And even the idea of the universal priesthood of the whole nation, however much ground it had lost by the temporary demands of a separate priesthood, retained enough to preserve its hold upon the consciousness of the people, and to point their longing hopes to the time of fulfilment, when they should enter upon the full (active) possession of all the privileges and blessings of the universal priesthood (1 Pet. ii. 5, 9).

§ 2. Birth from Israelitish parents secured to the new-born child a claim to be received into the membership of the covenant nation, but did not confer, or even guarantee, membership itself. On the contrary, a special act of initiation was necessary, viz., the rite of CIRCUMCISION (מוּלָה), which was also performed upon every stranger who desired to forsake heathenism and to be incorporated into the covenant nation (Gen. xvii. 27, xxxiv. 14 sqq.; Ex. xii. 43, 44). Circumcision had been instituted as a sign and seal of that covenant which God concluded with Abraham (Gen. xvii. 10–14). But as the Sinaitic covenant was neither an absolutely new one, nor essentially different from the one which God had previously concluded with the father of the nation, but was simply the renewal of that covenant as the basis of their national existence, the same covenant initiation and covenant seal was still retained for every individual, as that by which Abraham first entered into the covenant when he was called "alone" (Isa. li. 2).

As circumcision comes only so far into consideration in connection with the sphere of religious worship, that it attested the fact of membership in the covenant nation, and on that account was the *conditio sine qua non* of participation in certain sacrificial acts; an inquiry into the origin, essence, and significance of this institution would lead us too far away from our present object; and there is the less necessity for it here on account of what we have already written on the question (Hist. of the Old Covenant, vol. i. pp. 231 sqq. translation).[1]

But there were many NON-ISRAELITES (גֵּרִים) living in the land of Israel, for whose condition care was taken to make provision even in the earliest code of laws (viz., that contained in the middle books

---

[1] *Keil's* objections to my remarks, in his Bibl. Archäologie i. 311, do not really touch them ; and they are the more surprising, since his own explanation ("Its significance lay in the religious idea, that the corruption of sin brought into human nature by the fall was concentrated in the organ of generation, inasmuch as it is generally in the sexual life that it comes out most strongly; and, therefore, the first thing necessary for the sanctification of life is the purification or sanctification of the organ by which life is propagated") coincides so exactly with the first part of the results of my inquiry, that it might be called a brief summary of them.

of the Pentateuch). If they would allow themselves to be formally and fully incorporated into the covenant nation by receiving circumcision, a perfect equality with the Israelite by birth was guaranteed to them by the law in both religious and political privileges (Ex. xii. 48). They then ceased to be foreigners. At any rate, there can be no doubt that when we read in the Thorah of "the stranger that is within thy gates," or "in the midst of thee," etc., we have invariably to think of uncircumcised settlers, or foreigners who had not been naturalized. The rule with respect to their civil position is laid down in the fundamental principle, "One law shall be to him that is home-born, and unto the stranger that sojourneth among you" (Ex. xii. 49, cf. Lev. xxiv. 22 and Num. xv. 15, 16). And since they had, as strangers, no relations to fall back upon, they were urgently commended in Deuteronomy to the especial protection of the authorities, in common with widows and orphans; and because they had no inheritance in the holy land, and could not even acquire landed property, they were to be admitted to the festal and tithing meals along with the poor of the nation (Ex. xii. 48; Num. ix. 14; Deut. xiv. 28, 29, xvi. 10 sqq., xxvi. 11 sqq.), and were to share with them in the gleaning of the vintage, the fruit-gathering, and the harvest, and in the produce of the sabbatical year (Lev. xix. 10, xxiii. 22, xxv. 6; Deut. xxiv. 19 sqq.).

In return for these privileges, they were required, on the other hand, to submit to certain restrictions. For example, they were to abstain from everything which was an abomination to the Israelites, and consequently to renounce all idolatry, the eating of blood, etc. (Ex. xii. 19, xx. 10; Lev. xvi. 29, xvii. 8 sqq., xviii. 26, xx. 2, xxiv. 16 sqq.; Num. xv. 13 sqq.; Deut. v. 14); they were also to fast along with the Israelites on the great day of atonement (Lev. xvi. 29), and to keep the Sabbath as strictly as they (Ex. xx. 10, xxiii. 12). Their relation to the sacrificial worship was restricted to this, that they were allowed to offer all kinds of sacrifice to Jehovah (burnt-offerings, and peace- (or thank-) offerings, according to Lev. xvii. 8, xxii. 18, 25; and, according to Num. xv. 29, even sin-offerings also, as circumstances required), and to participate in the blessings which the sacrifice secured. They could take no part in the Passover without previous circumcision (Ex. xii. 48). But admission to the ordinary sacrificial worship at the tabernacle, was a necessary correlative to the unconditional law against serving and sacrificing to their former gods whilst in Jehovah's land.

§ 3. While the Israelite was thus marked and sealed in his own body as belonging to the covenant nation, the principle of separation from heathenism,[1] or the duty not to be as the heathen, was also symbolically manifested in other departments, chiefly in his daily food, but also to some extent in his CLOTHING (Num. xv. 38–40, cf. Lev. xix. 19 and Deut. xxii. 11). But as there is not the slightest connection between the latter and the sacrificial worship, it would be out of place to enter into any closer examination of the laws relating to that subject. There is all the more reason, however, why we should carefully examine the restrictions placed upon the Israelites in relation to their FOOD, inasmuch as they lay, on the one hand, at the foundation of the legal enactments with reference to the sacrificial worship, and were, on the other hand, the necessary result of the fundamental idea of that worship.

The former applies to the division of the *animal kingdom* into CLEAN and UNCLEAN; the Israelites being allowed to eat of the clean, whilst the unclean was prohibited (cf. Lev. xi.; Deut. xiv.). On the basis of the old Hebrew division of the animal kingdom into four parts, the law selects from the class of *land animals*, as clean or edible, none but those which ruminate and have also cloven feet, and pronounces all the rest unclean. The principal animals selected as *clean* are the ox, the sheep, the goat, and the various species of stags, and gazelles or antelopes; and as *unclean*, the camel, the hare, the badger, and the swine. Among *fishes*, the distinguishing characteristic of the clean is, that they have fins and scales; so that all smooth, eel-like fishes are excluded. In the case of the *birds*, there is no general rule laid down, but the unclean are mentioned by name,—nineteen kinds in Leviticus, and twenty-one (3×7) in Deuteronomy. The first heptad embraces the carnivorous and carrion birds,—eagles, vultures, ravens, etc.; the second, the ostrich and the different species of owls; the third, nothing but marsh-birds, and the bat. Of the fourth class, or the so-called

---

[1] Since circumcision was a sign and attestation of membership in the covenant nation, the importance of separation and distinction from heathenism was *eo ipso* expressed by it. It is true, this seems at variance with the fact that, according to Herodotus, the Colchians, Egyptians, and Ethiopians also practised circumcision. But among these nations circumcision was not a universal or national custom; for, according to Origen, it was only the priests in Egypt who submitted to it, and, according to Clemens Alex., only the priests and those who were initiated into the mysteries. In any case, the distinction between circumcised and uncircumcised in the Old Testament is uniformly equivalent to that between Israelites and non-Israelites (see *instar omnium*, Jer. ix. 25, 26).

swarming animals (שֶׁרֶץ), four species of locusts are the only exceptions to the universal sentence of uncleanness.

The distinction between clean and unclean animals, with the
command to abstain from eating the flesh of the latter, was never
merely a civil or medical arrangement, based upon sanitary considerations, in any of the nations in which it prevailed, and least of
all among the Hebrews. Such measures as these would have been
altogether foreign to the spirit of ancient legislation. Moreover,
the obligation to observe them was invariably enforced as a religious
duty, and never upon civil grounds. But to smuggle in laws of a
purely material and utilitarian tendency under the hypocritical
name of religious duties, for the mere purpose of facilitating their
entrance and securing a more spirited observance, would have
been a course altogether opposed to the spirit of antiquity, which
was far too naïf, too reckless and unreserved, to do anything of the
kind;—whilst the opposite course, of upholding religious duties by
political commands, is met with on every hand.

But the question as to the reason why certain animals were pronounced clean, and certain others unclean, is a somewhat different
one. This may undoubtedly be traceable to sanitary or other similar
considerations, lying outside the sphere of religion. The actual or
supposed discovery, that the flesh of certain animals was uneatable
or prejudicial to health, and a natural repugnance to many animals,
which sometimes could, and at other times could not, be explained,
may no doubt have been the original reason for abhorring or refusing
them as food. And if, either subsequently or at the same time,
some religious motive led to the establishment of a distinction among
animals between clean and unclean, *i.e.*, between eatable and not
eatable, nothing would be more natural than that all those animals,
whose flesh was avoided for the physical or psychical reasons
assigned, should be placed in the category of unclean, and that the
eating of them, which from the *one* point of view appeared to be
merely prejudicial to health, or repulsive and disgusting to natural
feelings, should, from the *other* point of view, be prohibited as sinful
and displeasing to God.

In heathenism there were two ways, varying according to the
different starting points, by which a distinction of a religious character might have been established in the animal world between clean
and unclean. *Dualism*, the characteristic peculiarity of which was
to trace the origin of one portion of creation to an evil principle,
whether passing by the name of Ahriman, Typhon, or anything

else, necessarily included in this category all noxious animals, and
such as excited horror or disgust, and prohibited the eating of them
as bringing the eater into association with the evil principle; and
Pantheism, which regards all life in nature as the progressive
development and externalization of the absolute Deity, necessarily regarded all noxious and repulsive objects in the animal creation as a deterioration of the divine life, and avoided them in
consequence.

But both these views are far removed from the Monotheism of
Israel, which recognised neither a dualism of world-creating principles, nor a self-development of God assuming shape in noxious or
disgusting forms of life, but only one holy God, who, by virtue of
His omnipotence, and in accordance with His wisdom, created the
world, and all that is therein, both good and holy. Yet even the
Monotheist could not deny the dualism of good and evil, noxious
and salutary, repulsive and attractive, ugly and beautiful, which
actually exists in the world. Moreover, his revelation taught him,
that degradation and corruption had penetrated, through the curse
of sin, into the world which God created good and holy (Gen. iii.
17, v. 29, ix. 5); and he could discern therein, not only the consequence and the curse, but also the image and reflection, of his own
sinful condition.

When the Israelites were commanded, by their own revealed
law, not to eat of the flesh of certain animals, but to avoid it as
unclean, the supposition is certainly a very natural one, that the
animals designated as unclean were those in which the consequences
or the reflection of human sinfulness and degradation were most
evidently and sharply defined, and that the command to avoid eating their flesh as an unclean and abominable thing, was intended to
remind and warn them of their own sin, and their own moral and
natural corruption; so that the real tendency of the laws of food
was so far a moral and religious one, resting upon a *symbolical*
foundation. And this is the most generally received opinion in
relation to the Mosaic laws of food.[1]

[1] The latest writer on Biblical Antiquities, *Dr Keil*, has nevertheless confounded the realist with the symbolical points of view. He says (vol. ii. p. 20),
" This distinction was based upon a certain intuitive feeling, awakened by the
insight of man into the nature of animals, and their appointment for him, before
that intuition had been disturbed by unnatural and ungodly culture. For as
the innate consciousness of God was changed, in consequence of sin, into a voice
of God in the conscience, warning and convicting him of sin and unrighteousness; so this voice of God operated in such a way upon his relation to the earthly

But these ideas, which generally and naturally suggest themselves, are not borne out, either by the specific marks of cleanness
and uncleanness mentioned in the law, or by the nature and character
of the animals specially designated as clean or unclean, or, lastly,
by the explanations of the lawgiver himself. To give only one or
two examples : Why should so useful, patient, obedient, and enduring an animal as the camel be better fitted to serve as a symbolical
representation of human sinfulness than the stubborn ox, or the
lustful, stinking goat? why the timid hare, more than the timid
antelope? or why the terribly destructive locusts less than so
many other kinds of the great mass of insects (*Sherez*)? And why
should the want of rumination and of a thoroughly cloven hoof—
the marks by which the uncleanness of the land animals was to be
recognised—exhibit so decided a picture of human sin, that every
animal not possessing these two marks was at once to be pronounced
unclean?

Moreover—and this is the most important fact—we never find
any such reason brought forward in the law, nor even remotely

creation, and especially to the animal creation, that many animals stood before
his eyes as types of sin and corruption, and filled his mind with repugnance and
disgust. It was not till after the further degradation and obscuration of his
consciousness of God that this repugnance became distorted in various ways
among many tribes, and along with this distortion the ability to select animals
as food, in a manner befitting the vocation of man, became lost as well. But,
for the purpose of bringing the human race back to God, the Mosaic law sought
to sharpen the perception of the nature of sin, and of that disorder which sin
had introduced into nature universally ; and to that end it brought out the distinction between clean and unclean animals, partly according to general signs,
and partly by special enumeration . . . , but without our being able by means
of our own reflection to discern and point out, in each particular instance, either
the reason for the prohibition, or the exact feature in which the ancients discovered a symbol of sin and abomination."—But to this it may be replied, that
if it was " the innate consciousness of God," the " voice of God " within him,
which first of all filled " the mind of man with repugnance and disgust" at the
unclean animals ; and if " this repugnance became distorted in various ways
among many tribes, in consequence of the further degradation and obscuration
of their consciousness of God ;" and if, " through unnatural and ungodly culture," the " intuition into the nature of animals and their appointment for man
was disturbed ;" or if, on the other hand, the original " selection of the clean
animals," which was restored by the Mosaic law " for the purpose of bringing
the human race back to God," was actually the " *proper* " one, in fact the one
" befitting *man's* vocation ;" it is difficult to understand how the Apostles could
feel themselves warranted in entirely abolishing the distinction between clean
and unclean animals,—not to mention any of the other objections to this mistaken view.

hinted at as the determining cause; whilst, on the contrary, a totally different reason is given in Lev. xx. 24–26 in clear and unmistakeable words. Thus in ver. 25 we read: "I am Jehovah your God, which have separated you from the nations. Ye shall therefore distinguish between clean beasts and unclean, and between unclean birds and clean; and ye shall not make your souls abominable by beast, or by bird, or by any manner of living thing that creepeth on the ground, which I have separated for you as unclean."—The leading thought in these laws of food, therefore, was *this*: because, and as, Jehovah had separated Israel from the nations; therefore, and so, Israel was to separate the clean animals from the unclean. Israel was thus to be reminded by its daily food, of the goodness of God in choosing it from among the nations, of its peculiar calling and destination, and of its consequent obligation not to be as the heathen were. The choice of clean animals for the sustenance of the natural life, was to typify in the sphere of nature, what had taken place among men through the selection and vocation of Israel: the heathen nations being represented by the unclean animals, and Israel by the clean. The fundamental idea of the Mosaic laws of food, therefore, was not *ethical*, but *historical*, having regard to the *history of salvation*.

The strongest confirmation is given to this view by the vision which Peter saw (Acts x. 10 sqq.), and which was intended to set before his mind the fact, that in Christianity the difference and opposition between heathen and Jews was entirely removed; so that the Apostle Paul was able to write to the Colossians (chap. ii. 16, 17): "Let no man therefore judge you in meat or in drink . . . . , which are a shadow of things to come; but the body is of Christ."

The circumstance that in the Mosaic law the vegetable kingdom is not divided into clean and unclean, as it is among other nations, but the animal kingdom alone, is to be explained on the ground that the sphere of animal life is the higher of the two, the one nearer to that of humanity, and therefore better adapted to exhibit relations and contrasts in the world of men; whereas in heathenism the distinction rested upon totally different (viz., physico-theological) principles, and therefore analogies could be found in the vegetable as well as in the animal world.

§ 4. But the discovery of the fundamental idea upon which the general symbolism of this question rests, by no means solves all the problems presented by the particular details. The question still remains to be answered, in cases where general signs are laid down as distinguishing clean from unclean, why the animals in which such signs were observed should be selected as clean, and all the rest pronounced unclean. *W. Schultz*, in his Commentary on Deuteronomy, expresses the opinion, that "it is easy to see that these signs were not in themselves the decisive marks of clean and unclean, but were abstracted after the distinction had been settled on other grounds;"—in other words, that in themselves they had no significance whatever. But how it is easy to see this, he has not informed us. There can be no question, indeed, that when the Israelitish lawgiver selected these signs, the custom already existed of avoiding the eating of the flesh of certain animals as injurious, repulsive, or disgusting; and from this he no doubt abstracted the common marks, that were henceforth to be the distinguishing signs of clean and unclean. But even then it may be asked, on the one hand, why he chose these particular marks as the criterion, rather than others which could be detected just as easily, and even presented themselves unsought;—why, for example, in the case of quadrupeds, he merely fixed upon rumination and cloven feet, and not also, or indeed primarily, upon the possession of horns, which would be the very first thing to strike the eye. There is the less reason for setting aside the omission of this sign as merely accidental and unimportant, from the fact, that the ancient Egyptians, among whom Moses had grown up and received his education, selected the want of horns as the leading sign of uncleanness in the case of quadrupeds (*Porphyr. de abst.* 4, 7). The circumstance, therefore, that Moses fixed upon rumination and a thoroughly divided hoof as the signs of cleanness, and not the possession of horns, is an evident proof that he must have had his own special reasons for doing so; and, with the wide-spread predominance of symbolism in all that concerned the worship of God, these reasons must be sought for in their symbolical significance: consequently, rumination and a thoroughly cloven foot must have possessed a symbolical worth which horns did not possess, in relation to the fundamental idea of the distinction to be made. But, on the other hand, it is quite conceivable, and even probable, that through the adoption of these marks of cleanness, which were taken from the leading representatives of the different classes of animals ordinarily used for food, certain animals may have been excluded, which would not have been placed in the category of the unclean, if sanitary, physical, or psychical considerations alone had prevailed. Thus, for example, pork and the flesh of the camel were eaten by other Eastern nations with great relish, and without the least hesitation.

If we examine the distinctive marks pointed out by the lawgiver, we shall see at once, that they all relate either to the *food* eaten by the animals, or to their mode of *locomotion*, or to both together. In the case of the *land animals*, as being the most perfect, this is particularly obvious; and here the two signs coincide. With the *water animals*, the question of food, which is brought less under the notice of man, is passed over, and that of locomotion is the only distinction referred to. Even in the case of the other two classes of animals, which are not indicated by any general signs, the questions of food and motion are evidently taken into consideration. With the *birds*, the food is clearly the decisive point, except that here it was impossible to point out any peculiarities in the *organs* of nutriment, which would be at the same time both universally applicable and symbolically significant. For similar reasons, the movements of the birds could not be adduced as furnishing marks of universal distinction. In the case of the *fourth class*, the infinite variety of species included, made it impossible to discover distinctive marks that should be universally applicable. At the same time, the name שֶׁרֶץ, *i.e.*, *swarmers*, leads to the conclusion, that their general movements were taken into consideration, as furnishing a common ground of exclusion.

The selection of food and locomotion as the leading grounds of separation in the case of every class, is by no means difficult to explain. For it is precisely in these two functions that the stage of animal life is most obviously and completely distinguished from that of vegetable life, and approaches or is homogeneous with that of man.

If, then, as Lev. xx. 24 sqq. unquestionably shows, the separation of the clean animals from the unclean was a type of the selection of Israel from among the nations ; and if, therefore, the clean animals represented the chosen, holy nation, and the unclean the heathen world, as the figurative language of the prophets so often implies; the marks and signs by which the clean and unclean animals were to be distinguished, must also be looked at from a symbolical point of view ;—in other words, the marks which distinguished the clean animals from the unclean, and characterized the former *as* clean, must have been a *corporeal* type of that by which Israel was distinguished, or at least ought to have been distinguished, *spiritually* from the heathen world. The allusion, therefore, was to the spiritual food and spiritual walk of Israel, which were to be consecrated and sanctified, and separated from all that was displeasing and hostile to God in the conduct of the heathen.

What we are to understand by *spiritual walk*, needs no demonstration: it is walking before the face of God—a firm, sure step in the pilgrim road of life. *Spiritual food* is just as undoubtedly the reception of that which sustains and strengthens the spiritual life, *i.e.*, of divine revelation, of which Christ says (John iv. 34), "My meat is to do the will of Him that sent Me." The two functions stand to one another in the relation of receptivity and spontaneity.

Let us apply this to the land animals. The first thing mentioned is their chewing the cud. Now, if this is to be regarded as a figurative representation of a spiritual function; if, for example, it is symbolical of spiritual sustenance through the word of God; the meaning cannot be better described than it is in Josh. i. 8: "This book of the law shall not depart out of thy mouth, but thou shalt meditate therein day and night, that thou mayest observe to do according to all that is written therein."—In the importance attached to the cloven hoof, this fact must have been taken into consideration, that the tread of animals so provided is surer and firmer than that of animals with the hoof whole. And no proof need be given of the frequency with which reference is made in the Scriptures to the slipping of the feet, or to a firm, sure step in a spiritual sense (*e.g.*, Ps. xxxvii. 31; Prov. v. 6; Heb. xii. 13, etc.).—For the birds no general marks of cleanness or uncleanness are given. But the determining point of view is nevertheless perfectly obvious. For example, all birds of prey are excluded, and generally all birds that devour living animals or carrion, or any other kind of unclean and disgusting food, as being fit representatives of the heathen world. In the case of the animals in the third and fourth classes, the common point which is placed in the foreground as distinguishing the unclean, is the singularity—so to speak, the abnormal and unnatural character—of their motion: their disagreeable velocity, their terrible habit of swarming, etc.

§ 5. The other *prohibitions of food* contained in the Mosaic law are based upon different principles, and are to be explained on the ground that the food forbidden was regarded either as *too holy*, or as *too unholy*, to be eaten;—the former on account of its relation to the sacrificial worship, the latter on account of its association with the defilement of death and corruption. The former alone comes under notice here. To this category belong the *blood* and the *fat* of animals. But so far as the fat is concerned, it must be remarked at the outset, that only the actual lobes or nets of fat, which envelope the intestines, the kidneys, and the liver (Lev. iii. 3, 4, 9, 10, 14, 15), are intended, not the fat which intersects the *flesh;* and also, that, according to Lev. vii. 23, this prohibition relates exclusively to the portions of fat alluded to in oxen, sheep, and goats, not to that of any other edible animals.

For the prohibition of the EATING OF BLOOD, Lev. xvii. 10 sqq. is the *locus classicus.* In ver. 11, a triple reason is assigned for the prohibition: (1.) "For the soul of the flesh is in the blood;" (2.) "And I have given it upon the altar to make an atonement for your souls;" (3.) "For the blood, it maketh atonement by means of the soul." According to *Delitzsch (Bibl. Psychol.* 196), the prohibition has a double ground here: "The blood has the soul in it, and through the gracious appointment of God it is the means of atonement for human souls, by virtue of the soul contained within it. One reason lies in the nature of the blood, and the other in the consecration of it to a holy purpose, by which, even apart from the other ground, it was removed from common use." But *Keil* opposes this. "It is not to the soul of animals as such," he says, "as the seat of a principle of animal life, that the prohibition applies, but to the soul as the means of atonement set apart by God" (*Biblische Archäologie* 1, 23). But if *Keil* were correct in saying (p. 24) that "in Lev. xvii. 11 the first two clauses do not assign two independent reasons for the prohibition, but merely the two factors of the foundation for the third clause, which contains the one sole ground upon which the prohibition is based" (which I do not admit, however); and if in Gen. ix. 4 ("but flesh in (with) the soul thereof, the blood thereof, ye shall not eat") the one sole reason for the prohibition were not the fact that the blood itself is animated, but its fitness as a means of atonement (which I am still less able to allow); even then the correctness of *Delitzsch's* opinion would be beyond all doubt, and that for the very reason which has led *Keil* to oppose it. For example, he adds (p. 23): "This is *clearly* evident from the parallel command in relation to the *fat* of oxen, sheep, and goats, or the cattle of which men offer an offering by fire unto the Lord (Lev. vii. 23, 25). This fat was not to be eaten any more than the blood, on pain of extermination (Lev. vii. 25, 27, xvii. 10, 13), either by the Israelites or by the strangers living with Israel." But *Keil* would not have spoken with such confidence if he had placed the relation between these two prohibitions (the eating of blood and of fat) clearly before his mind.

Even in the law of Leviticus (chap. vii. 23 sqq.) we find a very significant distinction between the prohibition of the eating of blood on the one hand, and that of fat on the other, which *Keil* has quite overlooked. According to Lev. vii. 23, it is only the fat of oxen, sheep, and goats that may not be eaten; the fat of other edible animals, therefore, such as stags, antelopes, etc., is not forbidden. But the prohibition of blood, instead of being restricted to that of oxen, sheep, and goats, extends to the blood of all animals without exception (ver. 26). Whence this distinction? The answer is to be found in ver. 25 : the fat of the oxen, sheep, and goats was not to be eaten, because it was to be offered as a fire-offering to Jehovah, *i.e.*, was to be burnt upon the altar. To understand this, it must be borne in mind that, according to the law of Leviticus, which was drawn up primarily with regard to the sojourn in the desert, the slaughter of *every* ox, sheep, or goat, even if it were only slain for domestic consumption, was to be looked at in the light of a peace- (or thank-) offering (Lev. xvii. 3–5) : hence *every* such slaughter was to take place at the sanctuary, the blood of the animal slain was to be sprinkled upon the altar, and the fat to be burned there also. The eating of fat, consequently, was prohibited only *because* and *so far* as it was to be offered to Jehovah; so that the fat of stags, antelopes, etc., might be eaten without hesitation.—It was altogether different with the law against eating blood. In this case there was no restriction or exception at all : no blood whatever was to be eaten, whether the animal from which it flowed were sacrificed or not sacrificed, sacrificial or not sacrificial. From this it necessarily follows, that the reason for prohibiting blood cannot have been the same as that for prohibiting fat. Had the prohibition of blood rested *merely* upon the importance of blood as a means of atonement; then, according to the analogy of the prohibition of fat, the blood of those animals only should have been forbidden, which really were offered as atoning sacrifices. But as it related to the blood of all animals, even to those that were neither sacrificed nor sacrificial, the principal reason for this prohibition must have been one entirely unconnected with the sacrificial worship. What it was, is clearly shown in Gen. ix. 4 and Lev. xvii. 11 : " For the soul of the flesh is in the blood."

That this is the correct view, is also evident from the parallel commands in the second law contained in Deuteronomy (Deut. xii.).

According to the law of Leviticus, the slaughter of an ox, sheep, or goat was to be carried out in every case like a sacrificial slaughter, and for that reason the eating of the fat of such animals was unconditionally forbidden.[1] The law in Deuteronomy, however, abrogated this command, as being unsuitable and impracticable in the Holy Land, especially for those who dwelt at a distance from the tabernacle, and allowed them at their pleasure to slay and eat oxen, sheep, and goats at their own homes, as well as antelopes or stags (Deut. xii. 15, 16, 20–24). But in the case of such private slaughtering, the blood was not sprinkled on the altar, nor was the fat burned upon the altar. As a matter of course, therefore, the command not to eat of the fat of the slaughtered animals was abrogated also;—and this is indicated with even superfluous emphasis by the repetition of the statement, that they might eat them like the hart and the roebuck (vers. 15, 22), of which they were never forbidden to eat the fat. But the eating of blood, whether the blood of oxen, sheep, and goats, or that of the roebuck and stag, remained as unconditionally forbidden as ever. Twice is it emphatically stated (vers. 16 and 24), that even in private slaughterings the blood was not to be eaten, but poured upon the earth like water. What *Keil* regards as the only reason for the prohibition, namely, the appointment of the blood as the means of expiation, was as much wanting here in the slaughtering of such animals as it had formerly been in that of the roebuck and stag. If, then, for all that, the law against eating blood still remained in its utmost stringency even in the case of private slaughterings, whether the animals in question

---

[1] *Keil* gives a different explanation (pp. 24, 25). "From the fact," he says, "that the general command in Lev. vii. 23, 'Ye shall eat no manner of fat of ox, of sheep, or of goat,' is more minutely expounded in ver. 25, 'Whosoever eateth the fat of the beast of which men offer an offering made by fire unto the Lord,' it seems pretty evidently to follow, that the fat of the ox, sheep, and goat, which was burned upon the altar when they were sacrificed, might be eaten in those cases in which the animal was merely slaughtered as food." But *Keil* has overlooked what he himself has stated two lines before; namely, that according to Lev. xvii. 3 sqq., the slaughter of such animals was to be regarded in *every* case as a *sacrificial* slaughter, and therefore, that instead of his view following "pretty evidently" from Lev. vii. 25, it is perfectly evident that the very opposite follows. So that, when *Keil* adds, that "in any case the inference drawn by *Knobel* from Lev. vii. 24 is untenable, viz., that in the case of oxen, sheep, and goats, slaughtered in the ordinary way, this (the application of the fat to ordinary use) was evidently not allowable;" it is obvious that it is not *Knobel's* inference, but *Keil's* condemnation of that inference, which is in any case untenable.

were adapted for sacrifice or not, it is evident that any reason for
such a law, based upon the appointment of blood as a means of
expiation, can only have been a partial and secondary one. There
must have been some other reason, and that a primary one, of
universal applicability; and this is indicated again in the second
giving of the law, viz., the nature of the blood as the seat of the
soul (ver. 23): "For the blood, it is the soul; and thou mayest not
eat the soul with the flesh." There is not the slightest allusion
here, any more than in Gen. ix. 4, to any connection between the
prohibition in question and the appointment of the blood as the
means of expiation, which was applicable only to animals actually
sacrificed, and to them simply *as sacrificed*.

We must maintain therefore, in direct opposition to *Keil*, that
it was to the *soul* of the animals expressly, as the seat or principle
of animal life, that the prohibition applied as a universal rule. In
the case of the blood of the sacrifices, it was merely enforced with
greater stringency, but had still the same reference to the soul as
a means of expiation sanctified by God. In Lev. xvii. 11, both
reasons are given; because, as the context shows, it is to the *sacrificial* blood that allusion is primarily made. But in what follows,
from ver. 13 onwards, the prohibition is extended from sacrificial
blood to blood of every kind, even that of animals that could not be
offered in sacrifice; and this extension of the prohibition is based
solely upon the nature of the blood as the seat of the soul (ver. 14),
and not upon the fact of its having been appointed as the means of
expiation.

B. THE PRIESTS

§ 6. Previous to the giving of the law, the priesthood in the
chosen family, just as in other kindred tribes, was not confined to
particular individuals; but the head of the family discharged the
priestly functions connected with the service of God, for himself
and his family (Gen. viii. 20 sqq.; Job i. 5). For this purpose,
Abraham, Isaac, and Jacob built altars in the different places
where they sojourned, and chiefly upon those spots in which Jehovah
had appeared to them; and there they offered sacrifices, and cleansed
and consecrated their households (Gen. xii. 7, xiii. 18, xxvi. 25,
xxxiii. 20, xxxv. 1, 2). On the institution of the paschal sacrifice
in Egypt, the father of every family discharged the priestly functions connected with that sacrifice (Ex. xii. 7, 22). After the

exodus from Egypt, all the priestly as well as princely authority culminated in the person of Moses. The hereditary priesthood of the heads of families was not abolished in consequence, any more than their princely rank (Ex. xix. 22, 24); but in Moses they both culminated in one individual head. It was in consequence of the request made by the people themselves to Moses (Ex. xx. 19), " Speak thou with us, and we will hear, but let not God speak with us, lest we die," and the divine approval of that request, that the priestly qualifications and duties were transferred from the people, and their representatives the elders, to Moses alone. At the completion of the covenant, therefore, we find Moses alone officiating as priest (Ex. xxiv. 6, cf. § 162 sqq.). But Moses could not possibly discharge all the priestly functions required by the congregation. On the contrary, his other duties already engrossed his whole time and strength; consequently he was allowed to divest himself of the priestly office as soon as the covenant was concluded, and to transfer it to his brother *Aaron*, who was then ordained, along with his sons Nadab and Abihu, Eleazar and Ithamar, as an hereditary priesthood. After the erection of the tabernacle they were duly consecrated and installed (Ex. xxviii. cf. § 165 sqq.).

But when preparation was made for removing from Sinai, the necessity was immediately felt for a considerable increase in the number of persons officiating in the worship of God. The tabernacle had to be taken down; all the different parts, as well as the various articles of furniture, had to be carried from place to place ; at every fresh encampment it had to be set up again : and for all this a very large number of chosen and consecrated hands were required. To this service, therefore, all the other members of the tribe to which Aaron belonged were set apart, viz., the tribe of *Levi*, —comprising the three families of the Kohathites, the Gershonites, and the Merarites. Henceforth, therefore, this tribe was removed from its co-ordinate position by the side of the other tribes, and was appointed and consecrated to the service of the sanctuary, that is to say, to the performance of all such duties connected with the tabernacle as were not included in the peculiar province of the priestly office, which still continued to be the exclusive prerogative of the family of Aaron (Num. i. 49-51, iii. 6-10, viii. 5-22).

After the sparing of the first-born in the night of the exodus from Egypt, they became the peculiar possession of Jehovah ; and consequently they ought properly to have been the persons selected for life-long service in the sanctuary. But for the purpose of giving greater compactness and unity to the *personnel* employed, the Levites and their descendants took their place (Num. iii. 12, 13, viii. 16–19). It was necessary, however, before this was done, that all the first-born should be redeemed by means of certain specially appointed sacrifices, and gifts to the tabernacle (cf. § 229).

In this way the persons officially engaged in the worship were divided into three stages. The lowest stage was occupied by such of the LEVITES as were not priests, who acted merely as attendants and menial servants. On a higher stage stood the Aaronites, as the true PRIESTS. And lastly, Aaron himself, and subsequently the successive heads of the family (according to the right of primo-geniture), represented as HIGH PRIEST, הַכֹּהֵן הַגָּדוֹל, the point of unity and the culminating point of all the priestly duties and privileges.

§ 7. What notion the Hebrew formed of the *priesthood*, cannot be determined with any certainty from the name כֹּהֵן, since the primary meaning of the root כהן is doubtful and disputed. On the other hand, Moses clearly describes the nature of the priesthood in Num. xvi. 5. On the occasion of the rebellion of the Korahites against the restriction of the priestly prerogatives to the family of Aaron, he announces to them, " To-morrow Jehovah will show who is His, and who is holy, that He may suffer him to come near unto Him; and whom He shall choose, him will He suffer to come near unto Him." There are four characteristics of the priesthood indicated here. The *first* is *election by Jehovah*, as distinguished both from wilful self-appointment, and also from election by human authority of any kind whatever. The *second* is the result of this election, viz., *belonging to Jehovah;* which means, that the priest, as such, with all his life and powers, was not his own, or the world's, but had given himself entirely up to the service of Jehovah. The *third* is, that as the property of Jehovah, the priest, like everything belonging to Jehovah, was *holy*. And this involved the qualification for the *fourth*, viz., *drawing near to Jehovah*, as the true and ex-clusive prerogative and duty of the priest.

All that is indicated here as composing the nature and purpose of the Levitical priesthood, has been already mentioned in Ex. xix. 5, 6, as characterizing the whole covenant nation when regarded in the light of its priestly vocation. As a *kingdom of priests*, Israel was Jehovah's *possession* out of, or before, all nations, and as such, a *holy* nation; whilst the basis of its *election* is seen in the deliver-ance from Egypt (ver. 4), and the design, that they might *draw near*, in the approach to the holy mountain (ver. 17). From this resemblance it follows, that the priesthood of the Aaronites in relation to Israel, was similar to that of Israel in relation to the heathen. The Aaronites were the priests of the nation, which had been called and appointed to a universal priesthood, but which was not yet ripe for such a call, and therefore still stood in need of priestly mediation itself.

What we are to understand by *coming near to Jehovah*, which was the true calling of the Aaronic priesthood, according to Num. xvi. 5, may easily be gathered from what goes before. The design and purpose of this priesthood was mediatorial communion with God, mediation between the holy God and His chosen people, which had drawn back in the consciousness of its sinfulness from direct communion with God (Ex. xx. 19). Like all communion, this also was reciprocal. Priestly approach to God involved both bringing to God, and bringing back from God. The priests brought into the presence of God the sacrifices and gifts of the people, and brought from God His gifts for the people, viz., reconciliation and His blessing.

§ 8. But from the very nature of such a mediatorial office, two things were essential to its true and perfect performance; and these the Aaronic priest no more possessed than any one else in the nation which stood in need of mediation.

If it was the consciousness of their own sinfulness which, according to Ex. xx. 19, prevented the people from drawing near to God, and holding direct intercourse with Him; the question arises, how Aaron and his sons, who belonged to the same nation, and were involved in the same sinfulness, could possibly venture to come into the presence of Jehovah. The first and immediate demand for a perfect priesthood, appointed to mediate between the holy God and the sinful nation, would be perfect sinlessness; but how little did the family of Aaron, involved as it was in the general sinfulness, answer to this demand!

Secondly, and this was no less essential, true and all-sufficient mediation required that the mediator himself should possess a doublesidedness; and in this the Aaronic priest was quite as deficient as in the first thing demanded, namely, perfect sinlessness. To represent the people in the presence of Jehovah, and Jehovah in the presence of the people, and to be able to set forth in his own person the mediation between the two, he ought to stand in essential union on the one hand with the people, and on the other with God; and in order fully to satisfy this demand, he ought to be as much divine as human. But the Aaronic priesthood partook of human nature only, and not at all of divine.

Both demands were satisfied in an absolutely perfect way in that High Priest alone (Heb. vii. 26, 27), to whose coming and manifestation the entire history of salvation pointed, who, uniting in His own person both deity and humanity, was sent in the fulness of time to the chosen people, and through their instrumentality (Gen. xii. 3, xxviii. 14) to the whole human race, and through whom, just as Aaron's sons attained to the priesthood by virtue of their lineal descent from Aaron, so, by means of spiritual regeneration and sonship (1 Pet. ii. 5, 9), the universal spiritual priesthood and "kingdom of priests" have been actually realized, the members of which are redeemed from sin, and partakers of the divine nature (2 Pet. i. 4), and of which, according to Ex. xix. 4–6, Israel was called and appointed to be the first-born possessor (Ex. iv. 22).

But as the manifestation of this priesthood could not be, and was not intended to be, the commencement and starting point, but only the goal and fruit, of the whole of the Old Testament history of salvation; and yet, in order that this goal might be reached, it was indispensably necessary that intercourse with God through the mediation of a priest should be secured to the chosen nation of the old covenant; the priesthood of that time could only typically prefigure the priesthood of the future, and could only possess in a symbolical and typical manner the two essential prerequisites, sinlessness and a divine nature. The former it acquired through washing and a sacrificial atonement, the latter by investiture and anointing on the occasion of its institution and consecration (Ex. xxix. cf. § 165 sqq.); and these were renewed previous to the discharge of every priestly function by repeated washings, and by the assumption of the official dress, which had already been anointed (Ex. xxix. 21). The sacrificial atonement, which was made at the first dedication, had to be repeated, not only on every occasion on which a priest was *conscious* of any sin or uncleanness, but also once a year (on the great day of atonement, cf. § 199), for the cancelling of all the sin and uncleanness of the entire priesthood which might have remained unnoticed; and this must be effected before any further priestly acts could be performed. Moreover, the demand for sinlessness had its fixed symbolical expression in the demand for physical perfection, as the indispensable prerequisite to any active participation in the service of the priesthood (Lev. xxi. 16–24).

§ 9. As the Levites and priests were separated by their vocation, and by their appointment to the service of the sanctuary, from the rest of the tribes, and did not receive, as the rest had done, a special allotment of territory in the Holy Land, where they could provide for their own wants by the cultivation of the soil, their *maintenance* had to be provided for in a different way. The tribe of Levi was to have no inheritance in the promised land, for, said Jehovah, " I am thy part and thine inheritance" (Num xviii. 20; Deut. x. 9, etc.). At the same time forty-eight cities were assigned to them as dwelling-places, distributed among all the tribes (that by their knowledge of the law they might be of service to all as teachers, preceptors, judges, and mediators: cf. Lev. x. 11); and thirteen of these cities were specially designated " cities of the priests" (Num. xxxv. 1–8; Josh. xxi.; 1 Chron. vi. 54–66).[1] But for their actual maintenance they were referred to Jehovah, in whose service they were to be entirely employed; so that it was only right that Jehovah should provide for their remuneration. This was done, by His assigning to them all the revenues and dues which the people had to pay to Him as the Divine King and feudal Lord of all. These included the first-fruits and tenths of all the produce of the

[1] As the priesthood was limited, after the death of Aaron's eldest sons, Nadab and Abihu, to the families of his other two sons, and therefore cannot have embraced more than from ten to twenty persons at the time of the entrance into the Holy Land, there is apparently a great disproportion between the number of priests' cities and the actual need,—on the supposition, that is to say, that these thirteen cities were intended to be occupied exclusively by priests. But for that very reason such a supposition is obviously a mistake. Even the so-called priests' cities were undoubtedly, for the most part, inhabited by Levites, and only distinguished from the rest of their cities by the fact, that one or more of the families of the priests resided there. Just as Jerusalem was called the king's city, though it was not inhabited by the court alone, so might these thirteen cities be called priests' cities, even if there were only one priestly family residing there. When we consider that the number of priests' cities was not fixed by the law, but was determined in Joshua's time (chap. xxi. 4), and that the number 13, which admits of no symbolical interpretation whatever, can only have been decided upon because of some existing necessity, it is more than probable that the number of priests at that time was exactly 13, and that at first there was only one priestly family in every priests' city. It is true, that if we deduct the home of the high priest, the one head of the entire priesthood, who dwelt, no doubt, wherever the tabernacle was, the number 12 remains, answering to the number of the tribes, which may be significant as a contingency, but was not determined on account of that significance, since the 24 orders of priests, which were afterwards appointed, do not appear to have been connected at all with the number of the tribes; nor was one priests' city taken from each tribe, but the selection was confined to the three tribes nearest to the sanctuary, Judah, Simeon, and Benjamin.

land, as well as the first-born of men and cattle, which were partly presented in kind, and had partly to be redeemed with money. Of all the sacrificial animals, too, which the people offered to Jehovah spontaneously, and for some reason of their own, certain portions were the perquisites of the officiating priest, unless they were entirely consumed upon the altar; and this was only the case with the so-called *burnt-offerings*.

All the first-fruits and first-born came directly to the *priests*. In these the Levites did not participate, because they had themselves been appointed as menial servants to the priests, in the place of the first-born who were sanctified in Egypt. On the other hand, the tithes fell to the share of the Levites, who handed a tenth of them over to the priests.

CHAPTER II.

THE PLACE OF SACRIFICE

§ 10. The patriarchs had erected simple altars for the worship of God in every place at which they sojourned (Gen. viii. 20, xii. 7, xiii. 18, etc.). Even the house of God, which Jacob vowed that he would erect at Luz (= Bethel: Gen. xxviii. 22), was nothing more than an altar, as the execution of the vow in Gen. xxxv. 1, 7, clearly proves. When the unity of the patriarchal family had been expanded into a plurality of tribes, houses, and families, and these again were formed by the covenant at Sinai into the unity of the priestly covenant nation, a corresponding unity in the place of worship became also necessary. The idea of the theocracy, according to which the God of Israel was also the King of Israel, and dwelt in the midst of Israel; the appointment and vocation of the people to be a " kingdom of priests," and a " holy nation" (Ex. xix. 6); the temporary refusal to enter upon the duties of that vocation (Ex. xx. 19); the consequent postponement of it till a future time; and the transference of it to a special priesthood belonging to the tribe of Levi;—all this was to have its symbolical expression in the new house of God. At the same time, it was necessary to create a fitting substratum for the incomparably richer ceremonial appointed by the law.

Moses therefore caused a sanctuary to be erected, answering to these wants and demands, according to the pattern which Jehovah had shown him on the holy mount (Ex. xxv. 9, 40), and by the builders expressly appointed by God, Bezaleel and Aholiab (Ex. xxxi. 2, xxxvi. 1, 2). To meet the necessities of the journey through the desert, it was constructed in the form of a portable tent, and consisted of the *dwelling* (הַמִּשְׁכָּן) and a *court* surrounding it on every side (הֶחָצֵר, Ex. xxv.–xxxi. and xxxv.–xl.).

The DWELLING itself was an oblong of thirty yards in length, and ten yards in breadth and height, built on the southern, northern, and western sides of upright planks of acacia-wood overlaid with gold. Over the whole there were placed four coverings. The inner one, consisting of costly woven materials (byssus woven in different colours, with figures of cherubim upon it), was so arranged as to form the drapery of the interior of the dwelling, whilst the other three were placed outside. In the front of the building, towards the east, there were five gilded pillars of acacia-wood; and on these a curtain was suspended, which closed the entrance to the dwelling, and bore the name of מָסָךְ.

The interior of the dwelling was divided into two parts by a second curtain, sustained by four pillars, and made of the same costly fabric and texture as the innermost covering. Of these two parts the further (or westerly) was called the MOST HOLY, קֹדֶשׁ קָדָשִׁים, and was a perfect cube of ten cubits in length, breadth, and height; so that the other part, or the HOLY, הַקֹּדֶשׁ, was of the same height and breadth, but twice as long. This inner curtain was called פָּרֹכֶת.

The COURT was an uncovered space completely surrounding the dwelling, 100 cubits long and 50 cubits broad, bounded by 60 wooden pillars of 5 cubits in height. The pillars stood 5 cubits apart, and the spaces between were closed by drapery of twined byssus. In the front, however, *i.e.*, on the eastern side, there was no drapery between the five middle pillars, so that an open space was left as an entrance of 20 cubits broad; and this was closed by a curtain of the same material and texture as the curtain at the door of the tabernacle, and, like the latter, was called מָסָךְ.

The position of the dwelling within the court is not mentioned. It probably stood, however, so as to meet at the same time the necessities of the case and the demands of symmetry, 20 cubits from the pillars on the north, south, and west, leaving a space of 50 cubits square in front of the entrance to the tabernacle.

§ 11. The ALTAR OF BURNT-OFFERING, מִזְבַּח הָעוֹלָה, stood in the

COURT. It was a square case, made of acacia-wood, lined within and without with copper, and filled with earth. It was five cubits in length and breadth, but only three cubits high. At the four corners there were four copper horns. About half-way up the chest there ran a bank, כַּרְכֹּב, all round the outside, evidently that the officiating priests might stand upon it, and so be able to perform their duties at the altar with greater convenience. From the outer edge of this bank a network of copper sloped off to the ground. The space underneath this grating was probably intended to receive the blood which remained over from the sacrifices.—There was also a LAVER, כִּיּוֹר, in the court, in which the priests washed their hands and feet,—a process that had to be repeated, according to Ex. xxx. 20, 21, every time they entered the Holy Place or officiated at the altar.

In the HOLY PLACE there were three articles of furniture :— 1. The ALTAR OF INCENSE, מִזְבַּח מִקְטַר קְטֹרֶת or מִזְבַּח קְטֹרֶת, made of acacia-wood overlaid with gold. It was one cubit in length, one in breadth, and two in height, and stood in the centre, before the entrance to the Holy of Holies. The upper surface, which was surrounded by a rim, and had gilt horns at the four corners, was called גַּג, a term suggestive of the flat roofs of oriental houses. The principal purpose to which it was applied was that of burning incense ; but there were certain sacrificial animals whose blood was sprinkled upon the horns.—2. The TABLE OF SHEW-BREAD, הַשֻּׁלְחָן, also constructed of acacia-wood overlaid with gold, a cubit and a half in height, two cubits long, and one cubit broad. Upon this was placed the so-called shew-bread (§ 159), which had to be changed every week.— 3. The SEVEN-BRANCHED CANDLESTICK, הַמְּנוֹרָה, of pure gold, and beaten work. From the upright stem there branched out, at regular intervals, three arms on each side, which curved upwards and reached as high as the top of the central stem. Each of these was provided with one oil lamp, so that there were seven lamps in a straight line, and probably at equal distances from one another. The height of the candelabrum is not given.

In the MOST HOLY PLACE there was only one article of furniture, viz., the ARK OF THE COVENANT or the ARK OF TESTIMONY, אֲרוֹן הָעֵדוּת, אֲרוֹן הַבְּרִית. It consisted of two parts. The ark itself was a chest of acacia-wood, covered within and without with gold plates, two cubits and a half long, and one cubit and a half in breadth and height. In the ark there was the testimony, הָעֵדוּת; i.e., the two tables of stone, which Moses had brought down from the holy mount, containing the ten words of the fundamental law, written by the finger of God. A plate of beaten gold, כַּפֹּרֶת, served as the lid of the ark; and at each end of this lid stood a cherub of beaten gold. The cherubim stood facing each other, and looking down upon the Capporeth, which they overshadowed with their outspread wings. With regard to the form of these cherubim, the figures of which were also worked in the *Parocheth*, the curtain before the Most Holy, and the inner covering of the tabernacle, all that we can gather from the description is, that they were probably of human shape, and that they had one face and two wings.

§ 12. On the DESIGN OF THE SANCTUARY,[1] the names themselves furnish some information. It was called the TENT OF MEETING, אֹהֶל מוֹעֵד ; and we may learn from Ex. xxv. 22, xxix. 43, what that name signifies. Jehovah says, that He will there meet with the children of Israel, and talk with them, and sanctify them through His glory. It is also called the DWELLING-PLACE, מִשְׁכָּן, as in Ex. xxv. 8, and xxix. 45, 46, Jehovah promises that He will not merely meet with Israel there from time to time, but dwell there constantly in the midst of them, and there make Himself known to them as their God. Lastly, it is also called the TENT OF WITNESS, אֹהֶל הָעֵדוּת, where Jehovah bears witness through His covenant and law that He is what He is, viz., the Holy One of Israel, who will have Israel also to be holy as He is holy (Lev. xix. 2), and who qualifies Israel for it by His blessing and atoning grace (Ex. xx. 24). In accordance with this design, as soon as it was finished, the glory of Jehovah filled the tabernacle (Ex. xl. 34 sqq.).

The tabernacle, then, must represent an institution, in connection with which Jehovah dwelt perpetually in Israel, to sanctify it— an institution, to establish which He had led them out of Egypt (Ex. xxix. 46); which was not established, therefore, till after the Exodus. This institution, as is self-evident, could be no other than the theocracy founded at Sinai, or the kingdom of God in Israel, the nature and design of which is described in Ex. xix. 4–6.

From this fundamental idea we may easily gather what was involved in the distinction between the *court* and the tabernacle. If the latter was the dwelling-place of Jehovah in the midst of Israel, the former could only be the dwelling-place of that people whose God was in the midst of it, just as the tabernacle was in the

---

[1] A more elaborate and thorough discussion of the meaning of the tabernacle and its furniture, is to be found in my *Beiträge zur Symbolik des alttest. Cultus* (Leipzig 1851).

midst of the court. And the fact that the people were not allowed
to *enter* the dwelling of God, but could only approach the door—
permission to enter being restricted to their consecrated representatives and mediators, the priests—irresistibly reminds us of Ex. xx.
19, and shows that the court was the abode of that people, which,
notwithstanding its priestly calling, was not yet able to come directly
to God, but still needed specially appointed priestly mediators to
enter the dwelling-place, to hold communion with God in their
stead, to offer the gifts of the people, and to bring back the proofs
of the favour of God.

But the dwelling-place of God was also divided into two parts:
the HOLY PLACE, and the MOST HOLY. These were two apart-
ments in one dwelling. Now, since the relation between the
dwelling-place and the court presented the same antithesis as that
between the unpriestly nation and the Aaronic priesthood—and
since the ordinary priests were only allowed to enter the Holy Place,
whilst the high priest alone could enter the Most Holy,—it is evident
that the distinction between the Holy and Most Holy answered
essentially to that between the ordinary priest and the high priest;
and therefore, that the abode of God in the Most Holy set forth the
highest culmination of the abode of God in Israel, which, for that
very reason, exhibited in its strongest form the fact that He was
then unapproachable to Israel. A comparison between the name
" Holy of Holies," and the corresponding " heaven of heavens," in
Deut. x. 14, 1 Kings viii. 27, also leads to the conclusion, not that
the Most Holy was a type of heaven in its highest form, but that it
contained the same emphatic expression of the Jehovistic (saving)
presence and operations of God in the kingdom of grace, as the
name " heaven of heavens" of the Elohistic presence and operations
of God in the kingdom of nature.

The division of the dwelling-place into Holy and Most Holy was
an indication of the fact, therefore, that in the relation in which
the priests stood to God, and consequently also in that in which the
people would stand when they were ripe for their priestly vocation,
there are two different stages of approachability. The constant
seat and throne of God was the Capporeth, where His glory was
enthroned between the wings of the cherubim (Num. vii. 89; Ex.
xxv. 22). But as the room in which all this took place was hidden
by the Parocheth from the sight of those who entered and officiated
in the Holy Place, the latter represents the standpoint of that
faith which has *not yet* attained to the sight of the glory of God,

and the *Most Holy* the standpoint of the faith which has *already* attained to sight (*vide* 1 Cor. xiii. 12).

The threefold division of the tabernacle contained a figurative and typical representation of the three progressive stages, by which the kingdom of God on earth arrives at its visible manifestation and ultimate completion. In the COURT there was displayed the existing stage, when Israel, as the possessor of the kingdom of God, still stood in need of priestly mediators; in the HOLY PLACE, the next stage, when the atonement exhibited in type in the court, would be completed, and the people themselves would be able in consequence to exercise their priestly calling and draw near to God; in the MOST HOLY, the last stage of all, when the people of God will have attained to the immediate vision of His glory. This triple stage of approach to God, which was set forth *simultaneously* in space in the symbolism of the tabernacle, is realized *successively* in time through the historical development of the kingdom of God. The first stage was the Israelitish theocracy; the second is the Christian Church; the third and last will be the heavenly Jerusalem of the Apocalypse. Each of the two earlier stages contains potentially within itself all that has still to come; but it contains it only as an ideal in faith and hope. For the first stage, therefore, it was requisite that representations and types of the two succeeding stages should be visibly displayed in the place appointed for worship.

§ 13. The principal object in the *court*, and that in which its whole significance culminated, was the ALTAR OF BURNT-OFFERING. The first thing which strikes the eye in connection with an altar is, that it represents an ascent from the earth towards heaven (בָּמָה = *altare*), a *lifting* of the earth above its ordinary and natural level. From the time that Jehovah ceased to walk with man upon the earth, and hold intercourse with him there, as He had done before the fall (Gen. iii. 8), and the earth was cursed for man's sin in consequence of the fall (Gen. iii. 17), and heaven and earth became so separated, the one from the other, that God came down from heaven to reveal Himself to man (Gen. xi. 5, xviii. 21), and then went up again to heaven (Gen. xvii. 22),—the natural level of the earth was no longer adapted to the purpose of such intercourse. It was necessary, therefore, to raise the spot where man desired to hold communion with God, and present to Him his offerings, into an altar rising above the curse. Whilst the name בָּמָה expressed what an altar was, viz., an elevation of the earth, the other and ordinary name of the altar indicated the purpose which it served:

it was a *place of sacrifice*, on which sinful man presented his *slain* offering for the atonement and sanctification of his soul before God.

But *the* altar which JEHOVAH caused to be built, was not merely the raising of the earth towards the heaven where God had dwelt since sin drove Him from the earth, but also the place where heaven itself, or rather He who fills heaven with His glory, came down to meet the rising earth;—not only the spot where man offered his gifts to Jehovah, but also the spot where God came to meet the gifts of man and gave His blessing in return. For Jehovah promised this in Ex. xx. 24: "In all places where I record My name, I will come unto thee and bless thee." But an altar, however high it may be built, does not reach to the heaven where God dwells. In itself, therefore, it merely expresses the upward desires of man. And these desires are not realized and satisfied, till God Himself comes down from heaven upon the altar.

According to Ex. xx. 24, 25, it was a general rule for an altar to be built of earth or unhewn stones, as still retaining their original form and component elements. It is true that this very composition of earth and stone represented the curse, which adhered to them in their existing natural condition. But man, with all his art and diligence, is unable to remove this curse. Consequently, no tooling or chiselling of his was to be allowed at all. Whatever he might do, he could not sanctify the altar which was formed from the earth that had been cursed. That could be done by none but God, who had promised " to record His name there" (Ex. xx. 24),—" to give the atoning blood upon the altar, to make an atonement for their souls" (Lev. xvii. 11). Jehovah appointed and consecrated the place where the altar was to be built; He gave to the blood of the sacrifice, that was sprinkled upon it, the atoning worth which it possessed; and He caused the smoke of the sacrifice which was consumed upon the altar to become a sweet smelling savour, as representing the self-surrender of man (Gen. viii. 21).

The elevated earth, which formed the altar in the court, was surrounded by a wooden chest covered with copper, to give it a firm cohesion and fixed form. By the square shape of the surrounding walls the seal of the kingdom of God was impressed upon it. The altar, therefore, was the evident representative of the Old Testament institution of atonement and sanctification, by which the expiation of sinful man and the sanctifying self-surrender of the expiated sinner were effected before God. This being its meaning, it could only stand in the court, the abode of the sinful, though reconcilable nation, which could not yet draw near directly to Jehovah, but still needed the mediation of the Levitical priesthood for the presentation of its sacrifices and gifts.

In our interpretation of the HORNS, which rose from the altar at its four corners, we need not refer, as *Bähr* (Symbolik 1, 472) and *Keil* (Arch. 1, 104) do, to passages in which the horn of the animal is mentioned as indicative of strength, or as its glory and ornament; nor to those in which the horn is used as the symbol of the fulness and superabundance of blessing and salvation; but, as *Hofmann* and *Kliefoth* have done, to such passages as Isa. v. 1, where the term horn is applied to an eminence running up to a point. For the idea of height is the predominant one in connection with the altar; and the only thing, therefore, that comes into consideration is, what the horn is in relation to the height of the animal, viz., its loftiest point,—and not what it is as an ornament or weapon. Still farther from the mark, however, is the allusion to the horn as a symbol of fulness; for the horn acquires this significance merely as something *separated* from the animal, or as a vessel shaped like a horn that has been *taken off*. The horns on the altar increased its height. Consequently, the blood sprinkled on the horns of the altar was brought nearer to God, than that which was merely sprinkled on the sides.

§ 14. Since the *Holy Place*, as we saw, was a part of the abode of God which the priests alone could enter, as the mediators of a nation which, notwithstanding its priestly calling, was still unpriestly, the three *articles of furniture* in the Holy Place, together with the offerings connected with them, foreshadowed typically what the nation, regarded as a priestly nation, was to offer to its God in gifts and sacrifices, and what qualities and powers it was to unfold before Him. And as the way to the Holy Place necessarily lay through the court, where atonement was made for the sinful nation, and where it dedicated and consecrated itself afresh to its God, and entered anew into fellowship with Him; the offerings in the Holy Place are to be regarded as symbols of such gifts and services, as none but a nation reconciled, sanctified, and in fellowship with God, could possibly present.

Of the three articles of furniture in the Holy Place, the ALTAR OF INCENSE was unquestionably the most significant and important. This is indicated not only by its position between the other two, and immediately in front of the entrance to the Most Holy, but also by its appointment and designation as an *altar*, on the horns of which the blood of atonement, that was brought into the Holy Place (§ 107), was sprinkled; inasmuch as this established an essential and necessary relation between it and the altar of the court on the one hand, and the Capporeth of the Most Holy on the other. It is true, the sacrifices which were offered upon this altar, and ascended to God in fire, were not the bleeding sacrifices of atonement, but the bloodless sacrifices of incense, which, as our subsequent investigation will show (§ 146), represented the prayers of the congregation, that had just before been reconciled, sanctified, and restored to fellowship with God, by the bleeding sacrifice of the court. The altar of incense stood in the same relation to the altar of burnt-offering, as the Holy Place to the court, as the priestly nation to the unpriestly, as the prayer of thanksgiving and praise from those already reconciled and sanctified to the desire and craving for reconciliation and sanctification, and as the splendour of the gold seven times purified, in which it was enclosed, to the dull, dead colour of the copper which surrounded the altar in the court. It was a repetition of the altar that stood in the court, but a repetition in a higher form.

The two other articles of furniture, the TABLE OF SHEW-BREAD and the CANDLESTICK, were offshoots, as it were, of the altar of incense, as their position on either side indicates ; and the peculiar form of each was determined by the offerings which it held ; for the bread required a table, and the lights a candelabrum. What was combined together in one article of furniture in the altar of burnt-offering in the court, was here resolved into three, which served to set forth the ideas in question in a much more complete and many-sided manner (cf. § 158 sqq.).

§ 15. In the MOST HOLY, as the abode of God in the fullest sense of the word, and in the most thorough unapproachableness, there was but one article of furniture, though one consisting of several parts, viz., the ARK OF THE COVENANT, with the CAPPORETH.

Hengstenberg's view, expressed in his Dissertations on the Penta-teuch (vol. ii. 525, translation), which may perhaps look plausible at first sight,—viz., that the covering of the ark, or of the law contained in it, by the Capporeth, was intended to express the idea, that the grace of God had covered or silenced the accusing and condemning voice of the law,—will be found, on closer and more careful investiga-tion, to be defective and inadmissible on every account (see my *Bei-träge zur Symbolik der Alttest. Cultus-stätte*, pp. 28 sqq.). I have the greater reason for still regarding the course of argument adopted as satisfactory, because *Keil* has been induced by it to give up *Hengstenberg's* view, and in all essential points to adopt my own. I will repeat the leading points of my argument here.

First of all, it must be borne in mind, that the ark of the covenant answered a double purpose : (1) to preserve the tables of the law, and (2) to serve as a support and basis to the Capporeth. Let us commence with the former. As the receptacle for the two tables of the law, it was called the " ark of the testimony," or " ark of the covenant." The tables of the law were named the testimony, הָעֵדוּת, because in them God furnished the people with' a testimony to His own nature and will. This attestation was the preliminary, the foundation, and the soul of the covenant which He concluded with His people. Hence the ark of the testimony was also called the " ark of the covenant," אֲרוֹן הַבְּרִית. In like manner, the tables of the law are also called " the tables of the covenant" (Deut. ix. 9, 11, 15), and the words engraved upon them " the words of the covenant" (Ex. xxxiv. 28). And, in certain cases, the former are designated in simple terms as "the covenant" (הַבְּרִית, equivalent to the record of the covenant: 1 Kings viii. 21; 2 Chron. vi. 11). There can be no doubt, therefore, that the tables of the law lying in the ark were looked upon as an attestation of the covenant concluded with Israel, and as that alone. But this record of the covenant did not lie naked and open; on the contrary, it was enclosed in an ark or chest,—the place of the lid being taken by the Capporeth. This showed that it was not only a treasure, but the most costly jewel, the dearest possession of Israel. And it was worthy of such estimation; for, having been written by the finger of God, it was a divine testimony, a pledge of the continuance and perpetuity of the covenant made with God, and a guarantee of the eventual fulfilment of all the promises attached to this covenant, and of all the purposes of salvation which it was designed to subserve.

The ark, with the testimony within it, was also a support to the Capporeth. For the Capporeth was not merely intended as a lid for the ark, but had an independent purpose of its own. This is evident from the name itself, which is derived from the *Piel* כִּפֶּר, and is to be rendered, not " *covering*," but " seat of atonement," ἱλαστήριον, *propitiatorium* (" mercy-seat," *Luther*, etc.). כִּפֶּר denotes not a local, material covering, but a spiritual one; and the object of this covering is always and everywhere the sin of man. For this reason, the name Capporeth cannot possibly be understood as denoting the fact that it covered the tables of the law. For the object to be covered by the Capporeth, *i.e.*, to be atoned for, could not be anything that came from God, and least of all God's holy law. Moreover, the law of God was to be anything but covered up, that is to say, covered up in any sense that would represent its voice as silenced.

The Capporeth, therefore, apart from the fact that it closed up the ark, must have been something in itself, must have had its own significance and purpose within itself. And though it did undoubtedly form a material, local covering to the ark, this can only have been of subordinate, collateral, and secondary importance.

§ 16. But what was this real, independent, primary, and principal significance of the Capporeth? Keil's interpretation (*Archäologie* i. 114) falls back into *Bähr's* error, of confounding the kingdom of nature with that of grace, or natural revelation with the revelation of salvation, and is altogether beside the mark. According to his view, " the Capporeth resembled the firmament, and bore the name Capporeth or mercy-seat, because the highest and most perfect act of atonement in the Old Testament economy was perfected upon it, and God, who betrothed Himself to His people in grace and mercy by an everlasting covenant, sate enthroned thereon." The latter part,—namely, that the Capporeth was the highest medium of atonement in the old covenant, and at the same time was the throne of Jehovah, which, though for the time unapproachable by the people, was nevertheless erected upon earth and in the midst of Israel,—is unquestionably perfectly correct; but for that very reason the Capporeth could not possibly represent the firmament. Or are we to suppose, that the highest and most perfect act of atonement in the old covenant ought properly to have been performed upon the firmament of heaven, but that, as this could not well be accomplished, a representation of it was placed as its substitute in the Holy of Holies? And was the true act of expiation in the fulness of time, of which this was only a shadow and type (§ 56), really performed above the firmament, *i.e.*, in heaven? Was it not rather accomplished on earth, in the land of Judæa? No doubt " that God, who betrothed Himself to His people in grace and mercy by an everlasting covenant," was enthroned upon the Capporeth. But this betrothal took place, not above the firmament, *i.e.*, in heaven, but on the earth, at Sinai. Jehovah came down for the purpose (Ex. xix. 20); and the glory of Jehovah entered the sanctuary, and took up its permanent place upon the Capporeth (Ex. xl. 34 sqq.; Num. vii. 89; Ex. xxv. 22). Unquestionably there is also a throne of God in the heaven of heavens, which stands upon the firmament; but the throne of God in the Most Holy Place on earth was so far from being a copy or representative of that heavenly throne, that it rather presented a contrast, and one as sharp as that between heaven and earth, nature and grace, Elohim and Jehovah.

This confusion of ideas, which *Keil* himself has generally kept distinct enough elsewhere (Arch. i. 94 sqq.), has evidently arisen from his being misled by the connection between the Capporeth and the figures of the two cherubim, and the fact that the latter are often represented as surrounding the throne of God in heaven. But if Jehovah, in addition to the throne in heaven, established one also for Himself upon earth, could He not surround the latter with cherubim also? Moreover, *Keil* has involved himself, without perceiving it, in the most striking self-contradictions. Figures of cherubim, precisely similar to those which stood upon the Capporeth, were also woven into the inner covering of the tabernacle, and into the curtain which separated the Holy Place from the Most Holy. Now if the Capporeth must represent the firmament of heaven because of the cherubim standing upon it, simple consistency requires that the entire space of the Holy and Most Holy should be regarded as a figurative representation of heaven. And this *Bähr* actually maintains, though *Keil* rejects such a view as thoroughly unscriptural, and decides correctly that the tabernacle was a figure of the kingdom of God in Israel (p. 95).

What the Capporeth was really intended to represent, is evident from its name, and was practically exhibited in the fact that the highest and most perfect expiation was effected upon it. It was called, and was primarily, a *means of atonement* (ἱλαστήριον, *propitiatorium*). By the circumstance that on the great day of atonement (Lev. xvi.) the blood of the holiest sin-offering was sprinkled upon it, just as the blood of the ordinary sacrifices on ordinary days was sprinkled upon the horns of the altar of burnt-offering in the court, or upon the altar of incense in the Holy Place, it was shown to be an *altar*,—but an *altar* that was as much higher and holier than the other two altars, as the Most Holy Place was higher and holier than the Holy Place and the court of the tabernacle.

But there were two other peculiarities connected with this altar. As the Capporeth acquired the form of an altar simply from its connection with the ark, inasmuch as without this support it would have been merely an altar-plate, and the essential characteristic, viz., that of elevation, would have been wanting; so this altar acquired its higher sanctity and worth, in part at least, from the fact that it contained within it the "testimony," the covenant, —that is to say, the record of the covenant, the costliest treasure in the possession of Israel. But in a still higher degree did its incomparable sanctity grow out of the fact, that the glory of Jehovah rested between the wings of the cherubim that overshadowed it, whereby the altar became the *throne* of God—the throne of grace. Now, since the support of the throne, together with the Capporeth as an altar-plate, enclosed the record of the covenant, or the covenant testimony and covenant pledge; the idea expressed was this, that Jehovah's being enthroned in this place was based upon, and rendered possible by, the covenant which God had concluded with Israel, and the institution of atonement which He had given (Lev. xvii. 11). With reference to the altar of burnt-offering, the promise had also been given (Ex. xx. 24), that Jehovah would come down to Israel there to receive their offerings, and recompense them by His blessing. But there He came invisibly, in a manner that could only be grasped by faith, not by sight; whereas upon the throne-altar in the Most Holy Place He descended, or rather was enthroned, in a visible (symbolical) form, viz., in the cloud, which represented the glory of Jehovah, and was visible to the eyes of those who were permitted to pass within the veil (Lev. xvi. 2, cf. § 199).

CHAPTER III

THE VARIOUS KINDS OF SACRIFICE

§ 17. The term *offering*,[1] when used in a general sense in connection with divine worship, usually denotes, according to its derivation from *offerre*, the *dedication* of any suitable possession to God, or to divine purposes. So far as etymology and the usage of the language are concerned, this idea is distinctly expressed in the Hebrew term קָרְבָּן, *Corban*, *i.e.*, presentation (equivalent to מַתְּנוֹת קֹדֶשׁ, "holy gifts," in Ex. xxviii. 38; *vid.* Mark vii. 11, "Corban, that is to say, a gift"). Such presents, which had all to be brought

---

[1] The German *Opfer* corresponds rather to our word sacrifice; but it was necessary to substitute the word offering here.—TR.

to the dwelling-place of God and delivered up in the court, inasmuch as they were gifts for God, might either be offered to God and to His sanctuary for a *permanent* possession or use—as was the case, for example, and chiefly, with all the offerings devoted to the erection, furnishing, and maintenance of the sanctuary (cf. Num. vii. 3, 11, 12, 13, 77, xxxi. 50), as well as with such objects of *vows* as became *Corban* in consequence of the vow (Mark vii. 11) —or the thing presented might be appropriated to and consumed in the service of God, or for His glory. The offerings of the latter kind were divided again into two classes, which differed essentially, according as they were laid upon the altar and offered directly to God, either in whole or in part, by being consumed in the fire, or else applied at once and entirely to the remuneration and maintenance of the priests and Levites as the servants of Jehovah (§ 69). The latter were regarded as the *taxes*, which the people had to pay to the God-King Jehovah, the true Owner of the land. They included the *first-fruits* and *tithes* of all the produce of the land, as well as the male *first-born* of man and beast. But the first-born of men and of the unclean animals—*i.e.*, of such as were not edible, and therefore not fit for sacrifice—had to be redeemed, whilst the first-born of clean animals, or those fit for sacrifice, were partly consumed upon the altar; so that, to a certain extent, they belonged to both classes (Num. xviii. 17, 18, cf. § 229). Thus, we find, there were *three classes of offerings:* (1) Corbanim for the sanctuary of Jehovah, or DEDICATION GIFTS; (2) Corbanim for the maintenance of the servants of Jehovah, or FEUDAL TAXES (first-fruits, tithes, and first-born); and (3) Corbanim for Jehovah Himself, or ALTAR-SACRIFICES. Of the last, some were called *most holy* (קֹדֶשׁ קָדָשִׁים), viz., such as were either consumed entirely upon the altar, or, so far as they were not consumed, were eaten by the priests, and by them alone. Cf. *Knobel* on Lev. xxi. 22.

In the present work we have to do with the gifts of the third class alone, *i.e.*, with the Corbanim which were placed either in whole or in part upon the *altar*. Even in the Thorah the name *Corban* is applied pre-eminently to these.

§ 18. *Hengstenberg* (Opfer, p. 4) very properly blames *Bähr*, and others who have followed him, for commencing their attempt to determine the nature and meaning of sacrifice, in the stricter sense of the term, with Lev. xvii. 11, where, as we have already seen (§ 11), the prohibition to eat blood is based upon the fact, that the soul of the flesh is in the blood, and Jehovah gave the blood to His people upon the altar, to make atonement therewith for their souls. In this passage they imagined that they had found "the key to the whole of the Mosaic theory of sacrifice." It is perfectly obvious, however, that Lev. xvii. 11 merely furnishes the key to the sprinkling of the blood in the case of the sacrifice of *animals*. But the question, whether, as has been maintained on that side, an explanation of the sprinkling of the blood prepares the way for understanding the other functions connected with the sacrifice of animals, or whether the animal sacrifices alone could lay claim to the character of independent offerings, whilst the bloodless (vegetable) gifts were merely to be regarded as accompaniments to the bleeding (animal) sacrifices, must be determined, even if it could be proved at all, from the special inquiry which follows afterwards, and therefore, even if correct, ought not to be laid down as an *a priori* axiom.

But what both *Hengstenberg* and *Keil* have adopted as the basis and key to the altar-sacrifices, both bleeding and bloodless, is certainly quite as inadmissible as that laid down by *Bähr*. The true basis is said to be found in Ex. xxiii. 15, "My face shall not be seen empty," or as it reads in Deut. xvi. 16, "Appear not empty before the face of Jehovah;" to which is added by way of explanation in ver. 17, "Every one according to the gift of his hand, according to the blessing which Jehovah thy God has given." It is really incomprehensible how these two theologians could fall into the mistake of regarding the passages quoted as the basis of the whole sacrificial worship ; for, according to both the context and the true meaning of the words, they have nothing to do with it, or rather, are directly at variance with its provisions. The amount of the sacrifices to be offered upon the altar (whether bleeding or bloodless) was not determined, in the majority of cases, as it is in Deut. xvi. 17, by the possessions or income of the person sacrificing. The command of the law of sacrifice was not "according to the gift of his hand, according to the blessing which Jehovah thy God hath given thee." The exact amount was prescribed in every case by the law; and the difference in the worth of the offerings was regulated, not by the wealth and income of the sacrificer, but partly by his position in the theocracy (*i.e.*, by the question, whether he was priest, prince, or private individual), and partly by differences in the occasion for the sacrifice.[1] But apart from this, how can our

---

[1] It is to be hoped that no one will be sufficiently wanting in perspicacity to bring forward as an objection to my statement the fact, that a poor man, who was not in a condition to bring the sheep which was normally required, was

opponents have overlooked the fact, that these passages do not refer to the altar-sacrifices in particular, which they ought to do to warrant such an application, and not even to the Corbanim in general, or as a whole. They apply exclusively and expressly to the first-fruits and tenths to be offered on the three harvest festivals; and they could not refer to anything else, even if no such statement had been made. How complete a mistake this *quid pro quo* is, is also evident from the fact, that if, instead of restricting the demand there expressed to the harvest festivals and the harvest gifts, we extend it, as *Hengstenberg* and *Keil* have done, to the sacrificial worship generally; then to enter the Holy Place, where the name of Jehovah dwelt, without offering sacrifice,—say even for the purpose of praying, or of beholding the beautiful service of the Lord (Ps. xxvii. 4, ciii. 4, and lxxxiv.; Luke ii. 27, 37, etc.),—would necessarily have been regarded as an act of wickedness and presumption.

§ 19. Since, therefore, neither the passages adduced by *Bähr*, nor those which *Hengstenberg* cites as containing the key to the nature and meaning of sacrifice, are available for the purpose, and since no others offer themselves, the only course left open is to take as our starting point the connection between the sacrifices in the more restricted sense of the word and all the rest of the offerings. We have to examine, therefore, (1) what they had *in common* with the other *Corbanim*, and (2) in what they *differed* from them.

The three classes of Corbanim (§ 17) were all holy gifts. They were called holy, because they were all related to Jehovah, whether they were offered and appropriated to Him directly and personally, or whether they fell to the portion of His servants the Levites and priests, or to His dwelling-place the sanctuary. In the case of all of them, those prescribed by the law (gifts of duty), as well as free-will offerings presented without constraint or necessity (spontaneous gifts), the real foundation of the offering was the consciousness of entire dependence upon God and entire obligation towards Him—a consciousness which is always attended by the desire to embody itself in such gifts as these. The main point was never the material, pecuniary worth of the gifts themselves, either in connection with their presentation on the part of man, or their acceptance on the part of God. The God whom the Israelite had recognised

allowed to offer a pigeon instead, and if this were impossible, to offer the tenth part of an ephah of wheaten flour. Lev. v. 11.

as the Creator of heaven and earth, could not possibly desire the offering of earthly blessings for their own sake ; He could not care about the gift, but only about the giver, that is to say, about the feelings, of which the gift was the expression and embodiment. Hence the possession, which the worshipper gave up, was the representative of his person, his heart, his emotions. In these gifts, which were his justly acquired property, gained by the sweat of his face and the exercise of his earthly calling, he offered, in a certain sense, an objective portion of himself, since the sweat of his own labour adhered to it, and he had expended his own vital energy upon it, and thereby, as it were, really given it life. In this way he gave expression to his consciousness of the absolute dependence of his whole life and activity upon the grace and blessing of God, and to his obligation to devote it entirely to God and to divine purposes in praise, thanksgiving, and prayer. He gave partially back to God, what he had received entirely from God, and had wrought out and acquired through the blessing of God. And in the part, he sanctified and consecrated the whole, or all that he retained and applied to the maintenance of his own life and strength, and with this his own life also, to the maintenance of which he had devoted it. "It is true (says *Oehler*, Reallex. x. 614), the impulse from within, which urges a man to the utterance of praise, thanksgiving, and prayer to God, finds its expression in the words of devotion ; but it is fully satisfied only when those words are embodied, when they acquire, as it were, an objective existence in some appropriate act, in which the man incurs some expense by self-denial and self-renunciation, and thus gives a practical proof of the earnestness of his self-dedication to God."

§ 20. If we proceed now to examine what it was, that constituted the essential *difference* between the Corbanim of the *third* class and those of the other two, we shall find it in the peculiar relation in which the former stood to the altar. For this reason we have designated the offerings of the third class *altar*-offerings. In material substance, it is true, they were essentially the same as those of the second class (the feudal payments). The objects presented were in both instances the produce of agriculture and grazing ; in both there were animal and vegetable, bleeding and bloodless, offerings ; and they were both alike the fruit and produce of the life and work connected with the ordinary occupation, or the means by which life was invigorated and sustained. But the difference was this : some went directly to the priests and Levites, whilst the others were given directly and personally to Jehovah, through the relation in which they were placed to the altar. For the altar was the spot *upon* which men presented their gifts to Jehovah who dwelt on high, and *to* which Jehovah came down to receive the gifts and bless the giver (Ex. xx. 24). All the *Corbanim* of the third class, whether animal or vegetable, were burned upon the altar in whole or part, and on that account are designated in the Thorah either אִשֶּׁה (firing, from אֵשׁ fire), or אִשֵּׁי יְהוָה (Jehovah's firing). What the purpose of this burning upon the altar was, is evident from the almost universal formula : לְרֵיחַ נִיחֹחַ אִשֶּׁה לַיהוָה (*i.e.*, firing to the savour of peace, of satisfaction, of good pleasure for Jehovah), Ex. xxix. 41; Lev. viii. 21, etc. (see also Gen. viii. 21). Jehovah smelt the vapour as it ascended from the burning,—*i.e.*, the essence of the sacrificial gift purified by fire from the merely earthly elements,—and found peace, satisfaction, good pleasure therein. The gift was intended for Him personally, and He accepted it personally, and that with good-will; and, according to Ex. xx. 24, He blessed the giver in consequence. But if, as we have seen, it was not the gift as such that Jehovah desired, but the gift as the vehicle of the feelings of the giver, as the representative of his self-surrender, the cordial acceptance of the gift on the part of God, expressed in the words רֵיחַ נִיחֹחַ, applies not to the gift in itself, but to the gift as the representative of the person presenting the sacrifice. The distinguishing feature which belonged exclusively and universally to the Corbanim of the third class, viz., that of burning upon the altar, was an expression therefore of the self-surrender of the worshipper, which was well-pleasing to God and accepted by Him, and which He repaid by His blessing.

But the Corbanim of the third class were placed in another relation to the altar, *so far as* their nature permitted, and one that was equally essential (in the case, that is, of the animal sacrifices), viz., by the sprinkling of the *blood* upon the altar before the sacrifice was consumed. The *design* of this we may settle now, without forestalling any subsequent inquiry, from the passage which has already been referred to in various ways, viz., Lev. xvii. 11; though *how* that design was, or could be, accomplished by such means, we must leave for a future section. This design is expressed in Lev. xvii. 11, in the words לְכַפֵּר עַל־נַפְשֹׁתֵיכֶם, *i.e.*, "to expiate (= to cover the sins of) your souls." The blood was the means of expiation, the sprinkling of the blood the act of expiation ; and Jehovah Himself, who appointed this as the mode of expiation for Israel ("And I have given it you"), acknowledged thereby its validity and force.

It is very apparent that the two acts—the sprinkling of the blood upon the altar, and the burning of the sacrifice upon the altar—were essentially and necessarily connected. The sprinkling of the blood, or expiation, was the means; the burning, or dedication to Jehovah, the end. In order that the second should be a " savour of satisfaction to the Lord," it was necessary that the first should precede it; the first, therefore, was the basis or prerequisite of the second.

It was entirely different with the Corbanim of the second class. It is true, they were also presented as feudal payments due to Jehovah; but instead of being retained, or *personally* appropriated by Him, they were handed over at once and without reserve to the priests or Levites. Even in their case the primary consideration was subjectively (so far as the act of offering was concerned), not the material gift in itself, but the consciousness of dependence upon God, and the sense of obligation towards Him, of which the gift was an expression; but objectively (so far as their application to the payment and maintenance of the priests and Levites was concerned) the material aspect once more presents itself. This distinction (viz., that they were not intended for Jehovah personally) then reacted upon the mode of presentation, so that there was no apparent necessity for either the burning as a symbol of direct personal appropriation on the part of Jehovah, or the sprinkling of blood as a symbol of the covering of sin preparatory to such appropriation. But with the altar-sacrifices, at least so far as they were personally appropriated by Jehovah, the loftier, ideal aspect of self-surrender was firmly retained to the end. For that reason they were holier than the others, requiring as a basis the sprinkling of blood, and as a consummation the burning upon the altar. They possessed and retained, from every point of view, a purely personal character: on the *objective* side, because they were to be set apart for Jehovah personally, and also because Jehovah desired a personal surrender, and not the mere material gift; on the *subjective* side, because in them the worshipper presented himself before Jehovah, with all his life and deeds, his hopes and longings, his thanksgiving and praise, his prayers and supplications.

Through this exclusively spiritual character the *altar-sacrifices*, as may easily be conceived, stand in a much closer relation to the equally spiritual character of *prayer*. They were indispensable to one another. For, on the one hand, a sacrifice offered *without* prayer, at least without the spirit of prayer, was a body without soul, an empty, lifeless, powerless *opus operatum;* and, on the other hand, prayer could not dispense with the accompaniment of sacrifice. Prayer in itself is merely an ideal expression of the need and longing for expiation and fellowship with God, and does not really set these forth; but in the sacrificial worship there is an embodiment, a visible and palpable expression, not merely of the subjective desire of the worshipper, but also of the objective satisfaction of that desire. I cannot help regarding it as a mistaken and misleading statement of *Hengstenberg's*, therefore, that sacrifice "was *in the main* an embodiment of prayer (Hos. xiv. 2; Heb. xiii. 15)." On the contrary, sacrifice was something different from and something more than prayer. It did not correspond to prayer, as the symbol to the idea; but it ran parallel to it, and required it as an accompaniment throughout its entire course. Moreover, "the main point in the sacrifice" was not, what prayer could have exhibited equally well, a subjective longing for the blessings of salvation, but an objective assurance of them. *Keil's* explanation, in which *Hengstenberg's* idea is adopted, but *without* the essential, though still not sufficient limitation, "in the main," is still more inadmissible. "Sacrifice," he says, "is the visible utterance of prayer as the most direct self-dedication of a man to God."[1] (Arch. i. 192.) But if sacrifice itself was in the main an embodiment of prayer, what necessity could there be for a special symbol of prayer to be associated with most of the sacrifices? For both *Hengstenberg* and *Keil* have thus correctly interpreted the *incense* which had to be added to every meat-offering, and thereby to every burnt-offering and peace-offering also, but which was not allowed to be added to the sin-offering.

§ 21. If we turn now to what was actually offered, to the *material substance* of the Corbanim, it is self-evident that the first and most important consideration was this, that the offering to be presented should be the *property* of the person presenting it, and should be properly acquired or earned.[2] How essential this demand was with reference to all the Corbanim, is evident from the nature of the case, and requires no proof. For instance, whereas in the first class the notion of property was without restriction, and embraced valuables of every kind (gold, silver, furniture, houses, fields, vine-

---

[1] *Vid. Delitzsch* on the Epistle to the Hebrews (p. 739): "The sacrifice, when offered in a right state of mind, had the self-dedication of the worshipper as its background, and his prayer as its accompaniment (Job xlii. 8; 1 Sam. vii. 9; 1 Chron. xxi. 26; 2 Chron. xxix. 26–30); but it was not the symbol of either self-dedication or prayer."

[2] Thus, for example, the gains of prostitution and the *merces scorti virilis* are forbidden to be offered (Deut. xxiii. 18).

yards, etc.), in the second it was restricted to the produce of agriculture and grazing, and in the third class was limited still further, —all garden produce, all fruits (except wine and oil), and all *unclean* animals being excluded, so that the only things left for this class of offerings were *oxen, sheep, goats,* and *pigeons,* as well as *wine, oil,* and *corn* (either *in natura,* or in the form of flour, dough, bread, cakes, etc.).

The fact that the Corbanim of the *second* class were limited to the produce of agriculture and grazing, but embraced all such produce, may be explained from their character as *feudal payments.* Agriculture and grazing were to be the peculiar and sole occupation of the Israelites in the land which their God had given them in fief ; hence their feudal payments were to be restricted to the produce of these.

But, in the case of strict *altar-sacrifices,* two other limitations were introduced. All kinds of property which *could* not serve the Israelite as *food* (*e.g.,* houses, clothes, furniture, etc.) were to be excluded, as well as every kind which *ought* not to be so used (viz., all unclean animals—the ass, the camel, etc.). In addition to these, every kind of property was to be excluded which had not been acquired by the worshipper himself in the sweat of his face, *i.e.,* by *his own diligence and toil,* and in the exercise of his own proper calling : for example, all edible game, such as stags, gazelles, and antelopes, and fruit which had grown ready to his hand, and could be eaten without the bestowal of any special labour or care (such as almonds, dates, pomegranates, etc.). Oil and wine were not included in them, because in their case it was not the grape and olive that were offered, but *juice* which had been procured in the sweat of the face.[1]

From what has been already said, it follows that both *Bähr* (Symb. ii. 316–17) and *Neumann* are in error, when the former

---

[1] It is true this last point could not be carried out in all its stringency and literality ; for a man who had no field or flock of his own (a labouring man, for example) could not offer bread that he had reaped, or cattle that he had reared. It was necessary, therefore, that he should be allowed to offer a sacrifice that he had *bought* (the purchase, at any rate, was made in such a case with money acquired by the sweat of his own face) ; and in the Holy Land this exception afterwards grew to be the rule whenever the person lived at such a distance from the sanctuary as rendered it difficult to bring the sacrifice with him. This exception was a compromise of a similar kind to that which allowed the poor man, who could not procure an expensive animal, to offer as a substitute an incomparably cheaper pigeon, or if that were impossible, the tenth part of an ephah of flour.

looks at the material of the altar-sacrifices exclusively in the light of a collection of the principal productions of the country, and a representation of the whole of the national property, whilst the latter merely regards it in the light of food. It is a sufficient reply to *Bähr*, that very many of the productions that were characteristic of the country, and much that represented the national wealth, could not be offered at all (*e.g.*, the ass, the grape, the fig, the pomegranate, milk and honey, etc.: Num. xiii. 23; Deut. viii. 7–9, xi. 7–9). And *Neumann's* assertion is no less inconsiderate; for if that had been the only regulating principle, stags, gazelles, and antelopes, as well as the numerous kinds of clean birds, together with vegetables, figs, dates, pomegranates, honey, etc., ought to have been offered as well.

To obtain a correct view of the material selected for the sacrifices, we ought to do as *Oehler* has done, viz., to combine the three aspects referred to, and to regard this as the principle of selection, that nothing was suitable to the purpose but personal *property* justly acquired, which was, on the one hand, the *fruit* of Israel's proper avocation (agriculture and the rearing of cattle), and on the other hand, the natural and legal *means* of sustenance, that is to say, of maintaining that avocation.

§ 22. From the rule thus laid down for the choice of the materials for the altar-sacrifices, it is perfectly obvious that in these offerings it was not the gift itself, but the giver, that was the primary object of consideration; in other words, that they represented a *personal* self-surrender to the *person* of Jehovah Himself. If this self-surrender to God was to be expressed, not merely ideally in thought, or verbally in prayer, but in a visible and tangible act; and if, moreover, as had been unalterably established since the occurrence related in Gen. xxii., this act was not to assume the form of a real *human* sacrifice; nothing remained but to select as a symbolical representation or substitute some other thing, which was evidently suitable for the purpose on account of the close and essential connection existing between it and the worshipper. But for this purpose it was not sufficient that the sacrifice should be merely the property of the person offering it; on the contrary, it was requisite that it should stand in a close, inward, essential relation, a psychical *rapport*, to the person of the worshipper. This was the case, on the one hand, whenever the material of the sacrifice was the result and fruit of his life-work, his true avocation, and thus in a certain sense was inoculated and impregnated with his own *vis vitalis;* and,

on the other hand, whenever it was appointed as the means of maintaining and strengthening his vital energy, that is to say, when it
impregnated *him* with its own *vis vitalis*. But, as the rule laid
down above evidently shows, both points of view were combined in
the material selected for the Mosaic sacrifices. To the cattle which
the Israelite had reared, to the corn which he had reaped, to the
wine and oil which he had pressed, there still adhered the sweat of
his toil. The acquisition and maturing of them had been dependent
upon his own unwearied care, his toil and exertion; and thus, in a
certain sense, one element of his own life had been transferred to
them, and penetrated into them. He had devoted a portion of his
life to the task of acquiring them; and they were consequently, as
it were, an objective portion of his own life. To recognise the full
importance of this connection, it must again be borne in mind, that
according to the law itself the whole of the earthly life-work and
vocation of the Israelite was restricted to agriculture and the rearing of cattle, and consequently that he devoted himself to it with
his whole heart, with undivided interest.

But wine, oil, corn, and cattle were not merely the result of
his toil and care, they were also and chiefly the fruit of the blessing
of GOD, a gift of God; and by virtue of what God had done, they
were appointed and suited to nourish and preserve his bodily life,
and to enable him to carry out his true vocation.

Keil disputes the correctness of this view of a *biotic rapport* between the sacrificer and his sacrifice; *Oehler*, on the contrary, admits
its truth. But when *Keil* argues, (1) that in that case the ass could
not have been excluded, and (2) that this principle is perfectly inapplicable to the vegetable portion of the materials of sacrifice,—it is a
sufficient reply to the former, that the ass was an unclean animal,
and therefore could not be used as food by the Israelites; and we
have already shown that there is no force whatever in the latter.

Neumann (p. 332), on the other hand, will not admit that the
question of *property* had anything to do with the choice of materials
for the altar-sacrifices; (1) "because dogs, asses, camels, houses,
and even wives, formed part of the property of an Israelite, and yet
were not offered in sacrifice;" (2) because " the ram, which Abraham sacrificed instead of his son, was hardly his own property;" and
(3) because "in the later period of the Jewish history the instances
were numerous enough, in which the people offered to their God
what had been contributed by foreign kings" (Ezra vi. 9; 1 Macc. x.
39; 2 Macc. iii. 3, ix. 16). *Keil*, who agrees with *Neumann* in his

rejection of our view, lays stress upon the last point only. The first needs no refutation on our part. To the second we reply, that this was before the standpoint of the sacrificial worship of the law had been reached; and the case in itself was so singular and extraordinary, that it cannot be regarded as supplying the rule for the rest. And to the third *Oehler* (p. 625) has already replied, that " in Ezra's time this was the necessary consequence of the poverty of the people (Ezra vii. 17, 22); but Nehemiah's directions (Neh. x. 33, 34) show how strong was the feeling even then, that it was the duty of the people themselves to provide for the expenses of their own worship." With regard to the later times of the Syrians and Romans, the custom at that time proves nothing; for many things were practised then, which were totally at variance with the spirit of the Mosaic legislation.

§ 23. The altar-sacrifices were presented under the aspect of *food*, not only subjectively, but objectively also; that is to say, they not only consisted of the materials which constituted the food of Israel, but they were also to be regarded as *food for Jehovah*. The latter would follow from the former as a matter of course, even if it had not been expressly stated. But it *is* expressly indicated, inasmuch as these sacrifices are spoken of as a whole, as the *bread, the food, of Jehovah* (Lev. iii. 11, 16, xxi. 6, 8, 17, xxii. 25; Num. xxviii. 2). Not, of course, that flesh, bread, and wine, as such, could be offered to the God of Israel for food (Ps. l. 12 sqq.). They were not to pass for what they were, but for what they signified; and only in that light were they food for Jehovah. That which served as the daily food of Israel was adopted as the symbol of those spiritual gifts, which were offered to Jehovah as food. We have no hesitation whatever in understanding the expression " bread of Jehovah" in the strict sense of the words; but we must keep well in mind, that in the case of the God of Israel the allusion could only have been to *spiritual*, and not at all to material food.

Jehovah, who, as the God of salvation, had entered into the history of the world, and moved forward in it and with it, stood in need of food in that capacity, but of spiritual food, the complete failure of which would be followed by His also ceasing to be Jehovah. That food Israel was to offer Him in its own faithful self-surrender; and the symbol of that self-surrender was to be seen in the sacrifices consumed upon the altar, and ascending as a " savour of satisfaction to Jehovah." If Israel had failed to fulfil its covenant obligation of self-surrender to Jehovah, it would have broken away from the covenant, and the covenant itself would have ceased; and had the covenant been once abolished, God would also have ceased to be the covenant-God, *i.e.*, to be Jehovah.[1]

§ 24. Our remarks, thus far, apply equally to all the materials of sacrifice, whether animal or vegetable. But there is one important point of view, from which there was an essential distinction between them, and which is adapted to throw light upon the question, why they stood side by side in the sacrificial worship; that is to say, why bloodless as well as bleeding sacrifices were required. Animals of the higher class, more especially domestic animals and cattle, stand incomparably nearer to man than plants do: their life rests upon the same psychico-corporeal basis, they are subject to the same conditions of life, they have the same bodily organs and functions, and need the same corporeal food as man. All this is wanting in the case of the plant; or rather, everything in it is precisely the opposite. An animal, therefore, is far better adapted to represent the *person* of a man, his vital organs, powers, and actions, than plants can ever be. On the other hand, the cultivation of plants, more especially the growing of corn, requires far more of the preparatory, continuous, and subsequent labour of man, and is more dependent upon him than the rearing of cattle. It was not upon the latter, but upon the former, that the curse was really pronounced in Gen. iii. 17–19 (cf. v. 29). The material acquired by agriculture, therefore, was far more suitable than the flocks to represent the *fruit*, or result of the life-work of man. And this distinction, as we shall afterwards show, was undoubtedly the principle by which the addition of the vegetable to the animal materials of sacrifice was regulated.

§ 25. The altar-sacrifices are thus divisible into *bleeding* (animal) and *bloodless* (vegetable) sacrifices.[2] The former may be grouped

---

[1] Compare with this what *Hengstenberg* says with reference to the shew-bread: "This was really the food which Israel presented to its King; but that King was a spiritual, heavenly one; and therefore the food offered to Him under a material form must be spiritual also. . . . . The prayer to God, 'Give us this day *our* daily bread,' is accompanied by the demand on the part of God, 'Give Me to-day *My* daily bread;' and this demand is satisfied by the Church, when it offers diligently to God in good works that for which God has endowed it with strength, benediction, and prosperity." (Diss. on the Pentateuch, vol. ii. pp. 531, 532, translation.)

[2] This distinction, however, is by no means coincident, as *Kliefoth* supposes, with that between the *expiatory* sacrifices ("by which forgiveness of sins and the favour and fellowship of God were secured") and *eucharistic* offerings ("in which, after reconciliation has taken place, God and man hold intercourse with

again in three classes: (1) SIN-OFFERINGS (חַטָּאת) and TRESPASS-OFFERINGS (אָשָׁם), the latter of which was merely one peculiar description of the former; (2) BURNT-OFFERINGS (עֹלָה); and (3) PEACE-OFFERINGS (שְׁלָמִים; *Luther*, "thank-offerings"). In the first, the *sprinkling of the blood* appears to have been the principal thing; in the second, the *burning upon the altar;* and in the last a new feature is introduced, which is wanting in both the others, namely, the *sacrificial meal.* In the different kinds of bloodless offerings we have to include, not only those which were burned upon the altar in the *court,* but those which were offered upon the altar, table, and candlestick of the *Holy Place.* The former were designated as *meat-offerings* and *drink-offerings* (מִנְחָה וָנֶסֶךְ), and consisted of corn (meal, bread, cake, etc.) and wine, with the addition of oil, incense, and salt. We find the same essential elements in the Holy Place, but distributed upon the three different articles of furniture—the incense upon the altar, bread and wine (meat- and drink-offerings) upon the table of shew-bread, and oil (light-offering) upon the candlestick.

Thus the whole of the Mosaic *Corbanim* may be classified as follows:—

OFFERINGS.

II. FEUDAL PAYMENTS, for the maintenance of the priests and Levites (first-fruits and tenths).	I. SACRED OFFERINGS, for the endowment of the sanctuary.	III. ALTAR-SACRIFICES, for personal appropriation on the part of Jehovah.	
1. Fruits. 2. Cattle. 3. Men.	A. *Bleeding.*	B. *Bloodless.*	
1. Clean. 2. Unclean.	1. Sin-offerings and trespass-offerings. 2. Burnt-offerings. 3. Peace-offerings.	(1). In the Court. Meat and drink-offerings.	(2). In the Holy Place. 1. Incense-offerings. 2. Light-offerings. 3. Meat-offerings.

one another in mutual fellowship of life"). Still less is he right in denying to the bleeding (expiatory) sacrifice the character of an offering altogether. This view is overthrown at once by the fact that all the sacrifices are called by the same name, *Corbanim.* Even the bleeding, expiatory, animal sacrifices were primarily offerings, or gifts; and this character of an offering was expressed in the burning (of their fleshy parts), to which they were subjected in the same way as the bloodless altar-gifts. Even in the case of those bleeding sacrifices in which the expiation reached its highest point, and everything else gave place to it (viz., in the case of the sin-offerings), the essential characteristic of an offering was invariably preserved through the burning of the fat (cf. § 142).

BOOK II

THE BLEEDING SACRIFICE

PART I

RITUAL OF THE SACRIFICE

§ 26. The ritual of the bleeding sacrifice may be arranged according to its salient points in the following manner:—

When circumstances demanded, or inclination prompted, the person presenting the sacrifice, having selected an animal in accordance with the legal directions as to both kind and mode, brought it before the door of the tabernacle, *i.e.*, to the altar of burnt-offering in the court, where he laid his hand upon it, and then slaughtered it on the north side of the altar. The sacrificer had now performed his part, and all the rest belonged to the province of the priest. The latter began by receiving the blood of the animal in a vessel, and applying it, either in whole or in part, and in various ways according to the nature and importance of the sacrifice, to the altar of the court (in certain cases also to the altar of the Holy Place, or the Capporeth of the Most Holy). He then flayed the animal, and having cut it in pieces, and washed the entrails and lower part of the thigh in water, burned either the whole of it except the skin, which belonged to himself, or only the fat, upon the altar of the court. It was only in the case of the burnt-offerings that the former was done; whilst the latter was the case with all the other kinds of sacrifice. But in the case of the peace-offerings, after the burning of the fat and the removal of certain portions, which fell to the lot of the officiating priest, the remainder was eaten at a sacrificial meal by the sacrificer himself and his family; and in that of the sin-offerings and trespass-offerings, the flesh was either burned without the camp, or (in certain cases) eaten by the priests in the Holy Place. With the burnt-offerings and peace-offerings, there

were also associated meat-offerings and drink-offerings; but never
with the sin-offerings and trespass-offerings.

Of the different points referred to here, we shall look, in the
first place, simply at those which mark the progressive steps of the
sacrificial ceremony as a whole, and only so far as they do this.
All the rest we shall defer till we come to our examination of the
various kinds of sacrifice.

CHAPTER I

THE NOTION OF EXPIATION

§ 27. The EXPIATION (Rabbinical: כַּפָּרָה) of the person sacrificing is what we meet with everywhere, not only as the first
intention, but to a certain extent as the chief and most important
end of the bleeding sacrifices in general. When the sacrifice of
animals is mentioned in the law, *making atonement* (לְכַפֵּר עָלָיו) is
nearly always expressly mentioned, and for the most part this
alone, as being the purpose, end, and fruit of the sacrifice. It is
perfectly obvious, indeed, that there were other ends to be attained,—
such, for example, as the self-surrender of the sacrifice *to* Jehovah
in the burning of the sacrificial gift, and the enjoyment of fellowship *with* Jehovah in the sacrificial meal; but the fact that these
ends could not possibly be attained in any other way than by means
of expiation, and on the basis of expiation, gave to the latter its
incomparable, all-surpassing importance, and its central place in
the plan of salvation, the progressive stages of which were symbolically represented in the sacrificial worship. The highest and
most difficult, in fact the only real enigma, which the saving
counsel of God had to solve in the whole history of salvation, was
the expiation of sinful man. Let this difficulty be overcome, and
every other difficulty falls with it to the ground, so that the way is
fully opened for the attainment of all the other blessings of salvation.
The question was not, how could man, who had been created *by* and
for God, attain to fellowship with God, and continue therein *as so
created* (there would have been no difficulty in this; in fact, it would
have followed, so to speak, as a matter of course); the question
was, whether, and how, *sinful* man, notwithstanding his sin, which
had severed all the bonds of fellowship with God, and rendered

their reunion impossible, could nevertheless attain to that fellow-ship again. Nothing but expiation, *i.e.*, the extermination of his sin, could render this impossibility possible. Consequently, the expiation of his sin was the Alpha and Omega for the wants and longings of a sinner desirous of fellowship with God; and for that reason, the law of sacrifice, which meets these wants and this longing with its institutions of salvation, reiterates again and again, and more than anything besides, its לְכַפֵּר עָלָיו or וְכִפֶּר עָלָיו הַכֹּהֵן ("to make atonement for him," or "the priest shall make atonement for him").

§ 28. Although the root כפר does not occur in *Kal* (for the כָּפַר in Gen. vi. 14 is probably a denominative verb from כֹּפֶר = pitch or resin, cf. *Fürst*, Lex. i. 621), the correctness of the generally accepted radical signification, "to *cover*," "to *cover up*," is fully established from the cognate dialects. This radical meaning has been retained in the *Piel*, only the notion of covering up has passed from the literal into a figurative sense. כִּפֶּר and כֻּפַּר are never used to denote any other than an *ideal* covering. In this sense it is chiefly em-ployed in religious phraseology, *i.e.*, in connection with divine worship. That which is covered up is *never* God, or anything godly,[1] but always something ungodly, displeasing to God, hostile to Him, provocative of His wrath and punishment; that is to say, sin, guilt, and uncleanness ("for sin," Lev. iv. 35, v. 13, etc.; "iniquity," Jer. xviii. 23; Ps. lxxviii. 38, etc.; "his ignorance," Lev. v. 18). If we find a number of other objects appended to כִּפֶּר (*e.g.*, "for the soul," or "for the souls," Ex. xxx. 15; Lev. xvii. 11, etc.; "for the children of Israel," Num. viii. 19; "for the house," Lev. xiv. 53, and many others), it is only in appearance that this is opposed to our assertion. All these objects come into con-sideration only so far as sin or uncleanness adheres to them; and it is not to them, but to the uncleanness adhering to them that the term כִּפֶּר applies. In such a case the covering becomes *eo ipso* an expiation, and the covered sin no longer exists as sin, but is an exterminated or expiated sin.

---

[1] It is incorrect, and likely to mislead, therefore, to speak of atoning the wrath of God, as *Delitzsch*, for example, does (Heb. p. 741): "it is the wrath of God excited by sin which is *atoned*, *i.e.*, appeased by the punishment of sin." On the contrary, we must distinguish between *expiation* and *reconciliation*. Accord-ing to the analogy of the ordinary expression, "to *reconcile* an enemy," we may also speak of reconciling the angry God, but never of *atoning* (expiating) God, or the wrath of God. The reconciliation of the angry person is effected through the expiation of that by which he has been offended, and his anger has been aroused.

We must here inquire, in the first place, however, by what
process of thought the covered sins were regarded as exterminated
or expiated. According to the general opinion, the covering removed
the sins from the sight of Jehovah ; Jehovah saw them no more ;
they no longer provoked His anger and His punishment ; and thus
they might be regarded as no longer existing, as exterminated, and
altogether removed from the wrath of God (*vid. Bähr*, ii. 204 ;
Ebrard, p. 42 ; *Kliefoth*, p. 31 ; *Oehler*, p. 630). In confirmation of
this view appeal is made to the expression in Lev. vi. 7, וְכִפֶּר
עָלָיו הַכֹּהֵן לִפְנֵי יְהוָֹה, where the sins are represented as being covered
up " before the face of Jehovah." But פָּנִים is *not* the face in the
sense of that which sees, but rather in the sense of that which is
seen, or is to be seen ; the expression employed to denote the
former is לְעֵינֵי יהוה. And when we find the forgiveness of sins
designated in Micah vii. 19 as a casting of the sins into the depths
of the sea, and in Jer. xviii. 23, " washing away (תִּמְחִי) the sins
before the face of Jehovah," answering as a parallelism to תְּכַפֵּר
עַל־עֲוֹנָם ; these are simply different *figures* for the same thing, from
which nothing at all can be inferred as to the meaning of כִּפֶּר,
although *Oehler* appeals to both these points. And when *Oehler*
goes on to remark, that " the immediate consequence is, that by
virtue of such a covering, the sinful man is protected from the
punishing judge," no objection can be made to this, unless, as is
done by *Delitzsch* (Heb. p. 387, 740), there is given to כפר itself
the meaning or force of a *protective* covering, or of a covering from
danger, namely, from the manifestation of the wrath of God. The
meaning of כפר, in the sacrificial terminology, cannot possibly be
that what is covered is to be *protected*, delivered, preserved. Such
a meaning would be perfectly inadmissible in connection with
the common expressions עַל־עֲוֹן, עַל־חַטָּאת (" for their sin," " for their
iniquity"), etc. ; for sin, iniquity, guilt, or uncleanness, is just what
is not to be *protected*, but, on the contrary, to be exterminated, set
aside, annihilated. No doubt the object of the verb כפר in the
sacrificial language, is for the most part the person of the sacrificer
himself ; in which case, the notion of protection, deliverance, preservation, and so forth, before the wrath of God would be perfectly
applicable. But the frequency with which the verb is connected
with sin, iniquity, etc., compels us to assume, that even where a
person is mentioned as the object, it is not the person himself, or in
himself, that is to be regarded as the object to be covered, but the
sin and uncleanness adhering to him. Moreover, when we observe

that very frequently, where the person of the sacrificer is mentioned as the object, there is added, as an explanatory apposition, either עַל־חַטָּאתוֹ ("concerning his sin"), Lev. iv. 35, v. 13; or עַל־שִׁגְגָתוֹ ("concerning his ignorance"), Lev. v. 18; or מֵחַטָּאתוֹ ("from his sin"), Lev. iv. 26, v. 6, 10, xvi. 34; or מִטֻּמְאוֹת ("from the uncleannesses"), Lev. xvi. 16; or, lastly, מֵאֲשֶׁר חָטָא (Eng. Ver., "for that he sinned"), Num. vi. 11; we must admit the correctness of the conclusion to which *Rosenmüller* and *Bähr* both came, that "the formula כִּפֶּר עָלָיו (Eng. Ver., "make atonement for him"), which occurs most frequently in the sacrificial ritual, is abbreviated from the more complete form כִּפֶּר עַל־נַפְשׁוֹ ("make atonement for his soul"), and that this again stands for כִּפֶּר עַל־חַטַּאת נַפְשׁוֹ ("make atonement for the sin of his soul").

But whether the word כִּפֶּר be understood as denoting a covering in the sense of withdrawing from view, or of protecting from danger, the use of the word in other connections—viz., in Gen. xxxii. 20; Prov. xvi. 14; Isa. xxviii. 18, xlvii. 11—seems to show that neither of these interpretations can be sustained. When Isaiah says, for example, וְכֻפַּר בְּרִיתְכֶם אֶת־מָוֶת ("your covenant with death shall be covered"), the meaning is not that the covenant with death shall be rendered invisible, for even as an invisible (secret) covenant it might answer its purpose quite as well; still less that it shall be protected from danger, for, on the contrary, it is to be rendered powerless and nugatory. But covering would only render it powerless and nugatory, provided it was a covering of a kind to suppress, restrain, and destroy the ability and effort to assist the ally. In the same way it would be opposed both to the meaning and the context, to imagine the words employed by Jacob, "I will cover his face with a present," as signifying either that he would protect Esau's face from danger, or that he would hide it from view by means of his present; on the contrary, Jacob's intention was to protect himself from the wrath of Esau, of which his face was the vehicle, and then to follow this "covering of his face" by actually "seeing his face." Nor can we interpret this passage, according to the analogy of the "covering of the eyes" in Gen. xx. 16, as indicating that it was Jacob's intention to "hold something before Esau's face which would prevent him from looking any longer at the wrong that had been done him" (*Hofmann*, Schriftbeweis ii. 1, p. 233); for in that case he would have followed the analogy of Gen. xx. 16, and said, אכפרה עיניו ("I will cover his eyes"), to say nothing of the fact that the meaning thus obtained could not possibly be applied to the sacri-

ficial כפר. Jacob determines to cover Esau's face, *not* that he may
no longer see the wrong that Jacob has done, but that the anger
depicted in Esau's face may be broken, that is to say, rendered
altogether powerless. And when it is stated in Prov. xvi. 14, that
" a wise man covers (יְכַפֶּר) the wrath of the king," the word is to be
understood in the same sense as Jacob's אכפרה. With this interpretation of the word כַּפֵּר, " a transition to the phrase כַּפֵּר הֹוָה (to cover
mischief) in Isa. xlvii. 11" is undoubtedly " possible," and a meaning may be obtained which shall be perfectly appropriate to the
parallel שַׁחַר רָעָה (" the dawning of evil").

In this way, then, we also understand the covering of sin in
the sacrificial worship as a covering by which the accusatory and
damnatory power of sin—its power to excite the anger and wrath
of God—is broken, by which, in fact, it is rendered both harmless
and impotent. And, understood in this sense, the sacrificial covering
was not merely an apparent, conventional, expiation of sin (which
would have been the case if it had been merely removed from the
sight of Jehovah), but a process by which it was actually rendered
harmless, which is equivalent to cancelling and utterly annihilating. Among other passages which show that the word כַּפֵּר must
be understood in this sense, we may cite Deut. xxi. 9, where the
נִכַּפֵּר in ver. 8 is followed by an explanatory תְּבַעֵר (thou shalt put
away).[1]

With this view the intensive force of the *Piel*, as determining or
modifying this signification, is firmly retained: it is so complete,
effectual, and overpowering a covering, that all real and active force
in that which is covered up is thereby rendered impossible, or slain.

Hofmann has a very peculiar notion with regard to כַּפֵּר. In his
opinion, it is a denominative from כֹּפֶר (a redemption fee), and signifies to give a covering, or payment; so that the means by which
the sin is expiated assumes the appearance of a " compensation,"
without which the sinner could not be set free from the captivity
of sin; in just the same sense in which payment is made as a redemption fee for deliverance from bodily captivity. But notwithstanding the amazing acuteness, and minute, hair-splitting cleverness,

---

[1] Since writing the above, I have found essentially the same view expressed
by *Kahnis* (i. 271), who says, " To expiate, literally to cover up, does not mean
to cause a sin not to have been committed, for that is impossible ; nor to represent it as having no existence, for that would be opposed to the earnestness of
the law; nor to pay or compensate it by any performance; but to cover it before
God, *i.e.*, *to deprive it of its power to come between us and God.*"

with which *Hofmann* has endeavoured once more to establish this
derivation and meaning, and to defend it against the objections of
Ebrard (pp. 41, 42) and *Delitzsch* (Heb. 386, 740), in the second
edition of his *Schriftbeweis* (ii. 1, 232 sqq.), he has not succeeded
even in rendering it plausible. He cannot adduce a single passage
from which this signification of כֵּפֶּר or its derivatives (כִּפֻּרִים and
כַּפֹּרֶת) can be proved;[1] and still less is he able to meet the important
fact, that the term כֹּפֶר, which is so common elsewhere, and which
is said to furnish the real key to the explanation of the sacrificial
worship, is not to be met with on one single occasion in connection
with the sacrificial worship, whereas the word כֵּפֶּר, which is said to
be derived from it, with its several derivatives, is perpetually employed, and occurs in connections of the most various kinds, which
would have furnished just as fitting an occasion for the use of כֹּפֶר,
if the two words had really been synonymous.

§ 29. The *subject* from whom the כַּפֶּר proceeded in connection
with the sacrificial worship, was always represented as either GOD,
or His servant and representative the priest; and the fruit and
effect of it as being the forgiveness of those sins (Lev. iv. 20, וְכִפֶּר
עֲלֵיהֶם הַכֹּהֵן וְנִסְלַח לָהֶם; also Lev. iv. 26, 31, 35, v. 10, 13, 16, 18,
vi. 7; Num. xv. 28), or the removal of that uncleanness (Lev. xii.
7, 8, וְכִפֶּר עָלֶיהָ וְטָהֲרָה, cf. Lev. xiv. 31, 53, xvi. 19), for which expiation was to be made. The *blood* alone is mentioned as the means
of *sacrificial* expiation (Ex. xxx. 10; Lev. vi. 30, viii. 15, xvi.
16, etc.); from which it follows, that it was the bleeding sacrifice
alone, and not the bloodless offerings also, which possessed an expiatory value. But *why*, or *in what way*, the blood was adapted to
be a means of expiation, we learn first of all in connection with the
publication of the command to abstain from eating blood in Lev.
xvii. 11 : " For the soul of the flesh is in the blood; and I have given
it to you upon the altar, to make an atonement for your souls : for
the blood, *it makes atonement by means of the soul.*" We adopt this
rendering of בַּנֶּפֶשׁ יְכַפֵּר, in common with *Bähr, Keil, Delitzsch*, etc.

[1] The only passage which could be adduced as favouring this meaning, viz.,
Ex. xxx.—where the census-tax, which is called כֹּפֶר נַפְשׁוֹ in ver. 12, is described in ver. 16 as כֶּסֶף הַכִּפֻּרִים, and in ver. 15 as serving לְכַפֵּר עַל־נַפְשֹׁתֵיכֶם—
only proves that on one occasion, under peculiar circumstances, and in a particular sense, the כַּפָּרָה, which, as a rule, was accomplished by the sacrificial blood,
was accomplished in a more literal sense by a money payment. But it by no
means follows from this, that on every occasion, whatever the means of expiation
might be, it must always be regarded in the light of a payment.

Ebrard (p. 44), on the other hand, adheres to the rendering adopted by the LXX. (ἀντὶ ψυχῆς), the *Vulgate* (*pro animæ piaculo*), and *Luther,* viz., "*for* (or *concerning*) the soul;" and assumes, in consequence, that according to the usual phraseology employed in connection with purchase and exchange, the animal soul is regarded as the purchase money paid for the redemption of the human soul. But this rendering is inadmissible, since כֹּפֶר (= to cover) is not one of the verbs denoting purchase or barter, and there is no allusion here to exchange. *Hengstenberg's* rendering, " for the blood expiates the soul," is still less admissible, as it has no analogy whatever in the usage of the language. For כִּפֶּר is never construed with בְּ *objecti* (in בַּקֹּדֶשׁ, Lev. vi. 30, xvi. 27, the בְּ is to be regarded as local), but only with עַל or בְּעַד, and sometimes also with a simple accusative. *Hofmann, Kliefoth, Bunsen,* and others, prefer to regard the בְּ as בְּ *essentiæ:* "the blood expiates *as* (in the character of) the soul." The objection made to this by *Delitzsch* (Psychol. p. 197), that the בְּ *essentiæ* never stands before a noun determined by an article or suffix, has been overthrown by *Hofmann,* who adduces several instances, in which, at all events, it stands before a noun with a suffix (Ex. xviii. 4; Ps. cxlvi. 5; Prov. iii. 26). I cannot admit that Ex. vi. 3 is a case in point; for even if *El Shaddai* might be regarded elsewhere as a proper name, the very use of בְּ *essentiæ* here would in itself contain an allusion to its appellative meaning. But although from this point of view also *Hofmann's* rendering appears perfectly justifiable, the instrumental force of the בְּ, as being the more usual one in connection with כִּפֶּר (Gen. xxxii. 20; Ex. xxix. 33; Lev. vii. 7, xix. 22; Num. v. 8; 2 Sam. xxi. 3), and therefore, at all events, the first to suggest itself, is certainly to be preferred.[1]

---

[1] *Even Hofmann* admits that this view has very much to support it in the frequent use of בְּ with כִּפֶּר, to denote the means employed in the process of expiation; but in his opinion there may be adduced *against* it the unnatural character of the fact, " that whilst on other occasions the sacrificial gift is the medium of the atoning act of the sacrificer, here the blood offered was to be rendered effective by something altogether different from him." Moreover, " in other places the blood and the soul are regarded as one." (Thus in Gen. ix. 4; Deut. xii. 23; and in our passage, Lev. xvii. 11.) But the blood is not otherwise distinguished from the soul, nor otherwise identified with it, than as a full purse is distinguished from and identified with the money that it contains. Since it was only the soul contained in the blood which gave its worth and significance to the blood itself, the latter might very well be called the soul, although the lawgiver was perfectly aware, and in ver. 11 has really stated, that the soul *may* be distinguished from the blood because the soul is *in* the blood. For it would be difficult for any one to persuade himself that the בְּ is a *Beth*

§ 30. There is something peculiar, however, in the slighting
way in which *Hofmann* speaks of Lev. xvii. 11. " It has sometimes
happened," he says (p. 237), " that the words of Lev. xvii. 11 have
been made the basis of the whole investigation with regard to the
nature of the bleeding sacrifice. . . . . When we read that ' the
blood, it expiates by means of the soul,' we learn nothing more than
we have already learned elsewhere." Again, at p. 239, he says :
" In this passage we neither find the blood and the soul of the animal treated as one ; nor are we told how far the blood, when it was
applied to the altar, had an expiatory effect ; nor is there anything
to lead to the conclusion, that every sacrifice, in connection with
which blood was applied to the altar, was intended as an expiation ;
or that the application of blood alone served as an expiation, to the
exclusion of all the rest of the sacrificial process."

But this is not a correct statement of the case. It is true that
we already know, from Ex. xxx. 10, Lev. vi. 30, viii. 15, xvi. 16,
that the blood was the medium of expiation ; and from Gen. ix. 4,
that the blood stands in an immediate and essential relation to the
soul. But that the blood, *as* soul, *i.e.*, as the vehicle of the soul,
was the *medium of expiation*, is stated first and *alone* in Lev. xvii.
11 ; and for that reason, this passage must be admitted to possess
an unparalleled and fundamental importance as a key to the meaning of the bleeding sacrifice.

It also follows undoubtedly from this passage, that any blood
which was sprinkled upon the altar, and therefore " every sacrifice
in which blood was applied to the altar," was intended as an expiation ; and also, that, as blood was applied to the altar in connection
with every animal sacrifice, expiation took place in connection with
them all ; and, *so far*, every kind of animal sacrifice might be designated as an *expiatory* sacrifice. But it does *not* follow from this,
that expiation was the sole object in every case, or an equally im-

essentiæ and not a *Beth locale* in the clause נֶפֶשׁ הַבָּשָׂר בַּדָּם הוּא. On the other
hand, I fully agree with *Hofmann*, in opposition to *Delitzsch, Knobel*, and *Oehler*,
that in ver 14, in the clause נֶפֶשׁ כָּל־בָּשָׂר דָּמוֹ בְנַפְשׁוֹ הוּא, the בְ is neither local
nor instrumental, since neither the one nor the other will give any tolerable
sense ; and that it is to be understood as בְ *essentiæ*, " the soul of all flesh is its
blood, as its soul," or, as *Hofmann* explains it, "it is true of the soul of all
flesh, that it is its blood, which constitutes its soul." But just as in this place
the context compels us to regard the Beth as essential, because this alone will
give any meaning ; so the current phraseology requires that in the word בַּנֶּפֶשׁ
in ver. 11 it should be regarded as instrumental, which gives a good meaning,
and is perfectly in harmony with the context.

portant object in them all. The words, " to make atonement for him " (לְכַפֵּר עָלָיו), are expressly used, in fact, not only in connection with the sin-offering (Lev. iv. 20, 26, 31, 35, etc.) and trespass-offering (Lev. v. 16, 18, vi. 7, etc.), but in connection with the burnt-offering also (Lev. i. 4). And if this is not the case with the peace-offerings, we must not conclude from that, that the law did not attribute to them any expiatory character at all. In proportion as the expiatory character of the different kinds of sacrifice diminished in importance, the eagerness of the law to give prominence to their atoning virtue diminishes also. The sin- and trespass-offerings are hardly referred to once, without an allusion to the atonement to be made. In connection with the burnt-offering, it is expressly mentioned only once, viz., at the very commencement of the sacrificial law (Lev. i. 4; compare, however, Lev. v. 10, xiv. 20, xvi. 24). And in the sections relating to the peace-offering (Lev. iii., vii. 11–21) it is not brought into prominence at all.

Thomasius (*Christi Person und Werk* iii. 1, p. 40) also adduces Ezek. xlv. 15 (see also ver. 17) as a proof of the expiatory character of the peace-offerings. But this passage cannot be accepted as conclusive. For although the meat-offering, the burnt-offering, and the peace-offering are classed together in ver. 15 (in ver. 17 the sin-offering also is mentioned), and the expression, " to make reconciliation for them " (לְכַפֵּר עֲלֵיהֶם), is applied in common to them all ; the introduction of the meat-offering renders this passage unserviceable for the end supposed. But we do not require any express or special proof passages. The question is settled already by Lev. xvii. 11. If all blood placed upon the altar was atoning blood, this must have applied to the blood of the peace-offerings also. And a still more decisive proof is to be obtained *per analogiam* from the entire ritual of sacrifice. If the sprinkling of blood in connection with the burnt-offering and trespass-offering served as an atonement (לְכַפֵּר עָלָיו), the sprinkling of the blood of the peace-offering, which was performed in precisely the same way, must necessarily have had the same significance.

On the other hand, it certainly cannot be directly inferred from Lev. xvii. 11, that it was the sprinkling of blood alone which possessed an expiatory worth, to the entire exclusion of all the rest of the sacrificial rites. Though this conclusion, which *Hofmann* disputes, is perfectly correct ; only it cannot be proved from Lev. xvii. 11. It may be inferred, however, on the one hand, from the fact, that the sprinkling of blood is frequently spoken of as making atonement, apart from any other portion of the sacrificial rite, whilst no other portion of that rite is ever mentioned as possessing atoning worth apart from the sprinkling of blood, and, on the other hand, from the impossibility of deducing the idea of expiation from any other part of the sacrificial ritual.

CHAPTER II

THE OBJECTS USED IN SACRIFICE

§ 31. We have already seen, chiefly from the statement in Lev. xvii. 11, that the *soul* of the sacrificial animal, which was brought to the altar in its blood according to divine direction, made expiation for the sinful *soul* of the person sacrificing, and procured the forgiveness of his sin. But neither this passage, nor any other, explains to us how, why, and by what process the *soul* of the sacrificial animal was adapted to serve as the means of expiation. The only way that we have, therefore, of obtaining an answer to this important question, is to ascertain what idea the Hebrew formed of the soul of the sacrificial animal in itself, and in its relation to the soul of man, and also through what process he imagined that soul to pass, before and during its appropriation as the medium of atonement.

A careful and thorough investigation into the *Old Testament* view of the nature and essence of the *soul* in itself, and in its relation to the other bases and powers of life in both the animal and the human spheres, cannot of course be undertaken by us here. We must be content to bring out those points which seem best adapted to further our immediate purpose.

The whole of the animal and human world is repeatedly comprehended in the phrase, כָּל־בָּשָׂר אֲשֶׁר בּוֹ רוּחַ (נִשְׁמַת) חַיִּים, " all flesh, in which is a (breath) spirit of life" (Gen. vi. 17, vii. 15, 22). Consequently, the nature of man, like that of the animal, consists of *flesh* (or body) and a *life-spirit*. But through the connection of the life-spirit with the flesh, through the indwelling of the spirit in the flesh, a *third* arises, viz., the *living soul* (Gen. ii. 7). Thus it is expressly stated in Gen. ii. 7, that God breathed into the body of the man, which had been formed from the dust of the earth, a " breath of life," and the man became thereby a living soul. But, according to Gen. vi. 17, and vii. 15, 22, a spirit or breath of life dwells in the animals also. Again, according to Gen. ii. 19, they too were formed from earthly materials. And lastly, they also proceeded as "living souls" from the creating hand of God (Gen. ii. 19, i. 20, 24). So that we may conclude that they too became "living souls," through the endowment of their material, earthly bodies with a "breath of life" (*vid.* Ps. civ. 30, 31 ; Job xxxiv. 14, 15 ; Eccl. iii. 21). In both instances the *nostrils* are mentioned as the seat of the spirit or breath (*vid.* Gen. vii. 22, ii. 7, בְּאַפָּיו). The meaning, however, is of course, not that the spirit of life, either in man or in the animal, is identical with the air which they breathe; but the obvious intention is to point out the spirit as the power, whose activity is manifested in breathing as the most striking evidence of existing life. But through the diffusion of this spirit-power throughout the flesh, there arises a third, viz., the living *soul*. The soul, therefore, is not something essentially different from the life-spirit, but merely a *mode of existence* which it assumes by pervading and animating the flesh; and regarded in this light, it has its seat, both in man and beast, *in the blood* (Lev. xvii. 11; Gen. ix. 4–6). Since the soul, therefore, represents in itself the unity of flesh and spirit, and as the incarnate life-spirit is the first principle, the seat and source of all vital activity, the whole man, or the whole animal, may of course be appropriately designated "a living soul," as is the case in Gen. i. 20, 24, ii. 7, 19.

§ 32. Now, if animals as well as men are "living souls," and in both this is dependent in the same way upon the indwelling of a "spirit of life" in the flesh, it might almost appear as though the Old Testament view rendered any essential distinction between man and beast impossible. But that is not the case. The essential distinction between man and beast, notwithstanding this apparent levelling on the part of the Hebrews, is no less certain, and is maintained with even greater sharpness, than was the case among other nations.

A comparison of Gen. ii. 7 with Gen. ii. 19 will be sufficient to show, that the author made an essential distinction between the animal and the human creation. It is true he uses the same expression, "God formed," with reference to both, and the result in both cases was a "living soul." But he makes a distinction even in the substratum for the formation of the body. In the case of the animals he says at once, "of the ground;" but in that of the man he says, "dust of the ground." In the former he speaks of the earthly material without selection; in the latter, of a nobler, finer, and as it were sublimated, earthly material. In the case of the former, too, there is no express reference made to the endowment of the earthly figure with a "breath of life;" though he can hardly have intended to deny that this was the case, since its result is admitted, viz., that the animal also became a "living soul." But he regarded it as too trivial and unimportant to be specially mentioned, and therefore embraced it in the one expression "formed;" whereas, in ver. 7, the "breathing in of the breath of life" becomes an independent act, and is described as the *acme* of the whole procedure.

In the first account of the creation, the formation of man is still more expressly distinguished from that of the animal. A simple command of God (i. 20, 24) calls the animals out of the earth as their material womb (rendered fruitful by the Spirit of God, which had moved upon the face of the primary chaotic matter); but in the creation of man God holds a formal consultation with Himself, and creates him in His own image. The creation ascends step by step; its last work is man; and he alone, of all creatures, bears in himself the image of God (i. 26, 27). Now, if we compare with this the two points in the creation of man in Gen. ii. 7, there can be no question that the endowment with the image of God is to be associated, not with the fact first named, "He formed," but with the second, "He breathed." The endowment of man with a spirit of life was at the same time an endowment with the image of God. The animals were also endowed, like man, with a spirit of life, and thus became a living soul; but man's spirit of life alone was impregnated with an essentially divine potency, by which the image of God was impressed upon his nature. And it is *this* potency which *we* are accustomed to call *spirit*, in distinction from body and soul, and because of the absence of which we deny that the animal is possessed of a spirit; whereas the Hebrew phraseology, employing the word spirit (רוּחַ), or breath (נְשָׁמָה), in a broader sense, attributes a spirit to the animal also.

Whether and how far that divine potency, which belonged to man alone, was obscured, weakened, suppressed, or even lost through the fall, we are nowhere expressly informed, either in the Pentateuch or any other part of the Old Testament. But that this did not take place without a considerable deterioration and alteration of its original standing and worth, especially from an ethical point of view, is presupposed by the whole of the Old Testament history and doctrine of salvation. But it is equally certain that its inalienable, so to speak its physical side—viz., self-consciousness, personality, freedom of choice, self-determination, and consequent responsibility for his actions—remained with man even after the fall (Gen. iv. 10; Deut. xi. 26; Josh. xxiv. 15, etc.); whereas the actions of the animal are determined by instinct, by the necessities of its nature, and it cannot direct or unfold its powers in any other way than that to which its nature impels, so that it is not, and cannot be, responsible.[1]

§ 33. " *Spirit*" or " *breath*" denotes the animal life (in man as well as the animal), so far as its activity is shown in the process of respiration. " *Soul*," on the other hand, denotes the same, so far as it is manifest in the circulation of the blood. As the spirit pervades the body, and, so to speak, becomes incarnate in it by means of the process of breathing, it becomes " *soul*," which has its seat in the blood, and, by means of the blood, penetrates and animates the whole body in all its members, the whole flesh in all its muscles and nerves. Hence the " *spirit*" is the potential, the " *soul*" the actual, principle of life; and it is not the spirit but the soul which connects the outer with the inner world (by its *receptive* activity), and the inner with the outer world (by its *spontaneous* activity). It is the sensitive principle, the seat of emotion, of liking and disliking, and the impelling power of motion and action. Through its mediation the impressions and influences of the outer world assume the form of perception. Through this the individual is affected agreeably or disagreeably from without, experiencing pleasure or pain. Through this also the individual manifests its power outwardly in movement and action. This impels it to do what yields it pleasure, to avoid what causes pain. It is also the seat and source of desire, both on its positive and its negative side, as affection or aversion, sympathy or antipathy. Hence, in the New Testament, whenever this is the only motive power by which any man's conduct is regulated, he is called a *soulish*, or psychical (Eng. Ver. " natural") man.

This is the common basis of the human and the animal souls. They have a common foundation—a common root and source. And both were originally dependent upon the primary moving of the Spirit of God, which moved upon the chaotic mass of earthly

---

[1] Such passages as Gen. ix. 5, vi. 7; Ex. xxi. 28; Lev. xx. 15, 16; Deut. xiii. 15, are not to be regarded in the light of *punishment* inflicted upon the *animal*. Gen. iii. 14 stands altogether by itself.

matter, out of which their corporeality was formed. But above this common natural basis, there rises the essential difference between the human and animal souls. Whereas the animal world was merely endowed with a spirit of life by a general creative operation of the Spirit of God upon the earthly material, out of which their bodies were prepared; the breathing of the spirit of life into the human form was the result of a direct, special, unique act of God, through which the general, earthly spirit of life was imbued with specific and divine powers; so that the spirit of life thus impregnated, rendered man not merely a living soul (Gen. ii. 7), but also the image of God (Gen. i. 27), and thereby stamped upon him on the physical (essential) side, as a copy of the divine nature, the indelible character of personality, with all its attributes, and on the ethical (habitual) side, as a (potential) copy of the divine character, the capacity to be holy as God is holy. For as man, by virtue of his personality, was able to mould himself otherwise than God had intended, and to will otherwise than God had willed; this side of his likeness to God could only have been imparted to him at first as a mere capacity, and not as a developed and inalienable reality. And the fact is recorded in Gen. iii., that the man did *not* progress from the potential holiness at first imparted, to an actual holiness of his own choosing; but, on the contrary, abused his freedom, and fell into unholiness and sin.

The following, therefore, we may regard as the result of our discussion thus far. The soul of the animal, like that of man, is the first principle, the seat and source, of the sensuous life in all its functions; in this respect, both are alike. But the difference between them consists in this, that if we look at the absolute condition of both, the soul of the animal is determined and sustained by instinct and the necessities of its nature, and therefore is not capable of accountability; whilst the soul of man, on the contrary, by virtue of the likeness to God imparted at first, is possessed of personality, freedom, and accountability; whereas, if we look at the condition of both, as it appears before us in reality, and as the practical result of that inequality, the soul of man appears laden with sin and guilt, and exposed to the judgment of God (Gen. ii. 17, iii. 16 sqq.), whilst the animal soul, because not responsible for its actions, may be regarded as perfectly sinless and free from guilt. The soul is in both the seat of pleasure and displeasure, and, as such, the impulse to all that is done or left undone; but in man alone can the pleasure or displeasure be regarded as sinful, and

the soul be designated as the birth-place and laboratory of sin;
since in it alone, and not in the animal soul, the element of personality, *i.e.*, of free self-determination and inalienable accountability,
is to be found.

We are all the more warranted, or rather compelled, to bring
forward this contrast—on the one hand, freedom from sin and guilt,
on the other, sinfulness and guilt—as of essential importance to our
question ; because, as לְכַפֵּר shows, in connection with every animal
sacrifice, though in different degrees, the point in question was the
expiation of the sin which clung to the soul of the person sacrificing. The sinless and guiltless soul of the animal was the medium
of expiation for the sinful and guilty soul of the person by whom
the sacrifice was offered.

§ 34. Before proceeding to the second question,—viz., what was
done to, and with, the soul of the sacrificial animal *before* and *for
the sake* of the expiation,—we must first of all consider the *choice of
the materials of sacrifice*, and what was *requisite* to fit them for the
purpose.

The material of sacrifice, so far as expiation was the object in
view, consisted of an *animal*. But *all kinds of animals* were not
admissible ; nor was *every individual* belonging to such species as
were admissible necessarily suitable for the purpose. The only
animals admissible were those which served the Israelites as *food*,
and had been *reared* by themselves (§ 21), and which therefore
stood in a *biotic* relation to the person presenting the sacrifice
(§ 22). We have already examined the meaning of these provisions, and have found that, whilst *all* the *Corbanim* were primarily
and chiefly representatives of personal self-surrender to Jehovah,
the altar-sacrifices possessed this character in an especial and exclusive manner. And another difference has also presented itself
(§ 24) ; viz., that the animal sacrifices set forth the person of the
sacrificer himself and his vital powers; the vegetable sacrifices, the
fruits and performances of those vital powers. And in connection
with this, it must also be borne in mind, that the laws of food sanc-
tioned and established the notion, that the clean, *i.e.*, the edible
animals, from which alone it was lawful to take those that were
sacrificed, were representatives of Israel as the chosen nation ; whilst
the unclean animals, on the other hand, were representatives of the
heathen world, which stood outside the sanctifying covenant with
Jehovah (§ 3; *vid.* Lev. xx. 24–26). If, as we have already seen
(§ 23), the altar-sacrifices were regarded as food for Jehovah

(לֶחֶם לַיהוָה), it follows as a matter of course, that Israel durst not offer to Jehovah such food as His own people had been forbidden to eat because it was unclean; and if the intention of such offerings was not to present earthly food, of which Jehovah had no need, but spiritual food, which alone is well-pleasing to Jehovah, and which was really requisite to His Jehovistic relation—in other words, the faithful self-surrender of the covenant nation,—all unclean animals were necessarily excluded, as being representatives of the heathen world. And the fact that even clean animals were not *all* admissible in sacrifice, but only such of them as were the objects of their own care and rearing, of their daily thought and need, had, as we have seen, its good and obvious foundation in the *spiritual* worth of this food of Jehovah, and in the personal self-dedication of the sacrificer, of which it was the representation.

With regard to the *sex*, both male and female were admissible; at the same time, the law for the most part gave express directions when a male animal was to be offered, and when a female, and proceeded generally upon the rule, that the male, as superior in worth, power, and importance, was to be used for the higher and more important sacrifices. The *age* of the animal was also taken into consideration: it was not to bear any signs of weakness about it, either because of its youth, or because of its age. As a general rule, it was required, that animals from the flocks should be at least eight days old (Lev. xxii. 27; Ex. xxii. 30); and in most cases it was prescribed, with regard to sheep and goats (Lev. ix. 3, xii. 6; Ex. xxix. 28; Num. xxviii. 3, 9, 11), and once with regard to oxen (Lev. ix. 3), that they should be a year old. But a still greater age is generally indicated in the case of oxen, by the use of the word פַּר and פָּרָה (as distinguished from the calf, עֵגֶל, Lev. ix. 3), without any limits being assigned. According to the rabbinical regulations, no animal was to be more than three years old.[1]—With regard to the *character* of the animal, bodily *faultlessness* was strictly required (Lev. xxii. 20–24). Both of these demands—viz., that of a vigorous age, and that of bodily faultlessness—were connected with the appointment of the animal as a medium of expiation. As so appointed, it was not to have the very same thing that it was designed to expiate in the person presenting the sacrifice. In man, no doubt, the infirmities, wants, and injuries, for which the expiation

---

[1] In Judg. vi. 25, the instruction to offer a bullock of seven years old was connected with the duration of the Midianitish oppression; and therefore, as an exceptional case, was not necessarily opposed to the rabbinical tradition.

was intended, were moral in their nature ; whereas an animal, not being an accountable creature, could have none but physical faults. But what sin is in the sphere of the moral spirit-life, bodily infirmities and injuries are in the sphere of the physical and natural life ; and, for that reason, bodily faultlessness and vital energy were adapted to copy and represent symbolically that spiritual purity and fulness of life, which were requisite in a perfect sacrifice as a medium of expiation, and as an antidote to ethical wants, infirmities, and crimes.

On proceeding now to examine what was done with the sacrificial materials so chosen and constituted, we find the whole process consisting of six leading stages : (1) The presentation of the animal, by bringing it to the altar in the court ; (2) the laying on of hands ; (3) the slaughtering before the altar ; (4) the sprinkling of blood against the altar ; (5) the burning of the flesh upon the altar ; and (6) the sacrificial meal which was held at the sanctuary.

CHAPTER III

THE PRESENTATION AND LAYING ON OF HANDS

§ 35. The BRINGING of the animal by the sacrificer himself is expressed by the verb הֵבִיא, and is to be distinguished from the "offering" of the animal (= הִקְרִיב), the latter term being used to denote the whole of the sacrificial rite. The place to which the sacrifice was required to be brought was the court of the sanctuary (Lev. i. 3, iv. 4, 14, etc.), as being the only spot where sacrifices were allowed to be offered (Lev. xvii. 1–6). The reason for this act lies upon the surface : the person presenting the offering showed thereby that he felt and desired to put into practice the wish, the need, or the obligation to renew, to fortify, and to give life, by means of such an offering, to his fellowship with that God who dwelt and revealed Himself there (§ 12). The presentation of the animal was followed, no doubt, by an examination on the part of the priests, to see whether it answered in kind and condition to the directions contained in the law (§ 34), inasmuch as it was necessary that this should be decided before any further steps could be taken.

§ 36. Of incomparably greater importance was the LAYING ON

OF HANDS, which was done by the sacrificer himself. This took place in connection with every kind of animal sacrifice (even in the trespass-offerings, § 122), except that of pigeons; and even then the omission was certainly made on outward grounds alone, and had therefore no decisive meaning. The standing expression applied to this ceremony, סָמַךְ אֶת־יָדוֹ (which led the Rabbins to call the act itself the *Semichah*), is stronger and more significant than our "laying on of hands:" it denotes a *resting, leaning* upon the hand. The choice of this expression, therefore, shows that it had reference to a most important act—an act which required the strongest energy and resoluteness both of mind and will,—for which reason the Rabbins expressly required that the Semichah should be performed with all the powers of the body (Maimonides, בְּכָל־כֹּחַ, cf. *Oehler*, p. 627).[1]

The *laying on of hands in general* denotes, throughout the Holy Scriptures, the transfer or communication of some supersensual element to or upon another, whether it be a power, gift, affection, or obligation : for example, in the act of blessing (Gen. xlviii. 13, 14; Matt. xix 13–15); in the communication of the Holy Spirit in general (Acts viii. 17 sqq., xix. 6), and especially in connection with consecration to any theocratical or ecclesiastical office (Num. xxvii. 18 sqq.; Deut. xxxiv. 9; Acts vi. 6; 1 Tim. v. 22); in the miraculous cures of Christ and His Apostles (Matt. ix. 18; Mark vi. 5; Luke xiii. 13; Acts ix. 12, 17); in the setting apart of a personal substitute (Num. viii. 10, xxvii. 18 sqq.; Deut. xxxiv. 9); in the sentence of a malefactor to execution (Lev. xxiv. 14 and Susannah ver. 34).[2] *Consecration*, therefore, to some new position in life, by one who had the power and the right to make the appointment, and to qualify and equip the other for it, is to be regarded as the general purpose of the imposition of hands. For *blessing* may be looked at

[1] According to the unanimous tradition of the Jews, a verbal confession of sins was associated with the imposition of hands; and, according to the Mishnah (cf. *Outram*, p. 170), it ran as follows :—*Obsecro Domine, peccavi, deliqui, rebellavi, hoc et illud feci, nunc autem pœnitentiam ago, sitque hæc (hostia) expiatio mea.* *Bähr* also admits that "the sacrificial ceremony can hardly have been performed in perfect silence; but, just as among the heathen, prayers or other formularies were repeated during the sacrifice." But the law of Moses never mentions any such custom; for Lev. xvi. 21 does not bear upon the point at all (§ 45), and the command in Lev. v. 5 and Num. v. 7 with regard to the confession of sin cannot be adduced as any proof of the custom, since it is not connected with the imposition of hands, but precedes the whole sacrificial ceremony.

[2] For a fuller examination of these passages, cf. § 45.

in this light, and *miraculous healing* also : the former is the consecration of the person blessed to the course and sphere of labour
which the person blessing intends for him ; the latter, the consecration of the person who has hitherto been ill or crippled, to a healthy
and vigorous life. What power, gift, affection, or obligation it was
that was communicated or transferred to this end through the imposition of hands, must be learned from the peculiar circumstances
under which, the purpose *for* which, or the psychical emotion and
decision *with* which it was performed in the cases referred to, as
well as in connection with the sacrificial ceremony.

§ 37. In *Bähr's* opinion (ii. 341), the *laying on of hands in connection with the sacrifice* was " nothing but a formal and solemn
declaration, on the one hand, that this gift was his actual property,
and on the other hand, that he was ready to give up this property
of his entirely to death, *i.e.*, to devote it to death for Jehovah." In
my *Mosaisches Opfer*, p. 65 sqq., I have, as I believe, already shown
this view, together with all the positive and negative arguments
adduced in its favour, to be perfectly groundless and untenable ;
and I therefore feel that I am relieved from the necessity of repeating my objections here.

Hofmann, on the other hand, in the first edition of his *Schriftbeweis* (ii. 1, pp. 153–4), has expressed himself as follows on the
significance of this ceremony :—" What the person offering the
sacrifice inwardly purposed to do, when bringing the animal to the
Holy Place, was to render a payment to God ; and he had full power
to appropriate the life of the animal for the rendering of this payment.[1] And the meaning of the imposition of hands was, that he
intended to make use of this power, and so inflicted death upon the
animal, by which he purposed to render payment to God."   Examples, analogies, and other proofs of this assertion, he did not think
of furnishing. In the second edition the passage is wanting, and
in the place of it we read (pp. 247, 248), that the laying on of
hands was " an appointment of the animal for a slaughter, the object of which (as *Delitzsch* admits) was twofold, viz., to obtain the
blood for the altar, and the flesh for the fire-food of Jehovah,
whether the intention was to supplicate the mercy of God towards
the sinner, *i.e.*, to make expiation, or (as in the case of the thank-
offering) to present thanksgiving and prayer for the blessings of
life."   But this correction has not really mended the matter.   For

---

[1] Strange to say, *Hofmann* bases this power upon the fact recorded in
Gen. iii. 21 ; cf. § 68.

if the "appointment for such a slaughter" was nothing more than the declaration, that by virtue of the power accruing to him from Gen. i. 26, he had determined "to do to this animal all that necessarily followed from his desire to obtain the mercy of God, or give glory to His goodness by thanksgiving and supplication" (p. 247), such a declaration was very superfluous; for it had already been sufficiently made in the simple act of bringing to the altar an animal that really belonged to him, and was entirely subject to his control. Nothing short of such a difference in the manner in which the imposition of hands took place, in the sin-offerings on the one hand, and the thank-offerings on the other, as would have shown that the former expressed a desire for the mercy of God, and the latter thanksgiving and prayer for the blessings of life, and thus would have introduced a new feature that was not already expressed by bringing the animal to the altar, could possibly deliver the laying on of hands, if so understood, from the reproach of a perfectly idle and unmeaning pleonasm. But if the appointment of the animal was something more than a simple declaration of the purpose for which it was offered; then, just as the imposition of hands in the ordination to an office was something more than the declaration that the person to be ordained was appointed to that office (viz., the requisite endowment with the Spirit of God), so must it also in this case have been intended to express a communication, both answering to, and qualifying it for the purpose to which it was devoted. But this is just what *Hofmann* denies.

§ 38. Whilst *Bähr* and *Hofmann* are thus unable to content themselves with the *traditional and orthodox view*, which has prevailed from time immemorial, and was adopted alike by the Rabbins and the Fathers of the Church, viz., that the laying on of hands was expressive of the transfer of sin and guilt from the person sacrificing to the animal sacrificed; that view has met with numerous supporters even in our own day. And even *Keil*, who in other respects has thoroughly given up the Church theory of sacrifice, has not been able in this particular point to break away from it; though, as we shall soon discover, he has involved his own doctrine in the most striking self-contradictions by thus stopping half-way (§ 53).

Modern supporters of this view start with the assumption, that the laying on of hands must denote, in the ritual of sacrifice, as in every other place in which it occurs, a communication or transfer, the object of which, here as everywhere else, was to be gathered from the feelings or intention of the person by whom the act was performed. Now, as the starting point in sacrifice was the consciousness of guilt, and the end the expiation of that guilt; as the soul of the sacrificer, therefore, was entirely filled with the desire to be delivered from its guilt and sin; the imposition of hands could only express the (symbolical) transfer of his sin and guilt to the animal to be sacrificed. But with regard to the special adaptation of this view to the various kinds of sacrifice, the advocates of this view differ from one another, and may be classified in two separate groups.

In the opinion of some, the laying on of hands had throughout the sacrificial ritual, in the burnt-offerings and peace-offerings, as well as in the sin-offerings and trespass-offerings, one and the same signification, viz., the transfer of sin or sinfulness from the person sacrificing to the animal sacrificed, since in every case it was preparatory to the expiation, and the expiation *alone*. This view formed one of the leading thoughts in my own *Mosaisches Opfer;* and among later writers it has met with approbation from *Hävernick, Ebrard, Kliefoth, Stöckl,* and others.

In the opinion of the others, on the contrary, the idea of the transfer of sin was expressed in the laying on of hands in the case of the sin-offerings and trespass-offerings only. In the burnt-offerings and peace-offerings they attribute to it a very different meaning. This remark applies to *Neumann, Delitzsch,* and *Keil* more especially, but also to *Gesenius, Winer, Knobel, Tholuck,* and others. *Keil,* who has gone most thoroughly into the question, expresses himself thus: " If the desire of the sacrificer was to be delivered from a sin or trespass, he would transfer his *sin* and *trespass* to the victim; but if, on the other hand, he desired through the sacrifice to consecrate his life to God, that he might receive strength for the attainment of holiness, and for a walk well-pleasing to God, he would transfer this *desire,* in which the whole effort of his soul was concentrated, to the sacrificial animal; so that in the latter, as in the former instance, the animal would henceforth take his place, and all that was done to it would be regarded as being done to the person who offered it. But if the intention was merely to express his gratitude for benefits and mercies received or hoped for, he would simply transfer this *feeling of gratitude* to the victim, so that it would represent his person only so far as it was absorbed (?) into the good received or sought for." *Delitzsch* expresses himself to the same effect: " By the imposition of hands the person presenting the sacrifice dedicated the victim to that particular object which he hoped to attain by its means. He transferred directly to it the substance of his own inner nature. Was it an expiatory sacrifice, *i.e.*, a sin-offering or a trespass-offering; he laid his sins upon it, that it might bear them, and so relieve him of them." *Delitzsch* does not go any further into a discussion of their meaning in the case of the burnt-offering and peace-offering. *Neumann* says, " The person presenting the sacrifice laid his hand upon the victim, to transfer to it his own individual determination by means of the appropriation. . . . Only, let it not therefore be supposed, that in *every case* it denoted a simple imputation of sins. If I brought a peace-offering to my God, the victim upon which I had laid my hand would carry my peace into His presence ; and if I brought an atoning sacrifice, it would express my desire to be delivered from my guilt and sin." *Hengstenberg* affirms, that " its signification in general was to show the *rapport* between the person sacrificing and the sacrifice itself. Anything more precise must necessarily be learned from the nature of the particular sacrifice. . . . In the sin-offering and burnt-offering the thought was expressed symbolically, ' That am I;' and in the thank-offering, on the other hand, ' That is my gift, my thanksgiving.'"

§ 39. According to the view last mentioned, therefore, the imposition of hands had a different meaning in every one of the different kinds of sacrifice ; just as it did not represent the same thing in a miraculous cure as in a simple blessing, nor the same thing in consecration to an office as in a sentence of execution. But are we warranted in resorting to such an analogy ? In the latter, the act has reference in every instance to a totally different department of life ; and in all the cases mentioned, the attendant circumstances, the occasions, and the subjects, differ entirely from one another. In the former, on the contrary, notwithstanding the difference in the sacrifices, the act itself is always confined to one and the same department, being performed with the same attendant circumstances, and on the same foundation ; and even the persons by whom it is performed are not distinguished in relation to that act by special and different endowments, or official positions, as is the case with a father who gives his blessing, with a worker of miraculous cures, a consecrating dignitary, or an accusing witness. But if, notwithstanding this, the imposition of hands in the different kinds of sacrifice effected the transfer of different objects, one would suppose that this difference would be indicated in some way, say, by a verbal declaration connected with the imposition of hands; yet of this there is nowhere the slightest trace.[1]

What can have been the object transferred in the case of the burnt-offerings and peace-offerings, if not the same as in that of the sin-offerings and trespass-offerings? *Delitzsch* leaves the question unanswered, and thus evades the difficulty of expressing a clear and definite opinion. According to *Neumann*, the peace-offering was thereby *commissioned* by the person presenting it to carry his peace before God (!). And yet none of the sacrificial rites which followed favour such a conclusion; for the sprinkling of its blood upon the altar served, according to Lev. xvii. 11, as a covering for sin; and the burning of the fat cannot have been intended as an execution of that commission, any more than the eating of the flesh. It is just as difficult to understand how *Hengstenberg* can maintain his distinction, seeing that the burnt-offering was undoubtedly quite as much a gift and offering as the thank-offering. *Keil's* distinction is perfectly incomprehensible. That the animal constituting the sin-offering or trespass-offering should, after I had transferred my sin or guilt to it, be treated itself as sinful or guilty, and that " what happened to it should be regarded as happening to the person offering the sacrifice," is perfectly intelligible. But when I had transferred my wish for powers of holiness to the animal selected as a *burnt-offering*, would the animal itself be regarded as *wishing* for such powers? or would the *thank-offering*, to which I had transferred my gratitude for benefits received or desired, be treated as *expressing thanks* for such benefits, and all that happened to it be looked upon as the fulfilment of my wish, or the result of my gratitude? Certainly not; for it was slaughtered immediately afterwards, and therefore could neither receive the power desired, nor manifest the gratitude that was felt. Moreover, in the presentation of a *thank-offering*, another feature was associated with the feeling of gratitude. The thoughts of the person offering the sacrifice were directed from the very first to the sacrificial meal, and to what was signified by that meal, namely, fellowship with God; so that the desire for this would fill and move his soul when laying on his hands, and even force itself into the foreground. Why then should not this be the object transferred? And just as the

---

[1] The peculiar and unparalleled case mentioned in Lev. xvi. 21 cannot serve as a proof, that the imposition of hands in connection with all the sin-offerings was accompanied by a verbal declaration; to say nothing of the burnt-offerings and peace-offerings. *Vid.* § 45.

want of expiation sought and found satisfaction, not only in the sin and trespass-offering, but in the burnt-offering and peace-offering also; so not in the burnt-offering only, but in the sin-offering, trespass-offering, and peace-offering also, did the striving after a self-surrender, that craved sanctification, seek and find satisfaction; the former being met by the sprinkling of blood, and the latter (though not in the same degree) by the burning upon the altar. Consequently, according to our opponents' premises, the imposition of hands would necessarily be preparatory not merely to the sprinkling of blood, but to the other sacrificial functions also; so that in the sin-offering, not merely the sin, but also the wish for sanctification would be transferred, and in the burnt-offering, not merely the latter, but the former as well. This, or something similar, is actually maintained by *Ewald* (Alterthk. p. 47). "The laying on of hands," he says, "indicated the sacred moment when the person presenting the sacrifice, just as he was commencing the sacred rite, laid *all* the feelings, which gushed from him in fullest glow, upon the head of that creature whose blood was to be shed for him, and to appear as it were before God."

In all the different varieties of sacrifice, the laying on of hands stood in the same local, temporal, and conditional, *i.e.*, preparatory, relation to the slaughtering, and the sprinkling of the blood. Are we not warranted, therefore, and even obliged, in every case, to uphold the same signification in relation to them? Take the burnt-offering, in connection with which, in the very front of the sacrificial law in Lev. i. 4, expiation is so evidently, expressly, and emphatically mentioned as one point, if not as the main point, and placed in the closest relation to the laying on of hands ("He shall put his hand upon the head of the burnt-offering; and it shall be accepted for him, to make atonement for him"). Is it really the fact that even here the imposition of hands stood in no relation whatever to the expiation? Certainly, if there were nothing else to overthrow such a view, the passage just quoted would suffice, and before this alone it would be compelled inevitably to yield.

§ 40. Let us now examine the other view, of which I was once a supporter, that the imposition of hands was intended to express the same simple meaning in connection with all the sacrifices, viz., the transfer of sin or sinfulness from the person sacrificing to the animal sacrificed. I will confess at the outset, that I am *no longer* prepared to maintain my old opinion in this particular form (§ 44 sqq.); but as the arguments of my opponents have not led me to this change in my views, my relinquishing that opinion has not made me insensible to the elements of truth which it contains.

We will compare it first of all with the view which *Keil* and *Delitzsch* oppose to it. In how much simpler, clearer, more intelligible, and concrete a form does it present the meaning of the ceremony in question! And what objection has been offered to it from this side? It is true, the *final* purpose in connection with the *burnt-offering* was the burning, and with the *peace-offering* the sacrificial meal; and consequently the ultimate intention of the person presenting the sacrifice was directed, in the former, to a complete self-surrender to Jehovah, in the latter, to fellowship with Him. But in the mind of the worshipper, the consciousness of his sin rose like an insuperable wall in the way of both: he knew that his self-surrender could never be well-pleasing to God, and that his longing for fellowship with God could never be satisfied, till atonement had been made for his sin. Even in the sacrifice of a burnt-offering or peace-offering, therefore, his desire was first of all directed to expiation; whilst his purpose of self-surrender, and the striving after fellowship with God, could only come to light when his sin had been covered and atoned for. Would not the longing for forgiveness, so long as it remained unsatisfied, stand in the foreground of his thoughts and feelings, and suppress for the time every other feeling? But if this question must be answered in the affirmative, every ground for our opponents' view is swept away. The only thing that could have favoured that view at all would have been, that the laying on of hands in the burnt- and peace-offerings should have taken place *after* the atonement was completed, and immediately *before* the burning or the sacrificial meal,—the animal of course having been killed in the meantime.

In the case of the *burnt-offering*, we appeal with conclusive force to Lev. i. 4; for it is not to the burning, but to the atonement, and to that alone, that the imposition of hands is there expressly represented as preparatory. Even in the burnt-offering it was requisite that all the desires and actions of the worshipper, all the co-operation and help of the priest, should be directed first of all to the making of atonement, before anything further or anything different could be undertaken; for the complete surrender, which was the ultimate purpose in the burnt- (or whole) offering, had necessarily to be preceded by complete expiation.

This applies to the *peace-offering* also. In the pious Israelite, the consciousness of his own sin and of the divine holiness was so clear and strong, that he was afraid lest he should die if he drew near to God and held communion with Him (Ex. xx. 19, xxxiii. 20, etc.); and consequently his longing for that communion, and for the joy which it inspired, was overpowered by the fear that he might not be able to stand. When he brought a peace-offering, therefore, hoping thereby to obtain communion—real house-and-table fellowship with God, how could it be otherwise than that the sinfulness which rendered him unfit for that fellowship should be present to his mind, and his whole soul be filled with the desire for expiation *before* anything else, and therefore in connection with the laying on of hands? And if the feeling of gratitude for benefits received, or the prayer for blessings desired, impelled him to present a peace-offering, would not the contrast between his own sinful unworthiness and the blessing enjoyed or hoped for so occupy and control his thoughts and feelings, that here also the consciousness of sin and the want of expiation would assert themselves, and fill his mind *before* everything else?

There is also another point of importance. If the imposition of hands, even in its preliminary signification, had respect to the objects which lay beyond the expiation, and, in the case of the burnt- and peace-offerings, to one of them exclusively, as our opponents maintain,—viz., in that of the burnt-offering to *self-surrender* in the burning, and in that of the peace-offering to *fellowship with God* in the sacrificial meal; we should expect to find an imposition of hands, or something answering to it, connected with the *meat-offering* also (especially when it was not introduced as a mere appendage to the bleeding sacrifice, but was an independent offering without the basis of an animal sacrifice: § 151 sqq.), inasmuch as the desire for sanctification and fellowship was as prominent a feature in these as in either the burnt- or the peace-offerings. But as *nothing* of the kind is to be found, we are warranted perhaps in drawing the conclusion, that the sacrificial imposition of hands had exclusive regard to the atonement, and *therefore* was admissible in the bleeding sacrifices alone.

§ 41. *Hofmann's* own view of the sacrificial imposition of hands we have already shown to be untenable (§ 37). In his arguments against my view and those of his other opponents, he really does nothing more than lay hold of certain expressions which are easily misunderstood, and are probably to some extent inappropriate or wrong, and then, having fathered upon them a meaning which does not belong to them, exhibit the absurdities to which this meaning leads. Thus he seizes upon the ambiguous expression of *Delitzsch* (p. 737), "By the imposition of hands the worshipper appropriated to himself the victim for that particular purpose to which he intended it to be applied," and observes, in reply (p. 247), "It is perfectly obvious that it was his own property; and that being the case, he did not require first of all to appropriate it to himself." But who cannot see that what *Delitzsch* means by "appropriating" is not appropriating it as property, but appropriating what was his property already to the purpose which, as a sacrifice, it was intended to subserve? Thus again he replies to *Kliefoth:* "But it was not a *real* transfer of sin and guilt; for it is impossible to see how they could ever be *really* transferred to an animal;" whereas *Kliefoth* means something entirely different. For, when he says (p. 52), "The imposition of hands was not a sign that the person laying his hands upon the head of another 'attributed' something to him; but invariably, wherever it occurs in the Scriptures, some real communication is made in consequence,"— he evidently refers to the imposition of hands *apart from* the sacrificial worship, and certainly does not mean to deny that in the purely symbolico-typical ceremonial it represents *symbolically*, what in other departments it *really* effects. It is much the same when *Hofmann* observes, in reply to *Keil* (i. 206), "Nor was it an appointment of the animal to be or to suffer anything in the place of the person offering it, either by causing it to be punished for his fault, which would be quite out of place in the thank-offering, or by transferring his own intention to it, when the slaughtering of the animal was really the commencement of its fulfilment." But the transfer of an intention is something very different from the fulfilment of that intention; and, so far as the supposed inappropriateness of this meaning to the imposition of hands in the case of the "thank-offerings" is concerned, *Keil* has fallen into just the same error as *Hofmann* here.

§ 42. *Hofmann* argues most warmly and elaborately against the opinion expressed by me in my *Mosaisches Opfer* (pp. 67 sqq.). "According to *Kurtz*," he says, "the imposition of hands always denoted the impartation of that which the one possessed and the other was to receive; consequently, in the case of sacrifice, as every sacrifice, in his opinion, was an expiatory sacrifice, it denoted the communication of the sinful affection to the animal soul, so that the death which took place was thereby rendered a representative death. An exchange of position was expressed by it: the soul of the sacrifice appearing as if laden with sin and guilt, and that of the person sacrificing as free from both." This view *Hofmann* now takes the trouble to expose, as leading to absurd consequences. " But how was it," he replies, " with the imposition of the hands when a person was blessing, or healing, or ordaining? Did he change places with the person upon whom his hands were laid, so that he lost the good which he conferred upon the other? In all these cases the imposition of hands was the act, which accompanied the conferring of whatever the person acting intended for the other. The internal process of intention and application was expressed in the corresponding pressure of the hand, applied to the head of the person for whom anything was intended, whether it belonged to the person officiating or not. The agent needed plenary power to communicate it, but there was no necessity for it to be his own; to say nothing of his parting with it by conferring it upon another, or exchanging it for what the other previously possessed. The person blessing did not transfer his own peace, nor the healer his own health, nor the person ordaining his own office : he simply made use of his own priestly character, his healing power, his official standing, to do to the other what this authority empowered him to perform."

I must acknowledge at the outset, that I now consider the expression, " a change of places," both inappropriate and liable to be misunderstood; and that, looking at the circumstances, it may properly be said, that by the imposition of hands the sacrificial animal was appointed to play the part of the sinner meriting punishment, *i.e.*, to bear the merited punishment in his stead, but not (what the expression might certainly be made to mean, though I never intended to say it) that the person presenting the sacrifice had henceforth to take the place which previously belonged to the animal sacrificed. But *Hofmann* does me a grievous injustice when he forces upon me the absurd assertion, that through the imposition of hands the person sacrificing not only transferred his sin and guilt to the sacrificial animal, but exchanged them for " what the other (viz., the animal) formerly possessed." I have undoubtedly said (p. 83), that " by the imposition of hands sin and guilt were symbolically imputed to the soul of the sacrifice ;" but not that, *vice versa* and *eo ipso*, the previous innocence of the animal sacrificed was imputed to the sacrificer. I have also said, it is true, that " henceforward the animal to be sacrificed passed for what HE was before, viz., laden with sin and guilt, and therefore took his place ;"

but not that the person presenting the sacrifice passed henceforward for that which the *animal* was before, and so took the place of the animal. And *Hofmann* has no right to father such nonsense upon me.

I grant that what the person acting conferred upon the other was not necessarily his own, in the sense of being his own property; but I have never said that the imposition of hands was the communication of something that was the *property* of the one and was to become the property of the other, but "of what the one *had* and the other was to receive." And certainly, in any case, I must first *have* what I am to impart to another. So that here also *Hofmann* twists my words, and then convicts me of talking nonsense.

Nor did I ever think of maintaining anything so foolish as that the person laying on the hand always, and under all circumstances, "parted with the *good* which he conferred upon the other," or that "the person blessing always transferred his own peace, the healer his own health, the ordainer his own office;" and this does not follow in any way from my explanation. Sin and guilt are not a "*good*," but an *evil;* and that makes an essential difference, which *Hofmann* is pleased to ignore. Where the imposition of hands denotes the communication of some *salutary* power or gift (as, for example, in blessing, in the communication of the Spirit, in ordination, or in the miraculous cures of Christ and His Apostles), which the agent desires another to possess, though without parting with it himself, we must regard such a communication as somewhat resembling a flame lighting a second flame without being extinguished, or the sun imparting light and warmth to the earth without thereby losing its luminous and warming power. But when, as in Num. viii. 10, it denotes the transfer from one person *to* another of a certain responsibility, from which the former desires to be free, the communication is to be regarded as exhaustive and complete; and the same would also be the case when it denoted (as in Lev. xxiv. 14 and Susannah 34, according to my opinion at that time) the rolling off or rolling back of a certain crime upon another. And it was upon the latter, not the former cases, that I rested my view, that the sacrificial imposition of hands, in which there was also the transfer of a responsibility and the rolling away of an evil, denoted the imputation of sin. It is only by generalizing, therefore, what *I* had particularized, that *Hofmann* has succeeded in stamping my view as absurd. How thoroughly unjust such generalization must be, is evident from *Hofmann's* observations in another way also;

for, in the reckless heat of his generalizing process, he brings forward a case as impossible, which is not only possible, but is mentioned in the Scriptures as having actually occurred. For in Num. xxvii. 18 sqq. and Deut. xxxiv. 9, Moses is said to have "transferred his own office to Joshua by the imposition of hands." And in how thoughtless and unfair a manner are the other two sentences composed! It is true, the person conferring the blessing does not "transfer his own *peace*, or the person effecting a cure his own *health;*" but the former imparts the blessing power, and the latter the healing power, entrusted to him, and that without suffering any loss in consequence, because it is in the very nature of such spiritual powers that they should not be exhausted through communication to others.

One more remark in conclusion. "In all these cases," says *Hofmann*, "the imposition of hands was the act which *accompanied* the appropriation of what the person acting intended for the other." Only *the accompaniment, then*, and not *the medium?* No doubt the latter would be inconvenient enough for *Hofmann's* theory of the sacrificial imposition of hands; but does this warrant him in diluting the mediation, which is so obvious in these cases, into a mere accompaniment? Was nothing more intended than a mere accompaniment, and not a real means of conveying the gift, when the Apostles communicated the Holy Ghost by the laying on of hands; or when, as is stated in Deut. xxxiv. 9, "Joshua was filled with the spirit of wisdom, FOR Moses had laid his hands upon him," and when Jehovah said to Moses, with regard to the same imposition of hands, "Thou shalt lay of thine honour upon him" (Num. xxvii. 20)?

§ 43. We have already seen in § 36, that the imposition of hands in all cases that were unconnected with sacrifice, denoted *dedication* to some new office, or some new position of responsibility. Was this also the idea when the imposition of hands was associated with the sacrificial worship? I do not imagine that any one will be able to answer this question in the negative. According to Lev. i. 4 (cf. § 39, 40), it denoted *the dedication of the sacrificial animal, as the medium of atonement* for the sins of the person whose hands were laid upon its head.

But on this common basis, as an act of dedication, there arises at once a considerable variety of divergences. In some cases the imposition of hands effected the *substitution* of one person for another (*vid.* Num. viii. 10, xxvii. 18; Deut. xxxiv. 9). What the person previously entitled, qualified, or required, was no longer able, or willing, or bound, to perform, was henceforth to be done by the other. In other cases, again, there was no room for the thought of any such substitution as this. Now, to which of these classes did the imposition of hands in the sacrificial ritual belong? We reply, without the least hesitation, to the former; and in this we may congratulate ourselves on the agreement of nearly all the commentators, who attribute a representative character to the sacrificial animal, though they do so in different ways, and who regard the imposition of hands as denoting dedication to this vicarious position.[1] And properly so. For if the assumption is warranted, that the God of Israel sought the sacrificial gift, so far as it was a gift, not for what it was in itself—*i.e.*, not as bodily food, and not on account of its material worth—and that Israel never imagined that it could serve its God with such gifts as these, but that, on the contrary, God sought the *giver* in the gift, and Israel represented thereby its own self-surrender;—if, moreover, it is also true that Israel, even on the ground of its laws of food (Lev. xx. 24–26, cf. § 4), was accustomed to regard the animals which were allowed to be offered in sacrifice as representatives of itself in contrast with the heathen world;—and if, lastly, it is evident from Lev. xvii. 11 that the animal, on account of the soul which dwelt in its blood, was also the medium of atonement for the soul of the person presenting it, which, as we shall presently see, it could only be through a vicarious expiation of his sins,—all this places it beyond the possibility of doubt that the animal sacrificed had also a representative character.

When Moses approached the end of his earthly course, he ordained Joshua as his successor, and substituted him for himself, by communicating of *his glory* (מֵהוֹדְךָ) to him (Num. xxvii. 20), and filling him with the spirit of wisdom (Deut. xxxiv. 9), through the laying on of hands. In Num. viii. 10, on the other hand, the substitution of the Levites in the place of the first-born of all the tribes, is described as effected through the laying on of the hands of the

---

[1] Even *Keil* admits, in various places, the representative character of the sacrificial animal by virtue of the imposition of hands, though this involves him in contradiction with his own fundamental view of the meaning of the sacrificial worship (§ 53, 69). Thus in the passage already noticed, when he says of the sin-, trespass-, and burnt-offerings, that " the sacrificial animal henceforth took the place of the person offering it, and what happened to it is to be regarded as happening to the sacrificer himself." But when he afterwards says that he admits the representative character of the peace-offering " only so far as the victim was absorbed in the good received or prayed for," I confess that I am perfectly unable to make out what the sentence means.

congregation, *i.e.*, of the elders as its representatives ; and what was transferred in this case, was the *obligation* of life-long service in the sanctuary, based upon the fact, that all the first-born belonged to Jehovah (§ 6).   In the one case, therefore, it was a good, a salutary power and gift, which was transferred ; in the other, a burdensome obligation.   Which of these two was analogous to the imposition of hands in the sacrificial ritual?   Certainly not the first.   For, according to the relation in which the imposition of hands is proved by Lev. i. 4 to have stood to the act of expiation, the idea was not the giving up of any good, but the getting rid of a certain evil. But was it analogous to the second ?   Undoubtedly it was.   As the debtor is under obligations to the creditor, the thief to the person robbed, the rebel to the king, in the sense of being bound to render to him, or suffer from him, according to the wrong that he has done ; so also is the sinner to his Lord and God.   This obligation was transferred by the person sacrificing to the sacrificial animal, that it might render or suffer all that was due from him to God, or, *vice versa*, on account of his sin ; and through this, the blood of the animal, in which is its soul, became the medium of expiation for the soul of the person sacrificing (§ 28).

§ 44. This was the meaning of the imposition of hands in the sacrificial ritual.   Consequently, I must candidly confess, that my previous opinion of this ceremony—viz., that it denoted a transfer of sin and guilt, a so-called imputation of sin, in sacrifices of every kind—cannot be sustained.   But so far from adopting in the place of it the opinion of *Neumann, Keil,* and *Delitzsch,* that the idea of the imputation of sin is to be restricted to the sin-offerings and trespass-offerings, I should be disposed to pronounce their opinion all the more untenable, just because of this unwarranted restriction (§ 39, 40).   Moreover, as I have already stated, no argument adduced by any one of my opponents—either *Hofmann* or *Hengstenberg, Keil, Delitzsch,* or *Oehler*—has brought me to the conclusion that my previous opinion was untenable.   What produced this conviction, was chiefly a more careful examination of Lev. xvii. 11, the very same passage which I had principally relied upon to support my previous opinion, and, in fact, a very simple argument (one so obvious, that I am puzzled to understand how it could ever have escaped my own notice, or that of my former opponents and supporters), *namely, that if the souls of the persons sacrificing, or, to speak with still greater precision, the sins adhering to or proceeding from their souls, were to be covered by the blood of the sacrifice, as*

Lev. xvii. 11 *states that they were, these sins could not have been communicated to the blood itself (or, more correctly, to the soul of the animal which was in the blood), but must have adhered to the soul of the sacrificer after the imposition of hands, as well as before.*

§ 45. The evidence adduced both by myself and others who held the same view, in support of the transference of the sins from the sacrificer to the sacrifice through the imposition of hands, I find on closer scrutiny to be insufficient. We will take first of all the argument based upon Lev. xvi. 21, which has been appealed to with the most confident assurance of victory (cf. *Tholuck*, p. 94 ; *Neumann*, 1853, p. 343 ; *Ebrard*, p. 49 ; *Delitzsch*, p. 737). The allusion is to the second goat presented as a sin-offering on the great day of atonement (after the first had been sacrificed in the ordinary way as an expiation), and the passage runs thus : " And let Aaron lay (וְסָמַךְ) both his hands upon the head of the live goat, and confess over him all the iniquities of the children of Israel, and all their transgressions in all their sins, and put (וְנָתַן) them upon the head of the goat," etc. All that *Hofmann* has said to weaken the certainly apparent force of this passage, is little adapted to do so. He says (p. 246): " Reference has been made to Lev. xvi. 21, as the passage where we are to learn the meaning of the imposition of hands in connection with the sacrifices. But why is it stated there, that the priest is to lay *both* his hands upon the head of the animal, which is an essentially different attitude, viz., that of a person *praying* over the animal? The act which we are considering corresponds to what followed afterwards, when he laid the sins of the congregation upon the head of the animal, that it might carry them into the wilderness." But who is likely to be convinced by the argument, that because the expression generally employed is " to lay *on the hand*," and here Aaron is *to lay on both hands*, therefore the ceremony referred to in the latter place is not the imposition of hands, but the attitude of prayer? If the difference between singular and plural be pressed at all, how is it possible to understand it in any other way than this, that the laying on of both hands denoted a greater amount of energy in the communication than the laying on of only one? Moreover, is not the very same act, which is designated in Num. xxvii. 18 as a סָמַךְ אֶת־יָדוֹ (" lay thine *hand* upon him "), afterwards described in Deut. xxxiv. 9 as a סָמַךְ אֶת־יָדָיו (" Moses had laid his *hands* upon him ")? Where are the proofs, then, that laying on the *hands* ever was or could be an attitude of prayer? And how weak and empty is the subterfuge, that it was

THE PRESENTATION AND LAYING ON OF HANDS

not the laying on of Aaron's hands, but what followed—viz., Aaron's laying the sins of the congregation upon the head of the animal—which corresponded to our ceremony! Is it not obvious that the latter was the necessary consequence and effect of the first? You have only to read the passage with the three consecutive verbs in the Perfect tense, to be convinced how utterly powerless the reasoning is. And by what means, if not by the laying on of the hands, are we to suppose that the sins were laid upon the head of the goat?

There is certainly more force in what *Bähr* has said (ii. 339) against the bearing of this passage upon the doctrine of imputation. "The goat," he says, "neither took the place of the high priest nor that of the children of Israel; it was not even put to death, but sent alive into the desert; in fact, it was not a sacrifice at all, and the treatment of it therefore proves nothing with regard to the ritual of sacrifice." In fact, everything connected with this imposition of hands was done in such a way, as to distinguish it entirely from the ordinary sacrificial ceremony. In addition to the circumstance pointed out by *Bähr*, it should also be remembered, that in every other case in which a sacrifice was presented for the whole congregation, it was not by the high priest, but by the elders as representatives of the congregation, that the laying on of hands was performed, and that this is the only occasion on which the ceremony is accompanied by a verbal declaration (וְהִתְוַדָּה) which serves to explain it. And this very circumstance, that a verbal explanation was thought necessary as an accompaniment to the act itself, is a proof that here, and nowhere else, the imposition of hands was to be regarded as a laying on of sin. We shall return to this passage at § 199.

§ 46. Again, Lev. xxiv. 14 has been misinterpreted in a manner that favours the doctrine of imputation. It is there commanded that, before stoning a blasphemer who has been sentenced to death, the witnesses of his blasphemy are to lay their hands upon his head. The same occurs in Susannah 34, when Susannah is condemned to death on account of her supposed adultery. The reason for this is thought to have been, that the capital crime committed within a community was supposed to reflect a kind of complicity in the guilt, a stain or curse upon the whole community, or, at all events, upon the witnesses of the act; and that this was to be rolled back upon the actual criminal. But no proof is to be found that such an idea was ever entertained. For the fact that the sins of forefathers continued to adhere to their descendants as guilt demanding punishment or expiation (2 Sam. xxi.), and the circumstance that the family of a criminal was regarded and punished as sharing in the guilt (Josh. vii.), had nothing in common with Lev. xxiv. 14. And Num. xxxv. 31–34, in which I once thought that I had discovered the key to Lev. xxiv. 14, has just as little bearing upon that passage. It is there commanded, that no ransom is to be accepted for the forfeited life of a wilful murderer, but he is to be executed forthwith. If this be neglected by Israel, the land is thereby defiled, and the blood which has remained unavenged will bring a curse upon the land, which will rest upon it until the demands of strict justice are satisfied. But this passage would only favour the view in question, provided the curse upon the land came from the crime of the murderer, which is evidently a misapprehension. It was not from the malefactor or his crime that it came, but from the neglect, on the part of the judges appointed for that purpose, to punish him for the crime.

Nevertheless, Lev. xxiv. 14 may help us to a correct interpretation of the sacrificial imposition of hands, or at least help to confirm the conclusion which we have already reached by a different method (§ 43). And it will do so all the more, if *Ewald* is really correct, as seems very probable, in stating that " the older sacrificial rite evidently furnished the model" for the judicial custom mentioned in Lev. xxiv. 14. In both cases it was a dedication to death which was expressed by the imposition of hands; with this difference, however, that the dedication in the case of the sacrificial animal signified a substitution of the animal for the person sacrificing it, whereas there could be nothing of the kind here, inasmuch as the act had reference simply and solely to the sin of the person about to be executed. " There is no transference here," as *Hofmann* correctly says, " of what is one's own to some one else; but the sin committed by the criminal is placed upon his own head, that it may come upon him in the punishment which he afterwards receives." On the other hand, the character of the transference, or assignment, was essentially the same in both. The idea in both cases was the assignment of an obligation or debt: in the former instance, that of another (§ 43); in the latter, his own, viz., the obligation to submit to death on account of the sin or crime that had been committed. In the former, the sinner himself devoted the animal to death for his own sin; in the latter, it was the witnesses of the crime who dedicated the criminal himself to death: for in the one, the sinner himself was his own accuser, because either he alone was aware of his sin, or he was best acquainted with it; in the other, it was the witnesses who (with the exception of the criminal himself) were the only persons aware of his crime, or those best acquainted with it.

§ 47. *Hengstenberg* adduces, as one of the principal arguments for a transference of the sins to the sacrificial animal, at any rate in the case of the sin-offering and trespass-offering, the names of the sacrifices themselves, חַטָּאת (= sin) and אָשָׁם (= guilt); and he has been followed by *Baumgarten* and *Keil*. Through the transfer of the sin, or trespass, he says, the animal became as it were a living sin or trespass. But *Oehler* (p. 649) has justly replied to this: " The name of the sin-offering, חַטָּאת, at all events, ought not to be adduced in support of such a view, since by a very simple metonymy (*vid., e.g.,* Micah vi. 3, where פֶּשַׁע also stands in connection with חַטָּאת) it is used to designate the sacrifice offered *for* the sin (עַל-חַטָּאת, Lev. iv. 3), on which account the LXX. generally render the name quite correctly, περὶ ἁμαρτίας." In addition to Micah vi. 7 (not vi. 3), we may adduce, in proof of the frequent occurrence of such a metonymy in the current phraseology, Isa. xl. 2, where the expression כָּל-חַטֹּאתֶיהָ can only be rendered " all the punishments" or " expiations for their sins," not all their " sins;" also Zech. xiv. 19, where, in the same manner, חַטַּאת מִצְרַיִם cannot mean the sin, but the punishment of Egypt. The thought, that through the " imputation of sins," the person to whom it was imputed actually became " sin," is, as it appears to me, a monstrous and inconceivable one, which presupposes that, at all events before the laying on of hands, the sacrificer was either " sin" himself, or equivalent to sin.

CHAPTER IV

SLAUGHTERING, AND THE SPRINKLING OF THE BLOOD [1]

§ 48. The imposition of hands was followed by the SLAUGHTER-ING (שְׁחִיטָה, 2 Chron. xxx. 17), by the hand of the person offering the

---

[1] The word *sprinkling* we have used here in its broadest sense ; so that it is, to be understood as including the application of the blood to the altar, and other *media* of expiation in every possible way (viz., literal sprinkling (הִזָּה), rinsing (זָרַק), and smearing with the finger).

sacrifice, and this again by the SPRINKLING OF THE BLOOD (וְזָרִיקָה)
by the hand of the priest.   If the conclusion which we have arrived
at above (§ 36, 43) as to the meaning of the imposition of hands
in connection with sacrifice be the correct one, viz., that according
to Lev. i. 4 it denoted the *consecration* of the animal to be the medium
of atonement for the sins of the person sacrificing, by means of a
substitutionary *transference* (as shown by the analogy of Num. viii.
10) of the obligation to do or suffer, in his stead, that which his God
demanded from him on account of his sin ; then the slaughtering
could only express the completion of the act, or the endurance of
the punishment, in order that the animal, or rather its blood, in
which was its soul, might thereby become fitted to be a medium of
expiation.   The *imposition of hands*, therefore, may be more exactly
defined as the consecration to death (according to the analogy of
Lev. xxiv. 14; cf. § 45), and that a *vicarious, penal death;* the
slaughtering, as the completion of this penal death, by which the
blood of the animal was fitted to become the medium of expiation ;
and the *sprinkling of the blood*, the completion of the expiation
itself.

This combination and this conclusion are so clear, firm, and
certain, that even if there were no other passage in the Old Testament in which death is represented as the wages of sin (Rom. vi.
23), the sacrificial worship itself would be sufficient to prove that it
is a genuine Old Testament doctrine.   But there are other passages
which can be shown to teach it.   It may be traced, in fact, to the
very first and fundamental beginning of divine revelation in the
primeval history of man.   For the declaration מוֹת תָּמוּת (" thou shalt
surely die"), in connection with the first sin (Gen. ii. 17, iii. 17),
taught it; and every one of the innumerable repetitions of מוֹת יוּמַת
(" he shall surely be put to death"), which occur in the law, confirmed the lesson taught.

The truth involved in Gen. ii. 17, iii. 17, that every sin, whether
small or great according to a human standard, is to be regarded as
rebellion against the will of God and an abuse of the image of
God, and therefore as deserving of death, but that a decree of
divine grace intervened, in consequence of which death does not
take place on the first sin, or *every* subsequent sin, but only when it
pleases God to cut off the man and the respite provided by that
sparing mercy (Gen. vi. 3) ; this truth is not only confirmed, but
explained and expanded by the Mosaic sacrificial worship on the
one hand, and the Mosaic jurisprudence on the other, or rather by

the supplementary or antithetical relation in which they stand the one to the other.

The eternal counsel of Divine Mercy devised a redemption from sin and its consequences. Death, indeed, as the necessary wages of sin, cannot be, and is not intended to be, averted in consequence, since the mortality which through sin has pervaded the corporeal life, must be brought, like an abscess, to a head, in order that in like manner it may then be overcome and removed by means of a curative process. On the other hand, not only is the approach of death retarded as long as God sees fit, that man and the human race may have time to manifest the subjective conditions of salvation, which the divine counsel of mercy demands, but death is divested of its eternal duration and rule ; for as death is in a man before he actually dies, so the man is in death after he dies. In the former case, death is a potentiality, bound and repressed by the vital energy ; in the latter, it is an unfettered power without him, and possessing unlimited supremacy over him. The author of the book of Genesis did not, of course, possess so clear and sure an insight into the relation between sin, death, and redemption, as has been made possible for man on New Testament ground ; but GOD possessed it, and even under the Old Testament it was by this that He regulated His treatment of man.

But whilst this general alteration of things removed the original necessity for *every* single sin to be immediately punished with death, and the divine provision intervened, that man might continue alive for a longer or shorter time notwithstanding his sinfulness and his many actual sins ; that provision did not extend to all actual sins, for example, not to such as threatened and endangered the very existence either of the moral world in general, or of the special theocratic plan of salvation, and therefore not to capital crimes. But in order that the consciousness might still be preserved, that strictly and originally every sin, even those which seemed the most trivial, deserved immediate death, and this law of nature was only interrupted by the sparing mercy of God ; the *institution of sacrificial expiation* was established, or rather permitted and *legitimated* by God,—an institution which stood in a typical relation to the complete salvation that had been predetermined in the eternal counsels of God, as the progressive development of the plan of salvation showed with growing clearness (Isa. liii.), and the event at Golgotha displayed in perfect light (cf. §57).

§ 49. *Keil* (i. 211), indeed, thinks that the scriptural proofs of the sacrificial death having been a penal death, are drawn by me among others, "*merely*" from two "*misinterpreted*" passages, viz., Rom. vi. 23 ("the wages of sin is death"), and Heb. ix. 22 ("without shedding of blood there is no remission of sins"). But I can safely affirm, that in this sentence both the "merely" and the "misinterpreted" are wrong. Where the misinterpretation of Rom. vi. 23 is supposed to lie, I cannot imagine, since I have understood the passage in just the same sense as *Keil* himself, who gives this exposition : "The wages of sin is the justly acquired and merited reward which follows sin." And *Keil* cannot deny that these wages "may be called a *punishment* so far as the reward is an evil and not a good." But in his opinion, "so long as it has not been proved from other sources that the sacrificial act (he ought to have said, the act of *slaying*) is to be regarded as a judicial act, there is no ground for applying Rom. vi. 23 to the sacrificial slaying." Very good; but where is the misinterpretation of Rom. vi. 23, if the explanation is correct, and it is only our application of the correct explanation which is inadmissible?

When *Keil* charges me, on the other hand, with misunderstanding Heb. ix. 22, the true ground for the charge is, that I have interpreted it in a different manner from himself. By the αἱματεκχυσία, for example, I understand the *pouring out* of the blood in the act of slaying. *Keil* understands it, in common with other expositors, of the *sprinkling* of blood, and consequently accuses *Bleek*, who gives the same explanation as I have done, of *counting* the passages in its favour instead of *weighing* them. Since then, *Lünemann* and *Delitzsch* have given the same interpretation of the passage. What *Keil* himself has adduced in opposition to this meaning, certainly does not seem adapted to prove it to be inadmissible. For instance, he says (i. 212): "The αἱματεκχυσία in the *Epistle to the Hebrews* cannot be understood as referring to the slaying of the sacrifice, because in the *whole of the law of sacrifice* the shedding of blood is nowhere referred to, and the slaying is never spoken of as a shedding of blood." But could not the writer of the Epistle to the Hebrews by any possibility gather *more* from the law of sacrifice, than is stated there *expressis verbis?* And is not the *slaying* of an animal *eo ipso* a shedding or pouring out of its blood ?[1]

---

[1] *Keil* closes his discussion of Heb. ix. 22 with this remark : "The expression αἱματεκχυσία relates to the pouring out of the blood on the altar, which appears to have been indispensable to the forgiveness of sin. And the shedding

However, I shall not dispute any further here, whether Heb. ix.
22 refers to the shedding of the blood or the sprinkling of the blood,
but will leave the decision of this controversy to the commentators
on the Epistle to the Hebrews; since, even if the latter were proved
to be the correct view, it would only show that the (possibly more
extended) view of the writer of that Epistle was in harmony with
our interpretation, though not the authoritative and genuine view
of the lawgiver and his contemporaries.

§ 50. As there is nothing at variance with the Old Testament
in the idea of death as a *penal suffering,* consequent upon sin and
indispensable to the expiation of sin; so also there is nothing at
variance with it in the other idea involved in our interpretation of
the *Shechitah* (the slaying), viz., that of *vicarious* suffering. This
even *Oehler* admits (p. 631); and the correctness of it is established
by the following passages.:

(1.) The vicarious death of an animal for a man is most clearly
expressed in Gen. xxii. 13, in the words תַּחַת בְּנוֹ, "in the stead of his
son." Abraham was to have offered his son as a burnt-offering,
and therefore to have given him up to death; but instead of his
son, he sacrifices, puts to death, a ram, according to the divine purpose, and under the direction of the word and providence of God.
It may be questioned whether this sacrifice was to possess an expiatory worth as well, and whether the slaying is to be regarded as a
death occurring as the wages of sin; but it cannot be disputed that
the severity of the test of Abraham's faith consisted not in the
הַעֲלוֹת (*i.e.,* in the burning) of his son, after he had been slain, but
in the *killing* of his son, which was indispensable to such a sacrifice,
and that the killing of the ram as an offering saved him from any
such necessity, and according to the gracious will of God was a
substitute for it: so that in this case, at all events, the death of an
animal did take place as a substitute for the death of a man, which
was strictly required. And that is all that is necessary for our
purpose.

(2.) To this we may add the ceremony prescribed in Deut. xxi.

of the blood of Christ is to be judged by the same rule. The satisfaction rendered by His death did not lie in the dying or shedding of blood *as such*, but
in the fact that He gave up Himself, or His life, as a *guilt*-offering for the sins
of the world." But who has ever maintained that the satisfaction rendered by
the *Old Testament sacrifices* consisted in the death *as such?* All that is maintained is, that it consisted in the death as *so appointed* by the imposition of
hands; and *mutatis mutandis* the same remark equally applies to the sacrifice of
Christ.

1–9, at the basis of which, even according to *Oehler's* decision, "there evidently lies the idea of *pœna vicaria*." (See also *Delitzsch* on Hebrews, pp. 742–3.) The blood of a murdered person demanded the blood of the murderer as an expiation (Num. xxxv. 33). But if the murderer could not be discovered, a heifer was to be killed, and the elders of the nearest town were to pray to God, that He would regard its death as representing the execution of the murderer who could not be found; that the innocent blood which had been shed might no longer lie uncovered, *i.e.*, unexpiated (ver. 8), in the land (because, according to Gen. iv. 10, so long as that was the case, it cried to heaven for vengeance); and that the city might not remain under the ban, which the murder committed in the neighbourhood had brought upon it. It is true, the object in this instance was not to cover or atone for the sin of the *murderer*, and therefore not to obtain blood as a means of expiation for that sin; so that, as a matter of course, the act of slaying could not be designated a שְׁחִיטָה. But the idea of a *pœna vicaria*, suffered by an animal instead of a man, is as evident *here* as in the sacrificial worship; the only difference being, that in the one case the punishment *could not* be inflicted upon the person who deserved it, because he was not to be found; and in the other case, it *was not* to be inflicted upon him, because the mercy of God had provided a means of expiation for his sin in the blood of the animal offered *by* him and dying *for* him.

(3.) A still further proof of the existence of the idea that an innocent person might die for a guilty one, and the latter thereby escape the punishment he deserved, is to be found in Ex. xxxii. When the people had sinned in the wilderness through the worship of the golden calf, to such an extent that the wrath of Jehovah was ready to destroy them altogether (ver. 10), and that even Moses ordered them to be decimated by the swords of the Levites to satisfy in some measure the just demands of that wrath (vers. 27, 28); he said (ver. 30), "I will go up unto Jehovah; peradventure I may be able to *make expiation* for your sin;" and then went before Jehovah interceding for the rest, and saying (ver. 32), "Now forgive them their sin, or else blot me out of Thy book." The meaning of this prayer is, that God might accept the punishment inflicted upon those who had been executed already, as an expiation or covering for the same sin on the part of those who were living still; and that if this did not suffice (since the latter had their own sins to atone for), that He would take his own life, the life of the innocent one, as a covering or expiation. No doubt Jehovah refused to grant this request, and said (ver. 33), "Whosoever hath sinned against Me, him will I blot out of My book;" but the existence of the idea of such a substitution in the religious consciousness of Moses is nevertheless unquestionable.[1] And more than that, the existence of a thought so opposed to all human notions of justice in the case of a man like Moses would be perfectly inexplicable and inconceivable, if it could not be traced to the manifestation of the very same idea in the sacrificial worship with the direct sanction of God.

(4.) To this we may add, that what Moses the servant of God offered, though God did not accept the offer, was to be actually performed by another, greater *Servant of Jehovah*—by one who, according to Isaiah's predictions in chaps. xl.–lxvi., was Moses' true antitype in the history of salvation in this as in everything besides, a Moses in higher potency,—and to be performed with the consent and approval of Jehovah (chap. liii.). Of this Servant of Jehovah it is stated in vers. 4 sqq., "He hath borne our griefs and carried our sorrows. He was wounded for our transgressions, He was bruised for our iniquities: the chastisement of our peace was upon Him; and by His stripes we are healed." And in ver. 10, with express allusion to the sacrificial worship, it is stated that God made "His life an offering for sin." Could there be a more obvious, more lucid, or more indisputable interpretation of the sacrificial slaying than this? The undeniable fact, that the later Jewish theory of sacrifice regarded the slaying as a vicarious penal death, might be despised as a rabbinical error; but the exposition of a prophet, like the writer of Isa. liii., instead of being thus lightly set aside, must be regarded as authentic. And even if the words of the prophet are not admitted to possess the character of an interpretation, at least they must have all the force of an *expansion* of the Mosaic view of sacrifice; and in that case they would at all events prove as much as this, that the foundation for such a view of the sacrificial slaying already existed in the Mosaic ritual of sacrifice.

§ 51. Whilst *Bähr* (ii. 343) attributes to the slaying a meaning in accordance with his general theory of sacrifice, viz., that it ex-

---

[1] *Hofmann* (p. 248) enters his protest against this view. "All that Moses really asks," he says, "is that if Jehovah will not forgive the nation, He may blot out his name from the book of life. He has no wish to live if his people are to forfeit their sacred calling, which they have received from God." But the answer given by God in ver. 33 requires our interpretation; for it presupposes that Moses had asked to be blotted out of the book, for the purpose of preserving those who had deserved it because of their sin. Cf. Rom. ix. 3.

hibited the completion of the self-surrender, for which the laying on of hands had already exhibited a willingness, and *Neumann* (l. c. 343) regards it as an acknowledgment on the part of the person presenting the offering, that he gave the animal entirely up, renouncing for ever both it and its life (both of them opinions which we do not feel it necessary to refute); *Delitzsch, Oehler,* and *Hofmann* do not allow it to have possessed any independent significance at all. *Oehler* says (p. 628), "In the Mosaic ritual the slaying was evidently nothing more than a necessary link in the process; it was simply the means of procuring the blood." *Delitzsch* again says (p. 426), "The *Shechitah* merely answered the double purpose of providing the blood, in which was the life of the animal, for the expiation of the soul of the sacrificer, and the flesh as fire-food for Jehovah;" and this *Hofmann* expressly approves and adopts in the second edition of his *Schriftbeweis*.

Delitzsch observes, at p. 744, "The killing was merely the means of procuring the blood and offering the sacrifice; and hence it was not called *killing*, but *slaughtering*." Let us look at this first of all. In opposition to the penal theory, *Delitzsch* lays stress upon the fact, that the killing of the sacrificial animal is always designated by the verb שׁחט, never by הֵמִית. In this he thinks that he can discover a proof that the idea of killing, as an act of significance in itself, was foreign to the sacrificial slaying, and the sole intention was to take away life, as the necessary step to another purpose, viz., the procuring of the blood or the flesh. This thought is derived, however, not from the Hebrew, but from the German idiom, where the notion of slaughtering certainly has received such an application. And the fact that the verb שׁחט is never used in ordinary life to denote a literal slaughtering for the purpose of cooking the flesh (טבח is the word generally used) ought to have created some distrust of this attempt to define the meaning of שׁחט. Moreover, we actually find this verb applied to the slaying of a man, where there could not have been any other object than to put him to death, namely, as punishment for a crime that was thought worthy of death (*e.g.*, Num. xiv. 16; Judg. xii. 6; 1 Kings xviii. 40; 2 Kings x. 7, 14, xxv. 7; Jer. xxxix. 6, xli. 7). שׁחט according to its etymology is related to שׁחה, שׁחח, שׁחת (*vid. Rödiger* in Gesenius Thes.), and its primary meaning was probably to throw down, to strike to the ground, to destroy, to lay in ruins. In the more developed stage of the language it became a technical term for the killing of an *animal;* from that it settled down into a

special term belonging to the sacrificial worship, and thus acquired
so definite and fixed a meaning, that people were afraid to apply it
to the slaughtering of an animal for the ordinary purposes of life.
From its original use, however, which was restricted to the killing
of an animal, it came also to be applied to the killing of a man,
when it took place, not in the mode adopted in an ordinary execution, but in a summary and informal manner, by striking to the
ground (as a beast is killed). Thus it is evident, that neither in
the derivation of the word, nor in its customary use, is there the
least warrant for attributing to it that exclusive reference to the
procuring of blood or flesh, which certainly has come to be associated with the German word *schlachten* (to slaughter).

§ 52. In opposition to the idea that the *Shechitah* had no independent significance of its own, there rises with irresistible force
the *solemnity* of the act, its firm incorporation into the sacrificial
ritual, and the necessity for its being performed on holy ground,
before Jehovah (Lev. i. 5, etc.), by the side of the altar, in the
presence of the priest, and with his indispensable, and therefore
certainly significant, co-operation. If it had been nothing more
than the means of procuring the blood and flesh for sprinkling and
burning upon the altar, it is difficult to see why it was necessary
that it should be performed on holy ground; why not at a man's
own home, from which the blood and flesh could easily have been
taken to the altar, without in any way detracting from the worth of
the sprinkling and burning. This was at all events indicated in the
original law (Lev. vii. 25, xvii. 3–5), where the slaughtering of *every*
animal, even for domestic and ordinary purposes, is ordered to be
carried out in precisely the same manner as a peace-offering (cf. § 5).

But what furnishes the strongest testimony against this attempt
to deprive the *Shechitah* of all independent worth, is the command,
that animals offered in sacrifice should be killed on the *north side
of the altar* only.

It is true, this command is particularly and expressly mentioned
only in connection with the burnt-offerings, sin-offerings, and trespass-offerings (Lev. i. 11, iv. 24, 29, 33, vii. 2); and the Rabbins
have inferred from this ("without reason," as *Keil* also says, i.
205), that the peace-offerings were to be slain on a different
side (viz., the south). But if the lawgiver had intended to make
the peace-offering an exception to this otherwise universal rule, he
would have indicated it, not by silence, but by an express command.
This silence is rather a direct proof of the contrary.

What the reason for this command was, it is impossible to determine with perfect certainty. But *Ewald's* opinion is assuredly wrong, that we may see in this "the remnant of an earlier belief, that the Deity resides either in the north or in the east, and that it is from thence that He comes." *Tholuck's* conjecture is a much more probable one, viz., that the *north* side (צָפוֹן, the hidden, dark, midnight side, hence the side pregnant with evil) was regarded as the gloomy and joyless one. Should this be accepted as the true explanation (and it would be difficult to find one more plausible), not only would it be a proof in itself of the independent worth of the *Shechitah*, but would throw a considerable weight into the scale in favour of the very same meaning which we obtained in § 48, 50, by a different process. But whatever may be the reason for the command, there must at all events have been *some* reason; and this is in itself a proof that the slaughtering, to which it referred, must have possessed some significance also.

A few commentators, indeed—*e.g.*, *Fr. v. Meyer* (on Lev. i. 11) and *Bunsen* (*ad h. l.*)—imagine that they can find a sufficient reason for the command in the external necessities of the case. On the eastern side, they say, there was the heap of ashes (ver. 16), on the western the tabernacle and the large basin (Ex. xl. 30), and on the southern the entrance; so that the only side left for the slaughtering was the northern side. But there is no force in this; for if there had been no other (symbolical) difficulties in the way, the southern side would have been the most appropriate, just because the entrance was there.

§ 53. That *Oehler* should see no meaning in the sacrificial slaughtering in itself, was a necessary consequence of his fundamental view of sacrifice; and in no other way could he possibly succeed in bringing the slaughtering into harmony with his explanation of the other parts of the sacrificial ceremony. This opinion is based upon the correct premiss, that if the sacrificial slaughtering had not the force of a *pœna vicaria*, we must give up all idea of discovering any symbolical meaning whatever. But with the independent position which it occupied, the solemnity with which it was performed in the Holy Place, etc., it is very hard to do the latter. Hence, even *Keil* acknowledges the necessity of attributing to it a significance of its own. The meaning which he has given, however, is more decidedly erroneous than even *Oehler's* negation of all meaning, since it drives him inevitably into partly open and partly latent opposition to the scriptural *data*, and also to his own interpretation of the other parts of the ritual of sacrifice. He commences (i. 206) with the admission, that " the slaughtering of the animal was a symbol of the surrender of life ·to death;" *only not* a surrender, he adds, " *to death as the punishment of sin*, . . . for although the death of the sacrificer, symbolized by the slaying of the victim, was a fruit and effect of sin, it did not come under the aspect of punishment, because sacrifice was an institution of divine grace, intended to insure to the sinner not the merited punishment, but, on the contrary, forgiveness of sins; whilst the death which follows sin is and remains, as a rule, a punishment *only* for that sinner for whom there is no redemption, and brings to those who are redeemed and forgiven deliverance from all evil, and an entrance into eternal and blessed life with God.[1] If, therefore, the object of sacrifice was the reconciliation of man to God, and his reception into a state of grace with all its felicitous consequences, which no one denies and there is no possible ground for denying, the death connected with the sacrifice can only be regarded as the medium of transition from a state of separation and estrangement from God into one of grace and living fellowship with Him, or as the only way into the divine life out of the ungodly life of this world. And even though the necessity for this way displays the holiness of the righteous God, who has appointed death as the wages of sin; yet a death which redeems man from sin, and introduces him into eternal life, cannot be called a punishment, since the idea of divine holiness and righteousness is by no means exhausted by the notion of punishment alone."

In examining this argument, even if we take no notice of the unhistorical blending of the Old and New Testament standpoints (for it is only the latter which teaches that death is the bridge for crossing from the ungodly life of this world into the godly life of eternal blessedness with God); and if we also pass over the doctrinal ambiguity, which both affirms and denies that death is the punishment of sin in the case of the redeemed, and ascribes to death, which is and remains under *all* circumstances the wages of sin, what belongs to redemption alone;—we shall still find this view in all respects untenable as applied to the ritual of the sacrificial worship. The death of the sacrificial animal is said to typify the death of the redeemed, which, however, is " not punishment for sin,"

---

[1] So far as these assertions are directed against the theory of penal death, we shall examine them by and by at § 65. Here we are only concerned to examine *Keil's* own view.

but rather " a passage into the divine life out of the ungodly life of this world." Now *Oehler* does not state, what alone would make good sense, that the holiness of the person sacrificing, *qua* redeemed, was " transferred to the victim," but, like *Keil* himself in his explanation of the imposition of hands in connection with the atoning sacrifice, maintains that " the sin and guilt" of the sacrificer *as* a sinner were so transferred; so that the animal was made " as it were incarnate sin," and its body " a body of sin." It is not by the atonement of sin, therefore, but by giving compensation for sins still unatoned for, that death is stamped as the " medium for the transition from a state of separation and estrangement from God into one of grace and living fellowship with God;" and yet, after all this, the sinner who is already perfectly redeemed, inasmuch as he has already entered " into a state of grace and fellowship with God," into " eternal and blessed life with God," is then for the first time to have expiation made for his sins. According to this theory of *Keil's*, the expiation, *i.e.*, the sprinkling of the blood, ought necessarily to have preceded the slaughtering; for it was through the expiation that the life of a sinner was *first* qualified for entering into a state of grace and fellowship with God, into eternal and blessed life with God. This no one has ever yet denied, or ever can deny.

By thus rejecting the true meaning of the sacrificial slaying, *Keil* is driven into opposition, partly to the biblico-orthodox doctrine, which he nevertheless still holds, and partly to his own interpretation of the other parts of the sacrificial ceremony. But it becomes still more striking, when we find in other parts of *Keil's* work the very same doctrine which he has here opposed and rejected when advocated by me, expressed in the very same words, and given as *his own* view of the sacrificial slaying. For example, whereas he affirms, at p. 207, that " the slaying typified the surrender of the life of the sacrificer to death, but *did not typify death as the punishment of sin;*" at p. 237 he says, " Now the ram of the trespass-offering stood for the person of the guilty man, and by being slain, suffered *death in his stead as the punishment for his guilt.*" At p. 228, again, he says, " By being slain, the animal of the sin-offering was given up to death, and *suffered death for the sinner, i.e.,* in the place of the person sacrificing, *as the wages of sin!*" and at p. 283, " By these attributes (*sc.*, freedom from blemish, and a fresh, vigorous fulness of life) the animal was perfectly fitted to bear as a sin-offering the guilt of the congregation imputed to it by the laying on of hands, and to *suffer death in a representative capacity as the wages of sin.*" So also at p. 384 : " As a sacrifice appointed by the Lord, the paschal lamb suffered death *vicariously, as the effect of sin, for* the father of the family who killed it for himself and his household."

Only on one or two occasions does it seem to have occurred to the writer that it was necessary to reconcile these self-contradictions. Thus at p. 213 he observes : " But the justice of God was made manifest through the grace that ruled in the sacrificial atonement, in *this respect :* expiation presupposed death ; without death, in fact, *i.e,* without dying spiritually, it is absolutely impossible to be received into the fellowship of divine mercy ; and without physical death there can be no entrance into eternal blessedness. And *herein lies the reason,* why every sacrifice of atoning worth was necessarily required to be a sacrifice by death, and why, in the performance of the sacrificial rite, the victim had to suffer death, before its blood could be sprinkled upon the altar." But even with reference to this exposition, which is not overburdened with superfluous clearness, we have several important queries to make. If expiation presupposed death, how could death even *before* expiation lead from the ungodly life of this world into the blessedness of life eternal, seeing that evidently this could only be said, if death, on the contrary, presupposed expiation ? " Only to a man redeemed and pardoned," says *Keil* himself, at p. 207, " could death bring redemption from all evil, and effect a transition into eternal and blessed life with God." But how is pardon itself secured ? Is it through physical death in itself ? Is it not rather through expiation, or the extermination of sin ? And yet, according to *Keil,* expiation presupposes death, which forms the passage to eternal life, instead of death presupposing expiation. How strange a righteousness of God would that be, which should be manifested in the reception of a sinner through death, *before* expiation, and therefore without expiation, into the blessedness of eternal life ? And yet *this* is said to constitute the reason why in the sacrificial ritual the victim was necessarily put to death, before its blood could be sprinkled on the altar! And if *this* was actually the reason why the sacrifices of an expiatory character (*i.e.,* according to *Keil,* the sin- and trespass-offerings) were required to be sacrifices by death, and why death necessarily preceded expiation,—where are we to look for the reason why the sacrifices, that were *not* expiatory in their character (viz., the burnt-offerings and thank-offerings), were also required to be sacrifices by death, and in their case also death necessarily preceded the expiation?

I am quite unable to find any reconciliation of the contradictions occurring here, in what *Keil* says at p. 228. "The sinner," he says, "certainly merited death, *and the victim taking his place had to suffer it in his stead,* because the mercy of God could not, and would not destroy, or even weaken, the holiness of the law; and therefore, even when the sinner was intended to discern in the death of the sin-offering what he himself would have deserved, if God had dealt with him according to His justice, the law contains no statement to the effect, that the sin-offering was in any sense a satisfaction," etc. (for the rest, see § 65, 67). On the contrary, the discrepancies appear rather to multiply. For how could the sinner discern in the death of the sacrificial animal what he himself would have deserved, viz., death as the punishment of sin, if that death was a symbol, *not* of death as the punishment of sin, but, on the contrary, of a death which redeemed from sin and introduced into the blessedness of eternal life? And how can it be said, that the victim had necessarily to suffer in the place of the sinner the death deserved by him as the punishment of his sin, if the death of the victim is not to be regarded as a penal death at all? And how is it possible to find the idea expressed in the institution of sacrifice, that the mercy of God could not destroy or weaken the holiness of the law which demanded death as the punishment of sin, if, as is stated immediately afterwards, the sacrifice had no satisfactory worth, and the grace of God out of *pure* mercy covered over the sin? Does not "pure" mercy in this way become an arbitrary mercy, opposing the demands of the holiness of the law, and not merely weakening, but actually abolishing it?

§ 54. We will now adduce two other examples, to show how the denial of a *satisfactio vicaria* in the Old Testament sacrifices, on the part of theologians who are generally anxious to adhere to the biblical and orthodox standpoint, is sure to drive them to inconsistencies and contradictions. *Delitzsch*, speaking of the imposition of hands which preceded the slaying, says (p. 737), "If it was an expiatory, *i.e.,* a sin- or trespass-offering, he laid his sins upon it, that it might bear them and carry them away from him." Now, if this be correct, it is placed beyond all doubt, that *between* the imposition of hands and the sprinkling of the blood (at any rate, in the case of the sin-offerings and trespass-offerings) something must have intervened, by which the sin imputed in the laying on of hands was overcome, wiped away, and changed into its opposite. For, just as sin could not be covered, expiated, wiped away by sin, so the blood of the animal, which after the imposition of hands was laden (as the vehicle of the soul) with sin and guilt, could not in that condition become the means of expiation. Something else must necessarily have been done to it in the meantime, by which the sin imputed to it, and by virtue of that imputation regarded as its own, had been conquered and wiped away, and by which it had been fitted to be used as a means of expiation; and there is nowhere else that we can look for this, but in the slaying which intervened, and which could only be a vicarious penal suffering, by virtue of which it suffered the death which the sacrificer deserved, and suffered it *for him.* The blood brought to the altar was then a proof that the merited punishment had been endured, and in that light was fitted to cover the sinful soul of the sacrificer himself.

Delitzsch, again, always lays great stress upon the necessity of acknowledging the representative character of the sacrificial animal. But as he is unwilling to acknowledge it in the שְׁחִיטָה, where it is primarily and chiefly appropriate, he is induced to place it in the sprinkling of the blood. Thus he says, at p. 741, " In Lev. xvii. 11 it is stated that the blood of the animal made expiation for the soul of the person offering it, by virtue of the soul which was contained in it: evidently, therefore, the soul of the animal took the place of the soul of the man; and when poured out in the blood, covered the soul of the man, which was deserving of death, before an angry God." And again, at p. 745: " The Old Testament sacrifice, *so far as it was expiatory,* was intended to be regarded as *representative.* There was no ritual manifestation, indeed, of the penal suffering, since the expiation was only effected through the blood, apart from the violent death; but the bleeding expiation, when understood typically, as it was intended to be understood, and has been prophetically expounded in Isa. liii., also pointed to a vicarious satisfaction to be rendered to the judicial righteousness of God." But the idea of representation in the first half of the sacrificial ceremony (*i.e., before* the burning) was evidently applicable to the slaying *alone, as* a penal suffering, and not at all to the atonement, *i.e.,* the sprinkling of the blood. The blood brought to the altar, or rather the soul which dwelt within it, was to cover the soul of the offerer *there.* How could it, then, take the place of the latter? For, where one person takes the place of another, the other is *not* there himself, but the representative is there *in his stead,* performing or suffering what the former ought to have suffered or performed.

§ 55. The meaning of the SPRINKLING OF THE BLOOD is self-evident, after what has been stated already. The person presenting the sacrifice was conscious of his sin or sinfulness; he knew that he was liable, in consequence, to death as the wages of sin. It is true, the divine long-suffering, which, notwithstanding the threat to the *first* sinner, "In the day thou eatest thereof thou shalt surely die," had preserved his life for a lengthened period, extended to him also as to *every other* sinner. Provided he did not commit, or had not committed, any sin which threatened to overturn and destroy the *moral* order of the universe generally, or the essential elements of its specifically *theocratic* order, and which it was necessary on that account for the judicial authorities of earth to punish with death, he need not immediately die. But, for all that, he was under sentence of death for every minor sin, and even for mere sinfulness, from which all actual sins proceed; and this sentence of death lay like a ban upon him, disturbing the peace of his soul, preventing him from the quiet and happy enjoyment of the blessings of life, causing him to see himself as an object of divine wrath, and even in this earthly life threatening him either with a quick and painful death, or with evils and calamities of every description. And with the Old Testament Israelite this was all the more the case, because his want of a clear perception of eternal life hereafter was accompanied with an equal want of any clear perception of retribution hereafter; and the whole weight of divine retribution to his consciousness, therefore, fell not in the life beyond, but in the life on this side the grave. To be delivered from this ban by the expiation, the wiping away, the forgiveness of his sin, was therefore the inmost desire of his soul, the most pressing need of his life. But from the very earliest times God had established an institution of grace, by which he could secure the expiation or forgiveness of his sins. Accordingly, relying upon the divine נְתַתִּיו ("I have given it," Lev. xvii. 11), he brought to the altar an animal from his own stall—a living, animated being like himself, a domesticated animal, which as such belonged to his own house, which had been tended by himself almost as one tends his own child, which was dear to him almost like a manservant or maid-servant, but which was not a sinful creature like himself, his servant, his maid-servant, or his child, but sinless, innocent, pure, without blemish, without fault or failing, and which, on account of all this, was apparently well fitted—at all events better fitted than any other gift which he could possibly offer as a recompense for his guilt—to redeem his soul which was under the death-ban of sin. And to that he set apart the animal, being directed to

do so by God Himself.   By laying his hands upon it he transferred
to it his own sentence of death, and caused it to suffer in his stead
the punishment, which he was conscious that he himself deserved
on account of his sins.   Upon this the priest, as the mediator between God and the nation, carried to the altar the blood which had
passed through death, the wages of sin, that on that spot where,
according to Ex. xx. 24 (cf. § 13), Jehovah had promised to come
to His people to bless them, he might cover and atone for the sinful
soul of the person presenting the sacrifice.

The imposition of hands was the qualification of the sacrificial
animal for the vicarious endurance of punishment; and the death
in which this was completed was the qualification of the animal
blood, in which its soul resided, for the act of expiation; and this
again was completed by the bringing of the blood thus qualified to
the altar, where it covered (ideally) the sinful soul of the person
offering it.   The imposition of hands did not deliver the person
sacrificing from his sin; for it was not a transference of his sin to
the sacrificial animal (§ 44), but only the communication of a substitutionary obligation, to suffer on his behalf what he had deserved
on account of his sin.   Even the slaying, in which it suffered death
vicariously for him, did not effect in itself an expiation or wiping
away of his sins, just as my pecuniary debts are not wiped out by
the fact of another having _earned_ the necessary money through the
labour of his hands.   The debts themselves can only be wiped out
by his covering them with the money which he has earned; and so
a debt of sin requires to be covered by the merit of the _suffering of
the sacrifice_ before it can be regarded as atoned for and wiped out;
in other words, the meritorious performance of the sacrifice must be
transferred to the sinful soul of the person presenting it, and personally appropriated to him (so as to be regarded as his merit, his performance), in the same way in which his obligation had previously
been imputed to the sacrifice.   And, according to Lev. xvii. 11, this
was done by means of the sprinkling of the blood, in which the sinless
and guiltless soul of the sacrificial animal covered (if only ideally) the
soul of the person offering it.   The merit acquired by the soul of the
victim, which in itself was pure and sinless and therefore liable to no
punishment on its own account, through its vicarious endurance of
death, now acted upon the sinful soul of the sacrificer as a covering
for sin, that is to say, it rendered his sin inoperative (§ 28).[1]

[1] Compare the pregnant words of _Kahnis_, i. 271: "The sacrificial blood
atones, so far as it is the life of the animal _in compendio_; for in the blood (Lev.

§ 56. But for this expiation to possess any objective validity, it was necessary that it should be performed at the altar (Lev. xvii. 11), and by the priest (Lev. i. 5, 11, etc.), not by the sacrificer himself ; and even that was insufficient unless the antecedents and preliminaries—viz., the presentation, the imposition of hands, and the slaying—had taken place before the altar and in the presence of the priest. *The latter* contains its own explanation ; for it is self-evident that an obligation or debt which I owe to any one must be discharged either in his own presence or that of his accredited agent, whether I discharge it in my own person or by deputy. *The former* proves that the sacrificial blood was not fully qualified for the purposes of atonement, either in itself, or through the imposition of hands and the infliction of death ; but that it acquired for the first time its objective, atoning power, through the fact that the priest, as mediator of the saving grace of God, brought it to the altar (*i.e.*, to the place of mercy and salvation, where Jehovah came to His people to bless them), and there it acquired a *divine* energy which supplied all its defects and endowed it with plenary power.

Substitution under any circumstances is of course a problematical thing, and its acceptance and acknowledgment are dependent upon the mercy of God (Ex. xxxii. 33). But the substitution referred to here, is in all respects so obviously insufficient, that we cannot speak of its possessing validity according to natural law, but only according to the law of mercy laid down by the divine plan of salvation. It is true, the sacrificial animal, as belonging to the flock and home, stood in a biotic *rapport* with the person presenting the sacrifice (§ 23) ; but the animal was not, what a thorough substitution would have required, *re vera* of his own nature—was not *re vera*, but only symbolically, his *alter ego :* there was altogether wanting an internal basis of substitution, a positive unity of nature and will, resting upon the nature and will of both. The animal, again, was certainly guiltless and sinless ; but only because it stood *below* the sphere of sin, not because it was elevated, or had raised itself, above that sphere. It is true, the obligation to suffer death for the sinner was transferred to it by the imposition of hands ; but this transference, again, was only symbolical and figurative, not literal and real. The animal was doubtless the property of the person sacrificing it ; consequently, he possessed the right and the

xvii. 11) is that life, which carries negatively the death that it has endured in our stead, and positively a pure life, which can be brought into fellowship with God." See also p. 585.

authority to offer up its life for his own good and salvation. But
for all that, it was a *forced*, and therefore an *insufficient* representation ; inasmuch as it was impossible, from a pneumatico-ethical
point of view, for the animal to declare its free-will to give itself up
to death for the sinner as the wages of his sin, being utterly destitute as it was of this pneumatic character, and of the least freedom
of will and purpose (§ 33) ; whilst from a psychico-physical point
of view, it would resist with all its might the attempt to use it in
this way as a means of atonement; whereas the sin to be expiated
had sprung from the soil of free personality, and therefore it was
requisite that the expiation itself should be the product of free personality, the sacrifice a voluntary one, the result of an independent and perfectly unconstrained resolution of the will. Again,
the sacrifice, it is true, was put to death. But *the* death which the
animal suffered, was not of the same kind or importance as that
which the sinner deserved ; for the life of an animal belongs to a
lower stage than that of man, and hence death to an animal is
something different from death to a man. Moreover, in the sacrificial worship, sin was considered, not as a violation of human
rights and claims (for in this respect it was liable to the penal juris-
diction of earthly magistrates), but as rebellion against God—both
God without us, *i.e.*, a resistance to the objective will and law of
God, and also God within us, *i.e.*, a violation of the image of God
in us, which in the form of conscience protests and strives against
sin. But if the foundation of all justice is the *jus talionis* (Ex. xxi.
23, soul for soul, eye for eye, tooth for tooth, etc.), and consequently
the violation of that which is violated must return upon the person
of the violator with all the force given to it by the greatness of
the injury, and the importance of that which is injured ; it is evident that, although the violation of earthly relationships may be
atoned for by earthly punishment (and in its most intense form
by capital punishment), yet sin, as an injury done to the eternal,
holy God, the Lord and Creator of heaven and earth, demands a
death which is not exhausted by earthly death (the only death possible to the sacrificial animal), and a punishment which continues
even in Sheol (as the abode of the departed human soul), yea,
to all eternity, because the God offended is an eternal God.

§ 57. The whole of the sacrificial ceremony, up to the act of
expiation itself, moved upon the basis of symbolism ; and the sacrificial blood, therefore, was capable of nothing more than a *symbolical atonement*. But Lev. xvii. 11 does not state that the atonement

was merely symbolized by the sprinkling of the blood; on the contrary, it assigns to it a real atoning power.   Whence did the sacrificial blood acquire this; and by what means did its *symbolical* atoning power acquire the potency of a *real* atonement, and the empty, powerless symbol a sacramental efficacy?

According to the principles of natural (so to speak, Elohistic) justice, the expiation of a sin can only be effected by personal satisfaction; that is, by the sinner himself enduring all the punishment deserved, in other words, an equivalent to the sin.   But it is altogether different with the principles of saving (Jehovistic) justice. For the divine plan of salvation has discovered a way by which the sinner, without completely exhausting the punishment of sin in his own person, may be freed and delivered.   It consists *objectively* in this, that a righteous being interposes for sinners, endures for them the merited punishment,—a righteous one, whose life is worth infinitely more than the life of all sinners together, whose temporary sufferings surpass in worth and importance even the eternal sufferings of the whole human race,—a righteous one, who, by placing himself in essential *rapport* with sinful humanity, becomes their true (not merely conventional) representative, their real *alter ego*, and thereby qualifies himself to endure the punishment of sin for them; and who undertakes all this of his own free-will.   It consists *subjectively* in this, that the sinner, on the other hand, is placed in a condition to enter into essential *rapport* with this righteous being by an unconstrained determination of his own will; so that, as the righteous one bears and exhausts the sinner's punishment as his own, he also may make the sin-exterminating merits, thereby acquired by the righteous one, into his own.

According to the counsel of God, the self-sacrifice of this righteous being could not, and was not intended to become a historical event until the fulness of time.   But to the consciousness of God, who is exalted above time and space, and to whom there is no past or future, but only an eternal now, this sacrifice, while to man still in futurity, was ever a present event; and therefore its fruits and its merits were objectively present also.   And *this* was the genuine and essential atoning power with which God endowed the sacrificial blood that was brought to the altar, as the place of salvation and of grace, so as to change the empty *symbol* into a true sacramental *type*.   Then, too, the saying applies: *accedit verbum* (Lev. xvii. 11, "I have given it") *ad elementum, et fit sacramentum*.   For even then God could appropriate the merit of that righteous one, which had already an objective existence to Him, to the covering of the sins of those who were subjectively fitted for it. But to prevent the delusion, that sin was a light thing in the estimation of God, that He could and would forgive sin and bestow His mercy without reserve, or without satisfaction being rendered to justice, an institution was provided in the sacrificial worship of the Old Testament for the sinner who desired salvation, that brought before his mind afresh, with every new sin for which he sought atonement, what his sin deserved, and he would have had to suffer, if he had been required to atone for it himself, and what must necessarily take place to release him from that obligation ; inasmuch as what God then directed to be done to the animal, was what would one day be done in the fulness of time to that righteous one, for the covering of the sins of all sinners who desired salvation and were fitted to receive it.

§ 58. Thus far we have taken our stand upon the New Testament, Gospel ground, that we might be able from this point of view to understand the meaning of the sacrificial expiation of the Old Testament, and see in what the objective atoning worth ascribed to it consisted. The question becomes incomparably more difficult, when we look at it from the legal standpoint of the Old Testament, and seek to discover the meaning attached to it by Moses and his contemporaries. Was the Israelite of that age also conscious of this typical import of the animal sacrifice; or, at any rate, was it possible for him to attain to this consciousness ?

In the first place, we may here point to the fact, that this typical import of the sacrifice actually did develop itself in the heart of Judaism, without any New Testament influence, and therefore out of the elements existing in the Mosaic ritual ; for not only is it expressed from the pre-Christian standpoint of an Isaiah (chap. liii.), but from the equally pre-Christian standpoint of many of the later Rabbins, who maintained very decidedly that the animal sacrifices would cease with the coming of the Messiah, because He would perform in the most perfect manner all that the sacrifices had been designed to accomplish.

We are warranted, therefore, in expecting and looking for the germs, or germinal elements, of this consciousness in Mosaism itself. Among these we notice first of all those shortcomings and defects in the animal sacrifices, which we have already pointed out, and which could not be overlooked even from the standpoint of an Israelite under the Old Testament. For the fact that the blood of bulls and goats could not take away sin (Heb. ix. 12), was one which must have forced itself upon the mind of every thinking man. It would also be brought before the Israelite by the fact, that atoning efficacy was not attributed to the blood of the animal, after or in consequence of the imposition of hands and infliction of death, but was acquired first of all from contact with the altar, upon which God came down to His people with power to bless and save (Ex. xx. 24).

But when this imperfection in his sacrificial worship was once clearly brought before his mind, and with it the contrast between the insufficiency of the means and the fulness of the promise, which insured an eventual and perfect efficacy to those means notwithstanding these defects; he could hardly fail to investigate and search for the explanation of this incongruity between the means employed and the effect produced. For ordinary purposes, the promise " This blood maketh atonement for your souls" was practically sufficient, provided it was received in simple faith; for the faith which laid hold of this word grasped at the same time the blessing of the sacrifice promised therein, which was really the same, even though its internal ground might not be perceived. But to any one who studied the secrets of the divine plan of salvation, and the sacred imagery of the ritual,—who did not " let the book of the law depart out of his mouth, but meditated therein day and night" (Josh. i. 8),—whose " delight was in the law of the Lord" (Ps. i. 2),—who prayed, " Open Thou mine eyes, that I may behold wondrous things out of Thy law,"—there must have presented themselves the first glimpses of a deeper knowledge, even if he perceived at the same time, that a more perfect insight could only be obtained after a further development of the sacred history and its accompanying revelation. Did not Moses himself point out the symbolical and typical character of the entire ritual appointed by him, when he distinctly stated that the eternal original had been shown to him on the holy mount? And what could be more simple, than to bring the germ and centre of the whole ritual into connection with the primary promises of the salvation to be secured through the seed of the woman, and the seed of the patriarchs? What more simple, than to connect the centre of his hopes and expectations with the centre of his worship—to imagine a hidden, even though incomprehensible, link between the two, and to seek in this link the solution of the sacred enigma?

But undoubtedly, for a clear perception and deep insight into the historico-typical import of the sacrificial atonement, and a full

solution of its enigmas, the way was first prepared through the prophetic standpoint of an Isaiah, and eventually completed in the
sacrifice on Calvary.

§ 59. The *juridical interpretation* of the Old Testament sacrifice,
in which the slaughtering is regarded as a *pœna vicaria* endured
by the sacrificial animal in the stead of the person offering it, has
been the one generally received from the time of the Rabbins and
Fathers—at least so far as the sin-offerings and trespass-offerings
are concerned; and even in the most recent times it has found
many supporters of note. Among these are *Gesenius, De Wette,
Winer, Hengstenberg* (in his Christology, and his Sacrifices of Holy
Scripture), *Scholl, Bruno Bauer, v. Meyer, Hävernick, Lange, Thalhofer, Stöckl, Tholuck, Ebrard, Knobel, Kliefoth, Keil, Thomasius,*
and *Kahnis.*

On the other hand, it has met with numerous opponents, especially in modern times; though the arguments adduced certainly
do not gain in importance from the fact, that for the most part
they are founded upon feelings altogether distinct from the subject
in hand, viz., an antipathy to the orthodox, New Testament doctrine
of reconciliation, as is undeniably the case with *Steudel, Klaiber,
Bähr,* and *Hofmann.* In the case of *Keil,* who repeatedly reverts
to the orthodox, traditional view, and thereby involves himself in
striking discrepancies, it is to be lamented that he should evidently
not have been conscious of the discrepancies, or he would certainly
have adhered throughout, and not merely in isolated passages, to
the old well-tried truth, instead of his new and untenable discoveries.
Neumann's views and words are so misty and obscure, that they
have consequently but little weight. But *Oehler* and *Delitzsch,*
who cannot certainly be supposed to have any ulterior end to serve,
have been led away to their negative position by attaching too much
importance to various plausible arguments.

§ 60. We will now examine the objections offered to the view
in question. *Steudel* adduces four objections in his *Vorlesungen
über d. Theol. des A. T.:* (1.) " Throughout the whole of the Old
Testament we never meet with any such idea as this, that the
pardon which God confers must be purchased first of all by substitution. He grants forgiveness at once, as soon as the sinner
repents; and that not merely according to the teaching of the
prophets (Ezek. xviii. 1 sqq., xxxiii. 14 sqq.), but according to the
teaching of the Pentateuch also (as in Deut. iv. 30, 31, xxx. 2 ; Lev.
xxvi. 40 sqq.), where the promise is given, that when the Israelites

turn to the Lord, He will also turn at once to them in mercy, and
bestow upon them all His blessing." To this I have already given
the following answer in my *Mos. Opfer*: How marvellous! whilst
some writers take the greatest offence at the wrathful Jew-God of
the Old Testament, who can only be appeased with blood, others
find in Him a loving Father, who forgives in the most indiscriminate
manner. God grants forgiveness, they say, without anything further;
in other words, without a sacrifice. But the whole law of worship,
which never promises forgiveness without anything further, but
always makes it dependent upon a sacrificial expiation, rises against
this. *Steudel* does indeed modify his "without anything further,"
by introducing the condition of repentance. But does not that
addition prove the very opposite of what it is meant to prove? It
proves, that is to say, that for the Israelite there was no forgiveness
without sacrifice; for conversion, turning to Jehovah, included the
offering of sacrifice. What could it mean but returning to the
theocratic union? And this could only be effected through sacrifice. What else could it mean than returning from a heathen to a
theocratic life, the central point of which was the sacrificial worship? What else, than resuming and faithfully performing the
theocratic duties that had been neglected, and which had their
centre in sacrifice? By what other means could the Israelite give a
practical demonstration of the earnestness, the genuineness, and the
permanence of his repentance, than by a faithful worship of Jehovah,
as demanded in the law, the very soul of which was sacrifice? If,
therefore, forgiveness could only be obtained by repenting and turning to Jehovah, by that very fact it was made dependent upon the
sacrifice, in which this was practically exhibited; and the entire argument is consequently reduced to this circle: an assumption that sacrifice did not involve substitution may be adduced as a proof that it did.

(2.) *Steudel* says, "It is just in connection with the more important sins that we never find the slightest intimation of their needing to be expiated by sacrifice. And yet if sacrifices were appointed
for the violation of precepts relating to outward acts, how important
must it have seemed, supposing substitution to have been the idea,
that sacrifices should be offered for moral offences in the strict sense
of the word, which were of much greater importance!" But the
most casual glance at the sacrificial law will show, that it was not
merely the violation of outward precepts, which the law undoubtedly
exhibits as equally important, and in certain circumstances more
important than many offences of a strictly "moral" character, that

had to be expiated by sacrifice, but offences of the latter kind as
well. In one respect, indeed, the statement is certainly correct.
There were certain offences of greater importance—those, for
example, which arose from wantonness and rebellion (Num. xv.
30, 31), whether they were violations of outward or of strictly
moral laws—which could not be expiated by sacrifice, but had to
be punished by extermination. The reason why the latter could not
be "bound" (as, *mutatis mutandis*, in the Christian Church), even
in the case of repentance, was, that the institution of sacrifice
under the Old Testament related to the earthly theocracy alone :
the sinner was excluded by his sin from membership in the covenant
and theocracy ; and the atoning sacrifice was intended to qualify
him for readmission, a thing which execution rendered *eo ipso* impossible. But the fact that the institution of sacrifice in the Old Testament contained no allusion to the life everlasting after death, may be
explained on the ground, that the standpoint of the Old Testament
did not furnish any clear or profound insight into the life eternal.

(3.) *Steudel's* third objection is this : "According to Lev. v. 11,
in cases of extreme poverty a bloodless sin-offering of meal might
be offered instead of the bleeding sacrifice. Hence the only correct
view of the sin-offering must be one, which regards it as of no
essential moment, whether the offering presented consisted of an
animal or of meal, and therefore does not recognise a *pœna vicaria.*"
But even *Bähr* (ii. 181) will not allow, that there is any force in
this argument. " *D. Strauss* is right," he says, " in pronouncing
this decision perfectly incorrect, and in saying, as he does in his
Streitschriften, p. 163, ' Whenever it was possible, whenever any one
was in a condition to bring a pair of doves, the sin-offering was to
be a bleeding one ; it was only in cases of extreme distress that
meal was allowed to be substituted ; but we have no right to allow
the nature of the substitute to exert any influence upon our interpretation of the thing itself, and to regard the characteristic which
was wanting in the former, as being necessarily absent from the
latter also.' " We cannot regard this argument, however, as *Bähr*
does, as sufficient in all respects to meet *Steudel's* objection, for the
substitute must be related in some way to the thing actually required, however inferior it may be in actual worth and importance.
Stones, for example, could never serve as a substitute for coffee,
though acorns might. And if, as a matter of course, even the
poorest of the people were to be furnished with the means of obtaining expiation ; in cases where it was absolutely impossible to

procure a sacrificial animal for the purpose, the substitute appointed would necessarily be, not an animal that *was not suitable for sacrifice*, but something which at all events *might be offered*. The symbolical manifestation of the *satisfactio vicaria* in the slaughtering of the animal would no doubt be wanting; but the *satisfactio* itself might be there, as the element of real satisfaction even in the animal sacrifice did not proceed from the slaughtering, but was communicated by the grace of God to the blood sprinkled upon the altar through a *donum superadditum*.

(4.) He argues, " On the great day of atonement (Lev. xvi.) the one goat upon which the sins of the people were actually laid, was sent away at perfect liberty into the desert, without any *poena vicaria*, whilst upon the other goat, which was sacrificed, the sins were not laid ; so that neither in the one instance nor in the other is substitution of any kind to be thought of." (For our answer to this, see § 199 sqq.)

§ 61. Whilst *Steudel's* objections, to which we have just referred, have not been repeated by any later writers, those of *Bähr*, in part at least, have met with great approval. They are the following :

(1.) " The juridical view, we are told, makes the act of slaying, by which the punishment was completed, the culminating point and centre of the whole of the sacred transaction. But this shows at once the fallacy of that view. For nothing is more obvious, than that the blood, and not the death, and the use made of the blood, the sprinkling therefore, and not the slaying, constituted the main feature and centre of the sacrifice. But the ritual law distinguishes the two, the slaying and the sprinkling, most sharply from one another, and states expressly that it was by the latter, and not by the former, that the expiation, the ultimate object of the sacrifice, was effected. In any case the sprinkling of the altar or Capporeth was not a penal act ; and it follows indisputably, therefore, that the notion of punishment can never have been the central point of the idea of sacrifice." Similar objections are made again and again by *Bähr*. For example, at p. 347 he says, " With this view, the sprinkling of blood—that main action, that culminating point of the whole of the sacrificial transaction—sinks into a mere accompaniment, a kind of supplement or appendix to the main action (the penal death) ; and it is impossible to see how, notwithstanding all that, it can have been, as the Scriptures so distinctly state, the *sine qua non* of the expiation." And again, at p. 280 : " He makes the death, and not the blood, the medium of expiation, contrary to the express declaration of Lev. xvii. 11. For, let any one only make the attempt to read at pleasure *death* for *blood*, *per synecdochen*, in this leading passage, and the words, otherwise so clear, become mere nonsense."—In *Oehler's* opinion, also, these objections are well founded. At p. 628 he says, "If the act of slaughtering were intended to represent the penal death deserved by the person offering the sacrifice; and if the shedding of blood, therefore, by the sacrificial knife were the true expiatory act; it ought to have been brought into greater prominence." And at p. 631: "It would be perfectly inexplicable, in that case, why the sacrificial ritual should represent the offering of the blood upon the altar, and not the slaughtering, as the real act of payment or of covering."

These objections have none of them any force at all, except on the assumption, that according to our view the slaughtering is regarded, or must be regarded, as the real act of expiation. But if it be shown that this is a misunderstanding, and if, moreover, it can be proved that the theory of a penal death can stand without any such assumption, and in fact, when rightly understood, actually excludes it, all these objections fall to the ground. Now I believe that I have already sufficiently, and for every unprejudiced reader, conclusively proved, that this is the case (compare more particularly § 55, 56, 57). After the explanations I have given there, I trust that it will be understood, that I also make, not the slaughtering, but the sprinkling of blood upon the altar, the main point, the kernel and centre of the sacrifice; and that I regard, not the death, but the blood which has passed through death, and is endowed for the first time with real atoning efficacy upon the altar, the true medium of expiation. To *Oehler's* remark, that according to my view the act of slaughtering ought to have been brought into greater prominence, I reply, (1) that I too regard the sprinkling of the blood as more important and more significant than the slaughtering, as is evident from what I have stated already; and (2) that the act of slaughtering in Lev. i., for example, where the burnt-offering is mentioned, is really brought into no less and no greater prominence than the sprinkling of the blood (vers. 5, 11, 15). This is also the case in chaps. iv. and v., where the sin-offering is referred to. For the slaughtering is never passed by unnoticed; and if it is simply mentioned without any further description of the manner in which it should take place, whilst the command to sprinkle the blood is followed by a minute description of the manner how, any one can see that such a description was quite as unnecessary in the case of the former, as it was indispensable in that of the latter. For the mode of slaughtering would be understood by everybody, and was just the same for one sacrifice as for another. There was no necessity, therefore, to describe it. And what would not be so naturally understood, namely, the catching of the blood by the priest, is distinctly and expressly enjoined. But the manner in which the blood was to be sprinkled was not so self-evident, and differed with different kinds of sacrifice. It was necessary, therefore, that this should be described with minuteness and precision. And if the person and place are described with the necessary fulness in connection with the sprinkling of the blood, a similar description is to be found with all necessary fulness in connection with the slaughtering also, since it is expressly observed, that it was to be effected by the person presenting the sacrifice before the altar, on its northern side (§ 53), and in the presence, as well as with the co-operation, of the priest who caught the blood.

But if *Bähr* means, that the sprinkling of the altar or of the Capporeth cannot possibly be regarded as a penal act, the "nonsense" must be put to his own account; for no one has ever asserted anything of the kind, and it does not follow either from my own exposition or from that of any one else. His *argumentum ad hominem* reads almost like a burlesque, when he advises that some one should just try for once to read at pleasure death for blood *per synecdochen* in Lev. xvii. 11. In my *Mos. Opfer* I have already replied to this, to the following effect: We cannot help imagining that the zeal of the esteemed author for his cause left him no time for reflection; otherwise we should set down as utterly unworthy, a line of argument, which might indeed dazzle and confuse a simple and unintelligent reader, but which has not the smallest shadow of force or of truth. To prove this, we need do nothing more than carry out the proposed *synecdoche*. Thus: Whosoever eateth the "death" shall be cut off, for the soul of the flesh is in the "death," and the "death" maketh an atonement for your souls: whosoever therefore eateth the "death" shall be cut off. No doubt this is mere nonsense; but we wash our hands in innocence, the "mere nonsense" belongs to the line of argument which led to it. The passage does not refer *ex professo* to sacrifice, but to eating; and for that very reason, not to eating death, but to eating blood. Sacrifice is only referred to for the purpose of explaining that the blood was not to be eaten because it was the medium of expiation. As a matter of course, therefore, the synecdoche could only be applied to those

words, which really relate to sacrifice : " I have appointed the blood
of the animal, as the seat of the animal soul, to be the medium of
expiation for your souls." If we make the proposed substitution
here, the words will read, " I have connected expiation with the
'death' of the sacrificial animal : the 'death' of the animal makes
expiation, covers your souls, viz., your sinful souls, and therefore
your death." This may possibly be an incorrect statement, but it
is by no means " mere nonsense."

§ 62. (2.) " It is thoroughly incompatible with the juridical view,
that the sacrificer himself, and not the priest as the representative
of God, should inflict the penal death. For if the sacrificing were
a penal act, God would certainly appear as the punisher, and the
sacrificer as the person to be punished." Even to later writers this
argument has appeared to be peculiarly forcible and conclusive.
We find it, for example, in *Hofmann* (p. 244) ; and *Oehler*
strengthens it by the emphatic inquiry : " Or does God really
appear as a judge, who commands the evil-doer to execute himself ? " It is quite out of place, however, to speak of self-execution,
since the animal to be slaughtered was not a symbolical *ipse ego* of
the person sacrificing, but a representative *alter ego*. But even if
we should regard it as a symbolical *ipse ego*, a symbolical " self-execution " would perhaps not be so absurd a thought after all ; for
when translated into its literal meaning, this symbol would express
the thought, as true as it is profound, that the sinner must punish
himself to escape the punishment of God. But this idea of the
sacrifice, as a symbolical *ipse ego*, is decidedly erroneous (§ 67, 69).
Kliefoth does me a great injustice when he says, that my " only "
reply to *Bähr's* objection, that God would necessarily have directed
the animal to be slain and the punishment to be inflicted by the
priest, is, that no doubt this might have been commanded, but God
ordered it otherwise. I have devoted almost two entire pages in
my *Mos. Opfer* to the proof, that the connection between punishment and suffering is a necessary one ; that punishment is the continuation of sin, its complement, which is no longer within the
sinner's caprice or power ; and that death is the finishing of sin,
comprehending all the punishment, according to the words of the
Apostle, " sin, when it is finished, bringeth forth death." Sin,
from its very nature, is a violation of the moral order of the world,
a pressure as it were against the law, which, because of the vitality
and elasticity of the law, produces a reaction, that falls upon the
sinner in the form of punishment. Sin, therefore, is a half, un-

finished thing, that demands completion; and that completion is to be found in death, which is not foreign to it therefore, or arbitrarily imposed from without. On the contrary, it is the sin itself that bringeth forth the death which existed in it potentially from the very first. From this point of view, therefore, we may say that God does not punish the sinner, but the sinner punishes himself; the recoil of the law, which reaches him as punishment, being evoked and determined by himself alone.

Kliefoth says nothing essentially different, at any rate, nothing better, when he supplies the supposed deficiency of my reply as follows: "That which slays the sacrifice is really the sin of the sinner which it has to carry." And I must pronounce it utterly erroneous, when he proceeds to observe that God Himself *cannot* possibly be represented as inflicting the punishment, since He puts no one to death, but lets the sin produce death by its own development; and as the sacrifice cannot put itself to death, since sacrifice is not suicide, there is actually *no one* left but the sacrificing sinner; and he therefore, as the cause of the death, *must* necessarily inflict it.—In opposition to this assertion, I still abide by my former argument (p. 76); viz., that inasmuch as this elasticity of the law, or of the moral order of the universe, is given to it by God, and is sustained by Him; or rather, inasmuch as God Himself *is* this moral order of the universe; He is also Himself the judge and punisher too. There is the same apparent discrepancy here which we find in the words of Christ, who says in John v. 22, that the Father hath given all judgment to the Son; and in John xii. 47 sqq., that the Father has not sent the Son into the world to judge the world; and that whoever does not believe is judged already, has judged himself. There is no intention to deny that God *can* be represented as the inflicter of punishment; but the same motive which led Christ, in John xii. 47 sqq., to transfer the act of judicial punishment from Himself to the sinner, may also have regulated the symbolism of worship. In the institution of sacrifice, for example, God appears as the merciful One, who desires not the death of the sinner, but his reconciliation and redemption (of course in a manner accordant with justice); whilst the sinner, on the other hand, appears as one who has brought death and condemnation upon himself through his sin, and is conscious of having done so. In this case it is peculiarly appropriate and significant, that he should accuse himself, pronounce sentence of death upon himself, and inflict it himself upon his symbolical substitute, which the plan devised by God has allowed him to choose.[1]

But those who accept the evangelical and prophetical teaching (Isa. liii.) respecting the sacrificial death of Christ, and admit the vicarious and penal character of His sufferings, and yet, for the reasons mentioned, deny all this in the case of the Old Testament sacrifices, should ask themselves the question, who it was that inflicted the death on Golgotha; whether it was God, or whether it was not rather the world whose punishment the Sacrifice had taken upon Himself?

§ 63. (3.) "The atonement," in *Bähr's* opinion, "can never have had God for its object, whilst in the juridical view the demands of divine justice are satisfied, and the wrath of God is appeased."—An argument without the slightest force, which rests entirely upon the inadmissible identification and interchange of reconciliation and atonement. (See § 28, particularly the note.)

(4.) " It is equally opposed to the thank-offerings, in which confessedly there is no idea of warding off a punishment, least of all the punishment of death, and in which God never appears as a judge to punish " (p. 281).—Again a perfectly futile argument, for the former cannot be admitted (§ 31, 41) ; nor can the latter be sustained.

(5.) " If the sacrificial death had been a penal death, every sin for which a sacrifice was offered would necessarily have been regarded as deserving of death ; and that no one can maintain. For sin-offerings were offered for sins of ignorance, and for not even purely moral, but theocratic offences " (p. 281).—The latter is palpably a mistake (§ 92) ; and the former may be met by the remarks in § 48 (cf. also § 56, 59), in connection with which we may refer *instar omnium* to Deut. xxvii. 26, " Cursed be he that confirmeth not *all* the words of this law to do them."

(6.) " The juridical view confounds symbolical substitution with real, religious with judicial. The sacrificial animal, in its estimation, was not a mere symbol, but a substitute for the person offering it ; so that the penal act itself was of necessity not a figurative, but a

---

[1] Cf. *Kahnis*, luth. Dogmatik i. 270 : " As every sacrifice was representative, the person offering it expressed, in the slaughtering of the animal, the sentence which he had previously pronounced upon himself, before venturing to hope for communion with God. After the man had thus practically declared, by the slaughtering of the animal, ' I am a sinner deserving of death in the sight of God,' the priest sprinkled," etc.

real one.   But in this way the sacrifice loses entirely its symbolico-religious character, and becomes a purely outward, formal, mechanical act."—That the former was not the case, has already been shown in § 56, 57; but even if it really were so, the latter would be a very superficial or a very inconsiderate expression.   Or does Bähr really mean that punishment inflicted before a worldly tribunal is a merely outward, formal, mechanical act, without any inward, essential, and moral signification ?

(7.) Lastly, we read at p. 347 : " The typology based upon the juridical view regards the sprinkling of the blood, as a type of the *imputatio justitiæ Christi et applicatio meritorum ejus*.   But how could this be effected by the sprinkling, not of the person offering the sacrifice, but of sacred places ?"   We find the same argument in *Oehler*, *Hofmann*, and *Keil*.   But it is a sufficient answer, to show that the application of blood to the altar was necessary, chiefly and primarily necessary (this has already been done at § 56, 57), and that it involved *eo ipso* an (ideal) application to the person of the sacrificer.   But the latter is unquestionably taught in Lev. xvii. 11, where it is distinctly affirmed, " I have given you the blood upon the altar, to make an atonement for your souls."   The souls of the persons sacrificing, therefore, were ideally upon the altar, and were there covered by the sacrificial blood ; a view which rests upon Ex. xx. 24 : cf. § 13.

§ 64.   We now turn to the forces with which *Neumann*, *Keil*, and *Oehler* have come to the help of *Bähr's* phalanx of objections.   Let us look first of all at *Neumann*.   " It would be foolish," he says, " if a sacrifice seeks and is the medium of forgiveness, to try to convince us that the forgiveness is secured through punishment, and that a punishment endured, not by the person seeking forgiveness, but by a creature having no share whatever in the guilt to be endured."   But who wants to convince Dr *Neumann*, that forgiveness was secured through punishment ?   So far as I know, all the supporters of the *satisfactio vicaria* have hitherto taught that forgiveness comes through mercy, but mercy is made conditional upon, and rendered possible by, the fact that the punishment of the guilty is sustained and endured by one who is innocent.   The idea that participation in the guilt to be punished was the necessary condition of a vicarious endurance of punishment, is absurd ; for the very opposite was the case ; and the prerequisite of substitution was, that there should *not* be participation in the guilt to be punished, since otherwise the substitute would have to undergo punishment, not *as* a substitute, but on its own account.   At the same time, substitution required an essential, internal *rapport*, a transfer of the obligation from the one to the other ; and this took place (at least symbolically) through the imposition of hands.   But we have already seen (§ 50) that the idea of vicarious suffering is a familiar one in the Old Testament, even apart from the sacrificial worship.   Moreover, if there were any force in this argument, the charge of absurdity would be just as applicable to the doctrine of satisfaction in the New Testament as in the Old, and yet the author has apparently no wish to abandon the former.[1]

§ 65. We will now examine the fresh arguments adduced by *Keil*.   (1.) At p. 207 he says, " Although the death of the sacrificer, typified by the slaughtering of the victim, was the fruit and effect of sin, it did not come under the notion of punishment; for sacrifice was an institution of divine mercy, which was intended to secure for the sinner, not the merited punishment, but forgiveness instead." —We have already seen, at § 53, how untenable and contradictory the results of *Keil's* own theory of the slaughtering of the sacrifice have been, and necessarily must be, in consequence of his rejection of the idea of punishment in death.   All that we have here to do with is the assertion, that sacrifice, as an institution of mercy, was intended to secure for the sinner, not punishment, but forgiveness instead.   But how inconsiderate this reply really is !   For that very reason, that the institution of sacrifice as a provision of mercy was intended to secure for the sinner, not punishment, but grace, and for the purpose of rendering this possible, it transferred the obligation to endure the punishment from the person sacrificing to the animal slain.   The same incautiousness meets us again at p. 211, note 3. " For when *Kurtz*," he says, " adds at last, that in the institution of sacrifice God appears as the merciful one, the exaltation of the

_____
[1] With reference to the prophetic intuition of the self-sacrifice of the Servant of Jehovah (Isa. liii.), *Neumann* himself proposes this question : " Can we have any doubt that the prophet regarded this sacrifice of the Servant of God as the punishment of our sins ?" and then replies, " Certainly we have considerable doubt, for, etc." I also not only doubt, but most decidedly deny that folly, to which *Neumann* seeks to forge the signature of the Church.   No one on our side has ever taught that our sins were *punished* in the sacrifice of Christ; but, on the contrary, it is always maintained that our sins, or rather we the sinners, *receive mercy* in that sacrifice.   And when *Neumann* afterwards states the following as the true meaning of Isa. liii. : " He endured the punishment which ought to have fallen upon humanity in the judgment of the Just One,"—I subscribe this meaning, and cannot see in what it differs from the orthodox theory of sacrifice.

divine mercy does not tally at all with the assumption, that the death
of the sacrifice represents the punishment of the sinner with death ;
for the mercy of God does not punish sin, but forgives it."—Most
decidedly, it is not the mercy of God which punishes, but His justice.
But why should it not be possible, and even *necessary*, for the justice
of God to find expression in the institution of sacrifice by the side
of His mercy; if, as *Keil* himself maintains (p. 228), mercy cannot,
and will not, forgive sins, without anything further, that is to say,
without justice being previously satisfied?

But when *Keil* still further maintains, at p. 207, that universally death, which entered through sin, is and remains a punishment *only* for that sinner for whom there is no redemption, this
no more needs any thorough refutation than the strange statement,
that " death delivers man from sin, and introduces him into eternal
life ; " for in the latter he ascribes to death what can only be
affirmed of Christ, the Redeemer from sin and death ; and with
regard to the former, we need only appeal to the terrors and bitterness of death, even to the pious Christian, as attested both by the
Scriptures and experience, to show that even to him death is still
the wages of sin, *i.e.*, punishment.   Moreover, here again *Keil* confounds, what ought to be carefully distinguished and kept apart
when the sacrificial worship is concerned, the death which comes
upon all men, both good and bad alike, on account of Adam's sin,
i.e., on account of the universal sinfulness of the human race (Gen.
iii. 19), and the death deserved afresh for every special sin (cf. § 48).
Keil is speaking of the former, whereas the institution of sacrifice
has simply to do with the *latter*.   Consequently his argument, even
if it were in itself as correct as it is weak and untenable, would necessarily fall wide of the mark.   And when *Keil* still further observes
(p. 207), that a death which delivers man from sin, and introduces
him into eternal life, cannot be called a punishment, " because the
idea of divine holiness and justice is by no means exhausted by the
notion of punishment,"—I must certainly leave this unanswered, because I do not understand it.   For though I might venture perhaps
to interpret the sentence *by itself*, I must confess that I cannot comprehend what it has to do with the context.

But (3) *Keil* seems to promise himself the most effect from his
reply on p. 213.   " Death," he says, " even regarded as the wages
or punishment of sin, is no extermination of sin, from which a
restitutio in integrum follows, since even after this punishment the
sin remains.   The injury that it has done to man, the desolation

brought by it into body and soul, is not removed, and the sinner sinks into eternal death, unless the mercy of God forgives the sin and quickens new life. So the fact that the authorities punish a thief or a murderer with death, does not restore what was stolen to its owner, or give back life to the dead. Death, therefore, regarded as punishment, cannot be described as the expiation of sin, since the punishment of sin neither cancels nor forgives. So also it furnishes no satisfaction for sin, but only for divine justice and objective right."—This is certainly *luce clarius!* And yet, strange to say, even *Oehler,* who is quite as decided an opponent of the theory of penal death as *Keil,* and a much more consistent one, thinks that " what *Keil* has said in opposition to the idea of the extermination of guilt by death, and a consequent *restitutio in integrum,* can hardly be regarded as decisive." Certainly I have sagacity enough to know that the execution of a murderer does not bring the murdered man to life again. But the fact is simply this, that Keil has not understood me. When I spoke of a *restitutio in integrum,* I did not mean the undoing of the deed by which the moral order of the universe had been disturbed, but the restoration of the disturbed order itself. And that I still maintain.

(4.) To this is added, what is really a surprising statement from such a quarter, that " the law, and in fact the whole of the Scriptures, contain neither a direct nor an indirect assertion to the effect that *the sin-offering possessed the character of a satisfaction.*" For how does this tally with the author's admissions on the very same page, that " the sinner deserved to die, and the victim which took his place had to suffer in his stead;" and that " the animal of the sin-offering suffered death in the place of the person sacrificing, as the wages of sin " ? If the victim *must* suffer death for the sinner, and in his stead, as the wages or punishment of his sin, and the design of the sin-offering—viz., the expiation or forgiveness of the sins of the person sacrificing—could not be secured without such a vicarious death, can it well be denied that such a death possessed the character of a satisfaction ? Moreover, at p. 237, the author expressly admits, at least in the case of the *trespass*-offering, what he here as expressly denies in the case of the *sin*-offering. " The trespass-offering," he says, " having been slaughtered, and having suffered death in the place of the person sacrificing, as the punishment for his guilt, and *satisfaction having thus been rendered* to justice," etc. And again, a few lines further on, he maintains that by the trespass-offering " *satisfaction* was rendered to divine justice," and that "the trespass-offering was a *work of satisfaction*, in consequence of which full pardon was granted to the guilty person on the part of God." It is true that at p. 228 he is speaking of the *sin*-offering alone, and at p. 237 of the *trespass*-offering only, the fundamental idea of which, according to *Keil's* theory (p. 223), is that of sufficiency or satisfaction, in marked distinction from the sin-offering. We shall show as we proceed that this theory is inadmissible (§ 95). But even if it were as well-founded as it is untenable, the self-contradiction we complain of would not be removed. For at pp. 223, 226, where he lays down the idea of satisfaction as the common fundamental notion of all the *trespass*-offerings, he understands by the word "satisfaction" something altogether different from what he does at p. 228, where he denies that the *sin*-offering had any satisfactory worth, and at p. 237, where he attributes such worth to the *trespass*-offering. In the former passage (pp. 223, 226) he defines the fundamental notion of the trespass-offering, as that of satisfaction for the violation of the rights of *others*, or of compensation (remuneration) for the purpose of recovering lost theocratic rights; so that it had regard to a satisfaction which the person sacrificing had to render to another, *along with* the sacrificial expiation; whereas in the latter (pp. 228, 237) he speaks of a satisfaction to be rendered to *divine* justice as such, and rendered, not by the offerer himself, but by the victim offered by him, "through its endurance of death in his stead, as the punishment for his sin or trespass." But here, according to *Keil's* own doctrine, sin- and trespass-offerings are not opposed to one another, but perfectly parallel and harmonious. If (according to p. 237) divine justice was satisfied through the vicarious endurance of death on the part of the *trespass*-offering, as a punishment for the guilt of the person sacrificing, that death, which the *sin*-offering endured vicariously for the person sacrificing and in his stead, must also be regarded as rendering satisfaction to the justice of God; and that all the more, because, according to *Keil's* own doctrine, the sin and guilt of the person sacrificing were imputed to the sin-offering as well as to the trespass-offering, through the laying on of hands (§ 38). There prevail throughout *Keil's* work, as we shall again have occasion to notice (§ 95), great obscurity and confusion with regard to the notion of satisfaction; and this is the cause of the present and other mistakes.

When *Keil* boldly appeals to the whole law, in fact to the whole Scripture, as bearing witness against the satisfactory import of the sin-offering, we cannot help asking whether he also intends to deny that there was any satisfactory import in the self-sacrifice of Christ? And yet, after what has been stated before, we must assume that he either denies all satisfactory import to the sacrifice of Christ, in opposition to both the Bible and the Church, or that he denies to that sacrifice the validity of a *sin*-offering, just as firmly as he attributes to it the exclusive validity of a *trespass*-offering. But we are forbidden to assume the former by the author's position in relation to both the Bible and the Church, and the latter by his definition of the sin-offering. For no one—certainly not *Keil* himself—would think of maintaining that the import and validity of the self-sacrifice of Christ are exhausted by the notion of " satisfaction for the violation of the rights of others, or a compensation (remuneration) for the recovery of lost theocratic rights." And what was the expiatory sacrifice of the great day of atonement, which undoubtedly shadowed forth the atoning sacrifice of Christ in a fuller, clearer, and more comprehensive manner than any of the Old Testament sacrifices? Was it a *trespass*-offering or a *sin*-offering (§ 202)?

§ 66. The first of Keil's arguments mentioned above is repeated with still greater emphasis by *Delitzsch*, p. 742, and with the greatest of all by *Oehler*, p. 631. The former says, "The animal sacrifice did not set forth in figure the events on Calvary, for this simple reason, that the institution of sacrifice was an institution of grace, in which, instead of justice punishing, grace forgave." But could grace do under the Old Testament what it cannot under the New, namely, forgive without the satisfaction of justice? And was not that institution, of which the proceedings upon Calvary were the kernel and centre, also an institution of grace? And if in the latter there was, for all that, an actual exhibition of penal suffering, why should there not be a symbolical (or typical) exhibition of it in the sacrificial ceremonies of the Old Testament? The institution of sacrifice in the Old Testament became an institution of grace, through the simple fact that the condition of pardon was the vicarious, penal death of the sacrifice.

In *Oehler* the argument runs thus: " In the Old Testament ceremonial God did not sanctify Himself by acts of penal justice : neither the house, in which His name dwelt, nor the altar, at which He met with the congregation, was a place of judgment. Whoever had sinned wantonly against the covenant-God and His ordinances, fell without mercy under the penal justice of God : for him there was therefore no more sacrifice, and for him the ritual of sacrifice was not designed. That ritual was a provision of divine *grace* for the congregation, which had indeed sinned in weakness, but was seeking the face of God."—The assertion, however, that the theory of a penal death makes the altar, or the house in which the name of God dwelt, a place of judgment, is one which could be made with justice, provided the act of slaying had really taken place *upon* the altar, or *in* the tabernacle. But it did not; and, as we shall presently see, *Oehler* is disposed to adduce this fact as an additional argument against the theory in question. But does not one argument cancel the other? The fact that the completion of the symbolical *pœna vicaria* took place *beside* the altar and not *upon* it, *before the door* of the tabernacle and not *within* it, *previous to* the act which expressed forgiveness and not *after* it, set forth the idea that mercy could only have free course after and in consequence of the satisfaction of justice. And why should not God be able to sanctify Himself in the sacrificial ritual also by "acts of penal justice," if such acts really are the preliminaries of mercy, if they promise it and render it possible, and if they are the necessary condition and basis of its manifestations? But what *Oehler* still further adds with regard to wanton sins against the ordinances of God, and sins committed in weakness, even if it had any force, would only affect the views we hold, provided it proved that sins of weakness, which admitted of sacrificial expiation as such, were *not* followed by judicial punishment at the hands of God, even when they remained intentionally unatoned for, in conscious contempt of the means of salvation that had been provided. Now it is evident that this was not the case, for the sinner offered sacrifice for the purpose of escaping the penal justice of God.

Oehler is quite wrong again, in my opinion, when he observes, at p. 629, "And if the slaying had been the real act of expiation, it would have taken place upon the altar itself, and not merely by the side." I have already abundantly and superabundantly shown, that according to our view the slaying was by no means the real act of expiation. But even if this had been the case, and if it would have been more in harmony with the idea for it to have taken place *upon* the altar than *by the side* of it, the actual impracticability would have been sufficient to prevent it. In conclusion, we may be allowed to take this opportunity of reminding our esteemed opponents of what we have written already at § 52.

§ 67. "The question as to the central idea of sacrifice," as

Delitzsch has very properly said, "may all be summed up in this: Why, and in what sense, was blood, *i.e.*, the life, when made to stream out by violence, the Old Testament medium of expiation?" We have already answered this question (§ 55 sqq.), and fortified it against all the objections and attacks with which we are acquainted. All that now remains for us to do, is to explain and examine the positive theories of our opponents.

Bähr's views are thus expressed at p. 210: "The *symbolical* character of the sacrifice consisted in the fact, that the offering of the *nephesh* in the sacrificial blood upon the altar, was a symbol of the self-sacrifice of the person sacrificing, and of his drawing near to Jehovah. As the offering of the animal blood was a surrender and giving up of the animal life to death, so the psychical, *i.e.*, personal, life of the individual sacrificing, which was opposed to God, was to be surrendered and given up, *i.e.*, to die; but as this is a surrender to Jehovah, it is no actual cessation of existence, but a dying, which becomes *eo ipso* a living. . . . The psychical ἀποθανεῖν is the condition of true life. The meaning of sacrifice, therefore, was briefly this: the psychical, sinful existence (life) was given up to God in death, for the purpose of obtaining true being (sanctification) by union with God." But to this more negative and subjective side there is added a positive and objective one (p. 211), viz., the reception and acceptance on the part of Jehovah, and the impartation of sanctification, the condition of true life, to the person thus surrendering himself. This latter element rendered the sacrifice a *sacramental* act, by which the blood appeared as the medium appointed by God, for covering sin or the soul, for bringing into union with God, and so producing sanctification. In the words of the law peculiar prominence is given to this sacramental character, especially in Lev. xvii. 11. The question, "how this sacramental character could be given to the blood," is answered by *Bähr* at p. 212, where he shows, (1) that the blood of the sacrifice, as the means of expiation and sanctification, was "something apart from the person for whom atonement had to be made, something different from himself, and in fact something appointed and chosen by God; (2) that it was nevertheless not something absolutely different, foreign, and opposed, but something related to him, analogous in its nature, homogeneous." If we add to all this the discussion as to the sprinkling of the blood, in p. 346 ("If, then, the blood represented the *nephesh* of the person presenting the sacrifice, the sprinkling of the blood upon one of the holy places (in this term *Bähr* includes all the vessels of the sanctuary) could have no other object, than the bringing of the *nephesh* to the place in which the holiness of God was manifested, that it might attest itself, and work efficaciously as such, *i.e.*, might sanctify him, and so destroy, cover over, what was sinful in him, make atonement for him "), we have the quintessence of *Bähr's* theory of sacrifice.

The simple fact that this theory has *never* met with approval, nor been adopted by any of the later commentators, may be regarded as a sufficient proof how little truth there can be in it, and may release me from the necessity of entering into so thorough a refutation here, as I have on a former occasion. Passing over, therefore, many other obscurities and self-contradictions, I shall simply point out in a summary manner how untenable its main propositions are. In the *first place*, then, it makes the soul of the sacrifice a figurative *ipse ego* of the person sacrificing, instead of a representative *alter ego*; whereas it is expressly stated in Lev. xvii. 11, that the animal soul, which was in the blood, covered the soul of the sinner upon the altar, and therefore in this, the culminating point of the sacrificial ceremony, even in its symbolical character, was regarded as another, and as entirely distinct from the soul of the person sacrificing. *Secondly*,—and this is connected with the former,—it makes the animal sacrifice, as *Delitzsch* expresses it, nothing more than the attendant shadow of the personal act of the man himself. *Thirdly*, as *Delitzsch* has also justly observed, " to die to oneself," or " to give oneself up to God through death," is an idea completely foreign to the whole of the Old Testament. *Fourthly*, the sacramental significance which it attributes to the sacrificial blood is not only entirely baseless, but is at open variance with the symbolical meaning which it is supposed to possess. *Fifthly*, and lastly, we may be allowed to point out, how *Bähr*, whenever he is speaking against the " juridical " view, cannot affirm with sufficient emphasis, that, in direct opposition to all the data of the law of sacrifice, it makes the act of slaying the real act of expiation, the kernel and centre, the climax and main point in the whole ceremony, and reduces the sprinkling of blood to a mere appendix and supplement; and yet, with his theory of the psychical or personal ἀποθανεῖν, he has plunged over head and ears into the very same, or even greater condemnation. Let any one read the whole of *Bähr's* exposition of the notion of sacrifice, and just observe how the word " death " and its various synonymes are crowded together: he is continually speaking of the surrender and giving up of life to death, of dying, of the cessation of life, of an ἀποθανεῖν, as the strictest and most essential idea of sacrifice. Now is not this making death the culminating point of sacrifice? The πρῶτον ψεῦδος of *Bähr's* theory is the thoroughly false position which he assigns to sanctification in relation to justification; and this *Kliefoth* also has observed. "The fundamental error in this view," he says, "is that it makes expiation and forgiveness the effect and consequence of sanctification, whereas the very opposite is the truth."

§ 68. We will now turn to *Hofmann*. At pp. 248-9 he writes as follows: " It was not the animal sacrificed, or the blood brought to the altar, which came between the sinful man and the holy God; but through the act of sacrifice the man produced the effect of a כֹּפֶר upon God (cf. § 28); with it he *interposed for himself*, the sinner, and *redeemed himself from guiltiness*." And again: " That authority over a living creature, which had its origin in the first forgiveness of sins on the part of God, was employed by man, who sacrificed in this way as an expiation, for the purpose of offering to God such sacrifice as was most closely related to him, the living one, and which he could not offer in any other way than by inflicting upon it the suffering, so painful for himself, of putting it to death. By this act, expressive both of faith in the revealed willingness of God to forgive sin, and of a consciousness of guilt, the man interposed for himself, the sinner, that he might be delivered from *his* guilt in consequence. As he could not come to God himself in such a way as that the death, through which he came to Him, should be the termination of that attitude towards God which sin had produced, and the commencement of a new one, he offered what was foreign to himself, and yet was really his own, and what participated in his attitude towards God only through its appointment as a sacrifice, so that with the death, through which it came to God, its relation to the sin of the sacrificer, that had cost it its life, was over, and he prayed to God that He would now bring his relation to Him to an end, whether that relation depended upon his sins in general, or upon some one particular sin."

The manner in which *Hofmann* explains the necessity for bringing the blood to the *altar* is also very peculiar. In the first edition (p. 152) he says, " The meaning of the sprinkling was this: the slaying of a living being, which took place as an atonement for the person presenting the sacrifice, was appropriated to the Holy Place in the blood, which had been its life. *It* was sprinkled, and not the person sacrificing, because it was he who made the payment,

and God to whom it was made.   The sin of the person sacrificing
made the Holy Place unclean, inasmuch as it was the place of his
connection with God.   Hence, what he had done for the restoration
of his fellowship with God was attributed to it, and the uncleanness
with which his sin had defiled it was thereby taken away.   The
very same thing, which was done on the yearly day of atonement
to every part of the sanctuary, including even the Most Holy Place
(Lev. xvi. 16 sqq.), was done to the altar of burnt-offering in connection with every sacrifice."—In the second edition I miss this
passage, which is remarkable for its clearness.   But the idea that
he has renounced the view expressed in it, is precluded by p. 258,
where he says, in perfect harmony with p. 164 of Ed. 1: " Now if
the procedure with the blood was the most distinctive peculiarity of
the sin-offering, the essential purpose must have been, to bring to
God what had been the life of the sacrificial animal, as a payment
rendered by its being shed, and by means of that payment to deliver
the abode and vicinity of God from the defilement which sin had
brought upon it."   For the correctness of this view, he appeals to
Lev. viii. 15, and xvi. 15.   Consequently, it appears as though
Hofmann only retained this view in connection with the sin-offering,
and had discovered that it was inadmissible in relation to the burnt-
offering and the thank-offering.

In all the rest, too, *Hofmann's* theory appears to be essentially
the same as before.   The sacrifice is still, in his estimation, an act
performed for God, or a payment made to God, with which the
sinner interposes for himself, and frees himself from the obligations
by which he is bound.   The idea of a *mulcta* is not yet fully laid
aside, and he still retains the indefensible allusion to Gen. iii. 21,
and the opinion, so irreconcilable with Lev. xvii. 11, that it was
not the soul of the sacrificial animal that was offered, but what *had
been* the soul or life of the animal, that in which the animal *had had*
its life.   Now, in the first place, so far as regards his fundamental
view of the sacrifice, as an act performed, or a payment made to
effect deliverance from liabilities which sin had imposed; this falls
along with the equally untenable interpretation of the כִּפֶּר (cf. § 28).
His reference to Gen. iii. 21, according to which the " first forgiveness of sins" was introduced by God's slaying animals and using
their skins " to clothe the nakedness of the first sinner, which had
been changed into a shameful nakedness in consequence of sin," for
the purpose of teaching him, that in future he and his descendants
could, and *might* deliver themselves from the liabilities produced by

sin through the slaying of animals, has not the slightest warrant, either in Gen. iii. 21, or in the whole of the sacrificial Thorah. For in Gen. iii. 21 there is nothing of the kind to be found, any more than in the Thorah itself, in which there is never the slightest allusion to any connection with the fact recorded in Gen. iii. 21 ; and the existence of any such connection is precluded by the fact, that the skins of the animals were not given back to the person sacrificing to be used as clothing, but in the case of the burnt-offering were assigned to the priest, the representative and servant of God (Lev. vii. 8), and in that of the sin-offering, when the priest himself was the person presenting it, were ordered to be burned along with the flesh outside the camp (cf. § 112).

Lastly, the interest which *Hofmann* has in still maintaining that the blood brought to the altar was not the soul of the sacrifice itself, but what *had been* its soul, may be very easily understood. At the same time, it is evident that he does so in the interest of his own singular theory of sacrifice, and not in that of any biblical *datum;* least of all, in that of the statement made in Lev. xvii. 11, which is in the most open and direct contradiction to what *Hofmann* maintains. For if, as is there stated, the blood was given upon the altar to make atonement for the soul of the offerer, and the atoning efficacy is attributed to the fact that the blood made atonement *through* the soul (or in *Hofmann's* words, *as* the soul, § 29), it follows as a matter of course, that what is intended is not the blood without the soul, but the blood as animated by the soul.

For this simple reason I cannot comply with *Ebrard's* expectation (p. 48), that I should willingly adopt the incidental (?) correction, that it was not the soul of the animal itself, but the slain and extinct life of the animal, in other words, the proof that the vicarious death had taken place, which was brought to the altar before the eye of God. For, according to Lev. xvii. 11, the blood of the sacrifice atoned, and could atone, only because, and so far as the soul which had endured the *pœna vicaria* was in it still; or, as *Neumann* expresses it (p. 352), " so long as the breath from above still moved within it," viz., the " breath of life" which made the animal also a " living soul" (§ 32). And in what sense the blood which had just flowed from the animal might be regarded as still being, as it were, the bearer and possessor of the soul, that is to say, as living blood, may be explained from the analogous phrases " living water" and " living flesh" (in distinction from cooked meat, 1 Sam. ii. 15). As *Oehler* observes (p. 630) : " Can it be surprising, then, that the fresh, steaming, and still fluid blood should be regarded as a blood with life and soul in it still?"

Lastly, with regard to *Hofmann's* view, that the sprinkling of the altar with the blood of the sacrifice served to deliver the former from the defilement, which the sin of the person sacrificing had brought upon it : this is erroneous only on the supposition that the intention of the sprinkling is limited to that; in which case it is decidedly erroneous. In Lev. xvii. 11 we do not read, " I have given you the blood upon the altar, to make atonement for the altar," but " to make atonement for your souls." But if the sin of the soul is expiated upon the altar, the sin is regarded as existing upon the altar and defiling it. But the sprinkling of blood, *i.e.*, the expiation, had reference primarily to the sin ; let this be conquered and exterminated, and then *eo ipso* the altar is delivered from its defilement. *Keil* and *Delitzsch* therefore are wrong in condemning *Hofmann's* view without reserve, that is to say, in opposing both what is false and what is true. That the blood of the sacrifice, when brought to the altar, purified the altar as well as the person sacrificing, is distinctly stated in Lev. viii. 15. Compare § 201.

§ 69. The principal points of *Keil's* theory of expiation are the following: " The bleeding sacrifice was also a sacrificial gift, and acquired its vicarious signification from the simple fact, that the faithful covenant-God appointed it, in His condescending mercy, as the vehicle of His grace (i. 205). By the laying on of hands there were transferred to the animal, as the representative of the person sacrificing, in the case of the sin- and trespass-offerings, the sin and guilt of the person sacrificing; in that of the burnt-offerings, his desire for sanctification; and in that of the peace-offerings, his gratitude for favours prayed for or received (p. 206). The slaying represented the surrendering to death of the life of the person sacrificing, but *by no means* to death as the punishment of his sin (p. 207) ; though, according to pp. 228, 237, 283, 384, it did set forth death as punishment for sins (§ 53). This death (which preceded expiation) still further represented death as the medium of transition from a state of alienation and separation from God into a state of grace and vital fellowship with Him, or as the door of entrance into the divine life out of the ungodly life of this world ;— as a death which redeemed from sin and introduced into the blessedness of eternal life, into which, therefore, in the case of the sin- and trespass-offerings at least, the soul which was laden with sin and guilt, or rather had become sin or guilt through the imposition of hands (p. 227), had already entered, even before the expiation or forgiveness of sins. The sprinkling of blood upon the altar, which then took place, denoted the reception of the person sacrificing into the divine fellowship; and this was "symbolically effected through the sacrifice, in such a manner, that by virtue of the substitutionary character of the sacrificial animal, the soul of the person sacrificing, which was offered up in the blood sprinkled upon the altar, was brought to the place of the Lord's gracious presence,—i.e., brought within the operations of divine grace, which (out of pure compassion, p. 228) covered or expiated, i.e., forgave sin."

As the refutation of this theory, in our account of which we have employed throughout the author's own words, is to be found in § 39, 40, and 65, so far as relates to the imposition of hands and slaying of the animal, we shall confine ourselves here to the meaning assigned to the sprinkling of the blood. The first thing which strikes us is that with *Keil*, just as with *Bähr*, the (symbolical) *substitution* which was maintained at first, and afterwards referred to again and again, is suddenly changed into a mere *similitude* of the person sacrificing, and the dissimilar *alter ego* becomes a similar *ipse ego*. But I cannot regard this alteration as an improvement, for it is obviously at variance with Lev. xvii. 11. It is distinctly taught there, that the soul of the sacrifice comes to the altar, as a most holy *means of atonement for* the soul of the sacrificer; whereas *Keil* maintains that it came as a *similitude* of the soul of the sacrificer, and therefore as being itself unholy and in need of expiation. Again, according to Lev. xvii. 11, the soul of the sinner was covered upon the altar by the *soul of the animal* which was in the sacrificial blood; whereas, according to *Keil*, "the *soul of the sacrificer*, which was offered up in the blood sprinkled upon the altar, was brought within the operations of divine grace, which covered sin;" so that, according to *Keil*, the soul of the sacrifice was that which had to be covered up, whereas, according to Lev. xvii. 11, it was that which effected the covering.

But, *secondly*, this sudden change of the dissimilar *alter ego* into a similar *ipse ego* is at variance (at least latently) in two respects with Lev. xxii. 20–24. For example, if, as *Keil* teaches, the sacrificial animal was intended to be not a dissimilar *alter ego*, but a similar *ipse ego*, it would be impossible to conceive, why the law should have demanded with such emphasis and stringency perfect spotlessness and faultlessness, as the *conditio sine qua non* of sacrificial fitness. If the person sacrificing came (as no one has denied that

he did, at least in the case of the sin- and trespass-offerings) as one
laden with sin and guilt, as blemished and unclean, as needing atonement and sanctification ; then, on the supposition that all that was
intended was, that there should be a symbolical representation of the
moral condition in this *ipse ego*, the law would never have demanded
such features in the animal sacrificed, as were expressive of a condition the very opposite to the existing moral condition of the person
presenting the sacrifice.   On the contrary, his sinfulness, his unholiness, and his need of expiation and sanctification, would have
been symbolized in the sacrificial animal by such a condition as could
truly be regarded as his likeness ; and the removal or negation of
that condition would have needed to be superinduced by the ritual
of sacrifice.   But in the actual law of sacrifice we find precisely the
opposite ; for all the regulations with regard to the nature of the
sacrifice were designed to exhibit it as innocent, holy, pure, faultless,
spotless, healthy and strong, and by that very sacrificial ritual (according to *Keil's* explanation) sin and guilt, uncleanness and unholiness, were imputed to it.

Thirdly, this view of the matter is altogether opposed to and
perfectly irreconcilable with *Keil's* own explanation of the previous
slaying of the sacrifice (§ 53) : The soul that had already been introduced through death, with all its sins unatoned for, into the
fellowship of the divine life, into the blessedness of life eternal, had
now to be torn away again from this *eternal* blessed life, and be *ex
post* atoned for again by being placed within the operations of divine
grace in the *earthly* kingdom of God (for that was the signification
of the altar, according to *Keil's* own correct interpretation : cf. i. 103,
104).

Fourthly, whilst *Keil* has correctly affirmed, on p. 228, that
" the sinner deserved death for his sin, and the victim which interposed for him had to suffer that death in his stead, because the
compassion of God neither could nor would either abolish or weaken
the holiness of the law,"—a few lines further down, this truth is denied again ; for there we are told, that " the soul of the man confessing his sin, which was represented by the blood of the victim,
could only be brought into the fellowship of divine grace, or into
the sphere of its operations, by means of the sprinkling of blood ;
and out of pure compassion that grace then covered up and exterminated sin." What becomes, then, of the firm demands of the
holiness of the law, which compassion neither could nor would either
abolish or weaken ?

Lastly, Keil's view of the sprinkling of the blood is proved to be perfectly untenable by the fact, that through the sprinkling of blood not only the sinful nation, or one particular individual belonging to it, but the defiled sanctuary and its furniture, could be and were commanded to be cleansed (§ 189). Now if, according to *Keil's* theory, the atonement for a sinful man was effected by the soul of the animal being brought, as a substitutionary representative of the soul of the man for whom atonement was to be made, to the place of the gracious presence of God—*i.e.*, within the sphere of the operations of divine grace,—then, in the same manner, when the polluted *altar* was to be expiated or purified, the blood of the sacrifice would necessarily be regarded as its substitutionary representative, placed within the sphere of the operations of divine grace (*i.e.*, upon the *altar*); which would be simply absurd.

§ 70. The views entertained by *Delitzsch* of the sacrificial expiation of the Old Testament may be gathered from the following passages of his Commentary on the Epistle to the Hebrews (p. 740): " That by which sin and uncleanness, or the person to whom it attached, was to be covered, could not be merely a symbol of the man himself; it must take his place not merely in a symbolical manner (as a substitute), but actually (as a representative in a legal sense)." And again at p. 742 : " *Satisfactio vicaria,* or, as it may also be called, *pœna vicaria,* is by no means strange, therefore, to the law (cf. Ex. xxxii. 30); though we are not to regard the slaying of the animal as an actual infliction of punishment. The animal sacrifice did not represent the proceedings upon Calvary, for this simple reason, that the institution of sacrifice was an institution of mercy, in which, instead of justice punishing, mercy forgave. As the event on Calvary is presupposed by the sacrament of the New Testament, though it is not repeated in that sacrament; so did that event form the mysterious background from which the divine appointment of animal sacrifice proceeded, though without there being any intention that the ritual should really depict it." Again at p. 426 : " Placed in the light of the New Testament counterpart, the surrender of the life of the sacrificial animal acquires a signification above the sacrificial ritual of the law. For in the latter the *Shechitah* was simply the means adopted for the double purpose, of obtaining the blood as the atonement of the soul of the sacrificer, and its flesh as fire-food for Jehovah. The offering up of the sacrificial animal was an involuntary submission to constraint on its part; and by the previous *Semichah,* or laying on of hands, an intentional signification was merely impressed upon it from without. But the death of Christ performed that, of which the sacrificial animal had without knowledge and will to serve as the means, in free, conscious self-determination; and unravelled the נְתַתִּיו ('I have given it', Lev. xvii. 11), in which the faith of the Old Testament had to rest." P. 745 : " Rightly understood, the sacrifice of the Old Testament, so far as it was expiatory, was intended to be substitutionary also. The penal suffering, it is true, was only exhibited typically, since the expiation was effected simply by the blood apart from the violent death ; but the bleeding expiation, when understood typically, as it was intended to be understood, and has been prophetically unravelled by Isa. liii., also pointed forward to a vicarious satisfaction to be rendered to the punitive justice of God."

It will be apparent, without further proof, that *Delitzsch's* view is the most like my own of all those that differ from it ; in fact, *Delitzsch* has undertaken to defend my view against *Bähr, Keil,* and *Hofmann,* and shown wherein, according to his opinion, it is superior to the theories of the above-named theologians (pp. 739, 740). He then sums all up in these words : " It is not to be denied, that the so-called juridical view defended by *Kurtz,* is the simplest, the most intelligible, and the most in harmony with the New Testament antitype." His objection to my view rests primarily upon certain difficulties connected with my explanation of the *Shechitah,* which he regards as insuperable. But if my new line of argument, which is modified in many respects and strengthened on the positive side, and my reply to his difficulties (§ 28, 30, 39, 40, 43, 44, 52, 54– 56, 66), are not altogether without force, I may possibly hope to see him take his stand still more decidedly and completely upon my side.

§ 71. *Oehler's* view is to be found at p. 632 of his solid and frequently cited work, which has rendered essential help to the study of this subject. He there says : " The real covering, that which atoned for the souls of the people, needed to be soul itself. A man might put his thanksgivings and his prayers into the form of a gift; but, as the gift of an unclean and sinful person, it would be itself unclean, and could only be pleasing to God so far as it presupposed the self-surrender of the person presenting it. For this reason, God appointed something in connection with the ceremonial of worship to represent this self-surrender. For the unclean and sinful soul of the worshipper, He substituted the soul of a clean and guiltless ani-

mal.   Offered in the blood of the sacrifice, the soul intervened between the person sacrificing and the holy God.   God thus beheld a
pure life upon His altar, by which the impure life of the person
approaching Him was covered over ; and in the same manner, this
pure element of life served to cover and remove the impurities that
were attached to the sanctuary.   Hence the importance of the blood
in the sacrifice was altogether specific.   It was not to be regarded
as the noblest gift consecrated to God ; but it was that which rendered the acceptance of all the gifts possible on the part of God,
since the self-surrender of the person sacrificing was accomplished
vicariously in it, and in it also the sinful soul of the person sacrificing was introduced into the gracious fellowship of God.   Because
the unfitness of a man to enter into the immediate fellowship of
God was asserted anew with every sacrifice ; therefore it was necessary that, with every sacrifice, the person offering it should be
covered by a pure life in the presence of God.   The importance
attached to this particular feature depended upon the question,
whether the expiation simply formed the *conditio sine qua non* for
the offering of the gift, or whether the whole of the sacrificial act
was designed as an expiation ; and this also regulated the proceedings in connection with the blood." But even this view, which does
away with a host of difficulties that beset all the rest, still leaves the
leading and fundamental question, how the soul of the sacrificial
animal, which was merely pure *on its own account*, could be regarded
as covering or atoning for the soul of the sinner, *i.e.*, as wiping away
sin, without violating the idea of divine justice, an insoluble
enigma, in which neither the imposition of hands nor the slaying
of the animal can receive its due importance, according to the place
assigned it in the ritual of sacrifice.   This point, however, has been
fully discussed in its proper place.

We conclude this chapter, therefore, with the firm and certain
persuasion, that the so-called juridical or " satisfactory " view of the
sacrificial expiation, of which the imposition of hands and slaying
of the animal formed the introduction, and which was represented
by the sprinkling of the blood, is not only, as *Delitzsch* says, and
even *Oehler* admits, " the simplest, the most intelligible, and the one
most in harmony with the New Testament antitype," but the *only*
one which is clear and intelligible, and the *only* one which is in harmony with the New Testament antitype.

CHAPTER V

BURNING THE SACRIFICE   THE SACRIFICIAL MEAL

§ 72. After the sprinkling of the blood was finished, the ritual of the bleeding sacrifice entered upon a new and different stage, viz., into one in which it rested upon the same basis, and moved within the same limits, as the bloodless sacrifices. For what now followed, viz., the *burning of the sacrifice* and the *eating of the sacrifice*, were processes to which the latter were subjected in essentially the same manner, and which constituted, in their case, the entire ritual. All that has hitherto been described in connection with the bleeding sacrifice (the imposition of hands, the slaying of the animal, and the sprinkling of the altar), was absent here; and necessarily so, because the very nature of the bloodless sacrifice furnished no substratum or point of contact for these ceremonies. The *bleeding* sacrifice was, in this second stage of its ritual, what the *bloodless* sacrifice was altogether, an *offering*, a *gift*, *food* (nourishment) for Jehovah (לֶחֶם אִשֶּׁה לַיהֹוָה, cf. § 23). Henceforth the whole ceremony has relation to the *flesh*, which is the food of man as much as bread and wine, and which, as food offered for Jehovah, could only be a symbol of what it was the duty and desire of the covenant-keeping, pious Israelite to offer as food to his God. It was different with the blood, which was the kernel and goal of the first stage of the sacrificial ritual. It is only in the most general manner that the *blood*, which was brought to the altar, could be designated a *gift for Jehovah*. For even though the sacrificer presented the animal, and brought it to the altar himself, he did not give it its atoning virtue and significance; nor did these exist already in the blood itself, but they were communicated to it by Jehovah alone (" I have given it," Lev. xvii. 11, cf. § 57). The *flesh*, on the other hand, as well as the bread and wine, already possessed the character of food, and therefore was naturally adapted to serve as a symbolical representation of the food to be offered to Jehovah. Again, neither literally nor generally could the atoning blood be designated as *food for Jehovah*. As blood is not a means of physical nourishment, and was not allowed to be used as food for man (Gen. ix. 4; Lev. xvii. 11; cf. § 5), it could not represent spiritual food, or food for Jehovah; consequently, we find that even the blood brought to the altar was there appropriated, not to Jehovah, but rather to

the offerer himself (§ 28).   The appropriation of the sacrificial gift
to Jehovah was effected solely through burning it upon the altar as
אִשֶּׁה לַיהוָה ; and as the blood could not be אִשֶּׁה לַיהוָה, so also it could
not be לֶחֶם לַיהוָה either.

§ 73. According to one view, which was formerly very generally
adopted, the BURNING OF THE FLESH OF THE SACRIFICE (for
which the expression used in the law is constantly הִקְטִיר, *i.e.*, to
cause to ascend in smoke or vapour, and *never* שָׂרַף) was a symbol of
the everlasting punishment of hell (Isa. lxvi. 24; Mark ix. 44, 46,
48; Rev. xx. 10). *J. D. Michaelis*, for example, expresses himself
thus in his *Entwurf der typischen Gottes-gelahrtheit* (§ 20): "To
show that sin was not expiated by death, but that there was also a
punishment after death; it was ordered that either the whole or
part of the sacrifice should be burned with fire.   The meaning and
intention of this command become still more obvious, when we
observe that the punishment of burning among the ancient
Hebrews was inflicted, not while the criminal was living, but after
his death; and that the punishment, which was inflicted after death
for the purpose of increasing the ignominy, showed, according to
the explanation given by Moses himself in Deut. xxi. 22, 23, that
the sinner had not suffered enough for his sin by being put to
death, but still remained accursed of God.   Consider, moreover,
how generally the idea of the punishment of hell was represented
in the ancient countries of the East under the image of fire; and
there will surely be no room to doubt, that the burning of the
sacrifices was intended to symbolize the punishments of hell."   *Von
Meyer* expresses a similar opinion.   In the *Blätter für höh. Wahrheit*
x. 51, 53, he says, with reference to the uninterrupted burning of
the fire upon the altar: "The slaughtering of the animal was the
death of the body, and the burning the punishment after death.
So long as the altar stood and burned for the consumption of the
sacrifices, the wrath of God on account of sin was not yet extinguished."   *De Maistre* also says, in his *Soirées de St Petersbourg* ii.
234: " The victim was always burned in whole or part, to show that
the natural punishment of crime was by fire, and that the substituted flesh was burned in the place of the flesh that was really
guilty."   But this view is decidedly and totally wrong.   It misapprehends the significance of the flesh, in regarding it as guilty or
sinful, and the purport of the fire as well.   It cannot be denied,
indeed, that fire is met with in the Scriptures as a figurative representation of devouring wrath, and of the torturing punishment of

hell. A glance at the concordances will show how frequently this is the case in both the Old and New Testaments. For all that, the view in question is a false one; because, through confining itself to the surface, it overlooks the deeper ground of this usage of speech, and its original unity with the still more common one, in which fire is a figurative representation of refining and sanctification. Fire is essentially the source of light and heat. But light and heat are the immediate and most important conditions of life. Without light and heat, all life becomes interrupted, becomes numbed and dies; but when nourished by light and heat, all life grows more cheerful, vigorous, and strong. The first thing noticed, therefore, in connection with fire, is its life-quickening, life-exciting, in a word, its animating power. The second is its power to refine. This is the second, because it is dependent upon the existence of a second thing, viz., of something ignoble, perishable, corrupt or corrupting, which is eliminated by the fire that refines the object. This second signification of fire, therefore, intervenes, when the perishable has infected and pervaded the imperishable. But it is identical with the first, since the eliminating and refining are *eo ipso* the restoring of the vital energy that has been interrupted. The *third* meaning of this element is that of consuming, torturing, damning; it is introduced in cases where the perishable has swallowed up the imperishable, and transubstantiated it into its own nature. A sufficient explanation of the connection between the second and third is to be found in 1 Cor. iii. 11 sqq., where the wood, hay, and stubble are said to be burned by it, whilst it refines and tests the gold, silver, and precious stones. Fire is the noblest, finest, keenest, and purest of the elements—I might, indeed, say the most godlike; for as nothing (morally) unclean can approach God, without receiving pain and condemnation in its accursed uncleanness, whereas the pure are happy in His presence, so nothing (physically) unclean can come into contact with fire without being consumed, whilst that which is pure receives thereby an elevation of its vital power. For this reason, fire is also employed in the Scriptures as the symbol and vehicle of the Holy Spirit; and this serves to explain the fact, that in all merely natural religions fire was regarded as the symbol, and even as the incarnation of Deity itself.—This view also misapprehends the meaning of death. It tears asunder the death of the body and eternal death as entirely heterogeneous; whereas here they ought to be regarded simply in their point of unity. In the death of the animal the death of the sinner was

symbolized in all its relations. The view in question, considered in
its typical bearing, would lead to *Aepin's* doctrine of an intensive
endurance of the punishment of hell on the part of Christ on His
descent thither, a notion which is neither doctrinally nor exegetically tenable. According to this view, again, the atonement made
was necessarily insufficient and nugatory, and for that reason was
abolished; whereas in Lev. xvii. 11, etc., it is accepted and declared to be perfectly valid. Moreover, how could *such* a burning
be regarded as a " sacrifice of a sweet-smelling savour to Jehovah "
(§ 20)? Equally irreconcilable with this view is the constancy
with which the function in question is designated by the verb הִקְטִיר.
" If," as *Oehler* has well expressed it—" if the fire on the altar was
a *penal* fire, and the burning sacrifice was as it were a burning in
hell; how could the smoke of the sacrifice be described as a smell
that was pleasing to God ?" Lastly, another thing which speaks
most decidedly and undeniably against this interpretation, was the
circumstance that the meat-offering, with its accompaniments (oil,
incense, and salt), was burnt in the same manner, and along with
the meat of the sacrifice. Now, the idea of punishment is absolutely untenable and absurd in connection with the burning of the
meat-offering, and still more with that of the accompaniments.
The meat-offering signified *good* works, the incense the prayers of
the believer, and the oil the Spirit of God. Both *Michaelis* and
v. Meyer admit this (§ 141 sqq.). Were these, then, also liable to
the punishment of hell-fire?

§ 74. All the commentators since *Bähr* are agreed in the opinion
that the burning of the sacrificial gift as a הִקְטִיר,—*i.e.*, as causing it
to pass away in smoke and vapour, or as sending it up to heaven,
where God dwells,—was intended to express the appropriation of
the gift to Jehovah. At the same time, there are many unessential
diversities along with this general agreement. According to *Bähr*
(ii. 347), " the primary intention of the burning was that the gift
might be consumed by fire, and so be entirely annihilated, as far as
the sacrificer to whom it belonged was concerned. This intention,
however, was merely a subordinate and negative one (there were
other ways in which it might have been annihilated); the gift
having been annihilated to the giver, was *eo ipso* to ascend to Him
who dwells on high. And the burning indicated for whom the gift
was intended, and whither it was directed ; this was, in fact, the
real and positive design of the act of burning. What was already
indicated to a certain extent by the altar upon which the gift was

offered, viz., its elevation towards Him who dwelt on high, **was**
first really completed by the fire through which it ascended."
Oehler expresses a similar opinion. At p. 632 he says: " The
burning denoted, on the one hand, the completion of the offering
on the part of the sacrificer, the gift being annihilated so far as he
was concerned. The main point, however, was not this, but the
acceptance of it by God, which was also completed in the burning."
But there is no warrant whatever for introducing a double reference, viz., the destruction of it to the person sacrificing, as well as the
appropriation of it to Jehovah. Wherever the former is indicated in
the sacrificial worship—as, for example, in connection with the flesh
of the peace-offering which was left over (§ 139),—the burning
is not a הַקְטִיר, but a שָׂרוֹף, and it takes place not on the altar, but in
a clean spot outside the sanctuary. Who ever thinks of a presentation, as being the annihilation of the *gift* itself to the person presenting it? It is simply an annihilation of his right of possession;
and *that* annihilation requires no peculiar form of expression, but is
effected *eo ipso* by the presentation itself.

We regard the appropriation of the gift to Jehovah, therefore,
as the real and only design of the burning. Through the burning
the gift was resolved into vapour and odour: its earthly elements
still remained, but its real essence ascended in the most refined and
transfigured corporeality towards heaven, where Jehovah was enthroned—a sweet odour of delight to Him, an אִשֶּׁה רֵיחַ נִיחוֹחַ לַיהוָה.

Kliefoth is wrong (p. 62) in "rejecting every interpretation
which supposes any kind of refining, purifying, or sanctifying
process to have taken place in connection with the burning of the
sacrifice." " It was pure in itself," he says, " and needed no refinement; and it was obliged to be clean, not merely as a means of
expiation, but as an object well-pleasing to God; in which, and
through the substitution of which, the person sacrificing also became well-pleasing. On the contrary, the burning by the fire of
the altar signified nothing more than that, pure and good as it was,
it was divested of its materiality by the fire of God, transmuted
from an earthly into a heavenly nature, transfigured, and so united
to God." But was not this " divesting of materiality," this " trans-
mutation of the earthly into a heavenly nature," this " transfigura-
tion in order that it might be united to God," in itself " a refining,
purifying, and sanctifying" process? Undoubtedly the sacrificial
animal was pure and spotless *in itself*, for that was the *conditio sine
qua non* of its fitness for sacrifice (§ 34),—and nothing had occurred

since (§ 44), by which its natural cleanness and spotlessness could have been altered. But it was not absolutely pure, in comparison, that is, with the holiness of God, to whom it was to be offered as a gift; but only relatively so, in comparison with the unclean, sinful man, whose sanctified self-surrender the surrender of the animal was intended to represent (§ 19). Although in this relation it was pure and faultless, without sin or blemish, yet with the stamp of the earthly it bore the faults and imperfections of everything earthly. Even of the holy angels of God it is said in Job xv. 15, "Behold, He putteth no trust in His holy ones; yea, the heavens are not clean in His sight" (cf. iv. 18, xxv. 5). If, then, even the heavenly creation is not to be regarded as clean in comparison with God, how much less the earthly creation, laden as it is with a curse! (Gen. iii. 17, v. 29.) And if anything earthly is to be offered to God, even though it be relatively the most holy and pure, it requires first of all to be purified, refined, and sanctified. The dross must be removed, and the true metal exhibited in its genuine refinement. And that was done by the purification and refinement effected by the fire.

But that fire, by which the sacrificial gift was appropriated to God in a refined and transfigured form, was not ordinary fire. It was *holy* fire: the very same which came out from God in connection with Aaron's first sacrificial service (Lev. ix. 24, cf. 2 Chron. vii. 1), and consumed the sacrifice, and which was henceforth *never* to be allowed to go out, that its character as fire of divine origin might be sustained. The refining and sanctifying power of which this fire was the symbol, was a power proceeding not from man but from God—the power of the Holy Ghost, which dwelt in the congregation, the fire-spirit of the law, which was proclaimed in fire on Sinai, and burned into the hearts with fiery glow, whose fundamental idea is the commandment, "Be ye holy, for I am holy" (Lev. xix. 2).

§ 75. It is of course self-evident, that the flesh of the animal, being given up to the holy fire of the altar, was not regarded as simple flesh, as what it was in itself, but rather in the relation in which it stood to the person sacrificing. But the question arises first of all, what kind of relation this was; whether it was that of *actual* substitution, in which another, *as another*, takes my place—does *instead* of me what I ought to have done, suffers *instead* of me what I ought to have suffered, so that, inasmuch as it has been done and suffered by this other, I am released from the responsibility to do or to suffer it myself; or merely that of an *ideal* representation, in which what the other does or submits to *as my representative* in my stead, does not release me, but, on the contrary, binds me to do it, or to submit to it myself as well. In the one case the representative is my real *alter ego*, in the other, my ideal *ipse ego*.

We have already shown, in the previous chapter, that in the first stage of the ritual of animal sacrifice, the representation could only be understood in the sense of an *alter ego*, and that *Bähr* and *Keil's* favourite interchange of this idea, for that of a symbolical *ipse ego*, is the fundamental error and the πρῶτον ψεῦδος of their so thoroughly mistaken theory of expiation. We must now proceed to inquire, whether consistency and unity of thought, so far as the whole of the ritual of sacrifice is concerned, require that in this second stage we should still firmly adhere to the idea of an *alter ego*, which is required in the first stage quite as much by the nature of the case as by the express statement of the law of sacrifice (Lev. xvii. 11).

If it were absolutely necessary to reply to this question in the affirmative, the burning of the flesh of the sacrifice could only be understood as signifying that the person sacrificing, after receiving expiation and forgiveness of sins through the completion of the sprinkling of blood, was conscious indeed of the obligation henceforth to cause all his members and powers, and all the activity of his life, of which they were the instruments, to pass through the refining fire of sanctification, and to present them, thus refined and sanctified, and consecrate them to God; but that, as he had not confidence in his own ability to perform this duty fully, he presented the sacrificial animal in the fire of the altar as a symbolical compensation for any defects.

But this view would throw the door wide open to the most momentous consequences, viz., to the danger of moral indifference; and would answer but little, or rather be altogether opposed, to the spirit of moral stringency and thoroughness which pervades the whole of the Old Testament. The exposure to damnation which follows sin, could be and was to be remitted to the penitent sinner desiring salvation, on the ground of the eternal, saving, counsel of God (§ 57), and in association with the symbolico-typical *satisfactio vicaria* of the sacrificial animal. But the obligation to a life and conversation thoroughly refined by the fire of the law, and to a self-sanctifying surrender and dedication of all his members and powers to Jehovah (cf. Rom. vi. 13), neither was nor could be intended to be remitted to the sinner, even after expiation had been secured. As justification necessarily presupposes repentance and faith, so is it on the other hand the basis and introduction to a sanctification and renovation of the whole future life, without which it is null and void. And whilst in itself this view is mistaken and contradictory, it has not the slightest link of connection or point of contact in the law of sacrifice. The warrant, to regard the death of the sacrificial animal as really and objectively vicarious, is found in Lev. xvii. 11, where God promises to give real atoning efficacy to the sacrificial blood which has passed through death ; but there is no promise to be met with anywhere to the effect that the burning of the sacrifice should possess, really and objectively, a similar representative character through direct communication from God.

§ 76. The body of the sacrificial animal, which was given up to the fire of the altar, cannot be regarded, therefore, as a substitutionary, objective *alter ego* of the person sacrificing, but only as his representative, subjective *ipse ego*. This is obvious from its character as a presentation, a gift, food, for Jehovah. Were the former the case, just as in the first stage of the ritual the sacrificial blood was the medium of expiation as the vehicle of the animal soul, the sacrificial flesh would also be the object of presentation as what it is in itself, viz., as the vehicle of corporeal, nutritive power. But the Old Testament revelation of God makes the firmest declaration to the contrary : " Will I eat the flesh of bulls, or drink the blood of goats ? " It is not about the gift for its own sake that Jehovah is concerned : " If I were hungry, I would not tell thee ; for the world is Mine, and the fulness thereof " (Ps. l. 12) ; but about the giver, who puts his love and attachment, his readiness to sacrifice his own entire being, into the gift, and in the gift surrenders himself. The character of the sacrificial flesh as a קָרְבָּן, a לֶחֶם לַיהוָה, is as decidedly at variance with the idea of a real and objective representation, as it demands and determines the character of one that is ideal and subjective.

But if the one half of the sacrificial animal, viz., the blood, be thus regarded as a substitutionary *alter ego*, and the other, viz., the flesh, as a representative *ipse ego*, does not this introduce an inadmissible duplicity into the sacrificial ritual, which completely destroys the unity of idea? It appears so unquestionably. But we must bear in mind that this duplicity is already there—that it is determined, established, and regulated by the duplex and antithetical character of the two different stages in the sacrificial ritual, viz., by the fact, that the blood is introduced, not as a gift and food for Jehovah, but as a real, objective means of expiation for the sinner, whereas the flesh to be burned is introduced, not as means, but as end—not as a gift of God for the sanctification of man, but as a gift presented to God by the self-sanctifying man, as a symbol of his sanctified self-surrender, an expression of his obligation to make such a surrender of himself.

Let any one present to his own mind the relation, in which the two stages of the sacrificial ceremony stood to one another. The essence of the קָרְבָּן, the sacrifice, as its very name denotes (הִקְרִיב = *offerre*), was the presentation, or gift; and the burning served to effect this. The act of expiation, the manipulation of the blood, therefore, is not expressed in any way in the name of the sacrifice; and this of itself is a proof that it was something distinct, independent, and superadded. In the idea, and possibly also in the history of the institution of sacrifice, the presentation or gift was the first and primary thing, even though the manipulation of the blood preceded the burning of the flesh in the ritual itself. Whether it was in connection with the very first act of sacrifice that was ever performed, or as the result of a later development of the institution of sacrifice, that the truth was discovered, that a gift or presentation could only be acceptable to God when preceded by the expiation and forgiveness of sin; it was certainly in consequence of, or in connection with this discovery, that the manipulation of the blood was added, and made the necessary preliminary of the presentation and gift, whilst in it the latter received its real and indispensable foundation.

That this was the course of development of the idea of sacrifice, —*in idea* at all events, and probably historically also,—is evident, as we have already stated, from the name itself. It is still further evident from the fact, that at all times there were offered in connection with the bleeding sacrifices bloodless offerings also, which bore the name, and possessed the character and force of sacrifice quite as much as the former, although their very nature precluded the possibility of their being employed to set forth an act of expiation. And, lastly, it is evident from the historical account contained in the book of Genesis: Cain presented merely bloodless offerings, viz., the fruits of the ground; Abel offered bleeding sacrifices, the firstlings of his flock and the fat thereof. But the application of the term *Minchah*, which was afterwards employed according to invariable usage to denote a bloodless gift exclusively, to Abel's offering as well as Cain's, is a proof to us that the two are looked at from the same point of view ; and therefore that the manipulation of the blood, which was usual in connection with the bleeding sacrifices at a later period, had not yet been introduced, or at all events that it cannot have possessed the same importance as in the sacrificial worship of later times.

Now, if the two stages of the ritual of sacrifice were thus both apparently and ideally distinct, different, and antithetical, in their relation to one another, so that each of them possessed its own independent and distinctive character, starting point, and goal ; there is the less reason for surprise that in each of the two stages the fundamental idea should have shaped itself differently according to the diversity in the characteristics of the two.

§ 77. We already know from § 23 and 72 that the sacrificial gift, which, after being refined by the fire of God, was appropriated to Him, was intended as food or *nourishment* for Jehovah, as the לֶחֶם לַיהוָֹה ; and in § 23 we have also shown in what sense it was meant that Jehovah needed such food for His existence. The sacrificial gift, namely, was the symbol of the self-dedication of the people in fidelity to the covenant, which was as it were the " daily bread" of Jehovah, because (according to the bold but apt words of *Hengstenberg*) " the prayer of man, ' Give us this day our daily bread,' had by its side the demand of God, ' Give Me this day My daily bread.'"

But as the food which God has given to man for his daily supply is twofold, animal and vegetable (Gen. ix. 3), the food which the Israelite offered to his God in the sacrificial gift was twofold also : flesh, in the bleeding sacrifice ; bread, wine, and oil, in the bloodless offering. This difference and antithesis, when transferred to the sphere of spiritual nourishment, must have its double signification even there. We have already briefly proved, too (§ 24), that the animal sacrifice represented the person of the man and his life's work ; the vegetable, on the other hand, the fruit and produce of that work. Here also, with regard to the former, we may remind the reader of what has already been stated in § 3, 4, with reference to the choice of clean animals as representing the chosen (holy) nation.

It was an essential defect in my former work, that I did not give sufficient prominence to the notion of nourishment, of the " bread of Jehovah." The consequence of this defect was a wrong interpretation of the flesh of the sacrifice, that was given up to the fire of the altar, which I here retract with all the greater earnestness because it has been adopted by other commentators. My former opinion was in substance the following : Blood and flesh are the two essential components of the animal.   The *blood* is the seat of the soul, and this is the impelling force of all vital activity.   The *flesh*, on the other hand (including bones, nerves, sinews, etc.), is the instrument of the soul, through which it receives all its impressions from without, and directs all its energy from within outwards,—the instrument, therefore, of all the soul's activity.   Hence the burning of the flesh of the sacrifice denoted a surrender and consecration of all the members and powers of the body to Jehovah, by means of the sacred fire which Jehovah Himself had given for that purpose, and through which they were refined and purified from all the dross of earthly imperfection, and in this transfigured form appropriated to Jehovah.   As the sprinkling of the blood was a figure of justification, so the burning of the flesh was a figure of sanctification.   It expressed the obligation of the person sacrificing, who had now obtained forgiveness of sins by means of the expiation, henceforth to consecrate to Jehovah all the energy of his life, all the members and powers of his body ; or, as the Apostle puts it in Rom. vi. 13, no longer to yield his members as instruments of unrighteousness unto sin, but to yield himself unto God, as one alive from the dead, and his members as instruments of righteousness unto God.

The allusion to justification in the sprinkling of the blood, and to sanctification in the burning of the flesh, I still hold most firmly. I cannot regard the latter any longer, however, as based upon the signification of the flesh as the complex of all the organs of the soul's activity, but trace it solely to the import of the sacred fire as a symbol of the refining, purifying, and sanctifying powers of God, which He had given to His people in the law.   For there is no trace anywhere of the flesh that was burned being regarded as the sum-total of the organs of the soul.   The utility of the flesh as food for man is the only point referred to ; and from this alone, therefore, can we determine the symbolical meaning of the flesh of the sacrifice that was burned.   In relation to food, the flesh itself is the principal thing ; in relation to activity, the bones and sinews.   Now, undoubtedly these were consumed as well as the flesh in the case of the whole- (or burnt-) offerings ; but in the other descriptions of sacrifice, the fat portions alone were placed in the altar-fire.   The fat portions were evidently regarded in this case as the best and noblest part of the whole, the *flos carnis*.   And they were so also from that point of view from which the flesh was regarded as food ; but they never could pass for the highest and strongest instruments of the soul's activity, even where the body was regarded as the organ of that

activity.   On the contrary, in this connection fat is the figure employed to represent inactivity, idleness, obstinacy (Isa. vi. 10).   Now,
if the flesh when burnt had been regarded as the organ of the soul's
activity, in the case of the sin-offerings and the trespass- and peace-
offerings, where it was of supreme importance that only the best of
the flesh should be burned, the folds of fat would certainly never
have been selected, but rather the organs of motion and action, of
seeing, hearing, etc.

In relation to the burning of the flesh of the sacrifice, therefore,
we simply adhere to the idea that it was *food* for Jehovah, but
without giving up on that account, what is perfectly reconcilable
with it, the allusion in the case of the flesh to a representation of
the person of the sacrificer, and in the bloodless offerings to the
fruits and results of his life's activity (§ 24).   The real sanctified *I*,
and the fruits of a sanctified activity, these are the food which
Jehovah desires, the nourishment which He needs in His capacity
as covenant-God, as the God of salvation, and which are in His
esteem a sweet savour of satisfaction and delight.

§ 78. To my former view *Hofmann* has replied (p. 241), " If
the blood of the sacrificial animal was not a symbol of the soul of
the sacrificer, the flesh could not represent his body, nor could the
burning of the former signify sanctification.   Sanctification and
justification do not stand in the same relation to one another as
body and soul; nor can we see why the sanctification of the body
should be symbolized, and not that of the soul."   I still agree, as I
formerly did, with *Hofmann*, in opposition to *Bähr* and *Keil* (§ 67,
69), that the blood of the sacrificial animal could not be a symbol
of the soul of the person sacrificing; and I also agree with him,
that the flesh of the former did not represent the body of the latter,
as the sum-total of the organs of his soul; but I still adhere to the
opinion that the " burning of the flesh signified sanctification."
For this meaning is unquestionably contained in the symbolical
worth of *fire*, which prevails throughout the Scriptures.   No doubt
flesh and blood, or body and soul, form the two essential halves of
the sacrificial animal, as justification and sanctification are the two
essential sides of redemption, of which the former was shown in
the manipulation of the blood, the latter in the burning of the
flesh.   But the fact that the former was intended to exhibit justification *really*, and the latter to exhibit sanctification *symbolically*,
precludes *Hofmann's* deduction, to the effect, that it necessarily
follows that sanctification and justification must stand in the same

relation as body and soul, and that sanctification must relate to the body, and justification to the soul.

But there is no force in *Kliefoth's* objection, that even in the burning the flesh was regarded as still animated (p. 63). "For this reason," he says, "the flesh of the sacrifice was always to be eaten on the same day; the eating was not to be separated so far from the act of slaughtering, etc., that the flesh could no longer be regarded as a living (?) part of the *victima*, of the personality sacrificed." The correct answer has been given already, viz., that in the burning of the flesh of the sacrifice the contrast between flesh and blood, or body and soul, was no longer the point considered. The flesh of the sacrifice was merely a gift, and in fact a gift which served as nourishment. But into this gift, which from its very nature (§ 3, 24) was better adapted to represent himself than any other gift could possibly be, the giver conveyed his love and gratitude, his attachment, his readiness to deny himself, his desire for a renewal of life,—in a word, himself and his whole personality; and bound himself to refine and purify himself by the fire-spirit of the law, just as the gift was refined by the altar-fire, and, thus refined, to consecrate and surrender himself, with all his thought, will, and feeling, to Jehovah, just as the sacrificial gift, ascending to heaven in the fire, was symbolically appropriated to Jehovah. This was the true and real "sweet savour to Jehovah," the designation so frequently applied in the law to the burning of the sacrifice.

§ 79. In conclusion, we have still to examine the SACRIFICIAL MEAL, which terminated the entire series of sacrificial acts. It is true, there was only one kind of sacrifice with which it was associated, viz., the peace-offering; but for all that, it formed an equally independent feature, and one that was quite as essential to the complete exhibition of the idea of sacrifice, as the sprinkling of the blood and burning of the flesh by which it was preceded. It is necessary, therefore, that we should examine it here.

After the portions of fat that were appointed for the altar had been burned, and the pieces that fell to the lot of the priests had been taken away, viz., the so-called wave-breast and heave-leg (*Eng. Ver.*, shoulder), the rest of the flesh was eaten, in the case of a peace-offering, by the person presenting it, and by the members of his household (together with the poorer Levites), in a joyous meal "before the Lord," that is to say, at the tabernacle (Lev. vii. 15 sqq., 31 sqq.; Deut. xii. 7, 17 sqq.).

About the meaning of the meal itself there can be no question. "To an oriental mind," says *Bähr*, ii. 373, "two ideas were inseparably associated in the notion of a meal: on the one hand, that of fellowship and friendship existing among the participators themselves, and also between them and the provider of the meal; and on the other hand, that of joy and gladness, so that even the highest and purest joy, viz., blessedness in the kingdom of heaven, is described under the figure of a meal (Ps. xxiii. 5, xvi. 11, xxxvi. 8; Matt. viii. 11, xxii. 1; Luke xiv. 15). And as what was provided for the meal in this case belonged, strictly speaking, to Jehovah, to whom it had been entirely given up through the act of presentation, all who took part in the meal ate with Him at His table. It was He who gave the meal; and this was a pledge of friendship and peace with Him."

This view was also adopted by me in my *Mos. Opfer;* and I attributed the following meaning, in consequence, to the sacrificial meal: The atonement was complete; the sin which had separated the sacrificer from Jehovah was covered, cancelled; the sacrificer had sanctified, consecrated, and surrendered himself and the fruit of his activity to Jehovah; and Jehovah now turned to him, welcomed him to His house and table, prepared for him a meal, and gave him meat and drink at His table. The sacrificial meal, therefore, was an expression and pledge, as well as an actual, symbolical attestation and enjoyment, of the blessedness offered to the covenant nation in fellowship with Jehovah. It exhibited the highest sacramental point of the whole process of sacrifice; or, to express the progressive stages of the sacrificial idea in doctrinal phraseology, just as the burning of the sacrifice answered to *sanctification*, and the sprinkling of the blood to *justification*, so the meal corresponded to the *unio mystica*.

It is quite in harmony with this explanation of the sacrificial meal, that, according to Deut. xii. 7, 18, the family of the person sacrificing took part in it, including even the servants, and also the Levites, who were supposed to be in need.[1] The meal, it is true, was prepared at the instigation and for the sake of the person sacri-

---

[1] In Deut. xvi. 11, 14, widows and orphans are also mentioned, as well as the strangers dwelling in the land, as taking part in the festal rejoicings of the harvest-feasts (Pentecost and the feast of Tabernacles). But I question whether it is meant by this, that they took part in the sacrificial meals, as *Hengstenberg* (p. 41) and *Oehler* (p. 642) suppose, since the sacrificial meal is not expressly named.

ficing, but not for him alone, since this would have robbed it of the essential characteristic of a social meal. The whole of the covenant-nation, in its normal relation to its covenant-God, had really a claim to share in the enjoyment of the happiness of which this divine meal was the symbol; so that, strictly speaking, if it had been practicable, the whole of the covenant-nation might and should have been invited; but as this was impossible, a small number of its members, chosen from the immediate circle of the person sacrificing, were invited to represent it, after the analogy of the paschal meal, at which every company formed a congregation by itself, or rather represented the whole congregation. The addition of the members of the family and of the servants also was all the more appropriate, since *they* participated in the reason for presenting the peace-offering, the flesh of which was eaten in the sacrificial meal (viz., in the divine blessings either prayed for or already received).

§ 80. But strong opposition has lately arisen from many sides to the view expressed above, that at the meal Jehovah was to be regarded as the host and provider of the meal. The principal objectors are *Hengstenberg* (p. 40), *Neumann* (*Sacra V. T. Salutaria*, p. 37 nota), *v. Hofmann* (ii. 1, p. 229), *Keil* (i. 251, 253–4), *Tholuck* (p. 88), *Ebrard* (p. 42), and *Oehler* (p. 642). On the other hand, *Kliefoth* (p. 65) and *A. Köhler* (*Herzog's* Cyclopædia) have adhered to the original view even in the face of this opposition.

Hofmann observes : " It was not the person offering who ate at the table of God ; but, on the contrary, it was he who invited Jehovah to his table. . . . . His ability to keep a feast in worship of God, and to invite God to it as a guest, he owed to the divine arrangement," etc. So *Oehler* again : " God condescended to become a guest at the table of the sacrificer, and received as the piece of honour the breast of the animal, which He then handed over to His servant the priest. In this sense, the meal was a pledge of the friendly and blessed fellowship which He was willing to maintain with His own people among whom He dwelt." *Keil* goes much deeper, and says, " The sacrificial meal cannot be looked at in this light, as though God provided the meal, welcoming all who took part in it to His table and home, and giving them to eat and drink of His own property ; but it is simply to be regarded as a meal in worship of God, in which God entered into association with His people, or with a certain portion, one particular family—not only receiving a part of the food destined for the meal, and giving it to His representatives, the servants of the sanctuary, to eat, but allowing the persons who presented it to eat the rest, along with their families, ' before Him,' *i.e.*, in His immediate presence.   Thus the sacrificial meal became a covenant meal, a meal of love and joy, which shadowed forth not only a fellowship of house and table with the Lord, but also the blessedness of the kingdom of heaven.   For by the fact that a portion was handed over to the Lord, the earthly food was sanctified into a symbol of the true, spiritual food, with which the Lord satisfies and invigorates the citizens of His kingdom."

I fully agree with *Keil* in his general view of the sacrificial meal, and of the symbolical importance of the flesh that was eaten in connection with it.   But for that very reason, I feel irresistibly compelled to regard God as the host; and just because *Keil* has not done this, he has involved himself in a striking self-contradiction, which is apparent in the concluding words of his explanation, where the food eaten at the meal is said to be a symbol " of the *true spiritual food* with which *the Lord* satisfies and invigorates the citizens of His kingdom;" and still more decidedly upon p. 385, where the flesh of the paschal meal, which he himself also regards as a sacrificial meal, is called " a means of grace, through which *the Lord* received His spared and redeemed people *into the fellowship of His house,* and gave them bread of life for the invigoration of their souls."   And at p. 386 he states in express words : " Through the oneness of the lamb to be eaten, the eaters were united into an undivided oneness and fellowship with the Lord, *who had prepared the meal for them.*" But is it not perfectly obvious, that I am received " into the house and table fellowship" of another, not by inviting *him,* but by his inviting *me*?   And how could the sacrificial meal be a meal of blessedness, or " *shadow forth the blessedness of the kingdom of heaven,*" if the meal was prepared, and the food given, not by God, but by the person sacrificing?   Was the latter the possessor and dispenser of the " true spiritual food"?   Was he not rather its needy recipient?   Or did a man bestow " the blessedness of the kingdom of heaven upon God"?   Was it not God who bestowed it upon man ?   The other commentators who have taken the same view, have succeeded in steering clear of such self-contradictions ; but they have robbed the sacrificial meal, in consequence, of that deeper and richer meaning, of which the Apostle makes use for the purpose of establishing its relation to the Lord's Supper (1 Cor. x. 16–21), and which is so closely connected with the parables of Christ in Matt. xxii. 1 sqq. and Luke xiv. 15 sqq.

§ 81. The first thing objected to by the opponents of our view, is the foundation upon which it rests; namely, that through the act of presentation the whole of the sacrificial animal was appropriated to Jehovah, and therefore was henceforth to be regarded as *His* property, and not as that of the person presenting it. " The slain-offering," says *Hengstenberg*, " was as such not a whole offering, and the parts eaten were those that were not consecrated to the Lord." *Keil*, again, says, " What was entirely appropriated to the Lord, and was to belong entirely to Him, had of necessity to be *entirely* given up to Him." And *Hofmann* observes : " The sacrificer did not eat what God left for him ; but, before he ate, he gave the best of his meal to God. The sacrificial animal did not become the property of God through the presentation, in any such sense as that it now, strictly speaking, belonged entirely to the altar ; but being intended as a thank-offering, it followed as a matter of course, that it belonged to the altar only so far as this destination involved. . . . . It was really the case, that the priest ate of the altar, or of the table of God, since the law assigned to him the breast and shoulder, which the person sacrificing was not allowed to eat, and which for that very reason were heaved and waved, *i.e.*, given up to God. But what was not so excepted, was intended from the very outset to be consumed with religious rejoicing, and was not merely given back by God for that purpose." I have no doubt whatever, that this view *may* be taken of the affair, but I cannot see that it *must* be. To *Hengstenberg* I reply, that the sin- and trespass-offerings were also as such not whole offerings; and yet the whole of the sacrificial animal was undoubtedly presented to the Lord, and appropriated to Him through the presentation. And to *Keil* : that by the simple act of presentation to the sanctuary, the sacrificial animal was both altogether designed for and altogether surrendered to the Lord ; and that the fact of the priest's receiving the animal, indicated the transfer of it from the possession of the sacrificer to that of Jehovah. And to *Hofmann* : that as the animal was presented as a thank-offering, even on the assumption that it thereby became the property of God, it follows as a matter of course, that only so much of it came to the altar as this destination involved, and that the rest was applied to the purpose to which it was devoted by virtue of its destination as a thank-offering. But if it be once admitted, that the priest ate from the altar, or from the table of God, what fell to him as his share of the thank-offering; I cannot see why the same thing might not be said with regard to the eating on the part of the person sacrificing, since the priest's portion was to be removed by the heaving and waving, as *Hofmann* himself affirms, not from being consumed by the fire of the altar, but from being consumed by the person sacrificing.

And when *Hofmann* still further observes (p. 230), " If this were not the case, the presentation of the firstlings could not be classed along with the thank-offerings ; for in the former, God was evidently invited as a guest, and the distinction between the two presentations consisted simply in the fact, that on the one occasion it was a religious meal, and on the other a social eating and drinking, from which God received His share;"—I cannot see any necessity which *compels* us to class together two things so heterogeneous in their nature and intention.   Still less can I understand how *Hofmann* could maintain that, in the presentation of the firstlings, " God was evidently invited as a guest;" since the firstlings, at least so far as they were not presented as a kind of peace-offering themselves—*e.g.*, the firstlings of the ox, the sheep, and the goat (§ 229, 230)—were not generally intended as a meal which the person offering them had to provide, but were delivered as feudal payments to the feudal Lord of the land, who remunerated His servants the priests with the proceeds.   And lastly, with regard to the stress laid by *Keil* and *Oehler* upon the custom of heaving and waving the breast and shoulder, the meaning of which custom they suppose to rest upon the assumption, that the host at the sacrificial meal was not God, but the person sacrificing, I hope to be able to prove in due time (§ 138), that the separation of the wave-breast and heave-shoulder was perfectly reconcilable with the opposite view.

With greater plausibility, perhaps, might those passages of Deuteronomy be adduced, in which the sacrificer is instructed to invite not only his family and his servants, but the (needy) Levites also, to participate in the sacrificial meal; inasmuch as it appears to have been left to his own free choice, *whom* he would invite, which certainly favours the view that he himself acted the part of host.   But even this argument cannot be regarded as conclusive. If the plan devised by God reached so far as to accept the best and noblest part of the sacrificial gift presented as a " sweet savour," a sign that they were welcomed as well-pleasing, and after having thus sanctified the rest, to give it back to the sacrificer for the preparation of a joyful meal, it is impossible to see why it may not also have reached *so* far, as to leave the offerer to make the selection of the guests to be invited.

§ 82. We have seen that the arguments adduced in support of the opposite view of the sacrificial meal, are all of them ambiguous and none conclusive. On the other hand, the proofs which we can furnish of the view we advocate, appear to leave no doubt as to its correctness. They are the following: (1.) Wherever in the law the peace-offerings are referred to, the term, offerings for Jehovah, or before Jehovah, is constantly applied to them *as a whole*, and not merely to that particular portion which was to be burned upon the altar, or assigned to the priest through the ceremony of waving (cf. Lev. ii. 1, 8, 11, 12, 14, iii. 1, 6, 7, 12, vii. 11, 14, 29, etc.). But what was offered to Jehovah and accepted by Him, became undoubtedly the *property of Jehovah* in consequence. (2.) It is evident from Lev. xxi. 22, when every part of the sacrifice which fell to the lot of the priest (the "*most holy*" flesh of the sin-offering, and the merely "*holy*" flesh of the peace-offering) is designated "*the bread of God*," that the sin-offerings, trespass-offerings, and peace-offerings, of which only the fat portions were enjoyed by Jehovah as "a sacrifice of a sweet smell," ought *properly* to have been *entirely* consumed in the altar-fire, as really was the case with the burnt-offering; but that God, according to His gracious arrangement, contented Himself with the fat portions, and gave up the rest of the flesh, partly to the priest and partly to the person sacrificing, to be devoted to other purposes. Now, whether we regard the genitive as *gen. obj.* or *gen. subj.*, in either case the expression "the bread of God" is a proof that the *whole* of the sacrificial flesh in the *peace*-offerings, as well as the sin- and trespass-offerings, belonged to God *after* and in consequence of the presentation. (3.) The view held by *Oehler* is thoroughly unsuitable and inadmissible. "God condescended," he says, "to become the guest of the person sacrificing; He received the breast as the portion of honour, and handed it over to His servant the priest." But if only the portion of honour was given up to God, and not the whole of the animal sacrificed, it was the fat which He Himself received that really constituted the portion of honour, and not the breast allotted the priest: moreover, neither God Himself, nor His servant and representative the priest, took part in the *meal;* for the latter was allowed to eat the breast and shoulder which fell to his share in any clean place, along with his sons and daughters (Lev. x. 14). (4.) If the person sacrificing was to be regarded as the host, there could be no reason whatever for the instructions to prepare the sacrificial meal "before Jehovah," *i.e.*, at the tabernacle, and therefore at the house of God; at all events, it would have been more appropriate to hold it in the house of the sacrificer himself. (5.) Another argument is furnished by the analogy of the paschal meal, which furnishes no appropriate sense, on the supposition that the master of the house invited God to his table, instead of God providing the food for those who partook of it (cf. § 186). (6.) It is evident, from 1 Cor. x. 18, 21, that we have the authority of the Apostle Paul in favour of our view.   In ver. 18 he affirms, that the ancient Israelites ("Israel according to the flesh"), who ate of the sacrifices, entered thereby into the fellow-ship of the altar; and from this premiss he deduces the further conclusion in ver. 21, that whoever took part in the sacrificial meals of the heathen as such, became a partaker of the table of demons, just as the Christian, when eating the Lord's Supper, became a partaker of the table of God. No proof surely is needed, that by the "Israel according to the flesh," we are to understand not the Israelitish priests to the exclusion of the people generally, but the nation itself; and consequently, that the eating refers not to the flesh of the sin-offerings, but to that of the peace-offerings. But if such eating brought the eater into the fellowship of the altar, or made him a participant of the table of God, it must have been regarded as eating at the table of God, and GOD must have been the provider of the food. This was also the case at the Lord's Supper, to which the Apostle regards the sacrificial meal as standing in a typical relation. The Christians presented the bread and wine, but they ate and drank of them, after they had been consecrated by the εὐλογία; they partook of them, however, as food given to them by God, through the eating and drinking of which they became partakers "of the table of the Lord."

§ 83. This view of the sacrificial meal, however, gives rise to a very peculiar difficulty. The surrender of the sacrificial animal to the fire of the altar represented, for instance, as we have seen above, and as nearly every other commentator admits, the self-surrender of the person sacrificing. This was most conspicuous in the case of the burnt-offering, when the whole of the body of the animal was consumed. But in the case of the peace-offerings also—when the greater part of the flesh had to be preserved for the sacrificial meal, and only the *flores carnis* therefore, viz., the fat portions, were to be burned as representing and sanctifying the whole— according to the universal laws of symbolism, precisely the same meaning must be attributed to the burning itself and the part to be burned. And if the flesh to be burned represented the person of the sacrificer himself, it seems as though it were hardly possible to ascribe any other meaning to the flesh that was eaten, since they were both parts of one and the same whole. But this would involve the strange conclusion, that in the sacrificial meal the person sacrificing was fed with that which represented himself, that is to say, with himself; a conclusion from which it is hardly possible to obtain any reasonable or tenable meaning. Hence all the commentators (§ 80), with the exception of *Kliefoth* (§ 84), drop the symbolical force of the sacrificial flesh as representing the person of the sacrificer, and either restore its original significance as spiritual food, or introduce a different meaning corresponding to its new destination.

But is not this mere caprice, which is perfectly inadmissible, and under all circumstances to be rejected? Apparently it is; but only in appearance. If we take a clear view of the whole condition of things, we shall see, that even with this dualistic view the unity of the idea is preserved, so that we obtain not two explanations which are mutually exclusive, but only two sides of the very same explanation.

Throughout the whole of the sacrificial ceremony, the flesh of the sacrifice continues to be *nourishment*, food, לֶחֶם. It was food for Jehovah, so far as it was burnt upon the altar; and food for the sacrificer and his household, so far as it was eaten by them at the tabernacle "before Jehovah." Since flesh and bread are the daily food of man, when the immediate object was to present to Jehovah food befitting Him, the food demanded by Him, these two were chosen as a symbolical representation of that food which is spiritual in itself, and therefore could not be actually presented in a form perceptible to the senses. It remained and signified what it always was, viz., nourishment or food; but inasmuch as it was intended to be food for Jehovah, its real character was *eo ipso* necessarily changed into a corresponding symbolical one. And since the remainder of the food, of which Jehovah received a portion as "a sweet savour," was given up to the sacrificer and his family, it received in consequence the character of such food as the person eating required, both from his nature and his position at the time. It thus came once more undoubtedly under the literal aspect of bodily food, but only to assume at once a symbolical character in accordance with the character of the eater as a justified and sanctified sinner, and with the solemnity of the meal, as an act of fellowship with Jehovah, and of participation in that blessedness which such fellowship affords.

The gift presented by the sacrificer was his own property; he put, so to speak, his heart, his feelings and emotions, his whole personality, into the gift. Thus the surrender of his property became a representative self-surrender : the body, the flesh of the sacrificial animal, became the symbolical representation of his own person ; and this was the nourishment which Jehovah demanded, this was the food which was to Him לְנִיחֹחַ, well-pleasing, the source of contentment and satisfaction. And in just the same manner the flesh, which was destined for the food of the sacrificer, and therefore was not given up to the altar-fire, received a symbolical dignity befitting the design and significance of the sacrificial meal.

If a friend presented me with a select portion of the produce of his vintage, his orchard, or his farm, upon which he had bestowed all his time and earnest attention, the gift would represent, in my estimation, his own personal devotedness ; and if I then invited him to my table and entertained him with his own gifts, he would partake of them, not as representing himself, but as my gifts to him, as representing my friendship and affection towards him. Precisely so was it with the sacrificial gift which God had received and accepted from the sacrificer, and with which He then entertained the giver himself. By the fact that he partook of the gift in the house and at the table of the Lord, he partook of it, not as *his own* gift, but as the gift of *God;* partook of it, not as what it *was* before, the representation of his own love and attachment to God, but as what it had become, the representation of the friendship and affection of God towards him.

§ 84. *Kliefoth* (pp. 63 sqq.) offers the most decided opposition to this idea of a transformation of the symbolical import of the sacrificial flesh, from a representation of the devotedness of the sacrificer to Jehovah, into a representation of the devotedness of Jehovah to the sacrificer,—from a feeding of Jehovah with the covenant-performances of Israel, into a feeding of Israel with the saving blessings of the house of God. He still maintains that the flesh must have had the same signification at the meal as in the burning; and he has set up a new interpretation for the former in consequence, viz., that "the sacrificial animal bore vicariously the sin of the person sacrificing, and made atonement for him; and God accepted this substitute, and in it the sacrificer, as an object of good pleasure. But it was also necessary that the person forgiven should be received again into the fellowship of His holy nation. When the sacrifice, therefore, had represented the sinner in the presence of God, to make atonement for him, it had also to represent him in the presence of the holy nation of God, to reconcile him with this as well, and restore him to its communion. . . . God had taken what was ideally the best of the animal, viz., the fat ; but He gave to His people what was humanly the best, viz., the flesh ; for it afforded pleasure to God, and advantage to the people of God, when an atoning sacrifice interposed for the sinner. This gift God bestowed upon the representatives of His holy nation, viz., the priests, and the smaller circle which more immediately surrounded the sacrificer himself, and stood towards him in the stead of the whole community, including, under certain circumstances, the sacrificer himself. These representatives of the holy nation then ate the sacrifice in a social meal. . . . In the sacrifice, the nation received the sinner whom that sacrifice represented, rejoiced in him again, incorporated him once more into its own body, allowed him again to share the benefits of its social life, and, in short, restored him to its fellowship. The consequence of this was, that such a sacrificial meal was a rejoicing before Jehovah (Deut. xxvii. 7) to all who participated in it."

This explanation has really much to commend it. If it were tenable on other grounds, we should regard it as a great recommendation, that it would enable us to look at the eating of the flesh of the sin-offering from precisely the same point of view as the eating of the flesh of the peace-offering. But the fact that the law itself never intended to place them in the same point of view, is shown clearly enough by the fundamentally different, and in many respects opposite treatment, which they received (cf. § 116). In the case of the peace-offerings, moreover, the eating of leavened bread along with them (§ 154) would present a difficulty which it would be very hard to remove. And here, again, we must point to the fact, that the priest did *not* take part in the sacrificial meal at the peace-offerings, but ate the portions which fell to him in his own family circle, whenever and wherever he pleased. And lastly, this explanation involves the incongruity, that the person sacrificing partook of what was the symbol of himself, in other words, was fed with himself. This difficulty did not escape *Kliefoth*, and he has endeavoured to remove it in a really ingenious, but hardly a satisfactory manner. "If a sacrificial meal," he says, "was to take place at all, the officiating priests, at any rate, would certainly partake of it, for it was really they who represented the nation as the holy nation of God. On the other hand, the circle of participants could be enlarged, especially when the notion of fellowship was placed in the foreground by the social meal. The greatest possible extension took place when the sacrificer himself was .added to the circle of participants. . . . And even then the fundamental idea, which we have already expounded, still remained: the person sacrificing received into himself the sacrifice which had made atonement for him. It is true he did not accept it in the same way in which God accepted it, namely, so as to give validity to its atoning virtue; but the sacrifice which God had accepted and reckoned to him as reconciliation, he received again at the hand of God, partook of it, and rejoiced in it, and in the reconciliation which he had obtained therein; whilst in that sacrifice he became himself well-pleasing to God, and, being reconciled in his own conscience, received it, with all that it had procured, as his own flesh and blood, and applied it to the improvement of his own life. In short, he ate the sacrifice along with the other participants, and in partaking of it, the sacrificer was received (by both the others and himself) as an object of good pleasure. And lastly, in thus joining in the meal, the sacrificer completed his own subjective appropriation of the sacrifice."

The leading fundamental mistake in this explanation is, that it confounds the subjective, ideal substitution set forth by the animal as a sacrificial *gift*, in the second stage of the sacrificial process, with the objective, real substitution exhibited in its first stage as a *medium of expiation* (cf. § 75, 76). Moreover, this still leaves the question unanswered, why, if the design of the eating of the sacrifice was primarily and universally restoration to the fellowship of the holy nation, it should have been restricted in the case of the sin-offerings to the smallest circle of participants, viz., to the priests alone (even to the exclusion of their families), and in that of the peace-offerings should have been extended to the largest possible circle. Lastly, according to this view, the admission of the person sacrificing to participate in the meal appears to be nothing more than an extraordinary arrangement made on his behalf, which might very well be dispensed with, and actually was dispensed with in the case of the sin-offering, without prejudice to the idea of the sacrificial meal; whereas in the law he is represented as the principal person in the case of the peace-offerings, and *his* eating is not only the most important point, but is actually indispensable, whilst the participation of the rest is a subordinate and entirely optional arrangement. (See § 116.)

PART II

VARIETIES OF THE BLEEDING SACRIFICE

CHAPTER I

DISTINGUISHING CHARACTERISTICS OF THE BLEEDING SACRIFICES

A. THE SIN-OFFERING, BURNT-OFFERING, AND PEACE-OFFERING

§ 85. The first thing which we select as distinguishing these three kinds of sacrifice, is the *difference in the ritual*. The presentation, imposition of hands, and slaughtering, were the same in all. But in the remaining functions, the *sprinkling of the blood*, the *burning*, and the *sacrificial meal*, we find characteristic differences, inasmuch as each one of these three stands out by itself as a peculiarly emphasized and prominent feature in one of the three kinds of sacrifice. The *sprinkling of the blood* was the culminating point in the *sin-offering*. In the others it evidently fell into the background, the blood being merely poured around upon the altar; but in the sin-offerings it acquired an incomparably greater significance, so indefinite and vague an application of the blood appeared insufficient, and the horns of the altar of burnt-offering, in which the whole worth of the altar culminated (§ 13), were appointed as the object upon which the blood was to be sprinkled. In some cases, indeed, even this appeared insufficient, and the blood was taken into the Holy Place, where it was sprinkled upon the horns of the altar of incense, towards the curtain before the Capporeth, and sometimes even upon the Capporeth itself, in the Most Holy Place.— The *act of burning*, again, was the culminating point in the *burnt-offering*. The gradations in this act were not shown, as in the sprinkling of blood, by an increase in intensity, but by increase in amount. For whilst in other kinds of sacrifice only certain select portions were laid upon the altar, in this the animal was entirely burnt.—Lastly, the *sacrificial meal* was the main point and real characteristic of the *peace-offering*. In the case of the burnt-offering, where everything was burnt, this could not possibly take place; and in that of the sin-offering, not only was it not allowed, but every one except a priest was strictly prohibited from even touching the flesh (Lev. vi. 27).

From this we obtain a by no means unimportant insight into the nature and distinguishing characteristic of the sacrifices. What we have already found to be the import of the sprinkling of the blood was the special object of the *sin-offering*, viz., expiation, justification. All the rest fell into the background beside this sharply defined purpose. In the *burnt-offering* the burning was the culminating point; and if the design of this act was no other than to give expression to the consciousness of the duty of sanctified self-surrender to Jehovah, this was also the chief purpose of this kind of sacrifice; it was the sacrifice of entire, full, unconditional self-surrender. In the *peace-offering* the meal was the principal feature; and if this represented the most intimate fellowship with Jehovah, friendly intercourse, house and table companionship with Him, we must seek in this the end and object of the sacrifice. The same progressive stages, therefore, which distinguish redemption and its symbolical correlate, the complete idea of sacrifice, incorporated themselves as it were in these three *varieties* of sacrifice: the stage of atonement, of *justificatio*, in the sin-offering; that of *sanctificatio*, in the burnt-offering; and that of sacramental fellowship, of the *unio mystica*, in the peace-offering.

The characteristic distinctions thus obtained are confirmed and extended, when we fix our eyes upon the *order of succession* of the different kinds of sacrifice. We should naturally expect, for example, to find the same order observed in the arrangement of the various kinds of sacrifice, as in that of the different sacrificial acts. And this was really the case. Where two of the sacrifices in question, or the whole three, were brought at the same time, the sin-offering always preceded the burnt-offering, and after this came the peace-offering; *e.g.*, Ex. xxix. 14, 18, 28; Lev. v. 8, 10, viii. 14, 18, 22, ix. 15, 16, 18, xii. 6 sqq., xiv. 19 sqq., xvi. 11, 15, 24. It cannot be fairly adduced as an objection, that in the account of the festal sacrifices in Num xxviii. and xxix., the burnt-offerings, which were only a multiplication of the daily burnt-offerings, are mentioned first, and the sin-offering not till afterwards; for there is nothing to compel us to regard this summary statement as describing the order in which the sacrifices were offered. The burnt-offering, as being the most common sacrifice, and one which was proved to be the leading sacrifice by the simple fact that it was multiplied in so significant a manner, especially at the feasts, might very properly be mentioned first (as is evidently the case in Lev. xii. 6, 8, compared with chap. v. 8, 10, xiv. 19 sqq.), without any regulative instructions being added with regard to the order of succession, which was sufficiently established already.

§ 86. Our insight into these sacrifices will be still further deepened and extended, if we notice the characteristic peculiarities connected with the *starting point* of the different kinds of sacrifice, and with the *motive* which prompted them. The first thing which strikes us in this respect is the following. Wherever *sin-offerings* are demanded by the law, we always find special faults or special circumstances mentioned, which lay under the curse of sin (§ 213), and needed to be expiated by sacrifice.[1] In the case of the burnt-offerings and peace-offerings these are entirely wanting. No special reasons are assigned for the *burnt-offering*. It was offered every day, and without any special occasion. It was different with the *peace-offering:* whenever this was required or presented, there was always some special reason assigned or assumed—some manifestation of divine mercy, either to be asked for, or already received. It follows from this, that the burnt-offerings had regard to the religious life in general; the other two, to the religious life in its particular manifestations. The *burnt-offering* was necessarily the expression of such religious feeling as a pious Israelite ought to maintain continuously and without interruption. This is in perfect harmony with what we have already ascertained to be the characteristic of the burnt-offering, namely, that it was intended as a symbolical manifestation and realization of the duty and readiness of the person sacrificing to make a complete and sanctified surrender of himself to Jehovah. The consciousness of this obligation would naturally be the deepest and most constant feeling in the mind of a truly pious Israelite. The idea of expiation might fall into the background by the side of it; but even this could not be altogether wanting, since all self-surrender rests upon justification. But the expiation was of a more general character, just as the sin to which it had regard was sin in general, and not any particular sin that could be mentioned by name. The expiation of the burnt-offering corresponded to the general consciousness of sin and unworthiness, as first produced by the demand for a perfectly sanctified self-surrender.—In the case of

[1] On the apparent exception in the case of the sin-offerings presented at the feasts, cf. § 105.

the *peace-offering* also, no particular sins are mentioned ; but here, again, the general consciousness of unworthiness, excited by the contrast to the blessings bestowed by God, came into prominence, and demanded the same general atonement which was also associated with the burnt-offering. The *sin-offerings*, on the other hand, had to do, not with sin in general, not with such sinfulness and infirmity as even the most pious were not free from, but with certain manifestations and effects of sin, which are mentioned distinctly by name. The allusion in this case was to sin that had grown into action, that had assumed a visible form ; to sin intensified, therefore, which necessarily demanded an intensified atonement. An actual separation from Jehovah had taken place, a positive breach of the state of grace had been committed ; consequently, the primary and pre-eminent object of the sacrifice was to reconstitute this state of salvation and of grace. In the case of the burnt-offerings and peace-offerings, the general sinfulness to be expiated was undoubtedly also something ungodly and displeasing to God, and therefore something which required to be removed or atoned for ; but it was merely a habitual distance, not an active departure from Jehovah : the sacrificer was still standing upon the foundation of salvation, upon which he desired to establish and fortify himself. This may serve to explain the fact, that the sin-offerings were always followed by a burnt-offering. The object of the former was to effect a restoration into a state of grace ; that of the latter, to secure the positive exercise of the duties and privileges thereby obtained. It also explains the fact, that it was only with burnt-offerings and peace-offerings that meat-offerings were associated—never with sin- (and trespass-) offerings. In connection with the former, the sacrificer always stood upon the ground of salvation. But this position needed to be attested by fruits of sanctification ; hence the addition of the meat-offerings. In connection with the latter, he had fallen from a state of grace. Their simple object was to reunite the broken bond, so that there could as yet be no allusion to fruits of sanctification.

§ 87. There is one point of peculiar importance which we must not pass over here, namely, the *relation between the sacrificial wor ship of the Mosaic, and that of the pre-Mosaic times.* And the first thing which strikes us is, that previous to the time of Moses we only read of *burnt-offerings* and *peace-offerings*, never of *sin- (and trespass-) offerings*. It is true that both of these have recently been disputed, and that in the most opposite ways. Whilst *Bähr* (ii. 363) denies that there ever were peace-offerings in the pre-Mosaic times, and recognises none but burnt-offerings as existing then, *v. Hofmann* maintains that, in addition to burnt-offerings *and* peace-offerings, sin- (or trespass-) offerings were just as common *even then* as in the Mosaic age, "only it was reserved for the Mosaic law to define more sharply the distinction between them" (p. 225).

It is easy enough to prove that there is no ground for *Bähr's* assertion. Even Abel's offering (Gen. iv. 4) must be regarded as the first step towards the development of the *slain- or peace-offerings* (for in the Pentateuch the two names denote one and the same thing; § 125). But we find them perfectly developed in distinction from the burnt-offerings in Ex. x. 25, when Pharaoh offers to allow the Israelites to go for a short time into the wilderness to serve Jehovah their God, *i.e.*, to offer sacrifice (chap. viii. 23), and Moses insists upon their being allowed to take all their cattle with them, for the purpose of presenting *slain-offerings* ("sacrifices," *Eng. V.*) *and burnt-offerings*. And the fact that, according to Ex. xviii. 12, Jethro, on meeting with Moses (before the giving of the law), offered *burnt-offerings and slain-offerings*, is a proof that the distinction between these two kinds of sacrifice was common to the Terahite family generally, and hence that its origin may be traced back to a time when that family was still undivided.

On the other hand, there is just as little foundation for *Hofmann's* assertion, that not only burnt-offerings and peace-offerings were known in the pre-Mosaic times, but sin- (or trespass-) offerings also. "No other argument can be adduced," he says at p. 225, "in favour of the opposite view, than that sin-offerings are never mentioned before the time of Moses ; an argument which causes all the less difficulty, since even Abel's offering was not a thank-offering as distinguished from a burnt-offering, nor Noah's a burnt-offering as distinguished from a thank-offering; and that in the account of the restoration of fellowship between Jehovah and Israel (Ex. xxiv. 5), burnt-offerings and thank-offerings only are mentioned." We readily admit that, in the time of Abel's and Noah's sacrifices, the distinction between burnt-offerings and peace-offerings had not yet been fully brought out. But it is indisputably evident from Ex. x. 25 and xviii. 12, that this had been done in the time of Moses and Jethro, and before the giving of the law. And when *Hofmann* proceeds, at p. 267, to explain the limitation of the sacrificial worship described in Ex. xxiv. 5, which also occurred before the giving of the law, to burnt-offerings and peace-offerings, excluding both sin- and trespass-offerings, on the ground "that the latter did not refer, like the former, to the general relation of sinful man to God, which was the only point contemplated when a new relation was established between man and God, to which sinfulness was to be no impediment," the worthlessness of this loophole is soon apparent. For if, when a general relation of fellowship was restored between God and Israel, it was only necessary to have in view the general sinfulness of humanity, and not special or individual sins, we cannot see why, when a particular relation of fellowship was restored between God and the family of Aaron (Lev. viii. 2 sqq.), or between God and the Levites (Num. viii. 8), and at the yearly renewal of the relation of fellowship between God and Israel at the feasts, it should have been necessary to keep in view anything more than the general sinfulness of man.   The fact is rather, that the omission of sin-offerings from the covenant-consecration of the people can only be explained on the supposition that, previous to the giving of the law of sacrifice, sin-offerings were as yet unknown (cf. § 163).

"But," observes *Hofmann* at p. 225, " are we to suppose that before this time sin never gave occasion for sacrifice? Is it not related of Abraham, that all over Canaan, wherever he settled for any lengthened period, he erected an altar for the purpose of regular and social worship? And is it not most likely that every separate expression of piety had its own sacrifice, and its distinctive characteristic found its fitting expression in some peculiarity in the sacrifice itself? The Mosaic law does not introduce the sin- and trespass-offerings in any special manner; but whenever they are referred to, it presupposes that, like the burnt-offerings and thank-offerings, they are already known."—Again mere arguments, of which one is as weak and worthless as the other. For with the very same arguments we might prove that the whole of the Mosaic ritual was known and carried out by Abraham, and that at the most it was reserved for the Mosaic law "to give it a sharper outline." And when *Hofmann* says, "It is impossible to see why sin-offerings should first have been introduced with the law of Moses, and in connection with breaches of its commandments; or how it could ever have been omitted when once sacrificial service had been established;" *Keil* has given a sufficient reply.   "As if," he says, "there had not been an atoning element in the burnt-offering as well."

Sin-offerings and trespass-offerings, as distinguished from burnt-offerings and peace-offerings, are undoubtedly to be regarded as a specifically Mosaic institution; and this is the only way of explaining their not being mentioned in the pre-Mosaic times, and their being altogether unknown in heathen lands both before and after the time of Moses. They were peculiarly theocratic in their character, and were connected with sins, to which the law first gave a distinctive character that specially demanded them. The fundamental law of Israel, so far as religion was concerned, was, " Be ye holy, for I am holy, saith Jehovah." This holiness, which was demanded by the law, and was the condition of theocratic fellowship, consisted in separation *from* the world *to* Jehovah, in being different from the heathen. Every transgression of the law, as the standard of that holiness, removed the Israelite from the sphere of the covenant with Jehovah into the sphere of heathenism ; he acted just as if there was really no theocratic law for him ; in other words, he acted like a heathen, placed himself on a par with the heathen, conducted himself as if he had not been dedicated to Jehovah—was not Jehovah's property and mancipium, but was a law to himself, and left to himself, just as the heathen were. Now, so far as these sins still admitted of expiation (§ 89 sqq.), being sins which received a peculiarly theocratic character from the theocratic position of the person committing them,[1] they necessarily required to be expiated by these peculiarly theocratic sacrifices. And this is in perfect harmony with what we have already discovered to be the distinctive characteristic of the sin-offering, viz., the heightening of the expiation, before which all the other features of this kind of sacrifice fell into the background. The importance and responsibility of sin, and its just exposure to curse and death, were heightened by the law. " Where no law is," says the Apostle (Rom. iv. 15), " there is no transgression ;" and (Rom. v. 13), " sin is not imputed where there is no law." The pre-Mosaic sacrifices answered to a consciousness of sin on the standpoint of " the law written in the hearts," and the Mosaic, to that produced by the " law of commandments contained in ordinances ;" and so far as particular sins belonging to this standpoint were concerned, the sin-offerings related specially to them. The former standpoint was the lower and more undeveloped of the two, and therefore the

---

[1] It might indeed be argued in opposition to this assertion, that not the Israelites only, but the גֵּרִים also were entitled and required to offer sin-offerings (Num. xv. 29). But there is no force in the objection. For inasmuch as they were equally bound down by a number of peculiarly theocratic laws (cf. § 2), it was really necessary that, so far as the transgression of those laws admitted of expiation at all, they should also be allowed to offer sin-offerings as an atonement for them.

institution of sacrifice connected with it was also more undeveloped, and the expiation especially more general and undefined. The latter was the more defined, more developed and higher of the two; and the whole of the institution of sacrifice, therefore, was more developed, and its individual features were expanded into independent, self-subsistent sacrifices, every one of which served as the representative of some one particular feature.

§ 88. In every one of the four varieties of sacrifice, account was taken of the need of expiation, and the necessity for sanctification of life. Both together constituted the essential nature and purpose of the sacrificial worship, and could not be omitted from any act of sacrifice, whose nature allowed of a manifestation of the two; though the emphasis might be differently laid according to circumstances,—the one being placed in the foreground in one case, and the other in another, or both being placed in the background, as in the case of the peace-offerings, and merely serving as a foil to the idea to be set forth in the sacrificial meal.

With this subdivision of the idea of sacrifice into sacrifices of various kinds, it inevitably happened, that when two or three of these were offered together, as was frequently the case, there was a repetition or crowding together of individual features. Thus, for example, when sin-offerings, burnt-offerings, and peace-offerings were presented at the same time, there was a triple reiteration of the ideas of expiation and self-surrender. The question might be asked, therefore, whether it would not have been more appropriate, either to combine the three in some one description of sacrifice in as complete a way as the sacrificial idea required, or else to limit every kind of sacrifice to that one feature, the necessity for which was peculiarly prominent at the time. But for many reasons, both internal and external, the latter would have been unadvisable and impracticable. And the former would have been both unnecessary and impossible;—impossible, because, for example, no sacrificial meal could have been held in cases where it was requisite that the whole should be burned; and unnecessary, because it was not desirable that an equally distinct and strong expression should be given to all three ideas in connection with every sacrifice. There was no other course open, therefore, than to arrange the sacrificial worship upon the plan which has actually been adopted in the law. This is done, not by a mechanical division, but by the same living individualization which we meet with on every hand through the spheres of both physical and spiritual life. Just as the separation of the human race, for example, into individuals, characters, temperaments, nationalities, is not effected by any mechanical division, so that one individual receives only one portion of what belongs to the idea of humanity, and another individual another portion; but by one in which every individual receives all that belongs to the idea of humanity, since without this he would cease to be a man, whilst the different elements vary in potency, something being prominent in this man which falls into the background in that, or a peculiar susceptibility for the development of *some one* organ or talent being apparent in this man, and of *some other* organ or talent in that;—so was it with the subdivision of the one sacrificial idea into sacrifices of various kinds. All that is essentially and indispensably necessary to the idea of sacrifice is found in every one, but in different degrees of potency.

The repetition of particular features, which was undoubtedly inevitable in consequence, but to which there are many analogies in other parts of the ritual, was so far from introducing any disturbance into the idea of sacrificial worship, that it rather served to bring to mind a thought essentially inherent in it; viz., the truth, that none of them could at once and for ever meet all demands, but that they all needed to be continually revivified or entirely renewed.

B. THE COMMON BASIS OF THE SIN-OFFERING AND TRESPASS-OFFERING

§ 89. The presentation of a trespass-offering, like that of a sin-offering, was always occasioned by special acts of sin, or at all events by special circumstances which were regarded as sin. The latter we shall consider more fully by and by (§ 213 sqq.). Our present task is to determine what special and actual transgressions were generally regarded as admitting and requiring sacrificial expiation, either by means of sin-offerings or trespass-offerings; after which we shall proceed to inquire which of them were expiated by sin-offerings, and which by trespass-offerings.

The sins which, as a general rule, admitted of sacrificial expiation, are represented in Lev. iv. 2, 22, 27 (where sin-offerings are referred to), and in Lev. v. 15 (which treats of trespass-offerings), as being those which were committed בִּשְׁנָנָה, *i.e.*, by mistake (*Ang.*, "in ignorance"). What is meant is evident enough, when we observe that in Lev. v. 17 וְלֹא יָדַע ("and knew it not") is substi-

tuted for בִּשְׁגָגָה (compare בִּלְתִּי דַעַת in Deut. iv. 42 and Num. xxxv.
11), and נֶעְלַם מִמֶּנּוּ ("hidden from him") in Lev. iv. 13, v. 2, 3, 4,
and that in Lev. iv. 14, 23, 28, the discovery of a sin that had been
previously unknown is given as an occasion and motive for offering
the proper sacrifice for the sin in question. From all these passages
it is perfectly obvious that the sins primarily regarded as admitting
of sacrificial expiation were such as had been committed unconsciously, unintentionally, or from haste, and therefore could not be
visited with judicial punishment. For this reason, in my *Mos.
Opfer*, p. 156, I followed *Bähr* ii. 388, in regarding such sins *alone*
as admitting of expiation, and all intentional and presumptuous sins
as excluded from it. I find the same view still advocated by some
of the latest commentators, *e.g.*, *Hävernick* (p. 192), *Welte* (p. 177),
and *Knobel* (p. 343). All the rest pronounce such a limitation too
narrow,[1] and include sins of *infirmity* among those that admitted
of expiation; whilst *Hofmann* (p. 251), *Keil* (1, 219), and *Delitzsch*
(p. 174), are unwilling to exclude even sins of infirmity committed
consciously and intentionally, or, as *Keil* expresses it, "those which
were committed with forethought and deliberate intention, or from
weakness of the spirit in its conflict against the flesh." But I must
still pronounce the idea of "sins of weakness" as one which it is
at variance with the Scriptures, and quite impracticable, to introduce,
for the purpose of determining the limits of the possibility of atonement. For the idea itself is so variable, elastic, and vague, that it
might be applied to almost *every* sin, especially if we include such
as have been committed "with forethought and design," and is perfectly useless, at all events, for legal purposes. Moreover, the word
בִּשְׁגָגָה precludes this explanation; for he who *errs*, *i.e.*, misses the
right way, does so, *not* from weakness, *i.e.*, because he has not
strength to keep in the well-known way, but because he either does
not know the way, or has missed it through inattention. Who, for

---

[1] Whether *Hengstenberg*, indeed, should be included in this number, is doubtful, on account of the self-contradiction into which he falls. On the one hand,
for example, he explains בִּשְׁגָגָה as meaning "sins of infirmity," and maintains
that "*Kurtz* is wrong in substituting unintentional, unconscious sins, for sins of
weakness" (pp. 17, 18). Yet, on the other hand, in the very same breath, he himself defines sins of infirmity as unintentional or unconscious; and says, "It was
for sins of infirmity that the Psalmist asked forgiveness when he exclaimed, 'Who
can understand his errors? Cleanse Thou me from secret faults,'—appealing to
the desperate *finesse* of sin, which understands in so masterly a way to render
itself invisible, to disguise itself, to assume the appearance of good, and which
we cannot escape, on account of this *finesse*, even with the most laudable zeal."

example, could refuse to class adultery among sins of infirmity, especially when it is not a premeditated act, deliberately planned, but simply the result of a temptation that was *not* sought, and a suddenly excited passion ?[1] And yet the law commanded that even such an adulterer should (not offer an atoning sacrifice, but) be stoned.[2]

§ 90. Nevertheless, I willingly admit that the category of unconscious and unintentional sins is not co-extensive with that of the sins that allowed of expiation; only the extension of the former to many sins committed knowingly and intentionally, which is unquestionably necessary, must not be deduced from the word בשגגה, for this merely denotes a sin committed through mistake, and is authoritatively interpreted by the law as meaning unconsciously or unintentionally. The following is rather the fact:—In those sections of the law of sacrifice, which point out, in a fundamental and general way, what sins may be and are to be expiated by sin-offerings (Lev. iv. 1–35), and what by trespass-offerings (Lev. v. 14–19), they are all characterized through such terms as בִּשְׁגָגָה, לֹא יָדַע, and so forth, as committed unconsciously and unintentionally. That was the rule therefore. But here also the maxim applied, that there is no rule without an exception. There were sins, for example, which could not be called unconscious or unintentional, but which were evidently so modified by other circumstances as likewise to admit of expiation by sacrifice. A few of such sins are mentioned in the law of sacrifice itself, in those sections where the sins, for which sin-offerings or trespass-offerings might be presented, are specially enumerated[3] (Lev. v. 1–13, and vi. 1–7);—for example, in chap. vi. 2, 3, the keeping back of something stolen, entrusted, lent, or found, accompanied by a denial on oath of its possession. These are all sins

---

[1] I do not expect any protest against this suggestion, at all events from *Hengstenberg;* for, in his opinion, even David's adultery was "chiefly a sin of infirmity" (p. 18), which I cannot dispute. But I certainly do dispute the assertion, that that was the reason why, according to the law, this sin of David's was not included among those that were to be punished with death, but those that were to be expiated by sacrifice. Undoubtedly, the sentence of death was not executed on David. The reason for this, however, was, not because the sin itself did not require it according to the law, but because there was no one in all Israel who was qualified to inflict the punishment prescribed in the law upon the anointed of the Lord, and the punishment therefore was necessarily left to the immediate judgment of God.

[2] The case recorded in Lev. xix. 20–22 is no proof against the validity of this rule.

[3] The connection between Lev. iv. and v., which is here assumed, we shall examine and justify below (§ 98, 99, 103).

which could not possibly be placed in the category of unconscious and unintentional sins. But there might be circumstances connected with them which mitigated the guilt, and rendered the sacrificial expiation admissible : for example, if the guilty person, as is expressly mentioned in chap. vi. 5, spontaneously acknowledged the crime which he had denied at first, and even denied on oath, and which could not be punished by the judicial authorities because it could not be proved, and if he voluntarily restored what had been taken fraudulently, together with the addition of a fifth of its worth. The case described in Lev. v. 1 also belongs to the same category, as the הִתְוַדָּה (" he shall confess") in ver. 5 clearly proves, viz., that of a person who was able to give evidence in connection with any matter that was the subject of judicial inquiry, and yet, after hearing the adjuration to all who knew anything about it, either from fear or a wish to please, neglected to do so.

In addition to these, there were no doubt included in the same class all sins that were not actually capital crimes, and for which, after they had been *civilly* expiated by the infliction of the punishment prescribed in the law, *religious* expiation was still demanded. It is true that there is only one case of this kind, in which the admissibility of and necessity for a sacrificial atonement is expressly mentioned (viz., Lev. xix. 20–22, cf. § 100); but this is quite sufficient to show the principle upon which it was founded, and to give it validity in all other cases of a similar kind. In the former case, it was by a voluntary, penitent confession, accompanied by a voluntary restoration, with compensation, in the latter, by the endurance of the civil punishment which the crime deserved, that the way was opened for a sacrificial atonement, and the intentional sins in question placed upon the same level in this respect with those that were unintentional.

Such sins, indeed, as the law visited with the punishment of death could not be atoned for by sacrifice, however sincere might be the sorrow, and however earnest the repentance : and that not because a person executed is no longer able to offer a sacrifice for himself; for sacrificial expiation, like absolution in the Christian Church, might have preceded execution. The reason was rather a purely internal one, based upon the peculiarity or imperfection of the Old Testament standpoint. Under the O. T. there was still wanting that clear insight into eternal life which has been opened to us by the New Testament revelation, and consequently the prerequisite which is essentially necessary to any combination of religious absolution from sin with the infliction of the capital punishment which the sin deserved, and which is requisite for the maintenance of the social, civil, and moral government of the world. In addition to this, there was the O. T. identification of State and Church, of the national community and the religious community, in consequence of which, absolute exclusion from the former (which execution involved) necessarily involved absolute exclusion from the latter also ; and *vice versa*, the restoration of the interrupted fellowship of religion and worship (which was effected by sacrificial atonement) necessarily involved *eo ipso* the restoration of social and national fellowship ; so that in capital crimes, and all such cases where the latter was inadmissible, the former was *eo ipso* the same.

§ 91. All sins were divisible into two classes, therefore,—those that admitted of expiation, and those that did not. Capital crimes were the only ones that were absolutely excluded. The *sins that admitted of expiation*, again, might be subdivided into those which from their nature could be expiated at once by sacrifice—viz., such as had been committed בִּשְׁגָגָה or בְּלֹא דַעַת, *i.e.*, without knowledge and will, without intention and forethought—and those which, although committed consciously and with forethought, and therefore in themselves not admitting of expiation, had yet been rendered expiable by other intervening circumstances. Among the latter were (1) sins which could not be proved, and therefore escaped judicial punishment, but of which a perfectly free, spontaneous confession had been made, dictated by penitence and a desire for atonement, and accompanied by a voluntary and superabundant reparation of the injury inflicted, so far as such reparation was possible ; and (2) sins which could be legally proved, and therefore were liable to punishment, but which had been legally atoned for by the endurance of the merited punishment. Of the former we have an example given in Lev. vi. 3 ; of the latter, in Lev. xix. 20–22.

But this really fourfold division, which we obtain from Leviticus, does not seem to harmonize very well with Num. xv. 27–31. It is stated there, for example, that for a sin committed " in ignorance " (בִּשְׁגָגָה) forgiveness might be obtained through the presentation of a sin-offering ; but that no expiation or forgiveness could be found for a sin committed " with a high hand " (בְּיָד רָמָה), because Jehovah was reproached thereby, His word despised, and His commandment brought to nought. On the contrary, he who committed such a sin was to be utterly cut off from the nation. The meaning of

בְּיָד רָמָה cannot be doubtful. It signifies "with hand raised," *i.e.*, with conscious rebellion against the will and commandment of God. The expression is not so clearly and sharply defined, indeed, that no difficulty could ever occur in deciding whether a particular sin belonged to this category or not. One might suppose, for example, that it would necessarily include a gross, premeditated robbery, as being a presumptuous rebellion against the seventh commandment; and yet, as Ex. xxi. 37 (xxii. 1) sqq. clearly proves, such a supposition would be just as erroneous, as the counter idea that adultery, even when caused by the strong temptation of sudden excitement, ought not to be included. But the ambiguity connected with the expression בְּיָד רָמָה is removed by the command, that any one who had so sinned should be cut off from the midst of the nation. From this it is perfectly obvious that a sin committed "with a high hand" was one which the law regarded as a capital offence, and consequently punished by death. The man who gathered sticks on the Sabbath (Num. xv. 32 sqq.), probably under the impulse of actual need, and the man who committed adultery in a moment of strong temptation, both of them sinned "with a high hand," and were to be put to death, though the one might plead his poverty, and the other the weakness of the flesh, in extenuation of his offence. The sanctity of the Sabbath, and the sanctity of marriage, were both of them fundamental laws of the theocratical commonwealth, the essential foundations of whose existence would be threatened and shaken if its laws were not observed; consequently any violation of them was a crime deserving of death—a transgression committed ביד רמה, "with a high hand."

A similar want of precision, to that which we find in ביד רמה, in ver. 30, is also inherent in the expression בשגגה, in ver. 27. According to its etymological signification, which corresponds entirely to the usage of the sacrificial law, the word denotes the unconscious or unintentional character of the sin in question (like וְלֹא יָדַע or בִּלְתִּי דַעַת); here, however, as the antithesis shows, it also includes such intentional sins as were liable to civil punishment, though not deserving of death, but which had been brought to the level of sins committed בשגגה, so far as the requirements of the sacrificial worship were concerned, by the endurance of the proper judicial punishment, and which might, by a more general use of the term, be even included among them.

§ 92. *Bähr* is not satisfied, however, with our admission, that the absolute exclusion of all intentional sins from sacrificial expi-

ation is untenable. He would rather extend the law of exclusion
to all breaches of the moral law, all moral transgressions in the
strict sense of the term, and so limit expiation to theocratical sins
alone, that is to say, to transgressions against the positively religious
law, the law of worship given to the people of Israel. I do not
think it worth while to refute this obviously erroneous assertion
with the same minuteness as in my former work, and shall content
myself with repeating the leading points in that refutation.

First of all, then, the distinction and contrast between positively religious (ceremonial) laws, and general, moral laws, upon
which his conclusion is based, is one that had no existence whatever to the Israelites. Moreover, it is evident that the כָּל־מִצְוֹת יְהוָֹה
(all the commandments of Jehovah), for the breach of which sin-
offerings were to be offered according to Lev. iv. 2, and trespass-
offerings according to Lev. v. 17, included the general moral laws,
and that the words of Num. xv. 27, 28, do not permit an exclusion
of moral transgressions generally, any more than these passages do ;
and also that the sins which required a trespass-offering, according
to Lev. vi. 1 sqq. and Lev. xix. 20 sqq. (e.g., theft, retention of
another's property with a denial of its possession, unchastity with
the bondmaid of another), did not belong to the category of positively religious transgressions, but of moral transgressions generally.

Lastly, we may also mention the characteristic circumstance,
that a *sin-offering* (and also a trespass-offering) always consisted of
one animal only ; there were *never* several animals slaughtered for
one and the same object, as was the case with the burnt-offerings
and peace-offerings, especially on the feast days (Num. xxviii. and
xxix.). So far as I know, *Hengstenberg* and *Ewald* are alone in
attempting any explanation of .this. " Hence it is evident," says
the former (p. 24), " that in the sin-offerings the objective feature
was of supreme importance, and that they were regarded chiefly as
the means of expiation established by God. With sacrifices of a pre-
eminently internal character, it was left to the worshipper to offer
as many animals as he pleased. There were no limits set to the
promptings of his own mind." In the sin-offering all the emphasis
and all the significance were concentrated upon the *act of expiation ;*
and this was an act of mercy on the part of God, in which everything depended upon the grace of God, and not upon the act of
man. In the burnt-offerings and peace-offerings, on the contrary,
the act of expiation was kept in the background ; and the idea of
presenting the *gift*, which was an act of man, came into prominence,

and was really the main point, the germ, and the goal in all sacrifices of this description. Hence in their case an expansion, a heaping up of the gifts, was admissible. *Ewald's* explanation, on the other hand, is perfectly forced and phantastical. " The number of the animals," he says (p. 67), " could not be increased, as in the case of the thank-offerings and whole offerings, at the will of the person sacrificing, as if he could thereby obtain greater favour from God : this one animal, indeed, he was required to bring, and that quite alone, as in solemn solitude and desolation, and as though there were no other resembling it, with which it could be associated or compared. But for that very reason, this gloomy severity might be relaxed in certain (?) instances, when the law allowed, or even prescribed, a whole offering in addition."

C. THE DIFFERENCE BETWEEN SIN-OFFERINGS AND TRESPASS-OFFERINGS

§ 93. All that we have hitherto ascertained, with regard to the fitness or unfitness of particular sins for expiation, is quite as applicable to trespass-offerings as to sin-offerings. But the question is more important and more difficult : *In what did the sins, for which a trespass-offering was adapted, differ from those which required a sin-offering ?*

There is scarcely a single question connected with the whole range of biblical theology on which there has been so much pure conjecture, and about the settlement of which theological science was so late in arriving at a correct conclusion, although the foundations for it evidently existed in the biblical text, and were not very difficult to find. Most of the opinions expressed need no refutation. For example, that of *Clericus* (on Lev. v. 16), who maintains that the difference is in the words only, and not in the thing itself ; or that of *Carpzov* (*App. crit. Antiqu.* p. 707), who contents himself with saying, " *omne istud differentiæ genus ex sapientissimo legislatoris arbitrio pendere ;* " or that of *Saubert* (de sacrif. vet.), who understands by אָשָׁם an intentional and malicious sin, and by חַטָּאת an unconscious one ; or that of *Michaelis*, who refers the former to sins of omission, the latter to sins of commission, in which he is just as arbitrary as *Grotius*, who does the very opposite. We may put *Abenezra* in the same class, when he refers the sin-offering to sins in which ignorance of the law could be pleaded, and the trespass-offering to those in which the law was

forgotten; and *Abarbanel* also, with other Rabbins, who maintain
that trespass-offerings were presented when the transgression was
doubtful, and sin-offerings when this was not the case. *Philo's*
opinion is quite as wide of the mark, viz., that the trespass-offering
was intended for cases, in which the sinner was impelled by his own
conscience to accuse himself of the sin. The same opinion, essentially at least, has been advocated by *Josephus,* and among modern
theologians by *Venema, Reland,* and others; and last of all by
Winer, who maintains (ii. 432), that "whoever brought a trespass-
offering was convicted by *his own conscience;* but he who brought
a sin-offering was convicted of a definite, but yet unconscious sin."
Bähr (ii. 412) is also of opinion, that this view comes the nearest to
the truth; though he admits that it by no means removes all the
difficulties, and that he does not see how they are to be removed.
Gesenius says that nothing more can be determined than that the
sin-offerings were presented in *gravioribus maxime delictis,* and the
trespass-offerings *in levioribus locum habuisse.* *Hengstenberg's* view
is by no means satisfactory (*Beitr. zur. Einl. ins alte Test.* iii. 214
sqq.; *Opfer,* p. 21). It amounts to the following: Every sin, even
when committed against a neighbour, was a robbery of God, and
as such demanded reparation. But the sacrifice could not satisfy
this demand. For the quieting, however, of anxious consciences,
and the stirring up of sleepy ones, the trespass- (or compensation-)
offering was introduced (according to Num. v. 5, 6, אשם literally
means compensation). "The sin was appraised, and in the sacrifice, to which the same value was ideally attributed, a restitution or
compensation was made for the robbery of God, which was connected with every sin. And as the principal object was to represent the idea that sin is a robbery of God, and to establish that
idea in the Church, the trespass- or restitution-offering was expressly instituted for a limited number of cases only." In opposition to this, we must repeat that אשם does not signify compensation
at all; that by this view the atoning force of the sin-offering is
destroyed; that if it were correct, every sin would have required
a trespass-offering; and that in that case the trespass-offering would
have been more important than the sin-offering, whereas, as the
ritual clearly proves, the opposite was really the case. *Ewald's*
view is still more decidedly false. "A simple sin-offering was
sufficient," he says; "and no further special act of penance could
intervene, either when the transgression of a single individual was
first of all observed by others, and then pointed out to him, or

when the transgression proceeded from the whole congregation, so
that no one felt himself to be more guilty than another; whereas,
on the other hand, if anything improper or unholy lay at the door
of an individual, of which he alone was conscious at first, or which
he felt at first as pressing upon him alone, without there being any
necessity for others to call upon him to offer an atonement for it,
the atonement could not remain so simple an act, but his atoning
sacrifice had to be increased in a peculiar manner into a trespass-
or penitençe-offering; and very frequently even this was not sufficient without compensation for an injury that might possibly have
been deliberately inflicted."

§ 94. Even the view which I have worked out in my *Mosaisches
Opfer* (pp. 197 sqq.) did not suffice, though *Oehler* (p. 642) thinks
he "must admit, that even if it did not quite hit the mark, it prepared the way for the correct view, which has been brought out
chiefly by the investigations of Rinck and Riehm." Their leading
thoughts are the following: (1.) Every sin is also a debt. As dis-
obedience against the commandment of God, it is sin; but as demanding compensation and restoration, it is a debt. (2.) At the
same time, there were many sins to which the term debt was pre-eminently applied, viz., those in which the idea of debt was specially prominent; and from that the offering connected with them received its
name (debt-offering). (3.) But the name אָשָׁם relates not only to
the *ethical* character of sin, as an injury done to the holy God and
a violation of His rights and claims, but also to its earthly, social
character, inasmuch as earthly, divinely instituted relations and
rights are thereby disturbed and injured. On both accounts compensation and restoration are requisite. Compensation, indeed, for
injury done to God, a sinner is never in himself able to render;
but compensation for the earthly injury, inflicted by his sin, is
often possible, and in such cases it was obliged to be rendered.
(4.) Compensation for the injury done to God was therefore made
by the sacrificial blood, which was placed by the sinner upon the
altar, and covered his sin before Jehovah; and compensation for the
earthly injury by a material reparation of the wrong that had been
done. The two kinds of compensation were most closely related to
each other; and for that reason the term אָשָׁם was applied not only
to the sacrificial animal, but to the material reparation also (Num.
v. 8; 1 Sam. vi. 4, 8). (5.) Sin-offerings were to be presented for
sins, whose earthly *asham* could *not* be paid by the sinner, any more
than the super-terrestrial (or ethical) one. Trespass- (debt-) offerings,

on the other hand, for sins whose earthly *asham* could be paid; so that, in this case, along with the ethical *asham*, for which the sacrificial expiation intervened, the earthly *asham* had really to be paid as well.

There is, for the most part, but little force in the objections made to this view by *Riehm*, *Rinck*, and *Keil*. At the same time, it would be useless to enter into any proof of this; since I no longer regard it as fully meeting every case, in which trespass-offerings were required and presented without any payment of the earthly *asham* being possible (§ 100, 101), and am ready to adopt, with a few slight modifications, the more correct explanation which *Riehm* has given. In his opinion, sin-offerings were presented for breaches of the covenant ordinances and commands, trespass-offerings for violation of the covenant rights; or, as he has since more correctly expressed himself,—in consequence of *Rinck's* objection, that the contrast between covenant rights and covenant commandments cannot be sustained, for the simple reason that the former were protected by the latter, and the violation of the one, therefore, was also a transgression of the other,—" Trespass-offerings were presented for such breaches of the covenant commands as were also violations of covenant rights, and sin-offerings for those transgressions of covenant commands to which the latter did not apply."

The only point that I should object to as untenable in this definition, is the emphasis laid upon the violated rights and commands, as *covenant* rights, and *covenant* commands. For although *Riehm* does not restrict these terms to specifically theocratical relations, but places them upon a more general moral basis, by including the legal relation in which individual Israelites stood to one another as members of the covenant, a limitation is still involved which is irreconcilable with the fact that, according to Num. xv. 29, the foreigners dwelling in the Holy Land, who were certainly not members of the covenant, could also present sin-offerings. Even *Oehler*, who defends *Riehm's* view, has silently removed this limitation; and *Knobel* (p. 397), who agrees with all the rest, pronounces the reference to the theocratical covenant incorrect, though the reasons which he has assigned are untenable. For his allusion to the offering of an אָשָׁם on the part of the Philistines for their detention of the ark which they had carried off (1 Sam. vi. 3), is out of place, since the Philistines did not offer an ethical, but a material אָשָׁם, *i.e.*, not a trespass-*offering*, but simply golden presents as a compensation; and the observation, that the graduations of both the atoning act and the atoning material, which existed in the case of the sin-offering, were wanting in that of the trespass-offering, proves too much, as Num. xv. 19 evidently shows, and therefore proves nothing.

§ 95. One objection offered to *Riehm's* definition by *Rinck*, and after him by *Keil*,—viz., that in the trespass-offering of a leper who was cured (Lev. xiv. 12 sqq.), and also in that of a Nazarite who had defiled himself (Num. vi. 12), there was no question of any violation of the rights of others,—is just as groundless, as their own explanation of this sin-offering, that it was a service rendered or payment made for reinstatement in the possession of the lost covenant rights, or the former state of consecration, is inadmissible (§ 101). Moreover, *Rinck* (p. 371) declares it to be incorrect to classify the sacrifices objectively, according to the differences in the sins, instead of subjectively, according to the kind of expiation; consequently, he finds the chief point and distinctive feature of the trespass-offering, not in the sin which required it as a violation of right, but in the *satisfaction* to be rendered *through* the sacrifice or in connection with it, and regards the following as the difference between the two, that " the trespass-offering bore the same relation to the sin-offering as *satisfactio* to *expiatio*." Appealing to the law of the trespass-offering in Lev. v. 17, which is couched in just the same terms as the directions for the offering of a sin-offering in Lev. iv. 27, he thinks that, as every sin, even where positive covenant rights were not concerned, was to a certain extent a violation of the rights of God; a trespass-offering (like a sin-offering) might be presented for every sin, according as the necessity for satisfaction or for reconciliation predominated. " In the trespass-offering the troubled soul brought a compensation for the injury according to the valuation of the priest; in the sin-offering, by the laying on of the hand it put itself on a level with the sacrificial animal, and received reconciliation through the priestly sprinkling of the blood."

Rinck very properly brings out the idea of *satisfaction*, *i.e.*, of compensation for the injury caused by the sin, as an essential feature in the trespass-offering; but the false application which he gives to this idea is evident from his statement, that the satisfaction was to be rendered *through* the sacrifice, *or in connection with* it; whereas, on the contrary, whenever it was rendered at all (and, as a matter of course, this *necessarily* took place wherever it was possible), it was always *in connection with* the sacrifice, and never *through* the sacrifice itself. The primary object of the sacrifice as such, even of the trespass-offering, was invariably expiation. Thus in Lev. v. 16, 18, vi. 7, xiv. 18, 21, etc., the words לְכַפֵּר עָלָיו are expressly applied to the trespass-offering, which is a sufficient proof of the incorrectness of the assertion, that sin-offerings and trespass-offerings stand in the same relation to one another as *expiatio* and *satisfactio*. Moreover, it is certainly folly to affirm that the satisfaction had to be exhibited *either* through the sacrifice, *or* in connection with it. The law must have applied either to the one alone, or to the other alone. If the *satisfactio* took place *in connection with* the sacrifice, the sacrifice must have had some other object besides satisfaction, and that can have been no other than *expiation* (כִּפְּרָה). And unity of idea required, that even where there was no satisfaction *connected with* the sacrifice, the sacrifice itself should still serve the purpose of *expiation*, and that in that case the element of satisfaction should not be exhibited *through* the sacrifice, but rather be omitted altogether; and this occurred, and could only occur, when satisfaction was impossible, *i.e.*, where the violation of the rights of others consequent upon the sin could not be repaired, and compensation could not be made for the injury inflicted.

The same objection applies in the main to *Delitzsch*, who writes (p. 743): "The fundamental idea of the sin-offering was the *expiation* or atonement; that of the trespass-offering, the *mulcta* or compensation." And when *Keil* compounds his definition from elements taken from *Riehm* and *Rinck*, and writes (p. 226), that "a trespass-offering was brought, when the object to be answered was a satisfaction for the violation of rights, *or* compensation (payment or service), for the purpose of obtaining a restitution of theocratical rights, which the person presenting it had lost," the dualism of heterogeneous principles (on the one hand, a wicked violation of right; and on the other, an innocent loss of right) is but little adapted to commend the definition, which may be proved to be false on other grounds as well (§ 101). But it is self-deception on the part of *Keil* (p. 223), when he imagines that he can reconcile this dualism, and elevate it to a higher point of unity, by calling the payment or service demanded for the restitution of complete theocratical right, *satisfaction*, and thus laying down "the idea of satisfaction as the fundamental idea common to all trespass-offerings." For no one can call the payment or service demanded of me for the restoration of a right, which has been lost without any fault of my own, a *satisfaction*. The payment, by which I redeem a right or a possession, is no satisfaction. For the notion of satisfaction always presupposes guilt. And if this be admitted, every ground is taken away (at least, so far as *Keil* is concerned) for placing the trespass-offering of the leper and the Nazarite in a different category from the other trespass-offerings (cf. § 101).

§ 96. In *Hofmann's* opinion (*Schriftbeweis*, Ed. 1), " חַטָּאָה was an action, אָשָׁם an existing condition of things. The former had taken place, the latter had grown. The one was conduct, by which the wrong-doer had violated his relation to the thing with regard to which he did wrong. The other determined the relation itself, which consisted of the fact that he had injured another, and was bound to make reparation" (p. 167). Again, in Ed. 2 he says, " Sin-offerings and trespass-offerings bore the same relation to one another, as the transgression of the law and an illegal condition of things: the latter were presented when, and only when, expiation was not excuse" (p. 265). " The conflict between an existing state of things and the law of God demanded a different kind of expiation (in the trespass-offering) from the expiation of an illegal action" (in the sin-offering). In reply to *Keil*, who objects that all conduct brings about an existing condition of things, and every existing condition of things proceeds from some conduct, from some action,—he still further observes : " He has not understood my meaning. I am not speaking of a condition of things that has resulted from an act performed, but of such a condition as might arise quite as easily *without* an action as *through* an action,—for example, in the case of the leper or the Nazarite."

But even with this supplementary restriction, the distinction laid down by *Hofmann* is quite untenable. For after the cure of an issue of blood in the case of a woman, or of seminorhea in that of a man, there was a " conflict between a continuous state of things and the law of God," and " a condition of things that had not resulted from an act performed," quite as much as after the curing of a leper ; and yet this condition of things was *not* atoned for and removed by a *trespass*-offering (Lev. xv. 15, 30), but a *sin*-offering was brought to expiate the existing uncleanness. These examples are sufficient to prove, that the distinction between a *state of things* at variance with the law, and an *action* opposed to the law, cannot be adduced as determining the difference between trespass-offerings and sin-offerings ; for in Lev. xv. *conditions* are mentioned at variance with the law, in which no *trespass*-offerings were presented, but on the contrary *sin*-offerings, although an issue of blood and *seminis emissio* were not *actions* opposed to the law, but

a condition of things at variance with the law. In order to antici-
pate any similar rebuke to that which *Keil* has received, I will just
add, however, that the last-mentioned incongruity certainly *appears*
to be removed, when *Hofmann* states, that in the word " *action*,"
which is inapplicable to these circumstances, he includes the term
" *occurrence*" (*Vorfall*), " *which was to him a consequence of sin.*"
But in this case he must allow, that the choice of the word " *action*," to determine the *general* rule for the sin-offering, was a very
unhappy one. Nor can I satisfy myself with the artfully turned
expression, " *an occurrence, which was to him a consequence of sin.*"
For a death which happened unexpectedly in the neighbourhood of
a Nazarite, and defiled him, was indeed an *occurrence*, but *not* an
occurrence which was *to him* a consequence of sin; it was only to
the deceased that it was that. The uncleanness resulting from the
infection of his own sinful and mortal nature with the impurity of
the corpse, was the only consequence of sin to the man himself.
The *uncleanness* which came upon him in this way, might indeed,
as every one would admit, be called a *condition* or *state of things*,
but never an *action*.[1] And if the *entrance* of this uncleanness be
designated an *occurrence*, I have no objection to offer, but would
simply remark, that on the same ground the *entrance* of any condition whatever could be, and should be, designated by the same
term.

§ 97. We now proceed to an independent examination of the
subject, and shall restrict ourselves first of all to the complex law in
Lev. v. 14–vi. 7, which undoubtedly refers to the trespass-offering,
and is to be regarded as the fundamental and normal passage in
relation to it. This passage is divided, by the repetition of the introductory formula in chap. v. 14 and vi. 1 (" And Jehovah spake
unto Moses, saying"), into two sections promulgated independently.
But, notwithstanding this, as the similarity of the opening words
(" If a soul commit a trespass, and sin" (v. 15), " If a soul sin, and
commit a trespass" (vi. 2)) clearly proves, they both treat of a common description of sins, namely, those which the Hebrew designated
as מַעַל.

The idea expressed by this word is very obvious. The original
meaning of מעל, like that of בגד, was to cover over; then to act in a
covered, deceitful, faithless manner. But in actual use בגד acquired
a different signification from מעל, inasmuch as Jehovah is almost

---

[1] It is hardly necessary to say, that the same remark applies, *mutatis mutandis*, to the commencement of the leprosy itself.

exclusively introduced as the personal object of the latter (מַעַל יהוה).
Only in Num. v. 12, 27, is the adulterous conduct of a woman
described as a מַעַל מַעַל בְּאִישָׁהּ (whereas in Ex. xxi. 8 the putting away
of a wife by her husband is condemned as בִּגְדוֹ בָהּ; an exception
which is evidently based upon the fact, that the relation of a wife
to her husband was regarded as analogous to that of the congregation to Jehovah). From this restriction of the personal object of
מַעַל to Jehovah, which is retained everywhere else,—and that not
merely where the faithlessness and wrong directly affected Jehovah
himself (as, for example, in the case of idolatry, of self-will in
connection with the service of Jehovah, or of the keeping back of
first-fruits, tenths, etc.), but also where they primarily affected a
fellow-citizen or fellow-man (cf. Lev. vi. 2 sqq.; Num. v. 6 sqq.;
Ezek. xvii. 20; Prov. xvi. 10),—it is evident that the distinction
between מַעַל and בֶּגֶד was this, that in the latter the wrong inflicted
was regarded simply as a violation of social fidelity between man and
man, in the former as a violation of the covenant fidelity of Israel
towards Jehovah. For, according to Lev. xix. 2, the fundamental
requirement of this covenant fidelity was, "Be ye holy as God
is holy;" and this holiness included fidelity to one's neighbour.
The Israelite, who acted faithlessly towards his neighbour, was
also faithless towards Jehovah, because unmindful of his covenant
obligations to Him. And whilst committing a בֶּגֶד בַּעֲמִיתוֹ, he rendered himself also guilty of a מַעַל בַּיהוָה. But before a בֶּגֶד בַּעֲמִיתוֹ
could be designated as a מַעַל בַּיהוָה, it was unquestionably necessary
that the person acting fraudulently should belong to the covenant
nation of Jehovah; not, however, that the person defrauded should
belong to it also, as *Riehm* supposes (p. 97). The instance which he
has quoted himself from Ezek. xvii. 20 ought to have convinced
him that this view is wrong; for there King Zedekiah commits a מַעַל
בַּיהוָה, through not keeping his oath to the heathen Nebuchadnezzar
(cf. ver. 13). The design of Jehovah in giving His law was not
merely to defend the rights " of the members of the covenant one
towards another," but quite as much to preserve the rights of a
heathen in relation to an Israelite. An Israelite could no more rob
and defraud a heathen without breaking the covenant, than he
could his fellow-countrymen and religious associates.

§ 98. Thus, the obligation to present a trespass-offering, which
is referred to in Lev. v. 14–vi. 7 (the basis of the law of the trespass-offering), presupposed a מַעַל בַּיהוָה, *i.e.*, a violation of the rights
and claims of others, regarded as a breach of covenant faithfulness

towards Jehovah. But every מַעַל בַּיהוָה could not be expiated by a trespass-offering. And the design of the passage before us is to give more particular information upon this point.

We will commence with the first, and, as we shall soon see, the leading section, in chap. v. 14–19. It mentions first of all one particular kind of sins, namely, those committed in connection with the holy things of Jehovah (מִקָּדְשֵׁי יְהוָֹה). This includes everything belonging to Jehovah, whether consecrated or laid under a ban (cf. Jos. vii. 1, מַעַל בַּחֵרֶם), those portions of both the bleeding and bloodless sacrifices which belonged to the priests (Lev. xxii. 14), and the first-fruits and tithes, which were set apart for the remuneration of the priests and Levites, and were to be looked at in the light of feudal payments to the divine King of Israel (Num. xviii. 13; Lev. xxvii. 30). But even this class of sins is restricted to those committed "through ignorance." For the expiation of such offences two things were enjoined: (1) the restitution of that which had been kept back, with the addition of a fifth part of its value; and (2) the offering of a ram without blemish, subject to the priest's valuation, as a trespass-offering. Thus along with, and previous to, the ethical אָשָׁם, there was a material one as well (for the material compensation for an injury is also called אָשָׁם in Num. v. 8; 1 Sam. vi. 4, 8).

So far everything is perfectly clear. But at ver. 17 a by no means inconsiderable difficulty seems to stand in our way. The rule for the presentation of a trespass-offering is thus expanded and made general: "If any one sin, and do one of all the commandments of Jehovah (אַחַת מִכֹּל מִצְוֹת יְהוָֹה), which he ought not to do, and knoweth it not (וְלֹא יָדַע), etc." This rule for the trespass-offering is almost exactly the same as that for the sin-offering in Lev. iv. 2, 22, 27, with this single exception, that instead of וְלֹא יָדַע ("and knoweth not"), we there find בִּשְׁגָגָה ("in ignorance"). The earlier commentators for the most part were at their wits' end here. *Bähr* (ii. 401) helped himself out of the difficulty by referring to the command that the animal to be offered should be valued by the priest, which is repeated in ver. 18 from ver. 15, and which was not given in the case of the sin-offerings. But it is also wanting in the case of many of the trespass-offerings; *e.g.*, in Lev. xiv. 12 sqq.; Num. vi. 12; Lev. xix. 20 sqq., etc. *Winer* refers to the condition introduced in Lev. iv. 23, 28 in connection with the sin-offering, "if it come to his knowledge" (אִם הוֹדַע אֵלָיו), which signifies an objective conviction; whereas, according to Lev. vi. 5, the trespass-

offering presupposed a free confession. But this leads to no conclusion, because the section in vi. 1–6 relates to a totally different
class of trespass-offering sins from those referred to in chap. v. 14–19
(§ 99), and an objective conviction is certainly not intended to be
excluded in vers. 14–19. The opinion expressed by me in my *Mos.
Opfer* (p. 210 sqq.) was also quite as wrong. I there stated that
the וְלֹא יָדַע ("and knoweth not") in chap. v. 17 had respect, not to the
sin committed, but to the commandment broken; and that whilst the
sins referred to in chap. v. 17 were such as had been committed in
ignorance of the command, in those referred to in chap. iv. 22, 27,
ignorance of the commandment could not be pleaded, but thoughtless-
ness, or the absence of intention (בִּשְׁנָגָה), in breaking the command.
This view, however, is precluded by the fact that in chap. v. 18 the
sin in question is called a שְׁגָגָה. The explanation of וְלֹא יָדַע given
by *Hofmann* is also inadmissible. He says (p. 259): "It is intended
to show, how it was that the sin had not been expiated *at once*. . . .
Whoever had remained *for a length of time* unconscious that he had
sinned against the law, was to bring a trespass- (debt-) offering,
apart from the expiation of the sin itself, for the fact that, although
unintentionally, he had allowed the debt to continue so long." But
even in cases where only sin-offerings, and not trespass-offerings,
were to be brought, it must frequently have happened that the
sinner was not conscious of his sin for a long time, and therefore
the expiation was neglected, or the "debt" continued, until he was
aware of it (cf. chap. iv. 13, 23, 28).—But there is no possible way of
escaping the conclusion that the וְלֹא יָדַע (" and knew it not") signifies
exactly the same thing as בִּשְׁנָגָה in chap. iv. 22, 27, v. 15.—*Riehm*
was the first to give the true explanation. " This passage," he says,
viz., chap. v. 17–19, " has not a new formula of introduction, and
therefore is immediately connected with what precedes (chap. v. 14–
16); so that the same *class* of sins is intended as before. A more
general application is given in vers. 17–19 to the special law contained in the preceding verses."

In determining the category of the trespass-offering, the law
started with unfaithfulness in connection with what belonged to
Jehovah. But the principle expressed required that it should embrace other analogous sins as well. Hence in vers. 17–19 there
follows a generalization of the rule laid down in vers. 14–16 for
circumstances of a particular kind. That the words, " If a soul
commit a trespass, and sin through ignorance " (ver. 15), are to be
understood as more precisely determining the expression, " If a soul

sin" (ver. 17), and therefore that they include fraudulent acts in connection with another person's property, is evident, so far as the *form* is concerned, from the close connection between this precept and the foregoing one, which is announced contemporaneously with it, and included in the same "the Lord spake" (ver. 14),—an argument that possesses all the greater force from the fact that it is also referred to in the second "the Lord spake," which follows in chap. vi. 1,—and so far as the *substance* is concerned, from the sameness in the expiation required.   *Keil* imagines, indeed (i. 221), that "as no reference is made to a material compensation, the sin alluded to must be of such a kind as to render such compensation impracticable." But that is a mistake ; for, since it is stated in ver. 18, that a ram is to be offered according to the valuation of the priest, there must have been some fixed standard of valuation, and that could only be the full compensation for what had been kept back, with the addition of a fifth, according to the directions of ver. 16, which we must assume to be equally applicable here.

§ 99. In proceeding now to examine the next section, Lev. vi. 1–7, which is introduced with a new and independent וַיְדַבֵּר יְהֹוָה ("the Lord spake"), we must endeavour to determine first of all the point in common between the two, and secondly, their antithetical relation.   Common to both is מָעַל מַעַל, which is placed in both instances at the head, and governs the entire section.   But it is quite a mistake on the part of some commentators to regard the antithesis between the two sections as consisting in the fact, that the first treats of fraud in connection with the property of Jehovah (ver. 15), the second in connection with that of one's neighbour (vi. 2) ; for this antithesis does not apply to the whole of the first section, but only to the first half (vers. 14–16) ; whereas the second half (vers. 17–19) undoubtedly includes in its אַחַת מִכָּל־מִצְוֹת יְהֹוָה (ver. 17) the breaches of the law mentioned in the second section (denial on oath of the possession of property stolen, found, obtained by fraud, or entrusted).   The real antithesis, which the commentators have overlooked, lies in the fact, that the frauds mentioned in the first section are such as have been committed בִּשְׁגָגָה (in ignorance, ver. 15), or, what is quite the same thing, those in which the plea "he knew it not" can be put in ; whereas in the second section (vi. 1–7) every mark of that kind is wanting, and from the nature of the sins mentioned, really impossible.

The relation between the two sections is therefore the following. In vers. 14–19, unconscious want of faithfulness in relation to the property of Jehovah is the first thing represented as demanding a trespass-offering; and then the same demand is extended to all *unconscious* acts of unfaithfulness, of whatever kind they might be. This absolves the whole sphere of the trespass-offering, so far as it is governed and affected by the general principle, that only such sins as have been committed "in ignorance" admit of sacrificial expiation. The trespass-offering, as thus bounded (v. 14–19), like the similarly defined sphere of the sin-offering (iv. 1–v. 13), is comprehended in one single וַיְדַבֵּר יְהֹוָה (iv. 1 and v. 14). But the truth, that from the complex character of earthly things there is no rule without an exception, applies even here. And the exception, which is admissible here, is expressed in a new law by a second (supplementary) "Thus saith the Lord." For example, in a conscious and intentional "trespass" there might be points introduced, by which the sin was modified and a classification with unintentional sins rendered possible, especially when the offender, who had at first denied, and that on oath, a sin which could not be punished because it could not be proved, afterwards repented and made a spontaneous confession. And this is what is added in chap. vi. 1–7. But this indulgence was not extended to conscious sin in connection with what belonged to Jehovah, because in that case fraud became sacrilege, which all legislators separate from ordinary theft as deserving of severer punishment. According to the spirit of the Mosaic law, it must be assumed that such sins were to be punished with death; and in Josh. vii. 15 this is confirmed by an actual fact.

A third passage, from which the law of the trespass-offering may be determined, is Num. v. 5–10. As nothing is said here of the two modifying circumstances (viz., the absence of intention on the one hand, and the confession of the crime on the other), under which a simple trespass-offering, accompanied with the restoration of the object of the fraud and the addition of one-fifth of the value, was admissible without any further civil punishment, an acquaintance with the two laws in Leviticus relating to the sin-offering is evidently presupposed; and so far as they relate to wrong done in connection with the property of another man, they are rendered still more precise by the addition of directions, which are wanting there, as to what is to be done with the material compensation, provided the person injured should have died in the interim.

§ 100. According to the laws hitherto examined, for every act of fraud committed by a member of the covenant in connection with the property of another, whether performed unconsciously and brought to his knowledge afterwards, or committed knowingly and afterwards repented of and voluntarily confessed, a trespass-offering was to be presented for the expiation of the faithlessness involved towards the holy covenant-God, and restitution to be made to the rightful possessor, accompanied with the addition of one-fifth of its value.

But if we look still further at the other cases in which trespass-offerings were also to be presented, we find that the definition of this kind of sacrifice which we have obtained from Lev. v., is not incorrect perhaps, but yet too limited; and it is evident that unfaithfulness in connection with the (material) property of another was not the all-embracing *genus*, but simply a *species*, though the *main* species, of the sins to be expiated by trespass-offerings, viz., that which gave rise to the entire institution, and which therefore constituted the standard *per analogiam* for every case that might be added afterwards.

The passage which comes closest to the fundamental passage in Lev. v., and is therefore to be explained most easily from the principle exhibited there, is Lev. xix. 20–22: " If a man lie with a woman, and have connection with her, and she is a slave נֶחֱרֶפֶת לְאִישׁ, and not redeemed nor emancipated, a punishment (בִּקֹּרֶת) shall take place: they shall not die, for she is not free; and he shall as his trespass (אֶת־אֲשָׁמוֹ) offer to Jehovah a ram of trespass." נֶחֱרֶפֶת לְאִישׁ cannot certainly signify here, that the maid is *despised* by her master; for in that case, as *Riehm* observes (p. 104), we should " expect לַאֲדֹנֶיהָ or בְּעֵינֵי אֲדֹנֶיהָ, and it would not have been necessary expressly to mention that they should not die." Nor can it mean " *betrothed* to a man," or even " to her master;" for as betrothed she would have been guilty of adultery, and therefore liable to be put to death; and it would be a perfectly unwarrantable exception, if only a free woman, and not also a slave, had to expiate with death any violation of conjugal fidelity, either as betrothed or married,— an exception precluded by the fact, that the children of maids were treated as legitimate. The expression in question must rather be rendered, as it has been by *Ewald, Hofmann, Bunsen,* and others, " *given up* to a man." According to Ex. xxi. 7–11, every maid was thus given up to her master, since he possessed the right, at any time and without reserve, to take her to himself, or give her to his son, as a concubine.

Hofmann (p. 260) is of opinion, that there is no ground for assuming that a maid of Israelitish descent is intended here; but there is certainly no ground for his own assumption, that only a foreign woman is intended, who had neither honour nor rights. The truth is, that the text does not exclude either; and the law, therefore, was equally applicable to the dishonouring of an Israelitish maid and to that of a stranger. But this is not the only violence which *Hofmann* has done to the same text, to force it within the limits of his own preconceived opinion respecting the trespass-offering. For example, בִּקֹּרֶת he renders inquiry, instead of vengeance, punishment. I do not of course dispute the fact, that it *might* from its etymology mean inquiry. But the fact certainly is, that the Talmud and the Rabbins understand it as meaning chastisement, scourging (hence the *Vulg. vapulabunt ambo*), with which *Fürst* (Lex. i. 214) compares the Æthiopic בקל and the Arabic מקר (both signifying " to beat"), and that this meaning at all events is more suitable to the text than the other. For what could be the object of an "inquiry in which the circumstances were examined, and judgment given accordingly," in this particular case, I certainly cannot see ; and the restriction which follows, "they shall not die," evidently presupposes corporeal punishment. *Hofmann* is still more decidedly mistaken, when he maintains that the wrong in this case was not a violation of her master's right of possession, and traces it rather to the fact, that " such a person abstracted from the nation of God what he expended upon the dishonoured stranger, who had not the control of her own body, but was without rights, and completely in the power of her master, and could not bear children either to him or to his nation ;" and also when he still further bases the necessity for a trespass-offering upon the fact, " that he had to free himself from the debt which he had incurred, on account of the reproductive power which had been squandered and lost to his family and nation." This may suit *Hofmann's* theory of the trespass-offering perfectly well; but it is so much the less in harmony with the law, which expressly allowed any Israelite to marry a woman of foreign descent, who had been taken in war, after she had cut off her hair, pared her nails, changed her clothes, and mourned a whole month for her father and mother. And it is well known that the lawgiver himself married first of all a Midianitish wife, and afterwards a Cushite. The marriages with foreign wives, which were untheocratical according to the law, were those in which the heathen woman remained a heathen still (Judg. iii. 6, 7 ; Ezra x. 18, 19).

The violation of another person's bondmaid, whether of foreign or Israelitish descent, is certainly presented in this passage in the light of an injury done to another's property, and therefore as a " trespass." Her master, as such, possessed the right to the entire possession of her person, since he could take her without hesitation to be his concubine. He was defrauded of this right when another seduced her; but it was not adultery so long as her master had not actually availed himself of the right, and therefore the punishment of death was not to be inflicted. But the violence done to the property of another had to be expiated, as well as the consequent sin against Jehovah. The latter was expiated through the trespass-offering. On the other hand, a *positive* compensation for the wrong was impossible. Hence there is nothing said about a valuation of the ram to be presented. But for a *positive* compensation there was substituted a *negative* one. If the wrong done by the seducer could not be met positively by something given to the person injured, it could negatively, by something inflicted upon the wrong-doer. The sensual pleasure which had been enjoyed could be covered and counterbalanced by corporeal punishment.

§ 101. There is more difficulty connected with Lev. xiv. 12 sqq., in which directions are given respecting the trespass-offering to be presented by the *leper* at his purification; and with Num. vi. 12, where the *Nazarite*, who had defiled himself by touching a corpse, and thereby had broken his vow, is ordered to present a trespass-offering at the renewal of his consecration.

Rinck and *Keil* (i. 221) have disputed the applicability of the idea of a " trespass" to these two cases. The notion of a violation of right *Keil* regards as quite foreign to them both. " The *leper*," he says, " had not brought upon himself the leprosy, which compelled him to abstain for a time from the public worship of God, but had been seized by it. Nevertheless he had been shut out by his leprosy, like an excommunicated person, from the possession and enjoyment of all covenant rights; and it was by means of sacrifice that he was to be reinstated in these rights, through a process of sacerdotal purification. To obtain these rights again, he was to bring a trespass-offering, as *payment* for them; upon which he was formally consecrated like a priest, and thus was restored to the fellowship of the priestly nation. So also the *Nazarite*, who had unawares become unclean through a sudden death occurring in his neighbourhood, had violated no law, but had simply interrupted the period of his vow, which never ought to have been interrupted, through the defilement that needed as such to be expiated by a sin-offering. The trespass itself he was required to make good materially, by commencing afresh the period of his vow, and by also bringing a lamb for a trespass-offering as *payment* or compensation for reinstatement in his former consecrated condition."

On the inadmissible dualism of heterogeneous principles, which is introduced by this doctrine into the laws of the trespass-offering, we have spoken already (§ 95) ;—here, therefore, we have simply to prove that the second principle is inadmissible also.

When *Keil* maintains that the leper had *not brought* his leprosy, nor the Nazarite his sudden defilement, upon himself ; we inquire, (1) how in that case the law could demand a *sin-offering* from him as well as the trespass-offering, seeing that the former undoubtedly presupposed moral guilt ; (2) how the leprosy could involve the *loss* of covenant rights, and a *payment* be demanded for reinstatement in covenant rights which had been lost without any fault of his own ; (3) how this payment could be made to consist of a *trespass-offering*, which served " to make atonement for him" (Lev. v. 16, 18, vi. 7, xiv. 18, 21) ; and (4) how nevertheless *Keil* himself can possibly speak upon the very same page of a " *trespass*" to be set right by the trespass-offering, just as he speaks at p. 237 of a " *fault* which was not of a material, but of a theocratico-ethical character," and also call the cured leper and the defiled Nazarite a " *guilty* person, who received *full pardon* at the hands of God, so that he was restored to full, unlimited possession and enjoyment of theocratic rights and blessings, and also of the *mercy of God*."

The leper had certainly brought his leprosy, with the consequent exclusion from the congregation, and the Nazarite his defilement, with the consequent disturbance of his vow, *upon himself ;*—not indeed by any special, sinful act of the will, but by the sinful *habitus*, which is inherent in human nature generally, and therefore was inherent in him as an individual, and *through* which he was predisposed to the leprosy or to defilement from a corpse, and *without* which neither one nor the other could have infected and clung to him. Even *Keil* himself, when treating *ex professo* of the Levitical purifications, can tell us much that is true and striking respecting the " connection between these defilements and sin," and point to the fact (p. 280), that these laws of cleanness were intended " to awaken and preserve in man the consciousness of sin and guilt, based as they were upon the assumption that human nature generally is infected, both body and soul, by sin," etc.

If, then, in consequence of this sinful corruption of his human nature, a member of the priestly nation (§ 1) was affected with leprosy, or a consecrated Nazarite defiled by touching a corpse ;— *in the first place*, the *sinful habitus* of his nature, which was thus brought to light, needed expiation ; and this was accomplished, as in every serious defilement, by a *sin-offering*. And *in the second place*, since the uncleanness of leprosy, or the contact of the Nazarite with a corpse, had caused a *disturbance* in the *covenant relation towards Jehovah*, inasmuch as leprosy excluded from the fellowship of the sanctuary, and the performance of God's *service* (עֲבֹדָה, Ex. xii. 25, 26, xiii. 5), which was obligatory upon every member of the covenant-nation, was rendered impossible, whilst the defilement of the Nazarite prevented the fulfilment of his vow, a wrong had been inflicted upon Jehovah, which also needed expiation ; and this was accomplished by means of a *trespass*-offering. And as the other trespass-offerings were to be accompanied with an augmented compensation for the material injury or loss occasioned by the "trespass," so the defiled Nazarite was to render the same, by commencing the whole period of his vow afresh. In the case of a leper this was impossible, and therefore was omitted. But in neither case could there be any idea of a priestly valuation of the animal of the trespass-offering according to the shekel of the sanctuary (cf. Lev. v. 15, 18, vi. 6), since the wrong done to Jehovah could not be compensated by money or money's worth, and therefore furnished no standard for the valuation of the sacrificial animal. Moreover, the two cases are analogous to the one quoted in Lev. v. 14–16, and therefore are to be regarded as a kind of " trespass in the holy things of the Lord."

§ 102. After all, the *idea of the trespass-offering* must be defined as relating to the violation of the rights and claims of others, or, as we might put it, to some kind of robbery committed upon others, not merely in material possessions and property which it would be possible to restore, but in rightful and obligatory services, based upon agreement or covenant, the neglect of which, from their very nature, could not always be compensated afterwards. In the case of the former, as a matter of course, the compensation (augmented by the addition of one-fifth of the value) necessarily preceded the offering ; whilst in that of the latter it could only be required when and so far as it was possible.

This expresses also the point of difference from the *sin-offering*, which was connected with all such sins as could not be regarded as a robbery (either of God as the covenant ally and King of Israel, or of a fellow-man), committed upon earthly possessions, or upon services required by duty or compact. The common canon for sin-offerings and trespass-offerings, which is expressed in essentially the same terms, for the former in Lev. iv. 22, 27, and for the latter in Lev. v. 17, enjoins that they shall both be presented on the breach of any one of all the commandments of Jehovah (אַחַת מִכָּל־מִצְוֹת יְהוָֹה). But the canon of the sin-offering in Lev. v. 17 is distinguished and restricted by the clause נֶפֶשׁ כִּי־תִמְעֹל מַעַל in ver. 15, which governs the entire section, Lev. v. 14–19; whereas in the law of the sin-offering no such restriction is laid down (cf. § 98, 99). The state of the case, therefore, is the following:—Originally and primarily a sin-offering was appointed for the transgression of any of the commandments of Jehovah; but in the further development of the laws in question, all such breaches of the commandments of God as could be looked upon in the light of a מַעַל were excepted from this rule, and a different kind of sacrifice, viz., the trespass-offering, appointed. This appears, therefore, as a subordinate species of sin-offering, modified in a peculiar manner.

This distinction between the sin-offering and trespass-offering in the law of sacrifice corresponds to the distinction in the usage of the Hebrew language between מִצְוֹת and מִשְׁפָּטִים. As the sin-offering was originally intended for all sins, so the term מִצְוֹת frequently denotes the whole of the commandments of God (= תּוֹרָה). But just as the subordinate idea of the trespass-offering developed itself from the primary idea of the sin-offering, and the trespass-offering assumed a settled form as an independent branch of the sin-offering, so that henceforth the two stood side by side; so out of the general idea of מִצְוֹת there sprang the special idea of מִשְׁפָּטִים, and the term מִצְוֹת came eventually to designate only such commandments as were not also מִשְׁפָּטִים (i.e., determinations of those rights, which in a theocratical commonwealth the one had to demand, and the other to receive, in their relation one to another), and the whole law is called הַמִּצְוֹת וְהַמִּשְׁפָּטִים, "the commandments and the judgments" (Lev. xxvi. 3; Num. xxxvi. 13).

The analysis here given is based upon the admirable work of *Riehm* (p. 106 sqq.); but I cannot follow him when he proceeds to maintain (p. 109) that "the word מִצְוֹת, in the laws of the sin-offering in Lev. iv. and Num. xv. 22, is to be taken in the more limited sense, as not including the מִשְׁפָּטִים." For in that case, in the description of the domain of the trespass-offering in Lev. v. 17, as distinguished from that of the sin-offering, the expression מִשְׁפָּטִים would necessarily have been employed, and the same term מִצְוֹת could not possibly have been used. *Riehm* himself has felt this; but he has by no means met the difficulty by his romantic supposition, that " in this passage the writer made use of a *formula* from the law of the sin-offering, for the purpose of generalizing the preceding command." In opposition to this erroneous view (but only in opposition to it), *Keil* is, in part at least, perfectly correct, when he replies at p. 226: " Although a distinction can be made between covenant commands and covenant rights, covenant rights are never opposed or placed in antithesis to covenant commands (? cf. the examples already cited, Lev. xxvi. 3; Num. xxxvi. 13); least of all in the precepts respecting the sin-offerings and tres-pass-offerings, where one species of the transgressions requiring a sin-offering is described as the doing of מִצְוֹת which ought not to be done." The true explanation is, that in both passages (in Lev. v. 17 as well as iv. 27) כָּל־מִצְוֹת includes all the commands of God without exception; but that in Lev. v. 17 the expression is limited to the מִשְׁפָּטִים by the clause, " if a soul commit a *trespass*," which has to be supplied from ver. 15, and in Lev. iv. is reduced to such מִצְוֹת as were not also מִשְׁפָּטִים by the introduction of exceptions that required a sin-offering (Lev. v. 14 sqq.).

§ 103. Lastly, we must also examine the previous section, Lev. v. 1–13. On account of ver. 6, " and he shall bring his trespass-offering unto the Lord for his sin," this section was formerly regarded as the introduction to the law of the trespass-offering, and even *Bähr* adopted this view. But I opposed it in my *Mos. Opfer* (p. 229 sqq.), and endeavoured to prove that it was intended to be regarded as a continuation of the section relating to the sin-offering. With the single exception of *Hofmann* (pp. 263–4), all the more recent expositors have adopted my view, and to some extent added force to my arguments. *Hofmann's* opposition to this view renders it necessary that I should enter into a more minute examination of this question.

The only objection that *Hofmann* is able to offer to our view is the expression, " he shall bring his trespass-offering," in ver. 6, which cannot have any other meaning than the same words in ver. 15 or chap. vi. 6. But there is a great difference between ver. 6 and the other two passages. For in both the latter, after the sacrificial animal to be offered has been mentioned, a second לְאָשָׁם is added to the expression אֶת־אֲשָׁמוֹ לַיהוָה, and it is *that* addition which distinguishes the sacrifice in question as a trespass-offering (cf. chaps. xix. and xxi.). In ver. 6, on the other hand, לְחַטָּאת is added in a similar way, and by this the sacrifice is distinguished as a sin-offering. Ver. 6, therefore, is to be rendered, "let him bring as his *asham* (= his debt) for his sin a female sheep as a *sin-offering;*" and ver. 15, and chap. vi. 6, " let him bring as his debt a ram for a *trespass-offering.*" For it is evident that in connection with the sin-offering there was also a debt, an *asham*, to be expiated, from the fact that in chap. iv., where the sins which required a sin-offering are mentioned, prominence is expressly given every time to the *asham* which was thereby to be expiated. And not only in ver. 6, but throughout the entire section, wherever the object of the sacrifice is expressly indicated, we find לְחַטָּאת, *never* לְאָשָׁם (vers. 7, 8, 9, 11, 12); and when in conclusion it is enjoined that neither oil nor wine is to be added, the reason assigned is that it is a *sin*-offering (כִּי חַטָּאת הִיא). It is true, this has not escaped the notice of our opponent. " Undoubtedly," he says, " this must also be borne in mind, that it is nevertheless stated in ver. 6, that the animal presented as a trespass-offering served לְחַטָּאת." But how thoroughly romantic is the explanation which *Hofmann* gives of this striking mode of expression! " All the cases enumerated in vers. 1–4," he says, " remind us so far of the cases classed together above, in which trespass-offerings were required, that in every instance a *condition of things opposed to the divine command had lasted for some time* before the expiatory payment was made. . . . There are faults which impress those who perceive them as demanding a trespass-offering, whereas from their true nature they require sin-offerings instead. For this reason it is said, ' let him bring his trespass-offering,' which is then treated as a sin-offering."

The following brief summary is given by *Hofmann* himself of the cases mentioned in vers. 1–4 : (1) When a man had omitted to furnish information which he was solemnly bound to furnish; (2) when a man had touched something unclean, and was not aware of it *till afterwards* (?); (3) when a man had thoughtlessly given his word on oath that he would perform a certain thing, and was not really conscious *till some time afterwards* that he had taken such an oath.—Here we must remark, however, that *Hofmann* added the " not till afterwards," and " not till some time afterwards," of which there is not a syllable in the text, from his own fancy, in order that the sin, which " from its nature required a sin-offering," might have to some extent the appearance which was requisite to enable him to state, on the basis of his theory of the trespass-offering (which we have already proved to be erroneous, § 96, 98), that it "impressed those who perceived it as requiring a trespass-offering." A man might abstain from giving the testimony demanded, or touch an unclean thing unawares, or promise something on oath without consideration, and become aware of it *immediately* after it had occurred. In the vast majority of cases, in fact, it would be so. But could such cases be regarded as studiously excluded from vers. 1–4, instead of being classified under them? Certainly not. So that there is not a word in the text about what, according to *Hofmann*, was to produce the (deceptive) impression, that the case referred to was suitable for a trespass-offering. And as *Hofmann* himself maintains that *from their very nature* all these cases required a sin-offering, there is no necessity to bring proofs of this fact.

§ 104. The other reasons adduced by *Riehm* and myself for not including Lev. v. 1–13 among the laws of the trespass-offering, are ignored by *Hofmann;* but they are clear and conclusive notwithstanding. They are the following: (1) The section is shown to be closely connected with the foregoing one, so that the two together make but one whole, by the fact that in the entire passage from chap. iv. 1 to v. 13 the introductory formula, "And Jehovah spake to Moses, and said," is only inserted once, viz., at the commencement in chap. iv. 1, and that it is not repeated at chap. v. 1; whereas the following section, again, is proved to be a new law by the repetition of this introductory formula in chap. v. 14. (2) As the sins mentioned in chap. v. 1–4 are introduced in other places as requiring, not trespass-offerings, but sin-offerings (particularly defilement, Lev. xii. 6–8, xv. 15, 30, etc.), so, on the other hand, the animals prescribed in chaps. v. and vi. (a ewe-sheep or goat) do not occur anywhere else in connection with the trespass-offerings, but only with the sin-offerings of the common people (Lev. iv. 28, 32). (3) In the sections relating to the *trespass-offerings*, we certainly never read anything about the exchange of the sacrificial animal (vers. 7 sqq.) for another of inferior value, or for bloodless offerings, *on account of the poverty* of the person presenting them; whereas there are unquestionably other places where this occurs in the laws relating to the *sin-offerings* (Lev. xii. 8, xiv. 21). The latter, which is the principal point, *Hofmann* does not refer to. On the other hand, he discusses the question, whether the exchange permitted in vers. 7 sqq. is to be restricted to the cases mentioned in vers. 1–4, or whether it is to be regarded as a general rule for all cases of sin-offering. He decides in favour of the former. For, in his opinion, the mode of transition in ver. 7 places it beyond the reach of doubt, that the subject of ver. 7 is identical with the subject of vers. 1–4. We may admit that this opinion is well founded, without on that account being forced to the conclusion, that the permission in question was only granted exceptionally in certain peculiar cases where sin-offerings *and* trespass-offerings were prescribed. *Hofmann* himself maintains, with perfect correctness, that the three cases cited in vers. 1–4 are "merely intended as specimens of a whole series of similar transgressions." And if this be the case, the three series of transgressions thus indicated may be regarded as *representing* the whole range of sin-offerings. Both here, and in Lev. xii. 8 and xiv. 21, the law mentions *poverty* on the part of the person presenting the offering as the sole and exclusive ground for the change; whereas *Hofmann* is obliged to seek for the main ground in the fact, that "all these faults admitted of an *excuse*," of which there is not a syllable to be found in any one of the passages. And the one excuse mentioned in connection with the faults named in chap. v. 1–4, might be pleaded in an equal measure, and for the most part undoubtedly in a still higher degree, in connection with *all* the sins committed "in ignorance," which are described in Lev. iv. as demanding a sin-offering. But the real reason why a modification was regarded as admissible in the sin-offerings and not in the trespass-offerings of the common people, on account of poverty, is to be found in the characteristic distinctions between the two; that is to say, in the fact that it was in the latter alone that there was any question of the robbery of earthly goods or sources, which demanded an equal restitution from both rich and poor.

§ 105. Hitherto we have spoken simply of such sin-offerings and trespass-offerings, as had to be presented for the expiation of particular offences that are mentioned by name. But in addition to these, *sin-offerings* had also to be presented on all the *feast-days* for the whole congregation, without any reference to particular sins. This raises two questions, that we must examine and endeavour to answer : (1) How is this fact to be reconciled with the assertion made in § 86, that both sin-offerings and trespass-offerings were invariably presented for the expiation of certain overt acts of sin, and not, like the burnt-offerings and peace-offerings, merely for the expiation of general sinfulness ? and (2) why were only sin-offerings presented at the feasts for the whole congregation, and not trespass-offerings also ?

The first of these two questions may be answered without difficulty. If, as we have seen in § 89-91, " ignorance," or "not
knowing," constituted the true, fundamental, and determining
characteristic of those sins which could be, and were to be, subjected to expiation by means of a sin-offering, as soon as the sinner
became conscious of them ; and if, on the other hand, there is
ample ground for the words of the Psalmist (Ps. xix. 12), " Who
can tell how oft he offendeth ? forgive my hidden faults," and the
lawgiver himself was conscious of their force ; he might assume
with undoubted certainty, that in every interval between the feasts,
a number of such sins had been committed, that were not expiated
because not known, and which were therefore made the subject of
a summary expiation (see especially Lev. xvi. 16, 21).

The second question is more difficult to answer. Among the
offences of the congregation which had remained undiscovered, and
therefore unexpiated, and which were to be subjected to a general
expiation at the feasts, it may certainly be assumed, that there
would be some which, from their nature, demanded a trespass-
offering. Why then was no trespass-offering presented for these ?

Of the two classes of sins to be expiated by trespass-offerings,
which are described on the one hand in Lev. v. 14–19, and on the
other in Lev. vi. 1–7, those of the second class, viz., those which
had been committed consciously, but had afterwards been repented
of and voluntarily confessed at the instigation of the sinner's own
conscience (§ 99), could not, of course, come into consideration ;
for they did not admit of expiation in themselves ; and when they
did so in consequence of the repentance and confession of the
sinner himself, they still stood in need of *special* expiation. But so
far as the sins of the first class were concerned, viz., acts of fraud
and robbery committed " in ignorance," no *trespass-offering* could
be presented at the feasts for offences of this kind which remained
unacknowledged and unatoned for, simply because it was essential to
the very nature of this kind of sacrifice, that the sacrificial expiation
should be based, so far as it was possible, upon a previous material
restitution. Thus, from the very nature of the case, trespass-offerings could *only* be presented for *acknowledged* sins. Hence for sins
which required trespass-offerings, but had not been acknowledged,
it was necessary that sin-offerings should be presented; and that
could be done, because the trespass-offering was merely a subordinate kind of sin-offering with peculiar modifications. In a summary act of sacrifice, the expiation effected by the sin-offering

might be regarded as comprehending that of the trespass-offering; but not *vice versa*. And the classified expiation for the acknowledged sins of individuals returned, so far as the unacknowledged sins of the whole congregation were concerned, to its original uniformity.

CHAPTER II

RITUAL OF THE SIN-OFFERING AND TRESPASS-OFFERING

§ 106. Before proceeding to an examination of the *ritual* of the SIN-OFFERINGS, we must first of all cast a look at the peculiar directions given with reference to the *materials* to be employed.

Apart from those sin-offerings which were presented in connection with Levitical purifications, as well as at the new moons and yearly feasts, or on occasions of special solemnity (*e.g.*, the consecration of the priests and Levites, of the tabernacle, etc.); a young bullock, *i.e.*, a bullock in the full vigour of youth (Lev. iv. 3), was offered for the expiation of the sins of the high priest, as the head and representative of the whole congregation.[1] And

[1] The rule in question commences thus: " If the priest that is anointed do sin to the inculpation of the nation (לְאַשְׁמַת הָעָם), etc." By the *anointed* priest, according to Lev. iv. 16, xvi. 32, xxi. 10, the high priest alone must be intended ; for he alone was consecrated by the complete anointing of his head (Lev. viii. 12), whereas his sons were merely sprinkled with anointing oil (Lev. viii. 30). This is the opinion of commentators generally. Yet what is most striking is, that no instructions are given respecting the animals to be offered by the ordinary priests, and yet *their* expiation would hardly be included in any of the other categories mentioned in Lev. iv. The commentators pass over this difficulty, as though it had no existence at all. But if their expiation could neither be placed on a par with that of the private individual, nor with that of the prince, no other course is open than to compare it to that of the high priest. Nevertheless we must adhere to the opinion, that Lev. iv. 3 refers to the high priest alone, to the exclusion of his sons. We are shut up to this not only by the settled usage of the expression " the *anointed* priest," but also by the phrase לְאַשְׁמַת הָעָם (to the inculpation of the nation). On this phrase *Knobel* has justly remarked : " The sin intended could only be one which he had committed in his official capacity as head of the nation." But the rest of the sentence is wrong : " to the exclusion of smaller *private* offences ; " for it is evident from Lev. x. 6, xxi. 10, 11, that even in the case of private offences, the high priest was still regarded as the anointed one, *i.e.*, in his official capacity. At all times, and under all circumstances, he was ever the high priest, the head and repre-

both for external and internal reasons, the demand could not be stretched any further, even in the expiation of the whole congregation, including the entire priesthood (Lev. iv. 13). On the other hand, a he-goat (שְׂעִיר עִזִּים) sufficed for the expiation of a prince (נָשִׂיא) of the congregation (Lev. iv. 23); and a she-goat or sheep for that of one of the common people (Lev. iv. 28, 32, v. 6). But in cases of extreme poverty, instead of the goat or lamb, two pigeons might be offered (one for a sin-offering, the other for a burnt-offering); and where even this could not be procured, a bloodless offering might be presented as a substitute for the bleeding sacrifice, viz., the tenth of an ephah of semmel (white) meal,— though without oil or incense, for the purpose of distinguishing it from the meat-offering, and so indicating its character as a sin-offering (Lev. v. 7, 11; cf. § 60).

The first thing which strikes us in these regulations is the graduation in the object sacrificed, according to the theocratical position of the person sacrificing; and an explanation of this is all the more requisite, from the fact that it does not occur in connection with any other kind of sacrifice. The explanation is no doubt to be found in the fact, that expiation by means of a sin-offering had reference to special sins, which are particularly named, and not merely to general sinfulness like the burnt-offering and peace-offering, and therefore bore a more individual, or more distinctly personal character; and also, that the higher the offending individual stood in the scale of theocratical office and rank, the greater was the moral guilt involved in his offence. The sins which required sin-offerings were such as had been committed directly and immediately against Jehovah, as the Holy One and Lawgiver in Israel, and against Him alone; whereas those which required trespass-offerings, being violations of merely earthly rights and claims, were committed primarily against the earthly holders of such rights and claims (including Jehovah also in the capacity of feudal Lord of the land). Fraud in connection with the property of another bore precisely the same character, whether the guilty person were a priest, a prince, or a private individual, and required the same material compensation in every case; so that the ethical compensation which

sentative of the nation, and on no occasion was regarded as acting without the anointing, and merely as a private individual. Hence an offence of the high priest always brought guilt upon the congregation (Lev. x. 16), just as a family was involved in the sin of its head (Josh. vii. 24), and a nation in the sin of its ruler (2 Sam. xxiv. 10 sqq.).

accompanied it, and was estimated according to it, was also the same for all in the case of the trespass-offering.   On the other hand, it made a difference of no slight importance, whether the priest or the common man had defiled himself in consequence of imprudence. (On the substitution of the bloodless offering for the bleeding sacrifice in the case of the sin-offering, we have said all that is necessary at § 60.)

§ 107. In the *ritual* of the sin-offering, the presentation, the imposition of hands, and the slaying of the animal presented no peculiar or unusual features, but in the *sprinkling of the blood* the distinctions are all the more surely and decidedly marked. Whereas in all the other kinds of sacrifice the blood was poured indifferently round about the altar of the fore-court, in the sin-offering, even of the lowest grade—those of the common people for example—it was not to be *sprinkled*, lest the intention should be overlooked, but *smeared* with the finger upon the *horns* of the altar (" and the priest shall put of the blood upon the horns," Lev. iv. 7, 18, 25, 30, 34).   This was also done in the case of the sin-offering of a prince of the congregation (Lev. iv. 25, 30, 34).   But in the sin-offering of the high priest, and that of the whole congregation, the officiating priest took the blood into the Holy Place, sprinkled (הִזָּה) some of it seven times with his finger before Jehovah against the *Parocheth*[1] (the curtain of the Holy of Holies), and then smeared it upon the horns of the altar of incense (Lev. iv. 5 sqq., 16 sqq.).   The blood which had not been used was poured out, in the case of all the sin-offerings, at the foot of the altar of burnt-offering, probably behind the lattice-work which surrounded it (§ 11).   The act of expiation was carried to a still higher point in the principal sin-offerings of the great day of atonement.   The blood was then taken into the Holy of Holies itself, and there sprinkled upon the Capporeth (§ 200).

All differences in the ceremonial, which coincided, as graduations of the expiatory act, with corresponding graduations in the material employed, according to the theocratical position of the person sacrificing, and which rested upon the same foundation

---

[1] According to *Hofmann* and *Knobel* אֶת־פְּנֵי פָרֹכֶת (Lev. iv. 6, 17) signifies *before* the Parocheth, *i.e.*, upon the ground in front of it. But this is improbable ; for in that case the most holy blood would have been trodden beneath the feet of the priests officiating in the Holy Place, or at any rate of the high priest when entering the Holy of Holies on the day of atonement, and would thereby have been profaned.

(§ 106), are to be accounted for from the differences in the signification of the sacred places and things which were immediately concerned (§ 12 sqq.). The fore-court was the place for the unpriestly
nation, or rather the nation that had not yet grown up to its priestly
calling (§ 1). For that reason the expiation of all the non-priestly
members of the nation, the prince as well as the beggar, was necessarily effected there. The Holy Place, on the other hand, was the
place where the priest *really* served Jehovah, and held communion
with Him, and where the priestly nation, according to its vocation,
ideally did the same. Here, therefore, the expiation of the priest
was effected, and also that of the nation as a whole, which still
retained its priestly character in its entirety and as distinguished
from the rest of the nations, though the individuals composing it
might have forfeited theirs. The expiation of the priestly nation
was effected in the Holy Place, to show that its ideal calling to the
priesthood, which had been disturbed by the sin to be expiated, was
restored, and that it still possessed the hope and claim to enter *really*
at some future day upon that priestly calling which it only possessed
ideally now. But the highest culmination in the process of expiation, which could only be effected once a year, and then by the
high priest alone, was assigned to the Holy of Holies, which was
closed even to the priests at every other time (Lev. xvi.), as a
typical sign that the nation would one day reach the summit of its
history, in consequence of that highest, most perfect, and primary
expiation of which this was but a feeble copy, and would then dwell
within the light of the now unapproachable glory of Jehovah.

The application of the blood to the *horns* of the altar may be
explained from the significance of the horns themselves, as the
elevated points, in which the idea of the altar culminated (§ 13).
It was done, as *Oehler* says, " to bring the atoning blood as near as
possible to God," and thus to increase its atoning efficacy. The
sprinkling seven times, whether against or in front of the curtain,
had reference not to the curtain itself, which was not an instrument
of expiation, but to the Capporeth behind it, which was thus to be
sprinkled not directly, but indirectly. In *Keil's* opinion, indeed,
" this affords but little explanation." But to my mind, if properly
understood, it explains everything. The sprinkling of the curtain,
which concealed the Holy of Holies, indicated that the ultimate
intention of the atoning act was to reach the highest and most perfect medium of expiation, but that in the present standpoint of the
plan of salvation there was still an obstructing veil between. This

sevenfold sprinkling against the *Parocheth* was not an independent
act of expiation, or so distinct from the smearing of the horns of
the altar of incense, that it would be right to speak of a twofold
expiation; but it was one with it, and to be understood as im-
pressing upon it the character of a substitute for the sprinkling
of the Capporeth, which was what was really necessary.   In connection with this it may still be maintained, that the *seven*fold
repetition of the act, which was not a leading but an auxiliary one,
was determined by the force of the number seven as the sign of
covenant-fellowship.

Lastly, so far as the arrangement was concerned, that all the
blood which was not used in sprinkling should invariably be poured
at the foot of the altar of burnt-offering, I cannot adopt *Keil's*
explanation, that " in this way the whole of the sacrificial blood was
brought to the place of God's presence, and thus it was indicated
that the soul was received not partially merely, but entirely into the
gracious fellowship of the Lord."   There are three reasons why I
cannot do so: *first,* because the idea that it was possible for only
one portion of the soul to be received into the gracious fellowship
of the Lord and the other to be excluded, is so unintelligible and
far-fetched, that there certainly could be no necessity for the law of
sacrifice to notice it at all; *secondly,* because the altar itself, and
not the foundation of the altar, or the ground upon which it stood,
was "the place of God's presence;" and when Jehovah promised
in Ex. xx. 24, "There will I come unto thee, and bless thee," He
certainly did not refer to the foundation of the altar, or the ground
upon which it stood; and *thirdly,* because even thus the end supposed would not be attained, inasmuch as this separation of the soul
would be most obviously expressed in the case of those sacrifices in
which the blood was brought into the Holy Place, and the smaller
portion of the soul would be brought into the higher fellowship
with God, represented by the Holy Place, whilst by far the larger
portion of the soul would only be brought into the inferior fellowship represented by the fore-court.—The pouring away of the remainder of the blood at the foot of the altar, was nothing more
than a fitting arrangement by which the blood was disposed of in a
sacred place, and thus saved from profanation.

§ 108. The directions given in the law, with reference to the
course to be adopted with the FLESH of the sin-offering, are quite as
peculiar as those relating to the blood, and still more complicated
and difficult to understand.

The BURNING upon the altar did not apply to the whole animal, as in the case of the burnt-offering, but was restricted, as in the case of the peace-offering, to the FAT PORTIONS (הַחֲלָבִים) alone. From repeated statements in the law of the sin-offering (Lev. iv. 10, 26, 35), it is evident that these were the very same portions as were burned in the case of the peace-offering (Lev. iii. 3–5, 9, 10, 15). Four different portions were included, when the sacrifice consisted of a bullock or a goat, viz. : (1) the fat which covered the viscera, *i.e.*, the great network of fat "which extended from the stomach over the intestines, and enveloped the latter ;" (2) the fat upon the intestines, *i.e.*, the fat "which had formed upon the intestines, and could easily be taken off ;" (3) the two kidneys, with the fat in which they were enclosed ; and (4) the יֹתֶרֶת עַל־הַכָּבֵד, also called יֹתֶרֶת מִן הַכָּבֵד, or merely יֹתֶרֶת הַכָּבֵד (Lev. viii. 16, 25, ix. 19, etc.). By the latter, *Gesenius, Bähr, Ewald, Keil,* and others understand, like the LXX. (λοβός), the great liver-lobe. But this, being a component part of the liver itself, could not be spoken of as " upon the liver," nor was it a fat portion like all the rest; moreover, it could not be obtained by merely loosening or peeling off, but only by cutting the liver in pieces. For this reason, it is more correct to regard it as the so-called small net or caul of the liver, " which commences between the two lobes of the liver, and stretches across the stomach to the neighbourhood of the kidneys" (*Luther, De Wette, Fürst, Knobel, Oehler, Bunsen,* etc.). In addition to these, when a sheep was sacrificed, there was (5) the fat tail, which frequently " weighs fifteen pounds and upwards in some species of oriental sheep, and consists entirely of something intermediate between marrow and fat."

§ 109. On the meaning of this selection, *Ewald* writes as follows (p. 45) :—" The different portions are generally called simply the fat, that is to say, the *internal* part; but, strange to say, the heart and the other blood-vessels are never included." In a note he adds, " where sheep are referred to, the tail is added : so thoroughly had the simple notion of fat, as such, gradually become predominant." The fundamental idea embodied in this opinion has been appropriated by *Keil* (i. 231). In connection with the view formerly advocated by myself, but which I now find to be erroneous, with regard to the flesh of the sacrifice (§ 77, 78), he says : " If the flesh of the victim generally represented the body of the person sacrificing as the organ of the soul, the fat portions of the inward part of the body, together with the kidneys, which were regarded as the

seat of man's tenderest and most secret emotions, could only represent the better part or inmost kernel of humanity, the psychical
body (σῶμα ψυχικόν), and the rest of the flesh merely the outer
man, the σῶμα χοϊκόν, a distinction analogous to that drawn by the
Apostle Paul in Rom. vii. 22, 23, between the inner man (ὁ ἔσω
ἄνθρωπος) and the members (τὰ μέλη)."

This explanation, with its contradictory consequences (§ 111,
114, 219), might well be regarded as the most unfortunate part of
Keil's sacrificial theory. For it is evident at the first glance, that
the selection of the altar-portion, as instituted by the law, is too
narrow for that theory on the one hand, and too broad for it on the
other.

In the first place, it is *too broad* for it. At p. 217, *Keil* has
faithfully reported that the *fat tail* was burnt along with the fat
from the inside, whenever a sheep was sacrificed. But when he
proceeds to the *explanation* of the burning of the sin-offering, he
stedfastly and consistently ignores the tail. He speaks everywhere
merely of "fat portions from the *inside*," of "*internal* fat." But
it is easy to see why the fat tail is so studiously avoided. For it
must be evident to any one, that the fat tail cannot represent the
"inner man," the "inmost kernel of humanity," the "inner, better
part of human nature," the "seat of a man's tenderest and most
secret emotions." And if *Keil's* interpretation of the fat portions
is inapplicable to the fat tail, it must also be regarded as erroneous so far as the other portions of fat are concerned. To *Ewald*,
with his historical and critical assumptions, this difficulty is by no
means an insuperable one ; but with *Keil's* historical views, there is
no way of overcoming it. Nothing is gained, however, by *ignoring*
an insuperable difficulty.—In the second place, the selection is also
too *narrow* for *Keil's* interpretation. For if the contrast between
the fat portions and the rest of the flesh is really to be understood
in the way he supposes, the heart, as being the central seat of the
inmost and noblest emotions, ought certainly to have been placed
upon the altar ; and it would have been far better to select the entrails themselves (the רַחֲמִים) as the seat of pity, love, compassion,
mildness, and goodness, instead of the net of fat which surrounds
them, and the liver itself, instead of the liver-caul. It is true, *Keil*
understands by יֹתֶרֶת, not the liver-net, but the liver-lobe. But this
is of no avail ; for in that case the liver itself would certainly have
been placed whole upon the altar, and not merely a portion of it.

We may also see how thoroughly wrong *Keil's* explanation is, if we inquire into the symbolical worth assigned to the fat from a *psychological point of view*. The conclusion to which our inquiry leads is, that the fat is the symbol of want of feeling or sensibility, obstinacy, and hardness of heart,—the very opposite of what *Keil* supposes it to indicate. It is quite enough to point to Isa. vi. 10, where a layer of fat, formed about the heart, is a sign and proof of the hardening of the heart. And according to the analogy of this passage, the folds of fat which envelope the entrails, kidneys, and liver, when looked at from the standpoint of psychological interpretation, can only indicate a quality that deadens and destroys all the nobler feelings and emotions, of which they are the symbolical expression.

But the simple contrast of σῶμα ψυχικόν and σῶμα χοϊκόν, of ὁ ἔσω ἄνθρωπος (the inner man) and τὰ μέλη (the members), and still more the parallel drawn between this antithesis and that of the outward flesh and the inward fat, can hardly be exempted from the charge of great obscurity, and a confusion of dogmatical, ethical, and psychological notions. The lobes of fat, the kidneys, the liver-lobe, and the fat tail represent, we are told, the ἔσω ἄνθρωπος (the inner man), and this is identical with the psychical body ; whereas the rest of the flesh represents " the members," as opposed to the psychical body. We will lay no stress upon the fact, that the σῶμα χοϊκόν (the earthly body) is not a biblical expression or idea, but one arbitrarily formed, and not very happily chosen in this connection.[1] But how is it possible to designate the " psychical body " (σῶμα ψυχικόν) as the innermost kernel of humanity, and to identify it with the "inner man"? Is not the " psychical (natural) body " distinctly spoken of in 1 Cor. xv. 42 sqq. as the corruptible and perishable part of man, and identified with the "outward man," the "members," the "flesh and blood," which cannot inherit the kingdom of God? Is not the real antithesis to the σῶμα ψυχικόν the σῶμα πνευματικόν or "spiritual body"? and the antithesis to the ἄνθρωπος χοϊκός, or "earthly man," the ἄνθρωπος ἐπουράνιος or "heavenly man"? Must not the σῶμα ψυχικόν, therefore, be rather identical with the σῶμα χοϊκόν (if indeed the expression be admissible at all)? How has *Keil*, then, come to identify it with the "inner man," notwithstanding the Scriptures? Whether we take the Bible, the rules of

---

[1] It is true we read in 1 Cor. xv. 47 sqq. of a πρῶτος ἄνθρωπος ἐκ γῆς χοϊκός (" the first man is of the earth, earthy "); but the Apostle neither speaks, nor could speak, of a σῶμα χοϊκόν.

language, or logic as our guide, if we seek for a contrast to the
"earthly body," must we not necessarily find it in the "spiritual"
or "heavenly body"? *Keil*, indeed, could not make use of this,
because his "psychical body" (= "the inner man") is still in need
of purification by fire, of separation from earthly dross. And this
difficulty is not removed by exchanging the "spiritual body" for
the "psychical body," in *Keil's* sense of the word, as equivalent to
the "inner man." The "earthly man" does require, indeed, such
purification and separation from dross, because the "spiritual" or
"heavenly body" is fettered and imprisoned within it; but *Keil's*
"psychical body," the idea of which is identified with that of the
"inward man," and *excludes the idea of the "earthly body" or the
"members*," neither requires nor admits of such purification.

The contrast between the "inner man" and the "members"
seems to present a far better antithesis than that between the
"psychical body" and the "earthly body;" and even if the former
be foreign to the Old Testament, so that it cannot be applied to the
interpretation of the ritual of sacrifice, the New Testament Apostle
has really adopted it. But the purpose to which *Keil* has applied
it, apart altogether from the inadmissible admixture of Old and
New Testament ideas, is a very unfortunate one. What the Apostle
understood by the "inner man" he tells us in what follows, where
he substitutes νοῦς (the "mind") for it, and draws a contrast between it and "the members." But do the fat tail, the net of fat,
the kidneys with their fat, and the lobe of the liver (?) really represent the νοῦς? We will even drop the fat tail and fat lobe, and
confine ourselves to the kidneys alone, which were regarded as "the
seat of a man's tenderest and most secret emotions," and for that
reason have probably led our author astray into his most unfortunate interpretation. But do the Old Testament כְּלָיוֹת (reins) correspond to the New Testament νοῦς? I think *not;* but rather the
לֵבָב (heart) as the seat of wisdom and knowledge. But the "heart"
formed part of the "remainder of the flesh," the "earthly body"
(σῶμα χοϊκόν), which "being corrupted by sin," and "exposed to
death," was not placed upon the altar. Even if we were willing,
however, from accommodation to the psychology of our author, to
allow the reins (כְּלָיוֹת) to be substituted for the mind (νοῦς), would
anything be gained by so doing? Again I say, *no;* for I cannot
escape from this alternative: *either* the kidneys stand *per metonymiam* for the movements and affections of the mind, of which they
were regarded as the seat,—and in that case the head, the heart,

the bowels, and even the feet, the eyes, the ears, etc., must do so too, and cannot be opposed to the kidneys, the liver-lobe, the net and tail of fat, as "the earthly body" to the "psychical body," nor as "the members" to the "inner man;"—or the kidneys, the liver, the fat tail, and the net of fat are regarded as "members" (μέλη), as well as the heart and entrails, the head, shoulder, leg, and foot,—and in that case they cannot serve, any more than the latter, as representatives of the "inner man."

§ 110. To arrive at the correct interpretation of the portions of fat, which were to be burned upon the altar "for a sweet savour unto Jehovah" (Lev. iv. 31), we must revert to the signification of the burnt sacrifice as לֶחֶם לַיהוָה, of which we have frequently spoken already (§ 23, 72, 77). From this expression we have already seen, that the psychological standpoint is not the true, scriptural point of view for the interpretation of the burnt sacrifice; and that the flesh was burned, not as being the organ of the soul, but as food for Jehovah, and food *alone*. But from this point of view the fat portions, as contrasted with the rest of the flesh, can only be regarded as the noblest, best, and most sublimated portion, the *flos carnis* (as *Neumann, Sacra V. T. salutaria*, p. 35, has well expressed it); and such passages as the following may be adduced as explanatory of the expression, and also of the question itself, viz.: Gen. xlv. 18, "the fat of the land;" Deut. xxxii. 14, "the kidney-fat of wheat;" Ps. lxxxi. 16, "fat of the wheat;" Num. xviii. 12, "fat of oil and fat of wine;" 2 Sam. i. 22, "the fat of the mighty," *i.e.*, the most distinguished heroes; Ps. xvii. 10, xxii. 12, 29, lxviii. 23; Amos iv. 1; Ezek. xxxiv. 16, 20; Zech. xi. 16, etc., "the fat" of the nation, *i.e.*, the rich and powerful among the people. Since the whole of the flesh was not to be placed upon the altar in the case of the sin-offering, for reasons to be examined presently, the fat portions only were to be burned, as being the first, best, and most distinguished part, and as representing the whole of the flesh. In these portions the whole of the flesh was sanctified and consecrated to Jehovah.

With regard to the *burning* of these *flores carnis* upon the altar, in the case of the sin-offering; it cannot have any other significa-tion than the burning of the same portions in the case of the peace-offering, and of the whole of the flesh (of which these were the first-fruits) in the case of the burnt-offering. What that meaning was, we have already shown and explained at § 75 sqq. It denoted the personal appropriation of the gift to Jehovah, and that gift was

food for Jehovah (לֶחֶם לַיהוָֹה), inasmuch as it represented the personality of the offerer himself, whose self-surrender was *the* food, which
Jehovah desired as the God of salvation, and of which in that capacity He ever stood in need. Its being presented to Him in the
holy fire of the altar pointed to the fact, that such surrender, however earnestly and honestly it might be meant, required, like everything earthly, to be purified by the fire of divine holiness, before it
could appear in the presence of Jehovah Himself (Isa. vi. 6, 7).

§ 111. The subject becomes much more difficult, when we
inquire why the *whole* of the flesh was not burned upon the altar
(as in the burnt-offering), instead of merely the first-fruits, since
there was no sacrificial meal in the case of the sin-offering, as there
was in that of the peace-offering.

In *Knobel's* opinion (Lev. p. 344), this question may be settled
by the simple remark, that " in the sin-offering and trespass-offering no flesh was burnt at all, because Jehovah accepts no food from
sinners." But Jehovah did accept the *fat portions* from sinners.
And if the burning of the whole animal (both fat and flesh) in the
case of the burnt-offering, and the very same fat portions in that
of the peace-offering was to be regarded as food for Jehovah, the
same action in connection with the sin-offering must certainly
possess the same signification.

Keil's answer to this question also embodies a similar idea. He
builds still further upon the basis of his mistaken interpretation of the
fat portion (§ 109), and proceeds thus (pp. 231–2) : " Consequently,
by the burning and complete consumption of the internal (?) portions
of fat, the inner and superior portion of human nature was committed to the sanctifying fire of divine love, and ascended thence
towards heaven purified, and in its glorified essence, as an offering
well-pleasing to the Lord. The outer man, on the contrary, the
σῶμα χοϊκόν, could not ascend to God in a glorified form, because
it was disordered by sin, and condemned to death. The flesh of the
sin-offering, therefore, might not be consumed upon the altar."

It is hardly necessary to say, that from the inadmissible assumptions contained in this reply, it cannot be correct (§ 109) ; but
even apart from these assumptions, it is altogether fallacious.   The
writer seems to have had such passages of the New Testament float-
ing before his mind as 1 Cor. vi. 13 and xv. 50, where we read of
" the belly, which God shall destroy," the " flesh and blood which
cannot inherit the kingdom of God," and the " corruption which
doth not inherit incorruption."   But it is very apparent, that we

have here to do with antitheses, to which the outward portions of
flesh and the inward (?) portions of fat in no way correspond.
According to the Apostle's doctrine, the outer man, the earthly
(psychical) body, is undoubtedly corrupted by sin and sentenced to
death ($\phi\theta o\rho\acute{a}$) ; but he also adds, that " this corruptible must put
on incorruption, and this mortal must put on immortality," and in
the former passage, that the same " members," which he contrasts
with the inner man in Rom. vii., are " members of Christ," and
that the same " body," which he regards in 1 Cor. xv. as given up
to $\phi\theta o\rho\acute{a}$, is nevertheless " the temple of the Holy Ghost which is in
you." Why then should " the outward man," the " earthly body,"
or the " members," not " ascend to God in a glorified form " in the
symbol of the sacrificial worship, and their symbols from the animal
world " be burnt upon the altar," if they both can be, and are,
members of Christ, and temples of the Holy Ghost? According
to *Keil's* own admission, the burning seemed to refine and glorify
the object burned, to remove the $\phi\theta o\rho\acute{a}$, or $\chi o\ddot{\imath}\kappa\acute{o}v$, that " in their
glorified essence they might ascend to God." Or does he possibly
regard the outer man, the body of a man, or his " members," as absolute $\phi\theta o\rho\acute{a}$, mere dross, and therefore incapable of being refined
and glorified? He cannot do this ; for it would call to mind Mani
and the Gnostics too strongly, and directly contradict in every point
the teaching of the very same Apostle, upon whose doctrines *Keil*
professes to have founded his theory.

Moreover, how did the case actually stand, *in the first place*, with
the *pigeons* that were offered as *sin-offerings*, with reference to which
Keil himself affirms (p. 218), that in all probability, after removing
the crop with its contents, which were thrown upon the ash-heap, just
as in the burnt-offering, the *entire* animal was burnt upon the altar?
In this case, at any rate, the " earthly body," $\sigma\hat{\omega}\mu\alpha\ \chi o\ddot{\imath}\kappa\acute{o}v$, could
be burnt upon the altar, and ascend to God in a glorified form !—
And how did it stand, *in the second place*, with the *burnt-offerings*?
In their case the inward (?) portions of fat were burnt upon the altar
along with the outward flesh,—that is to say, the " inner man " or
" psychical body " along with " the outer man " (the members or
" earthly body"),—and " being refined by the fire of divine love,
ascended to God in a glorified form." *Keil* will probably answer
that the sin and guilt of the person sacrificing were not imputed to
the burnt-offering, as they were to the sin-offering (§ 38). But to
that I should reply, (1) that it is not true, that by the imposition
of hands in the case of the sin-offering the outer portions of flesh

became the representatives of the " outer man ($= \sigma \hat{\omega} \mu a \; \chi o \ddot{\iota} \kappa \acute{o} \nu =$ $\tau \grave{a} \; \mu \acute{e} \lambda \eta$)," and the inner (?) portions of fat the representatives of the "inner man ;" but if they were so at all, they were so from their very nature, and from the natural contrast between them ;—(2) that even in the case of the burnt-offering a sprinkling of blood, *i.e.*, an expiation, took place, and therefore there must have been sin to expiate ;—and (3) that if the sin and guilt of the sacrificer were placed upon, or imputed to, the animal in the sin-offering, and thus the outer portions of flesh were infected with sin and uncleanness, the inner portions of fat and the outward tail of fat (which were burned upon the altar) must have been similarly infected with sin and uncleanness. Or does *Keil* really intend to maintain that the effect of the imposition of hands was restricted to the heart, liver, entrails, muscles, tendons and bones, and did not extend to the liver and kidneys, the net of fat, and the fat tail ?—How did it stand, *in the third place*, with the sin-offering of the red heifer (Num. xix.), where the very opposite took place, and the *inward* portions of fat *as well* as the outward flesh and bones were " burnt outside the camp as being corrupted by sin and liable to death, and thus given up to an annihilating death" ? (cf. § 219).—And how did it stand, *in the fourth place*, with the *blood* of the *ordinary* sin-offering (to say nothing at present of the blood of the red heifer, which was burnt along with the inner and outer portions of fat and flesh) ? Did the imposition of hands, by which the animal was laden with sin and guilt, and which made it as it were an incarnate sin (חַטָּאת), a " body of sin," exert the same influence upon the *blood* (which was also placed upon the altar), or not? Though *Keil* is always ready to affirm most unreservedly, that in the imposition of hands the sin and debt of the person acting were transferred and imputed to the sin-offering and trespass-offering, so that from that time forward it might be regarded and designated as an incarnate sin or debt (§ 46) ; yet he nowhere *expressly* states, whether he supposed this imputation to extend to the *whole* animal, or merely to its *blood* as the " vehicle of the soul," or only to the flesh as the " organ of the soul," and if the *latter*, whether to the outer portions of *flesh* and the inner portions of *fat*, including the outward tail of *fat*, or only to the first of these. But it must be patent to every one, that a discussion of these questions, a distinct and full answer to them, was indispensable as the foundation of his theory of the sin-offering. Yet he has not given one ; so that we are under the necessity of collecting his views from expressions scattered here and there. Let us endeavour therefore to supply the want in this way, as a reliable answer to these questions is absolutely necessary to enable us to understand and pronounce upon his theory.

When we read in different passages of his work, that by the imposition of hands sin and debt were transferred and imputed to the sin-offering and trespass-offering as such, and that it thereby became, as it were, an incarnate sin or debt, the most natural supposition is, that he regards the effect attributed to the imposition of hands as extending to the *whole animal*, and therefore to both flesh *and* blood. On the other hand, when we find it stated in a still larger number of passages, " that in the blood of the sacrificial animal (as the vehicle of its soul), the soul of the sacrificer was brought symbolically and vicariously to the altar as the place of the Lord's gracious presence, *i.e.*, within the sphere of the operations of divine grace, in order that its sin might be covered over by the grace and mercy of God, *i.e.*, forgiven" (§ 69);—we can draw no other conclusion than that the imputation effected by the imposition of hands affected chiefly, if not *exclusively*, the blood or soul of the sacrificial animal, which was in itself perfectly free from sin and guilt, from blemish of any kind ; and the latter would really be the only view in harmony with the facts. For the blood, which pervades the whole body even to its minutest fibres, is the seat of the animal's soul ; and the soul of the sacrificial animal, which was sinless and innocent in itself, but which after, and because of, the imposition of hands represented the soul of the sacrificer, with all its load of sin and guilt, was brought to the altar, in order that in it, or with it, the sins of the sacrificer might there be covered over. In any case, therefore, the sin of the person sacrificing must have been symbolically transferred to the *blood* of the animal,—and *to it alone*, not to the flesh and fat as well ; for the *blood* alone was the seat and vehicle of the soul, and not the bloodless flesh or fat, and the *soul* alone was the vehicle and cause, the bearer and confessor of sin, and not its organs (the flesh, bones, nerves, and sinews). We are certainly not wrong, therefore, in supposing the author's meaning to be, that by the imposition of hands the blood alone, as the vehicle of the animal's soul, was laden with sin and guilt, and not its flesh as well. And yet, when we read a little farther, and find the same author affirming that the flesh of the (slaughtered) animal (when drained of its blood) could not be placed upon the altar, because it was " unclean in consequence of the sin imputed to it" (p. 233), or because it was " laden with the sin imputed to it" (p. 231), we are obliged once more to assume, that he does *not* regard the sin of the sacrificer as imputed and transferred to the blood, because this was placed upon the altar, but as imputed to the flesh *alone*, and in fact to the *outward* flesh alone to the exclusion of the internal fat and the external tail.   Accordingly, at p. 412 he says, " The sacrificial *blood* did not defile in any sacrifice, but touching the *flesh* of the sin-offering did."

Thus from different passages of the same author we are brought by logical necessity to different and contradictory answers to the same question.   And we may venture even here to affirm, that the fundamental ideas upon which his theory of the sin-offering is based are as incorrect and deceptive, as they are necessarily obscure and contradictory.   (*Vid.* § 114.)

§ 112. The true answer to the question proposed at the head of the previous section, must be obtained from the design and disposal of the flesh, which was not burned upon the altar.   This was two-fold.   Sometimes it was *burned outside the camp* in a clean place, where the ashes of the sacrifices were also thrown, together with the hide, head, bones, entrails, and dung (Lev. iv. 11, 12, 20, 21 ; cf. xvi. 27).   This was done in the case of all the sin-offerings, whose blood was brought into the Holy Place (Lev. vi. 23), and therefore with the sin-offering of the priest and that of the whole congregation (including the priests).   But with all the sin-offerings, whose blood was not brought into the Holy Place, and therefore with those of the laity, whether prince or common man, it was *eaten in a holy place*, *i.e.*, in the fore-court, by the officiating priest and his sons ; his wife and daughters not being allowed to participate (Lev. vi. 18, 22).[1]

In addition to this we have the following directions (Lev. vi. 27, 28) : Whoever else touched the flesh was forfeited to the sanc-tuary (יִקְדָּשׁ),—probably in this way, that, like a man who had vowed himself to God, he had to redeem himself for a definite sum of money (Lev. xxvii. 2 sqq.).   If any one's clothes were sprinkled by the blood of the sin-offering, he was to wash them in a holy place.   And the pot, in which the flesh of the sin-offering was boiled, was to be broken if it were an earthen one, and carefully scoured out and rinsed with water if it were of brass.   Compare with this Lev. x. 16–20, the only passage which affords us any help

---

[1] If the officiating priests could not eat the whole, all that was left over was probably burned in a clean place outside the camp, as was expressly commanded in the case of the peace-offering (§ 139).

in the interpretation of these striking commands.   Aaron's sons had
offered the first sin-offering for the people (apart from the priests,
Lev. ix. 15), and, without Moses knowing it, had burned the flesh
outside the camp, just as Moses had commanded them to do with
the flesh of the sin-offering that they had offered for themselves.
When Moses discovered this, he reproved the priests, and said,
" Wherefore have ye not eaten the sin-offering in the Holy Place,
seeing it is most holy, and He hath given it you to bear (or take
away, לָשֵׂאת) the iniquity of the congregation, to make atonement for
them before the Lord ?   Behold, the blood of it was not brought in
within the Holy Place. Ye should indeed have eaten it in the Holy
Place, as I commanded." Aaron excused his sons on the ground that
they had offered their sin-offering and their burnt-offering on the very
same day, and then added, " Such things have befallen me : and if
I had eaten the sin-offering to-day, should it have been accepted in
the sight of the Lord ?"   And Moses was satisfied with this reply.

§ 113. *Cornelius a Lapide* (on Lev. x. 17) has given this explanation of the eating of the flesh of the sin-offering by the priests :
*Ut scilicet cum hostiis populi pro peccato simul etiam populi peccata
in vos recipiatis, ut illa expietis.   Deyling* follows him, and says
(Observv. ss. i. c. 45, § 2), *hoc pacto cum ederent, incorporabant quasi
peccatum populique reatum in se recipiebant ;* and *Hengstenberg* also,
who writes thus (p. 13) : " Both of these (the eating by the priests
in the one case, and the burning outside the camp in the other)
pointed to the fact that the uncleanness of the sacrificer was transferred to the sacrifice, and imbibed as it were by it. . . . The eating of the flesh by the priest was an act of worship.   It rested upon
the supposition, that the uncleanness of the sinner was transferred
to the sacrifice, and upon the idea, that for its complete removal it
was necessary that it should enter into a closer relation to the priesthood instituted by God, through which relation it was consumed by
the holiness conferred upon that office, in anticipation of a time
when both sacrifice and priesthood should be united in the same
person.   We meet with the same idea in Lev. x. 17.   Equally conclusive, too, is the circumstance that those sin-offerings, in which
the priests themselves were concerned, and therefore could not act
as representatives (?), had to be burned outside the camp.   Removal
from the camp, which was a type of the Church, was always a sign
of uncleanness under the Mosaic law."

But there are the gravest objections to this view. If the sinner's
uncleanness was transferred to the sacrifice, and imbibed by it as it

were, it is perfectly inconceivable that only the outer flesh should have been infected, and not the internal portions of fat as well. And if *Hengstenberg* admits this, I should ask him then how it is conceivable, that a gift which was saturated with uncleanness, and which not only represented sin, but was as it were a visible manifestation of it, could possibly be placed upon the altar, and designated in Lev. iv. 31 as a "sweet savour to Jehovah"? But if he does not admit it, the remarks which I have made in § 111 with reference to *Keil,* are equally applicable to him. Moreover, how could the flesh of the sin-offering be still regarded as laden with imputed sin, after the expiation of the sins imputed had been effected by the sprinkling of the blood (and that in the most forcible manner that could possibly be conceived)? But if the flesh of the sin-offering had been regarded as unclean, it could not have been designated as "most holy" (Lev. x. 17); and the priest, who had most scrupulously to avoid all contact with that which was unclean, could hardly have been commanded to eat it. The directions given in Lev. vi. 20, 23 speak quite as decidedly against the uncleanness of the sin-offering. The flesh was so holy, that not even the priest's relatives were allowed to eat of it, and it might only be eaten in the Holy Place. A layman, touching it by accident, was affected by its holiness, and was to be regarded as sanctified, dedicated to Jehovah. If a drop of the blood happened to be sprinkled upon the clothes of those who were present, they were to be washed in the tabernacle itself. All these directions are suggestive, not of uncleanness, but of the extreme purity and holiness of the sin-offering; and judging by their analogy, therefore, the breaking of the earthen pot, and the scouring of the copper vessel, in which the flesh had been boiled, are to be attributed, not to their defilement, but to their sanctification, and the importance of preventing the desecration of a sacred vessel by its being afterwards put to a profane use. *Hengstenberg* supposes, indeed, that he can dispose of all these instances by the simple remark, that "the uncleanness of the sacrifice was essentially different from that of the sinner; and sin transferred could never be exactly equivalent to indwelling sin." But the difficulty is not to be removed by such arbitrary assertions. Uncleanness is uncleanness, whether it has developed itself within the subject, or has been transferred to it from another unclean object. For example, according to Lev. xv., not only did a person's own sexual uncleanness require purification, but the uncleanness *transferred* to another also; and the distinction between personal and transferred uncleanness was not an essential one, but simply one of degree.[1] The $\pi\rho\hat{\omega}\tau o\nu$ $\psi\epsilon\hat{v}\delta o\varsigma$ in this view, however, is the dogmatically and exegetically inadmissible idea of a transference of the sin itself from the sacrificer to the sacrificial animal, whereas it was only the obligation to suffer or perform in the place of the sacrificer, what divine justice and holiness demanded on account of his sin, that was actually transferred (§ 43 sqq.). Again, the idea that the *clean* place outside the camp, where the flesh of the priest's sin-offering was burned, was strictly speaking an *unclean* one (an unclean clean place therefore!), is and remains a crying *contradictio in adjecto*, notwithstanding *Hengstenberg's* loophole, " that this belongs to the other side of the sacrifice."—This explanation, too, must also be pronounced untenable, because it gives a meaning to the eating of the flesh of the sin-offering by the priest, which is entirely inapplicable to the eating of the peace-offering, though there was a perfect analogy between them, and the only differences were those of degree (§ 118), and also because it places the burning of the flesh outside the camp in a totally different aspect from the corresponding burning of the flesh that was left over from the passover lamb, and from the peace and consecration services (Ex. xii. 10, xxix. 34; Lev. vii. 17, viii. 32, xix. 6).

§ 114. *Hengstenberg* is followed by *Keil* (i. 231), who says: " If the first part of expiation, namely, the forgiveness of sins, was effected symbolically in the sprinkling of the blood; the second part, viz., the extermination of sin and the sanctification of the pardoned sinner, was represented by the course adopted with the flesh of the sin-offering. . . . For as death merely puts an end to the continued activity of the sinner, but does not exterminate the sin, so (?) the flesh of the sin-offering, notwithstanding the death endured, was still laden with the sin imputed to it; and this also needed to be exterminated, if the expiation was to be complete. This extermination of the sin in the flesh was effected in the ritual

---

[1] Even the uncommon, though fruitless exertions made by *Keil* (i. 235), to convince us that " anything affected by sin and uncleanness might still be regarded as most holy, if we only put clearly before our mind the 'hieratic' notion of what is most holy," are only adapted to place the inconceivableness of most holy sin or most holy uncleanness in a clearer light, especially if we agree with *Keil* in regarding the sin-offering as becoming an " incarnate sin," and " a body of sin," which as such " was to be sentenced to the death of annihilation by fire" in the case of the sin-offerings of the priests and the congregation, and that " outside the camp, *i.e.*, outside the kingdom of God, from which every dead thing was taken away."

of sacrifice in a twofold manner. . . . This double procedure with the flesh of the sin-offering must be based upon one idea. . . . The eating of the flesh on the part of the priests was an act of worship according to Lev. x. 17, an official function, by which they were to bear the sin of the congregation,—an *incorporatio* therefore of the victim laden with sin, by which they exterminated the sin through the holiness and sanctifying power imparted to them by virtue of their office. . . . In those sin-offerings, on the other hand, in which they were themselves concerned, they could not act vicariously (?) . . . and as they needed expiation and sanctification themselves, they could not at the same time impart sanctification and expiation, but the sin could only be exterminated in fire by the burning of the flesh of the sacrifice that was laden with it. In both cases, therefore, the flesh, to which the sin was imputed, was destroyed ; in the first instance, by its sinful nature being swallowed up by the holiness of the priests,—in the second, by the manifestation of the fruit of sin, *i.e.*, of the death which sin produces. . . . For the priests themselves there was no one, in the economy of the old covenant, who could have borne and exterminated their sin by eating the flesh of the sin-offerings that were offered on their behalf. For this reason it was necessary that the flesh of the sacrifice laden with their sin, should be condemned as the body of sin to the death of annihilation, and be consumed by fire,—not upon the altar, however, since it had become unclean through the sin imputed to it, but outside the camp, *i.e.*, outside the kingdom of God, from which every dead thing was removed. At the same time, inasmuch as it was the flesh of a sacrifice, it was ordered to be burnt in the clean place to which the ashes were conveyed from the altar of burnt-offering, and not in any unclean place, that what had been set apart for a holy use might not become an abomination."

We observe here in the first place, that all we have said in § 113 with reference to *Hengstenberg's* theory, is equally applicable to this further expansion of it. The different points in this extension are quite as erroneous as the groundwork itself. And, first of all, we must condemn the confusion in language, which is apparent in the too comprehensive use of the word "*expiation*" on the one hand, and the too restricted use of the expression "*extermination of sins*" on the other, not merely because they are opposed to the forms of speech, but chiefly because of their obscurity, so far as the doctrinal idea is concerned. For instance, *Keil* divides the idea of expiation into two parts,—(1) forgiveness of sin, or justification, and (2) extermination of sin, or sanctification. Now this is opposed to the usage of the language; for the Latin word *expiatio* is admitted by all lexicographers to be *perfectly identical* with the German word *Sühnung* (expiation), and "forgiveness of sin," according to *Keil's* own view, is identical with the "expiation of sin." It is also *at variance with fact*; for לְכַפֵּר always relates to the sprinkling of the blood as such, and never to the *burning upon the altar* as such (it cannot, therefore, be regarded by him as a consecration of the gift already cleansed from sin by the sprinkling of the blood);—to say nothing of the possibility of its being applied to a "burning to annihilation," and "outside the kingdom of God, from which every dead thing had to be removed." There is something confusing, too, in the definition of sanctification as the *extermination of sin*. For the forgiveness of sin, or justification, might be defined in precisely the same way. And the definition is all the more inappropriate here, from the fact that the sin-offering had regard not to sinfulness in general, or to the sinful *habitus*, which is the object exterminated in the case of sanctification, but to certain acts of sin, the extermination of which is effected not by sanctification, but by justification.

But not only does *Keil* resolve expiation into two component elements—forgiveness of sin, or *justification*, and extermination of sin, or *sanctification*,—and regard the former as effected by the sprinkling of the blood, the latter by the course adopted with the flesh; he also resolves the latter again into two new elements: (1) the *purification* of the "psychical body," *i.e.*, of the better portion or inmost kernel of humanity, in the burning upon the altar; and (2) the *annihilation* of the body of sin (= σῶμα χοϊκόν, the earthy body). And this again is accomplished by a twofold process: (1) in the sin-offering of a layman, by the priests' *eating* the σῶμα χοϊκόν, or body of sin, and exterminating the sin through their official holiness; and (2) in the sin-offering of a priest, by the body of sin being removed from the kingdom of God, and sentenced to the death of annihilation by fire, that is to say, being burnt up. —But this resolution of the main idea of "expiation" into the antitheses which it is supposed to contain, presents many other difficulties besides those already discussed at § 109, 111, 113, which we must examine in order thoroughly to pronounce upon, *i.e.*, to condemn, this theory of the sin-offering.

The difficulties in question relate to the "second" element in the "expiation," namely, to the "extermination of sin," or sanctification, and the antitheses which it involves. The first of these antitheses is (*a*) the *purification of the inner man*, and (*b*) the *annihilation of the outer man*. The two together are said to complete the idea of sanctification, or the extermination of sin. This presents at once a difficulty which I cannot get over; for the idea of sanctification is that of purification, but not of annihilation; on the contrary, it rather excludes the latter. Nor can I understand the assignment of these two antithetical ingredients of sanctification to the inner and outer man. If the "inner man" be regarded as pure, as opposed to the outer man, and therefore pure from sin and corruption, I cannot see what there was that needed to be purified and burnt out by the altar-fire. But if, on the other hand, it be regarded as dwelling *in* the outer man, *in* the body of sin, and affected or infected by its sinfulness or sins, I cannot imagine how, according to *Keil's* theory, it could be placed upon the altar, since even then it would be "corrupted by sin," and "rendered unclean by the sin imputed to it." It would surely rather have needed "to be removed outside the camp, *i.e.*, outside the kingdom of God." There is the same internal contradiction in the second element of sanctification, viz., the annihilation of the outer man = $\tau\grave{\alpha}$ $\mu\acute{\epsilon}\lambda\eta$ = $\sigma\hat{\omega}\mu\alpha$ $\chi o\ddot{\iota}\kappa\acute{o}\nu$. If we take the idea of $\tau\grave{\alpha}$ $\mu\acute{\epsilon}\lambda\eta$ seriously, and therefore do not regard the outer man in a thoroughly Manichean fashion as essentially and altogether sin, but according to the teaching of both the Scriptures and the Church, as merely pervaded and defiled by sin, it is an object for purification, refinement, glorification, but not for destruction. But if we treat the idea of $\sigma\hat{\omega}\mu\alpha$ $\chi o\ddot{\iota}\kappa\acute{o}\nu$ seriously in this sense, that we regard it as mere corruption, mere dross, and therefore look upon the outer man (physically) as that part of us which becomes and remains the prey of corruption, or (ethically) as that which excludes and is excluded from the kingdom of God and eternal blessedness; the idea of destruction is certainly applicable, but not in any way that of sanctification, *i.e.*, of refinement, for the ore is the object for refining, but not the dross.

But even if we were willing or able to accept the *idea of annihilation*, which is inapplicable to the outer man, as the vehicle or means of sanctification, there is something in the antitheses, into which *this* idea is again resolved, which, in our opinion, is perfectly inconceivable; viz., (1) the annihilation of the outer man in the case of the *laity*, by its being *eaten* by the priests in the Holy Place, and (2) the annihilation of the outer man in the case of the *priests*, by its being *burnt* outside the camp, or the kingdom of God. The eating in the former case, and the burning in the latter, are said to signify the same thing, namely, annihilation, *i.e.*, sanctification; and even the object of this annihilation or sanctification is essentially the same, viz., the outer man, in the one case of the priest, in the other of the layman. Now, how is it conceivable that essentially the same end could be answered in essentially the same objects, when the one was received into the inmost centre of holiness, viz., into the priests, who were κατ᾽ ἐξοχήν the holy persons, the representatives of God, and the other removed from the kingdom of God to the place appointed for every dead thing, and disposed of there by being burnt with ungodly, *i.e.*, unholy fire? Even if recourse were had to the doctrine of modern physiology, that the process of digestion is a process of burning (which would hardly be advisable), there would still be the inexplicable incongruity, that the subject in the one case is holy, viz., the consecrated priests and they alone, to the exclusion even of the members of their families, and in the other case unholy, viz., profane fire; and again, that in the *former* the burning was to take place in the sanctuary itself, as the symbolical concentration of the kingdom of God, and could *only* be effected there; whereas in the *latter* it was ordered to take place not only outside the tabernacle, but even outside the camp, *i.e.*, the kingdom of God. And supposing it possible that the sacrificial law could have been capable of such self-contradiction, should we not expect to find the very opposite arrangement, viz., that the annihilation, *i.e.*, sanctification, of the outer man of the consecrated priests would have been effected in the sanctuary, and that of the outer man of the unconsecrated laity outside the camp?

§ 115. *Ewald* gives a different turn to the same fundamental idea of an *incorporatio peccati*: " According to the ancient belief," he says, " when this sprinkling of the blood was finished, with its most holy solemnity, the uncleanness and guilt were loosened and irresistibly enticed out of the object to which they adhered; and so we too must *evidently* understand the ceremony in the sense of antiquity. But shaken loose though it was, according to the same view, it passed first of all only into that body, whose blood had so irresistibly drawn it out: so that the remains of this body were now themselves regarded as having become unclean, and consequently were looked upon with all the horror which was felt towards anything unclean in the sight of God,—in fact, with even greater horror than usual; and it was just in this point that the night side of this entire class of sacrifices became most strikingly manifest. In perfect accordance with this idea, these remains were all burnt, exactly as they were—that is to say, without removing the filth belonging to them—far away from the sanctuary, in a common, though otherwise clean place, like any other object of disgust, that could not be got rid of and destroyed in any other way. . . . This burning was only carried out, however, in the case of expiatory sacrifices of the most solemn description. . . . . In ordinary cases the ceremony was *evidently* abbreviated in this way, that after the sprinkling of the blood the mercy of God was at once implored, to take away entirely the guilt which had thus been set in motion. . . . But when once they had got over the gloomy obligation to burn the remains of this sacrifice, and had learned, at least in ordinary cases, to solicit even without it the divine removal of guilt, so that the flesh destined to annihilation appeared as though rescued by superior mercy: they could venture still further, and it became legal in Jehovahdom, to take a portion of every sacrifice of this mournful description and throw it into the altar-fire. . . . . But the sacrificer himself durst not eat of it; nor was this ever afterwards allowed. . . . For this reason the flesh of the ordinary sacrifices was indeed preserved, but it was regarded as something miraculous, which had been preserved from destruction purely by the mercy of God, as a ' most holy thing.' Every one who touched the flesh with a common hand was regarded as forfeited to the sanctuary. None but priests of the sanctuary were considered qualified to consume the dangerous flesh ; but from them it was also expected that they should take it into themselves and consume it, and with it, as it were, the guilt that had been atoned for. . . . How difficult this was at first, we may learn from the book of Origins (*Ursprünge*) in the account of Aaron and his four sons."

So much of this view as is old, and admits of a refutation, has already received it in what has gone before, and will still further receive it in what follows. What is new is so unintelligible, fantastical, and arbitrary, as to admit just as little of refutation as of adoption. Even *Knobel* (p. 386) does not hesitate to throw away at once *Ewald's* notion of the dangerous character of the flesh, as a " romantic idea."

§ 116. *Kliefoth's* theory (pp. 67–70), according to which the eating of the flesh of the sin-offering by the priests is to be looked at in the same light as the sacrificial meal at the presentation of a peace-offering, and indicated, like the latter, the reconciliation of the sinner, and his actual reception into the fellowship of the holy nation, has been already discussed and shown to be inadmissible from the standpoint of the peace-offering (§ 84). We have now to examine it from the standpoint of the ritual of the sin-offering.

The chief fault in this view of *Kliefoth*, is the essential equality attributed to two different functions that admit of no comparison. If the eating of the sin-offering by the priests be compared to the eating of the peace-offering, the comparison in the case of the latter cannot extend to the true sacrificial meal, but must be restricted entirely to the eating of that portion of the peace-offering which was peculiar to the *priests*, viz., to the eating of the heave-shoulder and wave-breast. With the sacrificial *meal* connected with the peace-offering, the eating of the sin-offering by the priests had nothing in common. In the former, the sacrificer himself was the principal person concerned; next to him came his family, and then any one else that he chose to add out of the circle of his acquaintance. The eating in common was the chief thing, the institution of a lively, joyous, festal meal; and the participation of the priest in this meal was either not expected, or at all events was not essentially necessary. On the other hand, the sacrificer himself was most strictly forbidden to eat of the flesh of the sin-offering; none but the officiating priests were entitled to do so; a layman, who only touched the flesh, was forfeited to the sanctuary; and it was so far from having anything like the character of a common meal, that not even the priest's family was allowed to take part in it. But it certainly presented an essential analogy to the eating of the heave-shoulder and wave-breast by the priests, which merely stood upon a lower level on account of the inferior holiness of the peace-offering; so that the command that it should be eaten in the Holy Place, and by the officiating priests alone, was allowed to be so far modified, that a clean place could be substituted for the Holy Place, and their wives and daughters admitted to partake; a distinction corresponding to the respective epithets applied to them, of "holy," and "most holy."

Kliefoth endeavours, indeed, to bridge over the chasm between the non-priestly meal connected with the peace-offering, and the eating of the flesh of the sin-offering by the priests. But the arguments which he adduces can hardly be regarded as sufficient for the purpose.[1] There is something far more satisfactory in what the author

---

[1] For example, he says (p. 69): "As we found throughout the whole course of the sin-offering, that the activity of the sacrificer was to be confined to his

adduces in explanation of the omission of the sacrificial eating from those sin-offerings, in which the priests themselves were the sacrificers either in whole or in part;[1] and we can give unqualified assent (looking to the analogous procedure adopted in connection with the paschal lamb and the peace- and consecration-offerings), when he affirms that the burning of the flesh of such sin-offerings outside the camp had no religious (or symbolical) signification.

§ 117. That the *burning* (שׂרֵף) *outside the camp* had no symbolical signification, but only answered the purpose of preserving the flesh from putrefaction and profanation, because no one was allowed to eat it, had been maintained by *Bähr* (ii. 395) before *Kliefoth;* and all later writers, with the exception of *Hengstenberg, Keil,* and *Ewald,* have followed him in this. A still more generally received opinion, which *Ewald* is alone in rejecting, is, that this flesh, which was given up to be burned outside the camp, was not to be eaten by the priests, because the priests themselves were the sacrificers, or were associated in the sacrifice; since it was characteristic of the sin-offering, that the person presenting it was not allowed to eat of it. And no tenable objection can be offered to this, although the law itself lays no stress upon the point,[2] but always enforces the necessity for the burning outside the camp, on the ground that the blood of these sin-offerings had been brought into the Holy Place,— the meaning evidently being, that the flesh of these sin-offerings was holier than that of the others, and too *holy* even for the priests to eat (Lev. vi. 23, x. 18, xvi. 27). But these points of view do

penitence, and that in every act which was subservient to his expiation and restoration he was placed entirely in a receptive condition; so, in relation to the sacrificial meal (?), he was only to acknowledge to himself, what was accomplished thereby both for him and with him. On the other hand, the priests alone —those who were officially holy, and therefore actual priests,—to the exclusion even of their families, were to eat the flesh of the sin-offering; for it was in the very nature of a sin-offering that the sinner for whom atonement had been made, should be restored to holy fellowship, and indeed to the very centre of holiness."

[1] P. 70. "In these cases no sacrificial eating could take place, since the priests themselves were the sacrificers, and sacrificers were not allowed to participate. But even in these cases no sacrificial meal was necessary; for all that was requisite for the whole nation and the priesthood, was restoration to the fellowship of God, and the act of burning (*sc.* upon the altar) sufficed for that. A holier human fellowship, to which *these* sacrificers could have been restored, was nowhere to be found."

[2] See, however, the allusion to the meat-offerings of the priests in Lev. vi. 16.

not exclude one another; for the flesh would in this instance be *too holy* even for the priests to eat, inasmuch as they themselves take the position of unholy persons here, and persons needing expiation, —not, however, as *Knobel* supposes (p. 386), because this flesh could not be eaten by men at all, on account of its having been " touched by God."

But what was there in the character of the sin-offering which precluded the person presenting it from eating of the flesh? The true answer is simple and not far to seek :—because the eating of the flesh of the sacrifice by the person presenting it was the distinguishing characteristic of the peace-offering, and the sin-offering was to be a sin-offering and not a peace-offering ;—or, in other words, because, according to the arrangement of the institution of sacrifice, so as to embrace sacrifices of several different kinds, the sin-offering merely laid the foundation for the presentation first of a burnt-offering, and then of a peace-offering, so that it could not raise the person sacrificing to that culminating point in the symbolism of sacrifice, which was represented by the eating of the flesh of the peace-offering (§ 79 sqq.).

But the discovery of the reason why the person presenting a sin-offering was not allowed to eat of it himself, by no means solves the whole of the difficulty. We have still further to inquire, why the duty of eating was transferred to the *priests*, when the sacrifice was not offered by themselves? And if here we answer, with *Hofmann* (p. 281), " It was a rule, that what was offered in sacrifice belonged to the priest as a reward for his service, so far as it was not burned upon the altar," the question with which we started returns again, —why was not all the flesh placed upon the altar in the case of the sin-offering, but only a portion selected from the best of it? Here, again, the answer is easier and more simple than the far-fetched and, as we have already seen, erroneous replies of *Knobel, Keil, Hengstenberg, Ewald,* and *Kliefoth* would lead us to suppose. It is simply this : becase the sin-offering was not intended as a burnt-offering, the distinguishing peculiarity of which consisted in the fact that all the flesh was placed upon the altar; or because the sin-offering did not elevate the person presenting it to that height in the symbolism of sacrifice, which was expressed in the burning of the entire sacrifice; but this was first effected by the burnt-offering which followed and rested upon it.[1]

[1] See *Oehler's* excellent observations (p. 648): " If in the case of other kinds of sacrifice the previous expiation formed the *conditio sine qua non* for

§ 118. Now, so far as the *eating of the flesh of the sin-offering by the priests,* wherever it was admissible, was in itself concerned, this need not be looked at in any case in an essentially different light from the eating of the flesh of the peace-offering (viz., the wave-breast and heave-shoulder, § 132, 133). In making this assertion, indeed, we must notice the fact, that *Keil* has repeated with still greater emphasis the charge which he brought, not only against me, but against *Hofmann* also, viz., of having "confounded the sin-offering with the thank-offering." But, serious as this charge appears, there is really very little in it. For the distinctive independence of each of these two descriptions of sacrifice is fully brought out, and the boundary line between them immoveably fixed, if we keep firmly in mind the fact, that not only the priests but the sacrificers themselves were allowed to partake of the flesh of the peace-offerings; whereas of the sin-offerings the priests alone were permitted to eat, never the persons presenting them, not even the priests when they themselves were the sacrificers. The institution of a formal sacrificial meal by and for the sacrificer and his family constituted the one distinctive peculiarity of the peace-offering; and we affirm as decidedly as *Keil,* that this was not admissible in connection with the sin-offering. But the eating of the breast and shoulder by the priest, in the case of the peace-offering, differed from his eating the whole of the flesh of the sin-offering solely in these respects: *first,* that in the former a portion only was assigned to the priest, and in the latter the whole of the flesh (with the exception of the fat). But this may easily be explained, on the simple ground that in the former a meal had to be instituted for the sacrificer and his family, which was not the case in the latter;—and *secondly,* that in the sin-offering none but the officiating priests were allowed to eat the flesh, not even their families, and they were required to eat it in the Holy Place; whereas in the peace-offering even the female portion of their families might participate in the flesh assigned them, and it could be eaten in any clean place (Lev. x. 14). This also may easily be explained, on the ground that the former, being assigned solely and exclusively to the priests, was *most holy* (cf. § 149); whereas the latter, being participated in alike by both priests and sacrificer, was simply a *holy thing.* All the rest was essenti-

what was the chief thing in them, namely, the offering of the gift; in the sin-offering, on the contrary, the gift which followed served to confirm, and thus in a certain sense to complete, the expiation which this sacrifice was intended directly to effect."

ally the same in both: the priest as subject, the eating as the act performed, the flesh of the sacrifice as the object. We are perfectly justified, therefore, in adhering to the assertion, that there was no essential difference, but only a difference in degree, between the signification of the eating of the flesh of the peace-offering by the priests, and their eating the flesh of the sin-offering.

In proceeding to inquire what the eating of the flesh of the (sin- and peace-) offerings by the priests really signified, we must revert to the question, whether it was parallel and correlative to the true sacrificial meal, in which the flesh was eaten by the sacrificer himself, or to the burning upon the altar, which could be regarded in a certain sense as לֶחֶם יְהוָֹה, *i.e.*, as also an eating, namely, by Jehovah. I have no hesitation in giving an answer at once in the negative to the former, and in the affirmative to the latter, for the simple reason, that the priest officiated in the sacrificial ceremony as the servant and representative of God, who rewarded and entertained him on that account, supplying him, so to speak, with food from His own table. For, notwithstanding *Keil's* remonstrance, I must adhere to the assertion (the correctness of which is proved by the burnt-offering as the leading and normal sacrifice), that, strictly speaking, the whole animal ought to have been placed upon the altar as a gift and food for Jehovah; and that the only reason why this rule was ever departed from was, that here and there other circumstances intervened which required a part of the gift to be kept back from the altar.

The eating of the flesh by the priests, therefore, had no other signification than to set forth the idea, that the priests, as the servants of God and the members of the household of God, were supplied from the table of God. The priest received his portion of the food which the people offered to their God. And as the presentation of this food on the part of the people to Jehovah was a representation of their surrender of themselves to Him, the transference of a part of this food to the priests would also express the idea, that the people were bound to make a similar voluntary *surrender* of themselves, not only to God, but in gratitude and devotedness to the priests also, as the servants and representatives of God.

If any one choose to call the eating of the flesh of the sin-offering by the priests, when looked at from this point of view, an official eating, I have no objection to offer. But if the term "*official*" be used in the more comprehensive and literal sense, so that the eating is reckoned (as it is by *Hengstenberg* and *Keil*) among the official

functions of the priests, and regarded as co-ordinate with the sprinkling of the blood, and even designated (as it is by *Keil*) as a "second
stage of expiation," I must enter my protest against it in the most
decided manner.   It was dependent upon their office, but it could
never be regarded as a function of the office itself.   When the servant of a household partakes of the food assigned him from his
master's table, he eats, or rather receives it, in the capacity of a
servant; but eating it is certainly not one of the duties of his office.

§ 119.   As a proof of the assertion, that the eating of the flesh
of the sin-offering by the priests was an *official* act in the strict and
literal sense of the word, *Hengstenberg* and *Keil* refer us to Lev. x.
17 sqq.   It is necessary, therefore, that we should enter, in conclusion, into a closer examination of this passage.

Besides the meaning given to this passage by *Hengstenberg* and
Keil,—which cannot be the correct one, for the simple reason that it
gives a signification to the eating of the flesh of the sin-offering,
that we have already seen to be untenable and full of contradictions
from every point of view,—we have two others before us which are
worth examining more minutely.   One is supported by *Oehler*, who
says (p. 649): "When we read in Lev. x. 17, that the sin-offering was given to the priests to eat, to take away the guilt of the congregation, and to make atonement for it before Jehovah; as the
actual removal of the guilt and the atonement had already been
effected through the sprinkling of the blood, the expression must be
taken as declaratory.   The eating of the flesh on the part of the
priests, like the burning of the fat, implied an acceptance of the
sacrifice on the part of God, which served as a declaration and
proof, that the sacrifice had really effected the expiation designed.
So far *Philo* (*de vict.* § 13) was correct in his view, when he stated
that one of the reasons for this appropriation of the sin-offering was
to satisfy the person presenting it as to his having obtained forgiveness; 'because God would not have called His servants to partake
of such a meal, unless the sin had been completely forgotten.'"—I
have also no doubt that such a declaratory signification may be
attributed to the eating of the flesh by the priests, as well as to the
correlative eating of it on the part of God (§ 118).   But I cannot
admit that this is expressed in the words of Lev. x. 17.   If we once
take the words נָתַן לָכֶם to mean, "He has given it you *to eat*," and
therefore understand the clause, "to bear the iniquity of the congregation, to make atonement for them," as denoting the purpose
and effect of *the eating*, we must take them, not in a declaratory,

but in an effective sense, as *Hengstenberg* and *Keil* have done. For that is how the words read, and the passage affords us neither warrant nor occasion for changing the effective *reading* into a declaratory *sense*.

The other view we find in *Hofmann* (p. 281). He says : " It is not the eating of the sin-offering which is there said to be a bearing of the iniquity of the congregation ; but it is stated of the sin-offering itself, that God has given it to the priest to take away the iniquity of the congregation, to make atonement for it before Jehovah. Nor does this show why it was eaten, but why it was to be regarded as a specially holy thing. If the sin-offering, therefore, was given to the priest to make atonement for the congregation, which he could not otherwise have done, he was not to regard it as a Typhonic sacrifice, but as a holy thing, and not to shrink from partaking of it, but to make an actual use of his right to eat it as the reward of the expiatory duties of his office."   Although *Keil* has condemned this view as " perfectly arbitrary" (p. 235), *Hofmann* has inserted the passage *verbatim* in the second edition of his *Schriftbeweis*, without thinking it worth while to notice *Keil's* objections. And it seems to me that, at all events, he has done right to adhere to his own view. For there is really no force in *Keil's* assertion, that " Jehovah had not merely given the sin-offering to the priest, but had given it to him *to eat*, that by this eating he might bear the sin of the congregation."   Nor do we find any more trace of a proof of his own view, than of a refutation of the opposite. It is simply assertion *versus* assertion. And whilst *Hofmann* has given reasons for his opinion taken from the passage itself, I cannot discover any such in *Keil*.

The correctness of *Hofmann's* view becomes the more apparent, the more closely we examine the construction of the passage. Moses inquired, " Why have ye not eaten the sin-offering in the Holy Place ?" and met the supposed reply of the priests, that they had not done so because it was unclean, by asserting that, on the contrary, it was most holy. It was most holy, because God had given it to them, that thereby they might take away the guilt of the congregation, and make expiation for it before Jehovah. Now, since the previous question refers to the eating of the sin-offering, we might indeed suppose the אכל (eating) mentioned in the inquiry to be still understood in the נָתַן לָכֶם (has given you), and understand by this " giving," giving to eat, if that would give us a sense appropriate to the circumstances ; but there is nothing in the words to require this, nor could anything necessitate it except the actual occurrence of the word לֶאֱכֹל in the sentence. But as it is not there, and the insertion of it would not give us a sense in harmony with the circumstances, but one in all respects at variance with them, it is certainly most advisable to abstain from supplying anything, and to take נָתַן simply as it stands.

In reply to Moses' question and reproof, Aaron excused himself and his sons, on the ground that they had offered their own sin-offering and burnt-offering the same day, and had regarded the command to abstain from eating them as a command to abstain from eating the flesh of any sacrifice on that day, on account of the mourning of which the offering of a sin-offering was the foil. Now, though this reason for not eating might be one that was not supported by the law of sacrifice, and therefore might be an arbitrary extension of that law ; yet as it really proceeded from pious motives, it deserved to be excused, and that Moses did not refuse. But the same thing had happened to Moses here, which happened again on a different occasion (Num. xxxii. 6 sqq.), namely, that his rash and excitable character had led him to attribute wrong motives to the actions of óthers, because those actions did not correspond to his expectations. At the same time, in this instance he might certainly be excused, on the ground that it was unquestionably natural enough, with the Typhonic sacrifices of Egypt before him, to conclude that their reason for not eating had been based upon them.

The discrepancy which *Knobel* imagines that he has discovered between this passage and Lev. iv. 21, and on account of which he supposes it necessary to attribute the two passages to different authors, has been already proved by Hofmann to have no existence. " Of the sin-offerings," he says, " which the consecrated person (Aaron) presented, one for himself and one for the nation, he burned the flesh of the former, because he was not allowed to derive any other benefit from it than that which was derived by every one else for whom a sin-offering was presented, viz., the forgiveness of his sin. But the flesh of the other it was his duty to eat ; and it is not merely an oversight of the Elohist that it is so represented, since this sacrifice applied to the nation *in contrast to the priest*, and not, like the one prescribed in Lev. iv. 13–21, or xvi. 15, to the congregation generally, *i.e.*, to the *whole of Israel* (including the priests)."

§ 120. In the sin-offering of *pigeons*, which served in cases of

great poverty as a substitute for the sheep that should properly have
been offered, the ceremony was variously modified according to the
outward circumstances (Lev. v. 7 sqq.). Just as in the case of the
burnt-offering of pigeons (Lev. i. 15), the imposition of hands and
slaying of the animal by the person presenting the sacrifice were
omitted. The priest severed the head at the back of the neck, but
without entirely detaching it, and then *sprinkled* (הִזָּה) some of the
blood upon the wall of the altar (עַל־קִיר הַמִּזְבֵּחַ), and *squeezed out* the
rest of the blood at (אֶל) the base of the altar. With the pigeon
of the *burnt*-offering it was also commanded, that the crop should
be removed with the filth and thrown upon the ash-heap, that an
incision should be made in the wings, though without entirely separating them, and that the whole animal should then be burnt upon
the altar. These directions were probably equally applicable to the
pigeons of the *sin-offering* (cf. § 111).—But *Keil* is wrong in describing the ceremony connected with the *burnt*-offering of pigeons
as *perfectly* identical with that of the sin-offering, and in attributing
to the former what was restricted to the latter, and constituted its
distinctive characteristic as a sin-offering (cf. § 107), namely, that
the priest " sprinkled some of the blood of the latter upon the wall
of the altar, and let the rest flow out at the foot of the altar." The
law of the burnt-offering in Lev. i. 15 contains no allusion to the
sprinkling (הִזָּה) of the blood upon the *wall* of the altar, and a subsequent *squeezing out* of the rest of the blood at the foot of the altar,
but rather precludes this double process, by directing that the blood
shall be *squeezed out* against the wall of the altar, and thus combining the two acts into one.

§ 121. On the *ritual of the trespass-offering* we can be much more
brief. The animal appointed for this was, as a rule, a ram ; but
for the trespass-offering of the leper and the Nazarite, a lamb was
selected ; "no doubt," as *Oehler* supposes (p. 645), "to show the
inferiority of the אָשָׁם." We cannot determine with certainty why
a male sheep should be preferred to a female in this case, whereas
for the *sin*-offerings of the laity a female was preferred, whether
sheep or goat. *Riehm* (p. 117) conjectures that the violation of a
privilege had more of the character of violence in it ; and *Rinck* (p.
372), that the intention was "to give greater scope for the valuation." The exclusion of goats from the trespass-offering is attributed by *Knobel* to the character of the trespass-offering, as the
payment of a fine ; because in ancient times the sheep was the ordinary medium of payment, whether of fines or tribute.

The *valuation* of the ram by the priest (Lev. v. 15) was something altogether peculiar to this kind of sacrifice, and does not occur anywhere else. *Hengstenberg* observes on this point: "The ram of the אָשָׁם received an imaginary value through the declaration of the priest. This ram, it was said, which N. N. offers as compensation for his robbery of God, shall be equivalent to the amount of his robbery. The ram, which was presented as a compensation for the spiritual ὀφείλημα, was appraised as high as the amount that was given in compensation for the outward, material ὀφείλημα. By this symbolical act the idea of debt was most vividly impressed, and the necessity for making a settlement with God clearly placed before their eyes" (Dissertations on the Pentateuch, ii. 176, Eng. Tr. 1847). *Riehm* objects to this, because " such a mode of reckoning by imaginary amounts was foreign to the spirit of antiquity;" and he supposes the valuation to refer to the actual worth of the ram. " It was requisite," he says, " that the value of the ram, which depended upon the size, fat, etc., should correspond to the amount of the מַעַל." *Bunsen* takes the same view, and renders the passage, " according to thy valuation, worth at least two shekels." *Oehler* also supposes that " by the indefinite value fixed, viz., two shekels and upward, scope was given in the valuation, to bring the worth of the ram into a certain relation to the extent of the מַעַל committed." The actual worth of the ram has no doubt to be taken into consideration, but we must still maintain, with *Keil* (p. 236), " that the valuation had a symbolical meaning, since the actual worth of the different rams, all of which were without a fault, could not very greatly vary." In any case in which it was impossible to appraise the material מַעַל by money or money's worth, the valuation of the animal brought as a trespass-offering was, as a matter of course, omitted (Lev. xiv. 12 sqq.; Num. vi. 12; Lev. xix. 20 sqq.).

The offering of the animal sacrifice, which expiated the מַעַל *before God,* had to be accompanied by a material compensation to the injured person for the wrong that had been done through the מַעַל, increased by one-fifth of its worth. The addition of the fifth was to be regarded as a *mulcta,* so far as the wrong-doer was concerned, and afforded compensation to the injured person for the temporary loss of his rightful property; being, in fact, a kind of interest. The choice of a fifth as the particular price to be paid, is to be attributed to the symbolical meaning of the number five, as the half of the full number ten. In the case of an aggravated theft, on the other hand, the compensation demanded was either double, fourfold, or fivefold, according to circumstances (Ex. xxii. 1 and 4). Even in the case of taxes, a fifth was frequently the proportion fixed upon (Gen. xli. 34, xlvii. 24).

The suggestion of *Clericus* and *Rosenmüller*, that אוֹ (or) should be supplied, so as to leave it free whether a ram should be brought or the amount in money, is equally inadmissible, whether we consider the words or the circumstances, and is not worth refuting.

§ 122. The *imposition of hands* is never expressly mentioned in connection with the *trespass-offering;* and for that reason *Rinck* (p. 376) and *Knobel* (pp. 343, 396) maintain that it did not take place, and endeavour to explain the omission on the ground of the peculiar nature of this kind of sacrifice. The former maintains that "the idea of a sacrifice of compensation or restoration precluded it;" but we must bear in mind his distorted and mistaken opinion, that the relation between the trespass-offering and sin-offering was that of *satisfaction* and *expiation*. *Knobel*, on the contrary, says, that "as the payment of a debt, it was not subjected to the imposition of hands, which was expressive of a free gift;" but the imposition of hands was not expressive of the freedom of the gift, nor was the trespass-offering, as distinguished from the sin-offering, characterized by the want of freedom in the gift of the sacrificial animal presented as an expiation. The absence of any express reference to the necessity for the imposition of hands in the case of the trespass-offering, has been very well discussed and accounted for by *Keil* (p. 238): In Lev. vii. 1–7, for example, there is, no doubt, an omission of any such statement; but there is a similar omission in the case of the sin-offering in the corresponding passage, Lev. vi. 24–30. It is only in the section relating to the sin-offerings in Lev. iv., where the different cases are enumerated in which sin-offerings were to be presented, that it is mentioned at all; and if there is no allusion to it in the corresponding section relating to the trespass-offerings (Lev. v. 14 sqq.), this is to ·be explained from the fact, that the ceremony connected with the sacrificing of the trespass-offering is not described at all.—The relation in which the section referring to the trespass-offering (Lev. v. 14) stands to the earlier section on sin-offerings is that of a supplementary limitation, which provides in certain cases for the offering of a trespass-offering in the place of a sin-offering (§ 102). In accordance with this, which is its true intention, it is content with describing the cases in which that was to take place. It formed part of this, no doubt, to notice the payment of the six fifths as compensation, and the valuation of the sacrificial animal, but not to describe the rest of the ritual (the imposition of hands, the slaying, and the sprinkling of the blood). This is supplied afterwards in Lev. vii. 1 sqq.; and if the laying on of the hand is not specially mentioned, that is simply because the law assumed that the necessity for it was self-evident in the case of the trespass-offerings as well as in that of every other sacrifice.

In the *slaughtering* of the trespass-offering there was nothing peculiar (Lev. vii. 2); but the *sprinkling of the blood* was not carried out in the same intensified form as in the case of the sin-offering; and the reason for this, no doubt, was, that in the normal trespass-offering the trespass appeared to be lessened by the voluntary material restitution. The question, however, is not without its difficulties, how we are to understand the יִזְרֹק עַל־הַמִּזְבֵּחַ סָבִיב which was required in the case of the trespass-offering (as well as in that of the burnt-offering and peace-offering; *vid.* Lev. vii. 2). *Bähr,* *Keil,* and *Knobel* suppose it to denote a *sprinkling* upon the altar, or on the *walls* of the altar round about. But as the term הִזָּה, which is applied to the ritual of the sin-offering *alone,* and *never* used in connection with the trespass-offering, burnt-offering, and peace-offering, undoubtedly signifies sprinkling in the literal sense of the word, and hence the verb זָרַק must refer to the application of blood to the altar in some other form, the preference must certainly be given to the signification of pouring or swinging out, which is more in accordance with its use elsewhere, and also to *Hofmann's* view, according to which יִזְרֹק עַל־הַמִּזְבֵּחַ denotes a swinging about over the surface of the altar (p. 256). That something more is intended than a *sprinkling* upon the walls of the altar, or " upon the altar itself," as *Winer* supposes, is evident from the fact, that the blood could not have been all used up for that purpose; and yet we never read of any remainder having to be poured out at the foot of the altar, in connection with either the trespass-, the peace-, or the burnt-offerings, whereas this is *never omitted* in the laws relating to the sin-offering (Lev. iv. 7, 18, 25, 30, v. 9). It is quite as impossible to understand by it a pouring or swinging out of the blood against the outer walls of the altar, since in that case the blood would have run down the walls upon the bank which surrounded the altar, reaching about half way up (§ 11), and under the priests' feet. At the same time the סָבִיב, upon which such emphasis is laid, must not be overlooked. The blood was not to be poured upon the middle of the surface of the altar, where the altar-fire was burning, but by a twist of the hand was to be poured round in such a manner that it should fall upon the inner margin of the altar. So also the squeezing out of the blood of the pigeon offered as a burnt-offering עַל־קִיר הַמִּזְבֵּחַ, and the sprinkling of the blood of the pigeon offered as a sin-offering עַל־קִיר הַמִּזְבֵּחַ, hardly refer to the outer walls of the altar, but probably to their upper or inner surface. But when *Bähr* and *Knobel* appeal to the analogous expression עַל־קִיר הַמִּזְבֵּחַ in the case of the burnt-offering of pigeons, and take this as the rule by which to interpret the simple expression עַל־הַמִּזְבֵּחַ, I am compelled to maintain, *vice versa*, that the expression עַל־קִיר הַמִּזְבֵּחַ, which is always applied to the offering of pigeons, and that alone (i. 15, v. 9), must mean something different from the simple עַל־הַמִּזְבֵּחַ, which is *constantly* applied to the oxen, sheep, and goats, so that the evidence is in the very opposite direction.

With reference to the course to be adopted *with the flesh of the trespass-offering*, according to Lev. vii. 7 the law for the sin-offering was applicable to this also. It is true, that the only point expressly mentioned there is the eating of the flesh on the part of the priests, without admitting the female portion of their families,— so that the sacrifices alluded to were those that had been offered by laymen. Yet, as there can be no doubt that the sins which required trespass-offerings might be committed by priests, it follows as a matter of course, that in such cases also the law of the sin-offering determined the course to be adopted with the flesh. Now if the higher form of sprinkling was not adopted in the case of the trespass-offering, and those circumstances which rendered the flesh of the sin-offering most holy were wanting, and yet its flesh was also regarded as most holy, the only explanation that can be given of this is, that the trespass-offering, as a subordinate species of sin-offering, retained the character of most holy which was inherent in the latter, although the circumstances were wanting which had originally stamped that character upon the sin-offering itself.

CHAPTER III

RITUAL OF THE BURNT-OFFERING AND PEACE-OFFERING

§ 123. The most common name for the so-called BURNT-OFFER-
ING is עֹלָה. We may quietly pass by *Ewald's* interpretation of the
word, as meaning the "long burning," for the root of which he
invents a verb, עִל = עוּר, to glow, or burn, appealing as a matter of
fact to Lev. vi. 9, and still adhere to the old and traditional derivation from עָלָה, to ascend. In any case it is designated as the
ascending one *par excellence* (in distinction from the other kinds of
sacrifice, of which only the fat was placed upon the altar), because
the whole animal was burnt upon the altar with the exception of
the skin (Lev. i. 9, הַכֹּל), and this is expressed in the less common
name כָּלִיל, whole-offering (Deut. xxxiii. 10; Ps. li. 19; 1 Sam.
vii. 9). At the same time, it may be questioned, whether by this
term עֹלָה we are to understand an ascent to Jehovah through the
burning upon the altar, or simply the ascent to the top of the altar
itself (Lev. ii. 12). *Knobel*, who decides in favour of the latter,
traces the origin of the name to the fact, "that in the earliest times
the *whole*-offering was the only sacrifice presented;" in which case,
however, Gen. iv. 4 would have to renounce its claim to historical
credibility. In support of this explanation of the word, *Oehler*
appeals to the frequent combination of הֶעֱלָה עֹלָה with עַל־הַמִּזְבֵּחַ or
בַּמִּזְבֵּחַ (cf. Ps. li. 19). With very rare exceptions, he says, הֶעֱלָה is
the verb specially connected with the burnt-offering, just as הִקְרִיב,
הִגִּישׁ, זָבַח are connected with the other kinds of sacrifice. The other
allusion, viz., to the ascent of the smoke of the sacrifice, is supported
by *Jerome* (ad Ez. c. 45: *quod totum sacro igne consumitur*); the
Septuagint rendering (ὁλοκαύτωμα) is based upon it; and it is
decidedly the one most generally received by modern theologians.
Delitzsch, on the other hand, maintains that "in the Hebrew הֶעֱלָה
the idea of causing to ascend in the fire, and that of bringing upon
the altar, are merged into one another, and it cannot be maintained
that in ordinary usage either the one or the other prevailed" (Heb.
p. 313 A); and even *Hofmann* (p. 226) cannot dispute this. But
as the true and ultimate design of the sacrifice was not to raise it
upon the altar, but to cause it to ascend in the fire, that Jehovah
might partake of it, and be satisfied with the "sweet savour" (Gen.

viii. 21); and, moreover, as the still more frequent designation of the sacrifices as אִשֶּׁי יְהֹוָה, לֶחֶם יְהֹוָה, אִשֶּׁה לְרֵיחַ נִיחֹחַ outweighs the frequent combination of הָעֹלָה עָלָה with עַל־הַמִּזְבֵּחַ; the idea of causing to ascend in the fire is certainly to be regarded as at all events the leading idea. And the expression הַעֲלֵהוּ לְעֹלָה עַל אַחַד הֶהָרִים, in Gen. xxii. 2, is more favourable to this view than to the opposite one, since it shows in what sense הָעֹלָה עַל־הַמִּזְבֵּחַ is to be understood.

§ 124. We have already seen that no special reasons are mentioned for presenting the burnt-offerings (§ 86). They were neither consequent upon the commission of particular sins, like the sin- and trespass-offerings, nor upon particular manifestations of divine mercy, like the peace-offerings. For this reason no prominence was given to the act of expiation, nor was there any opportunity afforded for the sacrificial meal. On the other hand, the burning upon the altar is the culminating point, by which all the rest is regulated, and which marks it as an expression of perpetual obligation to complete, sanctified self-surrender to Jehovah (§ 74 sqq.).

It is incorrect, however, to affirm, as *Keil* has done, with reference to the offerers of this sacrifice, that "through the covenant which God had made with Israel, membership in the theocratic community was a prerequisite to the offering of a burnt-offering; so that it could *only* be presented by those who stood in covenant with the Lord, since none but those who were partakers of the grace of God could sanctify their lives to the Lord" (p. 241). For he has quite overlooked Lev. xvii. 8, and xxii. 18, 25, where reference is expressly made to burnt-offerings and sin-offerings that should be offered by strangers. From these passages it is very evident, that a simple acknowledgment of Jehovah as the only true God was quite sufficient, without any formal admission into the covenant of the theocracy, to entitle those who were not Israelites to participate in the sacrificial worship (cf. § 2).

Any kind of animal that was fit for sacrifice might be offered as a burnt-offering; but only the *males* of oxen, sheep, and goats (Lev. i. 10). In the case of pigeons the gender was a matter of indifference, because it was not outwardly visible, and did not affect the entire organism in any peculiar manner (ver. 14). "The choice of the male animal," says *Oehler*, p. 635, "pointed to the superior rank of this kind of sacrifice, just as male animals were selected for the higher description of sin-offerings." At the same time, the explanation already given by me, which *Oehler* admits and *Keil* quotes with approbation, viz., that the demand for a male animal was founded upon the peculiar idea of the burnt-offering, as a complete, earnest, energetic self-surrender, may be maintained as well. In the male sex all the limbs, bones, nerves, and muscles are stronger and more fully developed. Hence the male sex, since the form corresponds to the substance,—that is to say, since the powers of soul and spirit are strong and enduring in the same proportion,—is the prominent, vigorous, working sex, and in every language the idea of strong and energetic is expressed by the term *masculine*. *Kliefoth* also looks upon the demand for the male animal as founded on the character of the burnt-offering as a *whole*-offering, and explains it on this ground, that "the male animal was more an *entire* animal than the female." The ceremony with the *blood* was the same as in the case of the trespass-offering (§ 122). The directions how to prepare the flesh for burning upon the altar (Lev. i. 6–9) were based simply upon outward convenience, and therefore had no really symbolical significance. "Since the animal," says *Keil*, p. 242, "was to be offered as food for the Lord, it could not be burnt with the skin and hair upon it, but had first of all to be flayed. The cutting up of the animal, however, was for the purpose of burning, and was necessary, if for no other reasons, because it was impossible for a large animal to be laid upon the altar whole." And *Bähr* observes (ii. 366), that "the reason for commanding the hind-legs and entrails to be washed before they were burnt upon the altar, was simply that it was just these portions that could most easily be defiled by impurities." The assignment of the skin of the burnt-offering to the priest (Lev. vii. 8), was in accordance with the principle that they who wait at the altar are to be partakers of the altar (1 Cor. ix. 13). And if the burnt-offering, because it was a whole-offering, could not furnish the priest with food, its skin could be, and was to be, assigned to him for clothing.

§ 125. The specific name of the *fourth* kind of bleeding sacrifice is שְׁלָמִים. The singular שֶׁלֶם only occurs in Amos v. 22 as the name of a sacrifice. Where one single sacrifice of this kind is referred to, it is called זֶבַח שְׁלָמִים. This has generally been rendered a THANK-OFFERING, after the example of *Luther*, who followed *Josephus* (Ant. 3. 3, 1, χαριστήριος θυσία); or a PEACE-OFFERING, after the Septuagint (εἰρηνικὴ θυσία) and Vulgate (*sacrificia pacifica*); and lately a SAVING-OFFERING (*Heils-opfer: sacrificia salutaria*), after a rarer rendering of the LXX. (σωτήριον), which *Philo* (*de vict.*), and lately *Outram, Hengstenberg, Bunsen*, and others, have adopted. But as not one of these three names appeared to answer exactly in etymology and meaning to the idea of שְׁלָמִים, a number of other explanations have been attempted: such as restitution-offering (*Bähr*), payment-offering (*Ebrard*), finishing-offering (*Baumgarten*), offering of blessedness (*Neumann*).

There are two things connected with the interpretation of the word שְׁלָמִים, which have been especially the subject of dispute: (1) with reference to the form of the word, whether it is derived from the *Kal* שָׁלַם or שָׁלֵם = *integrum esse*, as *Keil, Oehler, Neumann, Hengstenberg, Tholuck, Kliefoth,* and others maintain; or from the *Piel* שִׁלֵּם = to compensate, repay, as *Bähr, Hofmann, Knobel,* and others suppose: and (2) with regard to the actual meaning, supposing the former derivation is to be preferred, whether it is the *terminus a quo* or the *terminus ad quem* which is designated as שְׁלוֹם.

In support of the derivation from the *Piel* שִׁלֵּם, and the consequent signification, thank-offering, offering of retribution or compensation, appeal has been made (by *Knobel* for example) to the fact that the *Piel* is frequently connected with the various kinds of sacrifice, belonging to the category of *Shelamim*, e.g., שִׁלֵּם נְדָרִים or שִׁלֵּם תּוֹדוֹת (Ps. lvi. 12; cf. Hos. xiv. 3, שִׁלֵּם פָּרִים); and also that nouns derived from Kal, so far as the form is concerned, by no means unfrequently revert to the *Piel* in their signification (*Ewald*, Gramm. § 150 *b*), a proof of which is to be found in connection with this verb in the word שַׁלְמֹנִים = *bribery*, in Isa. i. 23. "It is evident enough," says *Hofmann*, "that שֶׁלֶם means the same as שִׁלְמוֹן, which is formed from it, and which again is interchangeable with שִׁלּוּם (Micah vii. 3). A present made to a judge for a favourable decision, is called שִׁלְמוֹן in one instance and שִׁלּוּם in the other. Whether the present is made before the verdict, or afterwards, it is still a gift for a favourable sentence. . . . שֶׁלֶם denotes a gift from one who needs favour to one who grants it, whether the favour has been already granted, or is merely being sought. The שְׁלָמִים therefore were gifts presented to God, through which a man acknowledged that what good he possessed he owed to the favour of God, and what good he needed he must seek from that favour,—in a word, that they were χαριστήρια." The objection, that *Shelamim* were also presented in connection with prayers offered in circumstances of distress (Judg. xx. 26, xxi. 4; 1 Sam. xiii. 9; 2 Sam. xxiv. 25), is met by *Knobel* in this way: "Just as afflicted psalmists could associate the liveliest thanksgiving with earnest prayer, because they comforted themselves with the assurance of being heard (Ps.

xxxi. liv. lvii. lxxi.), so could others accompany their petitions with a thank-offering, and thus attest their gratitude beforehand, for the purpose of moving God the more readily to grant their request."

The possibility of שֶׁלֶם possessing the idea of compensation cannot be disputed; but to the application of this idea to the kind of sacrifice mentioned here there are many obstacles, which cannot be easily removed. It is always a much more simple course to retain the signification of the *Kal*, when the noun is derived from the *Kal* in form, and to regard it as a designation of the state of that אֲשֶׁר יָשְׁלַם. To this we are also led by the nearest cognate adjective שָׁלֵם, complete, uninjured, living in peace and friendship, friendly (Gen. xxxiv. 21); whilst the frequent expression שָׁלֵם עִם יְהֹוָה (1 Kings viii. 61, xi. 4, xv. 3) points us to Him, whose peace and friendship were sought through the Shelamim. The expression שְׁלוֹמִי, my friend, he who lives in friendship with me, must also be borne in mind (Ps. xli. 9). From this signification of the שֶׁלֶם, which is certainly the most natural one, there could be no reason for departing, and reverting to that of the *Piel*, unless the design and signification of this kind of sacrifice absolutely demanded it; for the word שִׁלְמוֹן, which is derived from שֶׁלֶם in form, need not have had the same meaning on that account in actual use, even apart from the fact that it would, at any rate, be a very doubtful thing to apply the idea of *bribery* to the *Shelamim*. And *Knobel's* argument, that *Shelamim* were offered even in circumstances of misery and distress, does not make this view by any means less doubtful. A psalmist, with his inward certainty of the approaching help of God, might perhaps express his gratitude in the simple prospect;[1] but he would do so as a poet, carried forward in spirit to the time when help had already arrived, or as a hero of faith moved by the Holy Ghost, and assured by the same Spirit that his petition would be granted. It is a very different question, however, whether what the inspired poet might do in thoughts and words in moments of special inspiration and elevation, could have the same legal or general force, as a rule and model for every individual in all the circumstances of this prosaic, every-day life, destitute as it is of any lyric flight, or theopneustic

---

[1] In the Psalms mentioned by *Knobel*, however, I cannot find one instance of present thanksgiving for that particular help, which is only solicited and hoped for, but merely a certainty and joyous anticipation of future thanksgiving answering to the certainty of future help (cf. Ps. liv. 8, lvii. 10, lxxi. 14 sqq.). But in Ps. cxviii. 21 we find what could be and was to be the object of thanksgiving in the very midst of suffering.

elevation *above* the simple necessities of the present time. For my own part, I have my doubts about it. And whilst *Hofmann* justly pronounces *Knobel's* opinion a "miserable evasion," we have all the more right to condemn it as arbitrary on his own part, and at variance with both grammar and facts, to place what has been received from the favour of God, and what has yet to be solicited from that favour, under the common point of view of a χαριστήριον, and thus in the strangest way to designate as *thanksgiving* not only praise for benefits already received, but prayer for benefits needed still. There is some sense in *Knobel's* "miserable evasion," but I can find none in *Hofmann's* evasion.

So far as the expressions שֶׁלֶם נְדָרִים and שֶׁלֶם תּוֹדוֹת are concerned, they unquestionably prove that the offering of *these* two kinds of *Shelamim* rested upon a moral and religious obligation. But as the same expressions are not applied to the third kind of *Shelamim* (the נְדָבוֹת), and according to this idea could not be applied to them, we have here a proof that the שְׁלָמִים could not derive their name from the verb שִׁלֵּם; otherwise this verb would have been equally applicable to the נְדָבוֹת. Even on this ground, therefore, it is evident that the meaning and purpose of the שְׁלָמִים do not necessitate, but rather preclude, our tracing the derivation to the *Piel* of שׁלם.

This becomes still more obvious if we institute a comparison between the name of the *Shelamim* and that of the other kinds of sacrifice. Just as the name עֹלָה (and more decidedly still the name כָּלִיל) pointed to what formed the distinguishing mark, the true purpose and culminating point of the burnt-offering, namely, the burning of the whole upon the altar (Lev. i. 9), and as the name חטאת pointed to the characteristic and most important feature of the sin-offering, viz., the act of expiation; so the name שְׁלָמִים also pointed to that which was the distinctive peculiarity of these sacrifices, to that which they contemplated more than any other kind of sacrifice, viz., the sacrificial meal.[1] But if it cannot be denied

---

[1] The other name זְבָחִים, or *slain-offering*, which is restricted in the Pentateuch to the *peace*-offerings, also points to the sacrificial meal. The verb זבח, for example, denotes the slaughtering of an animal with express reference to the meal which it is to furnish, especially the sacrificial meal, whilst slaughtering for ordinary meals is generally expressed by טבח, and שׁחט contains no allusion to a meal at all. At the same time, there is no reason for denying that in the later usages of the language the name זֶבַח is sometimes applied mistakenly to the bleeding sacrifices in general; for the most part, however, exclusively of the burnt-offering, which is only included in the phrase זֶבַח וּמִנְחָה.

(§ 79) that the meal was an expression and attestation of a condition of peace and friendship, of the maintenance and blessedness of fellowship, no other course is open than to trace the name of the שְׁלָמִים to the desire of the person presenting the sacrifice to see himself employed by means of the offering as שְׁלֶם יְהֹוָה, as שָׁלֵם עִם יְהֹוָה.

The recognition of this will furnish us at once with the true answer to the question mentioned above, whether the name of the *Shelamim* denotes the *terminus a quo* or the *terminus ad quem* of the offering. But if, according to what has been already stated, we must decide in favour of the latter, we cannot for all that fully agree with *Kliefoth*. "The *Shelamim*," he says (p. 75), "received their name from the *condition*, which they were to produce in the person presenting the sacrifice: they were to cause it to become *right* with him, to produce שָׁלוֹם between him and his God." For it was necessary that it should be right with him, and that he should stand in a relation of שָׁלוֹם towards his God, before he could even think of presenting a *Shelem* at all. If it had not been right between him and Jehovah,—if there had not been peace and harmony, but division and discord, between him and his God,—it would have been necessary that the cause of the discord should first be expiated by either a sin- or a trespass-offering. A *state* of peace and friendship with God was the basis, and *sine qua non*, to the presentation of a *Shelem;* and the design of that presentation, from which its name was derived, was the *realization, establishment, verification*, and *enjoyment* of the existing relation of peace, friendship, fellowship, and blessedness.

From what has been stated it is evident that the name most in accordance with the Hebrew, and most in harmony with the idea of this kind of sacrifice, is that of *peace-offering*. The expression *salvation-offering (Heils-opfer)* is too indefinite and ambiguous. At the same time it must be admitted, that the *sacrificia pacifica* of *Jerome* is likely to mislead. This *Gussetius* perceived, and hence he preferred the name *sacrificia pacalia; quibus pax cum Deo fovetur.*

§ 126. The peace-offerings may be divided, according to Lev. vii. 11 sqq., into three species: (1) זֶבַח הַתּוֹדָה, *i.e., praise-offerings;* (2) זֶבַח נֶדֶר, *votive offerings;* and (3) זֶבַח נְדָבָה, *freewill-offerings.* No one, so far as I know, except *Hengstenberg*, has disputed the admissibility of this threefold division. "*In vain*," he says (p. 36), "have *many* (?) *attempted* to change the generic name זֶבַח הַתּוֹדָה into that of a particular species." He even goes so far as to assert,

that "the words of Lev. vii. 11 sqq. do not favour it, but are *most
decidedly* opposed to it." But the most cursory glance at the passage in question shows how thoroughly groundless this confident
assertion is. Since the law of the *Shelamim* is announced in ver.
11, and this law commences in ver. 12 with the words אָם עַל־תּוֹדָה
יַקְרִיבֶנּוּ ("if he offer it for a thanksgiving"), and the offering is then
immediately designated as זֶבַח הַתּוֹדָה (sacrifice of thanksgiving),
and זֶבַח תּוֹדַת הַשְּׁלָמִים (the sacrifice of thanksgiving of his peace-
offerings), we should *necessarily* expect to find that *Shelamim* could
be offered for *other* reasons, which of course would not in that
case be called "sacrifices of thanksgiving." This expectation is
fully realized in ver. 16, where, after the materials and ritual of the
thanksgiving-offering have been described, we find these words:
וְאִם נֶדֶר אוֹ נְדָבָה זֶבַח קָרְבָּנוֹ ("but if the sacrifice of his offering be a
vow, or a voluntary offering"); so that two new species of *Shelamim*
are introduced which presented a common contrast to the thanksgiving-offering. In ver. 15, for example, it is stated that the flesh
of the thanksgiving-offering was all to be eaten on the same day
on which it was slaughtered; whereas, according to ver. 16, some
of the flesh of the votive and voluntary offerings might be eaten
on the second day. How, then, can any one think of the possibility
of identifying the thanksgiving-offering with the votive and voluntary offering, and regarding the former as the genus and the latter
as the two species? And what intolerable tautology would be contained in the designation זֶבַח תּוֹדַת הַשְּׁלָמִים, if שְׁלָמִים and תּוֹדָת were
perfectly equivalent terms! And when *Hengstenberg* maintains
that "only two classes of thank-offerings are *known* in Lev. xxii.
18, 21, the votive offering and the voluntary offering," the statement is correct enough if for *known* we substitute *named*. The
reason why only these two species of peace-offerings are named here,
is that this law merely supplies what was omitted in Lev. vii. 11
sqq., namely, a description of the materials allowable for these two
species, and of the fixed line of distinction between the two, which
arose out of the materials employed.—Moreover, as *Oehler* observes
at p. 638, the fact must also be noticed, that in Lev. xxiii. 37, 38
(also Num. xxix. 39) and Deut. xii. 6, an offering is mentioned distinct from both the נְדָרִים and נְדָבוֹת, where we cannot think of anything else than a זֶבַח הַתּוֹדָה, which, as being the leading and truest
peace- (slain-) offering (§ 128), is so designated *par excellence.*

§ 127. Most commentators follow *Philo* and the Rabbins, and
maintain that the *Shelamim* embraced not merely *thank*-offerings

in the stricter sense (for divine gifts already received), but also *supplicatory offerings* (for gifts first asked for at the time). Thus *Outram* (i. 11, § 1) describes the *sacrificia salutaria* as those *quæ semper de rebus prosperis fieri solebant, impetratis utique aut impetrandis;* and *Hengstenberg* (Beitr. iii. 36) says: "The *Shelamim* undoubtedly had salvation for their object; but, according to the variation in circumstances, they were offered either as incorporated thanks for what had been imparted, or as embodied prayers for what had yet to be received." *Scholl, Tholuck, Keil,* and others, agree with this; *Bähr* and *Kliefoth* being alone in disputing it.[1] *Bähr* observes: "*Scholl's* argument, that otherwise the Mosaic worship would have no supplicatory sacrifice at all, in the strict sense of the word, cannot have any force in itself; for, according to this method, what is there that could not be brought into the Mosaic worship?" To this I have already replied (M. O. pp. 134–5): "If the supplicatory offering rested upon a truly religious basis, and the idea to be expressed therein was really founded upon a religious necessity,—a fact which cannot be disputed, and which even *Bähr* himself admits, though he refers to the burnt-offering for the satisfaction of that want,—we are certainly warranted in expecting that the Mosaic economy, as a divine institute, would meet that want and satisfy it, and are bound to *look* for a provision answering to it. And we by no means agree with *Bähr* in the opinion, that ' it was characteristic of Mosaism, and a proof in its favour, that the supplicatory offerings so common elsewhere were not to be found in it; for it was so easy for magical notions to grow up, as to the power of these sacrifices to bind and compel the Deity, as was the case for the most part with heathen sacrifices.' What would not Moses have had to reject from the ceremonial of worship, if he had allowed himself to be deterred by such fears and impelled by such principles as these! The same magical notions of a force binding and compelling the Deity were to be feared in connection with all the rest of the sacrifices, and may spring up quite as easily with the most spiritual of all the forms of worship, viz., prayer. Moreover, it should be borne in mind, that support is by no means wanting to the notion of a power in *prayer* to bind and compel the Deity, and therefore in *sacrifice* also, the anticipated

---

[1] *Stöckl* (p. 263) describes the denial of the supplicatory offering as the "*sententia communis* of Protestant symbolism;" and yet the good man, as his book shows, has not read a single Protestant work on sacrifice, except *Bähr's Symbolik!* This is something more than *naïvete.*

operation of which is founded upon promises quite as express and
definite. We have only to remember how frequently, both in parables and without parables, the Redeemer attributes a compelling
(though certainly not a magical) power to prayer." Besides, the
presentation of *Shelamim* in times of trouble and distress (Judg.
xx. 26, xxi. 4; 1 Sam. xiii. 9; 2 Sam. xxiv. 25) is a sufficient proof
of the fact disputed by *Bähr*.

But the question is not without difficulty, whether the contrast
between the thank-offerings and supplicatory offerings is to be introduced into the three subordinate species of *Shelamim*, and if so,
how ? *Scholl* was of opinion, that as the " sacrifice of thanksgiving "
was undoubtedly a thank-offering in the literal sense, the supposition was a very natural one, that by נֶדֶר and נְדָבָה we are to understand two distinct kinds of supplicatory offerings. *Hofmann* objects
to this, on the ground that " the names do not harmonise with the
latter, since a vow might be quite as easily the payment of gratitude for a request obtained, as the attendant of a prayer for help
or blessing ; and a free gift might be so called for the simple reason
that it was prompted by nothing else than the will of the person to
present some offering." But the fallacy of these objections may
easily be detected. For according to the general usage of speech,
a vow can *only* be regarded as an " accompaniment of a prayer for
help," and never as " the payment of gratitude for a request obtained ;" and as it stands to reason that a spontaneous act must
have something to occasion it, some such occasion must be presupposed in connection with the presentation of a freewill-offering.
Hofmann does not tell us very distinctly where he would place the
supplicatory offerings, the existence of which he so firmly maintains.
But when he quotes with approval the words of *Hengstenberg* referred to above, saying " *Hengstenberg* is right in maintaining of the
Shelamim *generally*, that, etc.," it may probably be inferred that
he looks upon every one of the three species of " thanksgiving-offer-
ings " as adapted to serve equally as an expression of thanks for a
favour already granted, and prayer for one now first implored.
He has also stated this, in so many words, of the votive offering ;
but how he reconciles it with his explanation of the נְדָבָה as given
in the same place, I am quite unable to, discover. Nor can I see
how it is to be applied to the תּוֹדָה, the very name of which evidently
points to praise and thanksgiving for benefits received, and cannot
be interpreted as an expression of prayer and entreaty for future
benefits, without the greatest confusion of language.

§ 128. To arrive at a solution of the question before us, we will take the three species of Shelamim *seriatim*. The clearest and most systematic is the idea of the PRAISE-OFFERING, or זֶבַח הַתּוֹדָה. The verb הוֹדָה signifies *professus est, confessus est,* then *gratias egit, laudavit, celebravit;* hence תּוֹדָה = praise, thanksgiving. The *Todah*-offering, therefore, was a praise- or thank-offering in the literal sense; and in contrast to the vow- and freewill-offerings, would be presented whenever the reception of divine benefits impelled the pious Israelite to offer praise and thanksgiving to the Giver of all good gifts; and impelled him with the greater force, because of his consciousness that under all circumstances the blessing was undeserved, and he himself was but little worthy of such favour. It was this inward constraint of the pious heart that distinguished it from the נדבה; just as the absence of any previous vow, that thanks should be offered in a particular way *after* the blessing sought for had been obtained, distinguished it from the נֶדֶר.[1] The restriction of the praise-offerings, however, to benefits received, unhoped for and unasked, is too sweeping and unfounded (*Oehler,* p. 638, and *Kliefoth,* p. 78). It would confine the praise-offering in a most singular manner to far too narrow a circle, whereas it was evidently the leading, most literal, and most frequent *Shelem.* It was not the receipt of some unexpected good, but the receipt of it apart from any vow- or freewill-offering, which constituted the distinctive characteristic of the praise-offering. A plentiful harvest, for example, even if it had been both hoped and prayed for, but had not been the subject of any previous offering either vowed or actually presented, would certainly be a reason for presenting a praise-offering. So also the slain- or peace-offerings presented at the yearly festivals (Lev. xxiii. 19), and on special festal occasions (*e.g.,* Lev. ix. 18; Josh. viii. 31; 1 Kings viii. 63), were undoubtedly praise-offerings. The fact adduced above (§ 126) for a different purpose, viz., that in Lev. xxiii. 37, 38, Num. xxix. 39, and Deut. xii. 6, זְבָחִים are mentioned along with the votive and freewill-offerings, but distinct from them, by which, therefore, praise-offerings alone can be understood, is also a proof of our position.

---

[1] *Ewald's* opinion (p. 59), that the praise-offering differed from the others, not in the occasion, but in the solemnity of the offering itself, which was accompanied, he thinks, with songs of praise by learned vocal and instrumental performers, provided by the person presenting the sacrifice, to give greater solemnity to the offering, we may leave to its own merits.

§ 129. The votive and freewill-offerings present a common contrast to the praise-offerings. This is not only shown in the difference in the ritual (§ 139), but also proved by the passages just quoted, in which the generic name of this kind of sacrifice is applied to the praise-offerings, and the other two species are distinguished from them.

Now, first of all, so far as the VOTIVE OFFERINGS are concerned, the commentators have omitted for the most part to settle two questions, which are essential to a clear understanding of their position and meaning, viz.: (1) whether the votive offering itself was to be regarded as the object of the vow, or as an accompaniment merely; and (2) whether the votive offering was invariably offered *after* the blessing for which the vow was made had been received, or sometimes *before* it was received. *Kliefoth* is the only person, who has given any thorough answer to these questions; but unfortunately his answer is wrong. In his opinion, the presentation of the sacrifice was not in itself the object of the vow, but some other performance; *e.g.*, a gift to the tabernacle, abstinence from food and other enjoyments. The performance of the vow was *always* accompanied by this sacrifice, and it was after the receipt of what had been prayed for that both were presented. Examples of this are to be found, he thinks, in Num. vi. 13, 14; 1 Sam. i. 24; and 2 Sam. xv. 8. But the last of these examples is a proof of the very opposite. Absalom says there: "While I abode at Geshur in Syria, I vowed a vow, if Jehovah shall bring me again to Jerusalem, I will perform a service to Jehovah (וְעָבַדְתִּי אֶת־יְהוָֹה)." Now, whether this vow referred, as was probably the case, to the offering of sacrifice, or to the performance of any other service, the passage, at any rate, does not speak of a performance of the vow, *and* a votive offering connected with it. But the fact that in Num. vi. 14 a sin-offering and a burnt-offering are demanded along with and before the thank-offering, and that in 1 Sam. i. 24 *three* bullocks are offered, one of which was probably intended as a Shelem, is a proof that these two cases cannot serve as a model for the rest. In both instances the vow referred to is a Nazarite's vow, and the connection of the redemption of the vow with a sin-offering, burnt-offering, and peace-offering was consequent upon the peculiar and unique character of this kind of vow (cf. § 232). In addition to these passages, *Kliefoth* quotes Gen. xxviii. 20, Num. xxi. 2, Judg. xi. 30 sqq.; and here, too, there is not the slightest trace of a votive offering accompanying the performance of the vow. With the exception of Gen. xxviii. 20, they are not even supplicatory vows, and therefore have no bearing at all upon our subject. But when *Kliefoth* follows up the assertion that vows could be of a very different character, and that a votive offering was connected with all these vows, by stating that all these vows are regulated *minutely* in the law (Lev. xxvii. 1 sqq. ; Num. xxx. 1 sqq., vi. 1 sqq.; Deut. xii. 1 sqq.), it is a very singular fact that, with the exception of the law relating to the Nazarite vow in Num. vi., these *minute* regulations never mention a single votive offering to be connected with them.

On the other hand, I must support *Kliefoth* when he maintains, in opposition to *Hofmann*, *Oehler*, and others, that the votive offering was not presented till after the receipt of the blessing, the need of which had prompted the vow, and the acquisition of which it was intended to facilitate. This is so evidently and essentially a characteristic of the conditional or supplicatory vow (compare, for example, Gen. xxviii. 20 sqq.), that one would think the matter must be self-evident, and could admit of no doubt at all. But when, notwithstanding this, several commentators think it necessary to assume a previous presentation of the votive offering, this is to be attributed to the fact that, on the one hand, they are obliged to admit the existence of supplicatory offerings, and on the other hand, do not know how to arrange them in a natural manner; consequently they confound them most unnaturally with the votive offering, since at any rate the vow had a petition as a foil, though they ignore the fact that the performance of the vow was conditional upon the granting of the request.

The votive offering, therefore, if it was offered after the receipt of the blessing prayed for, was a *thank*-offering, as the praise-offering was; but it differed from this in the fact that it had been previously vowed, whereas the true praise-offering presupposed a blessing that had come from the pure, and nothing but the pure and unmerited grace of God, had been prompted by no promise of any performance in return, and therefore awakened livelier gratitude in proportion to the greater consciousness of unworthiness. Consequently, a higher place must be assigned to the praise-offering than to the votive offering in the scale of Shelamim.

§ 130. If, then, on the one hand, we must assume with certainty the existence of true *supplicatory offerings* in the Mosaic economy, *i.e.*, of such offerings as were not conditional upon the fulfilment of the prayer, but were connected with the prayer, to give it greater force; and if, on the other hand, neither the praise-offerings nor the votive offerings answer to this character; we necessarily expect to find it in the third and only remaining class of *Shelamim*. And there is really nothing to disappoint this expectation. The common contrast everywhere drawn between the praise-offering, on the one hand, and the FREEWILL-OFFERING and votive offering, on the other, is sufficient of itself to lead to this conclusion. If the presentation of a *Todah-* (praise-) offering had reference to a pure act of divine grace dependent on, and determined by, no service in return, we shall have to seek the common characteristic of the other two *Shelamim* in the fact that they were associated with an act of divine grace, which might be regarded as consequent upon some counter-performance of man. And this, in fact, is the one thing which was common to the votive offering and the supplicatory offering, which differed from one another simply in the fact, that in the former the sacrifice was not presented till after the blessing had been obtained, and in the latter was associated directly with the prayer. The former did not need to be presented, if the prayer was not granted; the latter had already been presented, even if the request continued unfulfilled. And just as the former presupposed a lower, and the latter a higher scale of piety and devotedness to God; so for the latter an animal of lower value might appear admissible. The fact that the directions in the law (Lev. xxii. 23, § 131) answer to this expectation, furnishes a fresh proof of the correctness of our interpretation of the נְדָבָה. It is also borne out by the *name* of this kind of *Shelem*. The argument which *Hofmann* has based upon this, in opposition to the classification of the *Neda-both* among the supplicatory offerings (namely, that the freewill-offering as such could not be prompted by anything but the desire of the person presenting it to offer something), we have already shown to have no force (§ 127). If we understand the name of the זֶבַח נְדָבָה, in the only way in which it can be understood, as antithetical to the זֶבַח נֶדֶר, and if the latter expresses the obligation to present the sacrifice referred to, the former must express the voluntary character of the offering, which might have been omitted without any sin, or the violation of any religious duty. And this was actually the case. For the vow once made, had to be performed without fail, as soon as the conditions were fulfilled; and therefore if the object of the vow was the presentation of an offering, this had to be presented without fail (Num. xxx. 3; Deut. xxiii. 22 sqq.). The supplicatory offering, however, *i.e.*, the strengthening of the petition by an offering presented at the same time, might be omitted without the violation of any religious duty; and therefore it was justly called a *freewill*-offering.

How vague, loose, and unsatisfactory the limitation given to the זֶבַח נְדָבָה by *Kliefoth* [1] and *Knobel* [2] appears by the side of this firm, certain, and clearly-defined explanation!—a charge from which my own explanation, as given in a previous work, is not altogether free.[3]

§ 131. With regard to the *materials* for the peace-offerings, no restrictions at all were laid down. Oxen, sheep, and goats, of either sex, might be taken (Lev. iii. 1, 6, 12, xxii. 19, etc.). Pigeons alone are nowhere to be met with as peace-offerings; and from this it may be inferred, that there was not the same stringent necessity for the offering as in the case of the sin-offering for example (cf. Lev. v. 7 sqq.). This wide range was probably allowed for the choice of the sacrificial animal (to judge from the analogy of Deut. xvi. 10), in order that it might be rendered proportionate to the magnitude of the divine gift to which it referred, or to the means of the person presenting it. Faultlessness was required in all the animals offered as *Shelamim*; and in the case of the freewill-offerings *only* could even animals with too short or too long a limb be admitted (*vid.* § 130). All the other requisites of cleanness were demanded even in this class of sacrifices (Lev. xxii. 22, 23).

The *laying on of hands*, the *slaughtering*, and the *sprinkling of the blood* were performed in just the same manner as with the burnt-offering and trespass-offering (Lev. iii.). We have seen (§ 30) that

---

[1] " There may be very various and manifold states of mind, in which a man is not conscious of any particular sin, but yet feels the need of making his peace with God. The outward events and inward conditions which might produce this are so manifold, that they could not be specified or fixed beforehand. Hence, in addition to the praise-offerings and votive offerings, the *Thorah* formed a third, open class of Shelamim."

[2] " The נְדָבָה was a sacrifice, which was not occasioned by any distinct act of divine mercy, nor by any particular promise, but sprang from the prompting of the heart itself, from a free, religious impulse (Ex. xxxv. 29, xxxvi. 3); as it were without the existence of any moral or legal obligation, though it always had especial reference to the goodness of God, and, as an acknowledgment of that goodness, was really a thank-offering " (p. 408).

[3] " The freewill-offerings could only have an anticipatory reference to acts of divine mercy, whether they related to some special manifestation of grace to be sought for, or, without any reference to particular blessings to be prayed for, were intended to secure the possession or continuance of prosperity in general " (M. O. pp. 138, 139).

even in the case of these sacrifices, an atoning efficacy was attributed to the sprinkling of the blood, and have shown in § 40 why an act of expiation was required in their case also. If, therefore, we must reckon the peace-offerings among the expiatory offerings in the broader sense, we cannot go so far as *Kliefoth*, with whom the distinction between this sacrifice and the sin- and trespass-offerings threatens to vanish altogether (§ 125), especially as he places the sacrificial meal of the *Shelamim* upon the same footing as the eating of the flesh of the sin-offering by the priests (§ 116). The former appears most distinctly, and in the most inadmissible way, in his examination of the votive sacrifices, where he has gone so far astray, in his endeavour to show that in the case of all the *Shelamim* there were certain circumstances existing, which introduced something wrong into the relation in which the sacrificer stood to God and his nation, and which had to be set right (שִׁלֵּם) by these sacrifices, as to pronounce vowing generally a sin, and to represent this as actually the view and teaching of the Thorah. "Vowing," he says, "came very near to a *venture*, by which God was tempted. The sinful man ought to have considered that he could not even perform his common duty uprightly. The Israelite should have rested in the full assurance, that as a member of the covenant nation he would receive all the blessings of God, even without any *presumptuous* promise; and if, notwithstanding that, he still made a vow, he placed himself in a wrong attitude to God and the people of God. . . . . And it was just this which was not right between the maker of the vow and God, and which had to be disposed of by a Shelem even after the vow had been paid." Whether, and if so how far, this view of a vow can be sustained on ethical and religious grounds, this is not the place to inquire. But when *Kliefoth* represents it as distinctly taught in the Pentateuch, and appeals to Num. xxx. 3 and Deut. xxiii. 21–23 in proof of this, nothing further is needed to refute this assertion, than to request the reader to examine the passages for himself.

§ 132. Of the *flesh of the peace-offerings* the same portions were burned upon the altar as in the case of the sin- and trespass-offerings (§ 108), namely, the *fat* portions (Lev. iii. 3 sqq., 9 sqq., 14 sqq.), and had just the same significance (§ 110). The reason why only the חֲלָבִים were burned upon the altar in the case of the peace-offering, is much simpler and more obvious than in the other cases (§ 111 sqq.). It is to be found partly in the appointment of the sacrificial meal in connection with the peace-offering for the wor-

shipper and his family, and partly in the necessity for allowing
the priest his portion as the servant of God. The significance of
the *eating of the flesh of the sacrifice by the priest* we have already
explained at § 118–9. On the other hand, we have to examine the
reasons for selecting the particular pieces assigned to him, and the
forms with which they were assigned. The two pieces set apart for
the priest were the *breast* (חָזֶה) and the *right leg* (שׁוֹק הַיָּמִין), Lev. vii.
30, 32.[1]

[1] According to *Ewald, Riehm, Knobel, Bunsen,* and others, Deut. xviii. 3 is
at variance with this, since according to that passage the part allotted to the
priests from the slain- or peace-offerings was not the wave-breast and heave-leg,
but a fore-joint, the two cheeks, and the stomach, the מֵאֵת זֹבְחֵי הַזֶּבַח in ver. 3
being evidently a more minute explanation of the אִשֵּׁי יְהֹוָה in ver. 1. But it
is perfectly inconceivable that the Deuteronomist should have been ignorant of
the directions of the Levitical Thorah, even if he had lived at a much later
period. And if they were known to him, there must have been some special
reason to induce him to make such an alteration; yet no one will ever succeed
in discovering any such reason. We should have to assume, therefore, in accordance with the Jewish tradition, which goes back to the Mishnah, *Josephus*
(Ant. 4. 4, 4), and *Philo* (de Sacerd. hon. § 3), that the זִבְחֵי זֶבַח are not
peace-offerings, but ordinary slaughterings, and that this supplementary law
was intended as an indemnity to the priests for the falling off in their revenues
in consequence of the repeal of the provisions of the earlier law in Lev. xvii.
1 sqq. by Deut. xii. 15. The term זֶבַח in Deut. xviii. 3 furnishes no evidence
against this view, since it is used in Deut. xii. 15 also, in connection with the
ordinary slaughterings; and the אִשֵּׁי יְהֹוָה in ver. 1 is rather a proof of the
opposite of what *Knobel* supposes it to teach. Ver. 3, for instance, commences
with the words, "And this shall be the priests' due *from the people*" (מֵאֵת הָעָם).
This is evidently intended as an antithesis to ver. 1, which states what they are
to receive *from Jehovah* ("They shall eat the offerings of Jehovah, and His
inheritance"). The difficulty started by *Bunsen* (p. 313), that "the law in Lev.
xvii. 1 sqq. was abolished in this book because of its impracticability, and such
an appointment as the Talmud discovers here, would only introduce another
impossibility in its stead," has been already met by *Oehler*, in *Herzog's* Real-
encyk. 12, 181–2, by the remark, that "the passage is far from containing any
allusion to an obligation to bring or send the portions mentioned to the sanctuary itself. Even the Jewish tradition classed these gifts among the קדשי
הגבול (*i.e.*, among those gifts to the priests which there was no necessity to
send to the priests officiating at the time, but which might be handed over to
any priest they chose). The gift might be sent to a priests' city, or to a priest
staying in the neighbourhood; and that the performance of the duty might be
omitted whenever there was no opportunity of carrying it out, is an assumption
that we are as fully warranted in making, as that the command to invite the
Levites to the feast of tithes was based, as a matter of course, upon the supposition that there were actually Levites in the neighbourhood." The question, why
these three pieces in particular should have been singled out for the priests, is

הָזֶה, from חָזָה = to split, divide (then to distinguish, to see), signifies "the *breast-piece*, which is called the *Brust-kern* (breast-kernel) in oxen, sheep, and goats, consisting for the most part of gristly fat, and forming one of the most savoury portions. . . . As Jehovah received the pure fat, as the best portion of all, so His servants received the finest breast-piece, which consisted of marbled and palatable gristly fat" (*Knobel*).—שׁוֹק, from שׁוּק שָׁקַק, to run, is understood by *Luther* and most modern commentators, after the example of the LXX. (βραχίων) and *Vulgate* (*armus*), as denoting the *fore-leg*, or rather the shoulder. But *Knobel* has justly objected to this rendering, on the ground that זְרֹעַ is the standing word for the fore-leg (Num. vi. 19; Deut. xviii. 3), and שׁוֹק must be understood as denoting the *hind-leg*, because it is even employed to designate the human thigh (Song of Sol. v. 15; Ps. cxlvii. 10; Judg. xv. 8). Moreover, the priest, to whom as the servant and representative of God the best portion belonged, would hardly have been put off with the shoulder, which is a poor joint in comparison with the leg; and it stands to reason that it is the thigh portion (the ham) that is intended, and not the shin-bone, which is almost bare. And under such circumstances *Hofmann's* far-fetched explanation, that the "shoulder" referred to the "burden of the office borne by the priest," smacks too strongly of the caprice of the ancient allegorists to lead us to alter our opinion. Still less, indeed, can we make up our mind to accept *Knobel's* explanation of the reason for selecting the hind-leg, viz., that according to the Old Testament idea, it was "from the hip that children issued (Gen. xxxv. 11, xlvi. 26; Ex. i. 5; Judg. viii. 30; 1 Kings viii. 19) and life proceeded, and therefore the hip was peculiarly the seat of vital power."—In the selection of the thigh for the priest the only point considered was the flesh, and the flesh was selected only to be eaten; hence the choice of the leg was determined solely by the fact that it contained the best and most savoury meat.—And the reason why the *right* leg was the one appointed for the priest, was simply that the right side is always regarded as the better of the two (Gen. xlviii. 13).

The breast and leg, which fell to the portion of the priests, are frequently designated, the former as the *wave-breast*, חֲזֵה הַתְּנוּפָה, the latter as the *heave-leg*, שׁוֹק הַתְּרוּמָה (Ex. xxix. 27; Lev. vii. 34, etc.), because they were subjected to the peculiar ceremony of *waving* or

answered thus by *Oehler* and *Schultz*: "Of every one of the three principal parts of the animal (the head, trunk, and legs) some valuable portion was to be set apart."

swinging on the one hand, and of *heaving* on the other. What the waving and heaving signified, however, has been by no means elucidated with perfect clearness and certainty by any previous investigations. It is true, that when we observe how the latest commentators (*Keil, Knobel,* and *Oehler*) arrive at the same results through the same means, and with what assurance they speak, whether in their affirmations or their denials, we ought properly to regard the question as set for ever at rest through their researches. But a more minute examination of their arguments, and of the relation in which they stand to the biblical fact, will show that they have helped forward only one part of the question, whilst they have thrown the other into still greater confusion, and removed it altogether away from its true solution.

§ 133. The ceremony of WAVING occurs not only in connection with the wave-breast of the peace-offering, but also "in the *Shelamim* offered at the ordination of the priests (Lev. viii. 25 sqq.) and at the consecration of a Nazarite (Num. vi. 20), in the meat-offering of jealousy (Num. v. 24), in the trespass-offering of the leper (Lev. xiv. 12), in the offering of the sheaf of first-fruits at the Passover, and also of the bread of the first-fruits and the lambs of the Shelamim at the weekly festival (Lev. xxiii. 11, 20)" (*Oehler*). The verb הֵנִיף, which it would be more correct and more intelligible to render *swing* than *wave*, is used to denote the backward and forward movement of a saw (Isa. x. 15) and of a threatening finger (Isa. xi. 15, xix. 16), and also the movement of a scythe, first from right to left, and then back again from left to right. The Talmud describes the sacrificial waving as a מוֹלִיךְ וּמֵבִיא, *i.e.*, a backward and forward motion, in which the proper direction was given to the piece of the sacrifice which lay upon the hands of the offerer by the hands of the priest placed underneath (*vid. Bähr* ii. 355). The later Rabbins, on the contrary, and most of the Christian archæologists, assume that the movement was in the direction of the four quarters of the globe, and suppose allusion to have been made to the omnipresence of God, to whom the gift was thereby to be consecrated. This view is certainly quite as reconcilable with the text of the Bible as the other; but no proper use can be made of the meaning which it gives, since it is impossible to see what an allusion to the omnipresence of God could do in this connection, inasmuch as "Jehovah dwelt in the sanctuary, and not in all the four winds of heaven" (*Keil*, p. 253). It is much more advisable, therefore, to keep to the simple explanation of the Talmud, as the latest expositors have done.

Even *Kliefoth* does this, though in a thoroughly untenable way. In his opinion, " the priest took hold of the offering which lay upon the hands of the offerer, and first drew it towards himself, and then pushed it back again towards the offerer" (p. 59). The meaning of this is said to have been, " that the priest first accepted the gift from the offerer in the name of God, and then it was given back to the offerer as a gift from God,"—a view which stands in direct and open contradiction to the statements of the text (Lev. vii. 34, x. 14, 15; Ex. xxix. 28), which show that the wave-breast was assigned to the priest and not to the offerer. The same rule applies to the waving of the Levites, to which he appeals; for they were not given back to the nation, but given to Aaron and his sons *as their own* (Num. viii. 19). What *Rinck* means by his " air purification," which was to be effected by the waving, it is impossible to tell. The true explanation is rather that of *Keil* (p. 250), that the waving was a movement towards the altar, or perhaps, better still, towards the door of the tabernacle, and thence back again towards the waving priest. The words " before Jehovah" (Ex. xxix. 26, etc.), which describe more exactly the purpose of the waving, are in perfect harmony with this, since they always contain an allusion to the tabernacle, when employed in connection with the ritual of worship. " The swinging in a forward direction," says *Oehler* (p. 640), " evidently denoted the presentation of the gift to God,—it was a practical declaration that, strictly speaking, it belonged to Him; whilst the movement back again denoted that God gave back the gift, and assigned it as His own present to the priest." This is essentially the same view as that expressed by *Hofmann* (p. 283) and *Knobel* (p. 412).

The statement in the Talmud, that with *every* waving the priest placed the pieces to be waved upon the hands of the offerer, and then put his own hands underneath and so completed the waving, has probably been too readily adopted by most of the later expositors. *Hofmann* is right, it appears to me, in rejecting it as having no support in the law itself. It is true, some have imagined that the requisite confirmation could be found in Ex. xxix. 24 and Lev. viii. 27, where the consecration of Aaron and his sons to the priesthood is described, and a waving of the right shoulder of the offering certainly does take place in the manner described. But on closer examination, these passages are rather adapted to sustain the very opposite conclusion. For if the animal offered in sacrifice received the name of " ram of the filling" (*sc.* of the hands, *vid.* § 170), it must have been something singular, which only occurred in connection with this sacrifice. And since it is stated immediately afterwards, in Ex. xxix. 26 and Lev. viii. 29, that Moses took the breast of the ram of the filling and waved it before Jehovah, this waving cannot possibly have been performed in precisely the same way as the previous waving of the leg, viz., in the hands of the persons to be consecrated. We shall not be wrong, therefore, if we assume that the introduction of the offerer in Lev. viii. 27 and Ex. xxix. 24 was occasioned by peculiar circumstances, and required to be expressly mentioned, because it was something extraordinary, a deviation from the usual mode of waving. (We shall find a proof of this in § 170.) This view is also at variance with the fact, that by the presentation of the sacrificial animal the offerer renounced all right of ownership, and assigned it absolutely and entirely to Jehovah, so that from that time forward it was to be regarded as no longer his own, but as Jehovah's property (§ 81, 82). The offerer, whose right of ownership in the animal had ceased, could not assign the breast-piece on his own account first to Jehovah and then to the priest; but the priest, to whom it was to be allotted according to the rules of the sacrificial worship, was required, before actually taking possession of it, to declare by the waving that it belonged to Jehovah, and that it was from Jehovah that he had received it.—On Num. vi. 19 cf. § 233.

§ 134. There is more difficulty in describing and explaining the HEAVING, which was performed upon the right leg. According to the Jewish tradition, the heaving was a symbolical ceremony, answering to the waving, in which the movement was in an upward direction, the gift being elevated therefore, and so consecrated to the God who was enthroned in heaven. This view continued the prevalent one till the most recent times. It was adopted by *Winer*, *Bähr*, *Hengstenberg*, *Kliefoth*, *Ewald*, and *Stöckl*; and, notwithstanding the very plausible objections offered by *Keil*, *Knobel*, *Schultz*, and *Oehler*, it is still retained by *Hofmann*, and in my opinion with perfect justice. For example, the writers named maintain that the waving is the only ceremony laid down in the Mosaic law as a special act of worship; that the heaving (lifting), on the other hand, simply denoted the *lifting off* or *taking away* of one portion from the rest, for the purpose of handing it over to Jehovah, to the sanctuary, or to the priests; that תְּרוּמָה is nothing more than " the *lifting off*, or the portion removed from a mass to be devoted to sacred purposes," and that it denotes in general " the holy offering."

Thus, says *Oehler*, שׁוֹק הַתְּרוּמָה was "the leg, which, after Jehovah had received His portion, and handed over the breast to the priest, was taken from what still remained, and handed over to the priest who officiated at the ceremony, as a mark of respect on the part of the offerer."

Of all the arguments adduced in proof of this, the weakest undoubtedly is the appeal to the Septuagint, in which the words תְּרוּמָה and הֵרִים are said to be understood in the same sense, inasmuch as they are rendered by ἀφαίρεμα, ἀπαρχή, ἀφαιρεῖν, περιαιρεῖν, ἀφορίζειν; for the Septuagint rendering of תְּנוּפָה and הֵנִיף is also ἀφαίρεμα, ἀφόρισμα, ἀπαρχή, ἀφαιρεῖν, ἀφορίζειν. Consequently the LXX. have evidently regarded הֵרִים and הֵנִיף, not simply as homogeneous, but as identical notions; and if anything is established by this fact, it is our own view, and not that of our opponents; for, whilst in the former הֵרִים and הֵנִיף are homogeneous notions, in the latter they are quite heterogeneous, and have nothing whatever in common. But there is still another consideration which favours our view. The idea of separation has two distinct aspects, a negative and a positive—that of separation *from* something, and that of separation *for* something. Now that the LXX., even when rendering the words הֵרִים and הֵנִיף by ἀφαιρεῖν and ἀφαίρεμα, or by ἀφορίζειν and ἀφόρισμα, looked more at the positive than at the negative side, is evident from the fact that, as a general rule, they rendered the Hebrew terms by Greek words which present the positive side alone,—*e.g.*, δόμα, εἰσφορά, ἐπίθεμα, δωρέομαι, προσφέρω, ἀποδίδωμι, ἀναφέρω, ἐπιφέρω, ἐπιτίθημι. And no proof is needed, that in doing so, they approach much nearer to our view than to that of our opponents.

Again, *Oehler* says, "there is not one passage in the Pentateuch, in which this signification of the word would not be found sufficient, without the slightest necessity for assuming that there was any special ceremony of heaving." But, *in the first place*, this assertion is incorrect; for in Num. xxxi. 50, 52, it is not sufficient,[1] inasmuch as the *officers* are there said to lift up *all* the gold, "which *every one*

---

[1] Strictly speaking, in Num. xviii. 17-19 also; for the first-born of oxen, sheep, and goats, which are here assigned as תְּרוּמָה, were not lifted from the mass, since this was not yet in existence, but only expected. And it will hardly be possible for any one to satisfy himself with the statement, that if such first-born were not taken out of a more numerous offspring of one particular animal, they might be regarded as a selection from the whole flock; for this command undoubtedly applied not merely to the possessors of whole flocks, but also to the possessors of one single animal.

had found," and not merely a select portion of it, as a heave-offering to Jehovah ; and in the *second place*, even if it were correct, it would prove nothing, as is evident from the simple fact, that in all the passages in the Pentateuch the idea of תְּנוּפָה and הֵנִיף may be expressed quite as well by ἀφόρισμα and ἀφορίζειν, or ἀφαίρεμα and ἀφαιρεῖν, the terms actually employed in the Septuagint along with others of a similar meaning.

Knobel says, " הֵרִים is never connected with אֶל־יְהֹוָה, or, like הֵנִיף, with לִפְנֵי יְהֹוָה, when sacrifices are referred to, but the invariable expression is הֵרִים לַיהֹוָה." To this it may be replied, (1) that הֵנִיף also is connected with לַיהֹוָה (Ex. xxxv. 22 ; Num. viii. 13) ; (2) that הֵנִיף also is never connected with אֶל־יְהֹוָה ; and (3) that the phrase הֵנִיף לִפְנֵי יְהֹוָה, which occurs so frequently, is as intelligible and appropriate a combination as the phrase הֵרִים לִפְנֵי יְהֹוָה would be unintelligible and unmeaning, and therefore we should never expect to meet with the latter. For, since הֵנִיף applied to Jehovah, who dwelt in the tabernacle in the midst of His people, לִפְנֵי יְהֹוָה is the most suitable, and therefore the most frequent indication of the personal object, both here and everywhere else, where Jehovah is regarded as dwelling *in the tabernacle. But הֵרִים applied to the " God who dwelleth on high," and therefore הֵרִים לִפְנֵי יְהֹוָה would be an unintelligible phrase; and even הֵרִים אֶל־יְהֹוָה would not be peculiarly appropriate, since the gift could not be reached up by the heaving to God enthroned in heaven.

§ 135. It is equally impossible to prove the necessity of accepting the meaning " lifting off " for תְּרוּמָה, on the ground that " the word is frequently used with מִן before the whole mass from which the heave-offering was heaved up, or taken away ;" for if only a part was to be consecrated to Jehovah through the ceremony of elevating, it is self-evident that it was taken *from* the whole. In all the passages cited by *Knobel* (Lev. ii. 9, iv. 8, 10, 19, vi. 8 ; Ex. xxix. 27 ; Num. xviii. 26, 30, 32), the whole, of which a part was heaved up, was already brought to the tabernacle itself, and consequently the elevation of the part to be lifted up coincided with the lifting of it from the whole, and the lifting off was *eo ipso* a lifting up, which was not the case with the horizontal movement of the waving, so that הֵרִים might very properly be connected with מִן, but not הֵנִיף. This argument could only be conclusive, however, if הֵרִים were also connected with מִן in cases where the lifting off took place outside the sanctuary, and the part lifted off was brought to the sanctuary afterwards. For example, מִן could be used in Num. xviii. 26, 30, 32, to denote the heaving of the priestly tithe, because the mass from which it was lifted, viz., the Levitical tithe, was already in the sanctuary; but it could not be applied in ver. 24 to the heaving of the Levitical tithe, which was taken from the entire mass outside the sanctuary. And just as in this case, so in every other instance, in which the lifting from the whole took place outside the sanctuary and therefore could *not* coincide with the elevating, the מִן which is thought to be so ominous, is entirely wanting; *e.g.*, in the heaving of the first-fruits in Num. xv. 19, 20, in the share of the booty which fell to the sanctuary in Num. xxxi. 28,[1] in the sacred gifts generally in Lev. xxii. 15 and Num. xviii. 19, and in the contributions towards the building of the tabernacle in Ex. xxxv. 5, 21, 22, 24. How natural would it have been, especially in the passages quoted from Ex. xxxv., to employ מִן, and write תְּרוּמָה מִן הַכֶּסֶף instead of תְּרוּמַת כֶּסֶף in ver. 24, if the argument of our opponents were a just one. For, although it certainly was not the intention of Moses that the Israelites should bring all the gold, silver, and brass, all the skins, all the linen and woollen clothes, all the shittim-wood, all the oil and all the spices and jewels which they possessed, but only a portion of them, yet the מִן is invariably wanting. Can this be merely accidental?

This also takes away the force of a fact mentioned by *Bähr*, upon which *Keil* and *Oehler* lay the greatest stress, and which the former cites with these words : " The same act which is designated הֵרִים מִ in Lev. ii. 9 is expressed by קָמַץ מִן in chap. ii. 2 ; again, for הֵרִים מִמֶּנּוּ in chap. iv. 8, we find הִקְרִיב מִזְבֵּחַ in chap. iii. 3; and, lastly, for כַּאֲשֶׁר יוּרַם in chap. iv. 10, we have כַּאֲשֶׁר הוּסַר in vers. 31 and 35 ; —a convincing proof, that הֵרִים מִן does not apply to any particular ceremony of heaving, but only to the lifting or taking away of the portions to be burned upon the altar." But by the laws of universal logic, we are not warranted in declaring, that because two ideas are applicable to the same object, they must on that account coincide with one another. If in the cases referred to הֵרִים is also הֵסִיר, or הִקְרִיב, or קָמַץ, it by no means follows that every הִקְרִיב, הֵסִיר and קָמַץ must be a הֵרִים also, and the two completely coincide.

And when *Knobel*, after reckoning up the cases in which a הֵרִים is mentioned in connection with worship, adds, that " there is no

---

[1] There is a מִן indeed associated with הֵרִים, but it stands before the offerer, and not the offering. No one, therefore, will be foolish enough to press this מִן in opposition to my assertion ; for in that case the offerers (= warriors) would have to be regarded as the mass, of which one portion was to be lifted off.

passage in the law in which it has a special ritual signification, but
it is always used in this general sense" (viz., lifting off),. we can
easily see, that this is a perfectly vague assertion ; for in all the passages, whether quoted by him or not, the word certainly *may* be
understood to denote a ritual elevation quite as naturally as a simple
and non-ritual selection ; in fact, as we have already observed, the
latter is *not* admissible, in one of the passages at least, viz., Num.
xxxi. 52.   And if I chose to meet his assertion, that the word has
not a ritual signification in any one of these passages, by a counter-
assertion that the word has a ritual signification in every one of
them, we should just have assertion for assertion, and the one
would still need to be proved quite as much as the other.   Our
opponents have hitherto failed to bring proofs on their side.   Let
us see now whether there has been greater success on ours.

§ 136.   *Oehler* acknowledges that " it cannot be disputed, that
in the later Jewish ritual there was a distinct ceremony of heaving,
but no such ceremony can be proved to exist in the Pentateuch."
This admission is based upon the rabbinical tradition, which goes
back to the earliest times.   Now we have no desire to question the
fact, that many things crept into the later temple worship, and still
more into the rabbinical tradition of the Talmud, to which no
reference is made in the ritual laws of the Pentateuch.   But in this
instance the unanimity and great antiquity of the tradition in question must not be underrated.   For if there is nothing at variance
with it either in the language or the facts of the Pentateuch, as is
evident from the foregoing proof of the futility of all the objections
that have been offered ; and if, on the other hand, the view we
hold can be shown to be in perfect harmony with the language,
the facts, and the laws of the Pentateuch, as will presently appear ;
there can be no reason whatever for disputing the correctness of
this tradition.

First of all, then, so far as the word is concerned, there is not
the slightest doubt that רוּם means *to be high*, and nothing else.
הֵרִים therefore signifies to *make high*, to *elevate*, to *raise on high*.
And it is *only* in this sense that it is ever met with in the whole
Hebrew thesaurus, apart from its application to the offerings of
divine worship.   What is there then to warrant us in rejecting this,
the only established meaning, and the only one in harmony with
the language, as soon as we come to the department of worship, and
in inventing a totally different meaning, which it never has anywhere else, and for which the fundamental idea of the root offers

no possible link of connection ?   Was the Hebrew language so poor
in words to express separation or cutting off, taking off and away,
that no other resource was left than to force this idea in connection with worship upon a word, with whose radical meaning it had
nothing whatever in common ?   Certainly not ; on the contrary, it
abounded in such words.   Then, again, how simple, natural, and in
accordance with the whole procedure, that *every* gift presented and
assigned to Jehovah, whether actually assigned to Him personally
by being burned upon the altar, or presented to Him to supply the
necessities of His dwelling-place or His servants, should be indicated symbolically as intended for Him, and consecrated to Him, by
being elevated in the place of His abode (either by *the side of* or
upon the altar).

If we examine the use of הֵרִים in the law of sacrifice, we meet first
of all with the three passages, Lev. ii. 9, iv. 8 sqq., vi. 8, the misunderstanding of which, in *Keil's* opinion, has been the principal cause
of the prevalent, but erroneous idea of a ritual elevation.   But this is
certainly an unfounded opinion ; for it is not from these passages
that the interpretation of הֵרִים as a peculiar ceremony has arisen,
but from those numerous passages in which the heave-leg and
heave-offerings (תְּרוּמֹת) are mentioned, and it is this which has suggested the necessity for understanding the הֵרִים in Lev. ii. 4, 6 in
the same way.   The relation between them is, in fact, the very
opposite : the rabbinical opinion is not based upon Lev. ii. 4, 6 ;
but, on the contrary, it is from this very passage that the opposition
to that traditional opinion has proceeded.   Let us look, however, at
the passages more carefully.   The command in Lev. ii. 9 and vi. 8,
that the priest is to heave a portion of the meat-offering (the so-
called *Azcarah*, cf. § 148) and burn it upon the altar, and again, in
Lev. iv. 8 sqq., that he is to heave all the fat of the sin-offering,
just as that of the peace-offering was heaved, and then burn it
upon the altar, can hardly be understood, as it is by *Keil*, as denoting a mere lifting off or taking away, since הֵרִים *never* means to
take away, but always to lift on high ; but rather, as it is by *Bähr*,
as relating " quite generally to the presentation of the gift upon the
altar, which was really an elevation."   And it would certainly never
have been understood in any other sense than that of simple elevation upon the altar, if the later passages in the law, with regard to
the heave-leg and heave-offerings, had not suggested the idea that
a special and ritual signification ought to be attributed to the heaving.   But cannot the simple and natural sense of a lifting of the

gift upon the altar for the purpose of burning, be made to harmonise
with the symbolical signification of the lifting as a dedication to
God, who dwells on high? I answer this question without hesitation in the affirmative. For the altar itself was a high place (בָּמָה),
and was required to be a high place (§ 13), because the gift upon it
was to be brought nearer to God, who was enthroned on high.

The actual fact, therefore, was as follows: the *heaving* or lifting
(הֵרִים) in the ceremony of worship always signified the offering or
presentation of the gift to God by lifting it up. Now, if the gift
was destined to be actually and personally appropriated to Jehovah,
i.e., to be burnt upon the altar, a special and independent ceremony
of lifting up was unnecessary, because this was already effected by
lifting it upon the altar itself. Everything that was brought to
the altar to be burnt was *eo ipso* lifted up; there was no necessity,
therefore, to embody this in an express command. But if the gift
was not destined to be burnt upon the altar, which was always the
case with offerings that were not appropriated to Jehovah personally, but was simply presented to Him for the maintenance of His
dwelling-place (the tabernacle) or of His servants (the priests and
Levites), it was requisite that a תְּרוּמָה should be performed by the
side of the altar as a special and independent rite. In the first
case the gift remained on high (*i.e.*, upon the altar), and was there
accepted by Jehovah Himself; in the second, it was taken down
again from the height to which it had been raised, and this was an
intimation that God renounced His own claim to it, and handed it
over to His servant, the priest, or to His house, the tabernacle.
Hence the signification of the heaving was essentially the same as
that of the waving (§ 133); the only difference being, that the *waving*
had reference to the abode of God in the tabernacle in the midst of
His people,—the *heaving*, on the contrary, to the abode of God in
heaven.

§ 137. The conclusion to which we have thus been brought is
confirmed in a most unquestionable manner, when we consider the
relation in which the *Thorah* places the הֵרִים to the הֵנִיף and the
תְּרוּמָה to the תְּנוּפָה. Who is there, who could observe with an unprejudiced mind, how the *wave*-breast and the *heave*-leg are constantly mentioned together and placed in the *same* category in the
case of the peace-offerings (Ex. xxix. 24; Lev. vii. 34, x. 14, 15;
Num. vi. 20), without the conjecture, or rather the certainty, irresistibly forcing itself upon his mind, that the תְּנוּפָה and the תְּרוּמָה
were homogeneous acts,—especially if he considers that in their

radical signification the two words הֵנִיף and הֵרִים are expressive of
thoroughly *homogeneous* ideas—the one denoting a movement from
right to left, the other a movement in an upward direction? And
when we observe still further how the תְּנוּפָה is evidently pointed out
in the text itself as a rite of consecration (Ex. xxix. 24 ; Lev. viii.
27), how can we any longer doubt that the תְּרוּמָה is to be understood
in the same way? Let any one read with an unbiassed mind Ex.
xxix. 27, " And thou shalt sanctify the breast of the wave-offering
and the shoulder (leg) of the heave-offering, which is waved and
which is heaved up, etc. ;" and how is it possible to attribute a ritual
signification to the waving, and none at all to the heaving? How
could two such heterogeneous ideas as that of *waving* (a solemn and
significant rite of consecration), and that of *lifting* (the simple and
unmeaning act of removing a portion from the whole), be placed in
such intimate and essential relation to one another? And how is it
conceivable that the heave-leg should have received its distinctive
name from the insignificant act of removing or separating a portion
from the remainder of the flesh, when the designation would indicate nothing peculiar or characteristic, seeing that the fat portions
which were placed upon the altar, and the breast which was waved,
were also removed and heaved (lifted) off the whole mass of the
flesh in precisely the same manner as the heave-leg?

Heaving and *waving*, therefore, were two essentially homogeneous rites of consecration, differing in unessential points alone. And
this alone will serve to explain the fact, that in a wider and less
stringent sense the two words could be used promiscuously, or identified and interchanged. Thus, for example, the freewill-offerings
for the building of the tabernacle are called תְּרוּמַת יְהוָֹה in Ex. xxxv.
5, 21 (cf. chap. xxxvi. 6), and תְּנוּפָה לַיהוָֹה in Ex. xxxv. 22 (cf.
chap. xxxviii. 24) ; and an offering of gold is referred to as תְּנוּפָה
in Ex. xxxv. 22, xxxviii. 24, whereas a similar offering is called
תְּרוּמָה in Num. xxxi. 52. In Num. xviii. 11, again, in the very same
verse the תְּנוּפֹת בְּנֵי יִשְׂרָאֵל are designated תְּרוּמַת מַתְּנָם ; and in Lev. ix.
21 the term waving is applied in common to the heave-leg and wave-
breast, and in Lev. x. 15 even to the fat portions burned upon the
altar. How hopeless do these facts render *Keil's* explanation :
" Since those portions of the sacrifices, which were waved, were
also regarded as sacrificial gifts to Jehovah, which He handed over
to the priests, every heave-offering might also be regarded as a wave-
offering,"—a consequence, the correctness and even the admissibility
of which is beyond the reach of my understanding ; for, so far as I

can see, the only thing that could follow is this, that every wave-offering might be designated a heave-offering, but not *vice versa*. But the former was the only one which would help *Keil's* views out of the difficulty.

§ 138. With reference to these two peculiarities and irregularities in the mode of expression, *Bähr* is of opinion, " that at all events as a rule the two movements were connected together, but the usage of speech was not always perfectly exact, and the two were frequently designated by one expression. If the movements had occurred separately, they would necessarily have had different objects; but this is hardly conceivable."—Whether the two forms of consecration were associated together in the other heave-offerings, we may leave undecided (I do not look upon this as improbable) ; but that in the case of the peace-offerings they were distributed between the breast and leg, is evident from the fixed and unchangeable designation of the one as the *wave*-breast, the other as the *heave*-leg. There is also another distinction, which is frequently overlooked. According to Lev. vii. 31, the wave-breast was to fall to the lot of Aaron and his sons, and therefore not to the officiating priest merely, but to the whole body of priests who were performing the service of the sanctuary at the time ; on the other hand, according to ver. 33, the heave-leg was to belong to that one particular son of Aaron who had attended to the sprinkling of the blood and the burning of the sacrifice, that is to say, to the officiating priest alone.

Thus we find a triple rite of consecration in the case of the peace-offering: (1) the lifting (heaving) of the fat portions upon the top of the altar (Lev. iv. 10), where Jehovah accepted them personally and enjoyed them in the fire-vapour; (2) the waving of the breast, which Jehovah handed over to Aaron and his sons (Lev. vii. 31); and (3) the heaving of the right shoulder, which Jehovah handed over to the officiating priest (Lev. vii. 33). Through these three ἀπαρχαί, which were taken from the whole mass, and, having been consecrated to Jehovah, were enjoyed partly by Himself and partly by His servants the priests, the rest of the flesh, from which they were separated, and which Jehovah handed over to the offerer (§ 82), was consecrated and sanctified also (Rom. xi. 16), and was then eaten by the latter along with his household and friends. Thus we see that in the case of the peace-offerings, all who were more or less concerned, Jehovah and His servants, the offerer and his household, derived from them food, satisfaction (נִיחֹחַ), and joy.

The only question that presents any difficulty is this, why was the breast waved and assigned to the priests in general, whilst the leg was heaved (lifted up) and fell to the lot of the officiating priest alone? I know no other way of arriving at an answer to this question, than that of tracing the relation of the breast, as half-fat, to the fat of the burnt sacrifice, and that of the leg, as the best of the flesh, to the flesh of the sacrificial meal. As the offerer of the sacrifice brought his whole family to the sacrificial meal, so Jehovah admitted *His* whole family, so to speak, *i.e.*, the whole of the priests performing service at the time, to participate in His enjoyment,—not indeed by assigning them a portion of the pure fat, which would have been thoroughly uneatable, but by assigning them the nearest to it, viz., the half-fat; and the reason why this was not heaved, but waved "before Jehovah," *i.e.*, moved towards the door of the tabernacle and then back again towards the priest (cf. § 133), was probably because the service of the priests in general had respect to God, who dwelt within the tabernacle. And as the wave-breast, as half-fat, was related to the meal provided for Jehovah ("the bread of Jehovah"), so the heave-leg, as the best of the flesh-meat, was related to the meal provided for the offerer. It was heaved (not waved), probably to exhibit its relation to the altar, upon which Jehovah's portion was burnt. Both of these are in perfect harmony with the fact, that the leg was allotted to the *officiating* priest alone; for *he* alone performed the loving service for the offerer of presenting his gift to Jehovah, and *he* alone performed the service at the altar, of sprinkling the blood and burning the sacrifice.

Thus the different mode of assigning the wave-breast and heave-leg to the priesthood was expressive of their double position, on the one hand as servants of Jehovah, and on the other as mediators of the people; and special regard was had to each of these two aspects of their official calling. But *Oehler* is wrong in supposing that the wave-breast was the piece of honour, which the offerer of the sacrifice presented to Jehovah, who accepted it, and then caused it to be eaten by His servant as His representative; whilst the heave-leg was the gift presented by the offerer directly to the priest. For, apart from the fact that after the presentation had taken place, the offerer had no longer any right of ownership in the animal, if the separation of a "piece of honour" for Jehovah could possibly take place at all, the term could only be applied to the fat, which Jehovah really accepted and partook of as *His bread*. And the heave-leg (even according to *Oehler's* own view of the תְּרוּמָה)

could not be regarded as a direct gift from the offerer to the priest, but, like all the תְּרוּמֹת, as really presented to Jehovah, and assigned by Him to the tabernacle or the priests.

§ 139. That the *sacrificial meal* had to take place at the tabernacle, is expressly commanded in Deut. xii. 7, 17 sqq., and was quite in harmony with its character as a hospitable meal, with which God refreshed and rejoiced the heart of the offerer. On the other hand, in Lev. x. 14 the priests are allowed to eat the wave-breast and heave-shoulder outside the sanctuary (though only in a clean place), and to bring the members of their families (sons and daughters) to participate. This is an indisputable proof that the eating of the flesh of the peace-offering on the part of the priests is not to be regarded as a participation in the sacrificial meal, as *Oehler* supposes, but only, like the eating of the flesh of the sin-offering, as an entertainment provided by Jehovah for the priests, as the servants of His house (*vid.* § 118).

On the other hand, the different grades of importance or holiness belonging to the three descriptions of peace-offerings (§ 126 sqq.) caused a difference undoubtedly, so far as the eating of the sacrificial flesh was concerned, which was equally applicable, whether it was by the priests or the offerer that the flesh was eaten. For example, according to Lev. vii. 15 sqq., xix. 6, 7, xxii. 30, the flesh of the *praise-offering* was to be eaten on the very same day on which it had been sacrificed. It is true, the same rule was binding generally in the case of the other two kinds of *Shelem*. But on account of the inferior importance of these two kinds, it was allowable to eat some of them on the second day, though none could be eaten on the third. All that remained had to be burned with fire (on the third day, probably like the sin-offering presented by a priest, § 112, 117) in a clean place outside the camp. Although it is not expressly stated, yet according to the analogy of Lev. viii. 32, Ex. xxix. 34, and xii. 10, this rule was probably applicable also to any of the flesh of the praise-offering which had not been eaten on the first day. So far as the purpose and meaning of this command are concerned, I cannot agree with *Oehler*, that the intention was "to prevent niggardliness" (since the sacrificial meal also possessed the character of a love-feast, *i.e.* was to embrace the poor and needy); for the simple reason, that the command applied, not only to the flesh set apart for the sacrificial meal, but also to the flesh which was assigned to the priests. What *Oehler* himself admits to be the *principal* reason, I am compelled to regard as the sole motive for the command, viz., " the putrefaction which would have taken place, and rendered the flesh unclean,—a danger which it was especially necessary to avoid in the case of the highest kind of peace-offering, viz., the praise-offering." It was on the same ground also that the commandments were based, that sacrificial flesh which had come into contact with anything unclean should not be eaten at all, and that any one who was levitically defiled was not to eat of the flesh of the peace-offering on pain of extermination (Lev. vii. 19 sqq.).

With reference to the *public Shelamim*, that is to say, the peace-offerings presented in the name of the whole nation, *Winer* has expressed the opinion, that in their case all the flesh was assigned to the priests. But this is expressly stated only of the two lambs which were to be offered as a peace-offering, along with the loaves of first-fruit at the feast of Passover (Lev. xxiii. 20); and *Keil* has justly objected to the extension of this rule to all the public *Shelamim*, on the ground that " it is at variance with Deut. xxvii. 7, where the *people* are commanded to offer thank-offerings at the solemn institution of the law upon Mount Ebal, and to rejoice before Jehovah, *i.e.*, to provide a solemn sacrificial meal from these thank-offerings. Again, at the consecration of Solomon's temple, the flesh of the 22,000 oxen and 120,000 sheep, which Solomon offered as a thank-offering (1 Kings viii. 63), could not possibly have fallen to the lot of the priests, but must have been employed in providing sacrificial meals for the whole of the assembled crowds. Moreover, no thank-offerings at all were prescribed for the regular weekly and yearly festivals (except the pentecostal offering already mentioned ; cf. Num. xxviii. and xxix.), so that the sacrifices slain at the feasts (Lev. xxiii. 27) are to be reckoned among those which were spontaneously offered."

BOOK III

THE BLOODLESS SACRIFICE

CHAPTER I

MATERIAL OF THE BLOODLESS SACRIFICE

§ 140. The bloodless or vegetable sacrifice, which was called קָרְבָּן like all the sacred offerings, and אִשֶּׁה יְהֹוָה or לֶחֶם יְהֹוָה like all the altar-sacrifices, is also designated מִנְחָה, *i.e.*, a gift, present, tribute, as distinguished from and opposed to the bleeding (animal) altar-sacrifice. In this broader sense[1] the word is not only used in the combination עֹלָה וּמִנְחָה (Ex. xxx. 9; Lev. xxiii. 37; Josh. xxii. 23, etc.), and זֶבַח וּמִנְחָה (Ps. xl. 6; Isa. xix. 21; Jer. xiv. 12, etc.; cf. § 125, note 2), but still more frequently stands quite alone. In a more precise and limited sense, again, the name is restricted to that portion of the bloodless sacrifice which consisted of meal, as distinguished from the libation of wine associated with it which is designated נֶסֶךְ (from נָסַךְ = to pour out). The complete offering is then called מִנְחָה וָנֶסֶךְ. In the Septuagint מִנְחָה is generally rendered θυσία or δῶρον θυσία (θυσίας); in the Vulgate, *oblatio sacrificium* or *oblatio sacrificii;* and by *Luther, Speis-opfer* (food-offering);—whilst נֶסֶךְ is rendered σπονδεῖον, σπονδή by the LXX., *libamentum, libamen* in the Vulgate, and *Trank-opfer* (drink-offering) by *Luther.*

We have already seen at § 21 that all tree-fruits were excluded from the *Minchah,* as well as garden-produce (vegetables, etc.). It was limited to the productions of agriculture and vine-growing, these being the characteristic employments of the nation in the Holy Land. At the same time, as the offering represented not only the fruits of

---

[1] In a still broader sense, also allowed by the etymology, the expression is applied on one occasion to a bleeding sacrifice, viz., to Abel's offering in Gen. iv. 3.

their labour, but also the presentation of food for Jehovah (§ 23),
it was not brought to the altar in the form of raw produce, but
dressed and prepared in the manner in which it served as the daily
food of man. Hence the food prepared from corn might be offered in very many different forms, whilst the drink-offering could
only be presented in one, viz., as a libation of wine.

In Lev. ii., for example, three leading descriptions of meat-
(food-) offering are mentioned: (1) in the form of *groats* (גֶּרֶשׂ כַּרְמֶל,
i.e., with the fresh ears roasted by the fire, and the dried grains
coarsely rubbed or crushed, ver. 14);—(2) as *white meal* (סֹלֶת, ver.
1; this was the term applied to the finest wheaten flour: barley flour
was only used in connection with the so-called jealousy-offering,
Num. v.: the groats and flour were covered with oil as well as
mixed with it, and incense was then laid upon them);—(3) in the
form of *loaves* or *cakes*, made of white meal mixed with oil. The
last was prepared in three different ways: (*a*) *Baked in the oven*
(תַּנּוּר, ver. 4): either in the form of חַלּוֹת or רְקִיקִים, both of which
were rubbed over with oil after they were taken out of the oven.
It is doubtful whether the name חַלּוֹת is derived from חלל, to pierce,
or from חלל = חול, to move round, to twist. In the former case it
would suggest the idea of loaves or cakes, with holes made in them
that the oil might penetrate them more easily; in the latter, which
is the more probable of the two, it would indicate their circular
shape (= כִּכָּר, 2 Sam. vi. 19). The name רָקִיק signifies something
beaten out thin and broad, corresponding probably to our *pancake*.
—(*b*) *Prepared upon the* מַחֲבַת (a flat iron plate: vers. 5, 6). The
difference between this and the previous sort was, that it consisted
of a thin layer of dough baked crisp, which was broken in pieces
(פִּתִּים) and dipped in oil.—(*c*) *Prepared* בְּמַרְחֶשֶׁת. Even the earlier
translators could not agree whether by this we are to understand
broiled upon the gridiron, or stewed in a saucepan (in oil), or fried
in a frying-pan (fritters or pancakes: *Knobel*).—The *oil* used in all
these preparations was olive oil. Nothing at all is said with reference to the colour of the *wine*.

§ 141. The meat-offering, as well as the drink-offering, appears
first of all in the light of *property*, especially of property acquired
by the labour and toil of the offerer, produced by his own diligence
and care (§ 21, 22). This idea of property, however, is certainly
not to be taken in the sense in which *Thalhofer* takes it, for the
purpose of serving the interests of Roman Catholicism, namely, as
relating to *punishment* (inflicted upon property) and *abstinence*.

" The notion of a *satisfactio vicaria*," he says, " was not applicable
to the bloodless sacrifices, since in their case the punishment was not
borne by another in the place of the man, but the man inflicted it
upon himself through abstinence : and this constitutes the leading
mark of distinction between the bleeding and the bloodless offerings;
—in the bloodless offerings the punishment of death was wanting,
and nothing remained but the punishment of property ; the man
feeling himself bound to an infirm nature, with which his spirit
could not hold unconditional intercourse, drew the latter away from
the former, and by abstinence subjected it to a punishment, which
was connected with guilt that lay at the foundation of this infirm
condition.   At the same time, in the bloodless offerings regard was
had, not so much to the *hereditary guilt*, as emphatically to *hereditary corruption;* for which reason the punishment was also distinguished in this case as the punishment of property alone, whereas
in that of the bleeding sacrifices it was the punishment of both
death and property."   But how very little the idea of abstinence
was associated with the sacrificial offering is evident from the peace-
offerings and the meat-offerings connected with them, which tended
rather to promote enjoyment, and summoned to rejoicing.   And the
very name of the Minchah shows how thoroughly it is opposed to the
idea of punishment; for who could regard a gift, a present, which
love and gratitude impelled him to present to an esteemed friend as
a punishment inflicted upon himself ? or who could associate such
an idea with the offering of a child, who brought the labour of his
own hands as an expression of his affection towards his parents ?

Moreover, the idea of property was only a subordinate one in
any case in connection with the sacrificial offering, and distinguished
the gift as one which stood in a close relation to the offerer, and so
fitted it to serve as an expression and representation of his own self-
surrender.   But the main point kept in view in determining the
constituent ingredients of the Minchah was that of *food*.   They
were the principal articles of daily consumption among the Israelites, with the exception of animal food ; and when offered upon the
altar of Jehovah, they were to serve as symbols of that food, which
Jehovah demanded of His people, and of which He stood in need
as the God of salvation (§ 23).   In contrast with the flesh of the
animal sacrifice, the offering of which represented more the self-
surrender of the *person* of the offerer to Jehovah, the vegetable
offerings, as we have shown at § 24, represented rather the fruit and
result of his life's work and the duties of his calling.

They were the signs of *spiritual* nourishment, of that spiritual food which the people had prepared, and which they were bound to present to their God as a covenant performance, a testimony to the keeping of the covenant, in which Jehovah rejoiced, which was to Him " a sweet savour," and which He partook of as His own nourishment, as the bread presented to Him by His people (Num. xxviii. 2, קָרְבָּנִי לַחְמִי). We find a confirmation of this in the words of Christ in John vi. 27, and chap. iv. 32, 33. In the first passage He says to the people, whom He had just been feeding in the desert, " Labour not for the meat which perisheth, but for that meat which endureth unto everlasting life, which the Son of man shall give unto you ;" and in the second He says, with reference to Himself, " I have meat to eat that ye know not of. My meat is to do the will of Him that sent Me, and to finish His work." The spiritual food of Christ, therefore, was to do the will of God, and accomplish the work entrusted to Him. And, according to chap. vi. 27, the *people* also were to procure this spiritual food, they *also* were to do the will of their God ; but as Christ had given them material food, it was *He* also who would give them spiritual food.

We may see from these passages, that according to the symbolical view and language of Hebrew antiquity, the faithful performance of the work assigned by God, with the faithful employment of the means and powers entrusted by Him, were regarded as a procuring and producing of *spiritual* food; and that towards the material food, the supply of which depended upon the help and blessing of God, it stood in the relation of type to antitype. The earthly calling of Israel was to cultivate the soil in the land assigned by Jehovah. The fruit of that calling, under the blessing of God, was corn and wine, their bodily food, that which nourished and sustained their corporeal life. The spiritual calling of Israel was to work in the field of the kingdom of God, in the vineyard of its Lord ; this work was the *covenant* duty of Israel. The result was spiritual bread, the spiritual nourishment which promoted and sustained their spiritual life, viz., the well-executed labours of their vocation crowned with divine blessing and success.

In addition to this there was another feature of importance, to which *Kliefoth* (p. 103), whose admirable exposition we insert *verbatim*, has directed particular attention. " Bread and wine," he says, " were not merely products of the soil, not merely articles of food growing up ready for man's eating through the goodness of God; they were *wrought out* by man himself, his production, acquired through his own labour in the sweat of his brow. *Yea more, they were also wrought by man;* they were not gifts of God remaining in their natural form, not raw productions, that is to say, but something which man had produced by his own diligence and skill out of the gifts of God and through the blessing of God. Thus the materials of the *Minchah* represented not merely everything that man receives through the goodness of God, but everything that he produces by his own labour out of the gifts of God, and through the assistance and blessing of God,—his labours and their results." And if the attempt is made to establish a difference in the symbolical significance of the bread and the wine, according to the light afforded by Ps. civ. 15, it must be sought in this, that the bread represented the strengthening, and the wine the refreshing side of the *Minchah;* in support of which, the proverb in Judg. ix. 13 may also be quoted, that wine " cheereth God and man."[1]

§ 142. The bloodless sacrificial gift came under the same point of view as the bleeding sacrifice, so far as the latter was a *gift;* and it was *entirely* a gift, when once the blood had answered its object as a means of expiation, and the flesh of the animal, together with the portion burnt, became the object of the sacrificial function. The one was quite as much a gift and food, and nothing more, as the other was. Just as a man who wished to spread his table abundantly would place not only bread and wine upon it, but animal food as well; so the Israelite also brought the same to his God as food and nourishment,—the *latter* representing the self-surrender of his personality, the *former* the self-surrender of the fruits of his labours and endeavours. But this parallel between the bleeding and the bloodless gifts has been sometimes misunderstood, and at other times denied ; misunderstood by *Bähr,* denied by *Kliefoth.*

Bähr is quite right in stating that the fundamental idea of the bloodless gift is related and parallel to that of the bleeding one; but he is altogether mistaken when he proceeds to say, " The very

---

[1] The view defended with such zeal by Roman Catholic theologians, that the bloodless sacrifice was a type of the Lord's Supper, we cannot possibly admit. The fact that the Old Testament *Minchah* was allotted exclusively to the priests after the burning of the altar-portion, and therefore was taken entirely away from the people, is a sufficient proof to the contrary. No doubt the sacrificial worship of the Old Testament does present a type of the Lord's Supper ; but this is to be sought for, not in the eating of the Minchah by the priests alone, but simply in the sacrificial meal (§ 82). The Apostle Paul finds it in this, and this alone (1 Cor. x. 16-21, cf. 1 Cor. v. 7).

appearance is a proof of this.   The bread (meal, corn) corresponded to the body of the animal, the oil to its fat, and the wine
to the blood, which was likewise poured upon the altar.   By virtue
of this relationship the bloodless offering might in exceptional cases,
as Lev. v. 11, be made a substitute for the bleeding sacrifice."
A more unfortunate appeal, however, is hardly conceivable than
that made to Lev. v. 11 here; for that very passage, if you only
read it to the end, proves the very opposite of what *Bähr* employs
it to prove.   For example, the verse closes with the words: " He
shall put no *oil* upon it, neither shall he put any frankincense
thereon, for it is a sin-offering."   Now it was indispensably essential
in the case of the bleeding sin-offering, that its *fat* should be placed
upon the altar.   How, then, could the oil of the bloodless offering
correspond to the fat of the bleeding one?   Still less, again, could
the wine correspond to the blood; for the man gave the wine upon
(or at) the altar as a gift and food for God, but the blood was
given by God upon the altar (Lev. xvii. 11) as a medium of expiation for the soul of man : the wine was regarded in the light of
food, but the eating of blood was most stringently prohibited.[1]

Kliefoth has fallen into the very opposite error (cf. § 25, note).
Whilst *Bähr* regards even the blood as a gift to Jehovah (§ 67),
Kliefoth will not for a moment admit that the flesh possessed the
signification of a gift; and whereas, according to *Bähr's* opinion,
the idea of self-surrender in the bleeding sacrifice absorbs the idea of
expiation, in *Kliefoth's* view the idea of expiation swallows up that
of gift.   The former can see nothing but self-surrender in the whole
of the animal sacrifice; the latter, nothing but a means of expiation.
Hence in the view of the former the bloodless sacrifice was really
parallel to the bleeding one, whilst in that of the latter it was in
direct contrast to it; in the one case everything answers the purpose of expiation, in the other all is gift and thanksgiving.

" The bleeding sacrifice," says *Kliefoth* (p. 87), " always served
as expiation (לְכַפֵּר?), the bloodless offering served just as invariably

---

[1] *Stöckl* (p. 293) also maintains, that as the bread corresponded to the flesh,
so the wine corresponded to the blood of the sacrificial animal; and he even goes
so far as to affirm that " the burning of the Azcarah was a symbol of the
latreutic side, and the pouring out of the wine of the propitiatory side, of the
ceremony."   " But," he adds at p. 295, " as the oil represented the Spirit of the
Lord, the might and power of God, so we shall hardly be mistaken in subscrib-
ing to the view, that the association of the oil with bread and wine involved a
reference to the subsequent transformation of these into the body and blood of
Christ."   (*Sic !*)

as thanksgiving (לְאַזְכָּרָה). It is evident, therefore, that in consequence of this distinction, all the processes that were common to
both the bleeding and bloodless offerings must have had a somewhat different signification in the latter from that which they had
in the former." But לכפר is invariably applied to the sprinkling of
the blood, and never to the burning of the sacrifice or the sacrificial
meal ; and if the ritual of the bleeding sacrifice in its second stage
had certain points in common with that of the bloodless offering
(§ 72), the inference must necessarily be drawn from this, that not
only the actions themselves, but the foundations upon which they
rested, and the conditions which they presupposed, must in both
cases have had the same signification. The burning of the sacrifice
in the case of the bleeding as well as the bloodless offering had its
signification simply in this, that it was to be " an offering made by
fire, of a sweet savour unto the Lord" (cf. Lev. i. 9, 13, 17, and
Lev. ii. 2, 9).

Again, it is perfectly inconceivable, how *Kliefoth* can have regarded it as a distinctive mark of the bloodless offering, in the first
place, that the giving to God was only a giving back, and therefore
every bloodless offering was לְאַזְכָּרָה, (*i.e.*, according to this mistaken
interpretation, *for thanksgiving*, cf. § 148) ; and in the second place,
that God never retained the gift of the bloodless offering, but
always returned it for the good of the offerer himself, and usually
in a symbolical manner for him to eat. As if the produce of the
flocks was not quite as much the gift and blessing of God as the
produce of the land, and the presentation was not quite as much a
grateful giving back to God in the one case as in the other. Moreover, did not God retain His own share of the food-offering, quite
as much as of the sin-offering, the trespass-offering, or the peace-
offering, and cause it to be burnt upon the altar as a savour of
satisfaction (cf. Lev. ii. 2, 9, 16) ?

§ 143. We have still further to speak of the things which were
commanded to be used as *accompaniments of the meat-offering*, and
also of those which were prohibited. And here the question must first
of all be discussed, whether the OIL was to be regarded as an accompaniment, or as a distinct portion of the meat-offering, like the bread
and the wine. *Hengstenberg* and *Keil* maintain the former; *Bähr*,
Neumann, *Kliefoth*, *Oehler*, and *Thalhofer*, the latter. The question
is not without its difficulties. The hypothesis that the oil (like the
incense) was to be regarded as a mere accompaniment to the meat-
offering, and (according to *Hengstenberg*), like the anointing oil, as a

symbol of the Spirit of God, through whose co-operation the spiritual
food was prepared, is favoured by the fact, that in the case of the
Minchah the oil is *never* found standing independently like the wine
by the side of the corn; but either the corn is mixed with it or
boiled in it, or the oil is rubbed over or poured upon the corn (Lev. ii.
1 sqq., vi. 21, vii. 10 sqq.; Num. xv. 4 sqq., etc.). These passages,
which are as lucid as they are numerous, must be taken as the rule
by which to interpret Lev. vi. 15, where the meal and the oil are
merely mentioned side by side, without its being expressly stated
that they were to be mixed together. And the command in Lev.
xiv. 10, that at the cleansing of the leper a log of oil should be
brought along with the *Minchah* of meal mixed with oil, cannot
possibly lead to any other conclusion; for this log of oil did not belong to the meat-offering, but was introduced for a totally different
purpose. It is true, *Neumann* repeatedly maintains, though without
any scriptural proof, that the oil is to be met with, not only as an
accompaniment to other sacrifices, but also as an independent portion of the sacrifice; but until he furnishes proofs, his assertion
can hardly be regarded as conclusive. Let any one read with an
unbiassed mind Lev. ii. 1, 15, where we find the meat-offering
mentioned for the first time in the law of sacrifice (" his offering
shall be of white meal (groats), and he shall pour oil upon it, and
put frankincense thereon"), and it will be impossible to have any
other impression, than that the oil was merely an accompaniment,
as well as the incense. The co-ordination of the oil and the incense
is still more obvious in Lev. v. 11, where oil and incense are forbidden to be added to the sin-offering of meal presented by the
poor man; and in Num. v. 15, where they are also prohibited in
the case of the offering of jealousy. The force of this co-ordination
is modified undoubtedly, but hardly destroyed, by *Oehler's* remark,
that the omission of oil, which renders food palatable, in the case
of both these sacrifices, may have been intended to answer precisely
the same end as the prohibition to mix a libation of wine with them,
and the command to select an inferior description of meal for the
jealousy-offering, namely, to give them a mournful character.

In support of the opposite view, that the oil is to be regarded
as co-ordinate with the corn and wine, and thus (in *Oehler's* opinion)
to be looked upon like them as a means of subsistence procured
through toil,—in which light it is frequently mentioned in the Old
Testament along with corn and wine as one of the leading productions of Palestine,—*Oehler* adduces the following arguments:

(1) " The oil, which is mentioned in the Scriptures as a symbol of the communication of the Spirit, is *only* the anointing oil, never the oil that was eaten." At the same time, he admits that, in the " case of need " referred to in Lev. ii., the use of the oil might be regarded as an anointing consecration of the meat-offering. (2) " It is perfectly obvious from Num. xv., especially from the quantities given there, that the oil of the meat-offering was co-ordinate with the wine of the drink-offering." But this conclusion is not quite so indisputable as *Oehler* supposes. The quantity of the meal, oil, and wine varied according to the quality of the sacrificial animal (§ 149) ; and though the quantity of oil and wine might be the same, it by no means follows that the position of the oil in connection with the meat-offering was precisely the same as that of the wine. It would only have been so if the oil could have been offered and used independently as well as the wine ; but this, as we have seen, was *never* the case.

After all, I must still adhere to the conclusion, that the oil in the case of the sin-offerings did not constitute an essential element, but was simply to be regarded as a significant accompaniment. In addition to the reasons already assigned, I am chiefly urged to this by the fact, that even if oil is frequently mentioned along with corn and wine, as representing the leading productions of Palestine, it is never met with as being of itself food and nourishment. Bread alone is mentioned on innumerable occasions as a representative of all kinds of food, and very frequently bread and wine, but never bread, wine *and* oil, or oil alone. And as it was in the usage of language, so is it also in daily life : bread is eaten by itself, and wine is drunk by itself ; but pure oil is never eaten or drunk as an article of food. It is always used either in the preparation of food or as an accompaniment of food, especially of food composed of meal, which is rendered more palatable in consequence. Now, if the idea of the *Minchah* was exhausted in that of the food which the Israelite offered to his God, and if oil was not food in itself, but only the means of rendering food palatable, the oil in the *Minchah*, in which it was used in the same way as in the preparation of food in ordinary life, could not be placed side by side with the bread and wine as the third essential ingredient.

§ 144. But the question still needs a somewhat careful examination : what was the *actual signification of the oil*, as the means of preparing, *i.e.*, of rendering palatable, the food offered to Jehovah ? Was it the same as it unquestionably possessed in the case of the

anointing oil, or was it a different one? *Neumann* (p. 340) arrives
at the conclusion, that it always signified "the gentle, invigorating
influence of an all-pervading, healing, peace-producing power," and
thinks that he is not wrong in recognising "in the mercy of God
the secret of the heavenly brightness of the oil." This explanation
is not the traditional one, it is true, but it is an orthodox one for all
that; for the Gospel of Nicodemus, the earliest testimony in, the
Christian Church, relates that, when Adam was drawing near to
death, he sent Seth to the tree of mercy for some oil to anoint him
with, that he might recover, etc. Now when sacrifice was offered
in connection with this oil, it represented the surrender of the soul,
which, sustained by the gentle power of this compassion, had found
in it the strength to draw near to the Lord, before whom nothing
unclean can stand.

Kliefoth (pp. 106, 120), on the other hand, finds a double signification in the oil. As the material employed in anointing, he regards it as the symbol of the Holy Spirit; as the material for
burning, he looks upon it as representing that part of human nature
which, when inflamed by the holy fire of God, gives out the light
of divine truth and knowledge; in distinction, that is to say, from
the active life of man set forth by the bread, it represented his life
of thought and knowledge. In the *Minchah*, however, it was not
the anointing material, but the burning material, the source of
light, that was employed; for it was placed in the fire, even the
altar-fire, the fire of God. This view also we must object to on
several grounds. The use of oil in daily life may be described as
threefold. In the *first* place, it was used for the *anointing of the
body*, by which the skin was to be rendered soft, smooth, blooming,
and shining, refreshed, strengthened, and invigorated. In this case
a virtue was ascribed to it which penetrated even to the bones
(Ps. cix. 18). Coincident with this in all essential points was the
use of oil in sickness, especially in the case of wounds, as a means
of lulling pain and restoring health (Isa. i. 6; Luke x. 34; Mark
vi. 13; Jas. v. 14). The *second* use of oil, viz., in the *preparation
of food*, is to be looked at from essentially the same point of view.
Here also the object was to anoint the food,[1] so as to make it
soft, palatable, and pleasant to the mouth. The *third* use also,
which was not less frequent or important, namely, as material for

---

[1] In Lev. ii. 5 and vii. 12, the cakes to be offered are expressly called
מְשֻׁחִים בַּשֶּׁמֶן, *oleo uncti.*

burning or giving light, may be looked at from the same point of view, as an anointing, for the purpose of enlivening, refreshing, invigorating. The thing to be anointed was the wick of the lamp. The wick would burn without oil, but only with a weak and miserable light, and very speedily its burning and illuminating power would burn itself out. It is very different when the wick is anointed with oil. Then it burns with a strong, bright flame, which is all the brighter and more lasting the more copious the anointing has been.

These three modes of using oil were all transferred to the symbolism of worship. The *first* was adopted in the anointing of the priests, the tabernacle, and the holy things (Ex. xxix. 22 sqq.; Lev. viii. 10 sqq.), in that of a leper who had been restored (Lev. xiv. 26 sqq.), in that of the king (1 Sam. x. 1; 1 Kings i. 33; 2 Kings ix. 1), and once also in that of a prophet (1 Kings xix. 16); the *second* is met with in the *Minchah* of the fore-court; and the *third,* in the *Minchah* of the Holy Place, viz., in the oil which was burnt in the seven-branched lamp.

We cannot possibly adopt *Kliefoth's* view, that the mixing or rubbing of the *Minchah* of the fore-court with oil was not to be regarded in the light of anointing oil, but in that of burning and illuminating oil. So thoroughly distorted is this view, that it does not for a moment appear to require a serious refutation. We adhere, on the contrary, to the conclusion, that the saturation of the *Minchah* of the fore-court with oil, whatever kind of *Minchah* it might be, expressed the thought, that the only spiritual food prepared by man that could be well-pleasing to God was that in which the Spirit of God had co-operated, and the only food that could be offered to Him was that which had been anointed with the oil of His Spirit. And though *Kliefoth* pronounces this view inadmissible, because in every case of anointing the oil was brought *to* the man from without and poured upon him, whereas the oil of the *Minchah* of the fore-court was brought *by* the man and proceeded from the man, this objection does not appear insuperable. For as the food was rendered palatable by the fact that the man who prepared it introduced, in addition to his own labour, the effects of the oil, which performed the most important part without any merit of his own, so the spiritual food prepared by him for Jehovah acquired its true fitness to give pleasure to Jehovah from the help and co-operation of the power of the Spirit of God, which came to his aid from the institutions of salvation. If the *salt,* which was also provided and added by the man, could be designated "the salt of the covenant of thy God" (Lev. ii. 13), the oil also may very properly be regarded as that of the Spirit of God.

Just as decidedly must I oppose *Kliefoth's* assertion, that there was no allusion to the Spirit of God in the oil of the lamp in the Holy Place. We will defer our reasons till a more suitable occasion (*vid.* § 160).

There is no foundation whatever for *Neumann's* objection, that even in the case of the anointing oil there was no allusion in the oil itself to the Spirit of God, since the essential element was not the oil, but the balsamic scents with which the oil was impregnated, and the substance of the glorified life (which was indicated by the mingled odours) was merely condensed by means of the oil, and so imparted to the anointed one. No doubt *Neumann* had Ex. xxx. 22 sqq. in his mind, where a description is given of the preparation of the holy oil from common oil and four fragrant spices for the purpose of anointing the tabernacle and its furniture, as well as Aaron and his sons (ver. 30, Lev. viii. 10 sqq.), but where it is also strictly forbidden to prepare or use such oil for the purpose of anointing anything else. Now, are we to suppose, notwithstanding this, that the oil with which the leper was anointed, or even that which was used in the anointing of Saul, David, Solomon, or Jehu, was this same holy oil? If not, and if it was simple, ordinary oil, without any admixture of such balsamic odours, either these anointings must have been all unmeaning and invalid, or *Neumann's* objection must be regarded as unfounded and vain.

§ 145. The description given in Lev. ii. of the different modes of preparing the *Minchah* is closed in ver. 11 by the general command, that every meat-offering was to be unleavened, and therefore neither *leaven* nor *honey* was to be used.

Leavened bread is more agreeable to the ordinary palate than unleavened, and more nutritious for ordinary digestions, provided the process of fermentation be stopped at the proper moment, and fixed by the force of heat in the baking. To understand the PROHIBITION OF LEAVEN, therefore, in the meal or bread, as used symbolically, we must go back and inquire what the leaven really was. Its component ingredients were the same as those of sweet dough, and it was once sweet dough itself; but through fermentation it was changed and corrupted, and thus became sour dough or leaven. Hence, as distinguished from sweet dough, it represented the old, corrupt, degenerate nature. And upon this was founded the first, prototypical prohibition of leaven at the exodus from Egypt in Ex. xii. (cf. § 175). Upon this Paul links his admonition to Christians in 1 Cor. v. 6 sqq., to purge out the *old* leaven, that they may become a *new* dough; and when the same Apostle writes in Gal. v. 9, "a little leaven leaveneth the whole dough," he intends thereby to warn the Galatians of the danger of falling back to the *old* legal standpoint of Judaism. Christ also refers to leaven as a representative of the old, degenerate nature when He says in Matt. xvi. 6 and Mark viii. 15, "Beware of the leaven of the Pharisees and Sadducees." And it is in this same light that we have to regard the leaven in the case of the *Minchah*. When the Israelite prepared spiritual food and presented it to his God, it was to be rendered palatable to Jehovah, not with the leaven of his own old nature, but with the oil of the Spirit of God. Making the meal palatable with oil and with leaven, were two opposite processes which precluded each other. In the former case the end was attained by a mild, quiet penetration into the food; in the latter, by a restless, fermenting disturbance and swelling up of the same. The leaven, which was dough itself, bore the same relation to the sweet dough pervaded with oil as the restless nature and driving of the natural man to the calm, mild bearing of a man sanctified and filled with peace by the Spirit of God.

The prohibition of HONEY stands side by side with that of leaven. The question, whether the honey of grapes or of bees is meant, there can certainly be no difficulty in answering. The prohibition applied to one quite as much as to the other. *Hengstenberg* (Diss. on Pentateuch, vol. 2, p. 533 transl.) supposes the allusion to be to the *delicias carnis*, to the pleasures of the world in themselves, to which no one was to give himself up who wished to prepare spiritual food acceptable to the Lord. In support of this he appeals to Hos. iii. 1 (*vid. Opfer*, p. 45). But as in the case of the leaven it was not the palatable taste imparted to the bread that was taken into consideration, so in that of the honey it would not be its sweetness, but the fact that, like leaven, it also tended to produce fermentation. In proof of this we may not only refer to the meaning which the verb הִרְבִּישׁ has in rabbinical phraseology (= *fermentescere*), and to the testimony of *Pliny* (H. n. 18, 11) as to this quality of honey, but above all to the Thorah itself, which embraces the prohibition of sour dough and honey under the common expression "made with leaven" (לֹא־תֵעָשֶׂה חָמֵץ, Lev. ii. 11).

These prohibitions of leaven and honey are then followed in ver. 13 by the *command*, that every meat-offering is to be *salted* with salt, and that no Minchah is to be without "*the* SALT *of the covenant of thy God*."[1] As the oil used in the preparation of the spiritual food for Jehovah brought in the Spirit of God as co-operating, so the salt, through its pungent and purifying power, warded off all putrefaction from the food, and ensured its lasting. In the corrosive and antiseptic property of salt there is hidden something of the purifying and consuming nature of fire; hence the Redeemer, in Mark ix. 49, combines the salting of the sacrifice with the purifying fire of self-denial. The power of salt to ensure continuance and render indestructible, is also shown in the epithet applied to an inviolable and permanent ordinance of God, "a covenant of salt" (Num. xviii. 19; 2 Chron. xiii. 5). And when the salt added to the *Minchah* is called the salt of the covenant of thy God, it is thereby stamped as a divine power proceeding from the covenant of God with Israel, and co-operating in the preparation of the food, so as to render it a βρῶσις οὐκ ἀπολλυμένη, ἀλλὰ μένουσα εἰς ζωὴν αἰώνιον (John vi. 27).

§ 146. There is a difference between the INCENSE, and the other accompaniments connected with the *Minchah*, viz., the oil and salt. The offering was so saturated and penetrated by the latter, that they were no longer outside or by the side of it, but only existed in it and with it;—the incense, on the contrary, though burned upon the altar at the same time as the *Minchah*, remains apart, accompanying but not pervading it. Connected with this is the fact, that only a small portion of the *Minchah* was placed upon the altar, and the rest was allotted to the priests; the incense, on the other hand, was to be entirely consumed (Lev. ii. 2, 16, vi. 15). Of the food intended for Jehovah, a portion was allotted to the priests for their board; but not even the priests could be fumigated with the incense burned for Jehovah (§ 149).

Whilst the fumigation of the fore-court was restricted to the substance of the incense, according to Ex. xxx. 34 sqq., three other fragrant substances were added for the fumigation of the Holy Place. There is the same distinction here, as between the anointing oil for the anointing of the sanctuary and the priests (Ex. xxx. 23), and

---

[1] That the salting mentioned in Lev. ii. 13 not only *could be* restricted to the *Minchah*, as *Oehler* maintains, but *was to be* so restricted, is evident from the words themselves, notwithstanding Ezek. xliii. 24 and Mark ix. 46; for the reading is not קָרְבָּנֶךָ as *Keil* and *Oehler* give it, but קָרְבַּן מִנְחָתְךָ בַּמֶּלַח תִּמְלָח.

the anointing oil for the anointing of the leper when cured (Lev.
xiv. 12, 15 sqq.). But the fundamental signification is undoubtedly
the same in both.

There is no other symbol of worship, the meaning of which is
so clear and unmistakeable, or so indisputably established by express
and authentic statements in the Scriptures themselves, as that of the
incense is. It was the symbol of *prayer*. In Ps. cxli. 2 prayer is
distinctly compared to incense, קְטֹרֶת. Isa. vi. 3, 4, is almost equivalent to an express interpretation. The seraphim praised God with
their thrice holy, so that the foundations of the thresholds of the
temple moved at the voice of their cry, and the house *was filled with
smoke*. The same may be said of Luke i. 10, where the people are
said to have prayed in the fore-court, whilst the priest was in the
Holy Place burning the incense. In Rev. v. 8 the four ζῶα and
the four-and-twenty elders are introduced with golden vials (bowls)
full of incense, " which are the prayers of saints." So, again, in
chap. viii. 3, 4, the incense is described as destined for the prayers
of the saints before the throne of God. According to Num. xvi.
46, 47, Aaron burned incense by Moses' directions, making atonement thereby for the people that were infected with the plague, and
so causing the plague to cease. But what else could the burning of
incense in this case represent, than the intercession of the high
priest? So also the burning of incense by Aaron in the Holy of
Holies on the great day of atonement, " that he might not die"
(Lev. xvi. 12, 13), could have this effect only as being the symbol
of prayer.

If we look now for the *tertium comparationis* between prayer
and incense, two things present themselves : the fragrance, and the
ascent of the incense in the smoke (cf. Rev. viii. 4). Both these
are to be connected together : the burning of the incense caused
the fragrance to ascend to Jehovah ; and here, as everywhere else
in the ritual of worship (§ 74), the holy fire by which the incense
was resolved into ethereal vapour had the force of purification.

Bähr's interpretation of the fragrance diffused by the burning
of the incense, as a symbol of the divine name (Symb. i. 462 sqq.,
ii. 327) or of the divine breath (der salom. Tempel, p. 181), needs
no further refutation. I think I have already answered it in a
most conclusive manner in my *Beiträge zur Symbolik des mos.
Cultus*, p. 41 sqq. And *Neumann's* contracted interpretation of the
holy incense as an " image of the soul glorified in God, and therefore of the priestly nature," in which prominence is given to the

"rough, sharp, bitter fragrance" as the essential and distinctive characteristic of the incense, whilst in further explanation a passage is quoted from the " Guide Book for the Easter Candle," published by the present Pope as a contribution to religious instruction in the States of the Church,[1] may be laid aside without hesitation for the explanation which is given of the incense in the Scriptures themselves, and which is just as simple and natural, as it is comprehensible and clear.

CHAPTER II

THE MINCHAH OF THE FORE-COURT

§ 147. Bloodless offerings were presented not only upon the altar of the fore-court, but also upon the altar, table, and candelabrum of the Holy Place. Hence we have to distinguish between a *Minchah* of the *fore-court*, and a *Minchah* of the *Holy Place*.

The law for the *Minchah of the fore-court* is laid down in Lev. ii. As we find in chap. i. the different kinds of burnt-offerings (oxen, ver. 3 ; sheep or goats, ver. 10; pigeons, ver. 14), in chap. iii. the different kinds of peace-offerings (oxen, ver. 1 ; sheep, ver. 6 ; goats, ver. 12), and in chap. iv. the various kinds of sin-offerings (a bullock, vers. 3, 14; a he-goat, ver. 23 ; a she-goat, ver. 28; a sheep, ver. 32), arranged according to the quality of the animal to be offered; so do we find in chap. ii. the different kinds of meat-offerings divided into offerings of meal, bread or cake, and groats (§ 140). Now if we compare together what is said of these three descriptions of Minchah, we are struck with the fact, that whereas the accompaniment of oil and salt, and the absence of honey and leaven, are expressly mentioned as common to them all, the accompaniment of incense occurs only in connection with the offerings of meal and groats, and is not mentioned at all in connection with the different offerings of cake or bread. If this omission was intentional and planned, so as to be equivalent to a

---

[1] The passage runs thus : *La Croce fatta sopra il cero con cinque grani d'incenzo significa, che i Cristiani in virtù delle cinque piaghe di Cristo devono portar volontieri la Croce, per dove il buon odore di una santa pazienza e rassegnazione.* *Neumann* seems to attach great importance to this book, as he frequently quotes it in proof of his explanations.

command to offer this kind of meat-offering without incense, the reason must have been, that in the case of the meal and groats the want of that fuller preparation, through which the cake-offerings had passed, was to be supplied by the introduction of the incense. And if it were so, from the explanations given in § 141, 146, there can be no great difficulty in discovering a suitable symbolical meaning. At the same time it may be more advisable, not to attribute any exclusive significance to this silence with regard to incense in the case of the offerings of bread or cake; since the loaves of shewbread offered in the Holy Place were by no means without their accompaniment of incense (Lev. xxiv. 7), although in name, in ingredients, and in mode of preparation they were essentially one with the חַלּוֹת mentioned in Lev. ii. 4.

§ 148. Again, the command to place a portion of the gift upon the altar, and then to cause it to ascend in smoke as an אִשֵּׁה יְהוָה through the altar-fire, is common to all three kinds. In the case of the meal-offering, a handful of the dough saturated with oil was ordered to be taken (ver. 2, cf. vi. 15, and ix. 17). Of the offerings of cake and groats the quantity was not fixed. But the analogy of Ex. xxix. 23 sqq. warrants us in assuming that a specimen of every kind of cake was placed upon the altar. The portion set apart for the altar bore the name of אַזְכָּרָה, which is rendered in the Septuagint μνημόσυνον, in the Vulgate *memoriale*, by *Luther* Gedächtniss; whilst *Bunsen* prefers the rendering *fire-portion*. The derivation ordinarily accepted, viz., from the *Hiphil* הִזְכִּיר, is rejected·by *Knobel*, on the ground that the Aramæan form אַזְכָּרָה for הַזְכָּרָה cannot be expected in the early Hebrew. Hence he invents for the *Kal* זָכַר the meaning *to think of* = to present with anything, and so gets the rendering *donation, gift, contribution*. But this meaning is quite foreign to זכר. And even though the Aramæan form be somewhat surprising, the derivation of such a form from the *Kal* is decidedly much more incomprehensible. Moreover, the derivation from the *Hiphil* is supported by the epithet applied to the meat-offering of jealousy in Num. v. 15, מַזְכֶּרֶת עָוֹן. If we adhere, therefore, to the derivation from הִזְכִּיר, the question arises, whether we should accept the primary signification, "to bring to remembrance," or the secondary meaning, to extol, or praise. The latter is adopted by *Bähr* (i. 411, ii. 428), who appeals to the common phrase הִזְכִּיר שֵׁם יְהוָה, and the rendering which he gives is *Lobpreis*, "praise." *Hofmann* follows in the same track, and explains it as meaning "the active praise of God." But *Oehler* justly objects, that the name *Azcarah* is also given to the altar-portion of the sin-offering in Lev. v. 12, and of the meat-offering of jealousy in Num. v. 26, where the idea of praise cannot possibly be thought of. *Kliefoth's* rendering, *thanksgiving* (*Danksagung*), has still less claim to adoption, for הִזְכִּיר never means to thank; and *Ewald's* translation, *Duft*, odour, is perfectly baseless. As we find in Lev. xxiv. 7 that incense was laid even upon the shew-bread, which was not burnt, but eaten by the priests after it had lain for a week upon the table of shew-bread, "that it might be an *Azcarah*, an offering made by fire unto the Lord," whilst in Isa. lxvi. 3 the presentation of incense is called הַזְכִּיר לְבֹנָה, the conjecture is a very natural one, that the name was originally given to the accompaniment of incense, and then was transferred to the offering of meal, which it accompanied. In that case the name (in the sense of praise) would be a very appropriate one, and the otherwise inexplicable fact would become intelligible, that the term was applied to the altar-portion of the meat-offering alone, and never to that of the animal sacrifice. But Lev. v. 12 and Num. v. 26 place difficulties in the way of this explanation, which it is very hard to overcome; since the altar-portion of the meal sin-offering and the meat-offering of jealousy, where the addition of incense is expressly prohibited as entirely at variance with the character and meaning of those offerings, is also called *Azcarah*. We must go back, therefore, to the rendering adopted by the earlier translators, to remind, to bring to remembrance; and understand the name *Azcarah*, as denoting that the offerer desired thereby to bring himself into gracious remembrance before God. The corresponding description of the offering of jealousy as מִנְחַת זִכָּרוֹן מַזְכֶּרֶת עָוֹן ("an offering of memorial, bringing iniquity to remembrance," Num. v. 15), may be regarded as a confirmation of this view. In both instances the offering of the *Azcarah* brings to remembrance the works of the person for whom they are burned upon the altar; with this difference, however, that in the latter the absence of the oil and incense calls to mind the doubtful and suspicious nature of the works in question.

§ 149. Whilst only a comparatively small portion of the meat-offering was thus burnt upon the altar, the accompaniment of incense was all consumed (Lev. ii. 12, 16, vi. 15). There cannot be any surprise felt at this regulation. For Jehovah might very well supply His servants the priests from the food which Israel offered to Him as the representative of its grateful self-surrender (§ 118); but incense, like the prayer which it represented, belonged to Himself alone.

After deducting the *Azcarah*, the *remainder of the meat-offering* in all its forms, as being most holy, was assigned to Aaron and his sons (Lev. ii. 3, 10), who were to eat it in a holy place, *i.e.*, in the fore-court (Lev. vi. 16, x. 12, 13). According to the more minute directions in Lev. vii. 9, 10, there was this distinction between them, that the remainder of the *Minchah* of cake was to be eaten by the officiating priest alone, whilst the *Minchah* of meal and groats[1] was to be eaten by *all* the sons of Aaron, the female members of their families being excluded (Lev. vii. 10). Hence it follows as a matter of course, and in Lev. vi. 17 it is even expressly stated, that the remainder of the *Minchah* of meal and groats had first of all to be baked, though without leaven. But if the *Minchah* was offered by a priest on his own account, it was all to be burnt upon the altar (Lev. vi. 23).

Both these directions present various analogies to those relating to the remainder of the animal sacrifice of the sin- and peace-offerings, *so far as* the latter became the portion of the priests. For example, they call to mind Lev. vii. 31, 33, where it is stated that in the case of the *Shelamim* the wave-breast was allotted to all the priests who were present at the sanctuary, whilst the heave-leg was the portion of the officiating priest alone ; but they differ from the rule relating to the peace-offerings (Lev. x. 14), and approximate to that of the sin-offerings (Lev. vi. 26, 29), in the fact that the remainder of the meat-offering, as being most holy, was to be eaten in a holy place, and only by the men. The same circumstance (cf. § 118) which gave to the priest's share of the peace-offering the lower character of holy, and to the priest's share of the flesh of the sin-offering the higher character of most holy, imparted the character of most holy to the meat-offering also. Just, for example, as that portion of the flesh of the sin-offering which was not placed upon the altar was assigned entirely and exclusively to the priests, so was it with the whole of the remainder of the meat-offering, strictly so called ; whereas the remainder of the flesh of the *Shelamim* was divided between the priests and the person presenting it. The rule that none of the meat-offering of a priest was to be eaten (Lev. vi. 16), tallied with the similar rule respecting the sin-offering of a priest, and rested upon the same ground (cf. § 117).

§ 150. The DRINK-OFFERING is nowhere mentioned in the true

---

[1] Of the two kinds of *Minchah* of meal mentioned in Lev. vii. 10, one mixed with oil and one *dry*, the latter must be understood as referring to the two cases in Lev. v. 11 and Num. v. 15, in which the addition of oil was prohibited.

law of sacrifice (Lev. i.–vii.) ; and throughout the whole of Leviticus it is only referred to in chap. xxiii. 13, 18, 37, in connection with such meat-offerings as were to be presented as an accompaniment to the burnt-offerings at the feasts. And there it is to be observed that the law commences in ver. 10 with the words, " *When ye be come into the land* which I give unto you," etc. In Exodus likewise the drink-offering is only mentioned in chap. xxix. 40, 41, as an accompaniment to the daily burnt-offering which was to be continued " *throughout your generations*," and in chap. xxx. 9, where burnt sacrifice, meat-offerings, and drink-offerings are forbidden to be offered upon the altar of incense in the Holy Place. In Numbers, bowls and cans for the drink-offering are mentioned among the vessels of the sanctuary in chap. iv. 7, and drink-offerings as well as meat-offerings are included in the sacrificial gifts to be offered by the Nazarite (chap. vi. 15). On the other hand, meat-offerings AND *drink-offerings* are described for the first time thoroughly and *ex professo* in Num. xv. 1–12 ; and here the law is also introduced with the words, " *When ye be come into the land of your habitations*, which I give unto you, and ye will make an offering by fire unto Jehovah, a burnt-offering or a slain-offering," etc. Then follow minute directions as to the quantity of meat-offering and drink-offering to be added to these bleeding sacrifices.

From the facts thus noticed the conclusion may apparently be drawn, that the lawgiver, for very obvious reasons, did not order a drink-offering to be connected with the meat-offerings presented in the desert, but deferred the obligation till after the settlement of the Israelites in the Holy Land.

But neither in Num. xv., nor even in Num. xxviii. and xxix., where a minute account is given of the daily, the sabbatical, and the yearly sacrifices, and of the meat- and drink-offerings to be appended to them, according to the rule laid down in the fundamental law in Num. xv.,[1] nor, in fact, in any of the canonical books of the Old Testament, are we expressly informed what was done with the wine set apart for the drink-offering. That it was offered

---

[1] For the bleeding sacrifice of a lamb or kid a *meat-offering* was required of the tenth of an ephah of white meal, which was to be mixed with a quarter of a hin of oil, and a *drink-offering* of a quarter of a hin of wine. When a ram was offered, the quantity was increased to two-tenths of an ephah of meal, a third of a hin of oil, and a third of a hin of wine ; and for a bullock to three-tenths of an ephah of meal, half a hin of oil, and half a hin of wine. The hin was nearly twice as much ($1\frac{2}{3}$) as the ephah, and according to the most probable calculation, held about 187 Rhenish cubic inches (*vid. Keil* ii. 142).

along with the meat-offering, and the presentation was effected by pouring it out, is evident from the independence and signification of the name נֶסֶךְ; and that it was *all* poured out, without the priests receiving any portion, may be inferred with tolerable certainty from Lev. x. 9 as compared with Lev. vi. 16, 23, x. 12, 13. For in the former passage the priests are forbidden to drink either wine or strong drink when they enter the tabernacle on pain of sudden death (such as befel Aaron's eldest sons, Nadab and Abihu). And as one characteristic of the *Minchah*, according to Lev. vi. 16, 23, was that the offerer did not partake of it himself, the same command must certainly be regarded as holding good in the case of the drink-offering also.

But nowhere in the Old Testament does there seem to be any hint, from which we can gather *where* the wine was to be poured. The first allusion to this occurs in the Book of Wisdom (l. 15). In the account of the official duties of Simon the high priest, it is stated with regard to the drink-offering, which the son of Sirach calls αἷμα σταφυλῆς (the blood of the vine), that ἐξέχεεν εἰς θεμέλια θυσιαστηρίου. But this statement is the less admissible, from the fact that it contradicts the rabbinical tradition (*Thalhofer*, p. 117), that the altar of burnt-offering in the second temple was hollowed out at the south-west corner, and that two pipes led from the altar to the brook Kedron, and that the wine and the blood left over from the sprinkling were poured into one of these, and the libation of water at the feast of Tabernacles into the other. Moreover, it appears to rest upon the utterly erroneous assumption (§ 142), that the wine of the *Minchah* corresponded to the blood of the animal sacrifice. Another statement occurs in *Josephus*, who says that the drink-offering was poured περὶ τὸν βῶμον (when the tabernacle was in existence, Ant. iii. 9, 4). It is quite an arbitrary assumption that this is identical with the εἰς θεμέλια θυσιαστηρίου of the Book of Wisdom. But *Josephus* probably selected his expression from, and understood it according to the analogy of, the sprinking of the blood in the case of the trespass-, burnt-, and peace-offerings, עַל־מִזְבֵּחַ סָבִיב. At the same time it may be questioned, whether he was led to identify the place at which the libation of wine took place with that where the blood was sprinkled by any ancient tradition, or merely by his own subjective notions. And even if we could safely assume the former, the question would still remain, what is the correct interpretation of the expression עַל־מִזְבֵּחַ סָבִיב (§ 122)?

The usual opinion of modern antiquarians, who think they can rely upon the Book of Wisdom and Josephus, is that the wine was poured out at the foot of the altar of burnt-offering, like the blood of the sin-offering which was left over after the sprinkling had been effected (§ 107). But I cannot help regarding this view as the least tenable of all. For the wine had nothing in common with the blood of expiation. It was nourishment, drink for Jehovah; and as it "maketh glad the heart of man" (Ps. civ. 15), so also it was to "cheer the heart of God" (Judg. ix. 13); consequently, like the flesh and bread, its proper place was the *top* of the altar, and not the foot. Wine intended for a king is not usually poured under the table, but placed upon the table. It is true, that after the necessary quantity of the *blood of the sin-offering* had been put upon the horns of the altar, the *remainder* was poured εἰς θεμέλια θυσιαστηρίου, but this was assuredly only for the purpose of disposing of *what was left over* of the most holy blood, in a suitable, *i.e.*, a holy place (§ 107). If this could serve as an analogy, therefore, for the libation of wine (though I can find no warrant for such a conclusion), the plan adopted would necessarily be this, that only an *Azcarah* of the wine would be poured *upon* the altar, and the remainder at the foot,—a possible thing certainly, but not a probable one. I must still most decidedly declare my adhesion to the view which *Thalhofer* pronounces long since antiquated, viz., that the wine was poured upon the flesh of the sacrifice as it lay upon the altar, in which case, of course, only a small portion would evaporate in the fire, whilst the greater part would soak into the earth which filled the altar-chest. We cannot, indeed, appeal to Num. xv. 5 (" wine for a drink-offering shalt thou prepare עַל־הָעֹלָה ") in support of our opinion, for עַל in this connection in all probability merely denotes the concomitance of the offering; but we may appeal to Ex. xxx. 9, which has hitherto been left unnoticed. The Israelite is there forbidden to offer either burnt-offerings or meat-offerings upon the altar of incense in the Holy Place; and then it is added וְנֵסֶךְ לֹא־תִסְּכוּ עָלָיו (" neither shall ye pour drink-offerings thereon "),—an indisputable proof, in my opinion, that the drink-offering was poured *upon* (עָלָיו), and not at the foot of the altar of the fore-court. In addition to this, we may also adduce the similar custom connected with heathen sacrifices, which even *Thalhofer* admits, and of which he quotes examples. At any rate, this view not only appears the most natural and obvious one, but the only one that has any significance. If all the altar-gifts were placed *upon* the altar, the drink-offering would certainly be no exception; and if the design of all was to serve, at least in part, as a "sweet savour" to Jehovah, this would not only be the best, but the only way of attaining that object in connection with the wine.

§ 151. In accordance with *Bähr's* example (ii. 191, 199), I have already maintained that the meat-offerings, apart from the peculiarly modified and qualified instance mentioned in Num. v. 15, were never offered by themselves, but always as an accompaniment, *i.e.*, in connection with some burnt-offering or peace-offering that had been presented before. *Hengstenberg* also observes (p. 42), that "the meat-offerings were connected with the bleeding sacrifices so as to form one whole, and never occurred independently;" and *Kliefoth* (p. 116), that " every *Minchah* offered in the fore-court was attached to a bleeding sacrifice;" so that both of them advocate the same view. *Thalhofer* has lately opposed this view with peculiar zeal, and evidently under the influence of the doctrinal desire to find an Old Testament type for the Romish theory of the unbloody sacrifice of the Lord's Supper. *Stöckl* naturally joins him, and even *Keil* describes it as one of the two leading errors of my former work.[1]

But various misunderstandings have crept into this discussion. In the first place, our assertion naturally related to the *Minchah* of the fore-court alone; and there was certainly no intention to deny the independence of the *Minchah* of the Holy Place. There was just as little intention to maintain, that the meat-offering was an accompaniment to the bleeding sacrifice in the same sense in which the incense, the salt, or the oil was an accompaniment to the meat-offering. Nor did I mean to dispute the fact, that the meat-offering was co-ordinate with the offering of flesh, which *Oehler* justly maintains, but simply to affirm its subordination to the sprinkling of the blood, and, since the latter was necessarily peculiar to the bleeding sacrifice, to that extent to maintain its subordination to the bleeding sacrifice itself. And though *Keil* argues (in the *Luth. Zeitsch.*), that we can no more draw the conclusion that the meat-offerings were mere accompaniments to the slain-offerings, from the fact that, according to Num. xv., no burnt-offerings or thank-offerings were to be presented without meat and drink-offerings, than we can take the many passages in the law which direct that a burnt-offering shall be added to the sin-offering

---

[1] The other is this, that I regard all the bleeding sacrifices as expiatory,—a view which I am still unable to give up: *vid.* § 30 and § 178, note.

as necessarily leading to the conclusion that the burnt-offerings were accompaniments to the sin-offerings ; yet it is very evident, that when and so far as a burnt-offering *necessarily* followed the sin-offering, it might unquestionably be called an accompaniment, in the sense already mentioned. *Keil's* argument in favour of the presentation of a meat-offering independently of any burnt-offering or peace-offering, on the ground that all the sacrifices are called by the collective terms זֶבַח וּמִנְחָה, is equally inconclusive ; for if this kind of proof were admissible, the expression מִנְחָה וָנֶסֶךְ would also prove that a drink-offering might have been presented without accompanying a meat-offering, a separation never recognised by the law. And when *Keil* appeals to the fact, that in the law of sacrifice, strictly so called (Lev. i.-vii.), the meat-offerings are treated as perfectly co-ordinate to the burnt-offerings, the thank-offerings, and the sin- and trespass-offerings, he seems to have over-looked Lev. vii. 11 sqq.; for there, even according to *Keil's* own view of the passage (p. 255), the meat-offering is really *subordinate* to the peace-offering. And is it not possible that two things should be co-ordinate, and yet be so closely connected that the one should never appear without the other ?

The assertion that, according to the Mosaic law, the meat-offering was always connected with a bleeding sacrifice, will be proved to be untenable, when instances are adduced in which a meat-offering is presented without a previous burnt- or peace-offering. In *Keil's* opinion, we find such instances " in the meat-offering which the priests had to present during the seven days of their consecration (Lev. vi. 20 sqq.) ; in the sin-offerings of the poor (Lev. v. 11 sqq.) ; and in the jealousy-offering (Num. v. 15, 25, 26)." But Lev. v. 11 is not a case in point ; for the offering mentioned there is not a meat-offering, but a sin-offering (although to a certain extent in the form of a meat-offering, *i.e.*, as meal, but without oil and incense ; § 60). There is apparently greater force in the appeal to the jealousy-offering in Num. v., since this really was regarded as a meat-offering (§ 235); but the thoroughly unique character of this sacrifice places it rather in the position of an exception, which does not affect the validity of the rule. Lastly, so far as the meat-offering of the priests is concerned, the force of the passage cited is a doubtful one, even apart from its questionable interpretation, because this meat-offering was undoubtedly preceded by a bleeding (burnt) sacrifice. We shall discuss this more thoroughly at § 156 and 167. No other examples have been cited of meat-offerings, either actually occurring, or supposed to occur, without the basis of a bleeding sacrifice. Hence, so far as *this* argument is concerned, the assertion might still hold good, that (apart from Num. v.) the meat-offering always followed a bleeding sacrifice, and was sustained by its expiatory worth.

§ 152. With regard to the law of the meat-offering in Lev. ii., *Keil* thinks it doubtful whether " the freewill meat-offerings appointed there could be offered independently or not, since we have no certain clue to the decision of this question." *Thalhofer*, on the contrary, lays the greatest stress upon this passage, and by comparing it with Num. xv., xxviii., xxix., arrives at the following result : that the Mosaic law recognised two kinds of meat-offerings, which differed in form and signification : (1) the so-called *Bei-opfer*, subordinate offerings, which could only be presented as an accompaniment to a burnt- or peace-offering (Num. xv., xxviii., xxix.) ; and (2) *independent meat-offerings*, which were *not* attended by a bleeding sacrifice (Lev. ii. 6, 7). This view of the question involves two assertions : *a.* that the meat-offering could be offered without resting upon the foundation of a bleeding sacrifice ; and *b.* that the meat-offerings presented by themselves and those accompanying a bleeding sacrifice were two different things. A further investigation of the question has convinced me, that the first point must be granted, but the second cannot be sustained.

Any one who reads with an unbiassed mind the introductory formula of Lev. ii., נֶפֶשׁ כִּי־תַקְרִיב, which runs parallel both in form and substance to the אָדָם כִּי־יַקְרִיב in Lev. i. 2, must certainly receive the impression that the passage treats of the presentation of a meat-offering as co-ordinate with that of a burnt-offering. But as we cannot infer from the introductory formula to chap. i. that the burnt-offering could *never* be offered in close connection with a previous sin-offering; so we cannot infer, as *Thalhofer* does, from the introductory formula to chap. ii., that the meat-offerings described there were always to be presented without a bleeding sacrifice preceding them. But if it appears from the later laws that the burnt-offering could be presented independently, *i.e.*, without resting upon the basis of any other sacrifice, the presumption is certainly a very natural one, that the same rule might apply to the meat-offerings described in chap. ii. This presumption is not proved to be erroneous by the fact, that the rule was afterwards laid down (Num. xv., xxviii., xxix.), that burnt-offerings and peace-offerings were never to be presented without a meat-offering following them ;—that would only be the case, provided it could be shown from subsequent laws that a meat-offering was never to be presented without a previous bleeding sacrifice. But it is impossible to prove this. On the other hand, the opinion derived from a comparison of Lev. ii. 1 with Lev. i. 2, that the meat-offering could be offered by itself as well as the burnt-offering, without the way being prepared by any other sacrifice, is a mere assumption, and not a necessary conclusion—conjecture, not certainty. To give this uncertain assumption the force of a certain result, we require different proofs from any that the introductory formula to Lev. ii. can possibly supply.

§ 153. *Thalhofer* images that he has obtained many such proofs from a comparison of Lev. ii. 6, 7, with Num. xv., xxviii., xxix. Irreconcilable contradictions, for example, between the meat-offerings described in the latter and those described in the former of these two passages, are supposed by him to lead irresistibly to the conclusion, that there were two different kinds of *Minchah*, one of which is referred to in Leviticus, and the other in Numbers.

If this were really the case, however, we should certainly expect to find, that separate names had grown up for these two different classes of meat-offerings, just as they did for the three classes of peace-offerings (§ 126). But there is not the slightest trace of anything of the kind. They always bear the same name מִנְחָה, and no distinguishing predicate is ever added. Hence we are not only *entitled* but *compelled* to assume that the very same class of meat-offerings is intended in Leviticus as in Numbers; a conclusion quite as little prejudiced by the distinction between the Minchahs of meal, of cake, and of groats in Lev. ii., as by the distinction between the burnt-offerings of bullocks, sheep, and pigeons in Lev. i.

But let us examine the supposed discrepancies. The *first* is, that the *Minchah* in Lev. ii. was furnished with an accompaniment of incense, to which no reference is made in Num. xv., xxviii., xxix. But we also find no allusion there to the salt to be added and the leaven to be avoided, the necessity for which even *Thalhofer* feels himself compelled to "transfer from Lev. ii. to Num. xv." And may not the lawgiver, who knew that in the original law of the meat-offerings in Lev. ii. he had pointed out the necessity for the Minchah of meal to have an accompaniment of incense, have assumed this in the latter case as well known and a matter of course?—The *second* is, that the meal *Minchah* in Num. is always accompanied by a libation of wine, which is not mentioned in Lev. ii. But are we really warranted in taking the absence of any express reference

to a drink-offering along with the meat-offering in Lev. ii. as leading to the conclusion, that no drink-offerings *could* be associated
with the meat-offerings in question? May not the lawgiver have
had his peculiar reasons for not mentioning on this occasion both
the meat-offerings and drink-offerings that were requisite to make
the bloodless offering complete, and for referring to the meat-
offerings alone? Is it not conceivable that in Lev. ii. he may have
intended to speak of the meat-offering alone, as being the essential
portion of the bloodless sacrifice, and that which constituted both
its antithesis to the bleeding sacrifice (in the one bread, in the other
flesh) and its distribution into the three different species (the *Minchah* of meal, cake, and groats)? Does not the entire organization
of the four first chapters of Leviticus really compel us to assume
this? As the libation of wine had no influence upon the classification of the bloodless sacrifices, it is quite subordinate and indifferent in relation to that particular point which the lawgiver there
had in view. He therefore passed it over on the same ground on
which he omitted so much in chap. i., iii., iv., that he afterwards felt
obliged to supply. Should there be any one who is still not satisfied,
we refer him to the conjecture noticed in § 150, that the meat-
offerings generally (the subordinate, as well as the independent
ones) were offered without the accompaniment of the libation of
wine during the journeying in the desert.

And what rational ground can we think of, that could have
induced the lawgiver to withdraw from the subordinate sacrifices
the accompaniment of incense, or (except in the case referred to)
from the independent *Minchah* the libation of wine?

§ 154. Again, *Thalhofer* lays stress upon the fact, that only the
first of the varieties of *Minchah* mentioned in Lev. ii., viz., the meal
Minchah, is referred to in Num. xv. xxviii. xxix. as an accompaniment to the burnt-offerings and peace-offerings, but never the cake
Minchah; and that the *Minchah* of groats is never mentioned in
connection with, or as resting upon, the basis of a bleeding sacrifice
at all. In this we think we must support him. *Kliefoth*, indeed,
maintains that the *Minchah of groats* described in Lev. ii. 14 sqq. is
to be regarded as the regular meat-offering connected with the two
Shelem lambs offered at the feast of Pentecost (Lev. xxiii. 19), a
combination which we shall afterwards show to be inadmissible
(§ 193). *Kliefoth* thinks he has found four examples of the occurrence of a *cake Minchah* as an accompaniment to a bleeding sacrifice;
but this is equally groundless. The first is said to be in Lev. vii.

12–14. "The meal Minchah," so *Kliefoth* affirms, "might indeed be associated with the burnt-offerings as well as with the votive and freewill peace-offerings, according to Num. xv. 3," but never with the praise—*Shelamim*. For the latter, on the contrary, Lev. vii. 12 sqq. prescribes a cake Minchah, which was a higher form of meal Minchah, just as the praise-offering itself was superior to the votive and freewill-offerings (cf. § 128 sqq.).

But this view is decidedly untenable. Lev. vii. 12 sqq. cannot possibly be combined with Lev. ii. 4 sqq. It is true the materials were essentially the same in both cases; viz., חַלּוֹת מַצּוֹת and רְקִיקֵי מַצּוֹת (§ 140). But the form and purpose of the offering are irreconcilably opposed to one another. According to Lev. ii. an *Azcarah* of the cakes was burnt upon the altar, and *all* the rest fell to the lot of Aaron and his sons, or, more strictly speaking, to the officiating priest (Lev. vii. 10). In Lev. vii. 12 sqq., on the other hand, no allusion whatever is made to an *Azcarah*; in fact, the context seems to preclude the presentation of anything of the kind. For instance, instead of the *Azcarah* a תְּרוּמָה is mentioned, which was offered to Jehovah, but which, instead of being burnt upon the altar, fell to the lot of that particular priest who had sprinkled the blood of the accompanying *Shelem*; and this *Terumah* was restricted to אֶחָד מִכָּל־קָרְבָּן, *i.e.*, in all probability (according to the analogy of Ex. xxix. 33) to a portion of each of the varieties of bread or cake offered, which included not merely unleavened cakes, but leavened bread as well,—another contrast to the stringent prohibition of leaven in Lev. ii. That the rest of the loaves and cakes were then eaten at the sacrificial meal, may be regarded as a matter of course.

But it is not with Lev. vii. 12 sqq. only that *Kliefoth's* view is at variance; it also gives an inadmissible interpretation to the words of Num. xv. 3. It is there commanded, "Ye shall make an offering by fire unto Jehovah, a burnt-offering, or a slain- (= a peace-) offering, for the consecration of a vow (לְפַלֵּא־נֶדֶר), or as a freewill-offering (בִּנְדָבָה), or at your feasts, etc." Now, no doubt the words לְפַלֵּא־נֶדֶר אוֹ בִנְדָבָה might be taken, as they are by *Kliefoth*, as epexegetical to the foregoing זֶבַח, and therefore so as to exclude praise-offerings. But it is more than improbable, that in this very passage, which is written for the express purpose of determining how large a quantity of meal, oil, and wine should be added to the bleeding sacrifices as a meat- and drink-offering, no reference whatever should have been made to the praise-offering, which was the most frequent and most important of all, and was really the only kind of *Shelamim* offered at the feasts. Now if we bear in mind that the generic names of the peace-offerings (שְׁלָמִים, and זְבָחִים) are used for the most part to designate the first, the most frequent, and the leading species, viz., the praise-offering, as being *the* peace-offering *par excellence,* and that in Lev. xxiii. 37, 38, Num. xxix. 39, Deut. xii. 6, the three classes of peace-offerings are mentioned side by side as שְׁלָמִים (or זְבָחִים), נְדָרִים, and נְדָבוֹת, it seems unquestionable that in this passage also, when the נֶדֶר and the נְדָבָה are mentioned along with the זֶבַח, we are to regard זֶבַח as the name of a particular species, and not as a generic name.

Keil's view of Lev. vii. 12 sqq. is also wrong in several respects. In one point we must unquestionably admit that he is correct ; viz., that the rest of the cakes and loaves were set apart for the sacrificial meal. And he may also be right in saying, that " what is stated here of the praise-offering, the first species of the *Shelamim,* we may accept without hesitation as the rule for the other two species, the votive and the freewill-offerings." But when he speaks of these cakes at the same time as the true Minchah of all the peace-offerings, he comes into evident collision with Num. xv., where a Minchah of meal, and *not* of cakes, which he erroneously restricts to the burnt-offerings (through overlooking Num. xv., and confining himself to Num. xxviii. and xxix., where the peace-offerings are not mentioned at all), is prescribed for the peace-offerings.

§ 155. *Thalhofer* has formed comparatively the most correct view of the injunctions in Lev. vii. 12–14. But even his view is not free from decided errors. He says that " with every burnt- and peace-offering there was associated a Minchah of meal as a subordinate offering with oil and salt, but *without* (?) incense, together with a drink-offering of wine. This Minchah of meal was *all* (?) burnt in the case of the burnt-offering, as well as in that of the peace-offering. This was all that was required in the case of the burnt-offering. But for the peace-offering, besides the general offering of the *Minchah* of meal, there was also a special accompaniment of unleavened pancakes, and cake, with leavened loaves, one portion of which was allotted to the officiating priest, whilst the remainder was used for the sacrificial meal."

This view I am quite prepared to adopt, except where I have inserted a note of interrogation. It seems to me probable that what is stated in vers. 12–14 respecting the praise-offering is also applicable to the other two kinds of *Shelem,* viz., that in addition to the general accompaniment of a meal-offering there was a special offering of cakes as well, and that the latter had reference simply to the sacrificial meal. The object of the lawgiver in Lev. vii. 12–20 was to lay down such regulations as the offerer of a peace-offering had to observe, in relation to that portion of the sacrificial gift which was assigned to him for the sacrificial meal. Now as these were not the same in all three kinds of *Shelem*, on account of the rapidity with which the flesh would decompose (§ 139), it was necessary that they should be separated. He commences with the most important and most frequent description, the praise-offering, referring first of all to the bloodless accompaniment, because what he has to say upon this point applies to all three *Shelamim*. He makes no allusion to the general accompaniment to all the peace-offerings, viz., the meal *Minchah*, because none of this was devoted to the sacrificial meal according to Lev. ii. 2, 3; but after an *Azcarah* had been offered upon the altar, *all* the rest was given to the priests. Moreover, in the form in which it was offered (viz., as meal or dough) it would have been unsuitable to the sacrificial meal, and would first of all have needed to be baked. For this reason, in the case of the peace-offerings also, along with the meal *Minchah* for the altar and the priest, there was a special accompaniment of unleavened cakes and leavened bread required for the sacrificial meal of the offerer. Now if the same rule did not apply to the two other kinds of Shelamim as to the praise-offering, this ought to have been pointed out with quite as much distinctness as it is in relation to the flesh (ver. 16 sqq.).

Hence this special accompaniment of cake and bread, of which no *Azcarah* was placed upon the altar, but which had reference simply to the sacrificial meal, is not to be looked at in the light of an ordinary meat-offering; nor is it called *Minchah*, but *Corban*. If it had been regarded as a *Minchah*, then, according to Lev. ii. 11, leavened loaves ought never to have been associated with it. A cake *Corban* of this kind, *along with* the legal *Minchah* of meal, is expressly mentioned in Num. vi. 15, 17, in connection with the peace-offering of the Nazarite. This passage serves in two ways to confirm our view. In the first place, it is stated in express terms, that it was not to be offered *instead* of the usual legal Minchah of cake, but *along with it;* and in the second place, it is not a *praise-offering*, but most undoubtedly a *votive offering* that is referred to here.

From all this it is obvious that the Corban of cake in Lev. vii.

12–14 *cannot* be identified with the Minchah of cake in Lev. ii. 4–10. The second example adduced by *Kliefoth*, viz., the offering of cake already mentioned, which accompanied the Nazarite's sacrifice (Num. vi. 15, 17), is still less admissible; for, as we have seen, it was also not a *Minchah* at all, and the peace-offering upon which it was based was not a *praise*-offering, as *Kliefoth* supposes, but a *votive* offering also.

A *third* example, adduced by *Kliefoth*, of the combination of a Minchah of cake with a bleeding sacrifice is Ex. xxix. (cf. Lev. viii.), where the *dedication* or so-called *filling* sacrifice, offered at the consecration of Aaron and his sons, is accompanied by a cake Minchah. That we have at last a real *Minchah* before us, of which, according to the directions in Lev. ii., an *Azcarah* was burned upon the altar, is apparently proved in the case of the former by ver. 23 sqq., and in that of the latter by ver. 26 sqq., where it is stated that a portion of each kind of cake was placed upon the altar along with the fat portions of the filling sacrifice. And yet this is a mistake. For if the portions placed upon the altar were to be regarded as an *Azcarah*, then according to the general rules laid down in Lev. ii. 10, vi. 14, and vii. 10, the remainder of the pastry could not have been used at the sacrificial meal by the offerers of the sacrifice (Aaron and his sons), whereas this actually was the case in Lev. viii. 3 (Ex. xxix. 32). The offering was not a *Minchah*, but simply a *Corban*, like the one described in Lev. vii. 12 (cf. § 170).

The *fourth* example adduced by *Kliefoth* is Lev. vi. 20 sqq., where we have an account of the Minchah which the high priest had to offer on the day of his anointing, or, more correctly (§ 178), the day after his anointing, and twice a day from that time forward. But this example also breaks down. For, even if we could regard the daily burnt-offering to which it was attached, but which had its own meal Minchah (Ex. xxix. 40; Num. xxviii. 5) and was the offering not of the high priest but of the whole nation, as its actual basis, it by no means corresponded to the rule laid down in Lev. ii. with regard to the Minchah of cake. For the whole of this high-priestly gift was placed upon the altar, and not merely an *Azcarah*. Moreover, it was restricted entirely to one of the three kinds of cake mentioned in Lev. ii., viz., to the second description (§ 140), which was baked upon the *Machabath* and broken in pieces.

§ 156. Taking all together, therefore, we must certainly admit that Lev. ii. is by no means exactly co-extensive with the cases in

which meat-offerings could be added to the bleeding sacrifices, and
therefore that the meat-offerings *might* be offered by themselves;
i.e., without special preparation being made through the atoning
medium of a bleeding sacrifice. Nevertheless, it is still true that
throughout the whole of the Old Testament not a single *datum* can
be discovered, to prove that such independent offerings were either
customary or frequent. And it is perfectly absurd for *Thalhofer*
to maintain that there was a complete antithesis between the Minchah as an accompaniment and the independent Minchah. The
rule for both is given in Lev. ii. It is true, the meal Minchah
was selected exclusively as the legal accompaniment to the normal
burnt-offerings and peace-offerings. But the material and ritual
of the meal Minchah were precisely the same, whether it was offered
by itself or in connection with a bleeding sacrifice. The fact,
however, that no burnt-offering or *thank*-offering could be offered
without the accompaniment of a meat-offering and drink-offering,
showed, as *Hengstenberg* truly observes (Passa, p. 158), "that self-
surrender does not consist in merely idle feelings, but must manifest
itself in diligence in good works." And the fact that the *Minchah*
never occurs as an accompaniment to a sin- or trespass-offering,
may be explained from the design and significance of both of these.
Sin-offerings and trespass-offerings were so exclusively restricted
to the expiation of particular sins, that there could be no allusion
even to the ideal offering of the fruits of righteousness.

As the *Minchah* of cakes and groats is never met with as the
accompaniment to a bleeding sacrifice, the validity of a sacrificial
offering that was to be presented by itself *must* be accorded to it.
But whether the meal Minchah, which holds a prominent position
in the sacrificial worship, as a constant accompaniment to all the
burnt-offerings and peace-offerings, could be offered by itself as
well, cannot be either affirmed or denied with certainty. The latter
would be perhaps the more probable conclusion. But so far as
the *Minchah of groats* is concerned, it is restricted by the epithet
מִנְחַת בִּכּוּרִים in Lev. ii. 14 to the first-fruits of the wheat harvest,
and is adopted here as the simplest and rudest form of preparation.
With the קָרְבַּן רֵאשִׁית in Lev. ii. 12 (cf. Num. xv. 19), which consisted of leavened loaves made of the first-fruits, it had so much in
common, that, like this, it was the freewill-offering of first-fruits
on the part of an individual; but it differed in this respect, that
it was a *Minchah* in the strict sense of the word, and therefore
an *Azcarah* of it was placed upon the altar; whereas this was not

allowed in the case of the loaves of first-fruits, which were leavened like ordinary bread (Lev. ii. 11), and consequently they too are called, not *Minchah*, but *Corban*.

§ 157. In conclusion, we have still to examine *Thalhofer's* assertion (p. 113 sqq.), that "of the meal Minchah prescribed by the law as an accompaniment to the burnt-offering and peace-offering, not merely an *Azcarah*, but *the whole* had to be consumed in the altar-fire." His proof of this assertion is really a curiosity. "If we bear in mind," he says, "that the accompaniment was a thoroughly essential ingredient of the burnt-offering, it is impossible to see how a portion could be assigned to the priests, seeing that it was in the very fact of its *being entirely burnt* that the real character of a burnt-offering was expressed." He does not fail to perceive, indeed, that if this kind of argument be applied to the meal Minchah, when offered as an accompaniment to the *Shelamim*, the distinguishing characteristic of which was the *eating*, the very opposite conclusion must be drawn; but he helps himself out of the difficulty by the hopeless subterfuge, that in applying Lev. ii. 3 to the peace-offerings, the priests "had evidently received too much of the bloodless gifts in comparison with the small share which they had of the bleeding sacrifices."

Keil (p. 256) also agrees with *Winer* (ii. 494), that the *Minchah* of the burnt-offering, like the burnt-offering itself, was *entirely* burned; inasmuch as this is involved in the very idea of a burnt-offering. But the independent character of the *Minchah* is to be firmly maintained, even when it stands as a necessary accompaniment to the burnt-offering; it still remains a מִנְחָה, and is not thereby raised to the footing of an עֹלָה or כָּלִיל, and therefore is to be measured by the standard, not of Lev. i., but of Lev. ii. An express testimony, however, to the fact that even of the *Minchah* of the burnt-offering, as prescribed in Lev. ii., only a handful was placed upon the altar, is furnished by Lev. ix. 17, on which *Thalhofer* naively remarks: "Lev. ix. 17 cannot possibly be adduced in opposition to our assertion; for most probably the allusion there is to an independent *Minchah*;" and this he supports by an argument as arbitrary as it is worthless, viz, that "this is indicated by the *Vav* with which the clause is introduced,"—an argument, of which, as *Thalhofer* himself adds, we need not trouble the reader with any further explanation.

But there is a statement of *Keil's* which also requires examination. At p. 256 he says: "If the rule laid down in Lev. ii. 3

and vi. 14 sqq. applied to all the public burnt-offerings, at the
yearly feast of Tabernacles alone there would fall to the lot of the
priests (during the week's festival) about six Dresden bushels of
white meal, mixed with about 250 Dresden quarts of oil, which had
to be eaten as unleavened bread. . . . . But the priests could not
possibly eat such a quantity as this in a week, even if they ate
nothing but unleavened oil-bread." To estimate properly the force
of this argument, we must first of all settle the question, whether
the priests were really obliged, as *Keil* assumes, to eat that portion
of the *Minchah* which was assigned to them, according to Lev. ii.,
on the very day on which it was offered. In Lev. ii. itself there
is not a syllable about any such obligation; nor is there in Lev. vi.
This was the case, undoubtedly, according to Lev. vii. 15, with the
flesh of the praise-offering; but there it was expressly commanded,
and the reason, no doubt, was the rapidity with which putrefaction
occurs in hot countries. But this does not at all apply to meal
mixed with oil. Consequently, it was in all probability left to the
option of the priest himself, in what time he could or would eat it
after it had been baked (Lev. vi. 17), the only thing required being,
that he should eat it in a holy place, *i.e.*, in the fore-court (Lev.
vi. 16). If, however, in opposition to this, we should be referred to
Ex. xxix. 34 and Lev. viii. 32, where the (cake) *Minchah* of the
consecration-offering of the priests is ordered to be eaten by Aaron
and his sons on the *self-same* day, after burning their *Azcarah* (Ex.
xxix. 33 sqq.; Lev. viii. 26 sqq.), and whatever is left is directed to
be destroyed on the following day by being burned with (common)
fire; this passage, if it bears upon our question at all, tells directly
against *Keil's* own view, and gives a totally different solution to the
example which he has adduced.

Lastly, with regard to *Thalhofer's* opinion, that the burnt-
offering of *pigeons*, which was offered for the most part by very
poor people only (Lev. xiv. 21 cf. v. 7), always remained without
the accompaniment of a meal Minchah; this is a perfectly arbitrary
and groundless assertion. For we have a proof of the very opposite
in Lev. xiv. 21, 31, where a leper who has been cured is directed,
in case of poverty, to present a burnt-offering of pigeons *along with*
a meat-offering, instead of the lamb usually required.

CHAPTER III

THE MINCHAH OF THE HOLY PLACE

§ 158. We must here refer to the results obtained in § 12–14, and expand those results by an inquiry into the signification of the gifts offered in the Holy Place.

If we compare the ritual of the Holy Place with that of the fore-court, we find first of all, that the independent bleeding sacrifice was entirely wanting in the case of the former (Ex. xxx. 9), and confined exclusively to the latter. It is true the most important part, viz., the atoning blood, was taken into the Holy Place whenever expiation was made for the priests or the ideally priestly nation, and there the atoning act was completed upon the horns of the altar of incense (§ 107). But even in these cases what gave to the blood of the sacrifice its validity as atoning blood, viz., the imposition of hands and slaughtering of the animal, belonged exclusively to the fore-court. The Holy Place represented that stage in the history of salvation, in which the great fact of vicarious suffering for the sins of the world lies in the past, and all that is needed is the personal appropriation of the atoning virtue of the blood that has been shed.—If we turn next to the gifts themselves, that were offered in the Holy Place, they were the same as those presented upon the altar of the fore-court, viz., bread, wine, oil, incense, and salt; but the form in which they were presented was modified in various ways, and the offering of flesh, which was the main thing in the gifts of the fore-court, altogether failed. The latter, as we have already seen, represented the self-surrender of the person as a person to be sanctified; the former, the surrender of the fruits of his sanctification, of the results of the sanctified work of his life and calling (§ 24, 141). Now, in the fact that only the latter was exhibited in the Holy Place and not the former, the idea was expressed, that the Holy Place represented that standpoint in the development of the history of salvation, in which personal self-surrender no longer needs to be expressly exhibited (because its complete and continuous accomplishment is the self-evident assumption of such a standpoint), and the fruits and results of the life's work alone need to attest their living and active existence.

Again, the bloodless offerings of the fore-court, meal (bread),

oil, and incense, appear continually intermingled, and are completed
in the same act and on the same holy altar; whereas those of the
Holy Place are divided into *meat*-offerings, *incense*-offerings, and
light-offerings. The bread and the wine were placed upon the
table; and if the accompaniment of oil and incense was not wanting
in the case of this bread, yet oil and incense, by being offered separately—the incense upon the altar of incense, and the oil upon the
candlestick—were raised from the subordinate position of a mere
accompaniment into that of an independent offering : they were no
longer merely means to an end which lay beyond them, but an end
in themselves. That is to say, even now the works of sanctification
to be offered require the co-operation of the Spirit of God, perpetuity through the salt of the covenant of God, and presentation in
connection with prayer. But by the side of this the incense was
also constantly burning by itself upon the altar of incense, and bore
witness to the fact, that the lives and actions of the saints of God
are a continual prayer, a praying without ceasing, and a praying
which needs no special stimulus, but which, being the breathing of
the spirit, is as natural, necessary, and indispensable a vital process,
as the breathing of the lungs is to the life of the body. Upon the
candlestick there burned, the whole night through, the oil of the
Spirit of God which dwelt in the congregation, bearing witness to
the word of the Lord : " Ye are the light of the world."

By this separation of the gifts, as *Kliefoth* observes, it was
possible to give a fuller expansion to the forms of presentation.
And the different elements were fuller, richer, and more developed.
Instead of the meal Minchah, which was the most common in the
fore-court, we find the cake Minchah, which was more perfect both
in form (חַלֹּת) and mode of preparation (מַאֲפֵה תַנּוּר). The incense
too was no longer the simple and ordinary kind, but compounded
with other and still more delicate perfumes. And the oil for the
lamps was the finest and purest olive oil that could possibly be obtained (Lev. xxiv. 2 ; Ex. xxvii. 20).

On the altar of burnt-offering only an *Azcarah* of the gift was
offered up; but the whole of the gift was invariably placed upon
the altar, table, and candlestick, in the Holy Place. Upon the
former a gift was offered up from time to time ; but upon the table
in the Holy Place the bread was always lying, whilst the incense
emitted its fragrance upon its altar from morning to evening, and
the light burned upon the candlestick the whole night through.
Bread and wine, which were offered in the fore-court as food for

Jehovah, needed to be purified by the fire of the altar before they could become " a sweet-smelling savour to the Lord;" but the loaves laid before Jehovah upon the table in the Holy Place, needed no such purification. It is true the accompaniment of perfume and the incense of the altar needed to be burned, as well as the oil of the candlestick: the burning in this case, however, did not denote purification, but was the only way by which the incense could be made to give out its fragrance and the oil its light. For it was not the incense itself in its concentrated form which was the symbol of prayer, but its perfume ascending to heaven; and it is not the mere possession of the Spirit of God which makes the congregation of saints the light of the world, but the fact that the Spirit *shines* through them.

§ 159. We will now examine one by one the offerings of the Holy Place; and first of all let us look at that which stood nearest to the *Minchah* of the fore-court, viz., the *face-loaves*, or, as the Hebrew name is rendered by *Luther* and others, the SHEW-BREAD (LXX. ἄρτοι προθέσεως, *Vulg. panes propositionis*). How this striking name arose, and what it signifies, we may learn from Ex. xxv. 30, where the shew-bread is mentioned for the first time. The command is given there, " Thou shalt lay upon the table face-bread before My face continually." לֶחֶם פָּנִים, therefore, is an abbreviation for לֶחֶם אֲשֶׁר לִפְנֵי יְהֹוָה: they were loaves that were laid before the face of God (*i.e.*, before the Capporeth as the throne of God in the Holy of Holies), that God might see them and rejoice in them. *Bähr's* interpretation of the name, viz., that it denoted that bread " by which God was seen, *i.e.*, with the eating of which the sight of God was associated, or through the eating of which a sight of God was obtained," is as unfounded and unscriptural as it possibly can be. There is no necessity to prove this here, though *Stöckl* has lately adopted this misinterpretation, and on the strength of it describes the shew-bread as " a splendid type of the N. T. Eucharist." It is sufficient to refer to Lev. xxiv. 8 : " Every Sabbath he shall set it (the bread) *before* Jehovah continually, *on the part of* the children of Israel, an everlasting covenant." The later name לֶחֶם הַמַּעֲרֶכֶת (Neh. x. 33), or הַמַּעֲרֶכֶת alone (2 Chron. ii. 4), points back to the directions in Lev. xxiv. 6, that the loaves were to be placed in two rows or piles (מַעֲרָכוֹת) upon the table in the Holy Place.

The number of loaves to be renewed every Sabbath corresponded to the number of tribes of Israel (Lev. xxiv. 5). They

were called חַלּוֹת on account of their shape (§ 140). For each
loaf two-tenths of an ephah of white meal was used. It is not
expressly stated anywhere that leaven and honey were to be avoided,
and oil and salt to be employed instead; but according to Lev. ii.
this is to be understood as a matter of course. Whether the loaves
were to be placed in two rows side by side, or in two piles one upon
another, cannot be determined with certainty, on account of the
fluctuating meaning of מַעֲרֶכֶת. The dimensions of the surface of
the table (two cubits long by one broad) render the latter the more
probable of the two. And the instructions in Lev. xxiv. 7, that
the incense to be added was to be laid עַל־הַמַּעֲרֶכֶת, also confirm
this. After the loaves had been laid upon the table from Sabbath
to Sabbath, they were taken away and fresh ones substituted.
Those which were removed were assigned to the priests, who were
required to eat them in a holy place, as being the "*most holy of the
fire-offerings of Jehovah*" (ver. 9). This epithet might appear
surprising, as none of the loaves were placed in the altar-fire; but
the explanation is to be found in the fact that their accompaniment
of incense was actually burned (probably upon the altar of burnt-
offering after the removal of the loaves, and before they were
eaten), and was called their *Azcarah* in consequence (ver. 7). This
places them in the same category as the remainder of the ordinary
meat-offering which was left over after the burning of the Azcarah
(§ 149).

A *libation of wine* in connection with them is not mentioned in
any of the passages which treat professedly of the arrangement of
the shew-bread (Ex. xxv. 30; Lev. xxiv. 5 sqq.; Num. iv. 7); but
it must certainly be taken for granted, on account of the frequent
allusion to the bowls and cans belonging to the table of shew-
bread (cf. Ex. xxv. 29, xxxvii. 16; Num. iv. 7).

§ 160. With regard to the *offerings of* OIL or LIGHT, directions are given in Ex. xxvii. 20, 21, xxx. 7, and Lev. xxiv. 3, 4,
that the high priest is to clean the lamps in the Holy Place every
morning, and fill them with the finest oil of pressed olives, and to
light them in the evening, that they may burn the whole night.
We have already shown at § 144, that the oil which imparted its
bright and lasting luminous properties to the burning wicks of the
seven-armed candlestick in the Holy Place, like the oil which was
mixed with the meat-offerings of the fore-court, may be regarded,
or rather, according to the laws of symbolism, must be regarded,
as anointing oil, and consequently as the symbol of the Spirit of

God. *Kliefoth,* it is true, as we pointed out there, has entered his protest against this view, but without convincing us of the incorrectness of our view or the correctness of his own. In this, however, we agree with him, that the juxtaposition of the twelve loaves of shew-bread and the seven burning lamps represented the *active* life of believers on the one hand, and their *intellectual* life on the other. This explanation, we are prepared to maintain with him, is sufficiently attested by such passages as Matt. v. 14–16; Luke xii. 35; Phil. ii. 15; Zech. iv.; and Rev. i. 12, 20. But the grounds upon which he defends this interpretation we must pronounce decidedly erroneous. For instance, he maintains that the oil had a double signification: that whilst as the anointing material it was undoubtedly a symbol of the Spirit of God, as burning or illuminating material it denoted that element in man which, being kindled by the holy fire of God, gives forth the light of divine truth and knowledge. But, in the *first* place, every symbol must receive, as far as possible, one uniform interpretation. *Secondly,* it was not the oil in the lamp that was lighted, but the wick, which burned brightly and permanently, however, only because and so far as it was supplied with oil; consequently the wick and not the oil would represent that part of human nature which, being inflamed by the holy fire, enlightens the darkness of the world. But the wick would give only a dull light, and be very quickly extinguished, if it were not fed or anointed with oil; and so the power of human thought and knowledge, even though enkindled with sacred fire, would never be able to enlighten the darkness of this world, if it were not anointed and fed with the oil of the Spirit of God. And *thirdly,* the passages adduced by *Kliefoth* himself do not sustain his interpretation.

He refers to Zech. iv. 12 and Rev. xi. 4; and we quite agree with him that the sons of oil mentioned there are the prophets; but the oil which they conduct to the Church of God, to render the wick in its candlestick burning and luminous, is not a human attribute of their own, but a divine attribute, which even the prophets did not derive from themselves, but received from God, that they might convey it to the Church. So again, the oil referred to in Matt. xxv. 1 sqq., which fails the foolish virgins at the end, and the want of which excludes them from participating in the marriage supper, because they know not how to supply it, cannot signify their own mental power—for in that case their difficulty as to the source of supply could not have been very great,—but must denote the Spirit of God, which, if despised and rejected in the day of grace, will not be found in the day of need. *Bähr's* interpretation, according to which the light burning in the Holy Place was a light proceeding from God and diffused by God, which served to enlighten the Church of God, falls to the ground with his similar and equally erroneous interpretation of the shew-bread and incense (§ 146),—a fall from which *Stöckl's* support will hardly protect it.

§ 161. With regard, lastly, to the INCENSE-OFFERING, we have little more to do than to refer to § 146 and 158. In the place of the simple incense of the fore-court, a fragrant material, composed of four separate ingredients (including frankincense), is described in Ex. xxx. 34–38 as being used in the Holy Place ; and the high priest was to renew and kindle it every morning and evening (Ex. xxx. 7, 8). At a later period this task might be performed by an ordinary priest (Luke i. 9, cf. Ex. xxx. 20). On the different ingredients of which this incense was composed, see *Keil*, pp. 90, 91. On a former occasion I gave it as my opinion, that the four ingredients represented the four component elements of perfect prayer (praise, thanksgiving, supplication, and intercession) ; but *Keil* has very properly observed (p. 107), that the fact of the anointing oil being similarly composed of four ingredients (Ex. xxx. 32 sqq.) is at variance with this, and forces us to regard the quadruple number of ingredients as being in both cases the stamp of the kingdom of God.

Stöckl (p. 303) separates himself entirely from the " *sententia communis* of Protestant symbolism," just as in other cases he is fond of speaking with the most innocent *naiveté* of the *isolated* standpoint of *Bähr*, the only Protestant whose work he has read upon the subject (§ 127, note). He cannot help admitting, however, that according to the clear statements of the Scriptures themselves, the incense was a symbol, not of the breath of God, but of the prayers of saints. But in so doing he runs against the words of Matt. ix. 16 : *Nemo autem immittit commissuram panni rudis in vestimentum vetus, tollit enim plenitudinem ejus a vestimento, et pejor scissura fit.* For nothing is more certain than that the offerings of the Holy Place must be regarded either as *all three* gifts proceeding from God to the holy nation, which is *Bähr's* view, or as *all three* offerings presented by the holy nation to Jehovah. At all events, this is demanded by " Protestant " hermeneutics, and is really a " *sententia communis* of Protestant symbolism."

The three offerings in the Holy Place, therefore, were the characteristic distinctions of that stage in the development of the priestly nation, which was represented by this division of the tabernacle, as a nation of uninterrupted *prayer*, of world-enlightening *knowledge*, and of successful *work* in the duties of its vocation.

BOOK IV

MODIFICATION OF THE SACRIFICIAL WORSHIP IN CONNECTION WITH SPECIAL SEASONS AND CIRCUMSTANCES

CHAPTER I

THE CONSECRATION OF THE PEOPLE, THE PRIESTS, AND THE LEVITES

A. COVENANT CONSECRATION OF THE PEOPLE

§ 162. The covenant consecration of the people at Sinai (Ex. xxiv.) took place after the solemn promulgation of the fundamental law, but before the erection of the sanctuary, and even before the publication of the law of sacrifice. After the people had unanimously declared their willingness to accept the duties and privileges of the covenant as expounded to them by Moses, and to regulate their conduct by them, Moses built an altar, which represented the striving of the people upwards, and the stooping of the gracious presence of God downwards. He then erected twelve pillars (probably round about the altar) as symbols of the nation. In this way was the fundamental idea of the future place of worship, viz., the gracious presence of God in the midst of the twelve tribes of Israel, first exhibited. Moses then sent some young men of the children of Israel to offer young oxen as burnt-offerings and peace-offerings; and taking one half of the blood, he sprinkled it upon the altar. After this he read the book of the covenant (Ex. xx.–xxiii.) to the people. When the people had repeated the promise, that they would live and act according to its precepts, he took the other half and sprinkled it upon them, saying, "This is the blood of the covenant which Jehovah concluded with you." Moses and Aaron then ascended the holy mountain, with Nadab and Abihu, Aaron's eldest sons, and seventy of the elders of Israel;

and when they had seen Jehovah, they partook of the sacrificial meal (Ex. xxiv. 1–11).

The question arises here, What was the position of the *young men* who offered the sacrifice? I have already given the following reply: The young men represented the sacrificing nation in the period of its youth, as a nation that had all the eagerness of youth to enter upon its course (Hist. of O. C., vol. ii. p. 143). *Keil* gave his full adhesion to this in his *Arch.* i. 261, but he has withdrawn it again in his commentary, on the strength of the objection adduced by *Oehler*, "that it could not be the nation which offered a sacrifice here on its own account, for the fellowship with God, which would enable it to approach God in sacrifice, had yet to be established." But this is incorrect, for the people had certainly been allowed to approach God in sacrifice before this. Abel, Noah, and Abraham had all done so, and even the Israelites themselves at the offering of the paschal lamb in Egypt. "Moreover," *Oehler* continues, "according to vers. 1 and 9, the nation already possessed its representatives in the seventy elders, and Moses alone officiated as priest; so that the young men must have officiated simply as the servants of Moses," that is to say, in the same manner in which the Levites assisted the priests afterwards. But it is not stated anywhere that the seventy elders took part in the actual duties of sacrificing; whereas in ver. 5 it is distinctly affirmed that the young men were to offer and slay the sacrifices. Now that was not the work of a servant, but an essential and independent function. Again, we never find the work performed or the help afforded by the Levites described as a הֶעֱלָה עֹלָת or זָבַח זְבָחִים שְׁלָמִים, as is the case in ver. 5, nor could it be so described. In the terminology of the Mosaic ritual the expression הֶעֱלָה עֹלָה is applied exclusively to the person sacrificing (*e.g.*, Lev. xvii. 8) or to the officiating priest (Lev. xiv. 20); and if the same expression is applied here to the young men *before* the issuing of the sacrificial law, it can only be in the same sense as in Gen. viii. 20, xxii. 2, 13. The young men undoubtedly appear as the sacrificers, and that in the *old* way, in which offerer and priest were united in the same person; but the old arrangement passes over into the new, inasmuch as the young men do not carry out the act of sacrificing any further than the point of slaying the animals, and then Moses steps in and performs the rest (viz., the manipulations with the blood) entirely by himself, the people and their representatives assuming only a passive and receptive attitude. In this there was a practical declaration of the fact that henceforth, according to the new order of things, every sacrificial transaction would require a specifically priestly mediation. The seventy elders, on the other hand, represented the *old* Israel, which was now born again into a *new, young* Israel, and therefore was represented by *young men* as well.

§ 163. It is still further striking, that no mention is made of a *sin-offering* in connection with this sacrificial transaction. If the period referred to were later instead of earlier than the promulgation of the law of sacrifice, we should necessarily expect to find the way prepared by a sin-offering, as was the case in all the festal and solemn sacrifices offered afterwards. Hence the absence of any sin-offering in this case furnishes conclusive evidence, that this kind of sacrifice was introduced for the first time by the sacrificial law, —a sufficient reason for its never being mentioned before (§ 87). The significance specially assigned to the sin-offering afterwards, must be sought for here in the sprinkling of blood in connection with the two other kinds of sacrifice. On the other hand, the peace-offering was already introduced in association with the burnt-offering, and it was necessary that both kinds should be offered together on this occasion, since the peculiar feature in the burnt-offering, viz., the burning of the whole, which was expressive of complete self-surrender, as well as the sacrificial meal, which was restricted entirely to the peace-offering, needed to be exhibited as an attestation of fellowship with God.

Now, since the sacrifice consisted not of one kind only, but of two kinds, viz., of burnt-offerings and peace-offerings, another question arises, namely, whether the blood used in the way described was the blood of the burnt-offering or of the peace-offering, or of both; and if the last, whether the two were mixed together, or each was taken by itself as "blood of the covenant." As the text (vers. 6–8) speaks only of blood generally, we are not warranted in restricting the proceedings described to the peace-offerings alone. But the other question, whether they were used separately or mixed together, must remain unanswered. And since the distinguishing feature in the two sacrifices is to be sought for, not in any similarity in the application of the blood, but in the different ways in which the flesh was disposed of, the answer to the question is of no essential importance.

The number of bullocks to be offered is not stated either for the burnt-offerings or the peace-offerings. They are simply spoken of in the plural number. As a very considerable quantity of blood would thus be obtained, the sprinkling of the people can hardly have been limited to their representatives, whether the young men who offered the sacrifices in their stead, or the seventy elders. It is more natural to suppose that Moses passed between the ranks of the assembled nation, and sprinkled the people themselves (though not of necessity every individual).

§ 164. The sprinkling of the altar with the blood of the sacrifice had for its object, here as everywhere else, the expiation of the offerer, *i.e.*, of the nation at large, and thus laid the foundation for the conclusion of the covenant. That such a foundation was needed, is apparent at once. Only a short time before, the people had said, " Speak thou with us, and we will hear ; but let not God speak with us, lest we die " (Ex. xx. 19). Sinful man cannot draw near to God, still less make a covenant with Him, without bringing to light the real character of his sin, as deserving death and a curse, and evoking the wrath and punishment of God. That which separates him from God, and renders any approach to God the cause of death and destruction, viz., sin, must first of all be rendered harmless and powerless. And this was accomplished through the medium of the כַּפָּרָה or sacrificial atonement.

But whereas in other cases the whole of the blood of the burnt- and peace-offerings was placed upon the altar, in this case only half of it was so applied, and the people themselves were sprinkled with the other half. *Hofmann* is right in disputing the expiatory cha- racter of this second sprinkling. " This was done," he says, " not to make atonement for the people, for atonement had already been made by the pouring out of the blood upon the altar, but to con- secrate them. The same life that had been offered as a mediation, and by the surrender of which expiation had been made for them, was now used to qualify them for the relation of fellowship with God, to consecrate the expiated nation into a sanctuary ; and for this reason the blood sprinkled upon the congregation was not called the blood of atonement, but the blood of the covenant. Otherwise, what need could there be for this unusual transaction ?"

The division of the blood into two equal portions does not relate to the fact that there were two parties to the covenant, Jehovah on the one hand, and the people on the other. Still less has it anything in common with the heathen custom of mixing the blood of two contracting parties together, as a symbolical representation of the idea that henceforth their lives and labours were one. On the con- trary, it was *one* blood which was sprinkled half upon the altar, as the place where Jehovah appeared (Ex. xx. 24), and half upon the people, with whom Jehovah was about to conclude a covenant. And when one half was put upon the altar, it was placed in relation not only to Jehovah, as a protection against His judicial wrath, but also to the nation, whose sin it was to cover or expiate there. And when the other half was sprinkled upon the people, not only was it thereby brought into connection with the people, but as it was taken from the very same blood, of which one half had been placed upon the altar, and as the same indivisible soul dwelt in the one half as much as in the other, the same relation to Jehovah which was established by the former half was equally valid and close in the case of the latter also. The same blood, *i.e.*, the same soul, which had expiated the sin of the nation upon the altar, was now to consecrate and unite the nation into covenant fellowship with God by the divine power which it had there acquired. If it had been intended, or *possible*, that the idea here referred to should be fully set forth, the whole of the blood ought first of all to have been placed upon the altar, and then, after it had been invested with saving power, and the gracious presence of God had been imparted to it upon the altar, it should have been taken away again and sprinkled upon the people. The correctness of this view is supported by the analogy which we find in the consecration of the priests, when, according to Ex. xxix. 21 and Lev. viii. 30, the blood was first poured out upon the altar, and after that as much as was necessary was taken off the altar again and applied to the sprinkling of Aaron and his sons (§ 171). But as this could not be done in the case before us, where so large a quantity of blood was required for the sprinkling of the people, in order to approximate as closely as possible to a full exhibition of the idea, one half of the blood was kept back, and with that the people were sprinkled; for notwithstanding the division, the half of the blood contained within it, whole and undivided, the very same soul which had acquired the divine powers of the altar in the other half.[1]

---

[1] The allusion to the sprinkling of the blood in Heb. ix. 19–21 deviates in several by no means unimportant points from the account given in Ex. xxiv. For (1) it speaks of Moses as using the blood τῶν μόσχων καὶ τράγων, whereas the Pentateuch only mentions τῶν μόσχων (*i.e.*, young oxen), and says nothing about τῶν τράγων, which are introduced in the Mosaic law as specifically sin-offerings. (2) Along with the sacrificial blood employed in the sprinkling, it mentions water, coccus-wool, and hyssop, as used for the same purpose. (3) It describes not only the whole nation, but the book of the covenant, and even the tabernacle and all the furniture of the priesthood, as having been sprinkled; whereas the latter were not yet in existence.

After the covenant of God with Israel had thus been concluded, negatively by expiation, and positively by the consecration of the people, the confirmation of the newly-established covenant fellowship followed in the sacrificial meal. It is, of course, very obvious that the whole nation could not be invited to this, but only a selection or representation; and it is perfectly intelligible that the representatives should have been chosen from the elders of Israel. But when the number is fixed at 70, not only is the symbolical value of this number (70 = 7 × 10) to be regarded as the reason, but its historical significance also, as seen in Gen. xlvi. 27. No explanation need be given of the fact that Moses took part in the meal; and the addition of the two eldest sons of Aaron had reference, no doubt,

But the author of the Epistle to the Hebrews cannot possibly be accused of any such anachronism as the statement last mentioned would contain, if it could be regarded as coinciding in point of *time* with the covenant consecration of the people. We are entitled, or rather compelled, to assume that he has disregarded the precise order of time, and introduced a fact which occurred at a later period, because it was subservient to the same idea and helped to exhibit it fully from every point of view. And if we are shut up to this conclusion by an otherwise unexampled and inconceivable anachronism, which could only have sprung from the most incredible ignorance on the part of the author, we are also warranted in disposing of the other discrepancies between the passage in question and Ex. xxiv. in precisely the same way.

The idea which the writer wanted to carry out and confirm in vers. 19–21 is clearly expressed in ver. 18, viz., that the old covenant could not be consecrated without blood. This consecration, however, was not completed and exhausted in the covenant consecration of the people (Ex. xxiv.); but that of the priests and Levites (Lev. viii. and Num. ix.), the former of which embraced the consecration of the sanctuary and its furniture, needed to be included. And this, it appears to me, is what the writer has done. But such a summary mode of putting the whole together necessarily involved certain incongruities, which could not fail to appear whenever the attempt should be made to separate the different points and arrange them in chronological order.

These three acts of consecration (of the people, of the priests with the sanctuary, and of the Levites) appear to me to be quite sufficient to sustain every particular mentioned by the author, with the sole exception of the sprinkling of the book of the covenant, which is not mentioned anywhere in the Pentateuch, and which the author therefore can only have derived from tradition; so that there is no necessity to bring in the ritual of the great day of atonement, which had nothing to do with the inaugural consecration, that was only once performed. From the covenant consecration of the people the author obtained the sprinkling of the whole nation (Ex. xxiv. 8); from the consecration of the priests, the sprinkling of the tabernacle and its furniture (Lev. viii. 10, 11, cf. Ex. xl. 9–11); and from that of the Levites, the sprinkling with water, coccus-wool, and hyssop (Num. viii. 7). It is true that in Num. viii. 7 we read of a sprinkling with *water* of purifying, מֵי חַטָּאת, but no reference is made to coccus-wool and

as *Keil* observes in his Commentary, i. 490, to their future election
to the priesthood.

B. CONSECRATION OF THE PRIESTS AND SANCTUARY.

§ 165. The command to consecrate the priests is contained in
Ex. xxix. 1–37 ; but the consecration was not to be carried out till
after the building and furnishing of the sanctuary had been completed, and the law of sacrifice had been proclaimed. After the
former had taken place, the consecration of the sanctuary was also
commanded in Ex. xl. 9–15 ; and after the promulgation of the
law, the double consecration (that of the priests themselves, and
that of the place and instruments of their official duties) was
effected, in the manner described in Lev. viii. 1–36.

The consecration of the priests consisted of two parts, each
comprising three distinct actions. The first embraced the washing,
clothing, and anointing of the persons to be initiated. The second
was a triple *sacrificial* action,—the sacrifice of a sin-offering, a
burnt-offering, and a peace-offering ; the last of which was desig-

---

hyssop. This difference, however, is quite irrelevant. Either the author had
in his mind, as *Delitzsch* supposes, a rod of hyssop, which was bound round
with coccus-wool and served as a sprinkling brush, such as we find used
on other occasions for the purpose of sprinkling water (Lev. xiv. 6, 7 ; Num.
xix. 18) ; or he was thinking (according to the analogy of Num. xix. 6, cf.
§ 221) of hyssop and coccus-wool as medicinal ingredients mixed with the
water, by which it was made into מֵי חַטָּאת, through the virtue of the one as a
medium of purification, and that of the other (*i.e.*, the wool soaked in coccus
juice) as a healing medicine. In either case, this account is to be regarded as a
fuller expansion of the brief description contained in the Pentateuch, for which
the writer might refer to legal analogies, and probably also to traditional *data*.
The diversity certainly is a more serious one, when we find the author of the
Epistle to the Hebrews referring expressly to the sprinkling of the sanctuary and
its furniture with *blood*, whereas the account in the Pentateuch only mentions a
sprinkling with *oil* (Lev. viii. 10, 11 ; Ex. xl. 9–11), and it is merely the priests'
clothes that are represented as being sprinkled with blood and oil (Lev. viii. 30).
But the supposition that the writer has supplemented the statement in the Pentateuch with traditional *data*, is rendered probable by the fact that *Josephus* (Ant.
3, 8, 6) perfectly agrees with him, and refers not merely to the priests *and* their
clothes, but also to τήν τε σκηνὴν καὶ περὶ αὐτὴν σκεύη as being sprinkled with oil
and sacrificial blood during the seven days of priestly consecration. Lastly, so
far as the goats connected with the bullocks are concerned, I am inclined to
assume with *Delitzsch*, p. 417, that " bulls and goats were a standing expression
with the author to denote all the bleeding sacrifices, just as δῶρά τε καὶ θυσίαι embrace the offerings of every description." But if this does not suffice, I still regard
it as more suitable to refer to the goat in Lev. ix. 3 than to that in Lev. xvi. 15.

nated as the true consecration-sacrifice. *Keil* is wrong, however, in drawing this distinction between the two, viz., that the former represented the qualification of the priests for the priestly office, the latter their installation in its dignity and privileges. For, on the one hand, washing and investiture had nothing to do with *qualification* for the priestly office; but, on the contrary, the investiture, as is expressly declared in Ex. xxix. 9, represented their *installation* in the dignity and privileges of the priesthood. It was the anointing alone which had to do with their qualification. And on the other hand, the sin-offerings and burnt-offerings themselves had nothing to do with their inauguration, but only the peace-offering associated with them.

The true explanation is rather this : both installation and qualification were represented in the first act, the former by the investiture, the latter by the anointing, whilst a clear ground for both was prepared by the washing; and the second act represented the same ideas, but through the medium of the sacrificial worship, the sin-offering setting forth the wiping away of sin, the burnt-offering the complete surrender of the entire person, though without any special regard to the specifically priestly service, whilst the peace- or consecration-offering expressed this appointment in the most decided manner.

§ 166. At the commencement of the ceremony Moses took Aaron and his sons to the door of the tabernacle, where they were subjected to a washing, most probably of the whole body. This removal of bodily uncleanness was " a symbol of spiritual purification, without which no one could approach God, least of all one who performed the duties of atonement" (*Oehler*, 178). The investiture of Aaron with the clothing prepared for him followed next ; this was equivalent to an investiture with the office itself, the official dress being a visible expression of the official character. Moses then took the anointing oil, which was composed, according to Ex. xxx. 23 sqq., of four strongly smelling spices (myrrh, cinnamon, calamus, and cassia) mixed with olive oil, and *anointed* first of all the dwelling-place and its furniture, then (by sprinkling seven times) the altar of the fore-court and all the rest of the utensils belonging to it, and last of all Aaron the high priest, pouring the oil upon his head. He then proceeded to the investiture of Aaron's sons; but no mention is made of their being anointed, either in Lev. viii. 13 or Ex. xxix. 8.[1]

---

[1] We must conclude, therefore, that Aaron alone was anointed, and not his sons, at the time of the investiture ; and we are confirmed in this opinion by

On the signification of the anointing oil, see § 144. The oil was a symbolical representation of the Spirit of God, with its enlivening, refreshing, healing, and enlightening power. Hence the anointing with oil indicated the communication of this Spirit, for the purpose of qualifying the person anointed for the office upon which he was about to enter (1 Sam. x. 1, xvi. 13). The four fragrant, spicy substances which were mixed with the oil, served to connect with the enlivening properties of the oil a capacity for diffusing fragrance also, and to heighten its quickening influence, by their power of arousing the vital energy. That there should be exactly *four* of these substances was not a mere accident; for four was the sign of the kingdom of God. The oil was applied to the *head* of the high priest, because the head is the true centre of spiri-

---

the fact that the high priest is frequently designated the "anointed priest," הַכֹּהֵן הַמָּשִׁיחַ, in distinction from the common priests (*e.g.*, Lev. iv. 3, 5, 16, xvi. 32). But this seems to be at variance with Ex. xxviii. 41, xxx. 30; Lev. vii. 35, 36, x. 7, where anointing is expressly ascribed to the common priests; whilst in Ex. xl. 15 Moses is commanded to anoint the sons of Aaron, *as he* had anointed their father. For this reason *Keil*, *Oehler*, and others are of opinion, that not only Aaron, but his sons also, were anointed at the time of the investiture, and that it is merely by accident that this is not mentioned in Ex. xxix. and Lev. viii. And since it is most decidedly assumed in Lev. xxi. 10, 12, that the high priest alone was anointed on the *head* and not the subordinate priests, the writers referred to are inclined to adopt the rabbinical notion, that whereas the oil was poured upon Aaron's head, it was only smeared upon the *foreheads* of his sons. But this solution is decidedly inadmissible. It is hardly conceivable, that if an anointing of the inferior priests was ordered to take place, and actually did take place, at this time, it could have been passed by without notice both in Ex. xxix. 8 and Lev. viii. 13 ; and this is perfectly *in*conceivable, if the anointing was to be carried out, and really was carried out, in a totally different manner from the anointing of the high priest. Moreover, justice is by no means done in this way to Ex. xl. 15 ; for the smearing of the forehead with oil is an *essentially* different kind of anointing from the pouring of oil upon the head. We must seek for a solution, therefore, which admits, on the one hand, that the high priest alone was anointed at the time of the investiture and not the inferior priests, and thus explains the fact that the former alone was called the "anointed priest;" but which, on the other hand, holds firmly to the opinion that the inferior priests were anointed as well, and that in the same way as the high priest. And such a solution we may obtain by comparing Lev. viii. 10–13 with ver. 30 (or Ex. xxix. 7, 8 with ver. 21). The anointing of the head was anointing κατ᾽ ἐξοχήν, and this was performed upon the high priest alone; hence he was also called the anointed priest κατ᾽ ἐξοχήν. But the sprinkling of the person and clothes with oil was an inferior kind of anointing ; and according to Lev. viii. 30 and Ex. xxix. 21, this was performed upon the high priest and the inferior priests as well.

tual life, and as such the noblest part of the body. And the oil was *poured*, not merely smeared or sprinkled, upon his head, to show that, for the discharge of the duties of his office, he needed, and would receive, the Spirit of God in richest *fulness*.

§ 167. The priestly *functions* connected with the sacrifice that followed, were naturally performed not by those who were just about to be consecrated to the priestly office, but by Moses, the mediator of the covenant. The former were rather the offerers of the sacrifice. As the sacrificial law had already been promulgated, its principles were no doubt adhered to in the proceedings on this occasion, which were peculiarly and singularly modified, only so far as this was required by the peculiarity and singularity of the object contemplated. Consequently, in this, as in all solemn sacrificial occasions, the first thing done was to present a *sin-offering*. " Not only the great importance of the occasion, but the position occupied by the priests in the theocracy, as the ἐκλογή of the covenant-nation, which had been chosen as a kingdom of priests, required that the highest kind of sacrificial animal, viz., an ox, should be chosen for the sacrifice" (*Keil*, 1, 262). And the fact that the blood of *this* sin-offering was not taken into the Holy Place, as was the case with other sin-offerings of either the high priest or the whole priesthood, but was merely smeared upon the horns of the altar of burnt-offering, as in the case of a prince or private individual, may be explained on the ground, that the offerers of the sacrifice were not yet in actual possession of the priesthood, but were just about to be initiated. It does seem indeed to be at variance with this, that after separating the portions of fat to be burned upon the altar, the rest of the flesh was not given up to the officiating priest (*i.e.*, to Moses), as on other occasions, to be eaten by him in a holy place, but as in the case of the priestly sin-offerings, whose blood was taken into the Holy Place, was burned outside the camp (§ 113 sqq.). *Hofmann* alone, it seems to me, has solved this problem satisfactorily. " As Moses was not a priest," he says, " but only consecrated the priest, he did not eat the flesh of the sin-offering, as the priest did afterwards, when he had offered a sin-offering for others. But on this occasion the flesh was burnt; for it was the attitude of the priest towards the nation which afterwards led to his eating the flesh of the sin-offering."

It is a mistaken view, therefore, on the part of *Keil*, when he maintains, that " this sin-offering became a *consecration-offering*, chiefly through the fact that the blood was *not* taken into the Holy

Place, as in the case of other sin-offerings of the same kind, but was merely placed upon the altar of burnt-offering, to purify, sanctify, and make reconciliation for it, as is distinctly stated in Lev. viii. 15" (i. 263). For the sin-offering presented here neither *was* nor *became* a consecration-offering; least of all did it become a consecration-offering *through the fact* that the blood was *not* taken into the Holy Place. Of the other fact, that the burning of the flesh was a complete deviation from the ordinary practice, not the slightest explanation is attempted. The true consecration-offering was neither the sin-offering nor the burnt-offering which followed it, but simply and solely the peace-offering, which concluded the whole ceremony, and for which the foundation had been laid by the previous sin-offering and burnt-offering, both negatively (namely, by the expiation effected in the sin-offering) and positively (by the complete self-surrender expressed in the burnt-offering). And when the sprinkling of the altar of burnt-offering with the blood of this sin-offering is represented in Lev. viii. 15 as a purification and sanctification of the altar, this is by no means to be regarded as an " installation of the persons to be consecrated in the privilege of approaching the altar and presenting the sacrifices of the congregation upon it;" it is rather to be interpreted according to the analogy of Lev. xvi. 16, and the explanation given at the close of § 68.

§ 168. In the ceremony connected with the *burnt-offering*, for which a ram was chosen on this occasion, there was no deviation from the ordinary custom. For it is undoubtedly an error on the part of *Keil*, to reckon it as one of the " peculiarities" in the offering of " all three animals," that " they were *offered* and *slaughtered* not by the persons to be consecrated, but by Moses, the mediator of the old covenant." For if this assertion were correct, there would be a complete departure from the most fundamental principles of the sacrificial law, which it would be absolutely impossible to explain and justify, and for which *Keil* has not been able to bring forward the shadow of an explanation, as there are not many persons who will be able to find any solution of the discrepancy in the fact, that " Moses was the mediator of the old covenant, through whose service Israel was consecrated as the congregation of God, and Aaron with his sons as priests of God." That all three animals were offered *for* the persons to be initiated, is placed beyond all doubt by the fact, that in the case of every one it is expressly observed, that Aaron and his sons laid their hands upon its head (vers. 14, 18, 22).

But if it was for them that the sacrifices were offered, they too were required to be the offerers and slayers of the sacrifice, unless the whole of the law of sacrifice was to be set at nought. This is so self-evident, that any express statement to that effect was perfectly unnecessary. When Moses is directed in ver. 2 to " take Aaron and his sons with him, and the garments, and the anointing oil, and a bullock for the sin-offering, and two rams, etc.," this does not surely imply that Moses is to " present" all these things himself. And it is quite as much at variance with the sense and the words, to interpret the words in vers. 15, 19, and 23, וַיִּשְׁחָט וַיִּקַּח מֹשֶׁה אֶת־הַדָּם (*Angl.* " and he slew it, and Moses took the blood"), as signifying that Moses slaughtered the animals himself. I will not lay any stress upon the fact that the Masoretic accentuation has guarded against this misinterpretation, but I do upon the fact that, according to the inviolable rules of grammar, the words must in that case read thus : וַיִּשְׁחָט מֹשֶׁה וַיִּקַּח אֶת־הַדָּם. In the order of words as we have them, on the other hand, a different subject from Moses must be given to וַיִּשְׁחָט (" he slew it"); and *Luther* gave it the correct interpretation when he rendered it as an impersonal verb, " they slew it" (*man schlachtete es*).

A ram was also selected, for the *peace-offering* or true *consecration-offering*. And here, again, the course adopted both with the blood (vers. 23, 24, 30) and the flesh (vers. 25–29, 31, 32) presents many points of peculiarity and divergence. After the ram had been killed, Moses took some of its blood and smeared it upon the tip of the right ear, the thumb of the right hand, and the great toe of the right foot, first of Aaron and afterwards of his sons. He then sprinkled the (rest of the) blood round about upon the altar of burnt-offering, and took the portions of fat and the right leg of the slaughtered ram, and one piece of each of the different kinds of cake, which had been offered along with the ram ; and having placed all this upon the hands of Aaron and his sons (probably one after another), he waved it as a wave-offering before Jehovah. After this he took it from their hands and burned it upon the altar. He next took the breast of the ram, which was his own portion, and waved it himself ; after which he took of the holy anointing oil and the blood upon the altar, and sprinkled the persons to be initiated, and also their clothes.[1] The remainder of the

---

[1] It is quite true that Ex. xxix. 21 mentions this sprinkling with blood and oil, *before* the directions as to the waving and burning of the altar-portions ; but that is, in all probability, simply for the purpose of placing together all that

flesh, together with the rest of the cake, was then appropriated to the sacrificial meal in the way described in connection with the praise-offerings. In this meal no one but the persons to be initiated took any part.

§ 169. The smearing of the three members of the body mentioned, *with the blood* of the consecration-offering, is unanimously regarded by commentators as a consecration of such members of the body as would be more especially called into exercise by the duties of the priestly vocation. The *ear* was to be consecrated to listen to the command and will of God, as the rule of their priestly walk and conduct; the *hand* and the *foot*, to observe the walk and conduct prescribed. There was no necessity to wet the whole ear, the whole hand, and the whole foot with blood, since the lap of the ear, the thumb, and the great toe represented the whole, of which they were the first and principal parts; whilst the *right* side was selected on account of its superiority to the left.

Simple and satisfactory as this explanation may appear, it is, for all that, not without its difficulties. For it cannot fail to strike us as a most significant fact, that in both accounts (Ex. xxix. 20 and Lev. viii. 24) the smearing of the ear, the hand, and the foot is represented as *preceding* the sprinkling of the altar with the blood, which was the real act of atonement. According to the analogy in other instances (*e.g.*, Ex. xxiv. 8), and the very nature of the case, we should expect to find just the reverse, since it was upon the altar of God that the blood received the divine and saving power which imparted to it all its fitness to be used as consecration blood. We should get rid of the difficulty most easily, if we were at liberty to assume that there is a *hysteron-proteron* in the biblical narrative, and that the smearing of the ear, the hand, and the foot were mentioned first, simply as being the *leading feature* in the consecration, whilst the sprinkling of the altar which preceded it in order of time was mentioned afterwards to give completeness to the account. But the *Vav consecutive*, וַיִּזְרֹק in Lev. viii. 24, and וְזָרַקְתָּ in Ex. xxix. 30, seem hardly to allow of any such solution; and it is rendered still more inadmissible by the fact, that in Lev. viii. 30 and Ex. xxix. 21 a second application of the blood to the persons to be initiated is mentioned, of which it is as expressly stated in the text, that it occurred *after* the sprinkling of

was done with the blood, before describing what was done with the flesh; whereas in Lev. viii. the order of succession is given according to the actual occurrence.

the altar, as it seems to be implied with reference to the other, that it was performed *before* the sprinkling.

Commentators have thought far too lightly of this difficulty. Thus, for example, *Bähr* (ii. 424), *Hofmann* (p. 285), and *Knobel* (p. 425) evade it; *Oehler* calls attention to it, but contributes nothing towards an explanation ; *Keil* alone has attempted this. " If then," he says, " those organs which would be actively employed in the service performed by the priests, were here brought into *rapport* with the sacrificial blood and endued with its power, the same organs were brought, *in* and *with* the blood sprinkled on the altar, within the sphere of that divine *vis vitæ*, which was in operation at the altar, and being pervaded by this, were sanctified and consecrated to the true and willing service of the Lord." But, on the one hand, the blood, even according to *Keil's* own view, had no power in itself, *i.e.*, before coming into contact with the altar, so as to be able to endue the organs to which it was applied with saving power ; on the contrary, that power was first communicated to it in consequence of its being placed upon the altar. And on the other hand, the idea that " *in* and *with* the blood," a portion of which had been smeared upon the ear, the hand, and the foot of the persons to be initiated, these very organs were themselves " brought within the sphere of the divine powers of life that were in operation at the altar," has too little to commend it, for it to be possible to yield an unconditional assent. And it seems to me, that the idea of a *rapport* being instituted between these leading organs of the priestly duties and the blood intended for the altar, which *Keil* is right in enunciating, may be held most firmly without supposing that the power which it could only acquire at the altar was already immanent in the blood, and without introducing the singular notion of an imaginary transposition of the members themselves to the altar in connection with the blood. It is far better to regard the vital powers acquired by the blood upon the altar, as working back upon that portion which had previously been removed and applied to the persons about to be initiated, by virtue of the unity and indivisibility of the soul which is in the blood. But even then the real problem remains unsolved, viz., why was not the application of the blood to the persons to be initiated deferred till *after* the sprinkling of the blood, and so much of the blood as was necessary for the purpose taken from the blood upon the altar, which would certainly have been simpler and more natural, and was perfectly practicable, as Lev. viii. 30 (Ex. xxix. 21) clearly proves ?

I confess that I cannot find any satisfactory answer to this question. At the same time, I have thought of the possibility of another view, to which I am led by an analogy in the course pursued with the flesh of this sacrifice. For instance, Moses took those portions of the fat and flesh which were intended to be burned upon the altar, laid them upon the hands of those who were about to be consecrated, and waved them before the Lord. If, as will be shown in § 170, this is to be interpreted as an investiture of the priests to be consecrated with the right of performing this part of the altar service, which henceforth belonged exclusively to them ; it might be conjectured that it was much the same with the application of the blood, which also preceded the sprinkling of the altar, viz., that the function of dealing with the blood at the altar service was thereby conferred upon the persons to be initiated, as a right belonging to them alone. With this explanation, the chief difficulty would undoubtedly be removed. Still, it must be admitted, that investiture with the right of sprinkling the blood might have been expressed more suitably in a different way, and that the reason why the ear and the foot were included is especially incomprehensible. And though unquestionably not the first application of the blood but the second is expressly designated a קִדּוּשׁ in Lev. viii. 30 and Ex. xxix. 21, yet looking at the analogous rite of consecration in the case of the restored leper (Lev. xiv. 17, 25), it is impossible to deny that even the first application possessed the character of consecration.

§ 170. There were many peculiarities also in the course adopted with the *flesh*. In the case of the ordinary peace-offerings, the heave-leg and a piece of *every kind of the cake* provided for the sacrificial meal (§ 155) fell to the lot of the priest who had attended to the sprinkling of the blood and the burning upon the altar ; whilst the wave-breast was assigned to the whole of the priests who were engaged in active service at the time. Here, on the contrary, the heave-leg and the selections of cake were included in the portions burned upon the altar ; and the wave-breast was assigned to Moses. " For the same reason," says *Hofmann*, p. 284, "for which Moses did not eat the flesh of the sin-offering (§ 167), the heave-shoulder also was not allotted to him." Moses had neither priestly office nor priestly character ; and if, notwithstanding this, he discharged the priestly functions in connection with the sacrifice, it was in consequence of a special commission from God, which applied to this case alone. For the same reason, he did not receive those portions of the sacrifice which specially belonged to the priests. At the same time, his labour was not to be left without reward, and this he received in the wave-breast. Now, if the conclusion to which we came before be correct (§ 138), viz., that the double portion assigned to the priests in the form of the wave-breast and heave-leg had respect to their double relation on the one hand as the servants of Jehovah, and on the other as mediators of the nation, and that the heave-leg had special reference to the latter, and the wave-breast to the former; it is easy enough to explain why the wave-breast was assigned to Moses on this occasion as the reward of his labour, and not the heave-leg, seeing that in the act of consecration he officiated purely under an extraordinary commission from God. On the very same ground on which none but the persons to be initiated were allowed to take part in the peace-offering (§ 172), the heave-leg, being the ἐκλογή of the *flesh* of the sacrificial meal (§ 138), could not be eaten by the non-priestly administrator (Moses). But if it could neither be used in the sacrificial meal, nor eaten by Moses, it necessarily fell under the category of the " bread of Jehovah," for which the whole of the sacrificial animal was offered, and as such was burned upon the altar along with the fat.

But, first of all, Moses placed so much of this offering as was to be burned upon the altar upon the hands of Aaron and his sons, and waved it before the Lord. This act was designated a filling, מִלְאִים; and the animal received the name of the *ram of filling*, אֵיל מִלְאִים, Lev. viii. 22, 28. This does not mean, as I myself formerly agreed with *Bähr* in maintaining, a present made by Jehovah to the priests about to be consecrated ; for, as *Keil* properly observes, " the expression מִלֵּא יָד לַיהוָה does not signify to offer presents to Jehovah, but to provide something to offer to Jehovah (1 Chron. xxix. 5; 2 Chron. xxix. 31; Ex. xxxii. 29). Hence, when Moses placed those portions which were to be offered to God in the hands of the priests, and then offered them symbolically to God before they were burned upon the altar, the intention must have been to deliver to them the sacrifices which they were henceforth to offer to the Lord, as a symbolical investiture with the gifts which they would be required as priests to offer to the Lord. It indicated the fact that from that time forward the right and the duty of officiating at the altar, and superintending the burning of the sacrifices, would belong to them alone." But when *Keil* adds, " they were to be invested, however, not merely with what they were to burn to the Lord, but also with what they were to receive for their service," *Hofmann* has pointed out the error involved in this. " It was not *merely* those portions," he says, "nor *all* those portions which afterwards fell to the lot of the priests, that Moses laid upon their hands, though this ought to have been the case, if the transfer to them of certain selections from the sacrifice had been the point really signified." *Only* so much of the sacrifice as was to be burnt upon the altar, and the *whole* of that, was placed in their hands; and thus the reference of the filling of their hands to the burning upon the altar was placed beyond all possible doubt. But *Keil*, on the other hand, has properly condemned the still more erroneous view expressed by *Hofmann*, that "the offering made by Moses for Aaron terminated with an offering by Aaron himself ;" for the whole terminated, not by Aaron attending to the burning upon the altar, but by Moses doing so (as he had previously performed the sprinkling of the blood). Moreover, "the true consecration of Aaron," in its complete and finished form, did not "precede the presentation of this offering ;" for the smearing of the ear, hand, and foot of the persons to be initiated, still needed to be followed by the sprinkling of their persons and clothes before the act of consecration was complete (Lev. viii. 30).

§ 171. The *sprinkling of their persons and clothes* was performed with blood from the altar, *and* holy oil. That the two were mixed together for the purpose of the sprinkling, as *Hofmann, Keil, Knobel, Oehler,* and others assume, is not expressly stated ; and the apparent analogy in the application of blood and oil to the cured leper, when the two were used separately, might be adduced in support of the opposite opinion (*vid.* Lev. xiv. 15 sqq., 25 sqq.). But the opinion mentioned appears to me the correct one, for the simple reason that the two are not said to have been used separately here as in Lev. xiv., and also because the oil is mentioned *before* the blood in Lev. viii. 30, whereas in Ex. xxix. 21 the blood stands before the oil, which could not be a matter of indifference unless they had been mixed together.

It may at once be granted that the sprinkling had reference "more particularly to the clothes," which were to be worn on all priestly occasions, and on them alone ;—provided only the necessary emphasis be laid upon the fact, that the clothes were sprinkled and consecrated *upon* and *with* the persons. The clothes represented the office filled by the person. The person and the clothes together represented the priest; therefore the consecration was performed upon both together. The atoning efficacy of the blood which had been attested upon the altar, was sufficient for the *covenant* consecration of the people : there was no necessity for any anointing with oil, because no special office was to be, or could be committed to the people generally. But in the *official* consecration of the priests, just because it had reference to the installation in a particular office, it was necessary that the sanctifying power of the anointing oil should be added to the atoning efficacy of the blood.

A peculiar, but certainly an incorrect explanation, has been given by *Keil* (i. 265) to this mixing of the blood with anointing oil. " The blood taken from the altar," he says, " shadowed forth the *soul* united to God by reconciliation ; the holy anointing oil was the symbol of the *Spirit* of God, the essential principle of all spiritual life in the kingdom of God. Consequently, by means of this sprinkling, the *soul and spirit* of the priests were endowed with the heavenly powers of divine life." I will only just point out in passing, how here again the leading idea of *Keil's* sacrificial theory (§ 70), viz., that the sacrificial blood was a symbol of the soul of the sacrificer, is proved to be an erroneous one ; for as the anointing oil was not a symbol of the spirit of the man presenting the sacrifice, but a representative of the sanctifying Spirit of God, so the blood could not be a type of the soul of the sacrificer, but could only represent the atoning power of another soul interposing for him with its purity, innocence, and holiness. And how marvellous an idea it would be, that the soul of the sacrificer should be " endowed" with itself ! It is equally wrong to separate the blood and the oil in such a way as to regard the former as a type of the soul of the animal operating upon the soul of the sacrificer, and the latter as a symbol of the Spirit of God operating upon the spirit of the sacrificer ; wrong, because the Hebrew psychology knows nothing of any such distinction between the soul and spirit of a man (§ 32, 23), and still more because the clothes which were also to be sprinked with blood and oil could not be separately endowed in this way according to soul and spirit (since there was neither soul nor spirit dwelling in them), but were only to be consecrated in a general manner as vehicles and *media* of the grace peculiar to the office.

§ 172. In the *sacrificial meal* there were only two distinctive peculiarities : one, that the leavened loaves prescribed in Lev. vii. 13 (cf. § 155) were omitted from the Corban of cakes connected with the sacrifice ; the other, that the right to join in the meal was restricted to the persons to be initiated to the exclusion of every one else, even of the members of their own families (Ex. xxix. 32). This restriction, however, may be very easily explained from the fact, that it was the sacrificial meal connected with a *consecration-offering*, which represented such a fellowship of the sacrificer with Jehovah, as precluded participation on the part of any one who had not been consecrated. And even the omission of leavened bread from the Corban of cake to be used at the meal, may be just as easily explained from the character of the meal, as the removal of all leavened bread from the paschal supper (§ 186).

The whole ceremony as thus described was repeated every day for seven successive days. This was expressly commanded with regard to the sin-offering (Ex. xxix. 36). In the case of the filling-offering, indeed, the filling of the hands is all that is expressly mentioned as having to be repeated for seven days (Ex. xxix. 35 ; Lev. viii. 33), but this necessarily presupposes a fresh presentation of the filling-offering ; and since the daily anointing of the altar is mentioned at any rate in Ex. xxix. 36, 37, the daily anointing of the persons to be initiated is also to be taken for granted as self-evident, together with their previous washing and investiture. During the seven days of consecration, the persons to be initiated were not to leave the fore-court either day or night (Lev. viii. 33). But on the *eighth* day the persons initiated entered upon the independent discharge of their priestly functions by offering for themselves a calf for a sin-offering, and a ram for a burnt-offering ; and for the people a goat for a sin-offering, a sheep for a burnt-offering, and a bullock and ram for a peace-offering (Lev. ix.).

There can be no doubt, according to Ex. xxix. 29, 30, and Lev. vi. 15, that the ceremony of consecration had to be repeated in the case of every new high priest, probably by representatives of the entire priesthood (say by the leaders of the different orders of priests). And the same remark applies in all probability, according to Lev. vi. 13, to the entrance of all the priests upon the duties of their office.

C. CONSECRATION OF THE LEVITES

§ 173. The consecration of the Levites, which took place at a later period, just before the departure from Sinai, was much more simple than that of the priests (*vid.* Num. viii. 5–22). The verb employed (טִהַר) distinguishes it from the act of priestly consecration (קִדֵּשׁ), showing that it was of a subordinate character, and wanting in all the features which constituted the specific peculiarities of the latter.

It commenced with the sprinkling of the persons to be initiated with water of purifying (מֵי חַטָּאת), the removal of all the hair upon their body, and the washing of their clothes. As they had no official costume, since they filled no particular office, but were merely servants and attendants, their ordinary clothes, at any rate, were to be cleansed and renewed. The shaving off of the hair, which was a kind of natural clothing, was also subservient to the same idea. The water of purifying was unquestionably no ordinary water, but water prepared expressly for this object; at the same time it was certainly not identical with the water of separation (מֵי נִדָּה, Num. xix. 9, cf. § 217), which was prepared from the ashes of the red cow and other ingredients, but was possibly just the same as the water prepared with cedar-wood, coccus, and hyssop for the sprinkling of men and houses that had been infected with leprosy (Lev. xiv. 5 sqq., 49 sqq.; cf. § 224).

After this triple form of purification, the substitution of the Levites for the first-born of all the people took place (§ 6). The Levites were brought before the door of the tabernacle, and the congregation—i.e., the elders as its representatives—laid hands upon their heads, to set them apart for the service of the sanctuary, as representatives of the whole congregation, in the place of the first-born out of all the tribes, upon whom the obligation originally devolved; whereupon the priests waved them before Jehovah, that is to say, in all probability, led them to the door of the tabernacle and back again to the altar of burnt-offering, to exhibit them as offered to the Lord by the congregation for the service of the sanctuary, and handed over by Him to the priests. In conclusion, two bullocks were sacrificed that had been presented by the Levites, one as a sin-offering, and the other as a burnt-offering.

CHAPTER II

ADAPTATION OF THE SACRIFICIAL WORSHIP TO SPECIAL PERIODS AND FEASTS

A. MOSAIC IDEA OF A FEAST

§ 174. The times of the Mosaic feasts are called מוֹעֲדִים and חַגִּים. The former (from יָעַד, to determine, to fix) served to characterize them as definite, established points or periods of time, connected with the natural, social, and religious life. In its more frequent allusion to the religious life, this expression was applied indiscriminately to every period of time that was specially marked by a more elaborate religious service, whether the object or occasion of the festival was joy and thanksgiving, or penitence and mourning, historical commemoration, or typical anticipation. The name חַג, on the contrary (from חגג, to wheel round, to dance, to rejoice), was much more restricted, and according to its etymological signification was applicable to *joyous* festivals alone (Deut. xvi. 11, 14).

The peculiar character of the Mosaic festivals was expressed *formally* in their being regulated as much as possible by the number seven, as the stamp of the covenant of God with Israel (seven being compounded of 3, the divine number, and 4, the world number), and *materially* by their being separated from the labours, toils, and cares of everyday life for the sanctification and consecration of the whole man to purposes of religion and the worship of God. The common starting point for the entire legislation with regard to the feasts, was the seventh day, or closing day of the week (שְׁבוּעַ), which was called for that reason the *Sabbath* (שַׁבָּת) κατ᾽ ἐξοχήν, and as such infolded prototypically within itself the fundamental idea of every festal celebration. In the epithet קֹדֶשׁ שַׁבַּת שַׁבָּתוֹן לַיהֹוָה (Ex. xxxv. 2), the negative side is expressed by שַׁבַּת שַׁבָּתוֹן, the positive by לַיהוָה. שַׁבָּת is a concrete form of intensification (= the rester); שַׁבָּתוֹן is an abstract (= rest). The combination of the two words expressed the strongest obligation to maintain a strict and absolute rest. The positive and special intention of the שַׁבָּת, which is expressed in the ליהוה, was the holy assembly (מִקְרָא קֹדֶשׁ, holy convocation, Lev. xxiii. 2), of which no precise account is to be found in the law, but which cannot be regarded in any other light than as a meeting of those members of the community who were near the sanctuary, for the sake of edification by means of sacrifice and prayer (compare the patriarchal expression, "to call upon the name of Jehovah"). No doubt this included the blessing of the people by the priest in the words prescribed in Num. vi. 24–26.

The further development of the idea of a feast, which sprang from the Sabbath-day, was carried out in three ways. The first was by the transference of rest (*mutatis mutandis*) from every seventh day to every seventh year, or the so-called *sabbatical year*, and from that still further to the *jubilee year*, which occurred every *seven times seven years*. The fundamental idea of the שַׁבָּת, as that which was to be observed, remained the same; the only change was in the subject for which it was a שַׁבָּת. In the *Sabbath of days* it was man and beast that were to rest after six periods of labour, and keep sabbath during the seventh. In the *Sabbath of years* it was the field that rested; for what a period of day and night is to man and beast, that a whole year with its summer and winter is to the field. In the *Sabbath of weeks of years* it was the altered condition of property, that had been occasioned by the commercial activity of the past jubilee period, which once more returned from a state of fluctuation to one of rest, *i.e.*, from the strange holder to its original possessor.

But between the changes of days and years there was an intermediate period, viz., the *changes of the moon.* This was not suitable, however, for a uniform organic incorporation in the system of sabbatic periods,—both because no special and peculiar subject for rest could be assigned it, and also because the number of months in the year was twelve and not seven. At the same time, so far as it was possible, the change of the moon was brought within the range of the sabbatical idea, viz., by a special festal prominence given to the seventh new moon of every year, and by the transference of festal ideas derived from other sources to the sphere of this particular month.

The idea of the Sabbath originated in the history of the creation. As God created the world, and all that it contained, in six days, so man and his beasts of burden were to rest after six days of work, and his field was to rest the seventh year after six years of labour. The observance of the Sabbath, therefore, was a confession of the God who by His almighty word created the heaven and the earth in six days out of nothing (Ex. xx. 8–11). And the acknowledgment of that God was the distinguishing characteristic of the religion of Israel; for all other religions either identify God and the world, or place eternal matter by the side of the eternal God. Whoever kept the Sabbath, therefore, declared by so doing that the God of Israel was the only true God, and acknowledged Him in word and deed as his own God. Whoever did not keep the Sabbath holy, despised and denied the God of Israel. Hence the Sabbath was a covenant-sign for Israel (Ex. xxxi. 12–17) on the side of nature, as circumcision was on the side of salvation. And whoever broke the Sabbath, though a member of the covenant, cut himself off from the covenant of God, and was liable to be put to death as a traitor to the theocracy.

These two aspects exhaust the meaning and validity of the

Sabbath and the sabbatical periods, as expressly described in the law. A further allusion has been found in Deut. v. 15, viz., to the exodus from Egypt. But this can neither be established as a fact, nor gathered from the words of the passage referred to; for what they enforce by a reference to the bondage of the Israelites in Egypt, is not the obligation to keep the Sabbath holy, but the right of man-servant and maid-servant to share in the Sabbath rest. Again, the allusion to the fall, which *Keil* follows *Hengstenberg* in adducing, is nowhere expressly stated. A latent existence no doubt it had, in the *relief* afforded from all the labour and toil of everyday life, which had their origin in the fall (Gen. iii. 17–19). And from this point of view, the earthly Sabbath reflected the Sabbath of God after the creation was finished,—a Sabbath in which man, beast, and field participated, in the fulness of their native glory and blessedness before the fall. And as every re-pristination of the lost blessings of creation, however transient, is at the same time a typical anticipation of their future restoration, the blessedness of the Sabbath rest, enjoyed by man, beast, and field, was a typical pledge and prophecy of the rest of the last time (Heb. iv. 9).

§ 175. But whilst in the observance of the Sabbath and the sabbatical times the acknowledgment of Jehovah on that side, on which He had revealed Himself as Creator of the heavens and the earth, with all that they contained, found an expression in accordance with the covenant; on the other hand, the acknowledgment of Jehovah as that God who had revealed and still continued to reveal Himself in the choice, guidance, protection, and preservation of Israel, also needed an embodiment, and found it in the three yearly feasts, *Easter, Pentecost,* and the *feast of Tabernacles,* in which the two ideas were united, on the one hand, of the redemption of Israel out of Egypt, and on the other hand, of the provision made for it in the Holy Land of everything required for its subsistence. They were memorial days of the historical facts by which the deliverance of Israel was effected, and also, in their connection with the time of harvest, thanksgiving festivals for the harvest blessings of the Holy Land. These three feasts were all, from their nature, festivals of rejoicing, and were called so (חַגִּים). But though moving in a different sphere from the sabbatical feasts, they were closely related to them both in form and substance. Preservation is only a continuance of creation. Hence they also bear on every side the stamp of the number seven. The two most important of these feasts—Easter and the feast of Tabernacles—commenced on the 15th of the first and seventh months respectively, that is to say, 2 × 7 days from the commencement of the month. And Pentecost was kept on the fiftieth day from the commencement of the Easter feast, *i.e.*, at the end of seven times seven days. But as the Hebrews had only lunar months, the 15th day of the month was the time of full moon. And this represented the culminating height and fulness of time. As the full moon with its soft light clothes the earth in a bright and joyous festal garment, so the feast in commemoration of the ways of God in nature and history spread a festal splendour over the earthly life, and made the feast-time a חַג, a bright and cheerful time of joy. It is true, this allusion is not mentioned in connection with the feast of Pentecost; but only because there were purely outward reasons why it could not be exhibited. And whereas we find the feast of Pentecost limited to one day, whilst Easter and the feast of Tabernacles occupied seven; this is to be explained on the simple ground, that in the case of those last named the historical and harvest feasts coincided, and that the feast of Pentecost was purely a harvest feast, and therefore was obliged to be satisfied with one day, which bore however a sabbatical character. But at the feasts of Easter and Tabernacles, all the seven days did not possess a sabbatical character with abstinence from work and holy meetings, but only the first, and (in the case of Easter) the seventh.

The common characteristic in the celebration of these three festivals was the obligation mentioned in Ex. xxiii. 17, xxxiv. 23, etc., to appear personally at the sanctuary before Jehovah, which was binding upon every adult male Israelite. The intention of these festal gatherings three times a year was not primarily a politico-national one (though even this is not to be excluded, on account of the theocratical character of the Israelitish commonwealth), but first and chiefly a religious one. Israel was to be brought thereby three times a year to the renewed consciousness that it belonged to the sanctuary, to be reminded of its covenant and feudal obligations towards Jehovah, the God and King of the land, to appear before Him and do homage to Him, and present its tribute as vassal in the first-fruits and tenths of its harvest-produce.

In the third place, the *atoning* and *sanctifying* power, exerted by the grace of God on behalf of His people, also needed a concrete expression in some one special feast-time; and this took place on the *great day of atonement*, which was observed on the 10th day

of the seventh month. It is true, the sacrificial atonement formed
the foundation of all the feasts—in fact, of all the worship, even
that which was performed daily at the tabernacle, viz., in the
sprinkling of the blood of the burnt-offering which was to be
offered every morning and evening, and was doubled every Sabbath ; and at all the new moons, as well as the three festal gatherings of the year, it was intensified in a still greater measure by
the multiplication of the burnt-offerings, and the addition of a sin-
offering for the whole congregation. But for all that, just because
expiation was the basis of all worship, the fundamental condition
of all fellowship with God, it also required a distinct, culminating
manifestation, or a festal day set apart exclusively for that purpose ;
and this was precisely the object and meaning of the yearly day of
atonement, which had also a sabbatical character on account of this
its great importance.

Again, the number of the yearly festivals in which work was
suspended and a holy convocation took place, was *seven ;* for in
addition to those already named (two at Easter, one at Pentecost,
one at the feast of Tabernacles, and one at the feast of Atonement) there were two others, one on the day of the new moon of
the seventh month, and one on the 22d day of the seventh month,
immediately after the expiration of the seven days of the feast of
the Tabernacles, the so-called עֲצֶרֶת, the concluding feast of the
whole festal period of the entire year (§ 196).

§ 176. This division of the feasts into three classes, which is
not only simple and natural, but clearly contained in the law itself,
has been set aside by *Ewald* for a classification which is most arti-
ficial and forced, and as unnatural as it is opposed to the clearest
data of the Scriptures. Yet even *Keil* has been sufficiently charmed
by its deceptive appearance of scientific accuracy to be led away
by it. According to his idea, the great day of atonement, together
with the three harvest and historical feasts, belonged to one common class, which " included all the yearly feasts that were sacred
to the memory of the mighty works performed by the Lord for the
founding, preserving, and inspiriting of His nation " (*Keil*, p. 354).
These annual feasts resolved themselves into two cycles, viz., that
of the Easter feast and that of the feast of Tabernacles, each of
them with a preliminary and a supplementary festival. In the
Easter cycle, the one day of the Passover formed the preliminary,
the seven days of unleavened bread the main festival, and the one
day of Pentecost the supplement. So again, in the autumn cycle,

the day of atonement was the preliminary, the seven days' feast of Tabernacles the main festival, and the Azereth the supplement.

But it can easily be shown that this arrangement breaks down on all hands. The first of these cycles, according to *Keil*, p. 354, had reference to the elevation of Israel, and its preservation as the people of God; the second, on the other hand, had for its object the continuance of Israel in the full enjoyment of the blessings of divine grace. But how inapt is this distinction and antithesis! The character of a harvest feast was common to them both, and both, therefore, had reference to the preservation of the people of God, and their enjoyment of the blessings of divine grace; and so also the remembrance of the saving deeds and miraculous guidance of God, by which the people had been raised into a nation of God, was common to them both.

In opposition to the view which prevailed till the time of *Ewald*, *Keil* argues as follows (p. 359) : "In the fundamental laws of the Pentateuch only three annual festivals, the feasts of *Mazzoth*, Harvest, and Assembly, are mentioned along with the Sabbath, as חַגִּים on which Israel was to appear before the Lord (Ex. xxiii. 12–17, xxxiv. 21–23) ; and the simple fact that neither the Passover nor the day of atonement is mentioned here, shows that however important they may have been in themselves, these two feasts were subordinate to the other three." But it seems to me that these very passages confirm the correctness of the opinion they are adduced to overthrow. In the first place, it is evident that they contain no allusion to *two* cycles of yearly feasts; in the second place, that they put the feast of Pentecost side by side with the feasts of *Mazzoth* and Tabernacles, as of equal rank and equal independence ; and in the third place, that the feast of Atonement, which is not mentioned, must possess a different character, and therefore belong to a different class. And it is surely a most hasty conclusion for *Keil* to draw, that because neither the Passover nor the feast of Atonement is mentioned in these passages, therefore these two feasts must have been subordinate to the other three. For the feast of Passover is not mentioned, simply because it was just as much identified with the feast of *Mazzoth*, as the feast of Booths (which is also not mentioned) with the feast of Assembly, and the feast of Weeks (which is not mentioned) with the feast of Harvest ; and the feast of Atonement is not mentioned, because it was not one of *those* festivals at which all Israel was to appear before the Lord. But even leaving this out of the question, the conclusion

itself, that " the Passover and the feast of Atonement were subordinate to the other *three*," furnishes sufficient evidence of the incorrectness of his own view and the correctness of the one which
he rejects. For in that case the feast of Pentecost must have belonged to the *principal* feast as much as the feasts of *Mazzoth* and
Assembly, and therefore cannot have been subordinate to the feast
of *Mazzoth*, but must have been co-ordinate with it.

    Keil adds still further : " Lastly, another argument against the
triple division is to be found in the fact, that the law has only *two*
different terms for the feasts, viz., מוֹעֲדִים and חַגִּים, of which the
former is applied to all the feast-times, whilst the latter is restricted
to the feasts of *Mazzoth*, of Weeks, and of Tabernacles." But here,
too, *Keil's* words seem to me to be adapted rather to refute what
they are meant to prove, and to establish what they are meant to
refute. For, according to his own account, the feast of Weeks, or
Pentecost, was called חג, as well as the feasts of Easter and Tabernacles. Is it not thereby made co-ordinate with them, especially
with the Easter festival, and that all the more decidedly, because
these three alone are so designated ? And how can any one adduce,
as a proof that there can have been only two and not three kinds
of feasts, the fact that only two epithets are ever applied to them,
when one of these epithets is common to *all* the feasts of these supposed two classes, and the other is restricted to one portion of the
second class ? It ought to be clear enough that such an argument
could only be a valid one if one of the two names were applied to all
the feasts of the first class, and to them exclusively, and the other
as generally and exclusively to all the feasts of the second class.

    But the distorted character of this arrangement appears still
more decidedly if we look separately at each of the two festal
cycles, which are said to form together the second class. But we
shall find a more suitable place for this as we proceed. Cf. § 181,
190, 196, 197.

B. DAILY, WEEKLY, AND MONTHLY SERVICE

    § 177. The public worship of God, however, the chief and
central point of which was always sacrifice, was not restricted to
the actual feasts. Every day, as God brought it round, demanded
the performance of this covenant duty ; but the celebration of the
feasts involved a more elaborate performance, regulated according
to the diversities in the character of the festal seasons.

The DAILY SERVICE consisted, so far as it was conducted in the fore-court, of the offering of a yearling lamb every morning and evening as a burnt-offering, along with the regular meat- and drink-offerings (§ 150, note; Ex. xxix. 38–42; Lev. vi. 9–12; Num. xxviii. 3–8); so that the morning sacrifice was burning the whole day, and the evening sacrifice the whole night, as an offering made by fire for a sweet-smelling savour to Jehovah. This daily burnt-offering was called the continual, standing sacrifice, עֹלַת הַתָּמִיד (Ex. xxix. 42; Num. xxviii. 6, 10, 15, 23, 24), and at a later period הַתָּמִיד alone (Dan. viii. 11, 12, 13, xi. 31). As this sacrifice was offered for the whole congregation, some provision must have been made for the performance by deputy of the laying on of hands and slaughtering, which ought to have been performed by the offerer himself. According to the early rabbinical tradition, the congregation chose so-called "standing men," אַנְשֵׁי מַעֲמָד, for that purpose. Attached to this sacrifice, which was offered for the congregation, was first of all the *Minchah* of the high priest, prescribed in Lev. vi. 20 sqq., which will come under review in the next section. And if private individuals had offerings of any kind to present on their own account, they were not presented till after the ordinary morning sacrifice. Even on the feast days, when the number of sacrifices offered for the congregation was increased in number and elevated in kind, the daily burnt-offering was not allowed to be omitted, but still formed the basis of the true festal sacrifices.

Even in the *Holy Place* daily service had to be regularly performed. Every morning fresh incense had to be kindled upon the altar of incense, and again every evening when the lamps of the seven-branched candlestick were lighted (Ex. xxx. 7, 8, cf. § 160, 161). This was the duty of the high priest, though according to later custom an ordinary priest might, and in fact generally did, officiate as his substitute.

§ 178. The *Minchah of the high priest* just referred to, which had to be offered every day, needs special investigation, as frequently it is either overlooked or its existence positively denied.

In Lev. vi. 20, for example, after the law of the daily burnt-offering (vi. 8–13) and the law of the meat-offering arising from it (vi. 14–18), it is stated that "this is the *Corban* of Aaron and his sons, which they shall offer unto Jehovah בְּיוֹם הִמָּשַׁח אֹתוֹ; the tenth part of an ephah of white flour as a continual *Minchah* (מִנְחָה תָּמִיד), half of it in the morning, and half thereof at night." The preparation of this Minchah is then still further described: the meal is to be mixed with oil, baked upon the *Machabath*, and then broken in pieces (פִּתִּים) before being offered (just as in Lev. ii. 5, 6, cf. § 140). Then follows the command that Aaron's successors are to do the same after their anointing. And in conclusion, it is designated a חָק־עוֹלָם, and the law is added that this *Minchah* (like every priestly *Minchah*) is to be "wholly burnt."

In the whole line of Jewish tradition these directions are understood as denoting that the existing high priest was to offer a *Minchah* of this kind for himself in connection with the daily burnt-offering of the people, for the first time immediately after the completion of his anointing or consecration, and twice a day from that time forwards. Later custom, on the other hand, allowed an inferior priest to act as his representative. It is in this sense, no doubt, that the expression in the Book of Wisdom (c. xlv. 14), θυσίαι αὐτοῦ ὁλοκαρποθήσονται καθ᾽ ἡμέραν ἐνδελεχῶς δίς, is to be understood; for *Keil's* solution, that the daily morning and evening *Olah* is intended, is overthrown by the term αὐτοῦ. *Josephus* (Ant. iii. 10, 7) speaks of the custom in very distinct and unmistakeable terms: "The (high) priest," he says, "offered out of his own resources, and that twice a day, meal of the weight of an *assarius*, kneaded with oil, baked, and roasted; one half he committed to the fire in the morning, and the other half in the evening. This view has been thoroughly defended by *Lundius* (*jüdische Heiligth.* iii. 9, § 17), and more recently by *Thalhofer* (p. 139 sqq.) and *Delitzsch* (pp. 315–6), and is accepted as the correct one by *Baumgarten, Oehler,* and others. On the other hand, it is disputed by *Keil*, who agrees with *Kliefoth* and *Knobel* in regarding the obligation to offer the *Minchah* in question as restricted to the consecration of the priests.

But this view is opposed first of all to the designation of this meat-offering as a "continual *Minchah*," which is analogous to the "continual sacrifice" and the "continual bread" (*i.e.*, the shewbread, Num. iv. 7), and must therefore be understood in the same way (Lev. vi. 9, 13). For *Keil's* idea, that the term "continual" relates to a continual offering during the time of anointing, which lasted seven days, is surely as inadmissible as *Knobel's*, that it denoted that every fresh high priest was to present it on his entrance upon office.

There is much more plausibility in *Keil's* appeal to the fact, that the expression בְּיוֹם הִמָּשַׁח אֹתוֹ cannot mean "the day *after* his consecration." But in the first place, it must be observed that the

explanation which *Keil* declares to be the only correct one, viz.,
" on the day of consecration, *i.e.*, during the *seven* days of consecration," is at any rate untenable. On the other hand, such passages
as Gen. ii. 4, iii. 5; 2 Sam. xxi. 12; Is. xi. 16, furnish unquestionable proof of the admissibility of the pluperfect rendering of the
infinitive after בְּיוֹם; or if any doubt should still be felt, it is completely removed, both substantially and grammatically, by Lev. vii.
36, which speaks of the priests as participating in the altar-sacrifices, "which Jehovah commanded to be given them of the children
of Israel בְּיוֹם מָשְׁחוֹ אֹתָם, a statute for ever throughout their generations."

But this view is rendered absolutely necessary by the fact, that
Moses evidently did not offer the *Minchah* described in Lev. vi. 20
sqq. for Aaron and his sons, as *Knobel* maintains, but they offered
it for themselves; whereas if it had been offered *during* the consecration, they could not have officiated themselves, but Moses must
have officiated for them. That they did officiate is not only distinctly
expressed in the terms יַקְרִיבוּ (ver. 20) and יַעֲשֶׂה (ver. 22), but necessarily follows from the fact, that this Minchah had to be entirely
burnt because it was offered by priests (vers. 22, 23). If Moses
had officiated as priest, according to Lev. ii. 10, all that was left
after removing an *Azcarah* would have been assigned *to him*, like
the wave-breast of the filling-offering at the consecration (Lev. viii.
29). But since Aaron himself officiated, his priestly consecration
must have been finished, and the reference therefore can only be
to a presentation made *after* the seven days of consecration.

In *Keil's* opinion, indeed, Lev. ix. 1 sqq. is at variance with the
conclusion, that this *Minchah* was presented on the eighth day (the
first after the termination of the period of consecration). But if
the omission of any allusion to this *Minchah* in Lev. ix. is a proof
that it was not offered on the eighth day, the same rule must apply
to the daily incense-offering, which is also not mentioned in Lev.
ix., but which was certainly offered on that day. Even the offering of the "continual sacrifice" is not professedly described; allusion is simply made in ver. 17 ὡς ἐν παρόδῳ to the " burnt sacrifice
of the morning." The ordinary and everyday functions of the
priests were never intended to be described in Lev. ix., though
they were certainly not omitted on the day referred to, but only
the sacrificial rites by which that day was distinguished above all
that followed.

But this argument of *Keil's* soon turns against himself. If the *Minchah* prescribed in Lev. vi. 20 was an essential element in the seven days' ceremony, as *Keil* maintains, why is there not a single syllable about it either in Ex. xxix. or Lev. viii., where *ex professo* the ceremony of consecration is more fully and elaborately described?

On the other hand, we cannot adopt the argument drawn by *Lundius*, and recently again by *Thalhofer*, from Heb. vii. 27, in support of the traditional view. For when it is stated there that the High Priest of the New Testament "needeth not daily, like those of the Old Testament, to offer up sacrifice first for His own sins, and then for the people's," the reference cannot possibly be to this daily *Minchah* of the high priest, because none but bleeding sacrifices, and in fact only sin-offerings, were really "offered for sin." The solution offered by *Keil* and others is still less admissible, viz., that the writer of the Epistle to the Hebrews "had the daily morning and evening (burnt-) offering in his mind;" for this was not a sacrifice "for his own sins," and was not followed by a second sacrifice "for the sins of the people."[1] The words of Heb. vii. 27 unquestionably allow, on the contrary, of no other allusion than to the sacrifice offered by the high priest on the great day of atonement (Lev. xvi.). It is true this was offered "yearly" and not "daily" under the Old Testament. But this difficulty has been satisfactorily set aside by *Hofmann* thus: "Καθ᾽ ἡμέραν stands before ὥσπερ οἱ ἀρχιερεῖς. The comparison is not between what Christ would have had to do and what the high priests have to do every day, but between what the high priests have to do and what Christ would have had to do every day. He would have needed to do day by day what He has now done once for all, since the expiation required is constant and ever new" (p. 405). See *Delitzsch, Hebräer-brief*, p. 317.

That this daily Minchah of the high priest was to be offered in

---

[1] Moreover, *Keil* appears to have quite forgotten with what warmth he has written in other places against the idea that the burnt-offerings were also *expiatory*. He has spoken of this as one of the two fundamental errors of my former work. But if the author of the Epistle to the Hebrews had written what *Keil* attributes to him, he would evidently have fallen into a far deeper error than I have. For I have merely ascribed to the burnt-offering an atoning efficacy in relation to general sinfulness; whilst I have restricted the expiation of actual sins to the sin- and trespass-offerings alone. And here *Keil* himself informs us, that in the Epistle to the Hebrews the burnt-offering is actually designated "a sacrifice for sins." Will he be consistent enough to charge him also with a "fundamental error"?

connection with the " continual sacrifice," may be gathered with
certainty from Lev. vi. 20, where it is stated that one half was to
be presented in the morning and the other in the evening; but
whether it preceded or followed the daily burnt-offering, is left undecided in the law. According to the Jewish tradition, it followed
the burnt-offering so far, that it was placed between the true
Minchah of the burnt-offering and its drink-offering. This order
of succession would evidently be based upon the idea, that the previous burnt-offering expiation formed the basis of the Minchah of
the high priest, and that the drink-offering was common to both.
I regard this view as the correct one. If the daily burnt-offering
was offered for the whole congregation, it applied to the high priest
as well, who was the head of the congregation. But to the general
Minchah he had to add a special *Minchah* for himself,—a *Minchah*
of cake too, which represented a higher mode of preparing the corn,
and pointed to the fact that he, in whom the holiness of the whole
community culminated, had to unfold and preserve in the duties of
his calling a more exalted holiness than could be demanded from
the whole nation.

§ 179. The observance of the SABBATH-DAY consisted *negatively*
in abstinence from all the labours of the earthly calling, and *positively* in a sacred assembly, the doubling of the two daily burnt-
offerings (Num. xxviii. 9, 10), and the placing of fresh shew-bread
in the Holy Place (§ 159).

Whilst the sacrificial worship of the Sabbath was merely a
doubling of the daily worship, that of the NEW MOON'S DAY (רֹאשׁ
חֳדָשִׁים) formed a link between the ordinary worship and its festal
elaboration at the yearly feasts, inasmuch as there was offered in
connection with the " continual sacrifice " a festal offering of two
young oxen, a ram, and seven yearling lambs as a burnt-offering,
also a buck-goat as a sin-offering, for the whole congregation (Num.
xxviii. 11 sqq.). On the other hand, the characteristics of the ordinary Sabbath (abstinence from work, and a holy assembly [1]) were
wanting, though a festal character was communicated to these days
(Num. x. 10) by the fact, that at the offering of the burnt- and

---

[1] "At a later period, however, the new moon is frequently placed as a feast
by the side of the Sabbath (Isa. i. 13 ; Hos. ii. 13; Ezek. xlvi. 1), and as one on
which ordinary avocations were suspended (Amos viii. 5), the pious in Israel
went to the prophets for edification (2 Kings iv. 23), many families offered
yearly thank-offerings (1 Sam. xx. 6, 29), great banquets were spread at the
court of Saul (1 Sam. xx. 5, 24), and at a still later period the more devout
fasted."—*Keil*, p. 368.

(freewill) thank-offerings of this day the silver trumpets were blown "that they might be לְזִכָּרוֹן לִפְנֵי אֱלֹהִים."

But the festal character, which was not fully manifested in the worship of the ordinary new moons on account of the absence of any *sabbatical* service, broke through even these restrictions on the SEVENTH NEW MOON of the year. As every seventh day and every seventh year, so also the seventh month of every year was to participate in the sabbatical character of the septimal divisions of time. But as no subject could be found to which this month bore any special relation, and the rest therefore could not be extended more widely than that of the weekly Sabbath, viz., to cattle and men, it would have been out of character to make the whole month a month of rest, as the analogy of the daily and yearly Sabbaths required. Consequently a sabbatical character, combined with a holy convocation and abstinence from all work, was given to the first day of the month alone; and in order to give prominence to the sacredness of character belonging to the entire month, all the principal feasts that were not necessarily bound down to any particular seasons, were assigned to this month, viz., the great day of atonement, the feast of Tabernacles, and, as the last glimmer of the departing festal time, the *Azereth*; so that in this month a שַׁבַּת שַׁבָּתוֹן accompanied with a holy convocation occurred no less than four times. In addition to the daily burnt-offering and the sacrifices appointed for the ordinary new moons, a bullock, a ram, and seven yearling lambs were offered as a burnt-offering along with the corresponding meat- and drink-offerings, and a he-goat as a sin-offering. The blowing of the silver trumpets also rose from the mere תָּקַע of an ordinary new moon to a loud, strong blast, a הֵרִיעַ (on the difference between the two, *vid.* Num. x. 7), and the first day of the seventh month was called in consequence יוֹם הַתְּרוּעַ, "the day of the trumpet-blast" (Lev. xxiii. 23 sqq.; Num. xxix. 1 sqq.). *Bähr* has erroneously interpreted this תְּרוּעַ as a "voice of Jehovah," by which God showed His people that the most important period of the year had now arrived. An admirable reply to this view has been given by *Keil* (p. 370), who also furnishes the correct explanation of the ceremony itself. "God," he says, " was thereby to be strongly, loudly, and continuously reminded of His people, that He might bestow His grace in greater energy for the sanctification of the month."

The observance of the *sabbatical* and *jubilee years* we need not dwell upon here, as they present no distinct peculiarities that have any bearing upon the sacrificial worship.

C. THE FEAST OF PASSOVER

§ 180. The institution of this festival is described in Ex. xii.
After nine plagues had been inflicted upon the Egyptians without
effect, Jehovah directed Moses to announce to the people, that the
tenth plague, viz., the destruction of all the first-born of Egypt,
both of man and beast, would at length overcome all the opposition
of the Egyptians to the departure of Israel (chap. xi.). This took
place in the first days of the month Abib (or the earing month),
which was afterwards called Nisan. The predicted plague was to
occur in the night between the 14th and 15th of that month; but
on the 10th every householder was to select a lamb without blemish,
and to keep it till the 14th day, when he was to kill it בֵּין הָעַרְבַּיִם,
i.e., between the two evenings (of the 14th and 15th). The lintel
and two upright posts of the house-door were then to be smeared
with its blood by means of a hyssop-bush, in order that when
Jehovah passed through Egypt to slay all the first-born, He might
pass over the houses of the Israelites. The lamb was to be roasted
whole, without breaking a single bone, and eaten the same night,
with bitter herbs and unleavened bread, by the entire family. If
any family should be too small for that purpose, it might join with
one of the neighbouring families. If a portion of the lamb should
be left, it was to be burned with fire. They were to eat it like
persons hurrying away, with a staff in the hand, and with the loins
girded and the feet shod. Moreover, as a memorial of the importance of the object and the greatness of the result, this festal meal
was to be repeated by all their descendants year after year, and
the remembrance of the event to be preserved by a seven days' festival, viz., from the evening of the 14th to the evening of the 21st,
during which time no leavened bread was to be found in any of the
houses. Persons who were levitically unclean were to be excluded
from the meal; but they were commanded, as well as any persons
who might be upon a journey, to keep a second festival on the 14th
of the following month. If any one should abstain from taking
part in it without such legitimate grounds, he was to be put to
death (Num. ix. 6 sqq.).

For the yearly commemoration of this event in the Holy Land,
it was prescribed in Deuteronomy (xvi. 5–7), in accordance with the
altered circumstances, that the lamb should not be slain in their
own dwellings, but at the place of the sanctuary alone, and that it
should be prepared and eaten there. In this command it was of

course assumed, that the blood could no longer be smeared upon the posts and lintel of the house-door, but, as in the case of all the other sacrificial animals, must be sprinkled upon the altar; for this could be the only object of the modification. The supposition that such was the ordinary practice, is expressly confirmed in 2 Chron. xxx. 16, xxxv. 11. That the fat was also burned upon the altar is not only very probable, but is firmly maintained in the Jewish tradition (cf. *Delitzsch über d. Pascharitus, Luth. Zeitsch.* 1855, 2). It cannot be deduced from Ex. xxiii. 18, however, as *Knobel* and *Delitzsch* suppose. This passage is rather to be explained after the manner of Ex. xii. 10. (*Vid. Hofmann*, p. 271, and *Keil's* Commentary *in loc.*)

Of the seven days of the commemorative festival, the first and last (the 15th and 21st of the month) were to be distinguished by a sabbatical observance, viz., abstinence from work and a holy assembly. On the first feast day probably, viz., the 15th of the month, or according to others the second (16th), the sheaf of first-fruits of the new harvest (a sheaf of barley, no doubt, since wheat did not ripen till later in the year) was offered and waved before Jehovah.[1] Along with this wave-sheaf—that is to say, before it—

---

[1] The day on which the wave-sheaf was offered has been a subject of dispute from the very earliest times, and continues so to the present moment. According to Lev. xxiii. 11, 15, it was to take place מִמָּחֳרַת הַשַּׁבָּת. This Sabbath was understood by the Bœthuseans as denoting the day following the weekly Sabbath which fell in the festal week (cf. *Lightfoot*, Opp. ii. 692, and *Ideler, Hdb. d. Chronol.* ii. 613); whereas *Philo, Josephus*, and the *Rabbins* are unanimous in regarding it as the first feast day, which had a sabbatical character (ver. 7), and consequently in assigning the offering of the sheaf to the second day of the feast. This view was also the prevalent one among Christian writers on biblical antiquities, and has been adopted by *Bähr* (ii. 620, 621) and *Keil* (i. 393, 394). But, in opposition to this, *Hitzig* has endeavoured to prove, (1) that the ancient Hebrews always commenced a new week with the new year, so that the Sabbaths of the first month invariably fell upon the 7th, 14th, 21st, and 28th; and (2) that the Sabbath referred to in vers. 11 and 15 can only have been the 21st, and consequently that the offering of the wave-sheaf ought to have taken place on the 22d. *Kliefoth* dropped the first part of this exposition, but adopted the second, and maintained that the Sabbath mentioned in ver. 11 could only refer to the last day of assembly mentioned just before in ver. 8, and not to the first day mentioned still further back in ver. 7, and therefore that the wave-sheaf was not offered till the 22d of the month. *Knobel*, on the other hand, approves of the first part of the theory set up by *Hitzig*, but disputes the second, and maintains that the wave-sheaf was offered on the 15th Abib.—Of these different views the Bœthusean must be set aside, since the offering of the sheaf of first-fruits had nothing to do with the weekly Sabbath. And the one which

there was offered a yearling as a burnt-offering, with the appropriate meat-offering (*two*-tenths, not one-tenth, of an ephah of meal)
and a drink-offering (a quarter of a hin of wine).   Before this
offering had been presented, neither roasted corn nor even bread
could be eaten from the new harvest (Lev. xxiii. 9–14).   Also on
each of the seven feast days a he-goat was offered as a sin-offering,
and two young bullocks, a ram, and seven yearling lambs as a

assigns the waving of the sheaf to the 22d Abib is equally inadmissible.   For,
according to this view, the celebration of harvest, which was certainly intended
to be an essential factor of the Easter festival, would really have taken place
after the feast, since the feast ended on the evening of the 21st, as is evident
not only from the name given to that day, עֲצֶרֶת (Deut. xvi. 8), but also from
the termination of the obligation to eat unleavened bread.   Moreover, Josh. v.
11, where it is stated that the Israelites who had just arrived in the Holy Land
ate *unleavened* bread of the corn of the land מִמָּחֳרַת הַפֶּסַח (which is no doubt
identical with מִמָּחֳרַת הַשַּׁבָּת in Lev. xxiii. 11), is a proof that this day was
within the seven days of *Mazzoth*.   For the idea suggested by *Kliefoth*, that
" what is intended is not the Easter cake, but the peculiar *Minchah* belonging
to the feast of Harvest," will not be likely to commend itself to any one who
observes that all the *Menachoth* were eaten by the priests alone, and not by the
people.   The choice simply lies, therefore, between the 15th and 16th Abib ; and
it is very hard to decide between them, as they are both exposed to peculiar
difficulties.   The assumption that the new year always commenced with the
first day of the week, and therefore that the 14th Abib invariably fell upon a
Sabbath, has against it the great improbability of the early Israelites ever doing
what such a custom would have involved, viz., of their having broken off the
last week of the year in the middle, and begun to reckon from the commencement again, as soon as the new moon announced the beginning of the year.
Nevertheless the biblical text appears to require this, and to exclude the traditional view.   Of the passages bearing upon the subject, Lev. xxiii. 15, 16
appears to me to stand in the first rank, and to possess great force.   The day
of Pentecost is fixed there in the following manner : " Ye shall count מִמָּחֳרַת
הַשַּׁבָּת, namely, from the day that ye brought the sheaf of the wave-offering,
seven whole Sabbaths (שַׁבָּתוֹת תְּמִימֹת) shall there be ; even unto מִמָּחֳרַת הַשַּׁבָּת
הַשְּׁבִיעָת shall ye number fifty days," etc.   Nothing is proved by *Keil's* appeal
to the parallel passage in Deut. xvi. 9, where the seven whole Sabbaths of
Leviticus are altered into " seven weeks " (שָׁבֻעֹת), not even that שַׁבָּת (= שָׁבוּעַ)
may also mean a week.   But if this were granted, *Hitzig* would still be right in
maintaining, that in that case שַׁבָּת then could only mean a week which closed
with a Sabbath-day.   And even if we gave this up as well, there would still
remain the leading proof in the passage, namely, that the מִמָּחֳרַת הַשַּׁבָּת in ver.
16 must signify the same as the same expression in ver. 15 and ver. 11, and
therefore that the Pentecost, as well as the day of the waving of the sheaf,
must always have been preceded by a שַׁבָּת, whether an ordinary Sabbath-day

burnt-offering, *after* the "continual sacrifice" (Num. xxviii. 17 sqq.).
The seventh day, with its Sabbath rest and holy assembly, brought
the whole festival to a close, and for that reason is designated עֲצֶרֶת
in Deut. xvi. 8. In the evening of this day, after sunset, and
therefore at the commencement of the eighth day, leavened bread
might be eaten again (Ex. xii. 18).

§ 181. The most common and general NAME of this feast is

or a high feast day with a sabbatical character. And as the latter was *never*
the case, we are necessarily shut up to the former. Again, Josh. v. 11 is apparently conclusive against the offering of the wave-sheaf on the 15th Abib,
although both *Bähr* and *Keil* adduce this passage in support of the opposite
view. The latter says, " our morrow after the Sabbath " was understood by the
contemporaries of Moses in Josh. v. 11 as equivalent to the " morrow after the
Passover ; " but he overlooks the fact, that it is stated immediately before, that
" they kept the Passover on the 14th day of the month at even," and therefore
the " morrow after the Passover," which follows directly afterwards, can only
denote the 15th of the month ; and, what is still worse, he also forgets that he
himself regards the name " Passover " as belonging (not only primarily, but)
exclusively to the 14th Abib, and upon that fact has founded his proof, that
the feast of Passover was the introductory festival to the feast of *Mazzoth*
(§ 181). I also regard the " Sabbath " in Lev. xxiii. 11 as confirmatory, though
not in the same degree as Lev. xxiii. 16 and Josh. v. 11. " *Sabbath* " invariably denotes simply the weekly Sabbath, and is never used in *this absolute manner*
to denote a great yearly feast day. At all events, whenever " the Sabbath "
stands, as it does here, without any further definition, we are always justified
in thinking first of the weekly Sabbath. I do not see that any great weight
can be attached to the argument adduced by *Knobel*, that Deut. xvi. 8 is a still
further proof, inasmuch as on the last day of the feast not only all " servile
work," but all " work " is prohibited, and thus the day is evidently signalized
as a weekly Sabbath ; for it does not appear to me that this distinction was
maintained with sufficient consistency (cf. Ex. xii. 16), however certain the
fact may be, that the command to abstain from work on the weekly Sabbaths
and the day of atonement (Lev. xxiii. 28 sqq.) was much more stringent than
on any other feast days (Ex. xii. 16). On the other hand, there seems to me to
be great importance in the remark made by *Knobel*, that " it is difficult to
understand why precisely the second day of the *Azyma*, when the people had
gone to their ordinary occupations, and had no occasion to assemble at the
sanctuary, should have been the one distinguished by the sacrificial gift peculiar to the festival. As if the people ought not to have been present when the
gift dedicated by them to Jehovah was solemnly presented ! " A holy convocation was appointed for the presentation of the loaves of first-fruits at the day
of Pentecost. And as we find from Num. xxviii. 11, 19, 24, that the number
of burnt-offerings to be presented was exactly the same on all seven days, but
that on the day of the wave-sheaf there were to be offered along with this a
special burnt-offering, meat-offering, and drink-offering, the second day, on
which there was no assembly, would have had a richer ceremonial than the first,
at which all the people were to appear at the sanctuary.

חַג הַמַּצּוֹת, or feast of unleavened loaves. It occurs four times in the Pentateuch (Ex. xxiii. 15, xxxiv. 18 ; Lev. xxiii. 6 ; Deut. xvi. 16). This name was given to the feast on account of the command to eat only sweet bread during the seven days that it lasted. On the other hand, the name חַג הַפֶּסַח, or feast of passing over, occurs only once in the Pentateuch, viz., Ex. xxxiv. 25. The name פֶּסַח (*Chald.* פַּסְחָא, LXX. πάσχα, *Vulg. Phase* or *transitus*) was derived, according to Ex. xii. 13, 27, from the fact that when Jehovah passed through the land, destroying the first-born of the Egyptians, He passed by the houses of the Israelites. The verb פסח signifies literally, " to stride " or " spring over" anything ; then, as that which a man strides over he does not trample upon, " to spare :" hence פֶּסַח also signifies sparing. What distinguished this feast from all others was, (1) the paschal meal with which it began, and (2) the eating of unleavened bread during the whole time that it lasted. From the former it received the name *feast of Pesach,* from the latter, *feast of Mazzoth.*

But it is quite a mistake to divide the feast of *Pesach* or *Mazzoth* into two different feasts, as *Keil* has followed *Ewald* in doing ; and altogether wrong to suppose that the former was merely a " preliminary festival," and the latter the " principal feast." On the contrary, nothing is clearer in the whole law of worship than that the paschal meal was the principal feast, and the eating of *Mazzoth* for seven days only a subdued echo of this leading feast. Even before the preparation of the Pesach meal all leavened bread had to be removed from the houses, and the Pesach meal itself was to be eaten with unleavened bread. It follows, therefore, as a matter of course, and is expressly stated in Ex. xii. 18, that the night of the Pesach meal belonged to the seven days of Mazzoth, and formed the commencement of them. The Pesach meal and the eating of the Mazzoth for seven days were a commemoration, not of the day of the exodus *and* the first seven days of their journey, but of the day of the exodus alone. And the appointment of seven days of *commemoration* for one *historical* day had its origin simply in the general character of a great festival, into which the commemoration of that one day was to be expanded. A space of seven days, neither more nor less, with the seal of the covenant number, was essential to the complete exhaustion of the idea of a high festival. But as the eating of the paschal lamb was the one, indivisible, and not to be repeated basis of the whole festival, and yet the festival itself was to be kept for seven days, this could only be done by the other essential part of the paschal meal, the eating of unleavened bread, being continued for seven days. This is really admitted by *Keil* when he says (p. 395), "The one day of deliverance became a seven days' festival of holy joy, sanctified by the sacred number seven, in which Israel rested from the oppression and toil of Egypt, and participated in the blessedness of divine repose." But holding to this, the correct view, how is it possible to place the *Pesach* and *Mazzoth* side by side as two distinct festivals, and to make the seven days' echo of the joy the *leading* festival, and the main celebration merely a preliminary feast?

"But in the law," says *Keil* (p. 393), "the *Pascha* in the evening of the 14th Abib is clearly distinguished from the seven days' feast of unleavened bread which followed: cf. Ex. xii. 18 ; Lev. xxiii. 5, 6 ; Num. xxviii. 16, 17. It is incorrect on the part of *Bähr*, therefore, to abolish this distinction, and to regard the names as simply two different names for one and the same festival."[1] It is difficult to understand, however, how Ex. xii. 18 can ever have been placed in the series of proof passages adduced in support of the distinction, since this is the very passage which furnishes the most unquestionable proof of the opposite. The words read thus : "On the fourteenth day of the first month, at even, ye shall eat unleavened bread until the one and twentieth day of the month at even." Consequently the time of the paschal meal is certainly to be reckoned among the seven days of Mazzoth. And just as Ex. xii. 18 furnishes a proof that the seven days' feast of *Mazzoth* included the paschal meal, so, on the other hand, in Deut. xvi. 2, where the seven days' offering of the festal thank-offerings is commanded in these terms, "Thou shalt sacrifice the Passover to Jehovah," we have a proof that even in the Pentateuch the name "Passover" was applied to the whole seven days' festival.

§ 182. The meal with which the festival began was called פֶּסַח (Ex. xii. 11), and the lamb that was eaten זֶבַח פֶּסַח (xii. 27) or זֶבַח חַג הַפָּסַח (xxxiv. 25). The first question that arises here is,

---

[1] It is with the greatest pleasure that I can appeal to *Hengstenberg's* energetic protest against this view (*Passah*, p. 146) : "From a mistaken view of Lev. xxiii. 5, 6, and Num. xxviii. 16, 17, many have assumed that in the books of Moses a distinction is made between the Passah and the feast of unleavened bread. This is not for a moment to be thought of. We have not two separate festivals there placed side by side, but simply the commencement and (? or) main portion of the feast *and* the whole feast. The ' feast of unleavened bread ' denotes the whole, including the paschal meal."

whether the *paschal lamb was to be regarded as a sacrifice*. Many
of the earlier Protestant theologians denied this on mistaken, pole-
mical grounds, connected with their opposition to the Roman
Catholic view of the Lord's Supper as a bloodless repetition of the
bleeding sacrifice of Christ (*vid.* History of the Old Covt., vol. ii.
p. 297). Among modern theologians, *v. Hofmann* is the only one
who has taken the same side; but he has done so in a totally different interest, and stedfastly kept his stand in spite of all opposition. The sacrificial character of the paschal lamb is defended,
first of all, by an appeal to the name זֶבַח, which is given to it. But
when *Hofmann* maintains, in opposition to this, that " this term
might be applied to any kind of sacrifice, as 1 Sam. xxviii. 24 and
Prov. xvii. 1 clearly prove," the true answer is not the one given
by *Keil* (p. 379), namely, that " זָבַח never means simply to *slay*,
like טָבַח and שָׁחַט, not even in Prov. xvii. 1, where זִבְחֵי רִיב are sacrifices of strife, *i.e.*, fat *sacrificial* portions eaten in a quarrelsome
house (?), or in 1 Sam. xxviii. 24, which is to be rendered: ' she
sacrificed the fatted calf to the king;'" but that given by *Harnack*
(*der christl. Gemeinde-gottesdienst*, p. 191): " The question is not
whether everything slaughtered was or could be called a *Zebach*,
but what act was it in connection with the O. T. theocracy and its
ceremonial law that was so described? Now it is only to the
bleeding offerings that the expression is there applied, and consequently the *Passah* must belong to this category also."

There can be no question whatever, that by *Philo* and *Josephus*,
and in the whole line of the Jewish tradition, the paschal lamb was
regarded as a sacrifice. And the Apostle Paul also refers to it
as a sacrifice in 1 Cor. v. 7: " For even Christ our Passover was
sacrificed (ἐτύθη) for us." It is true, that even here *Hofmann* has
succeeded in discovering two passages (Luke xv. 23; Acts x. 13),
in which θύειν is used of ordinary slaughtering. But in this case
also, the question is, not what θύειν might mean in ordinary phraseology, but what it did mean in the technical phraseology of religious
worship. And can any one really persuade himself that the Apostle
did not think, and did not wish others to know that he thought, of
the *sacrificial* death of Christ?

Again, the paschal lamb is called a קָרְבָּן in Num. ix. 7. It is
true, this passage unquestionably refers, not to the first celebration
of the Passover in Egypt, but to the first commemorative Passover
at Sinai. And upon this *Hofmann* founds his objection: " At all
events, a distinction must be made between the first זֶבַח־פֶּסַח and

the repetitions of it. In the former a lamb was slain to serve as
a meal, and that not a religious meal, but simply a meal appointed
by God. It was the repetition of it that was a religious festival.
But the lamb was not *offered* to God either here or there. It was
no *Minchah;* but in the repetitions of the festival it was applied in
a religious manner, and could therefore be called *Corban.*" But it
is evident at once, that this explanation is confusing rather than
enlightening. *Keil* has very justly described it as confusing on the
part of *Hofmann*, that he has opposed the application of the name
Minchah to the Passover ; for no one on the opposite side ever has
applied or could apply this name to it, inasmuch as every one knows
that in the whole Pentateuch except Gen. iv. 4, and the whole of
the later usage of the language, *Minchah* is only used of the *bloodless* offerings upon the altar. In *Hofmann's* opinion, the first Passover was not a religious festival, whilst the repetition of it was. But
why the former cannot also be called so, we are not told. Every
"performance of a divine command" is "religious service" in the
broader sense of the term ; therefore the slaying and eating of the
Egyptian Passover, which had been appointed by God, was so too.
And even in the more restricted sense it may be designated a religious service, an act of worship. For of all that distinguishes an
act of worship from ordinary actions, not a single essential point is
wanting here. It was appointed by God, and enforced by divine
promises to those who faithfully observed it, and by divine threat-
enings to those who despised and neglected it. The observance of
it was a practical acknowledgment of the God of Israel. It was
not an act to be performed this once only, but was to be repeated
year after year; and it is expressly described as עֲבוֹדָה, or the service of God (Ex. xii. 25, 26). It is true, it is not placed in any
direct relation to the sanctuary or the altar. But this does not
necessarily deprive it of the validity of an act of worship ; for that
was the case with circumcision also, and yet no one will deny that
this was an act of worship. In fact, the paschal supper in Egypt
has still stronger claims to the character of religious worship, than
the first circumcision in the grove at Mamre. For circumcision
continued even in later times, without any relation to the sanctuary
and altar ; whereas, as soon as a sanctuary and altar actually existed,
the Passover was placed in the closest and most essential relation
to them. In Egypt, however, this relation to the sanctuary and
altar was wanting, merely because it could not be manifested, as
Israel had neither altar nor sanctuary in the land of Egypt.

The paschal lamb is certainly never called a *Minchah;* but no one who knows what a *Minchah* is in the Mosaic phraseology would expect or require that it should be so called. According to Num. ix. 7, however, it both was, and was called, a *Corban.* Nevertheless *Hofmann* maintains that neither the Egyptian nor the Sinaitic Passover "was offered to God." But what is a *Corban,* if not an offering? And if it was an offering, who was there but *God* to whom it could be offered? Moreover, did not the men referred to in Num. ix. 7, who were prevented from taking part in the Passover at Sinai on account of a death in their neighbourhood, expressly describe the paschal lamb as a *Corban of Jehovah?* Now what has *Hofmann* done to evade the force of this passage? He changes the idea of "offering" at once into that of "religious application." Even the later Passover, he says, was not *offered* to God, but it was *applied* in a religious manner, and therefore could be called *Corban.* The text, indeed, is not favourable to this *quid pro quo;* for the men do not say, "Why may we not *apply the Corban of Jehovah* in a religious manner?" but rather, "Why should we not be allowed to *present* it (הַקְרִיב)?" Throughout the Bible, from Lev. i. 2 to Mark vii. 11, *Corban* invariably means something offered to God. And we shall therefore do right in adhering to our point, that at any rate the later Passover, being a *Corban of Jehovah,* was also "offered to God." And if these men, at the very first repetition of the Passover, speak at once of the paschal lamb as a *Corban,* we may certainly assume that they regarded the normal Passover in Egypt as *Corban* also. The act of bringing to the sanctuary and presenting upon the altar was certainly omitted, because the means of carrying it out were wanting. But did not the solemn selection and separation of the lamb, which took place four days before it was slain, mark it clearly enough as a *Corban of Jehovah*—as set apart for God, and for divine purposes?

Hofmann repudiates the idea that the paschal lamb was "offered to God, and the meal then arranged after the manner of the thank-offering meals." He says, "The animal was slaughtered for the express purpose of the meal, and not offered to God and then eaten at a meal." But how little penetration he shows in this distinction is very apparent. For has not *Hofmann* himself, when speaking professedly of the thank-offering meals, laid as strong an emphasis as possible upon the fact, that the animal slain as a thank-offering was not merely appropriated afterwards to the meal, but intended for it from the very first (*vid.* § 81)?

When *Hofmann* rejoins that "it was a meal commanded by God, and not an act of worship instituted by Israel for the purpose of laying before God its desire for deliverance : the slaying and the meal were not the spontaneous expression of this desire, but the fulfilment of a divine command;" so weak an argument hardly need be met by the remark, that subjective desire and an objective command, human need of salvation and the divine appointment of salvation, do not exclude, but demand one another. To meet the need of salvation spontaneously uttered by the Israelites, and to guide it into such modes of action as corresponded to His plan of salvation, God required and regulated in the law, not only the slaying and preparation of the paschal lamb, but the slaying and preparation of all the other sacrifices.

According to Ex. xii. 5, a male, unblemished lamb or kid of a year old was to be chosen for the first Egyptian Passover. What can have been the meaning and design of these requirements, if not to show that the Passover was a religious meal? If it had been only an ordinary meal, answering no other purpose than to strengthen the Israelites for their approaching journey, these regulations would really have been very superfluous. But we know what importance was attached to them in connection with the bleeding sacrifices, and how essential they were there (§ 34). The same remark also applies to the command in ver. 10, that none of the flesh of the paschal lamb was to be left till the morning, but whatever could not be eaten was to be burned with fire. Does not this remind us distinctly enough of the similar command with reference to the flesh of the sin-offering and peace-offering (§ 117, 139); and are we not warranted, nay, almost compelled, by this agreement to regard the paschal lamb as a sacrifice also? Another point to be observed is, that in ver. 6 the slaying of the lamb is designated שָׁחַט, the proper term for the slaying of a *sacrifice*. And when to all this we add the fact, that in every subsequent observance of the Passover the blood of the lamb was sprinkled upon the altar, and the fat portions burned upon the altar, I cannot understand how any one can still refuse to accord to the offering the dignity of a sacrifice. And in *Hofmann's* reply, that "the distinction between the first and every subsequent Passover comes all the more conspicuously to light in consequence, but the latter, to say nothing of the former, does not appear as an act of sacrificing," the demonstrative force of this fact is not really met, but evaded.

§ 183. If, then, the sacrificial character of the paschal lamb must be admitted, the question arises, to which of the classes of sacrifice otherwise occurring in the Mosaic economy does it belong? Strictly speaking, to none of them ; for the peculiarity belonging to the purpose of its institution gave a perfectly unique character to many portions of the ritual, with which it was accompanied. It stood nearest, no doubt, to the *peace-offerings ;* and since it has all the characteristic marks by which they were distinguished from the rest of the sacrifices, we feel perfectly justified in following nearly all the commentators, both earlier and later, and placing it among the *Shelamim.* It not only has the name *Zebach* (Ex. xii. 27, xxiii. 18), which is applied in the Pentateuch exclusively to the peace-offerings, but it has also the sacrificial meal in common with them alone ; and the directions in Ex. xii. 10, as to what was to be done with the flesh that remained over from the meal, correspond to those given with regard to what remained from the praise-offering, the most important description of peace-offering (§ 139). In answer to *Hengstenberg,* who opposes this, and regards it as a sin-offering—in fact, as the foundation, the root, and the centre of all other sin-offerings—we have simply to adduce the fact, that of all the distinguishing characteristics of the sin-offering, in name, object, and ritual, not a single feature appears in the case of the paschal lamb ; whereas, on the other hand, *all* the distinctive marks of the peace-offering are impressed upon it. And *Harnack's* emendation of the prevailing opinion, in which he endeavours to show that it comprised the nature of both sin-offering and thank-offering, is without foundation on the one hand, since the ritual of the Passover was wanting in every distinguishing mark of that of the sin-offering, and unnecessary on the other hand, for the one point which induced him to adopt this view, viz., the expiatory worth of the blood of the Passover, has its *analogon,* according to Lev. xvii. 11, in the sprinkling of the blood of the peace-offering. *Keil* has adopted it for all that.

§ 184. In the ritual of the Passover the first thing which strikes us is the instruction given in Ex. xii. 3, that the lamb to be used was to be selected on the 10th Abib, *i.e., four days* before it was to be slain. *O. v. Gerlach* attributes this simply to the hurry of their departure ; as if the choice of a lamb from the fold was an affair of so much time as to require four whole days! *Hengstenberg* goes much deeper than this. " The lamb," he says, " had to be selected four days before the feast, in order that they might accustom them-selves to regard it as a holy thing, and so the more easily forget its common nature in the light of the divine institution ; and still more, that their minds might be led for some time before the feast to take a right view of the great blessing to be conferred upon them, and be truly prepared for its reception." The correctness of this view can hardly be disputed. But it leaves the question unanswered, why exactly *four* days should have been fixed upon. Why not three, or seven? *Hofmann* was the first to examine this point, and he explains it thus in his *Weissagung und Erfüllung* (i. 123): "The lamb had to be chosen just as many days before it was wanted, as there had been דּוֹר (Gen. xv. 16) since the time when Israel was brought into Egypt to grow into a nation. Four days long did the sight of the lamb keep up the thought of the approaching deliverance, before it was dressed as a meal to give strength for the journey." But this allusion seems to me too far-fetched and obscure; and I prefer, therefore, to give the number four not a realistic, but a purely symbolical meaning. Four is the sign of the kingdom of God. And this was to be the characteristic number of the paschal lamb, on account of its connection with the history of the development of the kingdom of God. According to the Jewish tradition, this arrangement was confined to the first Passover in Egypt.

The slaying of the lamb was to take place on the 14th Abib, *between the two evenings* (Ex. xii. 6). According to the Samaritan, Caraitic view, which is generally regarded as the correct one by modern writers on Jewish antiquities, the expression בֵּין הָעַרְבַּיִם refers to the time between six o'clock and half-past seven,—the first evening commencing when the sun disappears below the horizon, the second at the time of total darkness. This is favoured by the nature of the case, and the analogy of the following passages: Ex. xvi. 12, 13, xxx. 8; Deut. xvi. 6. (*Vid. J. v. Gumpach, Alt-test. Studien, Heidelberg* 1852, pp. 224–37; and my History of the Old Covenant, ii. p. 301.)

§ 185. According to *Hofmann* (p. 272), even "*the smearing of the door-way* with the blood of the slaughtered animal was not the freewill expression of a desire for atonement, but the fulfilment of a divine command." But here too the contrast between a subjective desire and an objective command is an arbitrary invention of *Hofmann* himself, and is drawn not from the law, but from the air (cf. § 183); for the act of atonement in the ordinary sin-offerings, trespass-offerings, burnt- and peace-offerings, was not merely a "spontaneous expression of desire for atonement," but was quite as much the " fulfilment of a divine command" as the smearing of the door-posts with the blood of the Passover on the day of the exodus from Egypt.

Now since the paschal lamb was a sacrifice, as we have already seen at § 183, its blood was also expiatory, and the smearing of the door-posts with the blood is to be regarded as an act of atonement. This assumption is in harmony with the significance ascribed to the smearing. For example, according to Ex. xii. 13, 23, the blood was to be a sign and pledge to the inhabitants of the house, that when Jehovah saw it He would pass by and spare them from the plague which was about to fall upon the Egyptians. Israel needed an expiation, for it could not stand in its sin when God arose to judgment. But God desired to rescue and spare the Israelites for the sake of their calling, and because of their faith ; and for that reason He gave atoning efficacy to the blood of the sacrifice, which they slew at His command. This was to be appropriated by them in faith ; and as a proof that they had done so, they were to mark their houses with the atoning blood. And when the atoning blood of the sacrifice covered the posts and lintel of the door, the whole house, and everything within it, was thereby expiated and protected ; for the entrance represented the entire house. But the entrance to the house was formed by the two door-posts and the lintel which connected them ; the threshold was subordinate, and could be dispensed with. Hence the lintel only needed to be smeared, and not the threshold. Moreover, the latter could not properly have been smeared, as persons passing out and in would then have trodden upon the holy blood.

The command in vers. 6, 7, " *the whole assembly* of the congregation of Israel shall kill it, and take the blood and strike it on the two side-posts, etc.," is regarded by *Bähr* (ii. 633), *Hengstenberg* (Christol. iii. 525), *Keil* (i. 385), and others as a practical exemplification of Ex. xix. 6. " By this," says *Keil*, " the whole nation proved itself to be the kingdom of priests, which God had called it to be. For even if every Israelite was allowed to slay a sacrificial animal, the ceremonial connected with the blood was the exclusive prerogative of the priests." But they forget, in the *first* place, that it was through the conclusion of the covenant at Sinai that Israel was first consecrated, and qualified to act as a kingdom of priests ; and *secondly*, that even before the institution of the Passover, the ceremonial connected with the blood was performed not by specially consecrated priests, for there were none, but by the sacrificer himself, and therefore there was nothing peculiar and unusual in the instructions given in ver. 6. The design of these instructions was to lay stress upon the fact, that *no* Israelite was to be excluded, or to exclude himself, from participating in the paschal festival.

§ 186. If, then, the paschal lamb was a sacrifice, the *paschal meal* must be regarded as a sacrificial meal, and the same significance be ascribed to it as to every other sacrificial meal, viz., to set forth that fellowship with God which the sacrificial expiation had secured. *Hofmann*, indeed, cannot see any other purpose in the paschal meal than " to give them strength for their approaching journey." And if the bodily strength, which this meal was unquestionably intended to impart, in anticipation of the coming journey, be also regarded as a symbol of a corresponding spiritual invigoration, we are perfectly ready to adopt this view. But this was hardly the sense in which *Hofmann* understood it. In fact, with his denial of the sacrificial idea, he could not understand it in this way. But can it really be possible that in the sacrificial meal, the symbolical character of which is brought out so decidedly by so many significant points of detail, nothing more is to be found than the trivial advice, " Eat to-night till you are quite full, that you may be in a condition to start upon your journey to-morrow morning ? "

The instructions to *roast* the lamb (ver. 9), and not to boil it with water,[1] were not dictated, as *Bähr* (ii. 636) and v. *Hofmann* suppose, by the simple fact that this mode of preparation was better suited to the hurry of the whole proceeding; but are to be explained on the ground that in this way the character of the flesh would not be altered by any foreign substance, and the flesh, even when ready for eating, would still be the pure flesh of the lamb.

The further command, that *not a bone of the lamb was to be broken* (ver. 46), had a corresponding meaning. Of course, what is meant is simply dissection for the purpose of cooking, not for the purpose of eating. The lamb was to be placed upon the table as a perfect, undivided whole. The unity, represented in this way by the lamb, was transferred in a certain sense by the act of eating to those who partook of it. By eating of the one lamb as a divine repast, at the table of God, as His house and table guests, they

---

[1] If, notwithstanding this, we find the term בִּשֵּׁל applied in Deut. xvi. 7 to the preparation of the lamb, it must be borne in mind that there was a בִּשֵּׁל בָּאֵשׁ (2 Chron. xxxv. 13 ; cf. 2 Sam. xiii. 8), and that it is only בִּשֵּׁל בַּמַּיִם which is forbidden in Ex. xii. 9.

were joined together in a unity based upon the same fellowship with God (1 Cor. x. 17). For the same reason the head, the thighs, and the viscera were also to be eaten, of course so far as this was possible. And what remained from the meal was not to be kept for other meals, but burned the next morning (ver. 10). For if it had been spread over different meals, the idea of unity and completeness would have been destroyed, quite as effectually as if only the half of the lamb had been roasted. Moreover, it would have been brought in this way under the category of ordinary food, and so have lost the character of holiness. The burning in this case, as in the analogous cases connected with the peace-offering meal (§ 139), was simply a matter of necessity, and did not destroy the idea of unity. For, by being given up to the fire, it was withdrawn from all profane, everyday use, and annihilated as if it had never existed. In any case, the burning of the remaining flesh was an evil that was to be avoided as far as possible. Provision was made for this by the instructions in ver. 4, that if there should be too few in any house for one lamb, they were to join with a family in the neighbourhood. The prohibition in ver. 46, against carrying any part of it across the street from one house to another, also served to keep up the character of unity.

With reference to the *bitter herbs* (מְרֹרִים), which were to be eaten with the paschal lamb (ver. 8), I must still adhere to the opinion that they were to be regarded as an *accompaniment*. They were related, no doubt, to the bitterness of the bondage in Egypt, which is thus described in chap. i. 14 : " The Egyptians made their lives bitter (יְמָרְרוּ)." The eating of bitter herbs and the drinking of bitter water are also used in other places as a figurative representation of suffering and affliction (Ps. lxix. 21 ; Jer. viii. 14). But as an accompaniment to the sweet flavour of the lamb, they no doubt acquired the character of a *condiment*. The sweetness of the flesh was to be rendered still more palatable by the bitter vegetables ; for the bitterness was lost in the sweetness of the flesh, and it was through the former that the latter was rendered truly savoury. What the bitter condiment was to the sweet food, the remembrance of their sufferings in Egypt would be to their deliverance from bondage there. But there was something more intended than the mere remembrance of the oppression in Egypt. As bitterness and sweetness modified and supplemented each other in the meal, so the sufferings in Egypt and the deliverance from Egypt stood in a close and essential relation to one another. Without the former the latter

would never have taken place, and by the present consciousness of
the former the commemoration first acquired its true consecration
(cf. Heb. xii. 11).

The protest made by *Keil* (i. 386–7) against this view of mine
has not shaken my confidence in its correctness. In *Keil's* opinion,
" the words, ' *over* bitter herbs (עַל־מְרֹרִים) shall ye eat it,' show that
the bitter herbs were not to be regarded as an accompaniment, or a
condiment, modifying the sweetness of the meat, but as the true
basis of the meal, which was covered, or subdued as it were, by the
roast meat and the unleavened bread." But the expression עַל־מְרֹרִים
furnishes neither a confirmation of *Keil's* view nor an objection to
the traditional one. For it is so well known that in innumerable
instances עַל is used in the sense of *with, along with,* that it would
be quite superfluous to adduce passages in proof of this. And in
the present instance we are not only warranted, but compelled by
the very nature of the case, to take it in this sense. If a meal consists of roast meat and bitter herbs, it follows as a matter of course
that the meat is the principal thing and the herbs are the accompaniment, and not the reverse. I am just as little able to adopt *Keil's*
view, when he regards the bitter herbs as a symbol, not only of the
bitter sufferings endured by Israel in Egypt, but also of " the bitterness of life in this sinful world, which Israel in its natural state was
perpetually to endure, but which in its spiritual state it was to
overcome at every repetition of the feast of Passover, through the
flesh of the lamb that was slain for its sins;" for I cannot find the
slightest warrant for any such opinion in either the occasion or
purpose of the meal.

On the *command to eat only unleavened bread* at the paschal
meal, see the remarks in § 145. *Winer* refers to Deut. xvi. 3,
where the Passover bread is called the " bread of affliction," לֶחֶם עֹנִי,
and gives this explanation of the command : " The Israelites of a
later age could not be reminded in a more effectual manner of the
oppression endured in Egypt, than by having to eat for a whole
week such coarse and tasteless food." But to this *Bähr* very properly replies : " In that case the whole of the seven days' feast
would have been made into a time of chastisement and fasting ;
whereas, so far from being a feast of penitence and mourning, it
was really a חַג, or festival of joy. The meat-offerings and shew-
bread, which were intended, according to their symbolical worth,
as food for Jehovah, were also required to be unleavened. Was
it likely that they would be commanded to offer wretched and

tasteless bread to Jehovah?" But *Bähr's* own explanation (" it was called bread of affliction because it was bread which called to mind Egypt and the affliction endured by the nation there, but only inasmuch as it was eaten at the time of their deliverance and rescue from affliction") can hardly escape the charge of tracing the derivation of a name on the principle of *lucus a non lucendo*. *Hofmann* (*Weiss. u. Erfüll.* i. 124–5) gives the true explanation, which he discovers in the clause immediately following : "For thou camest forth out of the land of Egypt in haste, בְּחִפָּזוֹן, *i.e.*, in forced and anxious flight." The departure from Egypt was necessarily an עֱנִי, because it had to take the form of a חִפָּזוֹן, and Israel ate its last meal in Egypt "in affliction" (cf. Isa. lii. 12).

The command to eat the paschal meal in travelling costume, girt, shod, and with staff in hand (ver. 11), may be explained from the hurry with which, the very same night, the Israelites had to take their departure, being literally forced out by the Egyptians (vers. 12 sqq.).

§ 187. In immediate connection with the appointment of the first celebration of the Passover (Ex. xii. 14 sqq.), the *annual repetition* of it was commanded as a festival in commemoration of the deliverance from Egypt. The laws in the middle books contain no precise directions as to the mode in which this commemoration-feast was to be kept. But from Ex. xxiii. 17, where it is commanded that at the three principal feasts, and therefore at the feast of Passover, all the (adult) males are to assemble at the sanctuary, it may be inferred, that after the entrance of the Israelites into the Holy Land, the paschal meal was to be kept there, and there only. This is confirmed by Deut. xvi. 2, 5 sqq., where the *Passah* is ordered to be slain, prepared, and eaten, not in the towns where the people lived, but at the place of the sanctuary. The size of the *fore-court* of the tabernacle precludes the supposition that this is intended ; but the supposition is equally inadmissible, that reference is made to the *houses* and *inns* in Shiloh or Jerusalem, to which they were probably not to return till the morning after the Passover had been held (ver. 7). It would be more correct to suppose that the lamb was to be prepared and eaten in the open air, in the immediate vicinity of the sanctuary. This is also confirmed by 2 Chron. xxxv. 13. In the New Testament times, on the contrary, it was undoubtedly the custom to prepare the paschal meal in the houses of Jerusalem (cf. Luke xxii. 7 sqq.).

The reasons for this transference of the feast of the Passover from the dwelling-houses to the immediate vicinity of the sanctuary, are no doubt to be found in the sacrificial character of the paschal lamb. Sacrificial expiation and the sacrificial meal as such belonged to that place, which Jehovah had chosen, to cause His name to dwell there (Deut. xvi. 6), to meet with the children of Israel (Ex. xxv. 8), and there to dwell in the midst of them (Ex. xxix. 45, 46). At the first Passover in Egypt, these two leading branches of the festival necessarily took place in the houses, on the one hand because Israel was then without a sanctuary, and on the other because the existing circumstances positively demanded it. But even at the first commemorative festival at Sinai these reasons existed no longer. It was possible for the sacrifice of the Passover to be regulated by the ordinary laws relating to the sacrificial worship, and therefore this was required. The blood was to be sprinkled upon the altar of the fore-court, and the paschal meal to be held in the immediate neighbourhood of the sanctuary, according to the analogy of the meal connected with the peace-offering (§ 139). This assimilation of the paschal offering to the ordinary peace-offerings extended in all probability to the fat portions of the former (cf. § 169). It is true, this is nowhere expressly mentioned in the Old Testament; but it may be unhesitatingly assumed as a necessary consequence of the sacrificial character of the paschal lamb, and of the prohibition against eating the fat of the sacrificial animals (§ 5).

§ 188. As the Israelites in the meantime had renounced of their own accord their universal priesthood (Ex. xx. 19), and all specifically priestly functions had been transferred to the family of Aaron in consequence; consistency demanded that the sprinkling of the blood, even in the case of the paschal lamb, should henceforth be performed by the hands of the priests alone; and it is evident from 2 Chron. xxx. 16, xxxv. 11, that this was really the custom of a later age. At the same time, it is questionable whether this was, or even could be, carried out at once (i.e., at the first commemorative feast at Sinai). Considering, for example, the very small number of priests who were really able to officiate in the Mosaic times, or those immediately following, and on the other hand the number of lambs to be slain, actually amounting as they did to myriads, and the short time allowed for the slaying and sprinkling of the blood,—we must certainly decide that this was not the case. It is possible, therefore, that the outward circumstances of the time may have rendered it necessary to leave the sprinkling of the blood, in the case of the paschal sacrifices, to the heads of the families, until the priesthood had become sufficiently numerous to carry out the necessary consequences of Ex. xx. 19, as we find them afterwards carried out in 2 Chron. xxx. and xxxv., in the time of Hezekiah and Josiah.

Up to this point, but only so far, there may be a certain, though still a very limited amount of truth in the assertion made by *Philo*,[1] and certain modern scholars, to the effect, that at the offering of the paschal lamb, the head of every household officiated once a year as priest, as a sign and memorial that the priestly rights of the nation were only suspended, and would one day be restored in their fullest extent. The proof which *Philo* adduces in support of this view, when he cites as a peculiarly priestly function, what according to the Mosaic law was never performed by the priest, but by the sacrificer himself, viz., the slaying of the animal, is so obviously worthless, that even if we could understand *Philo's* falling into such a mistake, it would still be perfectly incomprehensible how *Hengstenberg* could do the same.[2] *Hävernick* and *Kliefoth* also hold fast to *Philo's* fundamental idea, though they reject his reasoning as unsound. The former maintains, that " apart

---

[1] *Philo, de vita Mos.* iii. p. 686, Ed. Frcf.: ἐν ᾗ (ἑορτῇ) οὐχ οἱ μὲν ἰδιῶται προσάγουσι τῷ βωμῷ τὰ ἱερεῖα, θύουσι δὲ οἱ ἱερεῖς, ἀλλὰ νόμου προστάξει συμπᾶν τὸ ἔθνος ἱερᾶται τῶν κατὰ μέρος ἑκάστου τὰς ὑπὲρ αὐτοῦ θυσίας ἀνάγοντος τότε καὶ χειρουργοῦντος. And again, *de decal.* p. 766: ἐν ᾗ θύουσι πανδημεὶ αὐτῶν ἕκαστος, τοὺς ἱερεῖς αὐτῶν οὐκ ἀναμένοντες, ἱερωσύνην τοῦ νόμου χαρισαμένου τῷ ἔθνει παντὶ μίαν ἡμέραν ἐξαίρετον ἀνὰ πᾶν ἔτος εἰς αὐτουργίαν θυσιῶν.

[2] Although *Bochart* (*Hieroz.* i. 2, 50, p. 376) and *Vitringa* (*Observv. ss.* ii. 3, § 10) had discovered and exposed *Philo's* error, yet *Hengstenberg* writes as follows, not only in the first edition of his Christology, but, without noticing my reply, in the second edition also: " And in order that the people might always remain fully conscious of this (viz., that the priests possessed rights that were only transferred to them, and therefore their mediation would at some future period disappear altogether); in order that they might know that they themselves were the real bearers of the priestly dignity, they *retained*, even after the institution of the Levitical priesthood, that *priestly* function which formed the root and foundation of all the others, viz., the *slaying* of the covenant sacrifice, of the paschal lamb, which formed the centre of all other sacrifices, inasmuch as the latter served only as a supplement to it. That even under the Old Testament dispensation this importance of the paschal rite was *duly* recognised, is seen from *Philo*," etc. (vol. ii. p. 470, Engl. translation). I am glad to find that *Keil* also rejects this view (i. 389). He is wrong, however, in citing it as adopted by *Bähr*. For *Bähr* is merely referring to the *first* Passover in Egypt, and agrees here *ad unguem* with *Keil's* own view, which we have already shown to be untenable (§ 185).

from the fact that at the Passover the head of the family always
officiated in an extraordinary manner, when holding the paschal
meal in *his own home,* in the family circle, and not, as in the case
of the other sacred meals, at the sanctuary (Deut. xii. 17, 18), and
therefore a reflection still remained of the privileges formerly conferred upon him by the Lord, and he stood out in patriarchal
dignity,—the Passover of later times is decidedly to be regarded as
a memorial festival in remembrance, and as a lively revival, of that
first festival, when Israel really obtained and celebrated its birth,
redemption, and acceptance with God. Thus the feast of Passover
was, and always remained, a commemoration of the old, original
destination of Israel to be a holy, priestly nation," etc. But these
two fresh arguments are also untenable, and the first has been
already refuted in § 187, the second in § 185.

Kliefoth's reasoning appears still more unsound. At p. 151
he says, " In the fact that all the Israelites were obliged to eat
unleavened bread, which *only* (?) *the priests* were allowed to eat on
other occasions, and that more stress was laid upon this eating of
what was unleavened at the yearly than at the first Passover, the
universal priesthood of all the Israelites was certainly expressed,
though only in an altered form." But it was only the unleavened
bread which had been offered to God as a *Minchah,* that none but
the priests were allowed to eat. The Israelites were never *forbidden*
to eat unleavened bread when and where they chose. And it by
no means follows, from the fact that they were commanded to eat
only unleavened bread during the seven days of the feast of Passover, that at other times the bread must all be leavened.

§ 189. In the *seven days' festival* that followed the Passover
(§ 180) there is one thing more that claims our special attention,
viz., the presentation of the *wave-sheaf* on the first day after the
proper Passover. With regard to this it was commanded in Lev.
xxiii. 10, that when they came to the Holy Land, a sheaf of the
first-fruits (עֹמֶר רֵאשִׁית) of the harvest was to be brought to the priest
on the day appointed, and to be waved by him. In connection
with this sheaf, probably as the basis of its presentation, a lamb
was also to be offered as a burnt-offering along with the customary
meat- and drink-offerings.

As the words read, they cannot be understood in any other way
than that the *sheaf* of first-fruits was to be presented and waved *as
a sheaf;* and then, according to the analogy in other cases, viz., the
similar offering of the bread of first-fruits at the day of Pentecost,

it must be assumed that the sheaf when waved fell to the portion of the priests. It was not regarded then in the light of a *Minchah*, but only in that of a *Corban*. Later Jewish tradition, as found in *Josephus*, Ant. iii. 10, § 5, and the *Mishnah*, Tr. Menachoth x. 1–4, undoubtedly regards the עֹמֶר רֵאשִׁית as a true Minchah, taking the word עֹמֶר as equivalent to עִשָּׂרֹן (a tenth of an ephah), and thus obtaining a basis for the identification of our עֹמֶר רֵאשִׁית with the מִנְחַת בִּכּוּרִים in Lev. ii. 14. Accordingly, on the 16th Nisan a sufficient quantity of barley ears for the measure proposed were dried in the fore-court of the temple; the grains were then bruised and cleansed from the bran; and after the groats so obtained had been prepared with oil, incense, and salt, and waved, a handful was burnt upon the altar, and the remainder was eaten by the priests.

This traditional idea of the Jews *Thalhofer* has attempted to justify, as supported quite as much by the text as by the actual nature of the case. But his arguments are anything but conclusive. The relation between the two ideas רֵאשִׁית and בִּכּוּרִים does not favour in the slightest degree the combination or identification of the עֹמֶר רֵאשִׁית in Lev. xxiii. 10 and the מִנְחַת בִּכּוּרִים in Lev. ii. 14. And though the word עֹמֶר was undoubtedly used according to Ex. xvi. 36 as synonymous with עִשָּׂרֹן probably because the average yield of a sheaf was a tenth of an ephah, there is nothing in this passage to warrant our taking it in that sense here. The *waving* of the sheaf, again, did not make it an altar-offering; for that only showed that it was offered to Jehovah for the priests (§ 133), and many offerings both were and were called תְּנוּפָה, although no part of them was placed upon the altar. It may be fully admitted that the offering of the wave-sheaf was the characteristic, and in a certain sense the main feature in the festal ceremony of this day; and yet it may be denied that this offering bore the character of an *altar*-sacrifice. And when *Thalhofer* observes that "sacrifice was the central point of the Mosaic worship, and it was only by sacrifice and its relation to sacrifice that anything could acquire a religious signification in Israel; even the Easter festival could only be raised into a feast of nature by a sacrifice,"—he forgets that this was fully met by the foundation laid for the offering of the wave-sheaf in the burnt-offering, and the accompanying meat- and drink-offering, which were to be connected with it.

The wave-sheaf falls rather under the general notion of first-fruits, with this simple exception, that it was not presented as the offering of first-fruits made by a single individual, but as the Corban of first-fruits of the entire harvest of the whole congregation. By the (preceding) accompaniment of a bleeding sacrifice, the congregation presenting the offering had been rendered acceptable to Jehovah, and their offering of first-fruits was thereby rendered acceptable also. The appointment of a burnt-offering is easily to be explained from the character and intention of this kind of sacrifice. But it might appear strange that as the harvest-feast had reference to the manifestation of divine goodness, a peace-offering was not added. Our astonishment disappears, however, when we consider that the blessing in question had not yet been received. The foundation had merely been laid for its reception. At the feast of Pentecost, after the ripening and ingathering of the harvest, the peace-offering was included also (§ 192).

But it is still a striking fact that the meat-offering was not to consist of *one*-tenth of white meal, according to the custom in other analogous cases, but of *two*-tenths ; whereas the measure of the drink-offering (a quarter of a hin of wine) was not doubled in the same way. This alteration of the rule adopted in other cases cannot have been made without reason. The cause is probably to be sought for in the nature of the sacrifice as a harvest-offering. The doubling of the quantity had respect to the meal only, and not to the wine, because the feast had reference to the corn harvest, and not to the vintage.

D. THE FEAST OF PENTECOST

§ 190. On the fiftieth day, seven full weeks therefore, after the offering of the sheaf of first-fruits (§ 180, note), the *feast of Weeks* (חַג שָׁבֻעוֹת, Deut. xvi. 9), also called the feast of Harvest (חַג הַקָּצִיר, Ex. xxiii. 16), and feast of First-fruits (חַג הַבִּכּוּרִים, Ex. xxiii. 16; Num. xxviii. 26), and by *Josephus* and the New Testament writers Πεντεκοστή (Acts ii. 1), was celebrated at the central sanctuary on the termination of the corn harvest. The feast lasted only one day, which had a sabbatical character (Lev. xxiii. 21; Num. xxviii. 26). The distinguishing feature in this festival was the offering of two leavened loaves of wheaten flour made from the first-fruits, together with certain bleeding sacrifices (Lev. xxiii. 17 sqq.).

The character of this festival, which had no historical associations, was that of an expression of gratitude for the harvest. Occurring as it did at the close of the harvest, which commenced at the feast of *Pesach* or *Mazzoth*, it certainly may be regarded as a *closing festival*: not, however, as even *Keil* follows *Ewald* in maintaining, as being the close of the feast of *Mazzoth*, but as closing the seven weeks' harvest which intervened. For the feast of Weeks had nothing to do with the feast of *Pesach* or *Mazzoth* either in substance or form; for it had no historical associations (connected with the deliverance from Egypt), and there was so far from being any enforcement of the obligation to eat unleavened bread, that, on the contrary, the loaves of first-fruits to be presented and eaten by the priests were actually required to be *leavened*. The feast of *Mazzoth* had its own closing festival on the seventh day of unleavened bread, which was specially distinguished by its sabbatical character and holy assembly, and is expressly designated עֲצֶרֶת in Deut. xvi. 8.

But the feast of Weeks is evidently pointed out as the concluding festival of the period of harvest, by the fact that neither the paschal meal, nor the beginning or end of the eating of unleavened bread, is the date from which it is reckoned, but the offering of the sheaf of first-fruits, as being the point at which the harvest just finished first really began (Lev. xxiii. 15, 16). The fixing of precisely fifty days from this presentation was determined not so much by the fact that so long a period was actually required for the harvest, as by the sacredness of the number seven which regulated all the festivals, and the resemblance to the sabbatical and jubilee years. The fifty days' harvest was as it were a jubilee period in miniature.

§ 191. With regard to the *loaves of first-fruits* or *wave*-loaves (לֶחֶם הַבִּכּוּרִים, Lev. xxiii. 20; לְ תְּנוּפָה, xxiii. 17), it is questionable whether they are to be regarded as meat-offerings in the strict sense (*Minchah*), or merely as an offering of first-fruits in the sense of Num. xv. 19 and Lev. ii. 12 (*Corban*). *Thalhofer* (p. 181) answers the former in the affirmative, and the latter in the negative; but with just as little reason as when he makes the same assertion with regard to the wave-sheaf of the feast of Passover (§ 189). For since these loaves were to be leavened, they could not be laid upon the altar, and therefore could not be regarded as meat-offerings in the true sense. For in Lev. ii. 11 it is laid down as a universal law: " Every meat-offering (כָּל־הַמִּנְחָה) that ye offer to Jehovah, ye shall make unleavened." It is true that in ver. 12 one exception to this rule is mentioned, viz.: " as a *Corban* of first-fruits ye may offer such to Jehovah;" but in this case the offering is called *Corban* and not *Minchah*. When we find, therefore, that notwithstanding this, it is commanded in Lev. xxiii. 16, with regard to the wave-loaves treated of in the whole section vers. 15–21—" Unto the morrow after the seventh Sabbath shall ye number fifty days, and ye shall offer *a new meat-offering* (מִנְחָה חֲדָשָׁה) to Jehovah," and that immediately afterwards in ver. 17 the offering of the wave-loaves is described (since an actual discrepancy between this passage and Lev. ii. 11, 12 is not for a moment to be imagined, and according to ver. 20 no part of them was really laid upon the altar), we must assume, either that the term *Minchah* is used in a general sense as equivalent to *Corban*, contrary to the ordinary usage, or that the " new Minchah" here refers not to the two wave-loaves themselves, but to the meat-offerings belonging to the bleeding sacrifices of this day, and that they are designated as " new," to show that they also were made from new flour, *i.e.*, the flour of that year.

In any case these two wave-loaves of Pentecost are most closely and intimately connected with the wave-sheaf of Easter, and bear the same relation to it which the close of harvest bears to its commencement. Hence the first-fruits were presented at Easter in the form in which the land had produced them, without any preparation on the part of man, viz., as a bundle of ears, and, as the barley was the first to ripen and the barley harvest was the first to be taken in hand, of barley ears; and at Pentecost in the completest form of human preparation and human food, viz., as leavened bread, and, as the wheat ripened and was harvested last, as bread made of wheaten flour.

Two-tenths of an ephah of white meal were used in the preparation of these two loaves. As an omer of ears probably yielded about an omer of grain or flour, it is a significant fact, that exactly double the quantity required for the Easter offering of first-fruits was ordered to be used for the wave-loaves; and this doubling of the quantity was also shown in the fact, that the flour was made into *two* loaves and not into *one* only. In the symbolism of the Hebrews, however, doubling always expressed a higher gradation, which rested in the present case upon the contrast between the beginning and the close of the harvest.—The two loaves of first-fruits, like the sheaf of first-fruits, fell to the share of the priests, after they had been waved as the sign that they were offered to Jehovah for His servants.

From the words of ver. 17, " Ye shall bring two wave-loaves *out of your habitations*," many commentators, especially the earlier ones (*e.g.*, Calvin, Osiander, C. a Lapide, etc.), supposed that the two pentecostal loaves were not one simple Corban presented for the whole congregation, but that *every* head of a family had to offer two such loaves, just as every one offered a lamb at the feast of Passover. But if that had been the case, supposing the command in Ex. xxiii. 14 sqq. to be at all scrupulously observed, the priests would have been obliged to receive and consume myriads of loaves on that one day; a thing perfectly incredible. The meaning of the words " out of your habitations" is rather, as *Keil* says (p. 398), " bread of the daily food of the household, not loaves separately prepared for holy purposes." No doubt leavened loaves of first-fruits may also have been presented by private individuals (Lev. ii. 12 and Num. xv. 19), but they were freewill-offerings and not connected with the day of Pentecost.

§ 192. In Num. xxviii. 27–30, two bullocks, one ram, and seven lambs are directed to be offered as a *burnt-offering*, in addition to the daily burnt-offering, along with the usual meat-offerings, and one goat as a *sin-offering*,—the same number, therefore, as on each of the seven days of the feast of Passover (§ 180). But when we find, on the other hand, that in Lev. xxiii. 18 one bullock, two rams, and seven lambs are ordered to accompany the two wave-loaves as a burnt-offering, one he-goat as a sin-offering, and two lambs as peace-offerings, the question arises, whether these two statements are to be kept apart as relating to two different offerings, or whether they are to be regarded as identical? If the latter, then the two lambs of the peace-offering alone are to be regarded as an accompaniment to the two wave-loaves, and the burnt-offerings and sin-offering as general festal offerings independent of the presentation of the wave-loaves. The difference arising from the fact, that in Num. xxviii. two bullocks and one ram are ordered, and in Lev. xxiii. one bullock and two rams, we should then have to admit to be an irreconcilable discrepancy, attributable to a copyist's error. This is the solution adopted not only by *Ewald*, *Knobel*, and others, but also by *Bähr* and *Kliefoth*. *Thalhofer* and *Keil*, on the other hand, follow *Josephus*,[1] and assume that there were two distinct offerings, one presented as a festal offering (Num. xxviii.), the other as an accompaniment to the wave-loaves (Lev. xxiii.).

Now I am fully aware that very powerful reasons, founded both

[1] According to Josephus (Ant. iii. 10, 6), the burnt-offering of the day in question consisted of three bullocks, *two* rams, and fourteen lambs, and the sin-offering of two he-goats. But his speaking of only two, and not three rams, must be regarded as a simple mistake.

upon analogy and symmetry, may be adduced in support of the first
view, and I dare not venture to reject it unconditionally. On the
other hand, I cannot give up the last view either, so unhesitatingly
as *Bähr* and *Kliefoth* have done. An expansion and elevation of
the accompanying sacrifices, such as the latter supposes to have
existed in the relation between the wave-sheaf of the Easter festival
and the wave-loaves of the Pentecost, may be explained without any
difficulty, from the fact, that at the close of the harvest, and when
it was all gathered in, the feeling of unworthiness and the obligation of gratitude would be incomparably stronger than when the
harvest began, with the corn but partially ripened. But what
weighs the most in my opinion is, that according to the opposite
view the wave-loaves must have been left without any burnt-offering
to accompany them,—an omission opposed to all analogy, especially
the analogy of the wave-sheaf (§ 190). If, then, according to Lev.
xxiii. 12, it was requisite that a burnt-offering should accompany
the usual meat-offering, we necessarily expect to find the same,
though in a still stronger degree, in connection with the offering of
the loaves. The two *Shelamim* lambs cannot be regarded as a substitute for this, but only as a still further expansion.

§ 193. In any case the two *Shelamim* lambs, which are no doubt
to be looked upon as praise-offerings, stood in the closest relation to
the two wave-loaves. This is evident from ver. 20 : " The priest
shall wave them with (עַל) the bread of the first-fruits for a wave-
offering before Jehovah, with (עַל) the two lambs; they (the loaves)
shall be holy to Jehovah for the priest." The notion that the
loaves were to be waved along with the lambs, and lying upon their
backs, is to be rejected as a rabbinical crotchet (Menachoth 5, 6).
At the same time, the ritual for the offering of these lambs certainly
presents a few singularities. Among these is the rule, that the
lambs were to be waved whole, and not merely the breast, as in the
case of the other *Shelamim ;* which is evidently to be accounted for
in this way, that as there was no sacrificial meal, the whole of the
meat fell to the lot of the priests. In all probability (at all events
the analogy of Lev. xiv. 24, 25 seems to point to this conclusion)
the waving took place *before* the slaughtering. *Keil's* opinion, that
the burning of the fat was omitted in the case of these *Shelamim*,[1]
certainly rests upon a misunderstanding. For in that case they

---

[1] At least this seems to be the meaning of his words: " the loaves of first-
fruits, together with these two lambs, were not burnt upon the altar, but sanctified to the Lord for the priests."

could not possibly have been called *Shelamim*. All that ver. 20
implies is, that the flesh of these lambs was not to be used as a
sacrificial meal for the persons presenting the sacrifice. They belonged to the same category as the first-born of the cattle that were
fit for sacrifice (Num. xviii. 17, 18, cf. § 229).

The absence of any direct allusion to the ordinary meat- and
drink-offerings in connection with the *Shelamim* lambs, is no proof
of their omission ; on the contrary, according to the invariable rule
laid down in Num. xv. 3 sqq., it is to be assumed as a matter of
course, that they were really added. And in fact, as even *Kliefoth*
supposes (p. 94), the meat-offering belonging to these *Shelamim*
lambs is in all probability what is meant by the " new Minchah" in
Lev. vii. 12 sqq., which is so called because it was to be made of
new corn. On the other hand, the accompaniments of cake and
bread, which properly belonged to the praise-offering, and were to
be eaten at the sacrificial meal (Lev. vii. 12 sqq.; § 154–5), were
probably omitted here, because no provision was made for a sacrificial meal in connection with the pentecostal lambs, the whole of
the flesh of which became the portion of the priests.

Kliefoth understands the affair somewhat differently. He supposes Lev. ii. 14–16 and Num. xv. 18 sqq. to relate to the pentecostal *Minchah*, and therefore connects them with this passage,
and makes the *Minchah* mentioned here a *Minchah* of groats. But
there is not the slightest occasion or warrant for connecting these
passages with the pentecostal *Minchah* of the congregation, either
in the passages themselves, or in Lev. xxiii. 15 sqq. On the contrary, the offerings referred to in both passages are spontaneous
offerings of first-fruits, not restricted to any particular day.

E. THE FEAST OF TABERNACLES.

§ 194. If the second feast in the wilderness was destitute of any
historical allusion, this was by no means the case with the third of
these festivals, which was associated with the feast of the autumn harvest (of fruit, oil, and wine). In its historical aspect this was called
the *feast of Tabernacles (lit. feast of Booths)*, חַג הַסֻּכּוֹת (Lev. xxiii.
34; Deut. xvi. 13; by *Josephus* and in the New Testament, σκηνο-
πηγία); and in its agricultural aspect, *feast of ingathering* (חַג הָאָסִיף,
Ex. xxiii. 16, xxxiv. 22). The first name it derived from the fact,
that during the seven days of its celebration, viz., from the 15th to
the 21st of the seventh month, of which the first day alone possessed
a sabbatical character with the suspension of labour and a holy as-

sembly, the Israelites were to leave their houses and dwell in booths.
These booths were constructed, on the first day, of branches newly
cut from various ornamental shrubs and fruit-trees (with the fruit
still hanging upon them), either in the court-yards and on the roofs
of the houses, or in the streets and public squares of the town (Lev.
xxiii. 40 sqq.; Neh. viii. 15, 16). It was the most joyous festival
of the whole year, and was called by the later Jews הֶחָג, *the feast*
κατ᾿ ἐξοχήν.

The design of their dwelling in booths for seven days is thus explained in Lev. xxiii. 43: " that your generations may know that I
made the children of Israel to dwell in booths when I brought them
out (בְּהוֹצִיאִי) of the land of Egypt."[1] Consequently from the very
earliest times the real design of their dwelling in booths was supposed to be to commemorate the sojourn of Israel in the wilderness
after the exodus from Egypt. But as the wilderness is so frequently described as a terrible place, where there was no water, but
serpents and scorpions, burning heat and drought (Deut. viii. 15),
and the life in the desert, therefore, as one full of privation and
danger, this hardly seems to suit the joyous character which is
so distinctly attributed to the festival.

So much is certain, that in connection with the feast of Taber-

---

[1] In complete disregard of the rules of the language, *Kliefoth* renders this
passage—" that your descendants may know, that by leading the children of
Israel out of Egypt I have brought them hither to dwell in booths ;" and then on
the ground of this rendering opposes any allusion in the festival to the sojourn
in the desert : (1) because Israel then dwelt in tents and not in booths ; (2) because the booths referred to were not constructed of such shrubs as grew in the
desert, but only of such as grew in the Holy Land and represented its loveliness
and fertility ; and (3) because the purpose of leading the Israelites out of Egypt
was not that they might dwell in the desert, but that they might be brought to
the promised land. But any allusion in the booths to their dwelling in the Holy
Land is certainly equally inadmissible. For (1) in the Holy Land they lived
not in booths, but in houses ; (2) the reading would in that case have been, not
הוֹשַׁבְתִּי " I *have* caused you to dwell," but " I *shall* cause you to dwell ;" (3) the
rendering given to בְּהוֹצִיאִי, "by leading out," is arbitrary and not admissible.
The dwelling in huts and the dwelling in tents do not present the strong and
exclusive antithesis that *Kliefoth* supposes, but they both present a common antithesis to dwelling in the houses of the towns and villages, and this alone comes
into consideration here. The omission of any allusion to the specific shrubs of the
desert is no argument against the traditional view. It would have been necessary to take a journey of several days into the wilderness before these could be
obtained, and that would certainly have been too much to demand. By employing fruit-trees of the Holy Land with the fruit still hanging upon them, a fitting
expression was also given to the agricultural character of the festival.

nacles, the sojourn in the desert was not to be looked at from this point of view, viz., as a state of privation and danger. At the same time, *Keil* does not quite hit the mark when he thinks to get rid of the contrast by observing, that " in the Scriptures the booth is not a symbol of privation and misery, but of defence, protection, and concealment from heat and storm. And the fact that God caused His people to dwell in huts during their wandering through the great and terrible desert, was a proof of the fatherly care of His covenant fidelity, etc." Undoubtedly the booth is often introduced in the language of poetry as a figure to represent protection and concealment, but only (and this *Keil* has overlooked) in contrast to the defenceless and unsheltered condition of the open field or desert. And where the booth stands, as it does here, in contrast to the firm, solid structure of a house, it cannot have this meaning.

We must look at the sojourn in the desert from a different side, therefore, if we would understand how it became the object of the most joyous and merry of all the festivals. To see this, we must first of all observe, that the introduction of the great and terrible desert mentioned in Deut. viii. 15 is quite out of place here. For the allusion can only have been to the first year of the sojourn in the desert, and in fact especially, if not exclusively, to the stay at Sinai, which lasted almost a year. For in the first place, the object commemorated by the festival must have been the year in which the covenant existed, and not the $38\frac{1}{2}$ years of its suspension ; and secondly, when the feast of Booths was instituted, and Lev. xxiii. 43 was spoken, the Israelites had seen nothing as yet of the great and terrible wilderness referred to in Deut. viii. 15, viz., the desert to the north of Sinai ; and that portion of the desert which they had hitherto passed through was comparatively rich in supplies of water and wide-spread oases with a more or less abundant vegetation ; whilst it was more especially true, that the places of encampment in the neighbourhood of Sinai had little, or rather nothing at all, of the terrible, barren, and revolting character of the northern desert. The contrast intended in Lev. xxiii. 43 is between their condition in Egypt and that at Sinai. In the former, the Israelite, with his oppressive and grievous bondage, could hardly take a single step without feeling the whip of his driver upon his back ; in the latter, he felt himself under God's open sky, free as a bird in the air, whilst he was surrounded by Nature in her grandest and most majestic forms (Ps. cxxiv. 7). His deliverance from the house of bondage in Egypt, which was commemorated in the feast of the Passover, was completed here ; it was here first that it became a *fait accompli*, when he entered the desert of Sinai and passed beyond the grasp of Egyptian despotism. It was the contrast between these two conditions that was commemorated in the feast of Tabernacles ; and to bring this to mind, even in the Holy Land, as long as the festival continued, the Israelites were to exchange their abode in close, dull, lifeless houses, for a temporary abode in booths of foliage that were fresh, free, and airy, and where all was green, fragrant, and alive.

§ 195. Now if this was the idea of their temporary abode in leafy bowers, this feast stands in a close and living connection with the Easter festival, whilst they mutually supplement each other. Did the one represent the deliverance from Egyptian bondage, the other represented the fruit of that deliverance—the fresh, joyous, and happy life resulting from the unrestricted enjoyment of the freedom they had wanted so long. And in no less admirable a manner does the historical bearing of the feast of Tabernacles link itself into a living unity with its agricultural aspect, as the feast of ingathering—the joyous time of the vintage and gathering of fruits, a time that ever overflowed with pleasure and delight. The combination of both these made it the most joyous festival of the entire year, Israel's true feast of blessedness in the full enjoyment of the material and spiritual blessings which the sojourn in the desert had brought and sealed,[1] and which the fruitfulness of the Holy Land poured out for them in richest abundance in the closing harvest of the year.

In accordance with this character, the festal sacrifices appointed for this feast were more numerous than those appointed for any other (*vid.* Num. xxix. 12 sqq.). On each of the seven days a he-goat was to be offered as a sin-offering, and as a burnt-offering two rams and fourteen yearling lambs. The number of the sacrifices remained the same for the whole seven days ; but the number of bullocks to be offered daily as a burnt-offering was diminished every day by one, so that whilst thirteen were offered on the first day, there were only seven on the last, and the whole number amounted to seventy.

---

[1] The later Jews, surprised at the want of any festival in commemoration of the giving of the law in the Mosaic cycle of feasts, sought to supply the want by forcing this meaning upon the feast of Weeks. But ought it not rather to be sought in the feast of Tabernacles ? According to our view of this festival, such a connection would be simple enough.

§ 196. In immediate connection with the seven days' observance of the feast of Tabernacles, viz., on the eighth day, the so-called עֲצֶרֶת or *concluding* feast was held. This feast had a sabbatical character with a holy convocation (Lev. xxiii. 36 ; Num. xxix. 35–38). This is generally regarded as the close of the feast of Tabernacles; but such a view is inadmissible. For in that case not only would it have been held on the seventh day, *i.e.*, on the last day of the feast, like the *Azereth* of the feast of the Passover, and not on the eighth day, but the obligation to dwell in booths would have applied to that day also. The fact that this was not the case, but that the dwelling in tents terminated the day before, is an un-answerable proof, that this *Azereth* was not a part of the feast of Tabernacles itself. And this is confirmed by a comparison of the festal sacrifices of this day with those of the seven days in which the booths were continued. If the view referred to were correct, either the diminution of the number of festal sacrifices would have proceeded in the same manner as on the other days, or else, what would have been still more appropriate on account of the sabbatical character of the day, it would have risen again to the same number as on the first day. But instead of that, the most simple offerings were appointed for this eighth day, namely such as were offered on the first day of the seventh month, which were far below those presented on the seventh or last day of the feast of Tabernacles both in number and character, viz., one he-goat as a sin-offering, and one bullock, one ram, and seven lambs as a burnt-offering.

This *Azereth* is rather to be regarded as the closing festival of the whole festal half of the year, in which the vanishing festal period brightened up once more, gathering all the festal allusions in softer radiance into itself, before it gave place to the other half, in which no feasts were held. Its immediate connection with the feast of Tabernacles, however, appears to have had this influence, that the feast itself had not an independent *Azereth* of its own, as the analogy of the Easter festival would seem to require, through the impartation of a sabbatical character to the seventh day.

F. THE DAY OF ATONEMENT.

§ 197. The design of the day of atonements or expiations (יוֹם הַכִּפֻּרִים, Lev. xxiii. 27), as the name itself shows, was the complete and all-embracing expiation, not only of the priesthood and the people, but also of the holy places, inasmuch as having been erected

in the midst of the sinful nation, they might be regarded as having
been contaminated and defiled by the impurity of the atmosphere
that surrounded them.　It was the highest, most perfect, and most
comprehensive of all the acts of expiation.　It was therefore unique
in its character; it took place only once in the entire year; it applied to all the sin and uncleanness of the whole year; and was
obliged to be performed by the high priest alone, in whom the
priestly dignity of the whole priesthood culminated, on the Capporeth
of the Holy of Holies, as the highest and holiest place of atonement.　But *Keil* (i. 404), *Knobel* (p. 486), and others are wrong in
restricting the expiations of this day to such sins as had remained
unknown, and therefore unexpiated, during the past year.　The
universality expressed so strongly in the words of Lev. xvi. 16,
"because of the uncleanness of the children of Israel, and because
of their transgressions in *all* their sins," is irreconcilable with this
idea; moreover, the sins which had remained unknown had already
been expiated once in the numerous sin-offerings of the feasts and
new moons.　The כִּפֻּרִים of this day applied rather to all the sins of
the whole nation without exception, known or unknown, atoned
for or not atoned for.　The observance of this day was founded
rather upon the feeling, that such expiation as the fore-court could
furnish was really faulty and insufficient, and that Israel had to
look for a higher and more perfect expiation, in which all the defects and insufficiencies of the existing means of atonement would
be fully remedied and supplied.　And this ultimate realization of
the idea of atonement was indicated, foreshadowed, and typically
guaranteed, by the ceremonial of this one day.　The intention of
the day was not to supplement and complete the public and private
expiations of the year, but to exhibit them in still greater potency,
and to impart to them a still higher validity.

In accordance with this intention, not only did the day of atonement assume the character of a high Sabbath (שַׁבַּת שַׁבָּתוֹן), distinguished by the suspension of labour and a holy convocation, but all
the people were commanded to afflict their souls (וְעִנִּיתֶם אֶת־נַפְשֹׁתֵיכֶם)
on pain of extirpation (Lev. xvi. 29, 31, xxiii. 27 sqq.).

The observance of this day was fixed for the tenth day of the
seventh month, so that it fell between the Sabbath of the new moon
and the feast of Tabernacles.　Its being placed in the seventh month
may be accounted for, on the ground that it possessed a sabbatical
character in the most eminent degree.　For the same reason it had
to be observed on one of the prominent points of this month.　But

as neither the first day of the month nor the day of the full moon was available for the purpose, the tenth of the month, which bore in the number ten the stamp of completion and perfection, was the only one which remained. And this suited all the better, because the feast of Atonement was thereby brought into the closest possible proximity to the feast of Tabernacles, and thus furnished a fitting basis to the feast of Israel's rejoicing by its most complete and comprehensive expiation; so that there was nothing to detract from the confidence and purity of their rejoicing, inasmuch as it rested upon the certainty, that they had obtained both reconciliation and fellowship with Jehovah.

Nevertheless it is certainly a mistake to bring down the great day of atonement to the level of a merely preliminary festival to the feast of Tabernacles, as *Ewald* and even *Keil* have done, making the latter the independent and principal feast, and the former the dependent and subordinate one, and thus robbing it of its character as a unique and independent festival, which governed the entire year. If the design had been to give any such position and significance to the day of atonement, the one unique act of expiation performed on that day would certainly have been made the commencement of the feast of Tabernacles, just as the seven days of the feast of unleavened bread were opened by the paschal meal. But even in that case it ought still to be designated as the *main festival*, and the rejoicing of the feast of Tabernacles as the result and fruit, and therefore as the after-feast; just as the paschal meal was the main festival, and the eating of unleavened bread for seven days the after-feast.

§ 198. The central point of the observance of this day was the כִּפֻּרִים, from which it derived its name, viz., the reconciliation of the priesthood, of the tabernacle and its furniture, and of the entire nation, which preceded the presentation of the ordinary festal sacrifices, and was to be performed immediately after the daily morning sacrifice (Lev. xvi.). To prepare for the performance of this, the high priest, whose function it was, bathed himself, and put on the peculiar *dress* prescribed for this day and for this purpose (Lev. xvi. 4). This dress had none of the splendour of his usual official dress, but was made entirely of white linen (בַּד), and consisted of four different articles (ver. 4)—a priest's coat (כְּתֹנֶת), drawers (מִכְנָסִים), a girdle (אַבְנֵט), and a turban (מִצְנֶפֶת).—Now, considering that the day of atonement was a day of self-humiliation and mortification, not for the people only, but also for the priesthood and the high priest himself, we cannot accept *Keil's* view, that this particular kind of dress was chosen because, having throughout the character of holiness, it was the " holiest and most glorious dress," holier and more glorious than the splendid official costume which the high priest wore on other occasions, and that he wore it that he " might appear before the Holy One as if cleansed from every blemish of sin, in the pure holiness of the greatest of the servants of God;" but we must still adhere to the explanation given by *Winer, Hofmann,* and *Baumgarten,* viz., that it is to be regarded as the plainer and more humble of the two.

The incorrectness of *Keil's* view is evident enough, from the simple fact that the high priest had to put on this dress when he offered the sin-offering for himself and his people, and therefore that he was not yet " cleansed from the defilement of sin," and had not yet " the pure holiness of the highest servants of God." It is evident also from the fact, that in that case the anointed (Ex. xxix. 21), or, as it was afterwards called, the " golden" dress, would have possessed the character of holiness and glory in a far lower degree; whereas evidently this twofold character was not weakened, but as a matter of course elevated and enhanced, by the addition of the gold, the precious stones, and the holy colours. In fact, according to this explanation, we ought, for the sake of consistency, to proceed to the absurd conclusion, that the ordinary official dress of the common priests was *much* holier and more glorious than the ordinary decorations of the high priest, since they bore an incomparably greater resemblance, in material, *colour,* and make, to the dress worn by the high priest on the day of atonement, than to his ordinary official dress, and, in fact, have been regarded by many commentators as precisely the same.

The evidence adduced by *Keil* in support of his view is very feeble. He supposes that the dress in question " is shown to be the *most glorious* in which the high priest could appear, by the epithet *holy garment,* which is expressly applied to it." It has not escaped his notice, indeed, that in Ex. xxviii. 4 the ordinary official costume of the priests is also spoken of as *holy garments;* " but," he says, " if in a law in which the Most Holy Place, where the Capporeth was, is invariably called simply הַקֹּדֶשׁ (vers. 2, 3, 16), it is stated with peculiar emphasis, with regard to the dress prescribed for this act of near approach to God, 'these are *holy* garments' (ver. 4), there can be no doubt that the predicate 'holy' is attributed to it in a higher sense than to the ordinary priestly costume, and is intended to designate it as the holiest costume of all." For all this, however, we still maintain with the most confident assurance, that the white linen dress, without any ornament of gold, jewels, and holy colours, was appointed to be worn in connection with the expiations of the day of atonement, because it was more in accordance with its character as a day of humiliation, penitence, and mortification. As a simple and less ornamental style of dress, it was opposed to the splendour and glory of the ordinary official decorations, and is to be regarded as a reduction of the decorations of the high priest to the style of an ordinary priest, in accordance with the humiliation and self-denial demanded by the day ; and the more elevated form of the cap (the turban) alone still served to indicate the elevation of the high priest above the rank of the common priests. On the other hand, to make the simplicity and absence of ornament fully complete, what little ornament there was on the dress of the common priests had to be laid aside ; so that a simple white linen girdle was substituted for the costly variegated girdle usually worn by the priests.

§ 199. Thus equipped, the high priest proceeded to the work of the day. He began by bringing a bullock for a sin-offering, and a ram for a burnt-offering, for himself and his house, *i.e.*, for the whole priesthood. Two he-goats were then brought for a sin-offering, and a ram for a burnt-offering, on the part of the congregation. Upon the former the high priest cast two lots before the door of the tabernacle, one designated לַיהוָה, the other לַעֲזָאזֵל. The goat upon which the lot " to JEHOVAH " fell was set apart to be slain as a sin-offering for the nation ; but the other one, upon which the lot " to AZAZEL " fell, was placed alive before Jehovah, לְכַפֵּר עָלָיו, to be sent into the desert " to *Azazel* " (vers. 7–10).

Before the high priest could proceed, as the head of the whole priesthood, to atone for the nation by means of the goat set apart for that purpose, it was necessary that he should first of all make atonement for himself and his own house, as both he and his house were involved in the general sinfulness (Heb. vii. 27). He therefore slew the bullock that he had already presented (ver. 11). But something more was needed for the atonement of this day than the application of the atoning blood to the horns of the altar of incense in the Holy Place, which was sufficient in the case of an ordinary sin-offering presented by the high priest (§ 107). On the present occasion it was requisite that this should be performed in the Most Holy Place, upon the highest medium of expiation, viz., the *Capporeth*. But the Most Holy Place was the abode of the unapproachable holiness of God, and was therefore closed not only against all the people, but against all the priests as well—the high priest alone being ever allowed to enter it, and he only on this particular day ; " for there," says Jehovah (ver. 2), "I appear in the cloud above the Capporeth." But as no sinful man can see God without dying, and the high priest had to officiate there on this one day because of his office and calling ; it was necessary that he should take peculiar precautions to avert this destruction from himself. He filled the censer with burning coals from the altar of burnt-offering, and, taking both hands full of beaten incense, he went with the two behind the curtain into the holiest of all, where he threw the incense upon the coals (without looking about him), that the cloud of incense might cover the Capporeth above the testimony, and by its effect in outwardly enveloping and inwardly (symbolically, § 146) appeasing, might protect him from the death that threatened him (ver. 13).[1] There can be no doubt, though it is not expressly stated, that he left the censer in the Most Holy Place until his last time of entering, in order that the production of smoke might continue, and the whole space be entirely filled with it.

---

[1] It is to be hoped that the dispute first commenced by *Vitringa* (Observv. ss.), and carried on with spirit by *Thalemann* and *Rau*, which has been continued even to our own day, whether the cloud mentioned in ver. 2, in which Jehovah appeared above the Capporeth, and the cloud of incense with which, according to ver. 13, the high priest was to cover the Capporeth, are to be regarded as identical or not, has been settled at last by the candid admission of *Knobel* and *Bunsen*, that the anti-traditional view is exegetically impossible. The cloud referred to in ver. 2, as well known, cannot be any other than that in which the glory of God is said to have appeared in Ex. xvi. 10, xix. 9, 16, and of which it is stated in Ex. xl. 34, 35, in connection with the erection of the tabernacle, that "the cloud covered the tent of the congregation, and the glory of the Lord filled the tabernacle ; and Moses was not able to enter into the tent of the congregation, because the cloud abode thereon, and the glory of Jehovah filled the tabernacle" (cf. 1 Kings viii. 11 ; 2 Chron. v. 13, 14). The cloud in ver. 13 is obviously distinguished from that in ver. 2 by the expression, " cloud of the incense " (already described). Moreover, the two stand in the most decided contrast to one another, for the cloud in ver. 2 threatens with death, and that in ver. 13 defends against it. In ver. 2 the reason why Aaron could not go *at any time* into the Most Holy Place is said to have been because God appeared there in the cloud. Now, if the cloud intended had been only the cloud of incense to be brought by Aaron, we should have to regard the appearance of God as dependent upon his bringing this cloud with him ; so that, *without* the cloud of incense, Aaron might have gone into the Most Holy Place at any time, which is the very thing expressly prohibited in the second verse.

§ 200. The danger of sudden death in consequence of the sight of the glory of God having thus been averted by that glory being enveloped in the cloud of the incense, the expiations of the day, the first stage of which was to unfold itself in the Most Holy Place, could now commence. First of all the high priest went again into the Most Holy Place with the blood of the bullock which had already been slain, and sprinkled some of it once *upon* the Capporeth towards the front,—at the foot, therefore, as it were of the glory of Jehovah which was enthroned upon it,—and then seven times in *front* of the Capporeth (ver. 14). As it was the blood of the bullock offered by Aaron for himself and his house, both acts had respect to the sins of the priesthood. The former, however, was intended chiefly as an atonement for the persons themselves, the latter as an atonement for the sanctuary (including of course the Most Holy Place), so far as they had been contaminated by the sinful atmosphere of the priests. This required a sevenfold sprinkling, because seven was the seal of the covenant, and the sanctuary was the seat of the covenant. The correctness of this view, in which I rejoice to have *Keil's* support (i. 405, 406), is evident from the object sprinkled, which was not the Capporeth itself, but the ground in front of it. The sevenfold sprinkling, therefore, had respect not to the Capporeth, but to the holy spot upon which it stood, and which became the Most Holy Place in consequence. *Delitzsch* opposes this view as irreconcilable with the wording of Lev. xvi., according to which the expiation of the priesthood and that of the sanctuary were coincident, inasmuch as any purification of the holy things from the uncleanness of Israel which attached to them, was at the same time an unlocking of the grace of God towards Israel, of which they were the vehicles. But what could be the intention of a double act of sprinkling, once upon the Capporeth, and then seven times in front of it, if the former of these two acts represented the expiation of the priesthood in and with the expiation of the sanctuary?

The sin which attached to the high priest, who was to make atonement for the people, and also the uncleanness which attached in consequence of this to the place of expiation, where atonement was to be made for the people, having thus been covered and rendered inoperative, it was now possible to proceed to the atonement for the *people*. For this purpose the high priest, probably leaving the bowl with the blood of the bullock in the Holy Place for subsequent use, went again into the fore-court, and after slaying the he-goat set apart as the sin-offering of the people, carried its blood also

into the Most Holy Place, where he performed just the same ceremony, and with just the same effect, for the people and their relation
to the Holy Place, as he had previously done with the blood of the
bullock for himself and his own relation to the sanctuary (vers.
15, 16 a).

The expiations now entered their *second stage*, the scene of which
was the *Holy Place*. This is summarily described in the following
words (ver. 16 b): " And so shall he do for the tabernacle of the
congregation, that dwelleth among them in the midst of their uncleanness." That we are to understand by אֹהֶל מוֹעֵד here, not the
whole of the tabernacle, but its most comprehensive part, the Holy
Place, cannot be doubted, on account of the obvious connection in
which it stands. And from the word כֵּן (so), which points to the
proceedings in the Most Holy Place described just before, it may
be inferred with certainty, that a sprinkling was to take place once
upon the altar of incense, and seven times *in front of it*, first with
the blood of the bullock, and then with that of the he-goat; whilst,
judging from the analogy in other cases (§ 107), it is more than
probable, that the former was applied not to the surface, but to the
horns of the altar (cf. Ex. xxx. 10). But the distinctive signification of the two kinds of sprinkling would be just the same here as
in the Most Holy Place. As the Holy Place, however, was acces-
sible to the common priests, it is expressly stated in ver. 17, that
during the performance of these acts no one but the high priest was
even to enter the Holy Place.

§ 201. The *third stage* of the expiations was carried out in the
fore-court, also by the high priest alone. " And he shall go," it is
stated in ver. 18, " unto the altar that is before Jehovah, and make
an atonement for it, and shall take of the blood of the bullock, and
of the blood of the goat, and smear it (וְנָתַן) upon the horns of the
altar round about. And (ver. 19) he shall sprinkle of the blood
upon it (עָלָיו) with his finger seven times, and hallow it from the
uncleanness of the children of Israel." The opinion expressed by
Bähr, Baumgarten, Delitzsch, Hofmann, Knobel, and others, that by
the " altar that is before Jehovah," in ver. 18, we are to understand
not the altar of burnt-offering, but the altar of incense, must be
rejected as a mistake. The expression " go out" (וַיֵּצֵא), which occurs
in ver. 18, after the acts of the high priest in the Holy Place have
been already described in ver. 16 b, must relate, not to his going
out of the *Most Holy Place*, but simply to his leaving the Holy Place.
It is true, *Hofmann* cites this very expression as an indisputable

proof of the opposite view, and says that this וצא evidently relates
to the clause in ver. 17, בְּבֹאוֹ לְכַפֵּר בַּקֹּדֶשׁ עַד־צֵאתוֹ (" when he goeth in
to make an atonement in the Holy Place, until he come out").
This is true enough, but the conclusion drawn from it is false for
all that. For the " going in" and " going out" in ver. 17 relate to
his going from the fore-court into the dwelling-place, and out of
the dwelling-place into the fore-court, and not to his passing from
the Holy Place into the Most Holy, and *vice versa*. Such a view
might indeed be rendered necessary if the reading were בְּבֹאוֹ בַקֹּדֶשׁ
לְכַפֵּר, instead of being as it is, בְּבֹאוֹ לְכַפֵּר בַּקֹּדֶשׁ. But with the words
as they stand, it is much more natural, according to the usage of
the language in other cases, to refer the going in and out to the
tabernacle as a whole. Moreover, the meaning of ver. 17 is certainly, not that just in those particular moments in which the high
priest was in the Most Holy Place no one was to enter the tabernacle, but evidently, that no one was to enter it at all during the
whole of the time that he was occupied within. There is nothing
in the fact, that the altar is spoken of as being " before Jehovah,"
to compel us to think of the altar of incense ; inasmuch as the expression " before Jehovah" occurs in innumerable instances, as
equivalent to, before the door of the tabernacle ; and the words
" from off the altar before Jehovah," in ver. 12, unquestionably
refer to the " altar of burnt-offering." Again, the appeal to Ex.
xxx. 10 loses all its force, if, as we have already shown to be
probable, ver. 16 *b* is to be taken in combination with it. And,
lastly, we may refer to ver. 20 (cf. ver. 33), where the different
stages are recapitulated, and consist of " reconciling the Holy Place
(*i.e.*, the Holy of Holies), the tabernacle (*i.e.*, the Holy Place), and
the altar." For in this passage it is obvious enough, that there were
three such stages and not *two*, and that what took place in the tabernacle (*i.e.*, the Holy Place) according to ver. 16 *b* could not be
identical with what is described in vers. 18, 19, as having been done
at the altar. But if, notwithstanding this, any one should still per-
sist in understanding by the altar in ver. 18 the altar of incense, and
regarding vers. 18, 19 as a further explanation of ver. 16 *b*, he would
set altogether at nought the וְכֵן יַעֲשֶׂה (" and so shall he do") in ver.
16 *b*. For this requires that the expiation in the Holy Place should
be performed in precisely the same manner as it had already been in
the Most Holy, viz., *once upon the altar* and seven times *in front* of
it, whereas vers. 18 and 19 would teach in that case that even the
sevenfold sprinkling was performed *upon* the altar in the Holy Place.

We most decidedly object to *Keil's* statement, that the high priest " first put the blood of the bullock and goat upon the horns of the altar of burnt-offering, and then sprinkled it seven times *upon the ground in front of the altar.* The text of ver. 19 is וְהִזָּה עָלָיו; and how any one can understand this to mean sprinkling "upon the ground in front of it," I cannot comprehend. But if the seven-fold sprinkling in the Most Holy Place certainly took place " *in front of* the Capporeth," and therefore that in the Holy Place was also performed *in front of* the altar of incense, it still needs to be explained, why the sprinkling in the fore-court should have taken place not *in front,* but *upon the top* of the altar. The answer is by no means difficult to obtain. The two compartments of the tabernacle were enclosed spaces, representing the abode of God in the midst of His people ; whilst the fore-court represented the abode of that nation which had its God in the midst of it (§ 12). In each of the former the entire space was the place of the revelation of God ; in the latter, the altar alone.

In *Delitzsch's* view, indeed, the altar of burnt-offering needed no further expiation, after the performance of the acts prescribed in Ex. xxix. 36, 37 ; " for," he adds, " how could any of the im-purity of Israel adhere to it, seeing that it flowed day after day with the blood by which Israel was reconciled ?" This remark is directed against *Hofmann's* view (§ 68), that all the sacrificial blood which came upon the altar did so merely for the purpose of cleansing it from the defilement brought upon it by the sin of the sacrificer. But *Hofmann* (on the common, though erroneous assumption, that on the day of atonement the altar of burnt-offering did not pass through the cleansing ceremony) has justly replied, that this rather tends to confirm his view, " inasmuch as it was by the daily offer-ings that the cleansing of the altar of burnt-offering was repeated again and again, so that it needed no such purification as the altar of incense on the great day of atonement."

But *Delitzsch's* opinion, that the altar of burnt-offering needed no further expiation after the expiation so fully performed at its consecration, and also *Hofmann's* opinion, that it needed no special expiation on the great day of atonement because it had been ex-piated again and again the whole year through, by means of the daily sacrifices, are both of them decidedly wrong. The *latter state-ment* is correct in itself, but does not prove what it is intended to establish. If, as *Hofmann* himself maintains, not only the sins which had been left without expiation during the year, but (according to ver. 16) even those which had been already expiated, were the objects of expiation on this day; then just in the same degree in which the priesthood and the people needed a new and higher expiation, was it requisite that the altar, at which they had been so imperfectly expiated, should be subjected to a similar expiation. The higher virtue ascribed to the sprinkling of the altar on this particular day rested upon the fact, that it was the same blood which had already been in the Most Holy Place, and had acquired the highest atoning power at the throne of God.—In opposition to the *former*, it is to be observed, that as the high priest was anointed (*i.e.*, consecrated) only once, but had to be expiated again and again, so the expiation of the altar of burnt-offering needed renewal and repetition, but not the anointing of the altar. Moreover, when we find that a special expiation had to be made for the priesthood before the expiation of the people, this is not to be understood as though the last expiation applied to the people only, to the exclusion of the priests; for in that case it would be impossible to understand, as *Hofmann* correctly observes, why a double act of expiation (distributed over the two he-goats) was requisite for the congregation, and only one for the priests. " The high priest began with the ceremony of expiation for himself and his house; not, however, as though the expiation for Israel had no further connection with him and his house, but because he durst not appear in the Most Holy Place as the representative of Israel without the cloud of smoke from the incense, nor, since both he and his house were sinful, without the blood of the appointed sin-offering" (*Hofmann*).

§ 202. After the completion of the atonement for the priesthood, the people, and the holy places, the second goat was brought, upon which the lot לַעֲזָאזֵל had fallen (ver. 8). According to ver. 5, both goats were set apart as a sin-offering (לְחַטָּאת). They are not to be regarded as *two* sin-offerings, however, but as forming *one* sin-offering together. This conclusion is not demanded, it is true, by the singular לְחַטָּאת; for that might very well be regarded as collective, and without the numeral אַחַת (*one*) there is nothing in ver. 5 to *force* us to adopt it. But the simple designation of both goats as sin-offerings requires it when we add the following circumstances: *first*, that the sin-offering is invariably spoken of in the singular number (§ 92); and, *secondly*, that nothing is done to this second goat which could possibly characterize it as an independent sin-offering. But *two* goats were requisite for this *one* sin-offering, because the ritual of this exceptional sin-offering rendered it necessary, that after the slaughtering and sprinkling of the blood the animal should either still be living, or be brought to life again. And as this could not possibly be represented by means of one single goat, it was necessary to divide the rôle, which this sin-offering had to play, between two goats, the second of which was to be regarded as the *alter ego* of the first, as *hircus redivivus*. Whilst the first goat, therefore, was slain as a sin-offering, and the people and sanctuary were expiated by its blood, the second goat was placed alive before Jehovah, and then kept to take the place of the other, after the latter had satisfied the demands of the day as far as it possibly could, and to carry on to completion the work which had been begun, but was not yet finished.

This second part of the expiation, which is not met with in any other sin-offering, is first of all summarily described in ver. 10 as being לְכַפֵּר עָלָיו לְשַׁלַּח אֹתוֹ לַעֲזָאזֵל הַמִּדְבָּרָה (" to make an atonement with it, and to let it go *la-Azazel* into the wilderness"), and is then described *in extenso* in vers. 20 sqq. as follows: the high priest laid both his hands upon the head of the live goat, and confessed over it all the iniquities of the children of Israel, and all their transgressions in all their sins, put them upon the head of the goat, and then sent it away by a man, who was standing ready for the purpose, into the wilderness, where it was to be let loose, in order that the goat might carry into the wilderness all their transgressions, which had been laid upon it.

The first question that arises here is, what are we to understand by *Azazel?* The different explanations which have been given may be divided into four classes. *First,* those which regard it as a description of the place to which the goat was to be taken; *secondly,* those in which it is taken to be a description of the goat to be sent away into the desert; *thirdly,* those in which it is regarded as a description of a certain evil dæmon dwelling in the desert, to whom the goat was to be sent; and, *fourthly,* those which treat it as an *abstract* noun, signifying " for complete removal."

§ 203. The last opinion is of comparatively recent origin. It is adopted by *Paulus, Steudel, Winer, Tholuck,* and *Bähr.* The design of the ceremony, as thus understood, has been most clearly explained by *Bähr.* "The true expiation," he says, "was effected by the blood of the first goat which was set apart for Jehovah; on the other hand, the ceremony with the other goat appears as a mere addition made for special reasons—a kind of complement to the wiping away of the sins, which had already been effected by means of the sacrifice. The whole ceremony had respect to the most comprehensive and highest form of expiation, beyond which no other was conceivable for Israel; and the true and essential purpose of the festival was to exhibit this in the clearest possible way. Hence, after the expiation had been accomplished by the sprinkling of the blood, the sin was still further to be carried away into the desert. What the first goat, which died as a sin-offering, was no longer in a condition to set forth, was supplied by the second, which was as it were one with the first, inasmuch as it carried the sin which had been covered entirely away, and that into the desert or desolate place, where it was quite forgotten; so that the idea of expiation or the extermination of sin was thereby rendered absolutely perfect (cf. Micah vii. 19)." *Tholuck* also observes : "As the two terms for the forgiveness of sins, כִּפֶּר, to *cover up*, and נָשָׂא, to *take away*, represent the same thing but under a different figure, so is it with the two symbols here, and that in such a manner, that the second is necessary to complete the first."

According to this view, the word is a *Pealpal* form of the Arabic עוּל = *removit*, and has been formed by modification from עֲזַלְזֵל. From a grammatical point of view this explanation is, no doubt, admissible, as the examples given by *Ewald* (Heb. Gram. § 157, 158) fully prove; though it cannot be denied, that the analogous forms are employed more for adjectives than for abstracts. And even from a material point of view, the objections raised by *Gesenius* in his *Thesaurus*, and *Hengstenberg* in his Egypt and the Books of Moses (pp. 169 sqq., Eng. transl.), are far from being conclusive; as for example when the former observes : "There is something cold and empty, and even incredible, in the supposition that this word, so singular and unparalleled in its kind, should have no other than the simplest and most obvious signification, for which the Hebrew language supplied so large a number of synonymes;" or when the latter maintains, that with any other explanation (than that which refers it to Satan) it would still be impossible to understand why the word should have been formed first of all for this particular occasion, as would then appear to be the case, and why it is never found elsewhere. Nor is there anything more conclusive in *Hengstenberg's* argument, that "if *Azazel* does not refer to Satan, there could be no reason for the casting of lots; and it is impossible, in that case, to understand why the decision should have been left to God,—why the high priest should not have set apart the one goat as a sin-offering, and the other to be sent away into the desert:

the very fact of the lots being cast presupposed that some personal
being stood in opposition to God, with regard to whom it was
necessary to uphold the supremacy of Jehovah, and to remove
every possibility of a comparison being drawn between them."
Here again *Hengstenberg* goes too far when he maintains, that
"even in ver. 8 it is impossible to tell what to do with such an
explanation as this : ' a lot for Jehovah and a lot for the complete
removal,' since the *lot* itself was not to be removed." Nor was it
the lot described as " for Jehovah" which was to be the portion of
Jehovah, but the goat upon which it fell ; and no one can dispute
the lawfulness of so simple a metonymy as the use of the lot for
the thing to be chosen by lot. At the same time, justice is not
done in this way to the antithesis between "Jehovah" and "Azazel."
And *Gesenius* is unquestionably correct in maintaining : " *Vi oppo-
siti exspectatur persona eaque talis, quæ Jovæ apte opponatur et con-
traria sit.*" And if לַעֲזָאזֵל were a *nomen actionis*, we should expect,
instead of לַיהוָה, to find לִשְׁחִיטָה or לִכְפָּרָה. A person and an action
never form a natural or appropriate antithesis.

§ 204. Of the three different interpretations in which the word
is treated as a *concrete noun*, we must at once reject the one which
regards it as a *description of the place* to which the goat was to be
taken,—whether it be looked upon as the name of a mountain in
the neighbourhood of Sinai, as it is by Ps. Jonathan, Abenezra,
and Jarchi, or as an appellative noun (= *recessus* from עזל, *remo-
vere*), as *Bochart, Deyling, Carpzov,* and *Jahn* maintain,—if only for
the simple reason, that the expression in ver. 10, "for Azazel into
the desert," *i.e.*, into the solitude for the solitude, would then contain
a most intolerable tautology. Moreover, a person and a place form
no truer antithesis than a person and an action. Hence modern
commentators have very properly given up this interpretation altogether. Even *Fürst*, who still adhered to it in his Concordance
from rabbinical sympathies, has dropped it in his Lexicon.

The notion that *Azazel* is intended as a *description of the goat
itself* is not much better. This is the view adopted by *Symmachus*
(τράγος ἀπερχόμενος), by *Aquila* (τράγος ἀπολελυμμένος), in the
Vulgate (*hircus emissarius*), and hence by *Luther* (*der ledige Bock* :
Angl. the scape-goat). It rests upon a thoroughly inadmissible etymology : עֵז = goat (? buck), and אזל = *abiit.* This view has long since
been antiquated, and regarded as no longer deserving of refutation ;
but *Hofmann* (Schriftb. i. p. 431) has revived it again and undertaken its defence. He derives עֲזָאזֵל from עָזַל = אָזַל, to go away, and

renders it " gone entirely away." " The phrase שַׁלַּח לַעֲזָאזֵל, in which ל is used in the same way as in the expression יֵצֵא לַחׇפְשִׁי in Ex. xxi. 2, signifies to drive away *as an exile* (*als Fernling*)." Now, if it could be proved that עֲזָאזֵל was a description of the goat to be led away into the wilderness, no doubt it would be allowable, and even necessary, to explain the words שלח לעזאזל in vers. 10 and 26 in this way. But that is just what is forbidden by the antithesis in ver. 8 between " the lot for Jehovah" and " the lot for *Azazel ;*" and it is self-deception on *Hofmann's* part to suppose that he has got over this antithesis by stating that " this signifies, not that the one *animal,* but that the one *lot,* was Jehovah's, and the other the exile's, the lot of the animal to be sent away." For הַגּוֹרָל לַיהֹוָה *is* no doubt the lot of Jehovah, but it *signifies per metonymiam* the animal to be assigned to Jehovah by lot. It was certainly not the lot, as the object *by* which the selection was made, that became the portion of Jehovah, but rather the lot as the object *for* which the lot was cast, viz., the animal. And if it was not the piece of parchment, metal, wood, or whatever may have been employed, but the goat upon which the parchment, etc., with the name of Jehovah upon it fell, that became the portion of Jehovah ; the same also applies, by virtue of the antithesis, to the " exile." It was not the piece of parchment which bore the name of exile that was to be devoted to exile, but the other goat; and this must be distinguished from the exile, quite as much as the first goat was to be distinguished from Jehovah.

§ 205. We have only one other view remaining, namely, that which regards *Azazel* as the *description of a personal being,* viz., an evil dæmon; and this has been very properly adopted by much the larger majority of the latest commentators, however otherwise divergent in their views,—*e.g.,* not only by *Hengstenberg* and *Keil,* but even by *Knobel* and *Bunsen,* by *Ewald, Diestel,* and *Fürst.* Nothing, in fact, can be more undeniable, than that the antithesis of ליהוה and לעזאזל in ver. 8 proves the latter to be a designation of some personal being, just as the former is. The same contrast renders it, still further, even more than probable that it is some *dæmoniacal* being that is referred to. And this is placed beyond all doubt by the fact that the desert is represented as his dwelling-place. For it is not in the New Testament that we first meet with the notion that the desert is the abode of dæmons and unclean spirits (Matt. xii. 43; Luke viii. 27; Rev. xviii. 2), but we find the same idea current even before the time of the captivity (Isa. xiii. 21,

xxxiv. 14, cf. Lev. xvii. 7).[1] Whether this idea is to be regarded
as an old Hebrew notion, dating from a period before the sojourn
in Egypt, or as one that originated in the intercourse with Egyptians, and if the latter, whether Azazel is to be regarded as a
Hebrew transformation of the Egyptian Seth or Typhon, who also
appears as an evil dæmon dwelling in the desert, is doubtful. *Hengstenberg* (Egypt and the Books of Moses, p. 170 translation) and
Hävernick (p. 203) support the latter view; but it is opposed, on
the other hand, by *Diestel* in his valuable treatise on Set-Typhon,
Azahel and Satan, on the ground that the Egyptological researches
of modern times have led to this result, " that the idea of Typhon
as an evil principle is to be assigned to a much later period than the
time of Moses, since the prevailing hatred felt towards Set in Egypt
arose *after* the time of the Ramessides, and therefore not earlier
than the 10th or 11th cent. B.C." We have neither time nor room
for settling this dispute. Nor does this seem indispensable to an
understanding of the Israelitish ritual. For even if the view upon
which it is based arose first of all in Egypt under the influence of
peculiarly Egyptian ideas, the form given to it in the festal ritual
of the day of atonement is certainly an independent, Mosaic one,

---

[1] *Hofmann* disputes this, but on insufficient grounds. He maintains that
the שְׂעִירִים (*Vulg. dæmones; Luther*, field-devils; *Eng. Vers.* devils), to which
the Israelites are forbidden to sacrifice in Lev. xvii. 7, correspond to the oxen
mentioned in 2 Chron. xi. 15 as objects of Jeroboam's worship, and that they are
both animal forms, representing the Deity, such as the Egyptians worshipped ;
and that the שְׂעִירִים in Isa. xiii. 21 are as truly animals as the בְּנוֹת יַעֲנָה mentioned in connection with them, and are as truly goats and not goat-legged
satyrs here, as in every other passage.—But the first reply to this is, that by
the שְׂעִירִים in Isa. xiii. and xxxiv. we cannot possibly understand ordinary *goats*
(for it is only of these that the name is used), since they are always domestic
animals, and we cannot imagine how they could ever come into association with
Iim and Ziim, or ostriches, and be introduced as living in desert places and ruins.
In Lev. xvii. 7 there is not the slightest warrant or occasion for thinking of
manufactured *images* of goats. And it is still more certain that *Hofmann's*
explanation of 2 Chron. xi. 15 is a misinterpretation. There is not a trace to be
found anywhere of the worship of goats having been introduced by Jeroboam
or his successors along with that of the calves, neither in the historical books of
Kings nor in the prophetical books of Hosea and Amos, which refer so frequently, so minutely, and at such length to the idolatrous worship of the
northern kingdom. The words " which he made," therefore, must be referred
merely to the " calves " mentioned in the latter passage, and the name שְׂעִירִים
must be regarded as a contemptuous epithet applied to heathen deities ; in connection with which it is to be borne in mind, that in both the Old and New

and is to be interpreted not according to Egyptian, but according to purely Israelitish ideas.

§ 206. If, then, we are thus brought to the conclusion, that by the Azazel of the day of atonement we are to understand a personal being, viz., an evil dæmon dwelling in the desert, the question arises, in what relation this notion is to be placed to the ordinary teaching of the Old Testament with reference to dæmons. With the comparatively slight development of this doctrine in the times before the captivity, and the marked reserve maintained in the inspired writings of those times with reference to this "mystery of iniquity," we must give up at the very outset all hope of any doctrinally clear and precise account of the notions which the early Israelite associated with this name. The occasional rays of light which the inspired writings throw upon this dark domain, without entering at all closely or professedly upon any description of its character, appear undoubtedly to warrant the assumption, that both tradition and the popular belief embraced a far more richly developed dæmonology than the inspired writers thought well to unfold

Testaments the heathen deities are looked upon as dæmoniacal beings having a real existence (vid. History of the Old Covenant, vol. ii. pp. 246–253, Eng. transl.). But if by the Seirim in Lev. xvii. 7 and 2 Chron. xi. 15 we are to understand dæmons, there is no possibility of attributing any other meaning to Isa. xiii. 21 and xxxiv. 15 ; and this interpretation becomes all the more certain, when we find the Lord Himself in the New Testament giving expression to the view that the desert is a favourite abode of dæmons. In Rev. xviii. 2, where the destruction of Babylon is spoken of, we have a passage of peculiar importance to the interpretation of Isa. xiii. 21 ; in fact, it is almost equivalent to a commentary upon these words of Isaiah. And this passage also proves that the juxtaposition of שְׂעִירִים and בְּנוֹת יַעֲנָה, to which the δαίμονες and ὄρνια ἀκάθαρτα correspond, does not necessitate our regarding the former as ordinary animals. But though undoubtedly the word שְׂעִירִים is an epithet applied to dæmoniacal beings, and both their existence and their abode in the desert are attested by Old and New Testament passages, this by no means compels us to picture them to ourselves as actually " goat-legged." This idea may have been current in the popular mythology, and the name may even have originated in this idea, and yet the name, when once current, may have been adopted by the language of revelation without the mythological representation of their bodily form being also accredited in consequence. It is much the same in this respect with the goats' legs of these dæmons as with the angels' wings of the Christian mythology. Supposing that a name for the angels had grown out of this idea, the language of revelation might have employed it without thereby adopting the idea to which it owed its origin. Christ could call the " prince of the devils " Beelzebub or Beelzebul, without giving His sanction in consequence to all the popular notions associated with the etymology of this name.

and accredit; but they are far too isolated and cursory to afford us any deep and comprehensive view.

A comparison of Lev. xvii. 7 with Isa. xiii. 21 will show at once, that according to the popular belief, there were many dæmons dwelling in the desert. Now if, on the one hand, the sameness of abode is a proof that Azazel was regarded as one of them, the prominence given to this one, on the other hand, shows that it was regarded as holding a distinct and exalted position among them; and we shall hardly be mistaken if we regard it as the culmination or head of the whole of the dæmon-world by which the desert was peopled. The ritual of the day of atonement places it in a distinct and peculiar relation to the sins of the nation. And this certainly suggests the thought, that there was a close connection between Azazel and the serpent in Paradise, by whose seductive influence upon the first pair sin entered the world of man. At the same time, it would be even more than precipitate to *identify* Azazel with the serpent in Paradise, or rather with the spirit of the fall, to which it served as the instrument, in such a way as to suppose that this identity was known to and present to the minds of the contemporaries of Moses. The serpent in Paradise was a hieroglyphic, which was not to be clearly understood till a future day,—a seed-corn of truth, which was not to be unfolded till the sun of revelation was about to reach the zenith of its glory. If the Mosaic doctrine of Azazel had been a conscious unfolding of the primeval account of the snake in Paradise, it would not only have been richer, clearer, and deeper than it is, but there would also of necessity have been marked and obvious points of contact between the two; but of this there is not the slightest trace.

And if the serpent of Paradise could not have formed the groundwork for the later view of the Azazel that dwelt in the desert, there is just as little reason to regard the latter as supplying the foundation for the still later teaching of the Old Testament respecting Satan. For the name never occurs again; nor is the desert ever expressly referred to as his peculiar dwelling-place. But whilst the account of the serpent in Paradise still remains altogether mysterious and enigmatical, and no marked or obvious points of coincidence are to be found between the Azazel of the desert and the Satan of a later date, it is easy to discover some very distinct lines of relationship between them. They are both personal, individual beings, and they both belong to the dæmon-world, and occupy a prominent and unparalleled position there. There can be

no ground, therefore, for denying *a priori* such a connection between
the two forms, as points to conscious identity.   However strange
the fact may appear, therefore, that the name Azazel never occurs
again in the later portions of the Old Testament, this may possibly
be explained to some extent on the supposition, that Azazel was
originally simply an adjective or common noun, and may still have
continued to be used in this form, whilst the name Satan grew more
and more into a proper name.   The fact that Satan is never referred
to in the Old Testament as dwelling in the desert, may be accidental,
and by no means warrants an unqualified denial of his identity with
Azazel.   On the other hand, the character of Satan as the enemy,
the calumniator, and the accuser of the righteous, corresponds precisely to the part assigned to Azazel in relation to the כִּפֻּרִים of the
day of atonement.   And even if the later doctrine concerning Satan
developed itself independently of the idea of Azazel, so much at
any rate is certain, that in Azazel we see the head of the dæmon-
world as opposed to God and hostile to salvation, so far as it was
at that time an object of thought at all; and this sufficiently explains the ritual of the day of atonement.

With regard to the etymology of the name עֲזָאזֵל, *Hengstenberg*
and *Knobel* are probably correct in taking it to be a *Pealpel* form
of the Arabic עזל = *semovit, dimovit, se separavit*, with an adjective
meaning, viz., " the entirely separate one," which is perfectly in
keeping with his dwelling בְּאֶרֶץ גְּזֵרָה (ver. 22), in a land cut off, or
separate.   *Diestel* and *Fürst* regard the existing form of the word
as a corruption of עֲזַאֵל, " power of God," or by another turn of
the expression, " defiance of God," and appeal to the fact that
among the heathen Shemites the name עַז occurs in various ways
as a name of Deity.   But the combinations of the names of angels
and dæmons with אֵל, the name of God, as the final syllable, are of
so late a date in Jewish history, that it is something more than
venturesome to transfer them to the Mosaic, or even an earlier age.

§ 207. One of the earliest explanations of the ceremony assumed that the second goat was meant as a gift or present for
Azazel, and was intended to prevent him from destroying the
efficacy of the sacrifices, offered for the expiation of Israel, by
means of his hostile influence.   According to the prevailing opinion,
the LXX. followed this interpretation.   In ver. 8 the rendering of
לַעֲזָאזֵל is τῷ Ἀποπομπαίῳ, the meaning of which, according to the
passages quoted by *Gesenius* from *Pollux, Suidas*, and *Harpocration*,
is = Ἀποτροπαῖος, Ἀλεξίκακος, *Averruncus*.   But as the LXX. have

rendered the Hebrew word in ver. 10 by εἰς τὴν ἀποπομπήν (and
in ver. 26 by εἰς ἄφεσιν), it seems to me more probable that their
'Ἀποπομπαῖος was used passively (= ἀποπεμπόμενος), and intended
as a name for the goat. There can be no doubt that *Josephus*
adopted this view, when he paraphrased the word thus in Ant. iii.
10, 3 : ἀποτροπιασμὸς καὶ παραίτησις τοῦ πλήθους παντὸς ὑπὲρ
ἁμαρτημάτων ἐσόμενος. Many of the Rabbins followed him, and
among more modern writers, *Spencer, Ammon,* and *Rosenmüller;*
also *Gesenius,* who speaks very confidently in his Lexicon of 1833,
where he says, " *Non dubitans reddo* ἀλεξίκακος, *averruncus, caco-
dæmonem in deserto habitantem, ex ritu illo vetustissimo et gentili
hostiis mitigandum intelligendum esse statuo.*" He repeats this
opinion, though not with the same confidence, in his Thesaurus,
and in the later editions of his Lexicon also.

But this view is so evidently at variance with the spirit of
Mosaism and of the Old Testament generally, that it is not deserving of any elaborate refutation, and in fact does not need one in
the present condition of the question (*vid. Bähr,* pp. 686, 687, but
more especially *Hengstenberg, l.c.* pp. 169 sqq.; the numerous objections adduced by the latter are not all equally conclusive). The
principal objections are the following : (1) In the very next chapter
(Lev. xvii. 7) sacrifices are forbidden to be offered to dæmons
(שְׂעִירִים). (2) Both the goats are described as sin-offerings in ver.
5 ; and, as *Hengstenberg* observes, the idea of a sin-offering presupposes holiness, the hatred of sin, on the part of the being to whom
it is offered. (3) The two goats form but *one* sin-offering (§ 202),
both are brought before Jehovah, and Jehovah's decision is sought
by lot as to what is to be done with them,—all of them *data*, which
entirely preclude our regarding one goat as a sacrifice for Jehovah,
and the other as an ovation for Azazel. (4) According to ver. 21,
the sins of the people were laid by the high priest upon the second
goat, that he might take them to Azazel. Now if the sins laid
upon it are regarded as already expiated, which they really were
by the offering of the first goat, the sending of them to Azazel was
an act of defiance and ridicule, rather than an ovation or an indem-
nification ; whereas, if we lose sight of the fact that the sins were
already expiated, the sending of these sins to Azazel was no doubt
an ovation for him, but at the same time it was an act of the
bitterest defiance towards Jehovah, and the most daring renuncia-
tion of His claims.

Even the modification, which *Witsius* gives to this view in his

Aegyptiaca (ii. 9, 3), does not render it any more acceptable. In his opinion, *non fuit caper emissarius diabolo oblatus, sed voluntate Dei expositus vexandus diabolo.* But *Bähr* justly objects to this, that "the text in that case would contain no allusion to what was really the principal thing, viz., the *vexari;* to say nothing of the fact that the idea of *vexari* is altogether foreign to the early Mosaism." Moreover, the goat laden with the sins of the people would then serve as the representative of the sinful nation, and the ceremony, in spite of the expiation already accomplished, would teach that vexation was still required,—a doctrine that would stand in the most direct opposition to the idea and purpose of the day.

§ 208. The question, why the sins of the people were laid upon the second goat, or rather, as this question is authoritatively answered by the text itself in ver. 22, why these sins were to be sent to Azazel, must form the backbone of every inquiry into the true meaning of this ceremonial. And here it is a matter of the greatest and most essential importance, whether the laying of the sins upon the second goat be regarded as dependent upon the previous expiation of the same sins by the sacrifice of the first goat, or whether the two acts be looked upon as equally independent, and having no relation the one to the other, so that in both of them there was precisely the same reference to the sins as such, *i.e.,* as not yet expiated. And the fact that care has not been taken to determine this at the very outset, or rather, that in most cases the question has not even been raised, has considerably obstructed the full, distinct, and thorough understanding of this singular ceremony, if not rendered it absolutely impossible.

We must once more insist, as we have already done, upon the fact, that when the sins were laid upon the head of the second goat, they could not be looked at in any other light than *as already expiated.* It is perfectly inconceivable that so important a transaction as the previous atonement for the whole congregation and the whole sanctuary through the blood of the first goat, which formed the basis of, and was presupposed by, all that followed, could possibly have been overlooked in what the high priest is described as performing in ver. 21. And this is both inconceivable and impossible if, as is generally admitted, the second goat is to be regarded as the continuation of the first, as the first called to life again, as its *alter ego,* occupying its place after its life had been taken, to carry on its work, and complete the task assigned it. Moreover, any such ignoring of the expiations described in vers. 15 sqq. as having

been effected through the blood of the first goat, in connection with
the laying on of the sins in ver. 21, would be equivalent to a direct
denial of the validity of those expiations, which nevertheless had
been carried to the highest possible point, would give the lie to the
promise of Jehovah in Lev. xvii. 11, and in fact would represent
the whole of the sacrificial ceremonial of the Old Testament as
destitute of power. Our view also receives an undeniable confirmation from the fact, that the laying on of hands is described in ver.
21 as performed by the high priest. Had it been to sin as such—
i.e., as committed by the nation—that reference was made, it ought
to have been laid upon the animal by the nation itself, or by its
natural representatives, the elders. If then, as was actually the
case, this was done by the high priest, who acted throughout the
whole of the sacrificial worship solely as the mediator of the grace
of God, and therefore as the representative of God Himself, and
who in this capacity, by means of the blood of the first goat, had
already covered, neutralized, and atoned for the very same sins
which he now laid upon the head of the second goat, it appears
self-evident that they could come into consideration here only as
covered and fully expiated. The view held by our opponents leaves
it perfectly inexplicable, why on this particular occasion it should
have been the high priest who put his hands upon the head of the
goat, and not, as in other cases, the elders in the name of the
whole congregation. Lastly, the only admissible explanation of
לְכַפֵּר עָלָיו in ver. 10 necessitates our view. At the same time, it is
still true, that with the great difficulty that presses upon this question, it needs a special and thorough investigation.

§ 209. According to ver. 10, after the lot had been cast upon
the two goats, the one upon which the lot of Azazel fell was placed
before Jehovah alive, לְכַפֵּר עָלָיו לְשַׁלַּח אֹתוֹ לַעֲזָאזֵל; and it was not till
after the expiation described in vers. 11–19 as effected with the
blood of the Jehovah-goat was completed, that it was brought
forward again. What was then done with it is described in vers.
20–22. Consequently, we have here an authentic commentary
upon ver. 10, *i.e.*, a detailed description of the purpose to which the
goat had been previously set apart, as described in that verse. And
if the לְשַׁלַּח אֹתוֹ לַעֲזָאזֵל is described in vers. 21 *b*, 22, we shall hardly
be mistaken in regarding the לְכַפֵּר עָלָיו as described in ver. 21 *a*,
after the command to bring up the goat has been given in ver. 20.
This making "atonement with it" is to be regarded as having been
effected by the high priest "placing both his hands upon the head

of the goat, and confessing over it all the iniquities of the children of Israel, and all their transgressions in all their sins, putting them upon the head of the goat." No other execution of this command is ever described, or even hinted at, nor is there room for it anywhere else.

But with this view, a meaning must undoubtedly be assigned to the expression לְכַפֵּר עָלָיו in ver. 10, which this familiar formula never has in any other connection. In other places, for instance, the עָלָיו invariably relates to the object of the expiation, either the person laden with sin, or the Holy Place that had been thereby defiled. And for this reason many commentators think that we ought to keep to the same meaning here; but they become involved in various contradictions and self-deceptions in consequence. Not one of them has been able to point out, even in appearance, *for what purpose, when,* and *by what means* the expiation of the goat took place. The goat, which according to ver. 5 had been offered as a sin-offering, was pure, holy, blameless, and spotless, and needed neither purifying nor expiating. The expiation of a sacrificial animal would be a *contradictio in adjecto ;* for the sacrificial animal as such was always the subject, never the object, of expiation. Moreover, under the Old Covenant expiation was always effected solely and exclusively by the sprinkling of blood ; but no allusion is ever made to the sprinkling of the second goat with atoning blood, nor can any place be found, in the whole of the compact and closely connected ritual, in which such sprinkling could be inserted.

Bähr (p. 684) maintains that "the formula in question, which occurs so frequently, is to be understood here in the same way as in every other connection, and to be rendered, 'to make atonement for it (the goat).'" But why so? "Expiation in this case bore some resemblance to that of the vessels and instruments of expiation in the sanctuary, which were consecrated afresh by the sacrificial blood; and this second goat was also, in a certain sense, an instrument of expiation, inasmuch as the sins were laid upon it, and it had to carry them away. To this purpose, therefore, was it consecrated."—But if such a consecration had been necessary, it would have been even more so in the case of the first goat. Moreover, a sacrificial animal was neither in a literal nor in a figurative sense a vessel of expiation, an instrument of expiation, or a place of expiation, like the altar or the sanctuary; nor did anything take place which could express or effect its expiation.

Keil (p. 410) opposes *Bähr's* view with some arguments[1] that miss the mark, and others which are quite conclusive (the only misfortune being, that the latter[2] apply as much to his own view as they do to *Bähr's*); but his own solution of the problem is altogether wide of the mark, and thoroughly incorrect. Thus at p. 406 he says: "This goat is not to be regarded as merely the bearer of the sin to be carried away; for it was not only set apart as a sin-offering, but by the lot it was placed on a perfect equality with the other, which was really sacrificed and placed like this one before Jehovah, to make atonement for it, *i.e.*, to make it the object of atonement." But the second goat was unquestionably *merely the bearer* of the sin to be carried away, for it is described as such, and only as such, in the record itself (ver. 22); and were it correct that it needed first of all to have expiation made for it, such expiation could have had no other object than to qualify it for what is expressly mentioned in ver. 22 as its peculiar duty. Again, it is quite wrong to state that the second goat "was placed before Jehovah *like the first*, to make atonement for it, *i.e.*, to make it *the object of atonement*;" for the *first* goat was never the *object* of atonement, that is to say, it was never appointed to have atonement made for it, but to be itself the subject or medium of atonement for the sinful nation and the polluted sanctuary. It is true, that with the πρῶτον ψεῦδος of *Keil's* theory of sacrifice, according to which the soul of the sacrificial animal was placed upon the altar as the substitutionary representative of the soul of the sacrificer requiring expiation, the sacrificial animal might in a certain sense be called the "object of expiation," and therefore this expression might be applied to the first goat; but even according to *Keil's* theory, the sacrificial animal (as a substitute for the sacrificer) could only become the object of expiation by its soul being brought within the range of the operations of divine grace, in other words, by its being placed upon the altar; consequently the second goat also could only become the object of expiation by its soul being brought within the

---

[1] For it is quite a misapprehension on his part, when he interprets *Bähr's* very clearly expressed opinion as implying that the first goat "was intended as a *symbol* of the sinful congregation, and the *second*, of the *vessels* (the altar, the tent of convocation, or the Capporeth), which had been defiled by the sin of the congregation." Such a thought certainly never entered into *Bähr's* mind!

[2] "The second goat," he says, "ought at any rate to have been sprinkled with the blood of the slaughtered goat, if it was to serve in any sense as an instrument of expiation, and as such was to be expiated itself." This is equally applicable to *every* view, in which the *goat* is regarded as the *object* of expiation.

range of the operations of divine grace, *i.e.*, by its being placed upon the altar. But that never was the case. Instead of this, it was taken body and soul into the desert, and so brought within the range of the operations of Azazel, *i.e.*, of the devil!

Hengstenberg, who also stedfastly maintains that ver. 10 relates to the expiation of the second goat, by a strange self-deception imagines that he has cleared up the subject, by affirming that through this act of expiation " the second goat was placed as it were *en rapport* with the first, and the qualities possessed by the first were transferred to the living goat" (p. 174). *Diestel* is also of opinion, that " we are probably to understand the matter in this way : the goat was to *bear* the sins of the whole nation, and became in consequence the object of the destroying wrath of God; but this destruction would prevent its continuing as a living goat, and therefore it was necessary that expiation should intervene to quench this wrath of Jehovah" (p. 195). But the propounder of this opinion hesitates, and adds immediately afterwards, " the ceremony by which this expiation was effected is certainly not mentioned." This is not the chief objection to the view in question, however, but rather the fact that it is full of internal contradictions. If, for example, we regard the expiation of the goat as taking place *before* the laying on of the sin of the nation, as *Diestel* appears to do, it is impossible to understand, (1) what there was to expiate in the pure, holy, innocent, and spotless sacrificial animal; and (2) how the sin, which was not to be laid upon it till afterwards, could thus have been rendered harmless beforehand. It would be a strange, unmeaning, and contradictory demand, to require a *clean* person, who was about to carry a very dirty object, and one that was sure to make him dirty, to wash himself carefully first of all![1] —If there is to be any sense at all in this explanation, we ought to understand the expiation of the goat as taking place rather *after* than before the sin of the people had been laid upon it. But even then it would be incomprehensible why sin, which had already been expiated in the highest, strongest, and most comprehensive manner through the blood of the first goat, should have to be subjected to a fresh, and in any case a weaker expiation.

§ 210. In such a state of things, we are obviously compelled to

---

[1] This also applies to *Hofmann*, who says in his *Schriftbeweis* (i. 431) : " The goat was first expiated, that it might take the sin of others upon it, and then laden with the sin of Israel." He gives another explanation, however, in his second edition (i. 289).

give up the conclusion drawn from לכפר עליו in ver. 10, that the second goat had to be expiated before it was sent away into the desert, as necessarily erroneous. No doubt, in other cases the preposition עַל with כפר always refers to the object of the expiation. But as the expiation of a pure, holy, and faultless sacrificial animal is a *contradictio in adjecto*, and pure nonsense; and again, as כפר is sometimes used absolutely, without the addition of the object of the expiation, to denote an expiatory action (ver. 32); we are warranted, or rather compelled, to regard the כפר in ver. 10 as absolute, and the עַל as used independently, and therefore to render it, as *Hofmann*, *Kliefoth*, and *Bunsen* have done, "to perform an act of expiation *over* it." This act of expiation must then be described in what follows, since it is something unusual and apart, and the description can only be sought and found in the laying on of the sins by the high priest in ver. 21. There is the less fear of our being wrong in this, from the fact that here, as in ver. 10, the sending into the desert was the object and effect of the action in question.

But how can that which is commanded in the first half of ver. 21 be regarded, or designated, as an act of expiation? The twisting of the laying on of the hand into the "attitude" or "position of a person praying over the animal," even if it were as correct in itself as it is obviously false and groundless, would never justify this, for the confession of sins in prayer is not an act of *expiation;* nor can the laying of the sins upon the head of the goat be regarded as in itself an act of expiation. And the difficulty would not be removed by our taking in the second half of the verse, as *Knobel* and *Hofmann* do, since the sending away of the sins could not be regarded as an act of *expiation*, inasmuch as the law recognises no other expiation than that effected through the sprinkling of blood. But the laying on of the sins, if taken in close and inseparable connection with the previous expiation effected by the blood of the first goat, might very properly be regarded as an act of expiation. And we are warranted in combining them together in this way by the ideal unity of the two goats (§ 202), the two together forming but *one* sin-offering. The laying on of the sins by the hand of the high priest could only denote an act, which presupposed and rested upon the expiation of the people and the sanctuary,—an act which might be omitted in the ordinary expiations, as being *implicitly* contained in them, but which it was necessary to set forth *explicite* on this particular day, when everything was

so arranged as to place the expiation *before the eye* as in every respect complete and all-sufficient.

But if this be the true interpretation of לְכַפֵּר עָלָיו in ver. 10, we
have here a fresh proof of the correctness of the view already
established, that the act of laying the sins upon the head of the
goat had regard to the sins *already expiated*, and that they were
sent into the desert to Azazel not as still unexpiated and deserving
the wrath and punishment of God, but as expiated, covered, and
deprived of all their power.—Consequently every interpretation of
the ceremony which ignores, denies, or disputes this, we must at
the very outset declare to be erroneous.

Diestel (pp. 195 sqq.) is quite in despair. He inquires: "Was
Azazel then supposed to be capable of producing certain evils and
plagues? If so, of what kind could they be, since all the plagues
of an extraordinary kind owed their origin exclusively to the wrath
of Jehovah?" In this extremity he helps himself by pronouncing
the view of Azazel, upon which this idea is founded, an effete, obscure, and incomplete theory, in a transition state, and one from
which the people might feel themselves repelled through the fear
that it would endanger a strict monotheism, and to which they might
be attracted on the other hand, as furnishing in a certain way points
of contact for a new formation, and still more as promising to give
a firm and objective hold to the consciousness of sin. The result
to which he is eventually brought is, that in Azazel we have before
us a figure which the people of Israel had received from the heathen,
and that in the ceremony before us Israel appears as rejecting it,—
the ceremony itself being a proof that the design was not to manifest any reverence, but on the contrary extreme disgust. But not
the least explanation is given, nor do we learn where the points of
contact for the new formation lie, or how the "effete, obscure, and
incomplete" theory could promise to give any fixed objective hold
to the consciousness of sin.

Knobel's explanation is much more lucid and complete, and
more deserving of approbation. "Through the sprinkling of the
blood," he says (p. 493), "the sins committed had been forgiven,
and punishment was averted in consequence; but these sins were
still actual facts, and separated Israel from the holy God. The
confession of these sins was an expression of Israel's repentance and
abhorrence of them. Jehovah accepted the good will for the deed:
He was ready to look upon the sins as set aside and removed along
with the goat, and Israel as free from sin; and He received the

nation, delivered from uncleanness and sin, into His fellowship once more, whilst the evil Azazel had to take to himself the evil of Israel thus sent to him by the goat. The sin-goat, therefore, embodied the idea, that Israel was delivered from all its sins, and received again into the fellowship of God." But there are two objections to this view: (1) The confession of sin ought in that case to have preceded the sprinkling of the blood, which secured the forgiveness and security from punishment, and not to have come afterwards; and (2) if the sin was covered, expiated, and exterminated by the sprinkling of the blood, it no longer separated the sinner from the holy God. And if, in addition to the neutralizing of the punishment due to the sins by the sprinkling of the blood, another special negation was still required as a fact, to open the way for the sinner to enter again into the fellowship of the grace of God, the latter ought not to have been omitted in the case of any expiatory offering for sin.

§ 211. *Hengstenberg* paved the way for the true vindication and explanation of the ceremony. In the first edition of his Christology (i. 1, 37) he maintained, that " by this act the kingdom of darkness and its prince were renounced; and the sins to which he had tempted, and by which he had sought to make the nation or the individual his own, were, so to speak, sent back to him. And in this way the truth was symbolically expressed, that he to whom God imparts reconciliation is free from the power of the wicked one." But *Tholuck, Bähr,* and others took exception to the idea of sending back the sins to Satan, which is altogether foreign to the Old Testament, and in fact to the Bible generally ; and *Hengstenberg* himself gave it up afterwards. In his *Egypt and the Books of Moses* he says, " The doctrinal significance of the symbolic action, so far as it has reference to Azazel, is this, that Satan, the enemy of the people of God, cannot harm those forgiven by God, but they, with sins forgiven of God, can go before him with a light heart, deride him, and triumph over him" (Robbin's translation, p. 161).

In my *Mos. Opfer*, p. 285, I followed *Hengstenberg*, and explained the meaning of the ceremony thus : The expiation to be effected on this day, being so decidedly complete and all-sufficient, was to be exhibited as too obvious and indisputable for even Satan, the accuser, to refuse to recognise it. Hence the sin was first atoned for in an ordinary, but an intensified form, and then sent to Azazel, that he might convince himself that they would no longer furnish him with a reason and cause for accusing Israel, or for exciting the

wrath and punishment of God on their account. Satan is introduced here, not as the author of sin, but rather as the accuser of
men on account of sin; and we may learn how familiar this idea
was not only to New Testament writers (Rev. xii. 10, 11), but in
Old Testament times as well, from the prologue to the Book of Job
and the vision of Zechariah (Zech. iii.).

This view of the matter, to which I still adhere, has since been
adopted by *Kliefoth* (p. 165). But *Keil* has only confused it, by
introducing extraneous and incongruous ideas. Thus at p. 407 he
says, " The goat was to carry the sins, which God had already forgiven to His Church, into the wilderness to Azazel, to bring them
back to the father of all sin, on the one hand as a witness, that by
his evil influence upon men he could not touch those who had received expiation from the Lord; and on the other hand, as a witness
to the congregation of Israel also, that those who were laden with
sins could not remain in the kingdom of God, but in case they were
not redeemed from them would be driven to the abode of evil
spirits." But if those sins which God had already forgiven were
laid upon the goat, the sending of them into the desert could not
possibly express the idea, that those who were laden with unexpiated
sins would be driven to the abode of evil spirits. And if the latter
is nevertheless to be retained, it must have been not sins that had
been expiated, but sins that were not expiated, which were laid upon
the goat and carried by it into the wilderness.

§ 212. After the high priest had sent away the second goat into
the wilderness, he went into the Holy Place of the tabernacle, took
off the linen clothes and left them there (ver. 23). He then washed
himself again (§ 198) with water in the fore-court, put on his ordinary high-priestly state clothes, and proceeded to offer his own
burnt-offering and that of the people; along with the flesh of these
he burnt upon the altar the fat portions of the two sin-offering
animals already slain, whilst he caused the rest of the flesh of the
two sin-offerings to be carried, along with the skins and the dung,
to the outside of the camp, and there burned with fire. It was not
till then, and only upon this basis, that the ordinary festal sacrifices
(Num. xxix. 7 sqq.) could be offered, viz., a goat for a sin-offering,
and an ox, a ram, and seven yearling lambs for a burnt-offering,
along with the customary meat-offering, and the day be concluded
with the daily evening sacrifice.

As soon as those *Cippurim*, from which the day derived its
name, had been completed, there no longer existed any reason why

the high priest should wear the linen clothes instead of the ordinary state dress (§ 198), and therefore his resumption of the latter requires no special explanation. We must, however, look somewhat closely into it, on account of the misinterpretation which *Keil* has given to the repetition of the washing (pp. 411, 412). According to *Keil*, the high priest cleansed himself, " by washing his body and his clothes (?) in a holy place from the uncleanness with which he had been defiled, by the act of laying the sins of the people upon the goat that was to be sent away into the wilderness." But by this view the author contradicts himself, for at p. 407 even he regards these sins as already atoned for, as those " which God had already forgiven to His congregation." *Bähr's* explanation of the renewal of the washing (ii. 685) must also be pronounced erroneous. He bases it upon Ex. xxx. 19 sqq., and infers, that because it is stated there that the priests had to wash themselves when they entered the tabernacle and when they approached the altar, Aaron also was required to wash himself first before he entered the tabernacle, and then again before he approached the altar. And *Keil* is quite right in his reply to this, that with *every* sin-offering, whose blood was brought into the interior of the tabernacle, the priest approached the altar of burnt-offering, after the sprinkling of the blood in the Holy Place had been effected, to pour out the remainder of the blood at the foot of the altar, and to burn the fat portions upon it, and that he did this without having first of all to perform a second washing. On the other hand, *Bähr* is also correct in maintaining, that this second washing is to be placed in the same light as the first washing which took place before the commencement of his duties. On both occasions the washing was connected with the putting on of fresh sacred clothes. With the old dress the old man was also to be laid aside, and this was symbolized by the washing of the body. It is true this presupposes that the high priest had defiled himself during the time that he had on the linen clothes, or at least might have done so. But this defilement could never have been contracted from the *holy* functions which he had performed in the meantime ; it could only have arisen from himself, from his own sinful human nature. The very same reason which *Keil* very aptly assigns for the striking fact, that notwithstanding the previous accomplishment of the highest, most perfect, and most comprehensive expiation by the sin-offerings of the high priest and the people respectively, another sin-offering occurred among the festal sacrifices, also serves to explain the necessity for this repeated washing:

" Because sin always surrounds the saint while here on earth, and defiles even his holiest resolutions and works, and he consequently needs forgiving grace for all his undertakings, these burnt-offerings and meat-offerings could not be well-pleasing to the Lord except upon the basis of a sin-offering."

In conclusion, the fact must also be borne in mind, that both the man who led away the living goat into the desert (ver. 26), and also the man who was commissioned to burn the flesh of the sin-offering outside the camp (ver. 28), were regarded as defiled in consequence, and were not allowed to enter the camp again till they had washed their clothes and bathed their bodies.   But here also *Keil's* explanation, viz., that " all contact with the sacrificial animals when laden with sin necessarily defiled," is not the true one; for, as we have already shown (§ 110, 114), this view involves the greatest absurdities.   That the man who took the goat into the desert became unclean in consequence, is intelligible enough; for he had been into the territory of Azazel, the unclean spirit κατ᾽ ἐξοχήν. And this also applies to the man who had to burn the flesh of the sin-offering outside the camp.   The camp, with the sanctuary in the midst of it, was *eo ipso* the place of purity; and all persons who were unclean in the highest degree, viz., all lepers, those who had an issue, and those who were defiled by corpses (Num. v. 1–3), had to live outside the camp during the period of their uncleanness. Distance from the camp was equivalent, therefore, to separation from the fellowship of the pure, and any temporary separation might easily lead to Levitical uncleanness, without the knowledge of the person defiled.   And the holiness of the day, which was carried to the highest pitch, required that the possibility of this should also be taken into account.

CHAPTER III

ADAPTATION OF THE SACRIFICIAL WORSHIP TO THE LEVITICAL AND PRIESTLY PURIFICATIONS

A. NATURE AND IDEA OF UNCLEANNESS IN CONNECTION WITH RELIGION

§ 213. The Mosaic law, in harmony with the views of nearly all ancient nations, particularly in the East, pronounced certain

conditions and functions of the human body unclean, and defiling
to others by contact; in other words, as shutting out from the
sanctuary and from participation in its worship. The different
forms of uncleanness, the lower grades of which could be removed
by simply washing with water, whilst the higher needed a sacrificial
expiation also, may be arranged in three classes: *first*, the uncleanness of human corpses and animal carrion; *secondly*, the uncleanness of leprosy in men, clothes, and houses; and *thirdly*, uncleanness
proceeding from both diseased and normal functions of the human
organs of generation. These conditions and functions, the whole
of which, with the single exception of conjugal intercourse,[1] were
involuntary and to a certain extent inevitable, are not treated in
the law as sinful in themselves, or as connected with special sins.
This is evident enough from the fact that marriage was encouraged
in every way by the law, and conjugal intercourse is spoken of as
a *duty* (Ex. xxi. 10), whilst the corpse of the most righteous man
was regarded as equally unclean and defiling with that of the
greatest criminal. Yet by requiring a sin- or trespass-offering for
the removal of the higher forms of uncleanness, it indicates a primary connection between them and sin, so far, that is to say, as the
processes occurring in the body are dependent upon the influences
and effects of the universal sinfulness. And it was this sinfulness,
when brought to light by its operations and consequences, though
for the most part independently of the will of the persons in question, which required sacrificial expiation by means of sin-offerings,
in the same manner as sinful acts unconsciously performed.

This is most apparent in the case of the uncleanness of *corpses*.
Death, with corruption in its train, is the inevitable issue of this
earthly, sinful life, according to the curse pronounced on sin (Gen.
ii. 17, iii. 19). And in death, what sin is and what it effects in

---

[1] *Sommer's* assertion, that the Mosaic law did not share the ordinary view of
the defiling influence of conjugal connection, but that it arose at a later date
(1 Sam. xxi. 5, 6 ; 2 Sam. xi. 4), and was wrongly transferred into the history
of the Mosaic times (Ex. xix. 15), could only be established by applying the
most obvious exegetical violence to Lev. xv. 18, which he was led to do, as we
shall presently see, by interests altogether apart from the subject itself. The
expression in Lev. xv. 18, as *Knobel* admits with laudable candour, can only
refer to actual intercourse, and not to involuntary emission, as Num. v. 13
clearly proves. And the same remark applies to the more concise expression in
Lev. xv. 24 (cf. Gen. xxvi. 10, xxxiv. 2, xxxv. 22 ; 1 Sam. ii. 22, etc.), and no
less to the somewhat more delicately expressed phraseology of ver. 33 (cf. Gen.
xxx. 15, 16, xxxix. 7, 12 ; Deut. xxii. 23, etc.).

the sphere of the spirit (the disturbance and destruction of life, the rending and dissolution of what God made one), come to light in the sphere of the body as well.—This was hardly less apparent in the case of *leprosy*, which was, so to speak, a living death,—the destruction of all the vital powers, a dissolution and putrefaction even in the living body, a death before death; so that, as *Spencer* says, the leper was a "walking tomb."

Lastly, so far as those functions and conditions of the *sexual life* are concerned, which are represented as rendering unclean, *Bähr* discovers a connection between these and sin and death. Generation and death, birth and corruption, are, in his opinion, the two poles, within which the sinful and accursed life of humanity moves. By generation and birth the sinful life of man, which is liable to death from the very first, is brought into existence; whilst by death, the wages of sin, and corruption, the completion of death, his life is brought to an end. Hence all the functions of the sexual organs, both normal and abnormal, which are related to generation and birth, come under the same aspect of uncleanness as death itself.—*Schultz's* reply to this view is not to the point. For when he objects that "the uncleanness of animals which were prohibited as food is not taken into account," this is just the redeeming point of *Bähr's* theory, that it clearly recognises the discordant nature of these two departments, and does not confound them with one another. And when he maintains that "generation and birth could not possibly defile, inasmuch as they were instituted by the blessing of God Himself," he overlooks the fact, that notwithstanding the blessing of God, in Gen. i. 28, which continued even after the entrance of sin, according to the intimations in Gen. iii. 16 both generation and birth were brought under the curse of sin, and affected by the influence of that curse.

On the other hand, we cannot deny the weight and importance of another argument, brought forward by *Sommer* (p. 240) and adopted by *Keil* (p. 280), in opposition to *Bähr's* view; viz., that the two supposed poles of human life, generation and death, birth and corruption, are placed by *Bähr* in a distorted relation to one another, which is concealed by the ambiguity of the word birth (*Geburt*, equivalent to giving birth, and being born). It is not begetting and dying, nor giving birth and falling into corruption, that are the two poles of sinful life, but being born and dying; and therefore, according to *Bähr's* assumptions, it is not that which begets and gives birth, but that which is begotten and born, which ought to be regarded as unclean, and subjected to washing either with or without a sin-offering.

§ 214. But what both *Sommer* and *Keil* propose to substitute for *Bähr's* theory is certainly even less tenable than that theory itself, and is to be regarded, not as progress towards an explanation of the matter, but as a retrograde movement. For example, *Sommer* maintains (pp. 201 sqq.) that "death produces two kinds of symptoms of corruption: on the one hand, the so-called death-spots upon the skin, and on the other, the corrupt secretions from the inside of the corpse. The spots upon the skin of the leper are analogous to the former, and certain secretions from the male and female sexual organs, which possess the nature of decomposition, and so indicate corruption, to the latter."—But even the analogy asserted to exist between the death-spots on the skin of a corpse and the spots upon the skin of a leper, is certainly a mistake. This might pass, however. But the parallel drawn between the sexual secretions and the corrupt secretions of a corpse is altogether unfortunate. An analogy of this kind might certainly be found in the *lochia*, particularly the white *lochia* of a woman in childbirth, and other diseased secretions from both male and female sexual organs, but not in the normal menstruation and the hemorrhage of women, for in this case there is not even an outward resemblance in the secretions; and it seems hardly credible that the law of Moses, which regarded the blood as the seat and bearer of the soul or life, and certainly was not acquainted with the chemical difference between the blood of menstruation and any other, should have treated the flow of red blood, with the true colour of life, as analogous to the pale, fetid secretions of a corpse. And it is least of all allowable to trace any analogy between the latter and the *emissio seminis* in a normal healthy intercourse, and on that account to attribute to such an *emissio* a defiling influence, as *Keil* does without hesitation. How can this be conceivable when the very opposite is the case, and the *semen virile* is the generator of life? This contradiction has not escaped *Sommer's* acuteness; but instead of altering his self-originated theory to suit the opposing *data* of the law (Lev. xv. 18) and history (Ex. xix. 15; 1 Sam. xxi. 5, 6; 2 Sam. xi. 4), he rather endeavours to set aside the latter in favour of the former by means of critical and exegetical arts. *Keil* cannot follow him in these operations, but he becomes involved in consequence in the very difficulties from which *Sommer* had succeeded in extricating himself.

There are other points also in which *Sommer's* theory proves to be untenable.   No one could deny, for example, that a hemorrhoidal discharge, which did *not* render unclean, belonged much more truly to *Sommer's* category than a normal and healthy menstruation ; or that the secretion of mucus, diseased matter, etc., from nose or mouth, from wounds and abscesses, which even corresponds to some extent in smell, colour, etc., to the secretions of a corpse, would have a much more suitable place in his category than either a voluntary or involuntary *emissio seminis.*   And yet not one of these is represented as defiling.   On the contrary, all the secretions to which the law attributes this result are those connected with the sexual life, whether they bear any resemblance to the secretions of a corpse or are as unlike as possible.   It is solely *in their connection with the sexual life,* therefore, that we must seek for the true cause of their uncleanness, and this is just the point in which *Bähr* is decidedly able to hold his ground against *Sommer* and his successors.

§ 215.   It is obvious enough from Gen. iii. 16, that according to the scriptural view the sexual life was not only morally, but also physically affected and changed by the curse of sin.   And this view has every claim to unhesitating adoption.   In whatever department of life sin has acquired moral supremacy, it has been invariably followed by a physical disturbance and change ; and what department of life is there in which either the one or the other has been more decidedly and more universally manifested, than in that of the sexual relation ?   Just as sin has produced mortality and sickness, as the precursor of death throughout the entire organism of man, so has it in an especial manner introduced diseased and deadly disturbance and disorganization into the sphere of the sexual life.   Medical science may be quite correct, from its own point of view, in pronouncing the menses and lochia of women, and the involuntary seminal emissions, etc., of men, necessary, and therefore normal and healthy functions ; but from a philosophical and theological point of view, they must for all that be regarded as equally abnormal and unnatural with the passing away of life into death and corruption, which is also normal according to the *dictum* of medical science.

Now the fact that the sexual organs themselves, and their functions in sexual intercourse, occupy, according to the *sensus communis* of all nations and all ages, an abnormal position, is attested by the circumstance that they have always been the objects of shame and secrecy.   In the Old Testament בָּשָׂר (flesh) is used to denote human nature in its mortal, lapsed condition, and *per emphasin* the sexual organs; and the priests who went up to the altar were required to wear drawers, that the nakedness of their flesh might not be turned towards the altar uncovered (Ex. xxviii. 42). And generation itself, which brings into existence a new life subject to sinfulness and mortality, is also in a certain sense a work of death. What observation teaches in many of the lower animals, viz., that the time of copulation is also the time of their death, has a certain analogy, so far as tendencies are concerned, in the higher animals, and even in man (*omne animal post coitum triste*); or rather, *vice versa*, the natural tendency to mortality, which is only dimly seem in the act of generation in man and the higher animals, has its perfect manifestation in those inferior organisms. The *emissio seminis* in the case of a man is the loss of a portion of his own *vis vitalis*, a surrendering of his own vital energy (אוֹנִי, Gen. xlix. 3), a disturbance and disorganization of his inmost vital marrow, however quickly restoration may occur ; and in the same way there are disorganizations of the sexual life in the menses as the necessary condition of conception, in the effects of pregnancy which disturb the normal life in so many ways, and in the lochia as the consequence of childbirth.

The double death-ban in which the sphere of human generation is involved, and which is apparent on the one hand in the fact that the parents can only beget a life that from the very first is sentenced to death, and on the other hand in the fact that generation itself is a disturbance and disorganization of their own life, is what places generation and the whole sphere to which it belongs in an analogous relation to death and corruption as the highest and most complete disorganization of all, and stamps it as having, though in an inferior degree, the same uncleanness which belongs to death and corruption as the wages and fruit of sin. But the life begotten did not need to be included in this declaration of uncleanness, which from its very nature applied to generation and childbirth alone ; in fact, it could not properly be so included. It is true the life begotten was from the very first involved in sin and death, and could not and would not escape from death as the wages of sin, or corruption as the completion of death ; but these had not yet manifested themselves in any phenomena which proved that death reigned in it also.

It was unquestionably the ban of death which reigns in the human body as the effect and consequence of sin, that stamped upon the phenomena apparent in the different departments of generation, leprosy, and decomposition the character of Levitical uncleanness. And the obligation resting on the Israelites, not indeed to preserve themselves free from such uncleanness, for that was impossible, but whenever it occurred to purify themselves, or to seek purification in a certain prescribed mode, was based upon the priestly character and consecration of the people as a covenant nation (§ 1), called to approach and hold communion with Jehovah, a holy God, who could tolerate no uncleanness that sprang from sin, but unfit to approach Him as long as the uncleanness continued. For a priest, in whom the priestly vocation was concentrated and intensified, and who was to hold constant and immediate intercourse with Jehovah, we can understand that the demand for purity and purification would be even stronger and more emphatic than for the rest of the nation (Lev. xxi. 22).

§ 216. As there were no special peculiarities in the sacrificial expiation required for sexual uncleanness, we need not dwell upon this (cf. Lev. xv.). Such expiation was not required, however, for any *emissio seminis*, either voluntary in sexual intercourse, or involuntary in nocturnal emission. In the latter case the man remained unclean until the evening, and was to wash his body with water ; in the former, both the man and his wife were to do this. The sexual flux (זוֹב) produced a higher stage of uncleanness. Those who were affected with it were to stay outside the camp during the whole time of their uncleanness (Num. v. 2), because their uncleanness would be communicated by contact both to persons and things. In this class were included menstruation, the continuous diseased flux in a woman, and diseased discharge from a man. In the last two cases the uncleanness lasted till the seventh day after the complete cessation of the discharge ; and in addition to the obvious washing the law required two doves to be offered on the eighth day, one as a sin-offering, the other as a burnt-offering, to wipe away the uncleanness. A woman, on the other hand, during the period of menstruation, was unclean for seven days in all, and when that time had elapsed, needed nothing more than to wash her body and her clothes. *Childbirth* produced uncleanness similar to that of menstruation, for seven days on the birth of a boy, and for fourteen on the birth of a girl. But ever after this time the woman had to remain at home in the blood of her purification, for 33 more days in the former instance, and 66 in the latter ; and then (after another washing) to offer a lamb as a burnt-offering, and a dove as a sin-offering, or in cases of poverty a dove for each.

The removal of the uncleanness produced by contact with a corpse, as well as the purification of a leper when cured, needs a thorough and separate examination on account of the peculiarities in the sacrifices required, and in the other means of purification prescribed.

B. REMOVAL OF UNCLEANNESS CAUSED BY TOUCHING A CORPSE.

§ 217. As the scriptural view regards all corruption in nature as primarily connected with the sinfulness of man (Gen. iii. 17 sqq., v. 29; cf Rom. viii. 19 sqq.), we may easily understand why the law placed not only human corpses, but also carrion, whether of clean or unclean, *i.e.*, edible or unedible animals, among the things that defiled. All contact with any such object rendered unclean till the evening, and required that both the person and the clothes should be washed (Lev. xi. 24 sqq., xvii. 15). This did not apply, however, to animals that had been slaughtered by man. Vessels, clothes, etc., were not defiled, as a rule, by contact with carrion; there were exceptions, however, in the case of eight creeping things that are mentioned in Lev. xi. 32 sqq. The uncleanness communicated by a *human córpse*, whether after a violent or a natural death (Num. xix. 16, 18, xxxi. 19), was much more intense in its character. Every tent or house in which there was a corpse, as well as all the people in it, and all the vessels that were standing about, were rendered unclean for seven days, during which time the people themselves were to remain outside the camp (Num. v. 1–3). Contact with a corpse found in the open country defiled for the same period; also contact with graves and the ashes of the dead. This uncleanness also passed from the persons affected by it to everything they touched; but in this case it only lasted till the evening. The uncleanness that proceeded directly from the corpse itself to persons and things, could only be removed by *sprinkling-water* prepared expressly for the purpose. And in the case of persons, a subsequent bathing of the body and washing of the clothes were also required. To obtain this sprinkling water (מֵי נִדָּה, *aqua impuritatis*) a spotless red heifer, that had never borne a yoke, was slain as a sin-offering outside the camp. The son or presumptive successor to the high priest (Eleazar) officiated on the occasion, and sprinkled some of the blood seven times towards the sanctuary. The cow was then burnt, along with the skin, the flesh, the bones, the blood, and the dung; and cedar-wood, coccus-wool, and hyssop were also thrown into the fire. All the persons who officiated at this ceremony became unclean till the evening, and were required to wash their bodies and their clothes. Whenever a death occurred, a clean man put some of these ashes into a vessel, poured fresh running water upon them, dipped a bundle of hyssop into the water, and sprinkled the persons or things to be cleansed on the third day, and again on the seventh. He also became unclean in consequence, and had to wash himself and his clothes. This ceremony of purification had to be performed not only by the Israelites, but also under similar circumstances by any foreigners who might be settled among them (cf. Num. xix.).

§ 218. *Bähr* (ii. 493 sqq.) has taken the first step towards an explanation of this ceremony, and in my opinion has for ever settled the most essential points. For the objections raised by *Hengstenberg* (in his Egypt and the Books of Moses, pp. 173 sqq., and his Commentary on Ps. li. 9), and the explanation which he offers instead, are altogether worthless and untenable; and I still regard the refutation which I gave in the *Studien und Kritiken* (1846, pp. 629–702) as perfectly conclusive (as *Keil* fully admits, pp. 286 sqq.), although *Hengstenberg* has thought proper to ignore it altogether, and to print his objections without alteration in the second edition of his Commentary on the Psalms.

The ultimate object of slaying and burning the red cow, was to obtain the means of purification in the form of a sprinkling water. Common water did not suffice, on account of the strength of the uncleanness to be removed. An alkali was wanted; the water needed to be mingled with ashes, and these were to be procured by the burning of the red cow. That this cow was slain as a sacrificial animal, in fact, as a sin-offering, is proved not only by vers. 9, 17, where it is directly called a sin-offering (חַטָּאת), but by the fact that the priest sprinkled the blood seven times towards the tabernacle. An expiatory significance must therefore be ascribed to this *sprinkling of the blood,* as in the case of every other sacrifice. But whose sin was it that had to be expiated by this sprinkling of the blood? Evidently that of the whole congregation, by which no doubt the animal had been presented, and the laying on of hands effected, through the medium of its representatives, the elders.

On the other hand, the *burning* of the red cow assumes a totally different aspect from the burning of the other sacrificial animals upon the altar. It is not described as a הַקְטִיר, but as a שָׂרֹף; it was neither placed upon the altar, nor in any relation to the altar; and, lastly, not only was the fat consumed, as in the case of other sin-offerings, or the whole of the flesh, as in the case of the burnt-offerings, but the skin, the blood, and even the *fæces* in the stomach and entrails, were all consumed together. The intention of the burning, therefore, can only have been to procure the ashes, to the exclusion of every other idea associated with the burning at other times. But it is a very significant fact, that a sacrificial animal which had been put to death by שְׁחִיטָה, and the blood of which had been used as a means of expiation, should have been selected for this purpose. Vicarious endurance of punishment and expiation based upon this were evidently presupposed by, and lay at the foundation of, the whole ceremony.

In the entire process we may discern two distinct elements, which are closely related, but must not be confounded : on the one hand, the *sentence of death* hanging over the whole congregation, and on the other, the *uncleanness* of the individual arising from contact with a corpse. The former assumed the aspect of a consequence of sin, and therefore required a sacrifice for its expiation ; the latter appeared merely as (secondary, not primary) defilement communicated to the individual, which did not require a sacrifice, but was removed by purification with water. As the uncleanness, however, was peculiarly strong and difficult to remove, washing with mere water was not sufficient ;—the cleansing power of the water needed to be strengthened, and the water therefore had to be made into a lye. But as the uncleanness which was to be washed away by the lye had arisen from the general sentence of death, which rests upon the whole human race, and consequently upon the congregation of Jehovah, but for which expiation had already been made by the sprinkling of the blood, it follows that the power by which the water was strengthened, was derived from the sacrifice offered for the cause of the defilement.

§ 219. The explanation which *Keil* has given of the burning of the red cow, as the wages of sin (p. 283), is quite inadmissible and contradictory. A few lines before he describes the slaying of the animal as the wages of sin ; and there he ought to have stopped (though he had already fallen into irreconcilable contradiction with his own previous theory of the sacrificial slaughter, cf. § 53), the more especially because he would thus have escaped the fresh self-contradiction, which appears in the fact, that by completely throwing overboard his own theory of the sin-offering, he is *obliged* to give up to the " death of annihilation" not only the " image of the outer man, the σῶμα χοϊκόν, corrupted by sin and exposed to death," viz., the flesh and bones, but also " the better part of human nature, the ἔσω ἄνθρωπος" (cf. § 109, 111, 114). This conclusion has not escaped his own observation. On the contrary, he has not hesitated to draw it expressly himself (p. 284). "The blood," he says, "as the vehicle of the soul, and the fat as the surrogate of the better *I* of the congregation, were given up to *annihilation* (?), just as the soul and the inner man are given up to death along with the body" (?). But if it was in the very nature of things, and therefore inevitable, that the better *I*, the ἔσω ἄνθρωπος, should be given up to annihilation with the death of the body, how could this be wanting in the case of the ordinary sin-offerings, and on the contrary, "the inner, better part of human nature, being purified by the sanctifying fire of divine love, ascend at once in transmuted essence up to heaven, and only the outer man, the σῶμα χοϊκόν, which as being corrupted by sin could not ascend in a glorified form to God, be given up to annihilation?" But the notion that the better part of man, the ἔσω ἄνθρωπος, was necessarily given up to "death," or rather to "annihilation," is as much opposed to the teaching of the Bible as to that of the Church; and what the author of this notion has added by way of explanation, viz., that "as the imperishable life-kernel of man is *preserved* in the dead corpse by the omnipotence of divine grace, and raised up again to a new and glorified life out of the ashes into which it (?) had fallen, so by the operation of the same omnipotent grace the imperishable remains of the red cow, which were not destroyed by the fire, but only changed (?) into ashes, furnished a powerful antidote against mortal decay (?)," only serves to heighten the obscurity and confusion. For the supposition that the inner, better part of human nature is to be at once and by the same act "*annihilated*" and "*preserved*," involves contradictions which no doctrinal system could reconcile. And every doctrinal system must firmly maintain, that it is not the imperishable life-kernel of man which falls into ashes, but the outer man alone, consisting of earthly flesh and bone, in which it is shrouded and concealed. At the same time, we simply protest in passing against the unhistorical commingling of the Old Testament and Pauline standpoints evinced in the fact, that the doctrine of the resurrection of the body, which was as yet undeveloped, is made the basis and starting point of the symbolism of this act of worship.

§ 220. The red cow, as we have seen, was intended as an antidote to the defilement of death, which was latent in the whole congregation in the form of universal liability to death, but was manifested in every actual death, and in that case infected all living persons who came into contact with it, and even clothes and other articles that might be touched by the corpse. This idea of an anti-dote against the defilement of death was the regulating principle of the whole institution, determining not only the choice of the sacrificial animal, but what should be added to it, and all that should be done with it.

In the first place, a *cow*, פָּרָה, was chosen; not a bullock, as in every other case in which a sin-offering was to be presented for the whole congregation. According to *Winer* (ii. 505), a cow was se-lected instead of a bullock, to distinguish this sin-offering, in which the animal was the medium of a holy purpose, from the other, in which it was presented before Jehovah in His sanctuary as the vehicle of exculpation. (*Keil* regards this as admissible, though he gives the preference to *Bähr's* explanation, to which we shall pre-sently refer.) The antithesis mentioned here, however, does not appear to me to be thorough enough to be regarded as answering to the contrast between a bullock and a cow. In *Knobel's* opinion, a somewhat inferior animal was chosen in this case, because only a greater or smaller number of persons within the limits of the nation were concerned, just as in Deut. xxi. 3 an עֶגְלָה is appointed for the expiation of a single city. But to this I cannot subscribe, just be-cause the עגלה in Deut. xxi. 3 was not a sacrifice (cf. *Keil* ii. 304); and, on the other hand, not only was the red cow offered in sacrifice for the *whole* congregation, because it was all involved in the ban of death, but the sprinkling water obtained from its ashes was applied to *every* individual in the congregation, because every one, with more or less frequency, was sure to be placed in circumstances that required its use. *Hengstenberg's* view, however, is certainly the most inadmissible, viz., that "because חַטָּאת, the Hebrew word for sin, is feminine, the animal which bore its image, and was ap-pointed to carry it in a representative character, was required to be the same" (Egypt and the Books of Moses, p. 175 Eng. tr.). The חַטָּאת הוּא in ver. 9, to which *Hengstenberg* appeals as "evidently" containing the reason, cannot be intended to explain the reason for the command in ver. 2, that the animal should be a cow. To make the physical gender of the sacrificial animal dependent upon the grammatical gender of the noun denoting the sacrifice, would have been a play upon words altogether foreign to the character of the lawgiver of the Old Testament, and one which, if adopted at all, ought to have been extended to every sin-offering, since they were all called חטאת. *Baumgarten's* explanation is no better. He traces

the command to select a cow, to the fact "that Israel is here regarded in its deepest corruption as a tempted and ruined woman."

The only admissible explanation is that of *Bähr*, which is quite
as natural as it is full of good sense, viz., that the choice of a cow
was dictated by the fact that the female sex, as distinguished from
the male, is the bearing or life-producing sex, and therefore presents
a fitting contrast to that life-destroying death whose defiling influence was to be thereby removed. *Delitzsch's* remark is good on this
point : " פָּרָה = the fruitful one, calls to mind the fruit-producing
power of life, which is the opposite of the withered impotence of
death."

§ 221. The cow was to be of a *red colour*, פָּרָה אֲדֻמָּה.   *Hengstenberg* misses the mark again here, in describing the red colour as the
symbol of sin (l.c. pp. 174 sqq.).   I have already given a thorough
examination (resp. refutation) to this idea (l.c. pp. 632–675) ; and
as no one but the author himself has repeated this mistaken opinion,
but, on the contrary, all subsequent writers have distinctly rejected
it, and agree with me in adopting the explanation given by *Bähr*, I
regard it as quite unnecessary to refute it again.   The colour red is
the colour of *life* in this connection, as it is in every other passage
of the Old Testament in which it is used in a symbolical sense.   I
still adhere to the opinion which I expressed in my *Mos. Opfer* (pp.
310, 311), that " the atoning, renovating power of the animal
resides in its blood ; the outer is the reflex of the inner.   Just as
in man the vital energy of the blood is manifested in the red
cheeks and lips, and in the flesh-coloured redness of the skin, so in
the red cow the blood was regarded as possessing such vigour, that
it manifested itself outwardly in the corresponding colour.   The
red hue of the cow was a characteristic sign of its fulness of life, and
fitted it to become an antidote of the power of death.

In this capacity, again, it was necessary that the cow should
also possess internally the greatest possible force and freshness of
life.   For this reason, not only was it to be like all other sacrificial
animals, without blemish or spot and in the full vigour of life, but
it was not to have *borne a yoke*, that is to say, its vital power was
not to have been consumed or diminished in any way whatever—a
requirement never made in connection with other sacrifices.

Still further to strengthen the idea already expressed in the
sex, constitution, and colour of the animal, three things were added
of homogeneous significance, viz., cedar-wood as the symbol of what
was imperishable (for proof passages, *vid. Knobel* on Lev. xiv. p.

476-7), hyssop as the means of purification (Ps. li. 7), and wool dyed
with coccus, as the colour of the most potent fulness of life. This
was the explanation first given by *Bähr*, who regards all three ad-
ditions as purely symbolical. But the emendation suggested by
Delitzsch deserves full consideration, the more especially because
the pleonasm contained in the red colour of the cow and the red of
the coccus-wool thereby disappears. " The three things," he says,
" which were thrown into the fire, were rather medicinal than symbolical : the cedar-wood was to impart to the ashes an odour of in-
corruptibility to counteract the odour of death ; the hyssop was
generally regarded in antiquity as a means of purification, and was
even taken internally for that purpose ; and in the coccus-wool the
juice of the coccus was probably looked upon as a medicinal element, for it used formerly to be employed as medicine for strengthening the heart." According to *Hengstenberg*, the coccus was a
symbol of sin, whilst the cedar and hyssop represented the exaltation and majesty of the Creator, as well as His condescension,—
those attributes, that is to say, which were peculiarly displayed in
the expiation and cancelling of sin, viz., majesty and compassionate
love. This explanation, the fallacy of which may be detected at once,
and which has never met with approval, has been thoroughly refuted
in the *Studien und Kritiken*, *l.c.* pp. 680-691.

The *ashes* procured by the process of burning were to be mixed
with *water*, to represent lye, which is used in cases when the uncleanness is too strong to yield to simple water ; and *running*, living
water was to be used for the purpose, to set forth the idea of an
antidote against the defilement of death and corruption.

The most remarkable feature connected with the burning of
the red cow, when measured by the plan adopted in other cases,
was the fact, that the *fæces* in the stomach and entrails were to be
burned along with the cow, as well as all the *blood* that remained
after the sprinkling was finished. The burning of both of these
rests upon one and the same basis. " As an image of life in the
plenitude of its vigour, the animal was consumed in all its fulness, and the completeness of its bodily frame" (*Hofmann*, p.
290). *Delitzsch* also observes (pp. 395, 396) : " The burning of the
blood may easily be explained, on the ground that the ashes of the
animal were to furnish the quintessence of a means of purification,
in which the blood, already endowed with atoning power through
the sprinkling of one portion towards the holy tent, formed the
most important ingredient."

§ 222. The most striking and most difficult points are these : (1) that the slaughtering, sprinkling of the blood, and burning of the cow took place outside the sanctuary, and in fact outside the camp; (2) that neither the high priest nor any ordinary priest officiated, but the presumptive successor of the former; (3) that not only all the persons employed in the sacrificial ceremony, but all who took part in the sprinkling, were rendered unclean in consequence until the evening, whilst only clean persons were qualified to officiate ; and (4) lastly, that the purifying water thus obtained was called מֵי נִדָּה = *aqua impuritatis*.

Keil's solution of these problems is for the most part a mistaken one, and founders on its self-contradictions. He is unquestionably right so far, that the appellation, *aqua abominationis s. impuritatis*, is to be explained according to the analogous appellation given to the sin-destroying sin-offering, viz., חַטָּאת. But this truth necessarily becomes an error in his hands, inasmuch as he gives the latter a decidedly mistaken interpretation, and transfers to the former the erroneous principle involved in the latter. As the sin-offering derived its name not from the fact that the sin of the sacrificer was imputed to it, and it became in a certain sense an incorporate sin, but from the fact that it was a sacrifice "for sin," an antidote to sin, and the means of its extermination (cf. § 47); so the purifying water was not called *aqua impuritatis* because impurity was regarded in any way as inherent in it or adhering to it, but because the object of its application was the removal of impurity. In the case of the sin-offering, the idea that it had become as it were an incorporate sin, had at least an apparent, if not a real basis, in the previous imposition of hands, the supposed vehicle of the imputation of sins; but in the sprinkling water every vehicle of this kind is wanting,—the defilement of death is not imputed to it, nor is it rendered an incorporate defilement in any other way. It is true, *Keil* supposes the sprinkling water to have been, and to have been called, *aqua impuritatis* on the very same ground on which ": not only the sprinkling of the blood, the burning of the cow, and the gathering of the ashes, but the sprinkling and even the mere touching of the purifying water, rendered the persons in question unclean till the evening." This is to be attributed, he supposes, not as *Bähr* and I maintain, to the reference of the whole ceremony to death and association with death, or to the existing uncleanness with which the persons officiating came in contact, but "to the fact that the ashes, as the residuum of the sin-offering, participated in the uncleanness of the sin imputed to it."

This view is fettered on all hands with impossibilities. We will look away from the fact that no sins ever were imputed to a sin-offering (§ 44 sqq.), and also from the fact that no uncleanness or defiling influence ever can have been inherent in the sin-offering as a "most holy" thing, either at the commencement, in the middle, or at the end of the process to which it was subjected (§ 113 sqq.); and even then a large body of incongruity still remains. (1) How could the ashes of the cow defile the officiating priest, when he had nothing whatever to do with them? Or was he really defiled by what *he* had to do, viz., to sprinkle the blood? But if so, how was it that the sprinkling of the blood did not defile the officiating priest in the case of any other sin-offering?—(2) If the sacrificial animal "suffered death as the wages of sin" for the sin imputed to it, then the sin imputed to it was covered, exterminated, forgiven, out of pure mercy through the sprinkling of the blood; and in that case "the wages of sin" were inflicted *once more* upon the slain animal in the process of *burning;* and even that did not suffice, but the ashes that remained still "participated in the sin imputed!" Does not this look as if the whole of the sacrificial worship was calculated in the most refined manner, not to exterminate sin, but to exhibit *luculentissime* the impossibility of exterminating it and the vanity of all the sacrificial functions, so as to drive the poor penitent sinner to despair instead of comforting and assuring him?—(3) But notwithstanding the fact that the ashes of the cow, and the sprinkling water prepared from those ashes, were themselves unclean, and all clean persons who came into contact with them were defiled, this very water was to cleanse those who were defiled, even though their defilement was of the most aggravated kind!—(4) If the ashes and the sprinkling water were themselves unclean, and rendered the clean unclean, why did the law lay such stress upon the fact, that *only clean* men should collect the ashes and prepare the water, and that it should be prepared in a *clean* place? In *Keil's* opinion, these directions were not at variance with his view; but this confidence may simply arise from his own self-deception. At all events, I do not see the force of his explanation, when he says that "these directions had reference to the destination of the ashes for holy purposes; whilst the uncleanness adhering to them was not physical but ethical, and resulted from the sin imputed to the sacrificial animal; so that when used in the way ordained by God, it effected a purification from the uncleanness of death adhering to sinners." And when he still further affirms that "a certain uncleanness adhered to the ashes of every sacrifice, so that the priest who carried them out of the camp to a clean place had to lay aside his priestly dress and put on other clothes" (Lev. vi. 11); the refutation is contained in the fact, that the ashes could only be carried to a "clean" place. That the priest had to put off his priestly dress and put on other clothes, cannot possibly be adduced as a proof of the uncleanness of the ashes, but may be explained on the ground, that the priest was not allowed to wear his official costume outside the sanctuary, much less outside the camp; whilst, on the other hand, the circumstance that the *priest* himself had to carry away the ashes to a *clean* place, serves rather as a proof that a residuum of the holiness belonging to the sacrificial animal as a medium of expiation adhered even to the ashes. And if what *Keil* says of the sacrificial ashes in general was *really* applicable to the ashes of the red cow,—namely, that they were only "the foul sediment of that which had *not* ascended to God in a transfigured essence, the remains of the sacrifices which had been consumed by the purifying fire of the altar,"—whence did these ashes acquire the purifying energy ascribed to them as the main constituent of the water of purification?

§ 223. No other answer can be given to the question, how the clean persons engaged in the preparation and application of the sprinkling water were rendered unclean, than that which *Keil* so groundlessly rejects, namely, that the defilement proceeded not from the purifying medium itself, but from the uncleanness to be thereby removed, on account of which, and in the very atmosphere of which, the means of purification were prepared and employed. For that very reason the high priest, who was not allowed at any time, or under any circumstances, to come into contact with the defilement of death (Lev. xxi. 10–12), could not officiate himself, as he invariably did when a sin-offering was presented for the whole congregation; whilst, on the other hand, the act itself was so important that an ordinary priest was not sufficient, and the priest who stood nearest to the high priest, viz., his son and successor, was therefore selected for the purpose. For the same reason, the whole transaction had to be performed outside the camp, "that the camp of Israel, not to say the sanctuary, might not be desecrated by being thus directly and intentionally brought into contact with death" (*Delitzsch*, p. 395). Nevertheless, as the sprinkling of blood, with its atoning virtue and effect, was absolutely necessary, in order to express this clearly the officiating priest was to sprinkle some of the blood of the cow seven times towards the sanctuary; "for since the defilement of death was not to be brought into any connection with the sanctuary, the blood of the animal that was appointed to remove this defilement was only applied to the sanctuary from a distance, in order that the sin-offering might receive its purifying or expiating virtue as it were through a power exerted from afar" (*Delitzsch*, *l.c.*). The sevenfold sprinkling in the direction of the tabernacle corresponded to the perfectly analogous sevenfold sprinkling towards the *Parocheth* in the case of those sin-offerings whose blood was brought into the Holy Place, and is not to be understood, in the one case any more than in the other, as a "merely preparatory, approximative restoration of the fellowship with the Lord which sin had destroyed" (*Keil*, pp. 284, 230). It referred in both instances to the place of expiation, which lay in that direction, but which for other reasons could not be approached at that particular time (cf. § 107).

C. CLEANSING OF A LEPER WHEN CURED

§ 224. The uncleanness of leprosy was distinguished from every other form of uncleanness by the fact that the person afflicted with it was not only excluded, like every unclean person, from the fellowship of the sanctuary, but though still alive was excluded like a dead person from both national and family fellowship. Consequently, the process of purification embraced a double restitution, and consisted, therefore, of two stages (Lev. xiv. 1–32).

The *first stage* (vers. 1–9) set forth his readmission to national fellowship, *i.e.*, the restoration of one who had passed as dead, to the fellowship of the living. This took place, as may be supposed, outside the camp; for it was not till this was effected that permission was to be granted him to enter the camp once more. The priest who was entrusted with the duty of declaring him clean, caused two clean living birds to be brought (the species is not given, and therefore was probably indifferent). One of these he killed above a vessel of living water (*i.e.*, water taken, not from a standing pool, but from a running stream or spring), allowing the blood to flow into the vessel. He then took the second live bird, dipped it along with a bunch of cedar-wood, coccus-wool, and hyssop into the water, and after sprinkling the person to be cleansed seven times, let the bird go into the open country,—in other words, return to its fellows and its own nest. In like manner, after the leper had shaved off all the hair from his body, and had washed his clothes and bathed himself, he was admitted into the camp, *i.e.*, to the fellowship of his own people.

The details of this ceremony of purification are for the most part clear and intelligible. Water is the means of purifying and enlivening (refreshing). In the case of river or spring water, this quality is stronger and less disturbed than in that of standing water. Blood is the symbol of life, and when mixed with water strengthens its significance as an enlivening, renewing, and refreshing medium of purification. This also applies to the cedar-wood, coccus, and hyssop that were added (§ 221). When covered with these signs and witnesses of life, the bird, hitherto bound and imprisoned, was once more let loose to return to its fellows, as an expressive representation of the cured leper, who also had been till now kept away from the fellowship of his nation, but who was now allowed to return with unfettered freedom, having been sprinkled with the water of purification and thereby cleansed, and, through the washing of his clothes, the shaving off of all his hair, and the bathing of his whole body, having been renewed in the whole outer man, and as it were new-born.

§ 225. The question, on the other hand, is a very difficult one, what was the signification of the bird that was slain, and what its relation both to the live bird and also to the entire ceremony of purification? From time immemorial (*vid. Origen*, hom. viii. in Lev.) the relation of the two birds to one another has been supposed to resemble that of the two goats of the day of atonement (§ 202). *Keil* accordingly still maintains, that "the *two* birds were symbols of the person who had recovered from his leprosy. And if it be admitted that the bird set at liberty was a sign that the man who was formerly a leper was now possessed of new vital power, delivered from the fetters of his disease, and free to return to the fellowship of his own people, the other, which was its counterpart, must also have been a symbol of the leper, and that in relation to his death." "Not, however," he adds (Note 4, p. 291), "in such a way as that the former was an image of the previous death-like condition of the leper, and the latter of his present free and living state; to which *Bähr* justly objects, that the qualities of cleanness and peculiar vitality expressly required, could not possibly represent a condition of uncleanness and death. On the contrary, though the slaying of the bird is not to be regarded as an actual sacrifice, since there was no sprinkling of blood towards the sanctuary, its violent death was intended to show, that on account of his uncleanness, which reached the very foundations of his life, the leper must inevitably have suffered death, if the mercy of God had not delivered him from this punishment of sin and restored to him the full vigour and energy of life."

But I am afraid the conviction that the difficult question is thus solved, and the true relation finally established, is not altogether free from self-deception. *Keil* has very properly stated that the bird slain cannot be regarded as a true sacrifice; but his subsequent explanation appears to me to go very far beyond the line that he has thus drawn for himself. For if the bloody death of this bird was really a symbolical expression of the fact, that the leper would necessarily have suffered death in consequence of his uncleanness, if the mercy of God had not delivered him from this punishment of sin; and if in reality " that act of divine mercy was shadowed forth in this institution, by virtue of which he needed only to go down to death in spirit, that his life might be renewed through the blood of the bird which was given up to death in his stead;" I cannot see in what the working of this non-sacrifice is supposed to differ from that of a true sacrifice, or what more the slaughtering and sprinkling of the blood in the case of a true sacrifice could possibly secure. But the analogy of the two birds to the two goats of the day of atonement is by no means so obvious, complete, or indisputable as *Keil* assumes. The two goats are expressly designated as *a* sin-offering; and by this a firm basis is supplied for the conclusion, that the second, living, goat was to serve as the former (slain one) revived, as *hircus redivivus*. In the case of the birds, on the other hand, there is no intimation of the kind. And *Keil* himself overthrows the analogy in its most essential features by adding, that " whilst one bird had to lay down its life, to shed its blood, *for* the person to be purified, the other was made a symbol *of* the person to be purified, by being dipped in the mixture of blood and water." Now in the case of the two goats, the second was a continuation, a revivifying of the first, and therefore was ideally identical with it. But, according to *Keil*, the first bird was the means to an end, whilst the second represented the end of the means, so that they represented two totally different things. How does this square then with *Keil's former* assertion, that " the *two* birds were symbols of the person recovered from his leprosy," and that, " if it be admitted that the bird set at liberty was a figure of the former leper, now delivered from the fetters of his disease, the second must have been a symbol

of the leper *likewise*"?   I can find nothing but an insoluble self-contradiction.   Or could the means by which a sick man was healed
possibly be a symbol of the person of the sick man himself ?   And
if one bird laid down its life *for* the person to be purified, in order
that the other might be made a symbol *of* the person to be cleansed
through being dipped in its blood, this *second* bird, *before* it was so
dipped, must have been a symbol of the leper while still unclean, and
can only have become a symbol of the cleansed leper *after* the dip-
ping.   But *Keil* himself declares the former impossible, inasmuch as
" the qualities of cleanness and peculiar vitality (demanded even in
the second bird) could not possibly represent a state of uncleanness
and death."

Bähr's opinion, therefore, that in the first bird it was not its death
that came into consideration, but only its blood, as setting forth the
full, undiminished vital energy of the one set free, is probably the
correct one ; and *Keil's* reply, that " in that case the slaughtered
bird would not be a symbol of the leper, but would be added simply
for the purpose of obtaining its blood," is to be regarded not as an
evidence against it, but as evidence in its favour.   Neither of the
two birds represented the leper as still diseased and unclean, and the
second alone represented him as recovered.   In the case of the first
bird, the only object was to procure the blood as a symbol of life, and
an animal of the same kind as the second was necessarily taken, in
order that its blood and life might be of the same kind as those of
the second bird.

§ 226. With the readmission of the leper as healed, the *second
stage* of restitution commenced, by which he was restored to the religious and ecclesiastical privileges of the clean, namely, into the
fellowship of the sanctuary (Lev. xiv. 9–32).

After seven days of preparation, during which he was allowed
to remain in the camp but still outside his tent or home, and after
a renewed washing, bathing, and shaving of the whole body, in order
that none of the old uncleanness might be carried over into the new
sphere of life, the true consecration commenced on the eighth day at
and for the sanctuary, by his bringing to the tabernacle a he-lamb
as a trespass-offering, and with it a log of oil ; also a ewe-lamb as a
sin-offering, and a male as a burnt-offering, together with three-
tenths of an ephah of white meal as a meat-offering.   In cases of
poverty two doves would suffice as a sin- and burnt-offering in the
place of the lambs, and the quantity of white meal required for the
meat-offering was then reduced to one-tenth.   The priest conducted

the person about to be consecrated up to the door of the tabernacle, and there waved the lamb of the trespass-offering and the log of oil. After this lamb had been slain in the ordinary way, he smeared the blood upon the tip of his right ear, the thumb of his right hand, and the great toe of his right foot. He then poured some of the log of oil into his left hand, and having sprinkled some of it with his finger seven times towards the door of the tabernacle, touched the three members, upon which the blood had already been placed, with the oil, and then poured the remainder of the oil in his hand upon the head of the person to be consecrated. After this, the sin-offering and burnt-offering were sacrificed in the usual way.

The first thing that needs explanation is the exclusion of the person to be received from his own home for seven days. The reason assigned by the Chaldee for this is : " *et non accedet ad latus uxoris suæ.*" This explanation is adopted by the Talmudists, and by *Bähr, Keil,* and others. It cannot have been from any fear of infection, however, as *Bunsen* assumes, but only to avert the opportunity and inducement to conjugal intercourse, which would have rendered him unclean till the evening, and so have interrupted the preparation for his consecration. *Sommer,* who denies that conjugal intercourse did render unclean, has to seek another explanation, and finds it in the fact, that " the leper, though recovered, was not restored to the congregation, and was therefore to be perpetually reminded that something was still wanting to his perfect restoration." *Keil* regards this explanation as quite admissible, and combines it with that of the Rabbins ; but in this I cannot follow him.

In contradiction to the practice adopted at all other trespass-offerings, *Bähr* maintains that the meat-offering is to be regarded as belonging to the trespass-offering. He has probably been led into this mistake by the fact, that in ver. 21 the meat-offering is mentioned between the trespass-offering on the one hand, and the sin- and trespass-offerings on the other ; whereas in ver. 10 it is mentioned in the series after the trespass-offering, the sin-offering, and the burnt-offering, and in both instances the true offering of the *Minchah* (vers. 20, 31) is connected, not with the trespass-offering, but with the burnt-offering. The mistake is a still more striking one when he adds, that " this meat-offering, moreover, was regulated entirely by the rule laid down in Num. xv. 4 ;" for neither ver. 10 nor ver. 21 is in harmony with this rule. In Num. xv. 4 one-tenth of white meal is ordered to be taken with the *lamb* of the burnt-offering, and not three-tenths as ver. 10 prescribes ; and nothing at all is said with reference to the Minchah of a burnt-offering of doves. This mistake, which at any rate is concealed in the case of *Bähr*, stares us boldly in the face in that of *Keil*, who expressly appeals to ver. 10 in support of the assertion, that the meat-offering consisted of one-tenth of white meal, and thus at very little cost disposes of the difficulty, that ver. 10 really requires not one-tenth but *three*-tenths of white meal, in direct contrast with Num. xv. 5 and chap. xxviii. xxix., and that it is only in ver. 21 that *one*-tenth is spoken of as sufficient for the poor man's burnt-offering of doves. This deviation from the general rule laid down in Num. xv. 5 can only be regarded as an exceptional case, and as warranted by the peculiar importance of this sacrificial act.

§ 227. We have already sufficiently explained in § 101 why a *trespass-offering* could be, and necessarily was, required in connection with this rite of reception. That the trespass-offering alone constituted the true *consecration sacrifice*, and not the sin- or burnt-offering, is indisputably shown in the previous waving, and the subsequent manipulation with the blood. The reason why a *trespass-offering* was selected for the purpose has been discussed in the main by *Hofmann*, who writes as follows (pp. 261, 262): "This sacrifice was required on account of the long estrangement of the leper from the sanctuary and the congregation. Compensation had to be made for the fact that he had been unclean so long, before the man who had become clean again could present a sin-offering as a recognised member of the congregation; and the blood, not of the sin-offering, but of the trespass-offering, was adapted to the purpose of his fresh consecration, because that which warranted a readmission to the sacred fellowship of the sanctuary was not a rite that had reference to sin as the cause of his disease, but one having reference to the condition induced thereby. So, again, it was from the consciousness of having been so long estranged from the sacred commonwealth that he needed to be delivered, before he could gain courage to pray for the forgiveness of the sin which had been the cause of his estrangement." All that I cannot subscribe to in this exposition is limited to two or three expressions, the unsuitable character of which has been already pointed out at § 28, 68, 96.

The smearing of the tip of the ear, the thumb, and the great toe, first with blood and then with oil, corresponds so strikingly to the similar proceedings at the consecration of the priests (§ 169, 171), that we must necessarily ascribe to them a common basis and

the same signification. The two parts of the consecration, which
were kept apart in the other case (the ear, hand, and foot being
touched with blood alone ; the persons and clothes with blood and
oil), are here simplified and combined into one. As there was
no official clothing in this instance, of course there could be no
sprinkling of the clothes. The most striking feature is the selection
of the ear, the hand, and the foot. This has been very properly
explained on the ground, that the consecration of the person to be
received was in this case also, in a certain sense, a consecration to
priesthood, inasmuch as the leper was once more to be incorporated
in the priestly nation (Ex. xix. 6), of which he had ceased to be a
member on account of his leprosy. But the difficulty arising from
the contrast to the covenant consecration of the nation (§ 163–4), in
which the sprinkling was effected with blood alone, and not with
oil, has been overlooked. This contrast, it appears to me, can only
be explained on the supposition, that the leper, as one who had
passed through both physical and civil death, had lost more by his
leprosy than the covenant consecration had conferred; that is to
say, had lost not only the covenant fellowship which that consecration imparted, but also the fellowship of the nation as chosen and
blessed in Abraham, which was of much earlier date ; and that he
needed therefore to be consecrated afresh, not only to the former
by the covenant blood of reconciliation (Ex. xxiv. 8), but also to
the latter by the oil of the *Spirit of God*.

§ 228. I cannot but regard it as erroneous and misleading on
the part of *Keil* (i. 293), to forsake the symbolism that has prevailed
thus far, and to express the singular opinion, that as this oil "was
presented by the person to be consecrated as an offering from his
own resources, it did not represent the spiritual power and gifts
with which God equipped those who were set apart to special
offices in His kingdom, but the divine spirit of life, which had been
breathed into him by the Creator, and which he therefore possessed
as his own property." But with this new interpretation the author
has overlooked the fact, that he falls into striking contradictions, not
only with the view held up in the Scriptures, but also with his own
assertions at other times. (1.) The fact that the person to be consecrated presented the log of oil himself, as a sacrifice from his own
resources, does not warrant the inference, that it represented the
subjective spirit of life breathed into him through his creation, and
not the objective Spirit of God without him ; for that oil with
which the *Minchah* was mixed or anointed was also offered by the

sacrificer himself from his own resources, and yet the thought expressed by the anointing of the meat-offering with this oil was not that " good works are performed in the power of the spirit of life imparted to him through creation," but, as *Keil* himself correctly maintains (p. 202), that they " are performed and rendered possible by the power of the *Spirit of God*, which was symbolized by the oil." (2.) It is equally a mistake to suppose, that only the holy anointing oil compounded of the four fragrant substances, and kept in the tabernacle, " shadowed forth the spiritual gifts and powers with which God endowed those who were set apart to special offices in His kingdom," and therefore that this holy oil had to be used for every official anointing, and never merely ordinary oil. For in Ex. xxx. 33 the use of *this* anointing oil is restricted to the consecration of the priests and holy vessels. " Whoever compoundeth any like it," it is expressly stated, " or whosoever putteth any of it *upon a stranger*, shall even be cut off from his people." On this *Keil* himself has properly observed (Comment., p. 533), " זָר, the stranger, was not merely the non-Israelite, *but the laity generally, or the non-priest*." Now, unless this commandment was broken, the oil with which Saul, David, Solomon, Jehu, Hazael, and Elisha were anointed to their royal or prophetic office, was not the holy anointing oil of the tabernacle, but ordinary oil; and *Keil* will hardly affirm that in these cases the persons anointed were to be endowed with their own spirit of life as originally created. (3.) The oil with which Jacob anointed the stone at Luz as a house of God (Gen. xxviii. 18, cf. xxxi. 13) was undoubtedly common oil out of his own resources, and yet Jacob wished to mark the spot as a place of the revelation, not of his own created spirit of life, but of the Spirit of God without him.

Again, *Keil* is very unfortunate in his further defence of this idea when he affirms here, as before with regard to the consecration of the priests (§ 171), that " as the sprinkling of the blood had reference to the *soul*, so the smearing with oil had reference to the spirit, which pervades both body and soul, and unites them into a human personality." Whereas at the consecration of the priests he supposed the soul of the man to be endowed with his own soul, which had been sanctified upon the altar, and his spirit with the objective, sanctifying Spirit of God, in this case he supposes even the spirit of the man to be endowed with his own spirit, " which had been pervaded by the Divine Spirit of grace through the waving and sprinkling of the oil before Jehovah." We have already shown at § 171 how impossible it is to reconcile this distinction of soul and spirit with the lucid psychology of the Old Testament.

Nevertheless the very point by which *Keil* has been led away is both true and well established. If this oil represented the objective Spirit of God, it necessarily belonged to Jehovah, and came from Jehovah. And this was really the case. For though the person about to be received presented it himself from his own resources, yet when he was anointed with it, it was no longer his own, but God's, and no longer common, but holy oil. To give it this character, it was waved before Jehovah, and sprinkled seven times towards the door of the tabernacle.

The directions with regard to the removal of the leprosy of clothes and houses (Lev. xiii. 47 sqq., xiv. 33 sqq.) we need not dwell upon here, as they have no connection with the sacrificial worship.

CHAPTER IV

ADAPTATION OF THE SACRIFICIAL WORSHIP TO CERTAIN PECULIAR CIRCUMSTANCES

A. PRESENTATION OF THE FIRST-BORN OF CATTLE

§ 229. From the time that the first-born of men and cattle were spared in Egypt, they belonged *eo ipso* to Jehovah (Ex. xiii. 14, 15). The whole tribe of Levi was substituted for the *first-born of man* of all the tribes, being set apart for service at the sanctuary, and handed over to the priests. Nevertheless the obligation still remained in force, as a perpetual reminder of the deliverance which Jehovah effected for His people out of the bondage of Egypt; but the presentation *in natura* was commuted into a redemption fee, which properly belonged to Jehovah, but was allotted by Him to the priests for their maintenance.

With the *first-born of animals*, everything depended upon whether they were fit for sacrifice (oxen, sheep, or goats) or not. In the latter case, according to Ex. xiii. 12, 13, xxxiv. 20, the first-born were to be redeemed with a sheep, or slain; but, according to a subsequent modification, they were always to be redeemed with money, according to the valuation of the priest, and with the addition of a fifth of their worth (Lev. xxvii. 27; Num. xviii. 15). But the first-born that were fit for sacrifice were to be presented as a heave-offering (תְּרוּמֹת הַקֳּדָשִׁים) within eight days of their birth, and actually offered in sacrifice (Num. xviii. 17 sqq.).

Keil (i. 335) treats these offerings of first-born as ordinary thank-offerings, presented by the possessors on their own account, and nothing more. "They were sacrificed as thank-offerings," he says, "upon the altar of the sanctuary; and, as in the case of all the *Shelamim*, the breast and right shoulder alone were assigned to the priest, the remainder of the flesh being left to the person presenting it, for a sacrificial meal" (Num. xviii. 17, 18; Deut. xii. 17, xv. 19, 20). But this is at variance, (1) with the general and fundamental law respecting the first-fruits and first-born, which the owner was never allowed to claim for his own enjoyment or use, but had to deliver up to Jehovah as a feudal tribute for the maintenance of the priests (Ex. xxii. 28, 29, xxiii. 19; Num. xviii. 12 sqq.; Deut. xv. 19, 20, etc.); (2) with the express and special command in Lev. xxvii. 26, that the first-born of cattle were not to be used as peace-offerings, because they already belonged to Jehovah; and (3), most of all, with Num. xviii. 17, 18, the very passage which *Keil* adduces *primo loco* in proof of his assertion, whereas, in the clearest words, it states the very opposite. The passage runs thus: "And the flesh of them shall be thine (the priest's), as the wave-breast and as the right leg are thine." This cannot obviously mean anything else than that, whereas the priest received only the breast and leg of the ordinary Shelamim, in the case of the offerings of first-born the rest of the flesh was to be his portion as well; and yet *Keil* affirms, as though it were self-evident, and any other meaning were perfectly inconceivable, that, "as in the case of all the Shelamim, only the breast and right leg were allotted to the priest, and the *remainder* of the flesh was left to the bringer of the offering for a sacrificial meal."

It is true he also adduces Deut. xii. 17, xv. 19, 20, as additional proof passages, but without even mentioning the apparent discrepancy between them and Num. xviii. 17, 18. In Deut. xii. 17, 18, for instance, it is expressly commanded, that both the tithes, the first-fruits, and the first-born, and also the peace-offerings, are to be eaten by the persons presenting them, not in their own homes, but only at the sanctuary. But it is very evident that in this command the principal accent is laid upon the fact, that this was not to be all disposed of in an arbitrary manner, like any private property, with which a man might do what he liked. And just as it is very certain that the meaning of the command is not, that all the tithes and first-fruits, and the whole of the flesh of the peace-offering, including the wave-breast and heave-shoulder, and even the fat portions, were to be eaten at the sanctuary by the persons presenting them, so also the meaning cannot be that they were to eat all the flesh of the sacrifices of firstlings. In the brief summary contained in Deut. xii. 17 sqq., the precise quantity that was to be eaten of each of the objects named must be gathered from other passages in the law, in which this point is specially and professedly treated of. Now the rule for the firstlings is given in Num. xviii. 17, 18. As the priests and Levites were allowed to devote a portion of the tithes assigned to them for their maintenance to a tithing feast for the offerers and their families at the sanctuary, so no doubt they might also devote a portion of the firstlings to the same purpose. The priests are not prohibited in Num. xviii. 17, 18 from using the flesh of the firstlings for a sacrificial meal, to which the bringers of the offerings might be invited; and Deut. xii. 17, 18 simply forbids the bringers of the offerings to slay and eat the firstlings in their own homes. Thus the two passages are in perfect harmony, and there is not the slightest necessity to twist the command in Num. xviii. 17, 18 into the very opposite.

§ 230. *Kliefoth's* views are much clearer and more correct. "The order of procedure," he says, "according to Num. xviii., was the following: the priests had to slay the animal at the altar of burnt-offering; the blood they poured out by the altar of burnt-offering; the fat portions they burned upon the altar as a savour of satisfaction to God; and the rest of the flesh then fell to their portion, to be used in the same way as the heave-shoulder and wave-breast of the *Shelamim*. There can be no doubt, therefore, that this was a real sacrifice: not only was it brought as near as possible to God, but it was also accepted by Him in the act of burning" (p. 99). We must pronounce it, however, a *ne plus ultra* of misinterpretation, when the same writer proceeds to affirm, that "for all that, it was not a *bleeding* sacrifice; although the material of sacrifice was an animal, and its blood was shed and brought to the altar, yet it was not an expiatory sacrifice."—And what is the proof of this unheard-of and contradictory assertion?—"There was no laying on of hands, it did not take the place of the offerer; therefore it did not serve לכפר. . . . It was a sacrifice, not of expiation, but of thanksgiving." But upon what does Lev. xvii. 11 make the

כַּפָּרָה ? Is it upon the imposition of hands? Is it not rather upon the sprinkling of the blood upon the altar? Unquestionably upon the latter alone. And how does *Kliefoth* know that this sprinkling of the blood was not preceded by the imposition of hands? It is certainly nowhere expressly mentioned. And so also in the case of the trespass-offering it is not expressly mentioned; and not even in that of the goat that was slain "for Jehovah" on the day of atonement: and yet here even *Kliefoth* does not hesitate to take for granted, that it was performed in connection with every animal altar-sacrifice.

The firstling sacrifices were no doubt *Shelamim*, like all the rest; but they were *Shelamim* offered, not by the original owner, who had no right, according to Lev. xxvii. 26, to use them as *Shelamim*, but by the priests, to whom all the first-fruits and firstlings were assigned as tributary payments. As the Levites, to whom the tithes were allotted, had to hand over the tenth to the priests, so the priests were required to hand over to Jehovah a portion of the firstlings assigned to them as a thank-offering for their priestly prerogative, viz., the fat portions which were burned upon the altar. They are to be regarded, therefore, as thank-offerings, or more correctly praise-offerings, presented by the priests for their priestly calling, and, like all praise-offerings, were raised upon the basis of an atoning act effected through the sprinkling of blood.

B. THE NAZARITE'S OFFERING

§ 231. The Nazarite's vow (נֶדֶר נָזִיר), as defined in the law, consisted of this: an Israelite, either man or woman, consecrated himself to Jehovah for a certain time as נָזִיר (from נזר = to be separated), and during his time of consecration abstained from all strong drink, and in fact from everything that came from the vine—from grapes, both fresh and dried, from must, wine, vinegar of wine, and from everything that could be made even of the skins and pips of the grapes. During the whole time he allowed no razor to come upon his head, and avoided all defilement through contact with a corpse, even that of his nearest relative. And if, nevertheless, he should be so defiled unawares, through the occurrence of a sudden death in his neighbourhood, he was obliged to have his head shaved, to bring two pigeons as a sin-offering and burnt-offering, for the priest to make expiation for him, and a yearling lamb as a trespass-offering, that he might be consecrated afresh. The time that had passed since the commencement of his vow all went for nothing, because the vow had been interrupted; and he had to go through the entire period of his consecration again.

When the time of his vow, the length of which was left by the law to the pleasure of the person himself, was at an end, the Nazarite had to offer a ewe-lamb, as a sin-offering for the sins that he might have committed unconsciously in his Nazarite condition, and this was followed in regular order by the offering of a he-lamb as a burnt-offering and a ram as a peace-offering. To the latter there was also added, besides the legal Minchah of meal, the usual Corban of cake (§ 155), to the exclusion, however, of leavened loaves. After the Nazarite's hair had been shaved off at the door of the tabernacle, and thrown into the fire in which the peace-offering was burning, the priest placed the boiled shoulder (זְרוֹעַ) and one peace of the Corban of cake upon the hands of the Nazarite, and waved them before Jehovah. They then belonged to the priest himself, together with the wave-breast and heave-leg. The sacrificial ceremony was closed as a matter of course by the sacrificial meal. With this the Nazarite was released from his vow, and once more permitted to drink wine.

§ 232. The positive side of a Nazarite condition was the consecration of the Nazarite to Jehovah; the negative, his separation from the world, with its enjoyments as well as its corruptions. The latter was expressed in the fact that the vow was irreconcilable with all defilement from contact with death, and also in the obligation to abstain from everything that came from the vine, as the general representative of the *deliciæ carnis* (Hos. iii. 1), and the intoxication of worldly pleasure (Hos. iv. 11; Prov. xx. 1): the former, in his allowing the hair of his head to grow, as the sign of "the consecration of his God upon his head" (ver. 7).

Hengstenberg (Egypt and Books of Moses, pp. 192–3, translation), starting with the assumption, that because in ordinary life the Israelites wore their hair cut short, to allow the hair to grow was an expression of indifference towards the demands of conventionality, and therefore a sign of mourning, regards this also as a sign of separation from the world. But the foundation upon which this view is based is decidedly erroneous. It is impossible to prove that allowing the hair to grow was a sign of mourning and separation from intercourse with the world; whilst, on the contrary, Jer. vii. 29 places it beyond all doubt that shaving off the hair was a sign of humiliation and sorrow. And the text itself is in many respects at variance with any such view. If, as *Keil* justly observes (i. 327), allowing the hair to grow was merely a sign of separation, we can see no reason why the hair should have been shaved off in case of defilement, since the defilement itself would have been sufficiently removed by the sin- and burnt-offerings (ver. 11). This view is equally irreconcilable with the description of the uncut hair in ver. 7 as "the consecration of his God upon his head" (נֵזֶר אֱלֹהָיו עַל־רֹאשׁוֹ). So again in vers. 9 and 18, on account of the uncut hair his head is called רֹאשׁ נִזְרוֹ, "his consecrated head;" and in ver. 11 the atonement offered as a fresh commencement of the period of his vow, and for the fresh growth of his hair, which had been shaved off on account of his defilement, is described as a sanctification (קִדַּשׁ) of his head. All this points to the fact that allowing the hair to grow had a positive and not a negative signification. "נֵזֶר," says *Keil*, "means *consecration*, or the sign of consecration. In this sense the anointing oil upon the head of the priest is called נֵזֶר (Lev. xxi. 12), also the diadem which was worn by the consecrated priest (Ex. xxix. 6), as well as that worn by the king (2 Sam. i. 10, etc.)." The uncut hair worn by the Nazarite in honour of the Lord was a similar sign of consecration. It was as it were the embodiment of his vow, the visible proof of his consecrated condition : for this reason, whenever his vow was broken, it had to be shaved off ; and for the same reason the supernatural power of Samson, which was a result of his consecrated condition, departed with his hair.

The hair did not acquire this meaning, however, as *Bähr* supposes, as a symbol " of the highest bloom or fulness of life, which the Hebrew regarded as holiness." This view is founded upon the groundless assumption, that in the estimation of eastern nations generally, and the Hebrew in particular, the hair is to the head what plants, trees, etc., are to the earth, and upon the fact that the vine which remained uncut in the sabbatical and jubilee years was called נָזִיר (Lev. xxv. 5, 11),—a fact which proves nothing, because, as *Keil* justly observes, " this biblical epithet for the vine was itself derived from the Nazarite institution, and the *tertium comparationis* consists in their not being cut, because they were separated from ordinary use as the property of Jehovah." Still less tenable is *Baumgarten's* explanation, founded upon 1 Cor. xi. 5, 7, where allowing the hair to grow is represented as " a sign of dependence upon another present power." The true point of view is that given by *Keil*, and founded upon ver. 7 : the uncut hair of the Nazarite was "the diadem of the consecration of God upon his head." For a rich, strong head of hair is an ornament not to a woman only, but also to a man (2 Sam. xiv. 25, 26), and still remains so, even where custom requires the cutting of hair, especially on the part of the men.

Now, if we consider the unmistakeable agreement which exists both in a positive and negative aspect between the character of the Nazarite and that of the priest,—in both, though in different forms, a consecration of God, a diadem (נֵזֶר) befitting a *king* upon the head; and in both, though in different degrees, the obligation to abstain from wine and strong drink (Lev. x. 8, 9), and to avoid all defilement from the dead (Lev. xxi. 1, 2, 11),—if we carefully consider all this, we shall hardly be mistaken in regarding the condition of a Nazarite as a kind of priestly position, as a visible manifestation in an intensified form of that priesthood, which is described in Ex. xix. 6 as מַמְלֶכֶת כֹּהֲנִים, and which was latent in the entire nation.

§ 233. The appropriateness of a *trespass-offering*, on the renewal of the vow which had been interrupted by an unexpected death, has already been pointed out (§ 101); and the fact that in this case the trespass-offering followed the sin- and burnt-offerings, whereas at the consecration of the restored leper it preceded it (§ 227), may be explained in *Hofmann's* words (p. 262): "It was just the opposite when the period of a Nazarite's vow was interrupted by a death occurring near him. It was then necessary that this occurrence, which was to him the consequence of sin, should be first of all expiated before he was in a condition to renew his vow. And the renewal of the vow was to be connected with a trespass-offering, because the payment of his vow was so much longer delayed; and this would leave him a debtor to God, unless a trespass-(debt-) atonement was made."

In the act of worship appointed for the *dissolution* of the vow at the close of the period of his consecration, the peace-offering with which it ended is the only point that causes any difficulty. *Keil* is wrong in calling this a "consecration offering," for there was no question of consecration in this case, but rather, so to speak, of unconsecrating. No proof is needed that it is to be regarded as a vow-offering, and not, as *Kliefoth* supposes, as a praise-offering. The cutting off of the Nazarite's hair, the sign of his consecration to God, as soon as that consecration came to an end, furnishes its own explanation; and the fact that it was thrown into the fire, and ascended in this as a "savour of satisfaction" to Jehovah, showed that the Nazarite condition had been well-pleasing to Him. The omission of the accompaniment of leavened bread, which was customary, according to Lev. vii. 13, with the Corban of cake appointed for the sacrificial meal, just as in the case of the consecration offering of the priest (§ 172), also attested the higher and as it were priestly character of that fellowship with Jehovah, which had been associated with the Nazarite's vow. A still further intensification was exhibited in the fact that the shoulder, already boiled, was assigned to the priest, in addition to the wave-breast and heave-leg, by waving upon the hands of the offerer. This was expressive of a closer and more intimate connection between the offerer and the priest as the servant of God.

C. THE JEALOUSY OFFERING

§ 234. If a husband had evident ground for suspicion that his wife had committed adultery, but was unable to bring legal proofs of the fact, so that civil punishment might be inflicted, he was warranted by the law (Num. v. 11–31) in leaving her to the special judgment of the omniscient God by means of a solemn act of adjuration at the tabernacle. To this end he brought the suspected wife to the priest, with a Corban of the tenth of an ephah of barley meal, though without the ordinary accompaniments of oil and incense. The priest took her into the court of the tabernacle, and having put some holy water (probably out of the laver of the court) into an earthen vessel, mixed it with dust from the floor of the tabernacle. After this, he led the woman before the Lord, *i.e.*, before the door of the tabernacle, and having uncovered her head, placed the Corban in her hands. He then took the water mixed with dust into his own hands, and commenced a solemn adjuration of the woman, pronouncing a curse upon her in the most terrible words in case she should be guilty, declaring that in consequence of the wrath and vengeance of God her belly should swell and her hip waste away; at the same time assuring her that the curse would take no effect provided she were innocent. The woman answered and confirmed the words of this adjuration by a second "Amen." After this the priest wrote the curses that had been uttered upon a slip (סֵפֶר), washed the words in the water, took the Corban from the hands of the woman and waved it before Jehovah, burned an *Azcarah* (§ 148) of the *Corban* upon the altar, and finally gave the woman the water to drink as curse-water, מֵי הַמָּרִים הַמְאָרְרִים (ver. 24), *i.e.*, as the water of bitter-making bitternesses.

§ 235. That the Corban of barley is to be regarded as a true meat-offering, there can be no possible doubt; for in vers. 15, 18, 25, it is expressly called a מִנְחָה, and according to ver. 15, an *Azcarah* of it was to be burned upon the altar. But *Bähr* is certainly wrong in describing it as the offering of the man and not of the woman. In the text it is expressly designated קָרְבָּנָהּ עָלֶיהָ, *her* offering, which is presented *on her account*. And the fact that it was regarded as *her* offering is unmistakeably proved by this circumstance, that she held it in her hand during the whole of the adjuration, and that the priest received it from *her* hand, before putting an *Azcarah* of it in the altar-fire. It is true it was the husband who furnished the barley meal, and brought it to the sanctuary. But there is nothing in this to warrant the supposition that it was to be regarded as *his* offering, i.e., as an offering presented *on his account*. From the very nature of the case, and the customs of the Israelites, even if it were *her* offering, the husband must necessarily furnish it. An Israelitish wife possessed no property, and was only entitled to the usufruct of her husband's. Hence, if she wished or was required to present an offering, it could only be done from her husband's property. Moreover, in this case the whole affair was opposed to her desire and will. As she was brought by her husband to the sanctuary without his asking whether she wished it or no, so her offering was also brought by him without any regard to her inclination. There is nothing at variance with this view in the fact that in ver. 15 it is called מִנְחַת קְנָאֹת, i.e., the offering of jealousy (*sc.* the husband's); for the husband's jealousy for the purity of his marriage was the occasion of her involuntary offering, an offering made on her account and presented for her.

But what was the purpose of an offering at all, especially a meat-offering? To this *Bähr* replies (ii. 445), "According to the Mosaic principles, every one who desired to draw near (קרב) to Jehovah to enter into any relation to Him as the Holy One, was required to bring a Corban (קרבן), and without this nothing could be undertaken in the presence of Jehovah." But this explanation falls to the ground with the erroneous assumption upon which it is based, that it was the offering of the husband and not of the wife; whilst it fails altogether to explain why it was a bloodless offering, and not a bleeding sacrifice, which would certainly have been more suitable for that purpose.

The true answer may be obtained from the name of the sacrifice in ver. 15, מִנְחַת זִכָּרוֹן מַזְכֶּרֶת עָוֹן, i.e., "a gift of memorial," by which Jehovah was reminded of the wrong (on the supposition, of course, that it had really occurred). The Minchah, as we saw at § 141, was a representation of the fruits of the life and labour of the offerer, that is to say, of the labour of his vocation in accordance with the covenant. Now the wife maintained that she had lived and acted in accordance with her vocation and with the covenant, and no human tribunal could convict her of a lie. The Almighty alone could judge justly, and therefore she was required to present herself at His tribunal, bringing a meat-offering as a sign and pledge that her life had been, as she maintained, one of fidelity to the law.

As a matter of course, therefore, it was necessary that her offering should be a meat-offering, and one presented without the usual basis of a bleeding sacrifice. This was no question of expiation. If the wife were guilty, there was no possible expiation for her crime; and if innocent, there was nothing to expiate, at all events, nothing in the circumstances which occasioned the whole affair.

§ 236. Starting with this view, it is easy to explain the separate data of the ceremony prescribed. *Barley meal* was to be used for the meat-offering, and not wheaten flour, as was usually the case. " Barley," says *Winer*, i. 307, " in the place of the customary wheat, pointed to the inferiority of the person who had fallen into such suspicion, for throughout antiquity this species of corn was regarded as *vile hordeum* (*Phœdr.* ii. 8, 9) and far inferior to wheat." The slighted barley answered to the ambiguous character of her calling and life. The husband had to furnish the offering from his own property; and with the conviction of the badness of his wife, it was natural, and even prescribed by the law, that he should take the worst kind of corn. The better, purer wheat would have been objectively less adapted to serve as a symbol of her life, even if she had not been really guilty of the crime of which she was accused; for in any case she had excited suspicion by improper behaviour, as it is distinctly shown in vers. 12–14 that the ceremony would not have been entered upon at all, unless the husband had been able to prove that his suspicions were well founded, and not purely imaginary. This ambiguous character of the offering, which corresponded to the ambiguity of the life of the woman to which it referred, also explains the prohibition of both *oil* and *incense*. Her works were to be presented in the offering; and whether they had proceeded from the Spirit of God, represented by the oil, or had been performed with uprightness of heart towards God, and in prayer, as represented by incense, was not only doubtful, but the presumption was the very opposite, and therefore these symbols were both omitted. The *uncovering* of her head pointed to this presumption; for the covering of a woman's head was the symbol of conjugal fidelity and chastity. An *earthen* vessel was prescribed on account of its worthlessness, and this again was expressive of the suspicion which the woman had drawn upon herself by her conduct. The *dust* of the floor of the sanctuary was related to the curse to be uttered over her; and *Bähr* has very aptly compared this with Gen. iii. 14, where the eating of dust is the consequence of the curse pronounced upon the serpent; also with Ps. lxxii. 9, and Micah vii. 17, where the eating of dust is introduced as a general sign of reprobation, cursing, and ignominy. The directions to take not ordinary water but holy water, and not ordinary dust but dust of the sanctuary, were also significant, since the tabernacle was the place where Jehovah dwelt in the midst of His people and revealed Himself, and therefore everything in it was brought into relation to Jehovah, the Holy One, so that the curse-water appeared the more potent in consequence. Although it was curse-water, it was still holy water; for the curse which it brought upon the guilty woman was the curse of Jehovah.

At first the priest acted as the attorney of the man in relation to the woman, who was suspected and accused but still maintained her innocence. In this capacity[1] he held in his hand the curse-water, the symbol and pledge of the curse which she had deserved in case she were guilty, and which would certainly fall upon her. The woman, on the other hand, maintained her innocence, and therefore held the symbol of her innocence, the meat-offering, the sign of good works, of righteousness before God, by which the curse would be rendered powerless and nugatory, provided she were really innocent, as she maintained. After the curse had been pronounced, and she had acknowledged and accepted it by her *Amen*, the offer-

---

[1] I still adhere to this opinion, though *Keil* has pronounced it erroneous. The man here appealed to the judgment of God, because his case could not be brought before an earthly tribunal. And the priest, as the servant of God and the mediator of the nation, took up the charge, and did all that his office prescribed to bring the matter to an issue. He may therefore be unquestionably designated the attorney of the husband who brought the charge. But his acting as attorney for the husband did not prevent him, when he had finished the husband's part, from also acting as the attorney of the wife who insisted upon her innocence, and taking up her cause as well. And this he did, when he took the meat-offering from her hands, and caused it to ascend to Jehovah in the altar-flame.

ing was taken from her and burned upon the altar; and upon this, she took the curse-water and received the curse which had been washed in it into herself. The symbol of her declared innocence was burned upon the altar, and the flame carried it to Jehovah, who judges righteously and tries the reins and the heart; and in the meantime the symbol of her guilt, as maintained on the other side, penetrated within, carrying with it the curse pronounced upon the guilty in the name of Jehovah. In this case none but Jehovah could decide, and He had undertaken the decision because of the importance of the matter. According to the wife's declaration, she was pure, and living in a good and just relation towards Jehovah, and therefore was qualified to present a meat-offering. The burning of this meat-offering was an appeal to Jehovah, the searcher of hearts. If her declaration of innocence were correct, God, as the protector of innocence, was invoked to accept of her innocence on this occasion; and if it were false, the presentation of the meat-offering contained an appeal to Jehovah, to punish the wickedness in accordance with the curse which the guilty woman had heard, approved, and acknowledged. Then after the whole affair had been given up to Jehovah, for Him to carry out, the woman drank the curse-water, the symbol and pledge of the penal justice of God.

The *drinking* of the curse-water was peculiarly significant. As an explanatory parallel, we may compare Ps. cix. 18, " As he clothed himself with cursing like as with his garment, so let it come into his bowels like water." In case she were innocent, as the priest at the very outset had assured her, the drinking would be followed by no disastrous results, would do her no harm, and she would conceive again. This last clause shows clearly in what the punishment of her crime would consist, provided the opposite were the case, and how the words relating to it are to be understood. Her belly (*i.e.,* her womb) was to swell, and her hip to waste away; both of them members which were most closely related to the sin in question, and were also the organs of childbirth. The wasting away of the hip and swelling of the belly, which only occur in extreme and decrepit old age, after the power of childbearing has gone, are in this case a terribly significant description of the curse of barrenness, the greatest reproach of an Israelitish wife.

§ 237. *Bähr* gave up the idea of this ceremony being intended as an ordeal, but it has been revived again by *Keil.* " This ceremony," he says (i. 298), "*was an ordeal,* a mode of procedure prescribed by the Mosaic law for leaving the decision as to the guilt

or innocence of the woman with God." But this view is founded
upon a mistaken notion as to the nature and design of an ordeal.
An ordeal expected and required an immediate decision on the part
of God, whether the accused were guilty or no, and that for the
purpose of judicial proceedings on the part of human authorities;
whereas in this case not only the decision, but the eventual punishment, was left to the judgment of God, and so far as any *discovery*
on the part of the human accusers and judges were concerned, the
whole proceedings were, for a time at least, entirely fruitless; and
even if the woman did not become pregnant again in the course of
time, this could not be regarded as an unquestionable proof of her
guilt, such as would warrant judicial proceedings, and the infliction
of the punishment of death as an adulteress. And even vers. 27,
28, where the law certainly declares, that the ceremony will not
remain without the intended effect, no more warrants the conclusion
that the lawgiver meant the rite to be regarded as an ordeal, than
1 Cor. xi. 27, 30 warrants the assertion, that the Apostle regarded
participation in the Lord's Supper as possessing that character.

I am equally unable to agree with *Keil* when he speaks of this
ceremony as a *sacramental* act. "This punishment (viz., barrenness) was brought upon the woman," he says, "by the curse which
was written down and washed with the writing in the water.
Hence the curse-drink cannot be regarded merely as a symbol and
pledge of the punishment, which Jehovah, the Holy One, caused
to follow the solemn adjuration. This view is based upon the same
severance of the visible and invisible, which is brought out most
prominently in the doctrine of the Lord's Supper as held in the
'Reformed' Church, and this is also connected with the opinion
that the rite was not an ordeal. The curse was communicated to
the woman in a real, so to speak a *sacramental* way; so that the
water was no longer simple water, but through the word and power
of God, which were *added* to the water in a *symbolical* manner by
the washing of the written curse, it acquired a supernatural power."

The first thing that strikes us here, is the obscurity of the explanation, which in the very same breath maintains the sacramental
character of the rite (in the sense of the Lutheran creed), and then
afterwards denies it. For it is a denial of it, when the author affirms,
that "the word and power of God were added to the water in a symbolical way by the washing of the written curse." A second mistake we find in the assertion, that *Bähr* and I are chargeable with
"the same severance of the visible and invisible which is brought out

most prominently in the doctrine of the Lord's Supper as held in the Reformed Church," and in the statement implied, that his own view holds fast to that union of the visible and invisible which is taught in the Lutheran dogma of the Lord's Supper. For this is not the case; on the contrary, *Keil's* theory no more corresponds to the relation between the visible and invisible as taught in the Lutheran doctrine of the Lord's Supper, than the view adopted by *Bähr* and myself, and his view represents the Reformed doctrine quite as decidedly as ours. Moreover, *Keil* has altogether overlooked the fact, that the Reformed doctrine of the Lord's Supper has been divided into two branches, the Zwinglian and the Calvinistic. The latter corresponds (if indeed things totally dissimilar can be compared) to what he *means*, viz., that a supernatural potency was communicated to the water *realiter;* the former to what he *says*, viz., that this power was communicated to the water in a *symbolical* manner.

But the relation between the visible and invisible in the Lord's Supper, is altogether incomparable to the relation between the visible and invisible in this ceremony. In the former it is the word of God, by whose operation the *materia cœlestis* unites with the *materia terrestris;* in the latter it was the priest's form of adjuration which *" was added to* the water in a *symbolical* manner,"— a *materia cœlestis* is never mentioned.

I conclude this inquiry, therefore, now as before, with the words of *Bähr* (ii. 447): " It was not the written words of the curse washed into the water that brought the evil upon the guilty woman. The curse-drink was merely a *symbol* and *pledge* of the punishment which Jehovah, the Holy One, would surely inflict upon the guilty woman after the solemn adjuration. The water in itself was altogether powerless; nor was any magical or miraculous potency communicated to it. But it was Jehovah from whom punishment was sought, provided she were guilty. It was He who suspended the punishment and the evil. Just as when His people, with whom He had entered into a covenant, went a-whoring after strange gods, He, as the jealous God, visited them with punishment and misery, so the wife who had committed adultery could and would experience His judicial righteousness: and just as He had blessed so many a barren woman with fruitfulness, so would the fruitful woman, who had brought the curse upon herself, be visited with barrenness."

INDEX

Twin Brooks Series

For a more detailed description of Baker Book House editions of theological classics, write:
Baker Book House, P. O. Box 6287, Grand Rapids, MI 49506.